Direct
18.00

W9-DHU-019

DISCARDED

UNIVERSITY OF WINNIPEG
515 PORTAGE & BALMORAL
WINNIPEG 2, MAN.   CANADA

BURT FRANKLIN: RESEARCH & SOURCE WORKS SERIES 329
Essays in Literature and Criticism 22

ILLUSTRATIONS

OF

SHAKSPEARE.

Published by T. Tegg Cheapside. Sept.r 1 1824.

PR
3004
.D6
1968

ILLUSTRATIONS

OF

SHAKSPEARE,

AND OF

ANCIENT MANNERS:

WITH

DISSERTATIONS

ON THE CLOWNS AND FOOLS OF SHAKSPEARE;

ON THE COLLECTION OF POPULAR TALES ENTITLED GESTA ROMANORUM;

AND ON THE ENGLISH MORRIS DANCE.

By FRANCIS DOUCE.

THE ENGRAVINGS ON WOOD BY JACKSON.

A NEW EDITION.

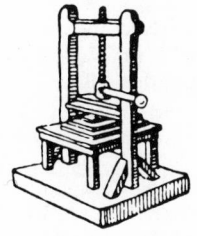

BURT FRANKLIN
NEW YORK

Published by BURT FRANKLIN
235 East 44th St., New York, N.Y. 10017
Originally Published: London 1839
Reprinted: 1968
Printed in the U.S.A.

Library of Congress Catalog Card No.: 68-58465
Burt Franklin: Research and Source Works Series 329
Essays in Literature and Criticism 22

PREFACE.

THE practice, and also the necessity of explaining the writings of Shakspeare, have already been so ably defended by former commentators, that no other apology on the part of those who may elect to persevere in this kind of labour seems to be necessary than with regard to the qualifications of the writer : but as no one in this case perhaps ever thought, or at least should think, himself incompetent to the task assumed of instructing or amusing others, it may be as well, on the present occasion, to waive altogether such a common-place intrusion on the reader's time. It is enough to state that accident had given birth to a considerable portion of the following pages, and that design supplied the rest. The late Mr. Steevens had

already in a manner too careless for his own reputation, and abundantly too favourable to his friend,
presented to public view such of the author's remarks
as were solely put together for the private use and
consideration of that able critic. The former wish of
their compiler has, with the present opportunity, been
accomplished ; that is, some of them withdrawn, and
others, it is hoped, rendered less exceptionable.

The readers of Shakspeare may be properly divided
into three classes. The first, as they travel through
the text, appeal to each explanation of a word or passage as it occurs. The second read a large portion of
the text, or perhaps the whole, uninterruptedly, and
then consult the notes ; and the third reject the illustrations altogether. Of these the second appear to
be the most rational. The last, with all their affectation, are probably the least learned, but will undoubtedly remain so ; and it may be justly remarked on this
occasion, in the language of the writer who has best
illustrated the principles of taste, that " the pride of
science is always meek and humble compared with the
pride of ignorance." He, who at this day can entirely
comprehend the writings of Shakspeare without the
aid of a comment, and frequently of laborious illustra-

tion, may be said to possess a degree of inspiration almost commensurate with that of the great bard himself. Mr. Steevens has indeed summed up every necessary argument in his assertion that " if Shakspeare is worth reading, he is worth explaining; and the researches used for so valuable and elegant a purpose, merit the thanks of genius and candour, not the satire of prejudice and ignorance."

The indefatigable exertions of Messrs. Steevens, Malone, Tyrwhitt, and Mason, will ever be duly appreciated by the true and zealous admirers of Shakspeare's pages. If the name of a celebrated critic and moralist be not included on this occasion, it is because he was certainly unskilled in the knowledge of obsolete customs and expressions. His explanatory notes therefore are, generally speaking, the most controvertible of any; but no future editor will discharge his duty to the public who shall omit a single sentence of this writer's masterly preface, or of his sound and tasteful characters of the plays of Shakspeare. Of all the commentators Dr. Warburton was surely the worst. His sentiments indeed have been seldom exhibited in modern editions but for the purpose of confuting them.

The wide dispersion of those materials which are essential to the illustration of inquiries like the present, will necessarily frustrate every endeavour at perfection; a circumstance that alone should teach every one discussing these difficult and obscure subjects, to speak of them with becoming diffidence. The present writer cannot flatter himself that he has uniformly paid a strict attention to this rule; the ardour of conjecture may have sometimes led him, in common with others, to forget the precepts he had himself laid down.

It may be thought by some, and even with great justice, that several of the corrections are trifling and unimportant; but even these may perhaps be endured wherever it shall be manifest that their object, and it is hoped their effect, has been to remove error and establish truth; a matter undoubtedly of some consequence in the school of criticism. One design of this volume has been to augment the knowledge of our popular customs and antiquities, in which respect alone the writings of Shakspeare have suggested better hints, and furnished ampler materials than those of any one besides. Other digressions too have been introduced, as it was conceived that they might ope-

rate in diminishing that tedium which usually results
from an attention to matters purely critical ; and that
whilst there was almost a certainty of supplying some
amusement, there might even be a chance of conveying instruction. Sometimes there has been a necessity for stepping in between two contending critics ;
and for showing, as in the case of many other disputes,
that both parties are in the wrong.

Some excuse may seem necessary for obtruding on
the reader so many passages from what Mr. Steevens
has somewhere called " books too mean to be formally
quoted." And yet the wisest among us may be often
benefited by the meanest productions of human in-
tellect, if, like medicinal poisons, they be administered
with skill. It had escaped the recollection of the
learned and accomplished commentator that he had
himself condescended to examine a multitude of
volumes of the above class, and even to use them with
advantage to his readers in the course of his notes.

With respect to what is often absurdly denominated
black letter learning, the taste which prevails in the
present times for this sort of reading, wherever true
scholarship and a laudable curiosity are found united,

will afford the best reply to the hyper-criticisms and impotent sarcasms of those who, having from indolence or ignorance neglected to cultivate so rich a field of knowledge, exert the whole of their endeavours to depreciate its value. Are the earlier labours of our countrymen, and especially the copious stores of information that enriched the long and flourishing reign of Elizabeth, to be rejected because they are recorded in a particular typography ?

Others again have complained of the redundancy of the commentators, and of an affected display of learning to explain terms and illustrate matters of obvious and easy comprehension. This may sometimes have been the case ; but it were easier to show that too little, and not too much, has been attempted on many of these occasions. An eminent critic has declared that " if every line of Shakspeare's plays were accompanied with a comment, every intelligent reader would be indebted to the industry of him who produced it." Shakspeare indeed is not more obscure than contemporary writers ; but he is certainly much better worth illustrating. The above objectors, affectedly zealous to detect the errors of other men, but more frequently betraying their own self-sufficiency and over-weening

importance, seem to forget that comments and illustrations are designed for the more ignorant class of
readers, who are always the most numerous ; and that
very few possess the happiness and advantage of being
wise or learned.

It might be thought that in the following pages ex-
emplifications of the senses of words have been sometimes unnecessarily introduced where others had already
been given ; but this has only been done where the
new ones were deemed of greater force or utility than
the others, or where they were supposed to be really
and intrinsically curious. Some of the notes will require that the *whole* of others which they advert to,
should be examined in Mr. Steevens's edition ; but
these were not reprinted, as they would have occupied
a space much too unreasonable.

At the end of every play in which a fool or clown is
introduced there will be found particular and discriminative notice of a character which some may regard
as by no means unworthy of such attention.

The Dissertations which accompany this work will,
it is hoped, not be found misplaced nor altogether

uninteresting. The subject of the first of them, though
often introduced into former notes on the plays of
Shakspeare and other dramatic writers, had been but
partially and imperfectly illustrated. The *Gesta Romanorum*, to which *The Merchant of Venice* has been
so much indebted for the construction of its story,
had, it is true, been already disserted on by Mr. Warton
with his accustomed elegance; but it will be found
that he had by no means exhausted the subject. The
morris dance, so frequently alluded to in our old plays,
seemed to require and deserve additional researches.

This preface shall not be concluded without em-
bracing the opportunity of submitting a very few hints
to the consideration of all future editors of Shakspeare.

It were much to be wished that the text of an author,
and more especially that of our greatest dramatic writer,
could be altered as seldom as possible by conjectural
emendation, or only where it is manifestly erroneous
from typographical causes. The readers of Dr. Bentley's notes on Milton will soon be convinced of the
inexpediency of the former of these practices, and of
what little importance are the conjectures of the mere

scholar, when unaccompanied by skill and judgement to direct them.

As the information on a particular subject has been hitherto frequently dispersed in separate notes, and consequently remains imperfect in each of them, would it not be more desirable to concentrate this scattered intelligence, or even to reduce it to a new form, to be referred to whenever necessary?

Although the strict restitution of the old orthography is not meant to be insisted on, nor would indeed accommodate the generality of readers, there are many instances in which it should be stated in the notes; and such will occur to every skilful editor.

Every word or passage that may be substituted in the text in the room of others to be found in any of the old editions should be printed in Italics, and assigned to its proper owner, with a reason for its preference to the originals. The mention of variations in the old copies must of course be left to an editor's discretion. No disparagement is meant to the memory or talents of one of the greatest of men, when a protest is here entered against " the text of Dr. Johnson."

It is to be regretted that all editions of Shakspeare, as well as of other dramatic writers, have not marginal references to the acts and scenes of each play. Those of Bell and Stockdale are, in this respect, pre-eminently useful. The time and trouble that would be saved in consulting them would be very consider-able.

The Edition of Shakspeare used in the compilation of this volume, and to which the pages cited refer, is the last published by Mr. Steevens himself, in fifteen volumes 8vo, 1793 ; but in order to facilitate a reference to most other editions, the acts and scenes of the plays are specified.

ILLUSTRATIONS

OF

SHAKSPEARE.

THE TEMPEST.

ACT I.

SCENE 1. Page 9.

ANT. We are *merely* cheated of our lives——

MR. STEEVENS has remarked that *merely* in this place signifies *absolutely*. His interpretation is confirmed by the word *merus* in Littelton's dictionary, where it is rendered *downright*.

SCENE 2. Page 10.

MIRA. . . . . . . a brave vessel,
Who had, no doubt, some *noble creatures* in her.

There is a peculiar propriety in this expression that has escaped the notice it deserved. Miranda had as yet seen no other *man* than her father. She had perceived, but indistinctly, some living creatures perish in the shipwreck; and she supposes they might be of her father's species. Thus she afterwards, when speaking of Ferdinand, calls him *noble*.

SCENE 2. Page 11.

MIRA. . . . . or *e'er*
It should the good ship, &c.

This word should always be written *ere*, and not *ever*, nor contractedly *e'er*, with which it has no connection. It is pure Saxon, æɲ. The corruption in Ecclesiastes cited in the note, is as old as the time of Henry the Eighth ; but in Wicliffe we have properly " *er* be to broke the silveren corde," and so it is given by Chaucer.

SCENE 2.   Page 20.

PRO. Bore us some leagues to sea; where they prepar'd
A rotten carcass of a boat, not rigg'd,
Nor tackle, sail, nor mast——

The present note is more particularly offered to the admirers of ancient romances, and to which class Shakspeare himself, no doubt, belonged. It is well known that the earliest English specimen of these singular and fascinating compositions is the *Geste of king Horn*, which has been faithfully published by the late Mr. Ritson, who has given some account of a French copy in the British Museum. He did not live to know that another manuscript of this interesting romance, in the same language, is still remaining in private hands, very different in substance and construction from the other. One might almost conclude that some English translation of it existed in Shakspeare's time, and that he had in the above passage imitated the following description of the boat in which Horn and his companions were put by king Rodmund at the suggestion of Browans,

" Sire, fet il purnez un de vos vielz chalanz
Metez icels valez ki jo vei ici estanz
Kil naient avirun dunt ascient aidanz
Sigle ne guvernad dunt il seint vaianz."   l. 58.

That is,

" Sir, said he, take one of your old boats, put into it these varlets whom I see here ; let them have no oars to help them, sail nor rudder to put them in motion."

SCENE 2.   Page 26.

ARI.   .   .   .   .   . sometimes I'd *divide*
And burn in many places; on the top-mast,
The yards and bowsprit, would I flame distinctly,
Then *meet and join*——

This is a very elegant description of a meteor well known to sailors. It has been called by the several names of the fire of

Saint Helen, Saint Elm, Saint Herm, Saint Clare, Saint Peter, and *Saint Nicholas.* Whenever it appeared as a single flame it was supposed by the ancients to be *Helena,* the sister of Castor and Pollux, and in this state to bring ill luck, from the calamities which this lady is known to have caused in the Trojan war. When it came double it was called Castor and Pollux, and accounted a good omen. It has been described as a little blaze of fire, sometimes appearing by night on the tops of soldiers' lances, or at sea on masts and sail-yards whirling and leaping in a moment from one place to another. Some have said, but erroneously, that it never appears but *after* a tempest. It is also supposed to lead people to suicide by drowning.

Further information on the subject may be collected from Plin. *Hist. nat.* l. ii. c. 37. Seneca *Quæst. nat.* c. 1. Erasm. *Colloq. in naufragio.* Schotti. *Physica curiosa,* p. 1209. Menage *Dict. etym.* v. *Saint Telme.* Cotgrave *Dict.* v. *feu, furole.* Trevoux *Dict.* v. *furole. Lettres de* Bergerac, p. 45. Eden's *Hist. of travayle,* fo. 432 b. 433 b. Camerarii *Horæ subsecivæ* iii. 53. Cambray *Voy. dans la Finisterre* ii. 296. Swan's *Speculum mundi* p. 89. Shakspeare seems to have consulted Stephen Batman's *Golden books of the leaden goddes,* who, speaking of Castor and Pollux, says " they were figured like two lampes or cresset lightes, one on the toppe of a maste, the other on the stemme or foreshippe." He adds that if the light first appears in the stem or foreship and ascends upwards, it is good luck; if *either lights begin at the top-mast, bowsprit* or foreship, and descend towards the sea, *it is a sign of tempest.* In taking therefore the latter position, Ariel had fulfilled the commands of Prospero to raise a storm.

SCENE 2. Page 28.

Ari. From the stili-vext *Bermoothes*——

The voyage of Sir George Sommers to the Bermudas in the year 1609 has been already noticed with a view of ascertaining the *time* in which *The tempest* was written ; but the important particulars of his *shipwreck*, from which it is exceedingly probable that the outline of a considerable part of this play was borrowed, has been unaccountably overlooked. Several contemporary narratives of the above event were published, which Shakspeare might have consulted ; and the conversation of the time might have furnished, or at least suggested, some particulars that are not to be found in any of the printed accounts. In 1610 Silvester Jourdan, an eyewitness, published *A discovery of the Barmudas, otherwise called the* ISLE OF DIVELS : *By Sir Thomas Gates, Sir Geo. Sommers, and Captayne Newport, with divers others.* Next followed Strachey's *Proceedings of the English colonie in Virginia* 1612, 4to, and some other pamphlets of less moment. From these accounts it appears that the Bermudas had never been inhabited, but regarded as *under the influence of inchantment*; though an addition to a subsequent edition of Jourdan's work gravely states that they are *not inchanted*; that Sommers's ship had been *split* between two rocks ; that during his stay on the island several *conspiracies* had taken place ; and that a *sea-monster in shape like a man* had been seen, who had been so called after the *monstrous tempests* that often happened at Bermuda. In Stowe's Annals we have also an account of Sommers's shipwreck, in which this important passage occurs, " Sir George Sommers sitting at the stearne, sceing the ship desperate of reliefe, looking every minute when the ship would sinke, hee espied land, which according to his and Captaine Newport's opinion, they judged it should be that dreadfull coast of the *Bermodes,* which iland were of all nations said and supposed to bee *inchanted and inhabited with witches and devills,* which grew by reason of accustomed monstrous thunder, storm, and *tempest,* neere unto those ilands, also for that the whole coast is so wonderous dangerous of rockes, that few can approach them, but with unspeakable hazard of *ship-wrack.*" Now if some of these circumstances

in the shipwreck of Sir George Sommers be considered, it
may possibly turn out that *they* are "the particular and recent event which determined Shakspeare to call his play *The
tempest*,"* instead of "the great tempest of 1612," which
has already been supposed to have suggested its name, and
which might have happened after its composition. If this
be the fact the play was written between 1609 and 1614
when it was so illiberally and invidiously alluded to in Ben
Jonson's Bartholomew-fair.

Scene 2. Page 30.

Pro. What is't thou can'st demand?
Ari. . . . . My liberty.
Pro. Before the time be out? no more.

The spirits or familiars attending on magicians were always impatient of confinement. Thus we are told that the
spirit Balkin is wearied if the action wherein he is employed
continue longer than an hour; and therefore the magician
must be careful to dismiss him. The form of such a dismis-
sion may be seen in Scot's *Discovery of witchcraft*, edit. 1665,
folio, p. 228.

Scene 2. Page 35.

Pro. . . . . . My *quaint* Ariel.

Quaint here means *brisk, spruce, dexterous*. From the
French *cointe*.

Scene 2. Page 35.

Cal. As wicked dew as e'er my mother brush'd
With raven's feather from unwholsome fen,
Drop on you both! a south-west blow on you,
And blister you all o'er!

The following passage in Batman *uppon Bartholome his
booke De proprietatibus rerum*, 1582, folio, will not only
throw considerable light on these lines, but furnish at the
same time grounds for a conjecture that Shakspeare was in-

* See Malone's *Shaksp.* vol. i. part i. p. 379.

debted to it, with a slight alteration, for the name of Caliban's
mother Sycorax the witch. " The raven is called corvus of
CORAX . . . . . . it is said that *ravens birdes* be fed with
deaw of heaven all the time that they have no black *feathers*
by benefite of age." Lib. xii. c. 10. The same author will
also account for the choice which is made, in the monster's
speech, of the *South-west wind.* " This *Southern wind* is hot
and moyst. . . . . . . *Southern winds* corrupt and destroy ;
they heat and maketh men fall into sicknesse." Lib. xi. c. 3.
It will be seen in the course of these notes that Shakspeare
was extremely well acquainted with this work ; and as it is
likely hereafter to form an article in a Shakspearean library,
it may be worth adding that in a private diary written at the
time, the original price of the volume appears to have been
eight shillings.

SCENE 2.   Page 36.

PRO. . . . . *urchins*
   Shall, for that vast of night that they may work,
   All exercise on thee.

Although *urchins* sometimes means hedge-hogs, it is more
probable that in this place they denote fairies or spirits, and that
Mr. Malone is right in the explanation which he has given.
The present writer's former note must therefore be cancelled,
as should, according to his conception, such part of Mr.
Steevens's as relates to the hedge-hog. The same term both
in the next act, and in the *Merry Wives of Windsor,* is used
in a similar sense.

Mr. Steevens in a note on this word in the last mentioned
play has observed that the *primitive* sense of *urchin* is a hedge-
hog, whence it came, says he, to signify any thing dwarfish.
There is however good reason for supposing it of Celtic origin. *Erch* in Welsh, is *terrible,* and *urzen,* a *superior intelligence.* In the Bas Breton language *urcha* signifies to *howl.*
" *Urthinwad Elgin,*" says Scot in his Discovery of witchcraft,
p. 224, edit. 1665, " was a spirit in the days of King Solomon,

came over with Julius Cæsar, and remained many hundred years in Wales, where he got the above name."

The *urchin* or *irchin*, in the sense of a hedge-hog, is certainly derived from the Latin *ericeus*; and whoever is desirous of more information concerning the radical of *ericeus* may be gratified by consulting Vossius's *Etymologicon* v. *erinaceus.* With respect to the application of urchin to any thing dwarf-ish, for we still say a *little urchin*, this sense of the word seems to have originated rather from the circumstance of its having once signified a fairy, who is always supposed to be a diminu-tive being, than from the cause assigned by Mr. Steevens.

It is true that in the ensuing act Caliban speaks of Pros-pero's *spirits* as attacking him *in the shape of hedge-hogs*, for which another reason will be offered presently ; and yet the word in question is only one out of many used by Shakspeare, which may be best disposed of by concluding that he de-signed they should be taken in both or either of their senses.

In a very rare old collection of songs set to music by John Bennett, Edward Piers or Peirce, and Thomas Ravenscroft, composers in the time of Shakspeare, and entitled *Hunting, hawking, dauncing, drinking, enamoring,* 4to, no date, there are, the *fairies* dance, the *elves* dance, and the *urchins* dance. This is the latter :

> " By the moone we sport and play,
>   With the night begins our day ;
> As we friske the dew doth fall,
>   Trip it little *urchins* all,
> Lightly as the little bee,
>   Two by two, and three by three,
> And about goe wee, goe wee."

SCENE 2. Page 40.

CAL. It would control my dam's God *Setebos.*

In Dr. Farmer's note it should have been added that the passage from Eden's *History of travayle* was part of Magel-lan's *Voyage*; or in Mr. Tollet's, that Magellan was included in Eden's collection.

SCENE 2. Page 42.

ARI. Those are pearls, that were his eyes.

We had already had this image in King Richard the third, where Clarence, describing his dream, says :

> " . . . . . in those holes
> Where eyes did once inhabit, there were crept
> (As 'twere in scorn of eyes) reflecting gems."

SCENE 2. Page 44.

MIRA. . . . . . . What is't, a spirit ?
Lord, how it looks about! Believe me, sir,
It carries a brave form.

The incident of Miranda's surprise at the first sight of Ferdinand, and of her falling in love with him, might have been suggested by some lost translation of the 13th tale in the *Cento novelle antiche,* and which is in fact the subject of *father Philip's geese,* so admirably told by Boccaccio and Lafontaine. It seems to have been originally taken from the life of Saint Barlaam in *The golden legend.*

ACT II.

SCENE 1. Page 54.

GON. How *lush* and lusty the grass looks !

Lush, as Mr. Malone observes, has not yet been rightly interpreted. It is, after all, an old word synonymous with *loose.* In the *Promptuarium parvulorum* 1516, 4to, we find " *lushe or slacke, laxus.*" The quotation from Golding, who renders *turget* by this word, confirms the foregoing definition, and demonstrates that as applied to grass, it means *loose or swollen,* thereby expressing the state of that vegetable when, the fibres being relaxed, it expands to its fullest growth.

SCENE 2. Page 76.

CAL. Sometime like *apes,* that moe and chatter at me
And after bite me ; then like *hedge-hogs,* which
Lie *tumbling* in my barefoot way——

Shakspeare, who seems to have been well acquainted with

Bishop Harsnet's *Declaration of Popish impostures*, has here recollected that part of the work where the author, speaking of the supposed possession of young girls, says, "they make anticke faces, *girn, mow and mop like an ape, tumble like a hedge-hogge,* &c." Another reason for the introduction of urchins or hedge-hogs into this speech is, that on the first discovery of the Bermudas, which, as has been already stated, gave rise in part to this play, they were supposed to be " haunted as all men know with *hogs* and hobgoblings." See Dekkar's *Strange horserace,* &c. sign. f. 3. b. and Mr. Steevens's note in p. 28.

SCENE 2. Page 77.

TRIN. A strange fish! Were I in England now (as once I was) and had but this fish painted, not a holiday fool there but would give a piece of silver: there would this monster make a man; any strange beast there makes a man : when they will not give a doit to relieve a lame beggar, they will lay out ten to see a dead Indian.

This speech happily ridicules the mania that appears to have always existed among our countrymen for beholding strange sights, however trifling. A contemporary writer and professor of divinity has been no less severe. Speaking of the crocodile, he says, " Of late years there hath been brought into England, the cases or skinnes of such crocodiles to be seene, and much money given for the sight thereof; the policy of strangers laugh at our folly, either that we are too wealthy, or else that we know not how to bestow our money." Batman *uppon Bartholome,* fo. 359 b.

SCENE 2. Page 82.

STE. This *mooncalf.*

The best account of this fabulous substance may be found in Drayton's poem with that title.

SCENE 2. Page 83.

STE. I was the *man in the moon.*

This is a very old superstition founded, as Mr. Ritson has

observed, on *Numbers* xv. 32. See *Ancient songs*, p. 34. So far the tradition is still preserved among nurses and school-boys ; but how the culprit came to be imprisoned in the moon, has not yet been accounted for. It should seem that he had not merely gathered sticks on the sabbath, but that he had *stolen* what he gathered, as appears from the following lines in Chaucer's *Testament of Creseid*, where the poet, describing the moon, informs us that she had

> " On her brest a chorle painted ful even,
> Bearing a bush of thorns on his backe,
> Which for his *theft* might clime no ner the heven."

We are to suppose that he was doomed to perpetual con-finement in this planet, and precluded from every possibility of inhabiting the mansions of the just. With the Italians Cain appears to have been the offender, and he is alluded to in a very extraordinary manner by Dante in the twentieth canto of the *Inferno*, where the moon is described by the pe-riphrasis *Caino e le spine*. One of the commentators on that poet says, that this alludes to the popular opinion of Cain loaded with the bundle of faggots, but how he procured them we are not informed. The Jews have some Talmudical story that Jacob is in the moon, and they believe that his face is visible. The natives of Ceylon, instead of a man, have placed a hare in the moon ; and it is said to have got there in the following manner. Their great Deity Budha when a hermit on earth lost himself one day in a forest. After wan-dering about in great distress he met a hare, who thus ad-dressed him : " It is in my power to extricate you from your difficulty ; take the path on your right hand, and it will lead you out of the forest." " I am greatly obliged to you, Mr. Hare," said Budha, "but I am unfortunately very poor and very hungry, and have nothing to offer you in reward for your kindness." " If you are hungry," returned the hare, " I am again at your service ; make a fire, kill me, roast me, and eat me." Budha made the fire, and the hare instantly jumped into it. Budha now exerted his miraculous powers, snatched the animal from the flames, and threw him into the moon, where he has ever since remained. This is from the information of a learned and intelligent French gentleman recently arrived from Ceylon, who adds that the Cingalese would often request of him to permit them to look for the hare through his telescope, and exclaim in raptures, that they saw it. It is remarkable that the Chinese represent the moon by a rabbit pounding rice in a mortar. Their mythological moon Jut-ho is figured by a beautiful young woman with a double sphere behind her head, and a rabbit at her feet. The period of this animal's gestation is thirty days ; may it not therefore typify the moon's revolution round the earth ?

Scene 2. Page 86.

Cal. Nor *scrape-trenchering*, nor wash-dish.

Scraping trenchers was likewise a scholastic employment at college, if we may believe the illiterate parson in the pleasant comedy of *Cornelianum dolium*, where speaking of his haughty treatment of the poor scholars whom he had distanced in getting possession of a fat living, he says, " Illi inquam, qui ut mihi narrârunt, quadras adipe illitas deglubere sunt coacti, quamdiu inter academicas ulnas manent, dapsili more à me nutriti sunt, saginati imò &c." It was the office too of apprentices. In *The life of a satirical puppy called Nim*, 1657, 12mo, a citizen describes how long " he bore the water tankard, *scrap't trenchers*, and made clean shoes."

ACT III.

Scene 1. Page 91.

Fer. This wooden slavery, than *I would* suffer.

The old copy reads *than to suffer*, which, however ungrammatical, is justly maintained by Mr. Malone to be Shakspeare's language, and ought therefore to be restored.   Mr. Steevens objects on the score of *defective* metre: but this is not the case; the metre, however rugged, is certainly *perfect*.

Scene 1.   Page 92.

MIRA. I am your wife, if you will marry me ;
    If not, I'll die your maid : to be your fellow
    You may deny me ; but I'll be your servant
    Whether you will or no.

Mr. Malone has cited a very apposite passage from Catullus, but Shakspeare had probably on this occasion the pathetic old poem of *The nut-brown maid* in his recollection.

Scene 2.   Page 94.

STE. Thy eyes are almost set in thy head.
TRIN. Where should they be set else? he were a brave monster
    indeed, if they were *set in his tail*.

The curious reader may nevertheless be gratified with a ludicrous instance of *eyes set in the tail*, if he can procure a sight of the first cut in Caxton's edition of *Æsop's fables*. In the mean time he is referred to the *genuine* chap. xx. of Planudes's life of that fabulist, which is generally omitted in the modern editions.

Scene 2.   Page 97.

CAL. What a py'd ninny's this? thou scurvy patch!

Dr. Johnson would transfer this speech to Stephano, on the ground that Caliban could know nothing of the costume of fools. This objection is fairly removed by Mr. Malone; besides which it may be remarked that at the end of the play Caliban specifically calls Trinculo a *fool*. The modern managers will perhaps be inclined for the future to dress this character in the proper habit.

Scene 2.   Page 100.

CAL. Will you *troll* the catch——

Troll is from the French *trôler*, to *lead*, *draw*, or *drag*, and this sense particularly applies to a catch, in which one part is sung after the other, one of the singers leading off. The term is *sometimes* used as Mr. Steevens has explained it. Littelton renders *to troll along his words*, by *volubiliter loqui sive rotundè*. *Trolling* for fish, is drawing the bait along in the water, to imitate the swimming of a real fish.

Scene 2. Page 104.

SEB. . . . . in *Arabia*
  There is one tree, the Phœnix' throne, *one phœnix*
  At this hour reigning there.

Bartholomæus *De propriet. rerum*, speaking of *Arabia*, says, " there breedeth a birde that is called *Phœnix;*" and from what has already been said of this book, it was probably *one* of Shakspeare's authorities on the occasion.

Scene 2. Page 106.

GON. Who would believe that there were mountaineers,
  Dewlapp'd like bulls, whose throats had hanging at them
  Wallets of flesh? or that there were such men,
  Whose heads stood in their breasts ?

The " dewlapp'd mountaineers" are shown to have been borrowed from Maundeville's travels, and the same author doubtless supplied the other monsters. In the edition printed by Thomas Este, without date, is the following passage : " In another ile dwell men that have no heads, and their eyes are in their shoulders, *and their mouth is on their breast.*" A cut however which occurs in this place is more to the purpose, and might have saved our poet the trouble of consulting the text, for it represents a complete head with eyes, nose, and mouth, placed on the breast and stomach.

ACT IV.

SCENE 1. Page 122.

CER.   Hail many-coloured messenger, that ne'er
       Dost disobey the wife of Jupiter ;
       Who with thy saffron wings upon my flowers
       Diffusest honey-drops, refreshing showers ;
       And with each end of thy blue bow dost crown
       My bosky acres——

An elegant expansion of these lines in Phaer's *Virgil. Æn.*
end of book 4.

> " Dame rainbow down therefore with safron wings of dropping
>   showres.
> Whose face a thousand sundry hewes against the sunne devoures,
> From heaven descending came——"

SCENE 1. Page 131.

ARI.   . . . . . so I charm'd their ears,
       That calf-like, they my lowing follow'd through
       Tooth'd briers, sharp furzes, pricking goss and thorns
       Which enter'd their frail skins.

Dr. Johnson has introduced a passage from Drayton's
Nymphidia, as resembling the above description.   It is still
more like an incident in the well known story of the *friar and
the boy.*

> " Jacke toke his pype and began to blowe
>   Then the frere, as I trowe,
>   Began to daunce soone ;
>   The breres scratched hym in the face
>   And in many another place
>   That the blode brast out,
>   He daunced among thornes thycke
>   In many places they dyde hym prycke, &c."

SCENE 1. Page 136.

CAL. And all be turn'd to *barnacles,* or apes.

Mr. Collins's note, it is presumed, will not be thought
worth retaining in any future edition.   His account of the
barnacle is extremely confused and imperfect.   He makes
Gerarde responsible for an opinion not his own ; he sub-

stitutes the name of Holinshed for that of Harrison, whose statement is not so ridiculous as Mr. Collins would make it, and who might certainly have seen the feathers of the barnacles hanging out of the shells, as the *fish barnacle* or *Lepas anatifera* is undoubtedly furnished with a *feathered* beard. The real absurdity was the credulity of Gerarde and Harrison in supposing that the barnacle goose was really produced from the shell of the fish. Dr. Bullein not only believed this himself, but bestows the epithets, *ignorant* and *incredulous* on those who did not ; and in the same breath he maintains that crystal is nothing more than ice. See his *Bulwarke of defence*, &c. 1562, Folio, fo. 12. Caliban's barnacle is the *clakis* or tree-goose. Every kind of information on the subject may be found in the *Physica curiosa* of Gaspar Schot the Jesuit, who with great industry has collected from a multitude of authors whatever they had written concerning it. See lib. ix. c. 22. The works of Pennant and Bewick will supply every deficiency with respect to *rational* knowledge.

ACT V.

Scene 1. Page 140.

Pro. Ye *elves* of hills——

The different species of the fairy tribe are called in the Northern languages *ælfen, elfen,* and *alpen,* words of remote and uncertain etymology. The Greek ολβιος, *felix,* is not so plausible an original as the Teutonic *helfen, juvare*; because many of these supernatural beings were supposed to be of a mischievous nature, but all of them might very properly be invoked to assist mankind. Some of the northern nations regarded them as the souls of men who in this world had given themselves up to corporeal pleasures, and trespasses against human laws. It was conceived therefore that they were doomed to wander for a certain time about the earth, and to

be bound in a kind of servitude to mortals.   One of their
occupations was that of protecting horses in the stable.   See
Olaus Magnus *de gentibus septentrionalibus,* lib. iii. cap. xi.
It is probable that our fairy system is originally derived from
the Fates, Fauns, Nymphs, Dryads, Deæ matres, &c., of the
ancients, in like manner as other Pagan superstitions were
corruptedly retained after the promulgation of Christianity.
The general stock might have been augmented and improved
by means of the crusades and other causes of intercourse with
the nations of the East.

SCENE 1.   Page 141.

PRO. . . . . . . you demy-puppets, that
>>By moonshine do the *green-sour* ringlets make,
>>Whereof the ewe not bites——

Green sour, if the genuine reading, should be given, as in
the first folio, without a hyphen ; for such a *compound* epithet
will not elsewhere be easily discovered.   Though a real or
supposed acidity in this kind of grass will certainly warrant
the use of *sour,* it is not improbable that Shakspeare might
have written *greensward,* i. e. the green surface of the ground,
from the Saxon ᵹᵽᴇᴀᵽᴃ, skin.

SCENE 1.   Page 158.

PRO. His mother was a witch ; and one so strong
>>*That could control the moon.*

So in a former scene, Gonzalo had said, " You are gentlemen of brave mettle ; you would *lift the moon out of her
sphere,* &c."   In Adlington's translation of *Apuleius* 1596,
4to, a book well known to Shakspeare, a marginal note says,
" Witches in old time were supposed to be of such power
that they could pul downe *the moone by their inchauntment.*"
In Fleminge's *Virgil's Bucolics* is this line, " Charms able arc
from heaven high to fetch the moone adowne ;" and see
Scot's *Discoverie of witchcraft* 1584, 4to, pp. 174, 226, 227,
250.

But all the above authorities are from the ancients, the system of modern witchcraft not affording any similar instances of its power. The Jesuit Delrio is willing to put up with any notice of this superstition among heathen writers, but is extremely indignant to find it mentioned by a Christian; contending that it exclusively belongs to the ancients. *Disquis. magic.* lib. ii. quæst. xi. The following classical references may not be unacceptable. The earliest on the list will be that in Aristophanes's *Clouds,* where Strepsiades proposes the hiring of a Thessalian witch to bring down the moon and shut her in a box that he might thus evade paying his debts by the month.

" Quæ sidera excantata voce Thessalâ
   Lunamque cœlo deripit."   Horat. *epod.* v.

" *Deripere lunam* vocibus possum meis."   Horat. *epod.* xvii.

" Et jam *luna negat toties descendere cœlo."*   Propert. II. *el.* 28.

" Cantus et *é curru lunam deducere* tentat
   Et faceret, si non ære repulsa sonent."
        Tibull. I. *el.* 8. and see *el.* 2.

. . . . " *Phœbeque serena*
Non aliter diris verborum obsessa venenis
Palluit, et nigris, terrenisque ignibus arsit,
Et patitur tantos *cantu depressa* labores
Donec suppositas propior despumet in herbas."＊   Lucan vi.

" Mater erat Mycale; quam *deduxisse canendo*
  Sæpe reluctanti constabat *cornua lunæ."*   Ovid. *Metam.* l. xii.

" Illa reluctantem *curru deducere lunam*
  Nititur" . . . .   Ovid. *epist.* vi.

" Sic *te* regentem frena nocturni ætheris
  Detrahere nunquam *Thessali cantus* queant."
        Senec. *Hippolyt.* Act. 2.

" Mulieres etiam lunam deducunt."   Petron. Hadrianid. 468.

In the same author the witch Enothea, describing her power, says, *"Lunæ descendit imago, carminibus deducta meis."* p. 489.

It is said that Menanda wrote a play called *the Thessalian,*

＊ The last line is a good comment on the "lunam despumari" of Apuleius speaking of the effects of magical mutterings.

in which were contained the several incantations used by witches to draw the moon from the heavens.

So when the moon was eclipsed, the Romans supposed it was from the influence of magical charms; to counteract which, as well as those already enumerated, they had recourse to the sound of brazen implements of all kinds. Juvenal alludes to this practice when he describes his talkative woman.

" .   .   Jam nemo tubas, nemo æra fatiget,
   Una laboranti *poterit succurrere lunæ.*"   *Sat.* vi. 441.

And see particularly Macrob. *Saturnal.* l. v. c. 19. It is not improbable that the rattling of the sistrum by the priests of Isis, or the moon, may be in some way or other connected with this practice, or have even been its origin.

In proportion to the advance of science, it will, no doubt, be found that the Greeks and Romans borrowed more than is commonly imagined from the nations of the East, where the present practice seems to have been universal. Thus the Chinese believe that during eclipses of the sun and moon these celestial bodies are attacked by a great serpent, to drive away which they strike their gongs or brazen drums; the Turks and even some of the American Indians entertain the same opinion. This is perhaps a solution of the common subject on Chinese porcelain, of a dragon pursuing a ball of fire, the symbol of the sun. The Hindoos suppose that a serpent, born from the head of a giant slain by Vishnu, is permitted by that deity to attack the sun. Krishna the Hindoo sun is sometimes represented combating this monster, whence the Greek story of Apollo and the serpent Python may have been derived.

THE FOOL.

The character of Trinculo, who in the *dramatis personæ* is called a *jester,* is not very well discriminated in the course of

the play itself. As he is only associated with Caliban and the drunken butler, there was no opportunity of exhibiting him in the legitimate character of a professed fool; but at the conclusion of the play it appears that he was in the service of the king of Naples as well as Stephano. On this account therefore, and for the reasons already offered in page 20, he must be regarded as an allowed domestic buffoon, and should be habited on the stage in the usual manner.

TWO GENTLEMEN OF VERONA.

ACT I.

Scene 1. Page 170.

Pro. For I will be thy *beadsman*, Valentine.

A beadsman is one who offers up prayers to heaven for the welfare of another. Many of the ancient petitions to great men were addressed to them by their " poor daily orators and beadsmen." *To count one's beads*, means, in the Romish church, to offer up as many prayers to God and the Virgin Mary as the priest or some voluntary penance or obligation shall have enjoined; and that no mistake may happen in the number, they are reckoned by means of certain balls strung in a kind of chaplet, and hence in the English language termed *beads*, from the Saxon beab, a prayer. There is much difference of opinion among ecclesiastical writers as to the origin of this practice. Some ascribe its invention to Peter the hermit in the eleventh century, others to Venerable Bede, misled probably by the affinity of the name. Monsieur Fleury more rationally conceives it to be not older than the eleventh century ; but the probability is, that it was imported into Europe by the crusaders, who found it among the Mahometans. The latter use it wherever their religion has been planted, and there is even reason for supposing that it originated among the natives of Hindostan. These chaplets made of beads are called *rosaries* when they are used in prayers to the Virgin. The term *bead*, as applied to the materials of which necklaces, &c. are made, seems therefore to have been borrowed from the chaplet of rosaries in question.

Scene 1. Page 171.

Pro. Over the boots? Nay, *give me not the boots.*

An allusion, as it is supposed, to the diabolical torture of the boot. Not a great while before this play was written, it had been inflicted in the presence of King James on one Dr. Fian, a supposed wizard, who was charged with raising the storms that the King encountered in his return from Denmark. In the very curious pamphlet which contains the account of this transaction it is stated that " hee was with all convenient speed, by commandement, convaied againe to the *torment of the bootes,* wherein he continued a long time, and did abide so many blowes in them, that his legges were crushte and beaten togeather as small as might bee, and the bones and flesh so brused, that the bloud and marrowe spouted forth in great abundance, whereby they were made unserviceable for ever." The unfortunate man was afterwards burned. But the above instrument of torture was not, as suggested in one of the notes on this occasion, " used only in Scotland ;" it was known in France, and in all probability imported from that country. The following representation of it is copied from Millæus's *Praxis criminis persequendi,* Paris, 1541, folio. This instrument of torture continued to be used in Scotland so late as the end of the 17th century. See *A hind let loose,* 1687, 8vo, pp. 186, 198, in the frontispiece to which work there is an indistinct representation of the boot. It is said to have been imported from Russia by a Scotchman. See Maclaurin's *Arguments in remarkable cases,* 4to, p. xxxvii.

SCENE 1. Page 171.

VAL. . . . . To be

> In love, where scorn is bought with groans : coy looks,
> With heart-sore sighs ; one fading moment's mirth,
> With twenty watchful, weary, tedious nights :
> If haply won, perhaps a hapless gain ;
> If lost, why then a grievous labour won ;
> However, but a folly bought with wit,
> Or else a wit by folly vanquished.

Thus explained by Dr. Johnson. "This love will end in a *foolish action*, to produce which you are long to spend your *wit*, or it will end in the loss of your wit, which will be overpowered by the folly of love ;" an explanation that is in part very questionable. The poet simply means that love itself is sometimes a foolish object dearly attained in exchange for reason ; at others the human judgment subdued by folly. He is speaking of love abstractedly, and not alluding to that of Proteus.

Scene 1. Page 178.

Speed. I thank you, you have *testern'd* me.

Mr. Holt White's information from a passage in Latimer's sermons, that the tester was then worth *more* than *six-pence*, is so far correct; but as an inference might be drawn from the quotation that it was actually worth *ten-pence*, it becomes necessary to state that at that time, viz. in 1550, the tester was worth *twelve-pence*. It is presumed that no accurate account of this piece of coin has been hitherto given; and therefore the following attempt, which has been attended with no small labour, may not be unacceptable.

The term, variously written, *teston, tester, testern*, and, in *Twelfth night, testril*, is from the French *teston*, and so called from the king's head, which first appeared on this coin in the reign of Louis XII. A. D. 1513, though the Italians seem previously to have had a coin of the same denomination. In our own country the name was first applied to the English shilling (originally coined by Henry the Seventh) at the beginning of the reign of Henry the Eighth, probably because it resembled in value the French coin above described; so that *shilling* and *teston* were at that time synonymous terms. Although the teston underwent several reductions in value, it appears to have been worth twelve-pence at the beginning of Edward the Sixth's reign, from three several proclamations in his second and third years for calling in, and at length annihilating, this coin, on account of the forgeries that had been committed; Sir William Sharington having falsified it to the amount of 12,000*l.*, for which by an express act of parliament he was attainted of treason. In the above proclamations the testons are specifically described as " pieces of xiid commonly called testons;" and in the last of them, the possessors are allowed twelve-pence a-piece on bringing them to the mint. Sir Henry Spelman, who has asserted in his glossary that the teston was reduced to nine-pence in the *first*

year of King Edward, must be mistaken. Stowe more correctly informs us that on the 9th of July 1551 (the *fifth* year
of the King's reign), the base shillings of Henry VIII. and
Edward VI. were called down to *nine*-pence, and on the
17th of August following to *six*-pence. He afterwards, under the year 1559, cites a proclamation for reducing it still
lower, viz. to fourpence halfpenny. We must conclude that
it again rose in value as the coin became improved ; for it appears from *Twelfth night*, Act II. Scene 3, that it was in
Shakspeare's time the same as the six-pence, and it has probably continued ever since as another name for that coin.

Scene 2. Page 185.

JUL. I see you have a *month's mind* to them.

There is a great deal of quotation given in the notes, but
nothing after all that amounts to an explanation of the term.
It alludes to the mind or *remembrance* days of our Popish ancestors. Persons in their wills often directed that in a
month, or any other specific time, from the day of their decease, some solemn office for the repose of their souls, as a
mass or dirge, should be performed in the parish church, with
a suitable charity or benevolence on the occasion. Polydore
Vergil has shown that the custom is of Roman origin ; and he
seems to speak of the month's mind as a ceremony peculiar
to the English. *De rer. invent.* lib. vi. c. 10.

ACT II.

Scene 2. Page 201.

JUL. Keep this remembrance for thy Julia's sake.
                         [*giving a ring.*
PRO. Why then we'll make exchange ; here, take you this.
JUL. And seal the bargain with a holy kiss.

This was the mode of plighting troth between lovers in
private. It was sometimes done in the church with great
solemnity, and the service on this occasion is preserved in

some of the old rituals. To the latter ceremony the priest alludes in *Twelfth night*, Act V. Scene 1.

> " A contract of eternal bond of love
> Confirm'd by mutual joinder of your hands,
> Attested by the holy close of lips,
> Strengthen'd by interchangement of your rings, &c."

Scene 4. Page 210.

Sil. That you are welcome?
Pro. . . . . . . *No*; that you are worthless.

Dr. Johnson has here inserted the particle *no*, " to fill up the *measure;*" but the measure is not defective though the harmony is. Mr. Steevens, disputing the suggestion of a brother critic, that *worthless* might have been designed as a trisyllable, asks whether *worthless* in the preceding speech of Sylvia is a trisyllable? Certainly not; but he should have remembered the want of uniformity of metre in many words among the poets of this period. Thus in p. 223, lines 8 and 9, the word *fire* is alternately used as a monosyllable and dissyllable; and where the quantity is complete, as in the present instance, the harmony is often left to shift for itself.

ACT III.

Scene 1. Page 232.

Duke. Why Phaeton, (for thou *art* Merop's son)

It is far more likely that Shakspeare found this at the end of the first book of Golding's *Ovid's metamorphosis*, than in the authorities referred to in Mr. Steevens's note.

Scene 1. Page 239.

Laun. There; and *Saint Nicholas* be thy speed.

The true reason why this Saint was chosen to be the patron of Scholars may be gathered from the following story in his life, composed in French verse by *Maitre Wace*, chaplain to Henry the Second, remaining in manuscript but never printed.

It appears from a passage in Ordericus Vitalis, p. 598, that the metrical legends of Saints were sung by the Norman minstrels to the common people.

> " Treis clers aloent a escole,
> Nen frai mie longe parole ;
> Lor ostes par nuit les oscieit,
> Les cors musca, la . . . .* prenoit
> Saint Nicolas par Deu le sout,
> Sempris fut la si cum Deu plut,
> Les clers al oste demanda,
> Nes peut muscier einz lui mustra.
> Seint Nicolas par sa priere
> Les ames mist el cors ariere.
> Por ceo qe as clers fist tiel honor
> Font li clerc feste a icel jor."

That is, " Three scholars were on their way to school, (I shall not make a long story of it,) their host murdered them in the night, and hid their bodies; their . . . . he reserved. Saint Nicholas was informed of it by God Almighty, and according to his pleasure went to the place. He demanded the scholars of the host, who was not able to conceal them, and therefore showed them to him. Saint Nicholas, by his prayers, restored the souls to their bodies. Because he conferred such honour on scholars, they at this day celebrate a festival."

It is remarkable, that although the above story explains the common representation of the Saint, with three children in a tub, it is not to be found in that grand repertory of Monkish lies, *The Golden Legend.* It occurs, however, in an Italian life of Saint Nicholas, printed in 1645, whence it is extracted into the Gentleman's Magazine for 1777, p. 158. There is a note by Mr. Whalley on *Saint Nicholas's clerks,* as applied to *highwaymen,* in King Henry the Fourth, part the first, vol. viii. p. 418, which, though erroneously conceived, would have been more properly introduced on the present occasion. Standing where it does, the worthy author is made responsible for having converted the parish clerks of

* A word defaced in the manuscript.

London into a nest of thieves, which he certainly never
intended. Those respectable persons, finding that scholars,
more usually termed clerks, had placed themselves under the
patronage of Saint Nicholas, conceived that *clerks* of any
kind might have the same right, and accordingly took this
saint as *their* patron; much in the same way as the wool-
combers did Saint Blaise, who was martyred with an instrument resembling a curry-*comb*, the nail-makers Saint *Clou*,
and the booksellers Saint John Port-*Latin*.

Scene 2.   Page 246.

Pro. Especially against his *very* friend. ˋ

Mr. Steevens explains *very* to be *immediate*. Is it not
rather *true, verus*? Thus Massinger calls one of his plays *A
very woman*. See likewise the beginning of the Nicene creed.

ACT IV.

Scene 2.   Page 257.

Host. . . . . . . the musick *likes* you not.

i. e. *pleases*, in which sense it is used by Chaucer. This
is the genuine Saxon meaning of the word, however it might
have been corrupted in early times from its Latin original
licet. In the next speech Julietta plays upon the word.

Scene 2.   Page 258.

Sil. What is your will?
Pro. That I may compass yours.
Sil. You have your wish; my will is even this;—

On which Dr. Johnson observes, "The word *will* is here
ambiguous. He wishes to *gain* her *will*; she tells him, if he
wants her *will* he has it." The learned critic seems to have
mistaken the sense of the word *compass*, when he says it means
to gain. If it did, his remark would be just. But to *compass*
in this place signifies, to *perform, accomplish, take measures
for doing a thing*. Thus in *Twelfth night*, Act I. Scene 2,

" that were hard to *compass*;" and in 1. *Hen.* VI. Act V.
Scene 5, " You judge it impossible to *compass* wonders."
Accordingly Sylvia proceeds to instruct Proteus *how* he may
perform her will. *Wish* and *will* are here used, as in many
other places, though inaccurately, as synonymous. If however Shakspeare really designed to make Proteus say that he
was desirous of *gaining* Sylvia's good will, she must be supposed, in her reply, purposely to mistake his meaning.

Scene 2.   Page 260.

> Sil. But since your falshood shall *become* you well
>   To worship shadows, and adore false shapes.

Dr. Johnson objects to the sense of this passage, and the
other commentators offer conjectural interpretations; yet
surely nothing is more clear than the sense, and even the
grammar may be defended. It is simply, " since your falsehood shall *adapt or render you fit* to worship shadows."
Become here answers to the Latin *convenire*, and is used
according to its genuine Saxon meaning.

Scene 2.   Page 260.

> Host. By my *hallidom*, I was fast asleep.

This Mr. Ritson explains, *by my holy doom*, or *sentence at
the resurrection*, from the Saxon haliȝbom; but the word
does not appear to have had such a meaning. It rather signifies
holiness or honesty. It likewise denoted a sacrament, a
sanctuary, relics of saints, or anything holy. It seems in
later times to have been corrupted into *holidame*, as if it expressed the holy virgin. Thus we have *so help me God and
hollidame*. See Bullein's *Book of the use of sicke men*, 1579, in
folio, fo. 2 b.

Scene 4.   Page 270.

> Jul. But since she did neglect her looking-glass,
>   And threw her *sun-expelling mask* away.

It was the fashion at this time for the ladies to wear masks,
which are thus described by the puritanical Stubs in his

Anatomie of abuses, 1595, 4to, p. 59. " When they use to
ride abroad they have *masks and visors made of velvet* wherewith they cover all their faces, having holes made in them
against their eyes, whereout they looke. So that if a man
that knew not their guise before, should chaunce to meet one
of them, he would think he met a monster or a Devil, for
face he can shew (see) none, but two broad holes against
their eyes, with glasses in them." More will be said on the
subject of this mode of disguising the female face in a remark
on *The merry wives of Windsor*, Act IV. Scene 2.

SCENE 4.   Page 271.

> JUL. . . 't was Ariadne, passioning
>   For Theseus' perjury and unjust flight.

A note is here inserted, " not" says its learned and classical
author, " on the business of Shakspeare," but to introduce a
conjecture relating to one of Guido's paintings commonly
supposed to represent Ariadne as deserted by Theseus and
courted by Bacchus, but which he conceives to have been
intended for Bacchus's desertion of this lady for an Indian
captive. An attentive examination of the print from Guido's
picture will, it is presumed, incline any one to hesitate much
before he shall decide on having discerned any traces of an
Indian prince s ; and this supposed character may rather
turn out to be Venus introducing the amorous Deity, attended by his followers, to Ariadne, forlorn and abandoned
by Theseus in the isle of Chios, according to Ovid, or Naxos
according to Lactantius. Nor is the female who accompanies
Bacchus " hanging on his arm," as stated by the critic. It
is impossible likewise to perceive in this figure the modest
looks or demeanour of a female captive, or in the supposed
Bacchus the character of a lover, insulting, according to
Ovid's description, his former mistress by displaying the beau-
ties of another. Boccaccio has very comically accounted for
Ariadne's desertion by Theseus, and her subsequent transfer

to Bacchus. He supposes the lady to have been too fond of
the juice of the grape, and that on her continuing to indulge
this propensity, she was therefore called the wife of Bacchus.
See *Geneal. deor.* lib. xi. c. 29.

SCENE 4. Page 274.

JUL. Her eyes are *grey as glass.*

This was in old times the favourite colour of the eyes in
both sexes :

" His eyen are *gray* as any *glasse.*"

Romance of Sir Isenbras.

" Her eyen gray as glas."

Romance of Libeaus desconus.

" Les iex *vairs* et rians com un faucon."

Roman de Guerin de Montglaive. MS.

And to come nearer to Shakspeare's time :—In the interlude of *Marie Magdalene,* a song in praise of her says, " your
eyes as *gray* as glasse and right amiable." The French term
ver or *vair* has induced some of their antiquaries to suppose
that it meant *green* ; but it has been very satisfactorily shown
to signify in general the colour still called by heralds *vair.*
It is certain however that the French romances and other
authorities allude occasionally to *green* eyes.

SCENE 4. Page 274.

JUL. My substance should be *statue* in thy stead.

In confirmation of Mr. M. Mason's note, it may be observed that in the comedy of *Cornelianum dolium,* Act I.
Scene 5, *statua* is twice used for a picture. They were synonymous terms, and sometimes a statue was called a picture.
Thus Stowe, speaking of Elizabeth's funeral, says that when
the people beheld " her *statue or picture* lying upon the coffin" there was a general sighing, &c. *Annals,* p. 815, edit.
1631. In the glossary to Speght's *Chaucer,* 1598, *statue* is
explained *picture*; and in one of the inventories of King
Henry the Eighth's furniture at Greenwich, several *pictures*

of earth are mentioned.   These were busts in *terra cotta* like
those still remaining in Wolsey's palace at Hampton Court.

ACT V.

SCENE 1.   Page 276.

EGL. That Silvia *at Patrick's cell* should meet me.

The old copy reads " at *friar* Patrick's cell," which Mr.
Steevens calls a redundance, justifying his alteration by a
passage in the next scene, where " At Patrick's cell" occurs.
But the old reading is right, and should not have been disturbed, there being no redundance when it is judiciously read.
Silvia is often used as a dissyllable, and must here be read
elliptically.   Besides, we had "*friar* Patrick's cell" before
in p. 263.

SCENE 4.   Page 280.

VAL. And to the nightingale's complaining notes
Tune my distresses, and *record* my woes.

It has been already observed that this term refers to the
singing of birds.   It should have been added that it was
formed from the *recorder*, a sort of flute by which they were
taught to sing.

SCENE 4.   Page 286.

JUL. How oft hast thou with perjury *cleft* the root?

The speech had been begun with a metaphor from archery,
and is here continued in the same strain.   *To cleave the pin*,
was to break the nail which attached the mark to the butt.

SCENE 4.   Page 290.

Mr. Ritson's reply to Mr. Tyrwhitt.

However ingenious and even just the system in this reply
may be, it is evident that Shakspeare was not governed by it;
but, on the contrary, that he *has* taken the liberties pointed

out by **Mr. Tyrwhitt.** The proof is, 1. From the circumstance that none of Shakspeare's contemporaries have used similar words in such a protracted form. 2. Because he has used other words in the same manner which are not reducible to **Mr. Ritson's** system ; such as *country, assembly,* &c. He never troubled himself about establishing a canon of which he was, in all likelihood, altogether ignorant ; but occasionally took such liberties as his verses required. This is clearly manifested by his various use, in many instances, of the self-same words.

THE CLOWNS.

The character of Speed is that of a shrewd witty servant. Launce is something different, exhibiting a mixture of archness and rustic simplicity. There is no allusion to dress, nor any other circumstance, that marks either of them as the domestic fool or jester.

MERRY WIVES OF WINDSOR.

ACT I.

Scene. 1.   Page 309.

Slen. She has brown hair, and *speaks small like a woman.*

It may be doubted whether the *real humour* of this speech
has been pointed out.   Does it not consist in Slender's cha-
racterizing Ann Page by a property belonging to himself,
and which renders him ridiculous ?   The audience would naturally smile at hearing him deliver the speech in an effeminate tone of voice.

Scene 1.   Page 314.

Fal. But not kiss'd your keeper's daughter.

This has the appearance of a fragment of some old ballad.

Scene 1.   Page 317.

Pist. He hears with ears.
Eva. The tevil and his tam! what phrase is this, *he hears with ear?*
Why it is affectations.

If, according to Mr. Henderson, Sir Hugh be justified in
his censure of this phrase as a pleonasm, we must also censure the parson in his turn for having forgot that the common prayer would have furnished an example of Pistol's language.   See also *Jerem.* xxvi. 11.

Scene 1.   Page 317.

Slen. Seven groats in *mill-sixpences,* and two *Edward shovel-boards*
that cost me two shillings and twopence apiece.

These sixpences were coined in 1561, and are the first
milled money used in this kingdom.   The invention is due
to the French, and was introduced here by a native of France,
who misapplied his talents by private coining, and suffered

the penalty of the law.   That seven groats could be lost in sixpences must be placed to the account of Master Slender's simplicity of wit.

With respect to the *Edward shovel-boards :*—Mr. Malone's inference from the reading in the old quarto that " Slender means the broad *shilling* of *one of our kings*," is sufficiently maintained by the other notes ; but that it was the shilling of *Edward the Sixth* there is no doubt, no *other* Edward having coined such a piece of money.   It still remains to explain how these shillings could have cost Master Slender two and twopence apiece ; because, if Dr. Farmer's quotation from Folkes had gone far enough, it would have appeared that the thick shillings mentioned by that writer were *pattern-pieces*, even originally of great rarity, and never in circulation. Folkes could have seen very few of such pieces, and it would be extremely difficult at present to find a single one ; whereas the common shillings of Edward the Sixth remain in great numbers.   We must suppose then that the shillings purchased of the miller had been hoarded by him, and were in high preservation, and heavier than those which had been worn in circulation.   These would consequently be of greater importance to a nice player at the game of shovel-board, and induce him, especially if an opulent man, to procure them at a price far beyond their original value.

SCENE 1.   Page 321.

BARD. . . .   And so conclusions *pass'd the careires.*

We are told that this is a technical term in the *manege ;* but no explanation is given.   It was the same as *running a career,* or galloping a horse violently backwards and forwards, stopping him suddenly at the end of the career ; " which career the more seldom it be used and with the lesse fury, the better mouth shall your horse have," says Master Blundeville in his *Arte of ryding,* b. 1. 4to, where there is a whole chapter on the subject, as well as in " *The art of riding,*" translated by Thomas Bedingfield from the Italian of Claudio Corte, 1584, 4to.

Scene 1.   Page 325.

SLEN. I hope upon familiarity will grow more contempt.

This is no more than a perversion of the common proverb, *Familiarity breeds contempt.*   Slender's school learning had furnished him on the occasion.   The phrase is still used in copy-books for children.

Scene 1.   Page 327.

SLEN. I bruis'd my shin the other day with playing at sword and dagger with a *master of fence.*

" *Master of defence,* on the present occasion, does not simply mean a professor of the art of fencing, but a person who had taken his *master's degree* in it," says Mr. Steevens, whose readers are under great obligations to him for pointing out one of the greatest curiosities extant on the ancient science of defence, in support of his position.   Yet it may be doubted whether the expression *master of defence* does not very often, and even on the present occasion, signify merely a *professor of the art.*   Numerous authorities might he adduced on this side of the question, but perhaps a single one that is apposite may suffice.   In Eden's *History of travayle,* 1577, 4to, speaking of Calecut in the East Indies, he says, " they have in the citie certayne *maisters of fence* that teach them how to use the swoord, &c."   The original Latin from which Eden translates has *lanista.*   Now it is not to be presumed that the last-mentioned *maisters of fence* had taken any degree.   It must be owned that the evidence of the manuscript cited by Mr. Steevens goes very far to show that none were allowed to practise as professors who had not taken a degree in some fencing school; an honour once conferred by king Edward the Sixth, and generally granted, though not till after many years' experience, by one who was himself a *master.*   Yet a person who had only a *provost's* degree might be allowed to teach, and *he* would be termed a *master of defence.*

SCENE 3.   Page 330.

HOST. What says my *bully-rook?*

Messrs. Steevens and Whalley maintain that the above term (a cant one) derives its origin from the *rook* in the game of chess; but it is very improbable that that noble game, never the amusement of gamblers, should have been ransacked on this occasion.   It means *a hectoring, cheating sharper,* as appears from *A new dictionary of the terms of the canting crew,* no date, 12mo, and from the lines prefixed to *The compleat gamester,* 1680, 12mo, in both which places it is spelt *bully-rock.* Nor is Mr. Whalley correct in stating that *rock* and not *rook* is the *true* name of the chess piece, if he mean that it is equivalent to the Latin *rupes.*

SCENE 3.   Page 333.

PIST. O base *Gongarian* wight!

It is already shown that this is the same as *Hungarian.* It simply means a *gipsy.* The parts of Europe in which it is supposed that the gipsies originally appeared were Hungary and Bohemia.   In Act IV. Scene 5, of this play, the host in the like cant language calls Simple a *Bohemian Tartar* ; and Munster in his *Cosmography* informs us that the Germans denominated the *gipsies Tartars.*

SCENE 3.   Page 333.

FAL. I am glad I am so acquit of this *tinder box.*

There is a great deal of humour in this appellation.   Falstaff alludes to Pistol's rubicund nose, which, like the above utensil, carried fire in it.

SCENE 3.   Page 333.

PIST. Young ravens must have food.

Either Shakspeare or the adage, if it be one, has borrowed from scripture.   See *Psalm* cxlvii. 9. or *Job* xxxviii. 41.

Scene 3. Page 337. Note 4.

To the instances adduced by Mr. Steevens in this note, of particular phrases in old theatrical characters, may be added that of Murley in *Sir John Oldcastle*, who is continually prefacing his speeches with " fye paltry, paltry, in and out, to and fro upon occasion." This practice has been revived in our modern comedies.

Scene 4. Page 347.

CAIUS. You are John Rugby, and you are Jack Rugby : come take-a your rapier, and come after my heel to de court.

It wås the custom, in Shakspeare's time, for physicians to be attended by their servants when visiting their patients. This appears from the *second part* of Stubs's *Anatomie of abuses,* sign. H. 4 b., where, speaking of physicians, he says, " For now they ruffle it out in silckes and velvets, with *their men attending upon them,* whereas many a poor man (God wot) smarteth for it." Servants also carried their masters' rapiers : " Yf a man can place a dysh, fyll a boule and *carrie his maister's rapier,* what more is or can be required at his handes ?"—Markham's *Health to the gentlemanly profession of a serving-man,* sign. F. 3.

ACT II.

Scene 1. Page 357.

MRS. FORD. . . . to the tune of *Green sleeves.*

Another ballad with this title, and which has an equally good claim to be the one alluded to as those already quoted, may be seen in Mr. Ellis's elegant *Specimens of the early English poets,* vol. iii. p. 327, edit. 1801.

Scene 1. Page 358.

MRS. PAGE. . . . for sure, unless he knew some *strain* in me that I know not myself——

The note seem to have wrested from this word its plain

and obvious meaning of *turn, humour, tendency*, in which it is often used by Shakspeare.

SCENE 1.   Page 359.

PIST. Hope is a *curtail dog* in some affairs.

A curtail or curtal dog is placed by Howel in the vocabulary at the end of his *Dictionary of four languages* among hunting-dogs, and is defined to be *a dog without a tail good for any service.* Yet we are not to suppose that the word uniformly signifies an animal with its tail cut off. It is in fact derived from *tailler court*, and applied to *any* animals that are defective, man not excepted. Thus in Greene's *Quip for an upstart courtier*, a collier is made to say, " I am made a *curtall* : for the pillory hath eaten off both my *eares*," sign. E. 2. Nashe, in his *Prayse of the red herring*, speaks of the *" curtaild skinclipping pagans."* fo. 20. Dr. Stukeley, in a manuscript note in his copy of Robin Hood's garland, states that " the *curtal* fryer of Fountain's abby is *Cordelier*, from the cord or rope which they wore round their wast, to whip themselves with. They were of the Franciscan order." But this is a mistake ; and the opinion of Staveley much more probable, who, in chap. xxv. of his *Romish horseleech*, says, that in some countries where the Franciscan friars, conformably to the injunction of their founder, wore short habits, the order was presently contemned and derided, and men called them *curtailed friars.*

SCENE 2.   Page 360.

FORD. Love my wife?
PIST. With *liver burning hot.*

It is here observed by Mr. Steevens, and elsewhere by Dr. Johnson, that the liver was anciently supposed to be the inspirer of amorous passions, and the seat of love. In conformity with this opinion, we are told in the English translation of Bartholomæus *De proprietatibus rerum*, lib. v. cap. 39,

THE CITY OF WINNIPEG WINNIPEG 2. MAN DISCARDED

that " the lyver is the place of voluptuousnesse and lyking of the flesh;" and again, " the liver is a member, *hot*, &c." There is some reason for thinking that the idea was borrowed from the Arabian physicians, or at least adopted by them; for in the *Turkish tales,* an amorous tailor is made to address his wife by the titles of " thou *corner of my liver,* and soul of my life!" and in another place the king of Syria, who had sustained a temporary privation of his mistress, is said to have had " his liver, which had been *burnt up* by the loss of her, cooled and refreshed at the sight of her." In *Twelfth night,* Fabian, speaking of Olivia's supposed letter to Malvolio, says, " This wins him, *liver and all.*"

SCENE 2. Page 367, 368.

PAGE. I have heard the Frenchman hath good skill in his *rapier.*

SHAL. In these times you stand on distance, your passes stoccadoes and I know not what. I have seen the time with my long sword I would have made you four tall fellows skip like rats.

The notes on these speeches are at variance on a supposed anachronism committed by Shakspeare in introducing the *rapier* in the time of Henry the Fourth. The same weapon is likewise found in *Richard II.* Act IV. Scene 1, where the controversy is renewed; and therefore it will be proper in considering this question to state the evidence and arguments in both places. It is maintained on one side that the *rapier* was not used in England before the reign of Elizabeth; and in support of this opinion a passage from Carleton's *Thankful remembrance of God's mercy* is offered; which, being only a second-hand and inaccurate statement from Darcie's *Annals of Elizabeth,* is not deserving of further notice. Darcie himself informs us that one Rowland York (who appears to have betrayed Deventer to the Spaniards in 1587) was the *first* that brought into England " that wicked and pernicious fashion to fight in the fields in duels with *a rapier called a tucke* onely for the thrust, &c." On this passage it may be remarked, that the *rapier* is not *generally* spoken of, but only a particular sort, the *tucke for the thrust.* On the same side Stowe is next cited, who mentions that the mode of fighting with the sword and buckler was frequent with all men till that of *the rapier and dagger* took place, when *suddenly the general quarrel of fighting abated,* which began about the 20th of Elizabeth (1578). Now here the date seems rather applicable to the cessation of the very popular combats with sword and buckler, and the substitution only, and, as it will presently appear, the revival of the rapier and dagger, as a more limited manner of fighting, from its superior danger. There is another passage in Stowe, p. 869, which not being already cited, and throwing some light on the nature of the rapier, may deserve notice. The historian relates that " Shortly after (referring to the 12th or 13th year of Elizabeth) began *long tucks* and *long rapiers,* and he was held the greatest gallant that had the deepest ruffe and longest rapier: the offence to the eye of the one, and the hurt unto the life of the subject that came by the other, caused her majesty to make proclamation against them both, and to place selected grave citizens at every gate to cut the ruffes, and breake the rapiers points of all passengers that exceeded a yeard in length of their rapiers, and a nayle of a yeard in depth of their ruffes." But this is likewise no evidence in favour of the *general* introduction of the *rapier* in the reign of Elizabeth, as Stowe merely refers to the *long foining or thrusting rapier.* The last quotation on this side of the question is from Bulleine's *Dialogue between soarnesse and chirurgi,* 1579, where the *long foining rapier* is also mentioned as " a *new* kind of instrument to let blood withall."

On the opposite side, Mr. Ritson produces a quotation from Nashe's *Life of Jacke Wilton,* who lived in the reign of Henry the Eighth, to show that *rapiers* were used at that period. This sort of evidence might appear, on a first view, inadmissible, on the ground that Nashe had committed an

error, very common with Shakspeare, in ascribing a custom
of his own time to a preceding one, if it were not supported
by the manuscript cited by Mr. Steevens in vol. iii. p. 327,
in which, but not in the quotation from it, it appears that the
rapier actually was in use in the time of Henry the Eighth ;
and therefore it is impossible to decide that this weapon,
which, with its name, we received from the French, might
not have been known as early as the reign of Henry the
Fourth, or even of Richard the Second. Shallow's ridicule
of *passes and stoccadoes* seems more objectionable, and may
possibly deserve the appellation of anachronism. It is not a
little remarkable that the *rapier* was an article of exportation
from this country in Cromwell's time. See *Oliverian acts*,
A. D. 1657.

Scene 1. Page 369.

> Ford. Though Page be a secure fool, and stands so firmly on *his*
> wife's frailty, yet I cannot put off *my* opinion so easily :
> she was in his company, &c.

This speech is surely not so obscure as the notes seem to
consider it. Ford says that *Page* makes a firm stand with
respect to, or on the question of, *his* wife's frailty. What follows better deserves explanation, because the grammatical
construction of the last sentence is, that *Page's* wife was in
Falstaff's company ; whereas Ford means to say, " I cannot
put off *my* opinion, i. e. of *my own wife,* so easily ; as *she* was
in Falstaff's company," &c. The emphasis should be laid on
the words *his* and *my,* and then the whole will be far more
intelligible.

Scene 2. Page 375.

> Fal. Your *cat-a-mountain* looks.

A term borrowed from the Spaniards, who call the wild
cat *gato-montes.*

Scene 2.   Page 375.

Fal. Your *red lattice* phrases.

Mr. Steevens, speaking of this external mark of an ale-house, says, " Hence the present chequers." But in reality the *lattice* is the younger of the two, as the reference in the note to the Pompeii plate in *Archæologia* demonstrates. Although the Romans were not acquainted with the game of chess, they certainly were with such a one as required a board with squares ; and in all probability this sign of a house of entertainment where table games were played, has been handed down to us from the ancients. The resemblance of *lattice* work, or *laths* crossing each other, to a chess or back-gammon board, might induce some ignorant painters to exhibit the former; but the *chequers* have once more reassumed their station. Nor was *red* always the colour ; for, in the cant language of jolly fellows, a red or *blue* lattice was termed *a free school for all comers.* See Heywood's *Philocothonista,* 1635, 4to.

Scene 2.   Page 376.

Quick. There is one mistress Ford, sir :—I pray come a little nearer this ways :—I myself dwell with master Doctor Caius.
Fal. Well, on : mistress Ford, you say——

Is it not more natural that Falstaff should, in this first instance, repeat the dame's own words, and say, " Well, one mistress Ford, you say."

Scene 2.   Page 389.

Ford. . . . an Irishman with my *aqua vitæ* bottle——

Irish aqua vitæ was certainly *usquebaugh,* and not *brandy,* as Mr. Malone has observed ; but Ford is here speaking of *English aqua vitæ,* which was very different from the other so called from the Irish words *uisge,* aqua, and *beatha,* vita. That the curious reader may judge for himself, and at the same time be furnished with the means of indulging any wish that he may have for tasting the respective sorts in their ge-

nuine form, the following receipts for making them are subjoined:—The first is from a manuscript monkish common-
place book, written about the reign of Henry the Sixth.
" For to make water of lyff, that ys clepyd aqua vitæ. Take
and fylle thy violle fulle of lyes of stronge vine, and put
therto these powdrys.   First powder of canel, powder of
clowes, powdyr of gyngevir, powdyr of notemugys, powder
of galyngale and powdyr of quibibis, poudyr of greyn de
parys, poudyr of longe pepyr, powdyr of blacke pepir, care-
wey, cirmowitteyn, comyn, fenyl, smallache, persile, sawge,
myntys, rewe, calamente, origaun, one ounce or more or
lesse as ye lykyth ; stampe hem a lytill for it will be bettyr,
and put hem to these powdrys, than set thy glas on the fyre
set on the hovel and kepe it wel that the eyre come not owte
and set ther undyr a viole and kepe the watyr."   The next is
from *Cogan's Haven of health,* 1612, 4to, chap. 222.   " To
make aqua vitæ.   Take of strong ale, or strong wine, or the
lees of strong wine and ale together, a gallon or two as you
please, and take half a pound or more of good liquorice, and
as much annise seedes; scrape off the bark from the liquorice,
and cut it into thin slices, and punne the annise grosse, and
steepe altogether close covered twelve houres, then distill it
with a limbecke or serpentine.   And of every gallon of the
liquor you may draw a quart of reasonable good *aqua vitæ,*
that is of two galons two quarts.   But see that your fire be
temperate, and that the heade of your limbecke bee kept colde
continually with fresh water, and that the bottome of your
limbecke bee fast luted with rye dough, that no ayre issue
out.   The best ale to make *aqua vitæ* of, is to be made of
wheate malte, and the next of cleane barley malte, and the
best wine for that purpose is sacke."   The last is a receipt
for making " Usquebath, or Irish aqua vitæ.   To every gallon of good aqua composita, put two ounces of chosen liquorice bruised and cut into small peeces, but first cleansed
from all his filth, and two ounces of annis seedes that are

cleane and bruised ; let them macerate five or six days in a
wodden vessell, stopping the same close, and then draw off
as much as will runne cleere, dissolving in that cleere aqua
vitæ five or sixe spoonefulls of the best malassoes you can
get : Spanish cute if you can get it, is thought better than
malassoes : then put this into another vessell, and after three
or foure dayes (the more the better) when the liquor hath
fined itselfe, you maie use the same : some adde dates and
raisins of the sun to this receipt; those grounds which re-
maine you maie redistill and make more aqua composita of
them, and of that aqua composita you maie make more *usquebath*."—Plat's *Delightes for ladies,* 1611, 24to. It is to be
observed, that *aqua composita* is wine of any kind distilled
with spices and sweet herbs. *Brandy,* or *burnt* wine, seems
first to occur in Skinner's *Etymologicon,* 1671, under the name
of *Brandewin,* from the Dutch or German, and soon after in
its present form ; yet *aqua vitæ* was continued a long while
afterwards.

SCENE 3.   Page 395.

HOST. *Cry'd game,* said I well?

The evidence, and indeed the sense, in favour of the phrase
to *cry aim,* preponderates so greatly, that one cannot hesitate in discarding the nonsensical expression of *cry'd game,*
which derives not the least support from any of Mr. Steevens's
quotations. The probability is very great that there was an
error of the press, and that the words should have been
printed according to the orthography of the time, " Cry'd I
ayme, said I well ?" A *g* might easily have crept in instead
of a *y.*

ACT III.

SCENE 1.   Page 398.

SIM. Marry, sir, the *city-ward*——

" The old editions read *pittie-ward,* the modern editors
pitty-wary," says Mr. Steevens, who in this edition has aban-

doned the best part of a former note where he had proposed
to read *petty-ward,* which is the right word, and of the same
import as the old one.   That such a word formerly existed is
demonstrable from its still remaining as a proper name, and
near Wimbledon is a wood so called, probably from the
owner.   Mr. Steevens mistakes in supposing *ward* to mean
towards in this instance, where it is put for the division of a
city; nor does his quotation from William of Worcester
assist him.   The *via de Petty* and the *Pyttey gate* might be
named after the hundred of Pyttey in Somersetshire.   In
Lyne's Map of Cambridge, 1574, we find the *petticurie.*

Scene 1.   Page 399.

Evans. I will knog his *urinals* about his knave's costard——

This utensil was the usual concomitant of physicians in
former times, as appears from most of the frontispieces to
old medical books and other ancient prints.

Scene 2.   Page 410.

Host. . . . . he smells April and May.

The same as if he had said he smells of *youth and courtship,*
symbolized by these months, the former of which in old
calendars is described in these lines :

" The next vi yere maketh foure and twenty,
   And fygured is to joly Apryll;
   That tyme of pleasures man hath moost plenty
   Fresshe and lovyng his lustes to fulfyll——"

and the latter in the following :

" As in the month of Maye all thyng is in myght,
   So at xxx yeres man is in chyef lykyng;
   Pleasaunt and lusty, to every mannes syght,
   In beaute and strength to women pleasyng."

Scene 2.   Page 412.

Host. I will to my honest knight Falstaff, and drink *canary* with
   him.
Ford. I think I shall drink in *pipe-wine* first with him; I'll make
   him dance.

It may be doubted whether the exact meaning of this

cluster of puns has already been given.   Mr. Tyrwhitt says
he cannot understand the phrase *to drink in pipe-wine*, and
suggests that Shakspeare might have written *horn-pipe wine*.
Now Ford terms canary *pipe-wine*, both because the *canary*
dance is performed to a tabor and *pipe*, and because the canary
bird is said to *pipe* his tunes.   Ford is speaking of Falstaff,
not of Page, as Mr. Tyrwhitt's note implies when it refers to
horns.   He says he will make him pipe and dance too.

SCENE 3.   Page 414.

MRS. FORD. How now, my *eyas-musket*?

There was no reason for disturbing the etymology of this
word given by Dr. Warburton, by substituting that of Dame
Juliana Bernes, which for ingenuity and veracity may be well
classed with many of those in *Isidore of Seville*, or *The golden
legend*.   Take an example from the latter.   " Felix is sayd of
fero fers, that is to saye, to bere, and of this word *lis, litis*,
whiche is as moche to say as stryfe, for he bare stryfe for the
fayth of our lorde."   Turberville tells us that " the first name
and terme that they bestowe on a falcon is an *eyesse*, and this
name doth laste as long as she is in the eyrie and for that she
is taken from the *eyrie*."   This is almost as bad as the lady
abbess's account.   *Eyrie* is simply the nest or *eggery*, and
has no connexion with the name of the bird.   *Eyas* or *nias*,
is a term borrowed from the French *niais*, which means any
young bird in the nest, *avis in nido*.   It is the first of five
several names by which a falcon is called during its first year.
The best account of this bird is in *La fauconnerie de Charles
d'Arcussa de Capre, seigneur d'Esparron*, 1643, 4to.   A *mus-
ket* is a sparrow-hawk, and is derived from the French *mouchet*,
and the latter probably from *musca*, on account of its diminutive form.   The humour therefore lies in comparing the
page to a young male sparrow-hawk, an emblem of his tender
years and activity.

ACT IV.

SCENE 2. Page 448.

MRS. FORD. . . . . . and her *muffler* too.

It would oppress the reader by citing authorities to prove that the muffler was a contrivance of various kinds to conceal a part of the face, and that even a *mask* was occasionally so denominated. From an examination of several ancient prints and paintings, it appears that when the muffler was made of linen, it only covered the lower part of the face; such it was in the present instance, for the old woman of Brentford would not want to conceal her eyes. It is otherwise in *King Henry V.* Act III. Scene 1, where Fortune's *blindness* is described, and there a linen bandage would be meant, but perhaps not very correctly called a muffler. The term is connected with the old French *musser* or *muçer*, to hide, or with *amuseler*, to cover the *museau* or *mufle*, a word which has been indiscriminately used for the mouth, nose, and even the whole of the face; hence our *muzzle*. It was enacted by a Scotish statute in 1457, that " na woman cum to kirk, nor mercat, with her face *mussaled* or covered that scho may not be kend." Notwithstanding this interposition of the legislature, says Mr. Warton, the ladies of Scotland continued *muzzled* during three reigns; and he cites Sir David Lyndsay's poem *In contemptioun of syde taillis*, in which the author advises the king to issue a proclamation that the women should show their faces as they did in France. *Hist. of Eng. poetry*, ii. 324.

The annexed cuts exhibit different sorts of mufflers. The first and third figures are copied from Jost Amman's *Theatrum mulierum*, Francof. 1586, 4to; the second, from Speed's Map of England, is the *costume* of an English countrywoman in the reign of James I.; the fourth is from an old German print; and the others from Weigel's *Habitus præcipuorum populorum*, Nuremb. 1577, folio; a work which, for the beauty of the wood-cuts, has never been surpassed.

In the reign of Charles I. the ladies wore masks which covered the eye-brows and nose, holes being left for the eyes. Sometimes, but not always, the mouth was covered, and the chin guarded with a sort of muffler then called a *chin-cloth*; these were chiefly used to keep off the sun. See Hollar's print of *Winter*. The velvet masks probably came from France, as they are mentioned in the *Book of values of merchandize imported*, under the administration of Oliver Cromwell. There was another sort called *visard masks*, that covered all the face, having holes only for the eyes, a case for the nose, and a slit for the mouth. They were easily disengaged, being held in the teeth by means of a round bead fastened in the inside. These masks were usually made of leather, covered with black velvet. Randle Holme, from whose *Academy of armory*, book iii. c. 5, their description is extracted, adds, that the devil invented them, and that none about court except w——s, bawds, and the devil's imps, used them, being ashamed to show their faces.

SCENE 2.   Page 450.

PAGE. Why this *passes!*——

The word had been already explained by Warburton in p. 329. Page, astonished at Ford's conduct, says it *exceeds every thing*. Such is the sense in the New Testament, "the love of Christ, which *passeth* knowledge," *Ephes*. iii. 19. The French often use *passer* in the same manner; and in *Hamlet* we have this expression, "I have that within which *passeth* show."

SCENE 2.   Page 452.

FORD. . . . his wife's *leman*.

Mr. Steevens derives it from the Dutch, a language whence we have borrowed few, if any words. The term is of Saxon origin, and *leveman* can be traced to an Anglo-Norman period. This was afterwards contracted into *leman*. The etymology is perhaps from leoꝼe, amabilis, and ꝏan, homo. The latter in Saxon denoted both man and woman ; so that *leman* was formerly applied to both sexes as a *person beloved*.

SCENE 2.   Page 455.

MRS. PAGE.   .   .   .   in the way of *waste*——

This expression is from the same *law* manufactory referred to by Mr. Ritson in the preceding note.   The incident in the present scene, of Falstaff's threshing in the habit of a woman, might have been suggested by the story of the beaten and contented cuckold in Boccaccio's *Decameron,* day 7. ver. 7.

SCENE 5.   Page 466.

SIMP. Pray you, sir, was't not the *wise woman of Brentford ?*

Mr. Steevens cites *Judges* v. 29, on this occasion : but the *wise ladies* there were of a very different character from the old woman of Brentford, even according to the Hebrew text : see the Vulgate and Septuagint versions, where the expression is still more remote.   The subject of these wise women will be resumed in a note on *Twelfth night,* Act III. Scene 4.

ACT V.

SCENE 1.   Page 475.

FAL. Hold up your head, and *mince.*

The word is properly explained by Mr. Steevens.   Thus in *Isaiah* iii. 16, " walking and *mincing* as they go."   Wicliffe has " with their feet in curious goyng ;" and Tindale, " tryppyng so nicely with their feet."   *To mince* is likewise to walk in a stately, or, as Littelton expresses it, *Junonian* step.

SCENE 2.   Page 477.

SLEN. I come to her in white, and cry *mum*, she cries, *budget.*

The word *mumbudget,* here divided, is used by Nashe in his *Have with you to Saffron Walden,* where, speaking of Gabriel Harvey, he says, " no villaine, no atheist, no murderer, but hee hath likened me too, for no other reason in the earth, but because I would not let him go beyond me, or *be won to put my finger in my mouth and crie mumbudget* when he had baffuld mee in print throughout England." *To play mumbudget*, is rendered *demeurer court, ne sonner mot,* in Sherwood's *English and French dictionary,* 1632, folio. *Mumchance* is silence; and a *mummery* was a silent masquerade. *Mumbudget* may be *silence in a budget,* a something *closed* or stopped up, Fr. *bouché.*

SCENE 4. Page 479.

MRS. PAGE. . . . hard by *Herne's oak*——

The tree in Windsor forest referred to in Mr. Steevens's note, was said, on newspaper authority in 1795, to have been cut down by his majesty's order, on account of its being totally decayed.

SCENE 5. Page 490.

PIST. *Vile* worm!

Old copy *vild,* which Mr. Malone shows to have been the *old* pronunciation. It may be added that it is likewise the *modern* in some of the provinces.

SCENE 5. Page 492.

[*Stage direction.*] " During this song, the fairies *pinch* Falstaff."

In the old collection of songs already cited in p. 7, there is one entitled " The fayries daunce," which bearing some resemblance to that by Shakspeare, may be entitled to the reader's notice :

> " Dare you haunt our hallowed greene?
>   None but fayries here are seene.
>   Downe and sleepe,
>   Wake and weepe,
>   Pinch him black, and pinch him blew,
>   That seekes to steale a lover true.
>   When you come to heare us sing,
>   Or to tread our fayrie ring,
>   Pinch him black, and pinch him blew,
>   O thus our nayles shall handle you."

Scene 5.   Page 500.

Page. What cannot be eschew'd must be embrac'd.

This is either a proverbial saying now lost, or borrowed from one of the following, " What cannot be altered must be borne not blamed;" " What cannot be cured must be endured."

TWELFTH NIGHT.

ACT I.

SCENE 1. Page 8.

DUKE.   How will she love, when the rich *golden shaft*
  Hath kill'd the flock of all affections else
  That live in her.

THIS *golden shaft* was supplied either from a description of
Cupid in Sidney's *Arcadia,* book ii., or from Ovid's *Metamorphoses,* translated by Golding, 4to, fo. 8, where, speaking
of Cupid's arrows, he says,

 " *That causeth love* is all of *golde* with point full sharp and bright.
 That chaseth love, is blunt, whose steele with leaden head is dight."

Milton seems to have forgotten that Love had only *one*
shaft of *gold.*   See *Parad. Lost,* iv. 1. 763.

SCENE 2. Page 11.

CAP.   .   .   .   she hath abjur'd the company
  And sight of men.

This necessary and justifiable change in the *ordo verborum*
from the reading in the old copy, and to which Mr. Steevens
lays claim, had been already made by Sir Thomas Hanmer.

SCENE 3. Page 21.

SIR TO.   .   .   .   Wherefore have these gifts a *curtain* before them?
  are they like to take dust, like mistress Mall's picture?

Mr. Malone's conjecture that curtains were at this time
frequently hung before pictures of value, is further supported
in Scene 5 of this Act, where Olivia, in unveiling her face,
mentions the practice.   In Deloney's *Pleasant history of
Jack of Newbery,* printed before 1597, it is recorded that " in

a faire large parlour, which was wainscotted round about, Jacke of Newbery had fifteene faire pictures hanging, *which were covered with curtaines of greene silke,* frienged with gold, which he would often shew to his friends and servants."

SCENE 3.   Page 23.

SIR AND. Taurus? that's *sides and heart.*
SIR TO.   No, sir, it is *legs and thighs.*

Both the knights are wrong in their astrology, according to the almanacs of the time, which make Taurus govern *the neck and throat.* Their ignorance is perhaps intentional.

SCENE 5.   Page 31.

SIR TO. . . . How now, *sot?*

There is great humour in this ambiguous word, which applies equally to the fool and the knight himself, in his *drunken condition.*

ACT II.

SCENE 3.   Page 51.

CLOWN. How now, my hearts? Did you never see *the picture of we three?*

The original picture, or sign as it sometimes was, seems to have been two *fools.* Thus in Shirley's *Bird in cage,* Morello, who counterfeits a *fool,* says, " *We be three of old,* without exception to your lordship, only with this difference, I am the wisest fool." In Day's comedy of *Law tricks,* 1608, Jul. says, " appoint the place prest." To which Em. answers, " At the *three fools.*" Sometimes, as Mr. Henley has stated, it was two asses. Thus in Beaumont and Fletcher's *Queen of Corinth,* Act III. Scene 1,

" NEAN. He is another *ass,* he says, I believe him.
UNCLE. *We be three,* heroical prince.
NEAN. Nay then we must have the *picture* of 'em, and the word *nos sumus.*"

Scene 3. Page. 53.

Clo. I did impeticos thy gratility.

This is undoubtedly the true reading, for the reason assigned by Mr. Malone. From the discordant notes on the passage, a question has arisen whether the fool means to say that he had put the sixpence into his own petticoats, or given it to his petticoat companion, his *leman*. Mr. Steevens has observed that " petticoats were not *always* a part of the dress of fools, though they were of idiots;" and on this assertion, coupled with another by Dr. Johnson, that " fools were kept in long coats to which the allusion is made," Mr. Ritson maintains that " it is a very gross mistake to imagine that this character (*i. e.* our clown's) was habited like an *idiot*." Now it is very certain, that although the idiot fools were generally dressed in petticoats, the allowed fool was occasionally habited in like manner, as is shown more at large in another part of this volume; which circumstance, though it may strengthen the opinion that the clown has alluded to his own dress, by no means decides the above question, which remains very equally balanced.

Scene 3. Page 63.

Sir To. Dost thou think because thou art virtuous, there shall be no more *cakes and ale* ?

The holiday cakes referred to in Mr. Letherland's note were the yule or Christmas cakes; those on the lying-in of the Virgin; cross-buns, and twelfth cakes. Mr. Lysons, in his account of Twickenham, mentions an ancient custom of dividing two great cakes in the church on Easter-day among the young people. This was regarded as a superstitious relic; and it was ordered by the parliament in 1645, that the parishioners should forbear that custom, and instead thereof buy loaves of bread for the poor of the parish.

SCENE 4.   Page 70.

DUKE. And the *free* maids that weave their threads with bones.

The private memoirs of Peter the wild boy, if they could be disclosed, would afford the best comment on the above disputed epithet, as applied to the *websters* in question.

SCENE 4.   Page 71.

CLO. And in *sad cypress* let me be laid.

Mr. Steevens has in this edition cancelled a brother commentator's note, which ought on every account to have been retained, and has himself attempted to show that a *shroud* and not a *coffin* of cypress or cyprus is intended. It is no easy matter, from the ambiguity of the word, to decide the question. The cypress tree was used by the ancients for funeral purposes, and dedicated to Pluto. As it was not liable to perish from rottenness, it appears to have been used for coffins. See Mr. Gough's Introd ction to *Sepulchral monuments*, p. lxvi. In Quarles's *Argalus and Parthenia*, book iii., a knight is introduced, whose

> " . . . . .   horse was black as jet,
> His furniture was round about beset
> With branches, slipt from the *sad cypresse tree*."

In further behalf of the wood, it may be worth remarking that the expression *laid* seems more applicable to a coffin than to a shroud, in which a party may with greater propriety be said to be *wrapped*; and also that the shroud is afterwards expressly mentioned by itself. It is nevertheless very certain that the fine linen called Cyprus, perhaps from being originally manufactured in the island of that name, was used for shrouds. In the churchwardens' accounts of St. Mary's, Cambridge, mention is made of *a sypyrs kyrcher belonging to the cross*. In this instance there being the figure of a dead body on the cross, the cyprus was designed as a shroud.

Scene 5. Page 88.

MAL. By my life, this is my lady's hand : these be her very C's, her
U's, and her T's, and thus makes she her great P's.

Mr. Ritson having with great probability supplied the
whole direction of the letter, there seems to be no foundation
left for Blackstone's conjecture. Malvolio had no motive for
any *coarse* allusion. With respect to the instance of the
letter in *All's well that ends well* not being recited literally
by Helen, it must be recollected that there was no reason for
making her do so, as she talks in *blank verse;* and it would
therefore have been improper that she should have given
more than the *substance* of the letter.

Scene 5. Page 93.

MAL. . . . and wish'd to see thee *cross-gartered.*

Of this fashion but few vestiges remain ; a circumstance
the more remarkable, as it must have been at one time extremely common among the beaux in Elizabeth's reign. In
the English edition of Junius's *Nomenclator,* 1585, 12mo,
mention is made of " hose garters, going *acrosse,* or over-
thwart, both above and below the knee." In the old comedy
of *The two angrie women of Abingdon,* 1599, 4to, a *serving-
man* is thus described :

" . . . . hee's a fine neate fellow,
A spruce slave, I warrant ye, he'ele have
His cruell *garters crosse about the knee.*"

Scene 5. Page 94.

MAL. I will be *point-de-vice* [*device*].

As the instances of this expression are of rare occurrence,
those which follow are offered as likely to be useful to the
author of any future work that may resemble the well-plan-
ned, but unfinished glossary of *obsolete and provincial words*
by the late Dr. Boucher. In the interlude of *The nature of
the four elements,* Sensuality, one of the *dramatis personæ,*
promises a banquet

> " Of metys that be most delycate,
> Which shall be in a chamber feyre
> Replete with sote and fragrāt eyre
> Prepared *poynt-devyse*."

In *Newes from the North*, 1579, 4to, mention is made of " costly banqueting houses, galleries, bowling-allees, straunge toies of *point-devise* and woorkmanship," sign. G. In an old and very rare satirical poem against married ladies, entitled, *The proude wyves paternoster that wold go gaye, and undyd her husbande and went her waye*, 1560, 4to, one of the gossips recommends her companion to wear

> " Rybandes of sylke that be full longe and large,
> With tryangles *trymly made poyntdevyse*."

Some further account of this piece may not be unacceptable. It is described in Laneham's *Letter from Killingworth* as forming part of Captain Cox the mason's curious library. In the appendix to Baker's *Biographia dramatica*, p. 433, a play under the same title is mentioned as entered on the Stationers' books in 1559 ; but from the correspondence in the date, it was, most likely, the present work, which cannot be regarded as a dramatic one. It describes the hypocritical behaviour of women at church, who, instead of attending to their devotions, are more anxious to show their gay apparel. One of these, observing a neighbour much better clothed than herself, begins her *paternoster*, wherein she complains of her husband's restrictions, and prays that she may be enabled to dress as gaily as the rest of her acquaintance. She afterwards enters into conversation with a female gossip, by whose mischievous instigation she is seduced to rebel against her husband's authority. In consequence of this, the poor man is first entreated, next threatened, and finally ruined. The author of this poem is not the first who has irreligiously made use of the present vehicle of his satire. One of the old Norman minstrels had preceded him in *The usurer's pater-noster*, which Mons. Le Grand has inserted among his entertaining *fabliaux*, and at the same time described some other similar compositions.

But to return to *point-device* :—There was no occasion for
separating the two last syllables of this term, as in the quotation from Mr. Steevens's text, nor is it done when it occurs
elsewhere in his edition. It has been properly stated that
point-device signifies *exact, nicely finical*; but nothing has
been offered concerning the etymology, except that we got
the expression from the French. It has in fact been supplied
from the labours of the needle. *Poinct* in the French language denotes a *stitch*; *devisé* any thing *invented, disposed,* or
arranged. *Point-devisé* was therefore a particular sort of pat-
terned lace worked with the needle ; and the term *point-lace*
is still familiar to every female. They had likewise their
point-coupé, point-compté, dentelle au point devant l'aiguille,
&c., &c. The various kinds of needle-work practised by our
indefatigable grandmothers, if enumerated, would astonish
even the most industrious of our modern ladies. Many
curious books of patterns for lace and all sorts of needle-
work were formerly published, some of which are worth
pointing out to the curious collector. The earliest on the list
is an Italian book under the title of *Esemplario di lavori :*
dove le tenere fanciulle & altre donne nobile potranno facil-
mente imparare il modo & ordine di lavorare, cusire, racca-
mare, & finalmente far tutte quelle gentillezze & lodevili opere,
le quali pò fare una donna virtuosa con laco in mano, con li
suoi compasse & misure. *Vinegia, per Nicolo D'Aristotile*
detto Zoppino, MDXXIX. 8vo. The next that occurs was
likewise set forth by an Italian, and entitled, *Les singuliers*
et nouveaux pourtraicts du seigneur Federic de Vinciolo Veni-
tien, pour toutes sortes d'ouvrages de lingerie. Paris, 1588,
4to. It is dedicated to the queen of France, and had been
already twice published. In 1599 a second part came out,
which is much more difficult to be met with than the former,
and sometimes contains a neat portrait, by Gaultier, of Catherine de Bourbon, the sister of Henry the Fourth. The
next is *Nouveaux pourtraicts de point coupé et dantelles en*

petite moyenne et grande forme, nouvellement inventez et mis en lumiere. Imprimé à Montbeliard, 1598, 4to. It has an address to the ladies, and a poem exhorting young damsels to be industrious; but the author's name does not appear. Vincentio's work was published in England, and printed by John Wolf, under the title of *New and singular patternes and workes of linnen, serving for paternes to make all sortes of lace, edginges and cut-workes. Newly invented for the profite and contentment of ladies, gentilwomen, and others that are desireous of this art.* 1591, 4to. He seems also to have printed it with a French title. We have then another English book of which this is the title: *Here foloweth certaine Patternes of Cut-workes: newly invented and never published before. Also sundry sortes of spots, as flowers, birdes and fishes, &c. and will fitly serve to be wrought, some with gould, some with silke, and some with crewell in coullers: or otherwise at your pleasure. And never but once published before. Printed by Rich. Shorleyker.* No date, in oblong 4to. And, lastly, another oblong quarto entitled *The needles excellency, a new booke wherin are divers admirable workes wrought with the needle. Newly invented and cut in copper for the pleasure and profit of the industrious.* Printed for James Boler, &c. 1640. Beneath this title is a neat engraving of three ladies in a flower garden, under the names of Wisdom, Industrie, and Follie. Prefixed to the patterns are sundry poems in commendation of the needle, and describing the characters of ladies who have been eminent for their skill in needlework, among whom are Queen Elizabeth and the Countess of Pembroke. These poems were composed by John Taylor the water poet. It appears that the work had gone through twelve impressions, and yet a copy is now scarcely to be met with. This may be accounted for by supposing that such books were generally cut to pieces, and used by women to work upon or transfer to their samplers. From the dress of a lady and gentleman on one of the patterns in the last mentioned book, it appears to have been originally published in the reign of James the First. All the others are embellished with a multitude of patterns elegantly cut in wood, several of which are eminently conspicuous for their taste and beauty.

It is therefore apparent that the expression *point-devise* became applicable, in a secondary sense, to whatever was uncommonly exact, or constructed with the nicety and precision of *stitches made or devised by the needle.*

ACT III.

Scene 1. Page 97.

Vio. Dost thou live by thy *tabor?*

This instrument is found in the hands of fools long before the time of Shakspeare. With respect to *the sign of the tabor* mentioned in the notes, it might, as stated, have been *the designation of a musick shop*; but that it was *the sign of an eating-house kept by Tarleton* is a mistake into which a learned commentator has been inadvertently betrayed. It appears from Tarleton's *Jests*, 1611, 4to, that he kept a tavern in Gracious [Gracechurch] street, at the sign of the *Saba.* This is the person who in our *modern* bibles is called the *queen of Sheba*, and the sign has been corrupted into that of the *bell-savage*, as may be gathered from the inedited metrical *romance of Alexander*, supposed to have been written at the beginning of the fourteenth century by Adam Davie, who, in describing the countries visited by his hero, mentions that of *Macropy* (the *Macropii* of Pliny), and adds,

> " In heore* lond is a cité
> On of the noblest in Christianté† ;
> Hit hotith ‡ *Sabba* in langage.
> Thennes cam *Sibely savage*,

---

* their.

† The mention of the region of Christianity is a whimsical anachronism as connected with the story of Alexander; but we must do our author the justice to admit that in *his* time the Ethiopians were Christians.

‡ is called.

> Of al theo world theo fairest quene,
> To Jerusalem, Salamon to seone *
> For hire fairhed †, and for hire love,
> Salamon forsok his God above."

Sibely savage, as a proper name, is another perversion of *si belle sauvage*; and though the lady was supposed to have come from the remotest parts of Africa, and might have been as black as a Negro, we are not now to dispute the superlative beauty of the mistress of Salomon, here converted into a Savage. It must be admitted that the queen of Sheba was as well adapted to a sign as the wise men of the East, afterwards metamorphosed into the three kings of Cologne.

Mr. Pegge, in his *Anecdotes of the English language,* p. 291, informs us that a friend had seen a lease of the Bell Savage inn to *Isabella Savage;* "which," says he, "overthrows the conjectures about a bell and a savage, *la belle sauvage,* &c." It is probable that the learned writer's friend was in some way or other deceived. The date of the instrument is not mentioned; and if the above name really appeared in the lease, it might have been an accidental circumstance at a period not very distant. Mr. Pegge was likewise not aware that the same sign, corrupted in like manner, was used on the continent.

SCENE 2.   Page 109.

SIR To. Go write it in a martial hand; be *curst* and *brief.*

Of the latter sentence Dr. Johnson has not given the exact explanation. It alludes to the proverb, " A curst *cur* must be tied *short.*"

SCENE 4.   Page 120.

SIR To. What, man! defy the Devil: consider, he's an *enemy* to mankind.

It was very much the practice with old writers, both French and English, to call the Devil, *the enemy,* by way of pre-emi-

* to see.   † fairness, beauty.

nence, founded perhaps on the words of Christ in *Luke* x.
19. Thus at the beginning of the *Roman de Merlin, MS.*
" Mult fu iriez *li anemis* quant n̄re sires ot este en anfer ;"
and see other examples in Barbasan's glossary to the *Ordene
de chevalerie,* 1759, 12mo, in v. *Anemi.* The cause of the
Devil's wrath in the above instance, was the liberation of
Adam, Noah, and many other saints and patriarchs from the
purgatorial torments which they had endured. In a most
curious description of hell in *Examples howe mortall synne
maketh the synners inobedyentes to have many paynes and
doloures within the fyre of hell,* b. l. no date, 12mo, the Devil
is thus referred to : " Come than after me, and I shal shewe
unto the *the ryght cursed enemye* of humayne lygnage." And
again, " About *the enemy* there were so many devyls and of
cursed and myserable soules that no man myght beleve that
of all the worlde from the begynnynge myght be yssued and
brought forth so many soules." Sometimes he was called
the *enemy of hell,* as in Larke's *Boke of wisdome,* b. l. no date,
12mo, where it is said that " *the enemye of hell* ought to be
doubted of every wise man." This note may serve also
in further explanation of the line in *Macbeth,* Act III.
Scene 1,

> " Given to the common *enemy* of man."

It is remarkable that the Devil should be likewise called *the
enemy of mankind* in the East. See Gladwin's *Persian moonshee,* part ii. p. 23.

Scene 4. Page 120.

FAB. Carry his water to *the wise woman.*

Here may be a direct allusion to one of the two ladies of
this description mentioned in the following passage from
Heywood's play of *The wise woman of Hogsdon;* " You have
heard of *Mother Notingham,* who for her time was prettily
well skill'd in *casting of waters* : and after her, *Mother
Bombye.*" The latter is sometimes alluded to by Gerarde the

Herbalist, who, speaking of the properties of vervain, says,
" you must observe *mother Bumbies* rules to take just so many
knots or sprigs, and no more, least it fall out so that it do
you no good, if you catch no harme by it." *Historie of plants,*
p. 581.

Lilly's comedy of *Mother Bombie* is well known. The
several occupations of these impostors are thus described in
the above play by Heywood: " Let me see how many trades
have I to live by : First, I am *a wise-woman,* and a fortune-
teller, and under that I deale in physicke and forespeaking, in
palmistry, and recovering of things lost. Next, I undertake
to cure madd folkes. Then I keepe gentlewomen lodgers, to
furnish such chambers as I let out by the night : Then I am
provided for bringing young wenches to bed ; and, for a need,
you see I can play the match-maker. Shee that is but one,
and professeth so many, may well be tearmed *a wise-woman,*
if there bee any." Such another character was *Julian of
Brentford,* mentioned in the *Merry wives of Windsor.* These
persons were sometimes called *cunning* and *looming* women.

SCENE 4. Page 121.

> SIR TO. Come, we'll have him in a *dark room,* and bound. My niece
> is already in the belief that he is *mad.*

The reason for putting Malvolio into a *dark room* was to
make *him* believe that he was *mad ;* for a *madhouse* seems
formerly to have been called a *dark-house.* In the next act
Malvolio says, " Good Sir Topas, do not think I am *mad,*
they have laid me here in *hideous darkness."* And again, " I
say this *house is dark."* In Act V. he asks, "Why have you
suffer'd me to be imprison'd, kept in a *dark-house ?"* In *As
you like it,* Act III. Scene 1, Rosalind says that " love is a
madness, and deserves as well a *dark-house* and a whip, as
madmen do." Edward Blount, in the second dedication to
his *Hospitall of incurable fooles,* 1600, 4to, a translation from
the Italian, requests of the person whom he addresses to

take on him the office of patron or treasurer to the hospital; and that if any desperate censurer shall stab him for assigning his office or place, he presently take him into *the dark ward*: and in the same work, certain idle fools are consigned to the *darksome guesthouse of their madness.*

SCENE 4. Page 124.

> OLI. I have said too much unto a heart of stone, and laid mine honour too unchary *on't.*

This is the reading of the old copy, which has been unnecessarily disturbed at Theobald's suggestion by substituting *out.* If might be urged that *laying honour out* is but an awkward phrase. The old text simply means, I have *placed* my honour too incautiously *upon* a heart of stone. The preceding note had shown that adjectives are often used adverbially by Shakspeare.

SCENE 4. Page 127.

> SIR TO. He is a knight, dubb'd with *unhack'd rapier,* and on *carpet* consideration.

The original word is *unhatch'd,* and if any alteration be admitted it should be *an hatch'd,* for the first reason assigned in Mr. Malone's ingenious note. Sir Toby says that his brother knight was no hero dubbed in the field of battle, but a carpet knight made at home in time of peace with a sword of ceremony richly *gilt or engraved.* In *Don Quixote,* the damsel whom Sancho finds wandering in the streets of Barataria disguised as a man, is furnished with "a very faire *hatched* dagger," chap. 49 of Shelton's translation. In *The tragical history of Jetzer,* 1683, 18mo, mention is made of "a sword richly *hatcht* with silver." Thus much in support of the above slight alteration of the old reading. The second conjecture of Mr. Malone, that *unhatcht* might have been used in the sense of *unhack'd,* deserves much attention; but there was no necessity for introducing the latter word into the text. To *hatch* a sword has been thought to signify to *engrave* it;

but it appears from Holme's *Academy of armory,* B. iii. p. 91, that " *hatching,* is *to silver or gild* the hilt and pomell of a sword or hanger."

With respect to *carpet* knights, they were sometimes called knights of the *green cloth.* For this information we are also indebted to Holme, who, in his above cited work, B. iii. p. 57, informs us that " all such as have studied law, physic, or any other arts and sciences whereby they have become famous and serviceable to the court, city, or state, and thereby have merited honour, worship, or dignity, from the sovereign and fountain of honour; if it be the King's pleasure to knight any such persons, seeing they are not knighted as soldiers, they are not therefore to use the horseman's title or spurs; they are only termed simply *miles et milites, knights of the carpet or knights of the green cloth,* to distinguish them from knights that are dubbed as soldiers in the field; though in these our days they are created or dubbed with the like ceremony as the others are, by the stroak of a naked sword upon their shoulder, with the words, *Rise up Sir T. A. knight.*"

ACT IV.

Scene 1.   Page 136.

Clo. I am afraid this great *lubber the world* will prove a cockney.

A typographical corruption seems to have crept into this place from similitude of sound; but a very slight alteration will restore the sense. The clown is speaking of *vent* as an affected word; and we should therefore read " this great *lubberly word* will prove a cockney," i. e. will turn out to be cockney language.

Scene 2.   Page 140.

Clo. For as *the old hermit of Prague——*

Not the celebrated heresiarch Jerome of Prague, but another of that name born likewise at Prague, and called *the hermit of Camaldoli* in Tuscany.

Scene 2. Page 141.

Clo. Say'st thou that *house* is dark ?

This Mr. Malone conceives to be *a pompous appellation for the small room* in which Malvolio was confined ; but it seems to be merely the designation of a madhouse. See the preceding note on Act III. Scene 4, p. 121.

ACT V.

Scene 1. Page 157.

Priest. A contract of eternal bond of love
Confirm'd by mutual joinder of your hands,
Attested by the holy close of lips,
Strengthened by interchangement of your rings ;
And all the ceremony of this compact
Seal'd in my function, by my testimony.

It will be necessary, for the better illustration of these lines, to connect them with what Olivia had said to Sebastian at the end of the preceding act :

" Now go with me, and with this holy man,
Into the chantry by : there *before him*
And underneath that consecrated roof
Plight me the full assurance of your faith ;
That my most jealous and too doubtful soul
May live at peace. He shall conceal it
Whiles you are willing it shall come to note ;
What time we will our *celebration* keep
According to my birth."

Now the whole has been hitherto regarded as relating to *an actual marriage* that had been solemnized between the parties ; whereas it is manifest that nothing more is meant than a *betrothing, affiancing* or *promise of future marriage,* anciently distinguished by the name of *espousals,* a term which was for a long time confounded with *matrimony,* and at length came exclusively to denote it. The form of betrothing at church in this country, has not been handed down to us in any of its ancient ecclesiastical service books ; but it is to be remembered that Shakspeare is here making use of foreign

materials, and the ceremony is preserved in a few of the
French and Italian rituals.

The custom of betrothing appears to have been known in
ancient times to almost all the civilized nations among whom
marriage was considered as a sacred engagement. Our northern ancestors were well acquainted with it. With them
the process was as follows : 1. *Procatio,* or wooing. 2. *Impe-
tratio,* or demanding of the parents or guardian. 3. The conditions of the contract. All these were sealed by joining the
right hands, by a certain form of words, and a confirmation
before witnesses. The length of the time between espousals
and marriage was uncertain, and governed by the convenience
of the parties ; it generally extended to a few months. Sometimes in cases of necessity, such as the parties living in different countries, and where the interference of proxies had
been necessary, the time was protracted to three years. The
contract of the affiancing party was called *handsaul* ; (whence
our *hansel*) of the agreeing party, *handfastening.* See Thor-
lacius *De borealium veterum matrimonio,* 1785, 4to, pp. 33,
42. Vincent de Beauvais, a writer of the 13th century, in his
Speculum historiale, lib. ix. c. 70, has defined *espousals* to be
a contract of future marriage, made either by a simple promise, by earnest or security given, by a ring, or by an oath.
During the same period, and the following centuries, we may
trace several other modes of betrothing, some of which it may
be worth while to describe more at large.

I. The interchangement of rings.—Thus in Chaucer's
Troilus and Creseide, book 3.

> " Sone after this they spake of sondry things
>   As fill to purpose of this aventure,
>   And playing *enterchaungeden her rings*
>   Of which I can not tellen no scripture.
>   But well I wot, a broche of gold and assure
>   In which a rubie set was like an herte
>   Creseide him yave, and stacke it on his sherte."

When espousals took place at church, rings were also interchanged. According to the ritual of the Greek church, the priest first placed the rings on the fingers of the parties, who afterwards exchanged them. Sometimes the man only gave a ring. In the life of Saint Leobard, who is said to have flourished about the year 580, written by Gregory of Tours he gives a ring, a kiss, and a pair of shoes to his affianced. The ring and shoes were a symbol of securing the lady's hands and feet in the trammels of conjugal obedience; but the ring of itself was sufficient to confirm the contract. In *The miracles of the Virgin Mary*, compiled in the twelfth century by a French monk, there is a story of a young man who, falling in love with an image of the Virgin, inadvertently placed on one of its fingers a ring which he had received from his mistress, accompanying the gift with the most tender language of respect and affection. A miracle instantly took place, and the ring remained immoveable. The young man, greatly alarmed for the consequences of his rashness, consulted his friends, who advised him by all means to devote himself entirely to the service of the Madonna. His love for his former mistress prevailing over their remonstrances: he married her; but on the wedding night the newly-betrothed lady appeared to him, and urged her claim with so many dreadful menaces that the poor man felt himself compelled to abandon his bride, and that very night to retire privately to a hermitage, where he became a *monk* for the rest of his life. This story has been translated by Mons. Le Grand in his entertaining collection of *fabliaux*, where the ring is called a *marriage ring*: but this is probably a mistake in the translator, as appears from several copies of the above *Miracles* that have been consulted. The giving of rings was likewise a *pledge of love* in cases where no marriage could possibly happen. In *The lay of Equitan*, a married woman and her gallant exchange rings,

> " Par lur anels sentresaisirent
> Lur *fiaunce* sentreplevirent."

In a romance written by Raimond Vidal, a Provençal poet of the thirteenth century, a knight devotes himself to the service of a lady, who promises him a kiss in a year's time when she shall be married. They ratify the contract by an exchange of rings. Mr. Steevens has on the present occasion introduced a note, wherein a ludicrous superstition is mentioned, in order to prove that "in our ancient *marriage ceremony*, the man received as well as gave a ring." But the passage which he cites from Lupton is wrongly translated from Mizaldus, who only speaks of *the* marriage ring : and so it is in Scott's *Discovery of witchcraft*, fo. 82. edit. 1584, 4to, where a similar receipt is given. Mr. Steevens was indeed convinced of this by the author of these observations, and in a note on *All's well that ends well* has retracted his opinion. No instance has occurred where rings were *interchanged* at a *marriage*.

II. The kiss that was mutually given. When this ceremony took place at church, the lady of course withdrew the veil which was usually worn on the occasion; when in private, the drinking of healths generally followed.

III. The joining of hands. This is often alluded to by Shakspeare himself. See a note in the *Winter's tale*, p. 17, Steevens's edition, 1793.

IV. The testimony of witnesses. That of the priest alone was generally sufficient, though we often find many other persons attending the ceremony. The words " there before him," and " he shall conceal it," in Olivia's speech, sufficiently demonstrate that betrothing and not marriage is intended; for in the latter the presence of the priest alone would not have sufficed. In later times, espousals in the church were often prohibited in France, because instances frequently occurred where the parties, relying on the testimony of the priest, scrupled not to live together as man and wife; which gave rise to much scandal and disorder. Excesses were likewise often committed by the celebration of espousals in taverns and alehouses, and some of the synodal decrees expressly enjoin that the parties shall not get drunk on these occasions.

The ceremony, generally speaking, was performed by the priest demanding of the parties if they had entered into a contract with any other person, or made a vow of chastity or religion; whether they had acted for each other, or for any child they might have had, in the capacity of godfather or godmother, or whether they had committed incontinence with any near relation of the other party; but the latter questions might be dispensed with at the discretion of the priest. Then this oath was administered—" You swear by God and his holy saints herein and by all the saints of Paradise, that you will take this woman whose name is N. to wife within forty days, if holy church will permit." The priest then joined their hands, and said,—" And thus you affiance yourselves;" to which the parties answered,—" Yes, sir." They then received a suitable exhortation on the nature and design of marriage, and an injunction to live piously and chastely until that event should take place. They were not permitted, at least by the church, to reside in the same house, but were nevertheless regarded as man and wife independently of the usual privileges: and this will account for Olivia's calling Cesario " husband;" and when she speaks of " keeping *celebration* according to her birth," it alludes to *future marriage.* This took place in a reasonable time after betrothing, but was seldom protracted in modern times beyond forty days. So in *Measure for measure,* Claudio calls Julietta his *wife,* and says he got possession of her bed upon a true *contract.* The duke likewise, in addressing Mariana who had been *affianced* to Angelo, says, " he is your *husband* on a pre-contract."

Before we quit the subject, it may be necessary to observe that betrothing was not an essential preliminary to marriage, but might be dispensed with. The practice in this respect varied in different times and places. The desuetude of espousals in England seems to have given rise to the action at law for damages on breach of promise of marriage. And thus much may suffice for a general idea of this ancient custom; the legal niceties must be sought for in the works of the civilians.

SCENE 1.   Page 159.

> SIR To. Then he's a rogue.   After a *passy-measure*, or a *pavin*, I hate a drunken rogue.

Florio, in his Italian dictionary, 1598, has "*passamezzo*, a *passameasure* in dancing, a cinque pace;" and although the English word is corrupt, the other contributes to show a part, at least, of the figure of this dance, which is said to have consisted in making several steps round the ball-room and then *crossing it in the middle*. Brantôme calls it " le *pazzameno* d'Italie," and it appears to have been more particularly used by the Venetians. It was much in vogue with us during Shakspeare's time, as well as the *Pavan*; and both were imported either from France, Spain, or Italy. In a book of instructions for the lute, translated from the French by J. Alford, 1568, 4to, there are two *passameze* tunes printed in letters according to the lute notation.

As to the *Pavan*, there is some doubt whether it originally belongs to Spain or Italy. *Spanish pavans* are certainly mentioned by Ben Jonson in the *Alchymist*, and by Brantôme in his *Dames illustres*, who adds that he had seen it danced by Francis I. and his sister, the celebrated Margaret of Navarre, and also by Mary Queen of Scots. There is good reason, however, for thinking the term is Italian, and derived from the city of *Padua*, where the dance is said to have been invented. Massa Gallesi, a civilian of the sixteenth century, calls it *saltatio Paduana*. In a catalogue of books that were exposed to sale at Frankfort fair, from 1564 to 1592, the following are mentioned : " Chorearum molliorum collectanea omnis fere generis tripudia complectens, utpote *Padoanas, passemezos,* allemandas, galliardas, branles, et id genus alia, tam vivæ voci quam instrumentis musicis accommodata. Antverpiæ, 1583, 4to." " Cantiones *Italicæ* quas *Paduana* Itali vocant, quatuor vocum. Venetiis, 1565, 4to." " Sixti Kargen, renovata cythara, hoc est, novi et commodissimi exercendæ cytharæ modi, constantes cantionibus musicis, *passomezo, podoanis,* gaillardis, Alemanicis et aliis ejusmodi pulchris exemplis, ad tabulaturam communem redactis. Argentorati, 1575, et Moguntiæ, 1569, folio." In Alford's *Instructions for the lute,* above mentioned, there is a *Paduane* and a *Pavane.* Randle Holme, in his *Academy of armory,* 1688, folio, book iii. c. 3, speaking of the *Pavan* as a tune, describes it as " the height of composition made only to delight the ear : be it of 2, 3, 4, 5, or 6 parts [it] doth commonly consist of three straines, each straine to be played twice over." In an old MS. collection of lessons for the virginals, there is one called " Dr. Bull's *melancholy* pavin." Mr. Tyrwhitt, therefore, is right in supposing that a jovial blade like Sir Toby would be naturally averse to these grave dances, and the dullness of the tunes belonging to them.

SCENE 1. Page 162.

DUKE. One face, one voice, one habit and two persons ;
A natural *perspective,* that is, and is not.

The several kinds of perspective glasses that were used in Shakspeare's time, may be found collected together in Scot's *Discoverie of witchcraft,* 1584, 4to, book xiii. ch. 19. They cannot be exceeded in number by any modern optician's shop in England. Among these, that alluded to by the Duke is thus described : " There be glasses also wherein one man may see another man's image, and not his own." It is to be observed that a *perspective* formerly meant a *glass* that assisted the sight in any way.

SCENE 1.　Page 169.

MAL. And made the most notorious *geck*, and gull.

Dr. Johnson rightly explains geck, a fool. It is so in all the Northern languages. In Saxon, ȝæc is a cuckow, whence *gouk, gawk,* and *gawky.* Mr. Steevens's quotations seem to exhibit the word in another sense, viz. a *mock* or *mockery.*

THE CLOWN.

The clown in this play is a domestic or hired fool, in the service of Olivia. He is specifically termed " an *allowed* fool," and " Feste the jester, a fool that the lady Olivia's father took much delight in." Malvolio likewise speaks of him as " a set fool." Of his dress it is impossible to speak correctly. If the fool's expression, " I will *impeticoat* thy gratility," be the original language, he must have been habited accordingly. Mr. Ritson has asserted that he has neither coxcomb nor bauble, deducing his argument from the want of any allusion to them. Yet such an omission may be a very fallacious guide in judging of the habit of this character on the stage. It must, however, be admitted, that where this happens there can be no clue as to the precise manner in which the fool was dressed.

MEASURE FOR MEASURE.

ACT I.

Scene 1. Page 180.

Duke. . . Then no more remains,
But that to your *sufficiency,* as your worth is able,
And let them work.

Sufficiency is, no doubt, *ability,* and not *authority,* as Warburton conceives ; and this shows that there is an omission
in the speech of what the duke would have added concerning
the authority which he meant to delegate. The most
rational addition is that suggested by Mr. Tyrwhitt. It is
remarkable that Dr. Johnson should contend for the introduction of a line of *thirteen* syllables !

Scene 1. Page 186.

Duke. *Mortality* and *mercy* in Vienna
Live in thy *tongue* and *heart.*

That is, " I delegate to thy tongue the power of pronouncing sentence of death, and to thy heart the privilege of
exercising mercy." These are words of great import, and
ought to be made clear, as on them depends the chief incident
of the play.

Scene 2. Page 191.

Lucio. Behold, behold, &c.

This speech should have been given to the *first gentleman,*
in order to correspond with the note, which is probably
right.

SCENE 2.   Page 191.

LUCIO. A *French crown* more.

The quotations already given sufficiently exemplify the
meaning; yet that which follows being remarkably illustrative, is offered in addition.   " More seeming friendship [is]
to be had in *an house of transgression* for a *French crown*,
though it be a *bald one*, than at Belinsgate for a boxe o'
th'eare." *Vox graculi, or Jack Dawe's prognostication*, 1623, 4to,
p. 60.

SCENE 2.   Page 192.

1. GENT. How now, which of your *hips* has the most profound
        sciatica ?

A most appropriate question to the bawd.   The author of
the facetious Latin comedy of *Cornelianum dolium* has named
one of Cornelius's strumpets *Sciatica*.   She thus speaks of herself; " In lectulo meo ægrè me vertere potui ; podagram, chira-
gram, et *hip*-agram (si ita dicere liceat) nocte quotidie sensi."

SCENE 2.   Page 195.

BAWD. What's to do here, *Thomas* Tapster ?

Why does she call the clown by this name, when it appears
from his own showing that his name was *Pompey* ? Perhaps
she is only quoting some old saying or ballad.

SCENE 3.   Page 201.

CLAUD. . . . . . for in her youth
    There is a *prone* and speechless dialect.

One of the old significations of this word appears to have
been *easily moving*, which is evidently the sense required in
this place.   See Cotgrave's *Dictionary*, in *prone*.

SCENE 4.   Page 203.

DUKE. Where youth and cost and witless bravery *keeps*.

Mr. Reed's explanation of this word as used for *dwells*, is
confirmed by another passage in this play, Act IV. Scene 1.

" .   .   . a breath thou art
  That dost this *habitation* where thou *keep'st*
  Hourly afflict."

Scene 5. Page 208.

Lucio. *For that, which if myself might be his judge,*
He should receive his punishment in thanks.

It has been conceived that there is here a transposition at
the press for " that for which." The emendation is more
grammatical than *harmonious*; but the expression is quite in
Shakspeare's manner. A few pages further on we have this
similar phraseology :

" Whether you had not sometime in your life
Err'd in this point *which now you censure him.*"

Scene 5. Page 211.

Lucio. Your brother and his *lover*.

This term was applied to the female sex not only in Shakspeare's time, but even to a very late period. Lady Wortley
Montagu in a letter to her husband, speaking of a young
girl who forbade the bans of marriage at Huntingdon, calls
her *lover*. See her works, vol. i. p. 238.

ACT II.

Scene 1. Page 216.

Escal. Let us be keen, and rather cut a little
Than *fall* and bruise to death.

On the very plausible authority of a passage in *As you like
it,* where the executioner is said to " fall his axe," the present
metaphor has been supposed to refer also to the punishment
of decapitation. If it be so, there is a manifest impropriety
in the expression " cut a little," as we are not to imagine that
Escalus would intend to chop off a criminal's hand, or to deprive him of his ears; both modes of punishment, which
though frequently practised in the reign of Elizabeth, seem
exclusively adapted to a community of barbarians. May not
the metaphor be rather borrowed from the cutting down of

timber, and Escalus mean to say, " Is it not better to lop off
a few branches, than to *fall* the whole tree ? "

SCENE 1. Page 217.

ANG. The jury, passing on the prisoner's life
      May, in the sworn twelve, have a thief or two, &c.

We have here one of Shakspeare's trips ; an English jury
in a German court of justice.

SCENE 1. Page 223.

CLO. Your honours have seen such dishes ; they are not *China
dishes*, but very good dishes.

We must not conclude with Mr Steevens that a *China dish*
was such an uncommon thing in the age of Shakspeare.   In
the first act of Massinger's *Renegado*, this article is mentioned, together with crystal glasses and pictures, as com-
posing the furniture of a broker's shop ; and it appears from
other authorities that China dishes were used at banquets.
During the reign of Elizabeth several Spanish carracks were
taken, a part of whose cargoes was *China ware of porcelaine*.
The recent seizure by Philip II. of Portugal and its colonies
led to this sort of commerce in the East Indies.   In Minsheu's *Spanish dialogues*, 1623, folio, p. 12, *China mettall* is
explained to be " the fine dishes of earth painted, such as are
brought from Venice."   It is very probable that we had this
commodity by means of our traffic with Italy, which also
supplied the term *porcelaine*.   China ware was so called from
its resemblance to the polished exterior of the *concha Veneris*
or some other similar shell, which, for reasons that cannot
here be given, was called *porcellana*. The curious reader may
find a clue by consulting Florio's Italian dictionary, 1598,
under the word *porcile*.   In the time of Cromwell a duty of
twenty shillings was paid on every dozen *China dishes* under
a quart, and of sixty on those of a quart and upwards.   See
Oliverian acts, A. D. 1657.

Scene 2.   Page 238.

Isab. . . . . . spare him, spare him;
He's not prepar'd for death! Even for our kitchens
We kill the fowl *of season.*

She means " not *before* it is in season; not *prematurely,*
as you would kill my brother."

Scene 2.   Page 240.

Isab. Could great men thunder
As Jove himself does, Jove would ne'er be quiet,
For ev'ry pelting petty officer
Would use his heaven for thunder; nothing but thunder.

This fine sentiment, which nevertheless contains a very
obvious fault in the mode of expressing it, appears to have
been suggested by the following lines in Ovid's *Tristia,* lib. ii.,
that Shakspeare might have read in Churchyard's translation :

" Si quoties peccant homines sua fulmina mittat
Jupiter, exiguo tempore inermis erit."

Scene 2.   Page 240.

Isab. Merciful heaven!
Thou rather with thy sharp and sulphurous bolt
Split'st the unwedgeable and gnarled oak,
Than the soft myrtle.

There is much affinity between the above lines and these
in Persius, sat. ii. :

" Ignovisse putas, quia, cum tonat, ocyus ilex
Sulfure discutitur sacro, quam tuque domusque? "

But although there were two or three editions of that author
published in England in the reign of Elizabeth, he does not
appear to have been then translated.

Scene 2.   Page 243.

Isab. . . . . prayers from *preserved* souls,
From fasting maids, whose minds are dedicate
To nothing temporal.

Here is no metaphor from *preserved fruits,* as Warburton
fancifully conceives. *Preserved* is used in its common and

obvious acceptation. Isabella alludes to the prayers of her fellow nuns in addition to her own.

SCENE 2. Page 246.

ANG. O cunning *enemy*, that, to catch a saint,
    With saints dost bait thy hook !

Enemy is here used for the *Devil*. See before in p. 62, 63.

SCENE 4. Page 260.

ISAB. . . . . Sir, believe this,
    I had rather give my body than my soul.

It is Isabella's purpose to give an evasive or ambiguous answer to Angelo's strange question, and she accordingly does so. Or, if it have any meaning, it may be " I would even consent to your terms if I could save my soul, or if my soul did not thereby incur perdition."

ACT III.

SCENE 1. Page 272.

DUKE. . . merely thou art *Death's fool;*
    For him thou labour'st by thy flight to shun,
    And yet run'st toward him still.

And in *Pericles*, Act III. Scene 2, " to please the *fool and death.*" One note may serve for both these passages.

Dr. Warburton had conceived an allusion in the first speech to certain characters of *death and the fool* in the old *moralities*, in which, most unquestionably, they are not to be found, at least, in any which now remain. It is in this place that the latter part of Mr. Steevens's note on the passage in *Pericles* should have been introduced, with the following additional circumstances that had probably escaped the learned commentator's recollection; that his informant concerning the skeleton character at the fair remembered also to have seen another personage in the habit of a fool: and that arriving when the performances at the booth were finished for

the evening, he could not succeed in procuring a repetition of
the piece, losing thereby the means of all further information
on the subject. It is therefore probable that the remainder
of Dr. Warburton's note is correct, although he may have
erred in his designation of this mummery. What connection
the subject in question has with the old initial letter of *death
and the fool,* and the *dance of death,* is shown in a note to
Love's labour lost, vol. v. p. 316, and in another on the passage
in *Pericles,* both of which should have been incorporated with
the present.

Mr. Ritson, in correcting a remark made by the ingenious
continuator of Ben Jonson's *Sad shepherd,* has inaccurately
stated that the figures in the initial letter were " actually
copied from the margin of an old missal." The letter that
occurs in Stowe's *Survey of London,* edit. 1618, 4to, is only
an enlarged but imperfect copy from another belonging to a
regular dance of death used as initials by some of the Basil
printers in the sixteenth century, and which, from the extraordinary skill that accompanies their execution, will ever rank
amongst the finest efforts in the art of engraving on blocks
of wood or metal. Most of the subjects in this dance of
death have undoubtedly been supplied by that curious pageant of mortality which, during the middle ages, was so
great a favourite as to be perpetually exhibited to the people
either in the sculpture and painting of ecclesiastical buildings,
or in the books adapted to the service of the church : yet
some of them but ill accord with those serious ideas which
the nature of the subject is calculated to inspire. In these
the artist has indulged a vein of broad and satirical humour
which was not wholly reserved for the caricaturists of modern
times ; and in one or two instances he has even overleaped
the bounds of decency. The letter in Stowe's *Survey* is
the only one that appears to have been imitated from the
above alphabet; and as it throws some light on that part of
the Duke's speech which occasioned the present note, it is

here very accurately copied. It is to be remembered that in most of the old *dances of death* the subject of the fool is introduced : and it is, on the whole, extremely probable that some such representation might have suggested the image before us.

SCENE 1.   Page 285.

CLAUD. . . . . . and the delighted spirit
    To bathe in *fiery floods*, or to reside
    In thrilling regions of *thick-ribbed ice ;*
    To be imprison'd in the viewless winds,
    And *blown with restless violence* round about
    The pendant world ; or to be worse than worst
    Of those that lawless and incertain thoughts
    Imagine *howling !*——

It is difficult to decide whether Shakspeare is here alluding to the pains of hell or purgatory. May not the whole be a mere poetical rhapsody originating in the recollection of what he had read in books of Catholic divinity ? for it is very certain that some of these were extremely familiar to him. Among them he might have seen a compilation on the pains of hell, entitled *Examples howe mortall synne maketh the synners inobedyentes to have many paynes and dolours within the fyre of hell* ; black letter, no date, 12mo, and chiefly extracted from that once popular work, the *Sermones discipuli,* which contains at the end a promptuary of examples for the use of preachers. From this little volume it may be worth while to select the following passage, as according in some degree with the matter of Claudio's speech :—" he tolde that he sawe in hell a torment of an *yzye ponde* where the soules the whiche therin were tormented cryed so horryble that they were herde unto heven," sign. B. iij. " And the sayde beest was upon a ponde full of *strong yse*, the which beest devoured the soules within his wombe in suche maner that they became as unto nothynge by the tormentes that they suffred. Afterwarde he put them out of his wombe *within the yse of the sayde ponde*," sign. G. iij. " The caytyve was in syke wyse, for she myght not helpe herself, the whiche herde terryble cryes and *howlynges of soules*," sign. H. And again, " And the devyll was bounde by every joynture of all his membres with great chaynes of yron and of copre brennyng. And of great torment and vehement woodnes whereof he was full he turned hym from the one syde unto the other, and stretched out his handes in the multytude of the sayde soules, and toke them, and strayned them in lykewyse as men may do a clustre of grapes in theyr handes for to make the wyne come forth. And in such maner he strayned them that he eyther brake theyr heedes, or theyr fete, or handes, or some other membres. Afterward *he syghed and blewe and dysperpeled the sayde soules* into many of the tormentes of the fyre of hell," sign. H. iiij.

The following lines from the sixth book of Phaer's Virgil might have furnished some materials on the occasion:

" . . . some *hie in ayer* doth hang in pinnes
    Some fleeting ben in *floods*, and deepe in gulfes themselves they tier
    Till sinnes away be *washt, or clensed cleer with purgin fire.*"

In the old legend of *Saint Patrick's purgatory* mention is made of a lake of ice and snow, into which persons were plunged up to their necks; and in the *Shepherd's calendar*, chap. xviii. there is a description of hell as " the rewarde of them that kepen the X comaundements of the Devyll," in in which these lines occur:

> "   .   . a *great froste* in a water rounes
> And after a *bytter wynde* comes
> Whiche gothe through the soules with yre ;
> Fendes with pokes pulle theyr flesshe ysondre,
> They fyght and curse, and eche on other wonder."

Chaucer, in his *Assemblie of foules,* has given an abridgement of Cicero's dream of Scipio ; and speaking of souls in hell, he says:

> " And breakers of the lawe, sothe to saine
> And likerous folke, after that they been dede
> *Shull whirle about the world* alway in paine
> Till many a world be passed."

It was not until the seventh century that the doctrine of purgatory was confirmed, when " they held that departed souls expiated their sins by *baths, ice, hanging in the air,* &c.," says a curious writer on this subject. See Douglas's *Vitis degeneris,* 1668, 12mo, p. 77.

With respect to the much contested and obscure expression of *bathing the delighted spirit in fiery floods,* Milton appears to have felt less difficulty in its construction than we do at present ; for he certainly remembered it when he made Comus say,

> "   .   .   .   .   .   one sip of this
> Will *bathe* the drooping *spirits in delight*
> Beyond the bliss of dreams."

SCENE 2.   Page 295.

ELB.   Bless you good *father friar.*
DUKE.   And you good *brother father.*

Mr. Tyrwhitt remarks that *father friar* is a blunder, and so indeed the Duke from his answer seems to consider it. Yet friars have often been addressed in this way ; and a few pages further Escalus calls the Duke *father,* who had just been introduced to him as a *friar.* The Duke, indeed, soon after uses the term *brother* when speaking of himself. Whilst the passage quoted by Mr. Steevens gives support to Mr. Tyrwhitt's observation that *friar* is a corruption of the French *frere,* it seems to disprove his assertion that Elbow's phrase is erroneous.

Scene 2.   Page 298.

> Lucio. What, is there none of *Pygmalion's images, newly made woman,* to be had now, for putting the hand in the pocket, and extracting it clutch'd?

None of the explanations of this speech are satisfactory, but least of all such part of a note by the author of these remarks, as refers to the *picklock,* which has been better accounted for by Mr. Ritson. It is probable, after all, that Lucio simply means to ask the clown if *he has no newly-coined money wherewith to bribe* the officers of justice, alluding to the portrait of the queen.

Scene 2.   Page 308.

> Escal. This would make mercy *swear and play the tyrant.*

The old belief certainly was that tyrants in general swore lustily; but here seems to be a particular allusion to the character of Herod, in the mystery of *The slaughter of the innocents,* formerly acted by the city companies in their pageants, and of which those for Chester and Coventry are still preserved in the British Museum. In this curious specimen of our early drama, Herod is made to swear by Mahound, by cockes blood, &c. He is uniformly in a passion throughout the piece; and this, according to the stage direction, " Here Erode ragis," is exemplified by some extraordinary gesticulation. See the notes of Messrs. Steevens and Malone on a passage in *Hamlet,* Act III. Scene 2.

Scene 2.   Page 310.

> Duke. . . .   and now is he *resolved* to die.

Mr. Reed has certainly adduced an instance which proves that *resolved* occasionally means *satisfied,* and we still talk of resolving difficulties, or a question in arithmetic; but in the passage before us it seems rather to signify *resolute, firm, de-*

termined. Thus the allegorical romance of *Le chevalier deli-beré* was translated into English in the reign of Queen Elizabeth, under the title of *The resolved gentleman*; and into Spanish by that of *Il cavalero determinado.*

ACT IV.

Scene 1.   Page 318.

Isab. And that I have *possess'd* him.

In the same sense Shylock says

" I have *possess'd* your grace of what I purpose."

It were better that Shakspeare should be thus made his own commentator where it can be done, than that he should be explained by quotations from other authors.

Scene 1.   Page 319.

Duke. . . . . volumes of report
        Run with these false and most contrarious *quests*
        Upon thy doings.

It is presumed that the sense of *messengers* annexed to this word by Mr. Ritson cannot be maintained, but that the very line he refers to establishes it to be *searches, inquiries.* Mr. Malone's note is, of the others, the most satisfactory. The Duke alludes to the false and various conclusions that result from investigating the actions of men high in office. There is an old pamphlet with the whimsical title of *Jacke of Dover, his quest of inquirie, or his privy search for the veriest foole in England,* 1604, 4to.

Scene 1.   Page 321.

Duke. Sith that the justice of your title to him
        Doth *flourish* the deceit.

That is, *decorate an action that would otherwise seem ugly.* Two metaphors have already been suggested; a third remains to be stated. *Flourish* may, perhaps, allude to the ornaments that embellish the *ancient* as well as modern books of penmanship. There are no finer specimens of beautiful writing extant than some of the reign of Elizabeth, who herself wrote a very elegant Italian hand in the early part of her life.

Scene 2. Page 322.

Prov. . . . and your deliverance with an *unpitied* whipping ; for you have been a notorious bawd.

Mr. Steevens makes *unpitied*, *unmerciful*; it is rather *a whipping that none shall pity*, for the reason that immediately follows.

Scene 2. Page 334.

Prov. Pardon me, good father, it is against my oath.

This is a very different provost from one of whom Fabian in his *Chronicle*, p. 187, relates the following story : " In the thyrde yere of the reigne of this Philip, *the provost of Paris*, having in his prison a Picard, a man of greate riches, whiche for felony or like crime, was judged to be hanged. The sayde provost for great benefit to him done and payment of great summes by the sayd Pycard, tooke an other poore innocent man, and put him to death, in steede of the sayd Pycarde. Of the whiche offence whan due proofe of it was made before the kynges counsayle, the sayde provoste for the same dede was put unto like judgement."

Scene 3. Page 335.

Clo. First, here's young master Rash, he's in for *a commodity of brown paper and old ginger.*

The nefarious practice of lending young men money in the shape of goods which are afterwards sold at a great loss, appears to have been more prevalent in the reign of Elizabeth than even at present. It is very strongly marked in Lodge's *Looking glasse for London and Englande*, 1598, where a usurer being very urgent for the repayment of his debt is thus answered, " I pray you, sir, consider that my losse was great by the commoditie I tooke up; you know, sir, I borrowed of you forty pounds, whereof I had ten pounds in money, and thirtie pounds in *lute strings*, which when I came to sell againe, I could get but five pounds for them, so had I, sir, but fifteene pounds for my fortie: In consideration of this ill bargaine, I pray you, sir, give me a month longer." But this sort of usury is much older than Shakspeare's time, and is thus curiously described in one of the sermons of Father Maillard, a celebrated preacher at Paris at the end of the fifteenth century, and whose style very much resembles that of John Whitfield. "Quidam indigens pecunia venit ad thesaurarium supra quem fuerunt assignata mille scuta; dicit thesaurarius, Ego dabo tibi, sed pro nunc non habeo argentum; sed expectes usque ad quindecim dies. Pauper dicit, Non possum expectare; respondet thesaurarius, Dabo tibi unam partem in argento et alia in mercantiis: et illud quod valebit centum scuta, faciet valere ducenta. Hic est usura palliata." *Sermo in feriam*, iiii. *de passione.*

SCENE 3.   Page 337.

CLO. . . . *ginger* was not much in request, for the old women were all dead.

This spice was formerly held in very great repute, and especially among elderly persons. Sir Thomas Elyot in his *Castle of health*, 1580, 12mo, says, it comforts the head and stomach, and being green and well confectioned, quickens remembrance, if it be taken in a morning fasting. Henry Buttes, who wrote a whimsical book entitled *Dyet's dry dinner*, 1599, 12mo, speaks much in its praise, and says that being condite with honey it "warmes olde mens bellyes." In Ben Jonson's masque of *The metamorphosed gipsies*, a country wench laments the being robbed of " a dainty race of *ginger*;" and in the old play of *The famous victories of Henry the fifth*, a clown charges a thief with having " taken the great race of ginger, that bouncing *Besse* with the jolly buttocks should have had." In Beaumont and Fletcher's *Knight of the burning pestle*, the citizen's wife gives a man who had been soundly beaten some *green ginger* to comfort him. Ginger was used likewise to spice ale. In Lodge's *Looking glasse for London and England,* the clown says, " Ile tell you, sir, if you did taste of the ale, all *Ninivie* hath not such a cup of ale, it floures in the cup, sir, by my troth I spent eleven pence, besides *three rases of ginger."* The numerous virtues of this root are likewise detailed in Vennor's *Via recta ad vitam longam.*

SCENE 3. Page 342.

PROV. One *Ragozine,* a most notorious pirate.

Some attempt to elucidate this name has been made in the first note to the Merchant of Venice, into which it is rather improperly introduced. Mr. Heath had supposed that *Ragozine* was put for *Ragusan, i. e.* a native of the city of *Ragusa* on the gulf of Venice, famous for its trading vessels ; but it was incumbent on that gentleman to have shown that the inhabitants of the above city were *pirates.* This however would have been extremely difficult, if not impossible ; for, on the contrary, Rycaut, in his *State of the Ottoman empire,* has expressly declared that the *Ragusans* never offered injury ; but that, on receiving any, they very patiently supported it. Wherever Shakspeare met with the name of *Ragozine,* it should seem to be a *metathesis* of the French *Argousin,* or the Italian *Argosino, i. e.* an officer or lieutenant on board a galley ; and, as Menage conjectures, a corruption of the Spanish *Alguasil.* See Carpentier, *Suppl. ad gloss. Dufresne,* under the word *Argoisillo.*

ACT V.

SCENE 1. Page 358.

ISAB. . . . but let your reason serve
To make the truth appear, where it seems hid ;
And hide the false, seems true.

The apparent difficulty in the last line proceeds from its elliptical construction ; yet the meaning is sufficiently obvious. Isabella requests of the Duke to exert his reason *to discover* truth where it seems hid, and *to suppress* falsehood *where it* has the semblance of truth. *Hide* is, doubtless, a licentious word, but was used for the reason suggested by Mr. Malone.

SCENE 1. Page 375.

LUCIO. Show your sheep-biting face, and be *hang'd an hour*.

There would have been little reason for dissenting from Mr. Henley's ingenious note, in which he supposes that this expression refers to the *pillory*, but for the subsequent remark by Lucio, " this may prove worse than *hanging."* It seems therefore more probable that " hang'd an hour" alludes to the *time* usually allotted for torturing the miserable object of the barbarous punishment by suspension, which is justly execrated by Randle Holme as " a dog's death," and always excites in the spectator a strange mixture of ludicrous and shocking sensations. It dishonours the living more than it degrades the criminal. The Turkish bowstring were much less offensive to the feelings of humanity : but the more solemn and decorous infliction of death, (if inflicted it must be,) would, as in military cases, be the stroke of the bullet, provided such a measure could be adopted without offending the soldier's honour. The pre-eminent mercy of the English law disdains to augment the horrors of premature dissolution by personal pain and torture ; its object is to prevent or diminish the commission of the crime. On this principle, one could wish that, on the close of the usual necessary and consolatory preparation for death, some mode of stupefying the offender were adopted ; that no sensation of torture on his part might be felt, nor any other on that of the spectator, than a satisfaction that the sentence of the law had been fulfilled. For this digression no apology can be necessary. As to Mr. Daines Barrington's supposition, that " the criminal was *suspended in the air by the collistrigium or stretchneck*," a very little reflection will suffice to show that it is

founded in error. Such a process would in *half an hour's*
time most effectually prevent a repetition of the ceremony.
The *collistrigium* was so called from the *stretching out or
projection of the neck* through a hole made in the pillory for
that purpose, or through an iron collar or *carcan* that was
sometimes attached to the *pillar* itself. No punishment has
been inflicted in so many different ways as that of the pillory;
and therefore the following varieties of it have been thought
worth exhibiting.

The first is from a manuscript of the Chronicle of Saint
Denis, in the British Museum, Bibl. Reg. 16. G. vi. It was
written in the thirteenth century. The second occurs in a

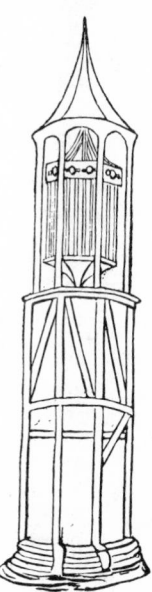

manuscript of Froissart, preserved in the same collection.
The third is copied from a print in Comenius's *Orbis pictus*,
and furnishes a specimen of the *carcan*, the woman being
confined to the pillar by an iron ring or collar. The fourth
is from a table of the standard of ancient weights and mea-

sures in the exchequer, and shows the mode of punish-
ing a forestaller or regrator in the time of Henry the

Seventh. The fifth exhibits Robert Ockam in the pillory
for perjury. The fact happened in the reign of Henry the
Eighth, but the cut is copied from Fox's *Martyrs,* published
long afterwards. The sixth and last figure represents an
ancient pillory that formerly stood in the market-place of the
village of Paulmy in Touraine. It is copied from a view of the
castle of Paulmy in Belleforest's *Cosmographie universelle,* 1575,

folio. Not long since there was remaining in the Section des halles at Paris an old hexangular building of stone, with open Gothic windows, through which appeared an iron circle or *carcan,* with holes for placing the hands and necks of several persons at the same time, in like manner as in the first and last figures. There is an engraving of it in Millin's *Antiquités nationales,* tom. iii. no. 34.

SCENE 1. Page 378.

> DUKE. Being criminal in *double* violation
> Of sacred chastity, and of promise-breach.

Mr. Malone thinks *double* refers to Angelo's conduct to *Mariana* and Isabel; but surely, however inaccurate the expression, it alludes to Angelo's *double* misconduct to *Isabella,* in having attempted *her* chastity, and violated his promise with respect to her brother. Thus in *Promos and Cassandra* :

> " Thou wycked man, might it not thee suffice
> By worse than force to spoyle her chastitie,
> But heaping sinne on sinne against thy othe,
> Hast cruelly her brother done to death."

In Cinthio Giraldi's novel, it is " Vous avez commis *deux crimes* fort grans, l'un d'avoir diffamé cette jeune femme, par telle tromperie que l'on peut dire que vous l'avez forcée : l'autre d'avoir fait mourir son frere contre la foy à elle donnée." Transl. by Chappuys, 1584.

SCENE 1. Page 385.

> DUKE. Thy slanders I forgive; and therewithal
> Remit thy other *forfeits*: Take him to prison.

Mr. Steevens has refined too much in supposing this word to mean *carnal offences.* It is simply *penalties.* The Duke remits all Lucio's offences except the injury done to the woman, and he is ordered to remain in prison until he marry her. *Forfeit* was also used in the French sense of the word, *crime, transgression.*

THE CLOWN.

The clown in this play officiates as the tapster of a brothel; whence it has been concluded that he is not a domestic fool, nor ought to appear in the dress of that character. A little consideration will serve to show that the opinion is erroneous, that *this* clown is *altogether* a domestic fool, and that he should be habited accordingly. In Act II. Scene 1, Escalus calls him a *tedious fool*, and *Iniquity*, a name for one of the old stage buffoons. He tells him that he will have him *whipt*, a punishment that was very often inflicted on fools. In *Timon of Athens* we have a *strumpet's fool*, and a similar character is mentioned in the first speech in *Antony and Cleopatra*. But if any one should still entertain a doubt on the subject, he may receive the most complete satisfaction by an attentive examination of ancient prints, many of which will furnish instances of the common use of the domestic fool in brothels. In *Twelfth night*, Act IV. Scene 1, Sebastian mistakes the clown for such a character as that before us, and calls him a *foolish Greek*, a term that is very happily explained by Dr. Warburton, whose note both communicates and receives support on the present occasion.

ON THE STORY AND CONSTRUCTION OF MEASURE FOR MEASURE.

Three sources whence the plot of this play might have been extracted, have already been mentioned, viz. Whetstone's *Heptameron*, 1582, 4to; his *Promos and Cassandra*, 1578, 4to; and novel 5, decad. 8, in Cinthio Giraldi. It is probable that the general outline of the story is founded on fact, as it is related, with some variety of circumstance, by several writers, and appears to have been very popular. It has therefore

been thought worth while to point out the following works
in which it occurs.

In Lipsii *Monita et exempla politica*, Antverp. 1613, 4to,
cap. viii. Charles the bold duke of Burgundy causes one of
his noblemen to be put to death for offending in the manner
that Angelo would have done; but he is first compelled to
marry the lady. This story has been copied from Lipsius
into Wanley's *Wonders of the little world*, book iii. ch. 29,
edit. 1678, folio; and from Wanley into that favourite little
chap book, Burton's *Unparalleled varieties*, p. 42. See likewise *The spectator*, No. 491. This event was made the subject of a French play by Antoine Maréchal, called *Le jugement
équitable de Charles le hardy*, 1646, 4to. Here the offender
is called Rodolph governor of Maestrick, and by theatrical
licence turns out to be the duke's own son. Another similar
story of Charles's upright judgment may be found in the
third volume of Goulart's *Thrésor d'histoires admirables*, 1628,
8vo, p. 373.

Much about the time when the above events are supposed
to have happened, Olivier le Dain, for his wickedness sur-
named the Devil, originally the barber, and afterwards the
favourite of Louis XI., is said to have committed a similar
offence, for which he was deservedly hanged. See Gode-
froy's edition of the *Memoirs of Philip de Comines*, Brussels,
1723, 8vo, tom. v. p. 55.

At the end of Belleforest's translation of Bandello's novels,
there are three additional of his own invention. The first of
these relates to a captain, who, having seduced the wife of
one of his soldiers under a promise to save the life of her
husband, exhibited him soon afterwards *through the window
of his apartment* suspended on a gibbet. His commander,
the marshal de Brissac, after compelling him to marry the
widow, adjudges him to death. The striking similitude of
a part of this story to what Mr. Hume has related of colonel
Kirke, will present itself to every reader, and perhaps in-

duce some to think with Mr. Ritson, (however they will
differ in *his mode* of expressing the sentiment,) that Mr.
Hume's narration is " an impudent and barefaced lie." See
The quip modest, p. 30. A defence also of Kirke may be
seen in the *Monthly magazine*, vol. ii. p. 544. Yet though
we may be inclined to adopt this side of the question, it will
only serve to diminish, in a single instance, the atrocities of
that sanguinary monster.

In Lupton's *Siuqila*. *Too good to be true*, 1580, 4to, there
is a long story of a woman, who, her husband having slain
his adversary in a duel, goes to the judge for the purpose of
prevailing on him to remit the sentence of the law. He obtains of her, in the first place, a large sum of money, and
afterwards the reluctant prostitution of her person, under a
solemn promise to save her husband. The rest, as in Belleforest's novel.

In vol. i. of Goulart's *Thrésor d'histoires admirables*, above
cited, there are two stories on this subject. The first, in
p. 300, is of a citizen of Como in Italy, who in 1547 was
detained prisoner by a Spanish *captain* on a charge of murder.
The wife pleads for him as before, and obtains a promise of
favour on the same terms. The husband recommends her
compliance, after which the Spaniard beheads him. Complaint is made to the *Duke* of *Ferrara*, who compels the captain to marry the widow, and then orders him to be hanged.
The other, in p. 304, is of a provost named *La Vouste*, whose
conduct resembles that of the other villain's, with this addition; he says to the woman, " I promised to restore your
husband; I have not kept him, here he is." No punishment is inflicted on this fellow.

The last example to be mentioned on this occasion occurs
in Cooke's *Vindication of the professors and profession of the
law*, 1646, 4to, p. 61. During the wars between Charles the
Fifth and Francis the First, one Raynucio had been imprisoned at Milan for betraying a fort to the French. His

wife petitions the governor Don Garcias in his favour, who refuses to listen but on dishonourable terms, which are indignantly rejected. The husband, like Claudio in *Measure for measure*, at first commends the magnanimity of his wife, and submits to his sentence; but when the time for his execution approaches, his courage fails him, and he prevails on his wife to acquiesce in the governor's demands. A sum of ten thousand crowns is likewise extorted from the unhappy woman, and she receives in return the dead body of her husband. The Duke of Ferrara, Hercules of Este, who was general for the Emperor, is informed of the circumstance. He first persuades the governor to marry the lady, and then orders him to be beheaded.

Towards the conclusion of this play Dr. Johnson has observed, that " every reader feels some indignation when he finds Angelo spared." This remark is rigorously just, and calculated to satisfy those moralists who would have preferred the catastrophe in some of the preceding stories. But in the construction of a play theatrical effect was to be attended to ; on which ground alone the poet may be defended. The other charge against him in Dr. Johnson's note is doubtless unfounded, and even laboriously strained. Shakspeare has been likewise hastily censured by a female writer of great ingenuity, for almost every supposed deviation from the plot of Cinthio's novel, and even for adhering to it in sparing Angelo.* It might however be contended, that, if our author really used this novel,† he has, with some exceptions, exerted

* Dr. Johnson in his dedication to the above lady's work, speaking of Shakspeare, says, " he lived in an age when the minds of his auditors were not accustomed to balance probabilities, or to examine nicely the proportion between causes and effects. It was sufficient to recommend a story that it was far removed from common life, that its changes were frequent, and its close pathetic." How much at variance is all this with the sentiments that follow on our play, and how it serves to mark the folly and absurdity of hireling dedications !

† It may well be doubted whether Shakspeare ever saw the story as related by Cinthio. There was not, as far as we know at present, any English trans-

a considerable degree of skill and contrivance in his alterations; and that he has consequently furnished a rich and
diversified repast for his readers, instead of serving up the
simple story in the shape of such a tragedy as might have
suited a Greek audience, but certainly would not have pleased
an English one in his time. In the novel, the sister, when
she solicits mercy for her brother's murderer and her own
seducer, (in the play Angelo is neither but in intention,)
justly urges that *excess of justice becomes cruelty*. He therefore who would refuse mercy to Angelo for an intentional
offence, has no right to censure him for severity to Claudio
who had committed a real one. In the novel, the sister is
actually seduced, and her brother murdered; and yet she
pleads for the offender. In the play, though Isabella believes
her brother to be dead, she reconciles herself to the sad event,
inasmuch as she knows that he suffered by course of law, as
well as by the cruelty of Angelo, from whose iniquity she
herself has happily escaped. She is stimulated to solicit this
man's life, from the suggestion and situation of her friend the
innocent Mariana, who would have felt more distress from
the death of Angelo, than the other parties discontent from
his acquittal. The female critic has likewise observed that
" *Measure for measure* ought not to be the title, since justice
is not the virtue it inculcates." But surely, if Angelo had
died, it would have been *outmeasuring measure*; as it is, the
administration of justice is duly balanced, and both he and
Claudio are equally punished in imagination. The Duke too,
who knew all the circumstances, deserves credit for some
ingenuity in his arrangements to protect the innocent, and,
if not rigidly to punish the guilty, at least to save a sinner.

lation of it in his time. He might indeed have seen the French version by
Gabriel Chappuys, printed at Paris, 1583, 8vo; but it is certain that his
chief model for the plot was the old play of *Promos and Cassandra*, a circumstance unknown to Mrs. Lenox. All must admit that the mode of saving
the deputy's life is much better managed by Shakspeare than by Whetstone.

Nor will any one contend that Angelo has escaped punishment : the agonizing state of uncertainty in which he long remained after the mock sentence, the bitter reproof of his colleague, and the still severer language of the Duke, will, it is to be hoped, conduce to satisfy every feeling and humane spectator of this fine play, that the poet has done enough to content even the rigorous moralist, and to exemplify, in his own divine words, that " earthly power doth then seem likest heaven's, when mercy seasons justice."

MUCH ADO ABOUT NOTHING.

ACT I.

SCENE 1. Page 395.

Enter LEONATO. . . .

THIS is the name of the injured lady's father in the novel of Belleforest which Mr. Steevens supposes to have furnished the plot of the play; a circumstance that tends very much to prove the justness of that gentleman's opinion.

SCENE 1. Page 396.

MESS. Without a *badge* of bitterness.

See a future note on *The taming of the shrew*, Act IV. Scene 1.

SCENE 1. Page 397.

BEAT. He *set up his bills* here in Messina.

This mode of expression will admit of a little more illustration than it has already received. The practice to which it refers was calculated to advertise the public of any matters which concerned itself or the party whose bills were set up; and it is the more necessary to state this, because the passages which have been used in explanation might induce the reader to suppose that challenges and prize-fightings were the exclusive objects of these bills. This however was not the case. In Northbrooke's *Treatise against dicing, dauncing, vaine plaies, &c.*, 1579, 4to, a work much resembling that extremely curious volume Stubbes's *Anatomie of abuses*, we are told that they used " to *set up their billes* upon postes certain dayes before, to admonish the people to make resort unto their *theatres*, that they may thereby be the better furnished,

and the people prepared to fill their purses with their trea-
sures." In the play of *Histriomastix*, a man is introduced
setting up *text billes for playes*; and William Rankins, another puritanical writer against plays, which he calls *the instruments of Satan*, in his *Mirrour of monsters*, 1587, 4to, p. 6,
says, that "players by *sticking of their bils* in London, defile
the streetes with their infectious filthines." Mountebanks
likewise set up their bills. "Upon this scaffold also might
bee mounted a number of *quacksalving emperickes*, who arriving in some country towne, clap up their *terrible billes* in
the market place, and filling the paper with such horrible
names of diseases, as if every disease were a divell, and that
they could conjure them out of any towne at their pleasure."
Dekkar's *Villanies discovered by lanthorne and candle-light, &c.*,
1616, 4to, sign. H. Again, in *Tales and quick answeres*,
printed by Berthelette, b. l. n. d. 4to, a man having lost his
purse in London "*sette up bylles* in divers places that if any
man of the cyte had founde the purse and woulde brynge it
agayn to him he shulde have welle for his laboure. A gen-
tyllman of the Temple *wrote under one of the byls* howe the
man shulde come to his chambers and told where." It appears from a very rare little piece entitled *Questions of pro-
fitable and pleasant concernings talked of by two olde seniors,
&c.*, 1594, 4to, that Saint Paul's was a place in which these
bills or advertisements were posted up. Thomas Nashe in
his *Pierce Pennilesse his supplication to the divell*, 1595, 4to,
sign. E. speaks of the " maisterlessemen that *set up theyr
bills in Paules for services*, and such as paste up their papers on every post, for arithmetique and writing schooles:"
we may therefore suppose that several of the walks about
Saint Paul's cathedral then resembled the present Royal Exchange with respect to the business that was there transacted;
and it appears indeed, from many allusions in our old plays,
to have been as well the resort of the idle, as the busy. The
phrase of *setting up bills* continued long after the time of

Shakspeare and is used in a translation of Suetonius published in 1677, 8vo, p. 227.

SCENE 1.   Page 399.

BEAT. . . . . challenged him at the *bird-bolt*.

In further exemplification of this sort of arrow, the following representations have been collected. A very sagacious *modern* editor of King James's *Christ's kirk on the green* has stated that the line "the bolt flew o'er the bire" is a metaphor of a *thunderbolt* flying over the cowhouse!

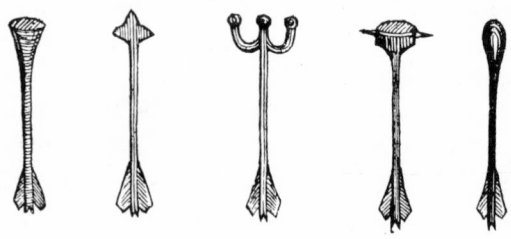

SCENE 1.   Page 412.

BENE. Prove that ever I lose more blood with love, &c.

There is a covert allusion in this speech that will not admit of a particular explanation. Debauchees imagine that wine recruits the loss of animal spirits. *Love* is used here in its very worst sense, and the whole is extremely gross and indelicate.

ACT II.

SCENE 1.   Page 429.

BEAT. . . . . that I had my good wit out of *the hundred merry tales*.

From the unfortunate loss of these *Merry tales*, a doubt has arisen from whence they were translated, it being pretty clear that they were not originally written in English. Two authorities have been produced on this occasion, the *Cent nouvelles nouvelles*, and the *Decameron* of Boccaccio.

Mr. Steevens is an advocate for the first of these, and refers to an edition of them mentioned by Ames. This, it is to be presumed, is the *Hundred merry tales* noticed under the article for James Roberts. To this opinion an objection has been taken by Mr. Ritson, on the ground that *many* of the tales in the *Cent nouvelles nouvelles* are " very tragical, and none of them calculated to furnish a lady with good wit." Now it appears that out of these hundred stories *only five are tragical*, viz. novels 32, 47, 55, 56, and 98. In the old editions they are entitled *Comptes plaisans et recreatiz pour deviser en toutes compaignies*, and *Moult plaisans á raconter par maniere de joyeuseté.*

Mr. Reed has " but little doubt that Boccace's *Decameron* was the book here alluded to." If this gentleman's quotation from Guazzo's *Civile conversation*, 1586, be meant to establish the existence of the above work in an English dress it certainly falls short of the purpose; because it is no more than a translation of an author, who is speaking of the *original Decameron.* But there is a more forcible objection to Mr. Reed's opinion, which is, that the first *complete* English translation of Boccaccio's novels was not published till 1620, and after Shakspeare's death. The dedication states indeed, that *many* of the tales had long since been published; but this may allude to those which had appeared in Painter's *Palace of pleasure*, or in some other similar work not now remaining. There are likewise two or three of Boccaccio's novels in Tarlton's *Newes out of purgatory*, which might be alluded to in the above dedication, if the work which now remains under the date of 1630 was really printed in 1589, as may be suspected from a license granted to Thomas Gubbin. There seems to have been some prior attempt to publish the *Decameron* in English, but it was " recalled by my Lord of Canterbury's commands." See a note by Mr. Steevens prefixed to *The two gentlemen of Verona.* There is a remarkable fact however that deserves to be mentioned in this place, which is, that in the proem to Sacchetti's *Novelle*, written about the year 1360, it appears that Boccaccio's novels had been *then* translated into English, not a single vestige of which translation is elsewhere to be traced.

A third work that may appear to possess some right to assert its claim on the present occasion is the *Cento novelle antiche,* which might have been translated before or in Shakspeare's time, as it has been already shown in a note on the story of *Twelfth night* that he had probably seen the 13th novel in that collection. It may likewise be worth mentioning that Nashe in his *Pappe with an hatchet,* speaks of a book then coming out under the title of *A hundred merrie tales,* in which Martin Marprelate, *i. e.* John Penry, and his friends were to be satirized.

On the whole, the evidence seems to preponderate in favour of the *Cent nouvelles nouvelles.* As the *greatest portion* of this work consists of *merry stories,* there is no impropriety in calling it *The hundred merry tales* ; the term *hundred* being part of the original title, and the epithet *merry* in all probability an addition for the purpose of designating the *general quality* of the stories. The *Decameron* of Boccaccio, which contains more tragical subjects than the other, is called in the English translation *A hundred* PLEASANT *novels.*

Whatever the *hundred merry tales* really were, we find them in existence so late as 1659, and the entire loss of them to the present age might have been occasioned by the devastation in the great fire of London.

SCENE 1.   Page 432.

> BENE. Come, will you go with me?
> CLAUD. Whither?
> BENE. Even to *the next willow,* about your own business, Count. What
> fashion will you wear the *garland* of?

It was the custom for those who were *forsaken in love* to wear willow garlands. This tree might have been chosen as the symbol of sadness from the verse in psalm 137, " We hanged our harps upon the willows, in the midst thereof ;" or else from a coincidence between the *weeping* willow and falling *tears.* Another reason has been assigned. The *Agnus castus* or *vitex,* was supposed by the ancients to promote chastity, "and the willow being of a much like nature," says an old writer, " it is yet a custom that he which is deprived of his love must wear a willow garland." Swan's *Speculum mundi,* chap. 6. sect. 4. edit. 1635. Bona, the sister of the king of France, on receiving news of Edward the Fourth's marriage with Elizabeth Grey, exclaims, " In hope he'll prove a widower shortly, I'll wear a *willow garland* for his sake." See *Henry the Sixth,* part iii. and Desdemona's willow song in *Othello,* Act IV. Two more ballads of a similar nature may be found in Playford's *Select ayres,* 1659, folio, pp. 19, 21.

Scene 1.   Page 438.

BEAT. Civil as an *orange,* and something of *that* jealous complexion.

This reading of the older copy has been judiciously preferred to *a* jealous complexion. *Yellow* is an epithet often applied to jealousy by the old writers. In *The merry wives of Windsor,* Nym says he will possess Ford with *yellowness.* Shakspeare more usually terms it *green-eyed.*

Scene 3.   Page 447.

BENE. . . now will he lie ten nights awake, *carving the fashion of a new doublet.*

The print in Borde of the Englishman with a pair of shears, seems to have been borrowed from some Italian or other foreign picture in ridicule of our countrymen's folly. Coryat, in his *Crudities,* p. 260, has this remaak; " we weare more phantasticall fashions than any nation under the sunne doth, the French onely excepted; which hath given occasion both to the Venetian and other Italians to brand the Englishman with a notable marke of levity, by painting him starke naked with a paire of shears in his hand, *making his fashion of attire* according to the vaine invention of his braine-sicke head, not to comelinesse and decorum." Purchas, in his

Pilgrim, 1619, 8vo, speaks of " a naked man with sheeres in one hand and cloth in the other," as a general emblem of fashion.   Many other allusions to such a figure might be cited, but it was not peculiar to the English.   In *La geographie Francoise,* by P. Du Val d'Abbeville, 1663, 12mo, the author, speaking of the *Frenchman's* versatility in dress, adds, " dans la peinture des nations on met pres de luy *le cizeau."*

The inconstancy of our own countrymen in the article of dress is described in the following verses from John Halle's *Courte of vertue,* 1565, 12mo.

> " As fast as God's word one synne doth blame
> They devyse other as yll as the same,
> And this varietie of Englyshe folke,
> Dothe cause all wyse people us for to mocke.
>
> For all discrete nations under the sonne,
> Do use at thys day as they fyrst begonne :
> And never doo change, but styll do frequent,
> Theyr old guyse, what ever fond folkes do invent.
>
> But we here in England lyke fooles and apes,
> Do by our vayne fangles deserve mocks and japes,
> For all kynde of countreys dooe us deryde,
> In no constant custome sythe we abyde
> For we never knowe howe in our aray,
> We may in fyrme fashion stedfastly stay."

Randle Holme complained that in his time (1680) English-men were as changeable as the moon in their dress, " in which respect," says he, " we are termed the Frenchmen's apes, imitating them in all their fantastick devised fashions of garbs."   *Acad. of armory,* book iii. ch. 5.

SCENE 3.   Page 452.

CLAUD. *Stalk on, stalk on,* the fowl sits.

It has been already shown that the *stalking bull* was equally common with the stalking *horse.*   It was sometimes used for decoying partridges into a *tunnelling net,* or cage of net work, in the form of a tun, with doors.   The process is described at large, with a print, in Willughby's *Ornithology,* 1678, folio, p. 34, where an account is also given of the *stalking-horse, ox, stag,* &c.

Howel in his *Vocabulary,* sect. xxxv. seems to have mistaken the *tun* or net into which the birds were driven, for the stalking bull itself. Sometimes, as in hunting the wolf, an artificial bush and a wooden screen were used to stalk with. See Clamorgan, *Chasse du loup,* 1595, 4to, p. 29.

SCENE 3. Page 455.

LEON. She tore the letter into a thousand *halfpence.*

Mr. Theobald explains this " into a thousand pieces of the same bigness," as if Beatrice had torn the letter by rule and compass. Mr. Steevens more properly supposes halfpence to mean *small pieces*; but his note would have been less imperfect if he had added that the halfpence of Elizabeth were of *silver,* and about the size of a modern silver penny.

ACT III.

SCENE 1. Page 469.

D. PEDRO. . . . the little *hangman* dare not shoot at him.

Dr. Farmer has illustrated this term by citing a passage from Sidney's *Arcadia*; but he has omitted a previous description in which Cupid is metamorphosed into a strange old monster, sitting on a *gallows* with a crown of laurel in one hand, and a purse of money in the other, as if he would persuade folks by these allurements *to hang* themselves. It is certainly possible that this might have been Shakspeare's prototype; we should otherwise have supposed that he had called Cupid a hangman metaphorically, from the remedy sometimes adopted by desparing lovers.

Scene 4. Page 488.

Marg. Clap us into *light o'love*.

When Margaret adds that this tune " goes without a burden," she does not mean that it never had words to it, but
only that it wanted a very common appendage to the ballads
of that time.   The name itself may be illustrated by the following extract from *The glasse of man's follie*, 1615, 4to.
" There be wealthy houswives, and good house-keepers that
use no starch, but faire water : their linnen is white, and they
looke more Christian-like in small ruffes, then *Light of love*
lookes in her great starched ruffs, looke she never so hie, with
eye-lids awrye."   This anonymous work is written much in
the manner of Stubbes's *Anatomie of abuses*, and for the same
purpose.

ACT IV.

Scene 1. Page 510.

Bene. Tarry, sweet Beatrice.
Beat. *I am gone, though I am here.*   There is no love in you—Nay,
I pray you let me go.

Though three explanations have been already offered, there
is room for further conjecture.   From the latter words of
Beatrice it is clear that Benedick had stopped her from going.
She may therefore intend to say that notwithstanding she is
detained by force, she is in reality absent ; her heart is no
longer Benedick's.

ACT V.

Scene 1. Page 524.

Leon. His *May of youth*, and bloom of *lustyhood*.

An allusion to these lines in the old calendars that describe
the state of man :

" As in the month of *Maye* all thyng is in myght
So at xxx yeres man is in chyef lykyng.
Pleasaunt and *lusty*, to every mannes syght
In beaute and strength, to women pleasyng."

In the *Notbrowne mayde* we have the expression *lusty May.*
Capel's edit. p. 6. Roger Ascham, speaking of young men,
says; " It availeth not to see them well taught in yong
yeares, and after when they come to *lust and youthfull dayes,*
to give them licence to live as they *lust* themselves." *Schole-
master*, 1571, fo. 13. See a former note in p. 45.

SCENE 1. Page 529.

CLAUD. If he be, [angry] he knows how to turn his girdle.

Mr. Holt White's ingenious note may be supported by the
following passage in Carew's *Survey of Cornwall*, 1602, 4to.
p. 76 : the author is speaking of wrestling. " This hath also
his lawes, of taking hold onely above girdle, wearing a girdle
to take hold by, playing three pulles, for tryall of the mas-
tery, &c."

SCENE 4. Page 554.

BENE. Prince, thou art sad; get thee a wife, get thee a wife; there
is no *staff* more reverend than one *tipp'd with horn.*

In this comparison the prince is the staff, and the question is what sort of a one is here alluded to. Messrs. Steevens, Reed, and Malone, conceive it to be the staff used in
the ancient trial by wager of battle; but this seems to have
but small claim to be entitled *reverend.* On the contrary, as
the combatants were of the meaner class of people, who were
not allowed to make use of edged weapons, the higher ranks
usually deciding the business by hired champions, it cannot
well be maintained that much, if any, reverence belongs to
such a staff. It is possible, therefore, that Shakspeare, whose
allusions to *archery* are almost as frequent as they are to
cuckoldom, might refer to the *bowstaff*, which was usually
tipped with a piece of horn at each end, to make such a notch

for the string as would not wear, and at the same time to strengthen the bow, and prevent the extremities from breaking. It is equally possible that the walking-sticks or staves used by *elderly* people might be intended, which were often headed or *tipped* with a cross piece of *horn*, or sometimes amber. They seem to have been imitated from the *crutched* sticks, or *potences*, as they were called, used by the friars, and by them borrowed from the celebrated *tau* of St. Anthony. Thus in *The Canterbury tales,* the Sompnour describes one of his friars as having " a scrippe and *tipped staf,*" and he adds that

" His felaw had *a staf tipped with horn.*"

In these instances the epithet *reverend* is much more appropriate than in the others.

Mrs. Lenox, assuming, with the same inaccuracy as had been manifested in her critique on *Measure for measure,* that Shakspeare borrowed his plot from Ariosto, proceeds to censure him for " poverty of invention, want of judgment, and wild conceits," deducing all her reasoning from false premises. This is certainly but a bad method of *illustrating* Shakspeare.

MIDSUMMER NIGHT'S DREAM.

ACT I.

Scene 1. Page 6.

Ege. Happy be Theseus, our renowned *duke*.

This is in reality no " misapplication of a modern title," as Mr. Steevens conceived, but a legitimate use of the word in its primitive Latin sense of *leader* ; and so it is often used in the Bible. Not so the instance adduced of *sheriffs of the provinces*, which might have been avoided in our printed bibles. Wicliffe had most properly used *prefectis*. Shakspeare might have found *Duke* Theseus in the *book of Troy*, or in Turbervile's *Ovid's Epistles*. See the argument to that of Phædra to Hippolytus.

Scene 1. Page 9.

The. You can endure the livery of a *nun*,
For aye to be in shady *cloister* mew'd.

The threatening to make a nun of poor Hermia is as whimsical an anachronism as any in Shakspeare.

Scene 1. Page 13.

Lys. Making it *momentany* as a sound.

Momentany and *momentary* were indiscriminately used in Shakspeare's time. The former corresponds with the French *momentaine*.

ACT II.

Scene 1. Page 30.

Fai. And I serve the fairy queen,
To dew her orbs upon the green.

Mr. Steevens in the happy and elegant remark at the end of his note on the last line, has made a slight mistake in substituting *Puck* for the *fairy*. When the damsels of old gathered the May dew on the grass, and which they made use of to improve their complexions, they left undisturbed such of it as they perceived on the fairy-rings; apprehensive that the fairies should in revenge destroy their beauty. Nor was it reckoned safe to put the foot within the rings, lest they should be liable to the fairies' power.

SCENE 1. Page 32.

PUCK. But they do *square*.

Dr. Johnson has very justly observed that to *square* here is to quarrel. In investigating the reason, we must previously take it for granted that our verb *to quarrel* is from the French *quereller*, or perhaps both from the common source, the Latin *querela*. Blackstone has remarked that the glaziers use the words *square* and *quarrel* as synonymous terms for a pane of glass, and he might have added for the instrument with which they cut it. This, he says, is somewhat whimsical; but had he been acquainted with the reason, he might have been disposed to waive his opinion, at least on the present occasion. The glazier's instrument is a *diamond*, usually cut into such a *square* form as the *supposed diamonds* on the French and English cards, in the former of which it is still properly called *carreau*, from its *original*. This was the *square* iron head of the arrow used for the cross-bow. In English it was called a *quarrel*, and hence the glazier's diamond and the pane of glass have received their names of *square* and *quarrel*. Now we may suppose without straining the point very violently, that these words being evidently synonymous in one sense, have corruptedly become so in another; and that the verb *to square*, which correctly and metaphorically, even at this time, signifies *to agree* or *accord*, has been carelessly and ignorantly wrested from its true sense, and from frequent use become a legitimate word. The French have avoided this error, and to express a meaning very similar to that of *to quarrel* or *dispute*, make use of the word *contrecarrer*.

Scene 1. Page 37.

Puck. The wisest aunt telling the saddest tale,
Sometime for three-foot stool mistaketh me;
Then slip I from her bum, down-topples she.

The celebrated duchess of Newcastle, in a poem of some fancy, entitled *The queen of fairies*, makes Puck or hobgoblin the queen of fairies' fool, and alludes to the above prank in the following lines:

"The goodwife sad squats down upon a stool,
Not at all thinking it was Hob the fool,
And frowning sits, then Hob gives her a slip,
And down she falls, whereby she hurts her hip."

The above dame is a farmer's wife who has been scolding because she was unable to procure any butter or cheese, and at Puck's holding up the hens' rumps to prevent their laying eggs too fast.

With respect to the word *aunt*, it has been usually derived from the French *tante*; but the original Norman term is *ante*. See examples in Carpentier *Suppl.* ad Ducang. v. *avuncula*. So the author of the old and excellent farce of *Maistre Patelin*,

"Vostre belle ante, mourut-elle?"

Scene 2. Page 39.

Enter Oberon and Titania.

Mr. Tyrwhitt's remark that the Pluto and Proserpine of Chaucer were the true progenitors of Oberon and Titania, may be perfectly true; but the name of Oberon as king of the fairies, must have been exceedingly well known from the romance of Huon of Bourdeaux, in which this Oberon makes a very conspicuous figure.

Scene 2. Page 41.

Tita. Met we on hill, in dale, forest or mead,
By paved fountain.

Milton, doubtless, had these lines in recollection when he wrote,

"To hill or valley, fountain or fresh shade."
Par. lost, b. v. l. 203.

SCENE 2.   Page 41.

TITA. *To dance our ringlets* to the whistling wind.

An allusion to what the country people call *fairy rings*, which they suppose to be the tracks of the dances of those diminutive beings.

SCENE. 2.   Page 43.

TITA. The *nine mens morris* is fill'd up with mud.

This game was sometimes called *the nine mens merrils*, from *merelles* or *mereaux*, an ancient French word for the jettons or counters, with which it was played. The other term *morris* is probably a corruption suggested by the sort of *dance* which in the progress of the game the counters performed. In the French *merelles* each party had three counters only, which were to be placed in a line in order to win the game. It appears to have been the *Tremerel* mentioned in an old fabliau. See Le Grand *Fabliaux et contes*, tom. ii. p. 208.

Dr. Hyde thinks the morris or merrils was known during the time that the Normans continued in possession of England, and that the name was afterwards corrupted into *three mens morals*, or *nine mens morals*. If this be true, the conversion of *morals* into *morris*, a term so very familiar to the country people, was extremely natural. The doctor adds, that it was likewise called *nine-penny*, or *nine-pin miracle*, *three-penny morris*, *five-penny morris*, *nine-penny morris*, or *three-pin*, *five-pin*, and *nine-pin morris*, all corruptions of *three-pin*, *&c. merels*. Hyde *Hist. Nerdiludii*, p. 202.

SCENE 2.   Page 44.

TITA. The *human mortals* want their winter here.

In the controversy respecting the immortality of fairies, Mr. Ritson's ingenious and *decisive* reply in his *Quip modest* ought on every account to have been introduced. A few pages further Titania evidently alludes to the *immortality* of fairies, when, speaking of the changeling's mother, she says, " but she, *being mortal,* of that boy did die." Spenser's fairy system and his pedigree were allegorical, invented by himself, and not coinciding with the popular superstitions on the subject. *Human mortals* is merely a pleonasm, and neither put in opposition to *fairy mortals*, according to Mr. Steevens, nor to *human immortals*, according to Ritson ; it is simply the language of a fairy speaking of men.

A posthumous note by Mr. Steevens has not contributed to strengthen his former arguments, as the authors therein mentioned do not, strictly speaking, allude to the sort of fairies in question, but to spirits, devils, and angels. Shakspeare, however, would certainly be more influenced by popular opinion than by the dreams of the casuists.   There is a curious instance of the nature of fairies, according to the belief of more ancient times, in the romance of Lancelot of the lake. " En celui temps," (the author is speaking of the days of king Arthur,) " estoient appellees faees toutes selles qui sentremettoient denchantemens et de charmes, et moult en estoit pour lors principalement en la Grande Bretaigne, et savoient la force et la vertu des paroles, des pierres, et des herbes, parquoy *elles estoient tenues en jeunesse et en beaulte,* et en grandes richesses comme elles devisoient." This perpetual youth and beauty cannot well be separated from a state of immortality.   Nor would it be difficult to controvert the sentiments of those who have maintained the mortality of *devils,* by means of authorities as valid as their own.   The above interesting romance will furnish one at least that may not be unacceptable. Speaking of the birth of the prophet and enchanter Merlin, it informs us that his mother would not consent to the embraces of any man who should be visible ; and therefore it was by some means ordained that a *devil* should be her lover. When he approached her, to use the words of the romance, " la damoiselle le tasta et sentit quil avoit le corps moult bien fait ; non pourtant les dyables n'ont ne corps ne membres que l'en puisse veoir ne toucher, *car spirituelle chose ne peut estre touchée, et tous diables sont choses spirituelles.*" The fruit of this amour was Merlin; but he, being born of woman, was but a semi-devil, and subject to mortality. A damsel with whom he had fallen in love, prevailed on him to disclose some of his magical arts to her, by means of which she deceived him, and preserved her chastity by casting him into a deep sleep whenever he importuned her. The romance adds, " si le decevoit ainsi *pource qu'il estoit mortel*; mais s'il eust este *du tout dyable,* elle ne l'eust peu decepvoir ; car ung dyable ne peut dormir."

SCENE 2.   Page 45.

TITA. Therefore the moon, *the governess of floods,*
    Pale in her anger, *washes all the air,*
    That rheumatic diseases do abound.

Thus in Newton's *Direction for the health of magistrates and studentes,* 1574, 12mo, we are told that " the moone is *ladie of moysture ;*" and in Hamlet, Act I. Scene 1, she is called " the *moist* star." In Bartholomæus *De propriet. rerum,* by Batman, lib. 8. c. 29, the moon is described to be " mother of all *humours,* minister and *lady of the sea.*" But in Lydgate's prologue to his *Storie of Thebes,* there are two lines which Shakspeare seems closely to have imitated ;

    " Of Lucina the moone, *moist and pale,*
        That many *showre fro heaven* made availe."

The same mode of expression occurs in Parkes's *Curtaine drawer of the world,* 1612, 4to, p. 48 : " the centinels of the season ordained to marke the *queen of floods* how she lends her borrowed light." This book deserves to be noticed for the good sense which it contains, and the merit of some occasional pieces of poetry.

SCENE 2.   Page 50.

OBE. I do but beg a little changeling boy
    To be my *henchman.*

Of all the opinions concerning the origin of this word, that of Sir William Spelman alone can be maintained. If instead of deriving it from the *German*, he had stated that it came to us through the *Saxon* Henʒeɾʒ, a *horse*, his information had been more correct. Although in more modern times the pages or henchmen might have walked on foot, it is very certain that they were originally *horsemen*, according to the term. Thus in Chaucer's *Floure and the leafe* :

> " And every knight had after him *riding*
> Three *henshmen*, on him awaiting."

If the old orthography *henxmen* had not been unfortunately disturbed, we should have heard nothing of the conjectures about *haunch* and *haunch*-men.

SCENE 2. Page 58.

Enter DEMETRIUS, *Helena following him.*

However forward and indecorous the conduct of Helena in pursuing Demetrius may appear to modern readers, such examples are very frequent in old romances of chivalry, wherein Shakspeare was undoubtedly well read. The beautiful ballad of the Nut-brown maid might have been more immediately in his recollection, many parts of this scene having a very strong resemblance to it.

SCENE 2. Page 61.

HEL. I'll follow thee, and *make a heaven of hell.*

Imitated by Milton :

> " The mind is its own place, and in itself
> Can make a *heav'n of hell*, a hell of heaven."
> *Par. lost*, b. i. l. 254.

SCENE 2. Page 62.

OBE. Quite overcanopied with *lush* woodbine.

See what has been already said on this word in p. 8; the meaning is the same as there. Theobald's amendment from *luscious* was probably in conformity with that passage; and the printers of the old editions not comprehending the meaning of *lush*, which even in their time was an antiquated word, ignorantly, as well as unharmoniously, substituted *luscious*.

Scene 3.   Page 68.

Her.   .   .   . in human modesty
Such separation, as, may well be said,
Becomes a virtuous bachelor and a maid.

That is, " *let there be* such separation," &c.   A comma
should be placed after *modesty*.

ACT III.

Scene 1.   Page 77.

Quin. When you have spoken your speech, enter into that *brake*.

It is submitted that *brake* cannot *in this instance* signify *a
large extent of ground, overgrown with furze,* but merely the
hawthorn bush or *tyring-house* as Quince had already called
it.

Scene 1.   Page 83.

Bot. Nay I can *gleek* upon occasion.

Again, in *Romeo and Juliet*, Act IV. Scene 5 :

" 1. Mus. What will you *give us?*
Pet.   No money, on my faith ; but the *gleek*."

On which consult Mr. Steevens's posthumous note in Mr.
Reed's last edition.

Mr. Pope had justly remarked that to *gleek* is to *scoff*.   In
some of the notes on this word it has been supposed to be
connected with the card game of *gleek* ; but it was not recollected that the Saxon language supplied the term Ԍliᵹ, *ludi-
brium*, and doubtless a corresponding verb.   Thus *glee* signifies *mirth* and *jocularity* ; and *gleeman* or *gligman*, a minstrel
or *joculator*.   *Gleek* was therefore used to express a stronger
sort of joke, a *scoffing*.   It does not appear that the phrase
to give the gleek was ever introduced in the above game, which
was borrowed by us from the French, and derived from an
original of very different import from the word in question.

Scene 1.   Page 84.

Tita. And light them at the fiery glow-worms *eyes*.

Dr. Johnson's objection to the word eyes, has been very

skilfully removed by Mr. Monck Mason; but this gentleman appars to have misconceived the meaning of Shakspeare's most appropriate epithet of *ineffectual*, in the passage from *Hamlet*. The glow-worm's fire was *ineffectual* only at the approach of morn, in like manner as the light of a candle would be at mid-day.

Scene 1. Page 88.

OBE. What night-*rule* now about this haunted grove?

Mr. Steevens has properly explained *night-rule*. *Rule* in this word has the same meaning as in the Christmas lord of mis-*rule*, and is a corruption of *revel*, formerly written *reuel*.

Scene 2. Page 89.

PUCK. An *ass's nowl* I fixed on his head.

The receipt for making a man resemble an ass, already given in a former note, must give place to the following in Scot's *Discoverie of witchcraft*, b. 13. c. xix. " Cutt off the head of a horsse or an asse (before they be dead), otherwise the vertue or strength thereof will be the lesse effectuall, and make an earthern vessell of fit capacitie to conteine the same, and let it be filled with the oile and fat thereof; cover it close, and dawbe it over with lome : let it boile over a soft fier three daies continuallie, that the flesh boiled may run into oile, so as the bare bones may be seene : beate the haire into powder, and mingle the same with the oile; and annoint the *heads of the standers by*, and they shall seem to have horsses or *asses* heads.

Scene 2. Page 95.

OBE. All fancy-sick she is, and pale of *cheer*.

Mr. Steevens deduces this word from the Italian *cara*; but it is from the old French *chere*, face. Lydgate finishes the prologue to his *Storie of Thebes* with these lines :

" And as I coud, with a pale *cheare*,
My tale I gan anone, as ye shall heare."

Scene 2.   Page 103.

Hel.   So with two seeming *bodies*, but one *heart*;
Two of the *first*, like coats in heraldry,
Due but to one, and crowned with one crest.

It may be doubted whether this passage has been rightly explained, and whether the commentators have not given Shakspeare credit for more skill in heraldry than he really possessed, or at least than he intended to exhibit on the present occasion.   Helen says, " we had two seeming bodies, but only one heart."   She then exemplifies her position by a simile—" we had *two of the first*, i. e. *bodies*, like the double coats in heraldry that belong to man and wife as *one person*, but which, like our *single heart*, have but *one crest*."

Scene 2.   Page 112.

Puck.   And yonder shines *Aurora's harbinger*,
At whose approach, ghosts, wandering here and there,
Troop home to church-yards.

Aurora's harbinger is Lucifer, the morning star.

" Now the bright morning star, *day's harbinger*,
Comes dancing from the East————" *

It was the popular belief that ghosts retired at the approach of day.   Thus the spirit of Hamlet's father exclaims,

" But soft, methinks I scent the morning air."

In further illustration see a subsequent note on *Hamlet*, Act I. Scene 1.

Scene 2.   Page 117.

Hel.   And, sleep, that sometime shuts up sorrow's eye.

Again, in Macbeth :

" Sleep, that knits up the ravell'd sleave of care."

---

* It has not been recollected to what poet these lines belong.

ACT V.

SCENE 1.   Page 145.

PHILOST. .   .   . I have heard *it* over,
And it is nothing, nothing in the world ;
Unless you can find sport in their *intents*,
Extremely stretch'd, and conn'd with cruel pain,
To do you service.

Dr. Johnson suspects a line to be lost, as he " knows not what it is to *stretch* and *con* an *intent*;" but it is surely not *intents* that are *stretch'd and conn'd* but the *play*, of which Philostrate is speaking.   If the line

" Unless you can find sport, &c."

were printed in a parenthesis, all would be right.   Mr. Stee-vens, not perceiving this, has endeavoured to wrest from the word *intents*, its plain and usual meaning, and would un-necessarily convert it to *attention*, which might undoubtedly be *stretch'd*, but could not well be *conn'd*.

SCENE 1.   Page 148.

PHILOST. The prologue is *addrest*.

We have borrowed this sense of the word (*ready*) from the French *adressé*.

SCENE 1.   Page 157.

MOON. This lantern doth the *horned* moon present.

But why *horned* ?   He evidently refers to the *materials* of which the *lantern* was made.

SCENE 2.   Page 168.

PUCK. By the triple *Hecat's team*.

By this team is meant the chariot of the moon, said to be drawn by two horses, the one black, the other white.   It is probable that Shakspeare might have consulted some trans-lation of Boccaccio's *Genealogy of the gods*, which, as has been already remarked, appears to have occasionally supplied him with his mythological information. As this is the first time we meet with the name of *Hecate* in our author, it may be proper to notice the error he has committed in making it a word of two syllables, which he has done in several other places, though in one (viz. I. *Henry Sixth*, if he wrote that play) it is rightly made a trisyllable :

> " I speak not to that railing Hĕcătē." Act III. Scene 2.

His contemporaries have usually‛ given it properly. Thus Spenser in the *Fairy queen*,

> " As Hĕcătē, in whose almighty hand." B. vii. Canto 6.

Ben Jonson has, of course, always been correct. Mr. Malone observes, in a note on *Macbeth*, Act III. Scene 5, that Marlowe, though a scholar, has used the word *Hecate* as a dissyllable. It may be added that Middelton and Golding have done the same; the latter in his translation of Ovid, book vii. has used it in both ways.

SCENE 2.   Page 168.

PUCK. I am sent with broom before,
       To sweep the dust behind the door.

In confirmation of Dr. Johnson's remark that fairies delight in cleanliness, two other poems shall be quoted. The first is the *Fairy queen*, printed in Percy's Ancient Ballads, iii. 207, edit. 1775.

> " But if the house be swept,
> And from uncleanness kept,
> We praise the household maid," &c.

The other is the *Fairies farewell*, by Bishop Corbet, printed also in Percy's collection, iii. 210, from his *Poetica stromata*, 1648, 18mo. It is also in a preceding edition of the bishop's poems, 1647, 18mo.

> " Farewell rewards and fairies !
> Good housewives now may say ;
> For now foule sluts in dairies
> Doe fare as well as they :

And though they sweepe their hearths no less
Than mayds were wont to doe,
Yet who of late for cleanliness
Finds sixepence in her shoe?"

Scene 2.   Page 170.

OBE. To the best *bride bed* will we,
Which by us shall *blessed* be.

Mr. Steevens remarks that the ceremony of blessing the
bed was observed at the marriage of a *princess*. It was used
at *all* marriages. This was the form, copied from the Manual
for the use of Salisbury.   " Nocte vero sequente cum
sponsus et sponsa *ad lectum pervenerint,* accedat sacerdos et
benedicat thalamum, dicens : Benedic, Domine, thalamum
istum   et omnes habitantes in eo ; ut in tua pace consis-
tant, et in tua voluntate permaneant : et in amore tuo vivant
et senescant et multiplicentur in longitudine dierum.   Per
Dominum.—Item *benedictio super lectum.*   Benedic, Domine, hoc *cubiculum,* respice, quinon dormis neque dormitas.
Qui custodis Israel, custodi famulos tuos in hoc lecto qui-
escentes *ab omnibus fantasmaticis demonum illusionibus* : custodi eos vigilantes ut in preceptis tuis meditentur dormientes,
et te per soporem sentiant : ut hic et ubique defensionis tuæ
muniantur auxilio.   Per Dominum.—Deinde fiat benedictio
super eos in lecto tantum cum Oremus.   Benedicat Deus
corpora vestra et animas vestras ; et det super vos benedic-
tionem sicut benedixit Abraham, Isaac, et Jacob, Amen.—
His peractis *aspergat eos aqua benedicta,* et sic discedat et
dimittat eos in pace."   We may observe on this strange
ceremony, that the purity of modern times stands not in need
of these holy aspersions to lull the senses and dissipate the
illusions of the Devil.   The married couple would, no doubt,
rejoice when the benediction was ended.   In the French romance of *Melusine,* the bishop who marries her to Raymon-
din blesses the nuptial bed.   The ceremony is there represented in a very ancient cut, of which a copy is subjoined.
The good prelate is sprinkling the parties with holy water.

Sometimes during the benediction the married couple only
sat upon the bed; but they generally received a portion of
consecrated bread and wine. It is recorded in France, that
on frequent occasions the priest was improperly detained till
the hour of midnight, whilst the wedding guests rioted in the
luxuries of the table, and made use of language that was extremely offensive to the clergy, and injurious to the salvation
of the parties. It was therefore, in the year 1577, ordained
by Pierre de Gondi, archbishop of Paris, that the ceremony
of blessing the nuptial bed should for the future be performed
in the day time, or at least *before supper*, and in the presence
only of the bride and bridegroom, and of their nearest relations.

There is a singularity in this cut which may well excuse a short digression. This is the *horned* head-dress of the bride, a fashion that prevailed in England during the reign of Henry the Sixth, and for a short time afterwards. Lydgate has left us an unpublished ditty, in which he complains of it. As it is, like most of his other poetry, very dull and very tedious, a couple of stanzas may suffice; each concludes with a line to recommend the *casting away of these horns.*

> " Clerkys recorde by gret auctorite,
> Hornys were yove to beestys for diffence;
> A thyng contrary to femynyte
> To be made sturdy of resistence.
> But arche wyves egre in ther violence,
> Fers as tygre for to make affray,
> They have despyt and ageyn conscience
> Lyst nat of pryde ther *hornys cast away.*

> Noble pryncessys, this litel shoort ditee
> Rewdly compiled lat it be noon offence
> To your womanly merciful pitie,
> Thouh it be rad in your audience;
> Peysed ech thyng in your just advertence,
> So it be no displesaunce to your pay,
> Undir support of your patience
> Yevyth example *hornys to cast away.*"
>
> *Harl. MS.* No. 2255.

In France, this part of female dress was a frequent subject of clerical reprehension. Nicholas de Claminges, a doctor of the Sorbonne, and contemporary with Lydgate, compares it to the horns of oxen. " Tenduntur hinc et inde mira et inaudita deformitate gemina cornua bipedali prope intervallo à se distantia, majorique latitudine caput fœmineum diffundunt quam bubalinum longitudine distenditur. Auro ac gemmis omnia rutilant. Stibio et cerusa pinguntur facies; patent colla; nudantur pectora." Nicolai de Clemangiis *opera,* Lugd. Batavor. 1613, 4to, p. 144. And again, in his letters, " quid de *cornibus* et caudis loquar, quas illic jam vulgo matronæ gestant, qua in re naturam videntur humanam reliquisse, bestialemque sibi ultro adscivisse.   Adde quod *in effigie cornutæ fœminæ Diabolus plerumque pingitur."*   We cannot but admire the pious writer's ingenuity in the latter declaration, and how well it was calculated to terrify the ladies out of this preposterous fashion.

SCENE 2.   Page 171.

OBE.   With this field-dew *consecrate*
Every fairy take his gait ;
And *each several chamber bless,*
Through this palace with sweet peace.

Thus in the *Merry wives of Windsor*, Act V. Scène 5 :

" Search Windsor castle, elves, within and out :
Strew good luck, ouphes, on every sacred room."

In the first line of Oberon's speech there seems to be a covert satire against holy water.   Whilst the popular confidence in the power of fairies existed, they had obtained the credit of occasionally performing much good service to mankind ; and the great influence which they possessed gave so much offence to the holy monks and friars, that they determined to exert all their power to expel the above imaginary beings from the minds of the people, by taking the office of the fairies' benedictions entirely into their own hands.   Of this we have a curious proof in the beginning of Chaucer's admirable tale of the *Wife of Bath* :

" I speke of many hundred yeres ago ;
But now can no man see non elves mo,
For now the grete charitee and prayeres
Of limitoures and other holy freres
That serchen every land and every streme.
As thikke as motes in the sonne beme,
Blissing halles, chambres, kichenes, and boures,
Citees and burghes, castles highe and toures,
Thropes and bernes, shepenes and dairies,
This maketh that ther ben no faeries :
For ther as wont to walken was an elf,
Ther walketh now the limitour himself."

The other quotation from Chaucer, which Mr. Steevens

has given, is not to the present purpose. The *fairies' blessing* was to bring *peace* upon the house of Theseus ; the *night-spell* in the *Miller's tale,* is pronounced *against the influence of elves,* and those demons, or evil spirits, that were supposed to occasion the night-mare, and other nocturnal illusions. As this is a subject that has never been professedly handled, it may be worth while to bring together a few facts that relate to it ; to do it ample justice would require an express dissertation.

A belief in the influence of evil spirits has been common to all nations, and in the remotest periods of the human history. The gross superstitions of the middle ages, which even exceeded those in Pagan times, had given birth to a variety of imaginary beings, who were supposed to be perpetually occupied in doing mischief to mankind. The chief of these were the *Incubus,* or *night-mare,* and certain *fairies of a malignant nature.* It therefore became necessary to check and counteract their operations by spells, charms, and invocations to saints. Some of these have been preserved. The lines given to Mad Tom in *Lear,* beginning

"Saint Withold footed thrice the wold,"

is on of them ; and in the notes belonging to it, as well as in those by Mr. Tyrwhitt on the *Canterbury tales,* vol. iv. 242, others have been collected. To these may be added the following in Cartwright's play of *The Ordinary,* Act III. Scene 1 :

"Saint Francis, and Saint Benedight,
Blesse this house from wicked wight,
From the night-mare and the goblin,
That is hight *good fellow Robin.*
Keep it from all evil spirits,
Fayries, weezels, rats and ferrets,
From curfew time
To the next prime."

This indeed may be rather considered as satirical, but it is a parody on those which were genuine. Sinclair, in his *Satan's invisible world discovered*, informs us that " At night, in the time of popery, when folks went to bed, they believed the repetition of this following prayer was effectual to preserve them from danger, and the house too."

> " Who sains the house the night,
>   They that sains it ilka night.
>   Saint Bryde and her brate,
>   Saint Colme and his hat,
>   Saint Michael and his spear,
>   Keep this house from the weir ;
>   From running thief,
>   And burning thief ;
>   And from an ill Rea,
>   That be the gate can gae ;
>   And from an ill weight,
>   That be the gate can light
>   Nine reeds about the house ;
>   Keep it all the night,
>   What is that, what I see
>   So red, so bright, beyond the sea ?
>   'Tis he was pierc'd through the hands,
>   Through the feet, through the throat,
>   Through the tongue ;
>   Through the liver and the lung.
>   Well is them that well may
>   Fast on Good-friday."

As darkness was supposed to be more immediately adapted to the machinations of these malicious spirits, it was natural that, on retiring to rest, certain prayers should be chosen to deprecate their influence, which was often regarded as of a *particular kind.*   To this Imogen alludes when she exclaims,

> "To your protection I commend me, Gods !
>   From fairies, and the *tempters of the night*
>   Guard me, beseech ye ! "
>
> *Cymbeline,* Act II. Scene 2.

So Banquo in *Macbeth* :

> " Restrain in me the *cursed thoughts that nature*
>   *Gives way to in repose.*"

An ancient hymn by Saint Ambrose goes to the same point :

> " Procul recedant somnia
> Et noctium phantasmata :
> Hostemque nostrum comprime
> Ne *polluantur corpora*."

The demon who was supposed to have particular influence in these nocturnal illusions, was Asmodeus, the lame devil of whom Mons. Le Sage has made such admirable use.   In expelling him, the sign of the cross was most efficacious ; a very old practice on similar occasions, as we learn from the following lines in Prudentius :—

> " Fac, cum *vocante somno*
> *Castum petis cubile*
> Frontem, locumque cordis
> *Crucis* figura signes.
> Crux pellit omne crimen,
> Fugunt crucem tenebræ :
> Tali dicata signo
> Mens fluctuare nescit.
> Procul, ô procul *vagantum*
> *Portenta somniorum*,
> Procul esto pervicaci
> Præstigiator astu."

Relics of saints, images of the holy Virgin, sanctified girdles, and a variety of other amulets were resorted to on the same occasion, exhibiting a lamentable proof of the imbecility of human nature.

Scene 2.   Page 172.

Puck. *Give me your hands*, if we be friends.

Thus in the *epilogue* to Stubbes's excellent play of *Senile odium*,

> " .   .   . jam *vestræ quid valeant manus*
> Nimis velim experiri : ab illis enim vapulare, munus erit."

LOVE'S LABOUR'S LOST

ACT I.

SCENE 1. Page 181.

KING. Let fame, that all hunt after in their lives,
Live register'd upon our *brazen tombs*.

IT was the fashion in Shakspeare's time, and had been so
from the thirteenth century, to ornament the tombs of eminent persons with figures and inscriptions on *plates of brass*:
to these the allusion seems rather to be made, than to monuments that were entirely of brass, such being of very rare
occurrence.

SCENE 1. Page 182.

LONG. Fat paunches have lean pates.

From the Latin *pinguis venter non gignit sensum tenuem.*
See Ray's *Proverbs*. The rest of Longaville's speech, " and
dainty bits," &c. merely repeats the same sentiment for the
sake of a rhime.

SCENE 1. Page 183.

BIRON. If study's gain be *thus*, and this be so.

Mr. Ritson would read, *If study's gain be this*. There is no
occasion for any change. *Thus* means *after this manner* ; but
the poet would not write *this,* in order to avoid a cacophony.

SCENE 1. Page 191.

KING. This *child of fancy,* that Armado hight,
For interim to our studies shall relate,
In high-born words, the worth of many a knight
From *tawny* Spain, lost in the world's debate.

The context seems to indicate that *child of fancy* is here
used precisely in the sense in which Milton applied it to
Shakspeare, from whom he probably borrowed it. The

meaning of this controverted speech may be as follows:
" this child of *invention* shall relate to us, in his bombastic
language, the worthy deeds of many a Spanish knight which
are now forgotten amidst those topics that engage the attention of mankind." The expression *tawny Spain* may refer to
the Moors in that country; for although they had been expelled from thence almost a century before the time of Shakspeare, it was allowable on the present occasion to refer to
the period when they flourished in Spain; or he might only
copy what he found in the original story of the play.

Scene 2.   Page 198.

ARM. Why, sadness is one and the self same thing, dear *imp*.

This word, which is well explained by Mr. Ritson, was
often, as in the present instance, used to *pages*. Thus Urquhart in his *Discovery of a jewel*, &c. p. 133, calls a person
of this description " a hopeful youth and tender *imp* of great
expectation."

Scene 2.   Page 200.

MOTH . . . the *dancing horse* will tell you.

The best account of Banks and his famous horse Morocco
is to be found in the notes to a French translation of Apuleius's *Golden ass* by Jean de Montlyard, Sieur de Melleray,
counsellor to the Prince of Condé. This work was first
printed in 1602, 8vo, and several times afterwards. The
author himself had seen the horse, whose master he calls a
Scotishman, at Paris, where he was exhibited in 1601, at the
Golden Lion, Rue Saint Jaques. He is described as a
middle-sized bay English gelding, about 14 *years old.* A few
quotations from the work itself may not be unacceptable.
" Son maistre l'appelle *Moraco* . . . . . . Nous avons
vu son maistre l'interroger combien de francs vaut l'escu: et
luy, donner trois fois du pied en terre. Mais chose plus
estrange, parce que l'escu d'or sol et de poids vaut encor
maintenant au mois de Mars 1601, plus que trois francs:

l'Escossois luy demanda combien de sols valoit cest escu *outre* les trois francs; et Moraco frappa quatre coups, pour denoter les quatre sols que vaut lescu de surcroist." In which remark the counsellor shows himself less sagacious than the horse he is describing. He proceeds: " Après un infinité de tours de passe-passe, il luy fait danser les *Canaries* avec beaucoup d'art et de dexterité." The rest of the numerous tricks performed by this animal are much the same as those practised by the horses educated under the ingenious Mr. Astley. We also learn from this French work, that the magistrates, conceiving that all this could not be done without the aid of magic, had some time before imprisoned the master, and put the horse under sequestration; but having since discovered that every thing was effected by mere art and the making of signs, they had liberated the parties and permitted an exhibition. The Scotchman had undertaken to teach any horse the same tricks in a twelvemonth. It is said that both the horse and his master were afterwards burned at Rome as magicians; nor is this the only instance of the kind. In a little book entitled *Le diable bossu,* Nancy, 1708, 18mo, there is an obscure allusion to an English horse, whose master had taught him to know the cards, and which was burned alive at Lisbon in 1707; and Mr. Granger, in his *Biographical history of England,* vol. iii. p. 164, edit. 1779, has informed us that within his remembrance a horse which had been taught to perform several tricks was, with his owner, put into the Inquisition. The author of the life of Mal Cutpurse, 1662, 12mo, mentions her " fellow humourist *Banks the vintner in Cheapside,* who taught his horse to dance and shooed him with silver." In the eighth book of Markham's *Cavalarice or the English horseman,* 1607, 4to, there is a chapter " how a horse may be taught to doe and tricke done by *Bankes his curtall.*" It is extremely curious, and towards the end throws light upon the second line of Bastard's epigram quoted by Mr. Steevens.

SCENE 2.   Page 203.

ARM. *Green, indeed, is the colour of lovers.*

Green eyes, jealousy, and *the willow,* have been mentioned
as the subjects of this allusion; but it is, perhaps, to *melancholy,* the frequent concomitant of love.   Thus in *Twelfth
night,* " And with a *green* and yellow *melancholy* ;" certainly
in that instance, the effect of love.

SCENE 2.   Page 206.

DULL. *She is allowed for the day-woman.*

See more on the word *dey* in Mr. Tyrwhitt's edition of
The Canterbury tales, iii. 287, who supposes that a *dey* originally meant a day labourer, however it came afterwards to be
applied to the *dairy* : yet this conjecture must give way to
Dr. Johnson's statement that *day* is an old word for milk.
The doctor has not indeed produced any authority, and the
original Saxon word seems lost; but in the Swedish language, which bears the greatest affinity to our own of any
other, as far as regards the Teutonic part of it, *dia* signifies
to milk, and *deie,* in Polish, the same.   *Die,* in Danish, is *the
breast.*   The nearest Saxon word that remains is *diende,
sucklings;* and there can be no doubt that we have the term
in question from some of our northern ancestors.   The *dey*
or dairy maid is mentioned in the old statutes that relate to
working people ; and in that of 12 Ric. II. the annual wages
of this person are settled at six shillings.

ACT II.

SCENE 1.   Page 221.

PRIN. *Good wits will be jangling: but gentles agree.*

These alliterative and anapæstic lines are in the manner of
Tusser, who has many such ; for example,

" At Christmas of Christ many carols we sing."

It will be admitted that the construction of this sort of verse is rather less adapted to a court than a cottage ; but it is presumed that none will be inclined to find Shakspeare guilty of such poetry, which a good deal resembles the halfpenny book style of

> " Here's N. with a nag that is prancing with pride,
> And O. with an owl hooping close by his side."

Scene 1.   Page 222.

Bovet. His heart like an agate with your print impressed.

An allusion either to the figures of the human face often found in agates and other stones, or to an engraved gem.

ACT III.

Scene 1.   Page 225.

Moth. Master, will you win your love with a French *brawl*.

The word *brawl* in its signification of a dance is from the French *branle*, indicating a shaking or swinging motion. The following accounts of this dance may be found more intelligible than that cited from Marston. It was performed by several persons uniting hands in a circle, and giving each other continual shakes, the steps changing with the tune. It usually consisted of three *pas* and a *pied-joint*, to the time of four strokes of the bow; which being repeated was termed *a double brawl*. With this dance balls were usually opened. *Le branle du bouquet* is thus described in *Deux dialogues du nouveau langage François, Italianizé,* &c. Anvers, 1579, 24mo:—" Un des gentilhommes et une des dames, estans les premiers en la danse, laissent les autres (qui cependant continuent la danse) et se mettans dedans la dicte compagnie, *vont baisans par ordre toutes les personnes qui y sont* : à sçavoir le gentil-homme les dames, et la dame les gentils-hommes.   Puis ayans achevé leurs baisemens, au lieu

qu'ils estoyent les premiers en la danse, se mettent les derniers. Et ceste façon de faire se continue par le gentilhomme
et la dame qui sont les plus prochains, jusques à ce qu'on
vienne aux derniers."—P. 385. It is probably to this dance
that the puritan Stubbes alludes in the following words:
" for what clipping, what culling, what *kissing and bussing,
what smouching and slabbering one of another*: what filthy groping and unclean handling is not practised every where in these
dauncings? Yea the very deed and action itselfe which I
will not name for offending chaste eares, shall bee purtrayed
and shadowed foorth in their bawdy gestures of one to
another."—*Anatomie of abuses,* p. 114, edit. 1595, 4to. And
John Northbrooke, another writer *ejusdem farinæ,* in his invective called *A treatise wherein dicing, dauncing, vaine plaies
or enterludes,* &c. 1579, 4to, exclaims that "the Pagans were
better and more sad than wee be, they never knewe this newe
fashion of dauncing of ours, and uncleanely handling and groping, and *kissings,* and a very kindling of lechery: whereto
serveth all that *bassing,* as were pigeons the birdes of Venus?"
And again; " they daunce with disordinate gestures, and with
monstrous thumping of the feete, to pleasant soundes, to wanton songues, to dishonest verses, maidens and matrons are
groped and handled with unchaste hands, *and kissed and dishonestly embraced,*" fo. 64, 66. Amidst a great variety of
brawls mentioned in the very curious treatise on dancing by
Thoinot Arbeau, entitled *Orchesographie,* Lengres, 1588, 4to,
there is a *Scotish brawl,* with the music, which is here given
as a specimen of an old Scotish tune.

The facetious macaronic poet Antony Sablon, or de Arena,

whose work Camden says he " kept as a jewel," has left the
following description of a brawl:—

Modus dansandi branlos.

" Ipse modis branlos debes dansare duobus,
    Simplos et duplos usus habere solet.
Sed branlos duplos, passus tibi quinque laborent.
    Tres fac avantum, sed reculando duos,
Quattuor in mensura ictus marchabis eundo,
    Atque retornando quattuor ipse dabis."

This dance continued in fashion in our own country so late
as the year 1693, when Playford published a book of tunes
in which a *brawl* composed by Mons. Paisable occurs; and
see many of the little French pieces in the *Theatre de la foire,*
1721.

SCENE 1.   Page 225.

MOTH. *Canary* it with your feet.

The *canary* was another very favourite dance. In the
translation of Leo's *Description of Africa,* by Pory, 1600,
folio, there is an additional account of the *Canary islands,* in
which the author, speaking of the inhabitants, says, " They
were and are at this day delighted with a kind of dance which
they use also in Spain, and in other places, and because it
took originall from thence, it is called *the Canaries."* Thoinot
Arbeau likewise mentions this opinion, but is himself, in
common with some others, inclined to think that the dance
originated from a ballet composed for a masquerade, in which
the performers were habited as kings and queens of Morocco,
or as savages with feathers of different colours. He then describes it as follows :—A lady is taken out by a gentleman,
and after dancing together to the cadences of the proper air, he
leads her to the end of the hall; this done he retreats back to
the original spot, always looking at the lady.   Then he makes
up to her again, with certain steps, and retreats as before.
His partner performs the same ceremony, which is several
times repeated by both parties, with various strange fantastic
steps, very much in the savage style. This dance was some-

times accompanied by the castagnets.   The following *Canary*
tune is from Arbeau.

SCENE 1.   Page 236.

COST. Guerdon,—O sweet guerdon!

Mr. Steevens deduces this word from the middle age Latin
regardum.   It is presumed that few, if any, words are derived from the Latin of that period, which itself was rather
corrupted by the introduction of terms from the living languages of Europe Latinized by the Monkish writers.   *Guerdon*, as used by us, is immediately from the French: not
equivalent, as some have imagined, with *don* de *guerre*, but
formed from the Teutonic *werd* or *wurth*, i. e. *price, value*.

SCENE 1.   Page 237.

BIRON. This *wimpled*, whining, purblind, wayward boy.

If, as Mr. Steevens observes, the advocates for Shakspeare's
learning, on a presumption that he might have been acquainted with the Roman *flammeum*, or seen the celebrated
gem of the marriage of Cupid and Psyche, had applauded
the choice of his epithet, it is certain they would have shown
very little skill or critical judgment on the occasion.   By
wimpled, Shakspeare means no more than that Cupid was
hood-winked, alluding to the usual representation in paintings where he is exhibited with a bandage over his eyes.   It
may be observed here that the blindness of the God of love
is not warranted by the authority of any ancient classic
author, but appears to have been the invention of some
writer of the middle ages; not improbably Boccaccio, who in
his *Genealogy of the Gods* gives the following account:
" Oculos autem illi fascia tegunt, ut advertamus amantes

ignorare quo tendant; nulla eorum esse indicia, nullæ rerum distinctiones, sed sola passione duci."—Lib. ix. c. 4.

The oldest English writer who has noticed the blindness of love is Chaucer, in his translation of the *Roman de la rose*:

> " The God of love, *blind as stone.*"

But this line is not in the French original. Shakspeare himself has well accounted for Cupid's blindness:

> " Love looks not with the eyes, but with the mind,
> And therefore is wing'd Cupid painted blind."
>
> *M. N. Dream*, Act I. Scene 1.

SCENE 1.   Page 240.

BIRON. And I to be a corporal of the field.

Dr. Farmer's quotation of the line from Ben Jonson, " As corporal of the field, maestro del campo," has the appearance, without perhaps the intention, of suggesting that these officers were the same : this, however, was not the fact. In Styward's *Pathway to martiall discipline*, 1581, 4to, there is a chapter on the office of *maister of the campe,* and another on *the electing and office of the foure corporalls of the fields*; from which it appears that " two of the latter were appointed for placing and ordering of shot, and the other two for embattailing of the pikes and billes, who according to their worthinesse, if death hapneth, are to succeede the great sergeant or sergeant major."

SCENE 1.   Page 241.

BIRON. . . . . like a *German clock.*

Such part of Mr. Steevens's note as relates to the invention of clocks may, in a future edition, be rendered more correct by consulting Beckman's *History of inventions.* It is certain that we had clocks in England before the reign of Elizabeth; but they were not in general use till that time, when most, if not all, of them were imported from Germany. These clocks resembled what are still made for the use of the lower classes of people by several ingenious Germans established in London.

SCENE 1.   Page 242.

BIRON. Some men must love my lady, and some Joan.

Alluding to the homely proverb, " Joan's as good as my
lady in the dark :" and in Markham's *Health to the gentlemanly profession of serving men,* sign. I. 3, we have, " What
hath Joan to do with my lady ?"

ACT IV.

SCENE 1.   Page 243.

PRIN. . . . . my friend, where is the bush
That we must stand and play the murderer in ?

The practice of ladies shooting at deer in this passage alluded to, is of great antiquity, as may be collected from
Strutt's *Sports and pastimes of the people of England,* p. 9.
The old romances abound with such incidents ; but one of
the most diverting is recorded in *The history of prince Arthur,* part 3, chap. cxxiv. where a lady huntress wounds Sir
Lancelot of the Lake, instead of a deer, in a manner most
" comically tragical."

SCENE 1.   Page 246.

COST. God-dig-you-den all.

" A corruption," says Mr. Malone very justly, " of God
give you good even." Howel, at the end of his *Parley of
the beasts,* has an advertisement relating to orthography, in
which, after giving several examples that the French do not
speak as they write, he observes that " the English come not
short of him (the Frenchman) ; for whereas he writes, *God
give you good evening,* he often saies, *Godi, godin."* But the
whole of what Howel has said on this subject is unfairly pil-
laged from *Claude de Sainliens,* or, as he chose to call himself
in this country, *Hollyband* ; who after very successfully re-
torting a charge made by the English, that Frenchmen do
not sound their words as they spell them, is nevertheless

content to admit that his countrymen do *sometimes* **err, as** when they say *avoo disné*, for *avez vous disné?* See his treatise *De pronuntiatione linguæ Gallicæ*, Lond. 1580, 12mo, p. 81. This person was a teacher of languages in London, and wrote several ingenious works, among which is the *first* French and English dictionary, 1580, and 1593, 4to ; afterwards much amplified by Randle Cotgrave, and by him rendered the best repertory of old French that is extant. It is in other respects an extremely valuable work.

Scene 1.   Page 49.

Bovet. A phantasm, a *Monarcho*.

Another trait of this person's character is preserved in Scot's *Discoverie of witchcraft*, edit. 1584, p. 54, where, speaking of the influence of melancholy on the imagination, he says, "the Italian, whom we call here in England *the Monarch*, was possessed of the like spirit or conceipt." This conceit was, that all the ships which came into port belonged to him.

Scene 2.   Page 526.

Enter Holofernes.

A part of Mr. Steevens's note requires the following correction:—Florio's *First fruites* were *printed* in 1578, 4to, by Thomas Dawson. In 1598 he dedicated his Italian and English dictionary to Roger Earl of Rutland, Henry Earl of Southampton, and Lucy Countess of Bedford. As to the edition of 1595, mentioned by Mr. Steevens, does it really exist, or has not too much confidence been placed in the elegant but inaccurate historian of English poetry? See vol. iii. p. 465, note (h).

Scene 2.   Page 262.

Hol. *Dictynna*, goodman Dull ; *Dictynna*, goodman Dull.

It is possible, as Mr. Steevens has remarked, that Shakspeare might have found Diana's title of *Dictynna* in Golding's Ovid ; but there is reason for supposing that he had seen an English translation of Boccaccio's *Genealogy of the Gods*, though we have it not at present. E. Kerke, in his notes on Spenser's *Shepherd's calendar*, quotes this work; yet he might have used the original. From the same source it was possible for Shakspeare to have acquired the present information, as well as what other mythology he stood in need of. The Latin dictionaries of Eliot and Cooper would likewise supply him with similar materials.

Scene 3. Page 274.

BIRON. Thou mak'st the *triumviry*, the corner-cap of society,
  The shape of love's Tyburn that hangs up simplicity.

An allusion to the gallows of the time, which was occasionally *triangular*. Such a one is seen in some of the cuts to the first edition of Holinshed's *Chronicle*, and in other ancient prints.

Scene 3. Page 276.

BIRON. By earth she is *but corporal*; there you lie.

This is Theobald's alteration from the old reading, which was, "She is not, Corporal, there you lie," and has been adopted by the modern editors from its apparent ingenuity. A little attention may serve to show that no change was necessary, and that the original text should be restored. Theobald says that Dumain had *no post in the army*, and asks what wit there is in calling him corporal. The answer is, As much as there had already been in Biron's calling himself *a corporal of Cupid's field*; a title equally appropriate to Dumain on the present occasion. To render the matter still clearer, it may be observed that Biron does not give the lie to Dumain's assertion that his mistress was a *divinity*, as presumed by the amended reading, but to that of her being *the wonder of a mortal eye*. Dumain is answered sentence by sentence.

Scene 3. Page 276.

DUM. Her amber hairs for foul have amber *coted*.

Mr. Steevens's explanation of *coted*, and of the whole line, is inadmissible. *Foulness* or *cloudiness* is no criterion of the *beauty* of amber. Mr. Malone has partly explained *coted*, by *marked*, but has apparently missed the sense of it here when he adds *written down.* Mr. Mason has given the true construction of the line, but he mistakes the meaning of *coted*, which, after all, merely signifies to *mark* or *note.* The word is from the French *coter*, which, in like manner as Mr. Malone has well observed of the English term, is the old orthography of *quoter.* The grammatical construction is, " her amber hairs have marked or shown that [real] amber is foul in comparison of themselves."

SCENE. 3.   Page 291.

LONG. Some tricks, some *quillets*, how to cheat the Devil.

The objection to Warburton's derivation of *quillet* from the *French* is, that there is no such term in the language : nor is it exclusively applicable to law-chicane, though generally so used by Shakspeare. It strictly means a *subtilty*, and seems to have originated among the schoolmen of the middle ages, by whom it was called a *quidlibet.* They had likewise their *quodlibets* and their *quiddities.* From the schoolmen these terms were properly enough transferred to the lawyers. Hamlet says, " Why may not that be the scull of a lawyer ? where be his *quiddits* now, his *quillets*, his cases, his tenures and his tricks ? " The conjectures of Peck, and after him of Dr. Grey in a note to Hudibras, seem to merit but little attention.

SCENE 3.   Page 294.

BIRON. Still climbing trees in the *Hesperides*.

An error is here laid to Shakspeare's charge, of which he is ,·ot perhaps guilty. The expression *trees in the Hesperides* must be regarded as elliptical, and signifies *trees in the gardens of the Hesperides.* Shakspeare is seldom wrong in his mythology, and, if he had doubted on the present occasion, the dictionaries of Eliot or Cooper would have supplied him with the necessary information. The first quotation in the note from Greene, is equally elliptical; for this writer was too good a scholar to have committed the mistake ascribed to Shakspeare : so that the passage, instead of convicting the latter, does in reality support him. As to the other quotation from *Orpheus and Eurydice,* the learned critic himself lays but little stress on it; or indeed might, on reconsideration, be disposed to think the expression correct. It would not be difficult to trace instances in modern authors of the use of *Hesperides* for *gardens of the Hesperides.* See Lempriere's excellent classical dictionary, edit. 1792, 8vo.

ACT V.

Scene 1.   Page 302.

Hol. His humour is lofty, his discourse peremptory, his *tongue filed.*—

Mr Steevens has remarked that Chaucer, Skelton, and Spenser are frequent in their use of this phrase, but he has offered no explanation. It signifies *polished language*; thus Turbervile, in his translation of *Ovid's epistles,* makes Phyllis say to her lover—

> " Thy many smooth and *filed* wordes
> Did purchase credites place."

Scene 1.   Page 306.

Arm. . . . . a sweet touch, a quick *venew* of wit.

The *cut and thrust* notes on this occasion exhibit a complete *match* between the two great Shakspearean *maisters of defence.* " A venew," says Mr. Steevens, " is the technical term for a *bout* (or *set-to,* as he had before called it in vol. iii. p. 317,) at the fencing school." On the other hand, Mr. Malone maintains that " a venue is *not* a *bout* at fencing, but a *hit* ;" and his opponent retorts on the ground of *positiveness* of denial. As the present writer has himself been an amateur

and practitioner of the noble science of defence, he undertakes on this occasion the office of umpire between the sturdy
combatants.

The quotations adduced on either side are not calculated to
ascertain the clear and genuine sense of the word *venew*, and
it is therefore necessary to seek for more decisive evidence
respecting its meaning. Howel in his *Lexicon tetraglotton*,
1660, mentions " a *veny* in fencing; venue, *touche*, toca ;"
and afterwards more fully in his vocabulary, sect. xxxii. " A
foin, *veny*, or stoccado ; la botta; la *touche*, le *coup*." In Sir
John Harrington's *Life of Dr. Still*, is the following expression, " he would not sticke to warne them in the arguments
to take heede to their answers, like a perfect fencer that will
tell afore-hand in which button he will give the *venew*."
Nugæ antiquæ, vol. ii. p. 158, edit. 1804, by Park. In Ben
Jonson's *Every man in his humour*, Act I. Scene 5, Bobadil, in answer to Master Matthew's request for *one venue*,
says, " Venue ! fie : most gross denomination as ever I heard ;
O, the *stoccata*, while you live, sir, note that." On this passage, Mr. Reed, in a note on the play of *The widow's tears*, Dodsley's *Old plays*, vol. vi. 152, observes that " the word appears
to have been out of fashion with the fantastic gallants of the
time very early." Its occurrence however so late as the time
in which Howel's dictionary was published seems to render this
ingenious remark very questionable, and suggests another explanation of Bobadil's wish to change the word, namely, his
coxcombly preference of the terms of the Spanish and Italian
schools of fencing to those used in the English, which, it is
presumed, were more immediately borrowed from our Gallic
neighbours. That the terms *stoccado* and *imbrocato* denoted
a *hit* or thrust, may be collected from many passages in Vincent Saviolo's *Use of the rapier and dagger*, 1595, 4to ; and
in Florio's Italian dictionary, 1598, folio, *stoccata* is rendered, *a foyne, a thrust given in fence* ; and *tocco, a venie at
fence, a hit.* All the above circumstances considered, one

should feel inclined to adjudge the palm of victory to Mr. Malone.

It is however remarkable enough that Mr. Steevens is accidentally right in defining a *venew* a *bout*, without being aware of the signification of the latter word. Florio renders *botta*, a *blowe*, a *stroake*. In the best of all the ancient French treatises on the art of fencing, entitled *Traicté sur l'espée seule, mere de toutes armes,* &c., by Henry De Sainct Didier, Paris, 1573, 4to, it is said, " *bottes* en Napollitain, vaut autant à dire, que *coups* en François." He then mentions five sorts of *bottes,* viz. *maindrette, renverse, fendante, estoccade,* and *imbroucade.* Nevertheless the word *bout* had been used in the sense of a *set-to* in Shakspeare's time. In *The first part of King Henry the Sixth,* Act I. Scene 5, Talbot says to the Pucelle, " I'll have a *bout* with thee." It retained, however, its original meaning long afterwards. Howel, and Sherwood likewise in his English dictionary at the end of Cotgrave have " a boute, coup," and so it is defined by Skinner: but the following passage from the account given by Sir Thomas Urquhart in his singular book entitled *A discovery of a most exquisite jewel found in the kennel of Worcester streets,* &c. 1652, 12mo, of the combat between the admirable Crichton and the celebrated Mantuan duellist, will put the matter beyond all doubt. " Then was it that to vindicate the reputation of the duke's family and to expiate the blood of the three vanquished gentlemen, he alonged a *stoccade de pied ferme*; then recoyling, he advanced another thrust, and lodged it home; after which retiring again, his right foot did beat the cadence of the blow that pierced the belly of this Italian, whose heart and throat being hit with the two former stroaks, these *three franch bouts* given in upon the back of other . . . . . by them he was to be made a sacrifice of atonement for the slaughter of the three aforesaid gentlemen who were wounded in the very same parts of their bodies by other such *three venees* as these." The same mode of expression is also used by the same writer in a subsequent account of a duel between Francis Sinclair, a natural son of the Earl of Caithness, and a German, at Vienna; where it was agreed that he who should give the other the first *three bouts,* should have a pair of golden spurs, in the event of which combat Sinclair " gave in two *venees* more than he was obliged to."

On the whole therefore it appears that *venew* and *bout* equally denote a *hit* in fencing; that both Mr. Steevens and Mr. Malone are right in this respect; but that the former gentleman is inaccurate in supposing a *venew* to mean a *set-to,* and the latter equally so in asserting that " a *venew* is *not* a *bout."*

SCENE 1.   Page 311.

> DULL. I will play on the tabor to the worthies, and let them dance the *hay.*

This dance was borrowed by us from the French. It is classed among the *brawls* in Thoinot Arbeau's *Orchesographie,* already mentioned in page 135.

SCENE 2.   Page 312.

> ROS.   For he hath been five thousand years a boy.
> KATH. Ay, and a shrewd unhappy gallows too.

This description of Cupid is borrowed from some lines in Sidney's *Arcadia,* B. ii. See them already quoted on another occasion by Dr. Farmer in *Much ado about nothing,* Act III. Scene 2.

SCENE 2.   Page 316.

> Ros. That he should be my *fool,* and I his *fate.*

Dr. Warburton's conclusion that *fate* here signifies *death* is not satisfactory. Death would be an awkward character for Rosaline to assume, but that of *dame fortune* infinitely more natural.

It must be owned that destiny and fortune are, strictly speaking, very different characters; yet they have sometimes been confounded. Even Pindar, as Pausanias observes, has made fortune one of the *Parcæ.* In *Julius Cæsar*, the expression, " he is but fortune's *knave*," seems to resemble the present, and to mean, " he is the servant of fortune and *bound to obey her.*"   Shakspeare is very fond of alluding to the *mockery* of fortune.   Thus we have

> " O I am fortune's fool."   *Romeo and Juliet.*
> " Ye fools of fortune."   *Timon of Athens.*
> " I am the natural fool of fortune."   *King Lear.*

In the last of which passages a pointed allusion is made to the *idiot fool.*   Sir J. Suckling uses the same expression in his play of *The goblins*; and Hamlet speaks of " the fools of nature," precisely in the same sense.

SCENE 2.   Page 327.

BOVET.   Fleeter than arrows, *bullets*, wind, thought, swifter things.

The word *bullets* is doubtless an interpolation in the manuscript by some ignorant person who thought it more appropriate than *arrows,* on account of the substitution of fire-arms for archery.   It might very properly be omitted in the text, without any diminution of editorial accuracy.

SCENE 2.   Page 330.

BOVET. Fair ladies mask'd are roses in their bud ;
        Dismask'd their damask sweet commixture shown,
        Are *angels vailing clouds,* or roses blown.

Of the several explanations here offered of *vailing,* Dr. Johnson's is the best.   The poet compares a lady unmasking to an angel dispelling the clouds in his descent from heaven to earth.   The term is from the old French *avaler* to *put* or *let down*; the true etymology of which appears in the phrase *à mont et à val*, from top to bottom, from *mountain* to *valley,* which very often occurs in old romances.   In that of the *Saint Graal,* MS. we have " et avalerent aval le vessel."   In Spenser's *Shepherd's calendar,* under January, " By that the welked Phœbus gan *availe.*"

SCENE 2.   Page 339.

BIRON. *Three pil'd* hyperboles.

So in Fennor's *Compter's commonwealth,* 1617, 4to, p. 14,

we have " *three pil'd,* huge Basilisco oaths, that would have torne a roring-boyes eares in a thousand shatters."

SCENE 2.   Page 345.

COST. You cannot *beg us,* sir.

It has been already stated that it was not the next relation only who begged the wardship of *idiots* in order to obtain possession of their property, but any person who could make interest with the sovereign to whom the legal guardianship belongs. Frequent allusions to this practice occur in the old comedies. In illustration of it, Mr. Ritson has given a curious story, which, as it is mutilated in the authority which he has used, is here subjoined from a more original source, a collection of tales, &c., compiled about the time of Charles the First, preserved among the Harleian MSS. in the British Museum, No. 6395. " The Lord North begg'd old Bladwell for a foole (though he could never prove him so), and having him in his custodie as a lunaticke, he carried him to a gentleman's house, one day, that was his neighbour. The L. North and the gentleman retir'd awhile to private discourse, and left Bladwell in the dining roome, which was hung with a faire hanging; Bladwell walking up and downe, and viewing the imagerie, spyed a foole at last in the hanging, and without delay drawes his knife, flyes at the foole, cutts him cleane out, and layes him on the floore ; my L. and the gentl. coming in againe, and finding the tapestrie thus defac'd, he ask'd Bladwell what he meant by such a rude uncivill act ; he answered S^r. be content, I have rather done you a courtesie than a wrong, for if ever my L. N. had seene the foole there, he would have begg'd him, and so you might have lost your whole suite." The same story, but without the parties' names, is related in Fuller's *Holy state,* p. 182. Powel, in his *Attourney's academy,* 1630, 4to, says, " I shall neede to give you this monitorie instruction touching an *ideot*; that you be assured that yourselfe is somewhat the wiser man before you goe about to *beg him*, or else never meddle with him at all, lest you chance to play at handy-dandy, which is the gardian or which is the foole? and the case alter, *è converso, ad conversum.*" In *A treatise of taxes*, 1667, 4to, p. 43, there is the following passage : "Now because the world abounds with this kind of fools, (Lottery fools,) it is not fit that every man that will may cheat every man that would be cheated ; but it is rather ordained that the sovereign should have the guardianship of these fools, *or that some favourite should beg the sovereign's right of taking advantage of such men's folly, even as in the case of lunatics and ideots.*" To this practice too, Butler alludes, in *Hudibras*, part iii. canto 1, l. 590.

> " Beg one another idiot
> To guardians, ere they are begot."

Mr. Justice Blackstone, in treating of idiots, has spoken of it ; and adds in a note, that the king's power of delegating the custody of them to some subject who has interest enough on the occasion, has of late been very rarely exerted.

Scene 2.   Page 350.

> Biron. The pedant, the braggart, the hedge-priest, the fool and
> the boy :—
> Abate a throw at *novum*; and the whole world again,
> Cannot prick out *five* such, take each one in his vein.

The game of *novum* or *novem*, here alluded to, requires further illustration to render the *whole* of the above passage intelligible. It is therefore necessary to state that it was *properly* called *novum quinque*, from the two principal throws of the dice, nine and five ; and then Biron's meaning becomes perfectly clear, according to the reading of the old editions. The above game was called in French *quinquenove*, and is said to have been invented in Flanders.

Scene 2.   Page 351.

> Pageant of the nine worthies.

The *genuine* worthies were Joshua, David, Judas Maccabeus, Hector, Alexander, Julius Cæsar, Arthur, Charlemagne, and Godfrey of Bulloigne, or sometimes in his room **Guy of Warwick.** Why Shakspeare, in the *five* of them only whom he has introduced by name, has included Hercules and Pompey, remains to be accounted for. It was a great pity to omit, on this occasion, the very curious specimen of an ancient pageant given by Mr. Ritson, who, in stating that nothing of the kind had ever appeared in print, seems to have forgotten the pageants of Dekker, Middleton, and others, a list of which may be found in Baker's *Biographia dramatica*, vol. ii. 270.

SCENE 2.   Page 353.

BIRON. Your nose *smells* no, in this, most *tender smelling* knight.

He is addressing, or rather ridiculing Alexander. Plutarch in his life of that hero relates, on the authority of Aristoxenus, that his skin " had a marvellous good savour, and that his breath was very sweet, in so much that *his body had so sweet a smell* of itselfe that all the apparell he wore next unto his body, tooke thereof a passing delightfull savour, as if it had been perfumed." This Shakspeare had read in Sir Thomas North's translation.

SCENE 2.   Page 353.

COST. Your lion, that holds his *poll-ax* sitting, &c.

The clown's Cloacinian allusion to the arms of Alexander is a wilful *blunder*, for the purpose of introducing his subsequent joke about Ajax. These are the arms themselves copied from the *Roman des neuf preux*, Abbeville, 1487, folio, showing that the chair is not a chaise-perçée.

The modern *patent Bramahs* were in Shakspeare's time called *Ajaxes*. Thus in *The hospitall of incurable fooles*, 1600, 4to, fo. 7: " Whoever saw so many odd mechanicks as are at this day, who not with a geometricall spirite like Archimedes, but even with arte surpassing the profoundest Cabalistes, who instead of a pigeon loft, place in the garrets of houses, *portable* and commodious *Ajaxes*." The marginal explanation comes *closer* to the point. Again, " the Romans might well be numbered amongst those three-elbowed fooles in adoring Stercutio for a God, shamefully constituting him a patron and protector of *Ajax* and his commodities," fo. 6.

SCENE 2. Page 360.

Cost. I will not fight with a *pole*, like a *northern man*.

On this passage Dr. Farmer says, " *Vir borealis*, a clown, See glossary to Urry's Chaucer." The Doctor's notes are generally clear and instructive, but in this instance he is obscure. It is presumed that he intends to refer the reader to the word *borel* in Urry's glossary, where it is properly explained *a clown*. Whether *borel* be derived from *borealis* may be questioned; but Shakspeare in all probability was unacquainted with this word and its etymology. Does he not refer to the particular use of the quarter staff in the Northern counties?

SCENE 2. Page 367.

Prin. As *bombast*, and as lining to the time.

Bombast is from the Italian *bombagia*, which signifies all sorts of cotton wool. Hence the stuff called *bombasine*. The cotton put into ink was called *bombase*. " Need you any inke and *bombase* ?" Hollyband's *Italian schole-maister*, 1579, 12mo, sign. E. 3.

THE CLOWN.

The clown in this play is a mere country fellow. The term *fool* applied to him in Act V. Scene 2, means nothing more than a *silly fellow*. He has not sufficient simplicity for a natural fool, nor wit enough for an artificial one.

It will probably be discovered at some future time that this play was borrowed from a French novel. The *dramatis personæ* in a great measure demonstrate this, as well as a palpable Gallicism in Act IV. Scene 1, viz. the terming a *letter* a *capon*.

MERCHANT OF VENICE.

ACT I.

Scene 1. Page 397.

Salar. There, where your *argosies*, with portly sail
Like signiors and rich burghers *of* the flood,
Or as it were the *Pageants* of the sea,
Do overpeer the petty traffickers.

Argosies are properly defined to be " ships of great bur-
then," and so they are described almost wherever they are
mentioned. Mr. Steevens has quoted Rycaut's *Maxims of
Turkish polity*, to show that the term originated in a corruption of *Ragosies*, i. e. ships of *Ragusa*. However specious
this may appear, it is to be observed that Rycaut, a writer at
the end of the seventeenth century, only states it as *a matter
of report*, not as a *fact*; and he seems to have followed the
slight authority of Roberts's *Marchant's map of commerce*. If
any instance shall be produced of the use of such a word as
ragosie, the objection must be given up. In the mean time
it may be permitted to hazard another opinion, which is,
that the word in question derives its origin from the famous
ship *Argo*: and indeed Shakspeare himself appears to have
hinted as much; for the story of Jason is twice adverted to
in the course of this play. On one of these occasions Gra-
tiano certainly alludes to Antonio's argosie when he says,

" We are the Jasons, we have won the fleece."
                                        Act III. Scene 2.

Gregory of Tours has more than once made use of *Argis*
to express a ship generally. With respect to *Ragozine*, it
has been contended in a former note, page 89, that this

name ought not to have been introduced in the discussion of the present subject.

Mr. Steevens remarks that both ancient and modern editors have hitherto been content to read " burghers *on* the flood ;" and, on the authority of a line in which we have " burghers *of a city,*" he has substituted " burghers *of* the flood." He might have been less inclined to this new reading, had he recollected that the " signiors and rich burghers *on* the flood" are the Venetians, who may well be said to live *on* the sea. It would be difficult to discover who are the signiors and burghers *of* the flood, unless they be whales and porpoises.

In calling argosies *the pageants of the sea,* Shakspeare alludes to those enormous machines, in the shapes of castles, dragons, ships, giants, &c., that were drawn about the streets in the ancient shows or pageants, and which often constituted the most important part of them.

SCENE 1.   Page 399.

SALAN. Now, by *two-headed Janus.*

Dr. Warburton's note may well be spared in all future editions. If Shakspeare have shown a knowledge of the antique, which he might have obtained from his dictionary at school, the Doctor has, unluckily, on this occasion proved himself less profound in it than Shakspeare, or he would not have ventured to assert that the heads of Janus were those of Pan and Bacchus, Saturn and Apollo, &c. It is presumed that these heads will continue to perplex the learned for many generations.

SCENE 2.   Page 410.

POR. If a *throstle* sing.

Notwithstanding the apparent difference in opinion between Messrs. Steevens and Malone respecting this bird, they are both right. The throstle is only a variety of the thrush, as will be seen by consulting Mr. Pennant's Account of English birds. In *The new general history of birds,* 1745,

12mo, there is an account of "the song-thrush, or throstle;" and see Randle Holme's *Academy of armory,* book ii. ch. 12, no. lxxiii.

SCENE 3. Page 413.

Enter SHYLOCK.

His stage dress should be *a scarlet hat lined with black taffeta.* This is the manner in which the Jews of Venice were formerly distinguished. See Saint Didier *Histoire de Venise.* In the year 1581 they wore *red caps* for distinction's sake, as appears from Hakluyt's *Voyages,* p. 179, edit. 1589. Lord Verulam, in his Essay on usury, speaking of the witty invectives that men have made against usury, states one of them to be "that usurers should have *orange-tawny bonnets,* because they do *Judaize."*

SCENE 3. Page 414.

SHY. He lends out money gratis, and brings down
The rate of usance here with us in Venice.

" It is almost incredyble what gaine the Venetians receive by the usury of the Jewes, both pryvately and in common. For in everye citee the Jewes kepe open shops of usurie, taking gaiges of ordinarie for xv in the hundred by the yere; and if at the yeres ende the gaige be not redemed, it is forfeite, or at the least dooen away to a great disadvantage : by reason whereof the Jewes are out of measure wealthie in those parties."—Thomas's *Historye of Italye,* 1561, 4to, fo. 77.

SCENE 3. Page 416.

SHY. He stuck them up before the *fulsome* ewes.

Fulsome has, doubtless, the same signification as the preceding epithet *rank,* the physical reason for its application being very generally known. " Ικτιδος *pellis.* Proverbium apud Germanos in vilissimum quodque et maxime *fœtidum* scortum. Nam Ictis, id est sylvestris mustela cum graviter exarserit, male olet." Erasmi *Adagia.* Spenser makes one of his shepherds speak thus of a kid :

"The blossoms of lust to bud did beginne
And spring forth *ranckly* under his chinne."

Fulsome is from the Gothic *fuls*, i. e. *foul, fœtid*. That it sometimes had another root, viz. *full,* is manifest from the line in Golding's *Ovid,* whose expression "fulsome dugs" is in the original " *pleno* ubere," but is of no service on the present occasion, though quoted by Mr. Steevens.

SCENE 3.   Page 418.

SHY. About my money and my *usances*.

Mr. Steevens asserts that *use* and *usance* anciently signi-fied *usury,* but both his quotations show the contrary. Mr. Ritson very properly asks whether Mr. Steevens is not mis-taken; and Mr. Reed, maintaining that he is right, adduces a passage which *proves* him to be *wrong.* A gentleman, says Wylson, borrowed 1000 pounds, running still upon *usury* and *double usury.* " The merchants termyng it *usance* and *double usance,* by *a more clenly name,*" i. e. *interest,* till he owed the usurer five thousand pounds, &c. The sense was obscured by the omission of an important comma after the word *name.* Mr. Malone's note was quite adequate to the purpose of ex-planation.

SCENE 3.   Page 421.

SHY. . . . . . seal me there
    Your single bond; and in *a merry sport,*
    If you repay me not, &c.

Thus in the ballad of *Gernutus*:

" But we will have *a merry jeast*
    For to be talked long ;
You shall make me *a bond,* quoth he,
    That shall be large and strong."

ACT II.

SCENE 1.   Page 423.

MOR. But let us make incision for your love,
    To prove whose blood is *reddest,* his, or mine.

Dr. Johnson's observation that " red blood is a tradition-ary sign of courage" derives support from our English Pliny,

Bartholomew Glantville, who says, after Isidorus, " *Reed* clothes ben layed upon deed men in remembrance of theyr *hardynes* and *boldnes*, whyle they were in theyr bloudde." On which his commentator Batman remarks: " It appereth in the time of the Saxons that the manner over their dead was a *red* cloath, as we now use black. The *red* of *valiauncie*, and that was over kings, lords, knights and valyaunt souldiours."

SCENE 2. Page 426.

LAUN. Do not run; scorn *running with thy heels*.

Mr. Steevens calls this *absurdity*, and introduces a brother critic, Sir Hugh Evans, who had maintained that " he hears with ears" was *affectations*: both the parties had forgotten their Bible. As to the proposed alteration "*withe* thy heels," it might be asked, who ever heard of a person *binding* his *own heels* to prevent running? Mr. Malone has well defended the consistency of Launcelot's speech. It may be added that in *King Richard II.* Act V. Scene 3, we have " *kneel* upon my *knees*."

SCENE 2. Page 427.

LAUN. Well, my *conscience* says—Launcelot, budge not; budge, says the *fiend*; budge not, says my *conscience*.

It is not improbable that this curious struggle between Launcelot's conscience and the fiend might have been suggested by some well-known story in Shakspeare's time, grafted on the following Monkish fable. It occurs in a collection of apologues that remain only in manuscript, and have been severally ascribed to Hugo of Saint Victor, and Odo de Sheriton or Shirton, an English Cistercian Monk of the 12th century. " Multi sunt sicut mulier delicata et pigra. Talis vero mulier dum jacet mane in lecto et audit pulsari ad missam, cogitat secum quod vadat ad missam. Et cum *caro*, quæ pigra est, timet frigus, respondet et dicit, Quare ires ita mane, nonne scis quod clerici pulsant campanas propter oblationes? dormi adhuc; et sic transit pars diei. Postea

iterum *conscientia pungit eam* quod vadat ad missam. Sed
caro respondet, et dicit, Quare ires tu tam cito ad ecclesiam ?
certè tu destrueres corpus tuum si ita manè surrexeris, et hoc
Deus non vult ut homo destruat seipsum ; ergo quiesce et
dormi. Et transit alia pars diei. Iterum *conscientia pungit
eam* quod vadat ad ecclesiam ; sed *caro* dicit, Ut quid ires
tam cito ? Ego bene scio quod talis vicina tua nondum
vadit ad ecclesiam ; dormi parum adhuc. Et sic transit alia
pars diei. Postea *pungit eam conscientia* ; sed *caro* dicit,
Non oportet quod adhuc vadas, quia sacerdos est curialis et
bene expectabit te ; attende et dormi. Et sic dormiendo
transit tempus. Et tamen ad ultimum verecundia tacita
atque coacta, surgit et vadit ad ecclesiam, et invenit portas
clausas." Then follows the moral of the fable, in which the
church is repentance, the bells the preachers. The lazy flesh
prevails over conscience, till, on the approach of death, fear
dictates the sending for the priest. An imperfect confession
of sins takes place ; the party dies, and the miserable soul
finds the gates of heaven shut.

SCENE 5. Page 443.

SHY. The *patch* is kind enough.

It has been supposed that this term originated from the
name of a fool belonging to Cardinal Wolsey, and that his
parti-coloured dress was given to him in allusion to his name.
The objection to this is, that the motley habit worn by fools
is much older than •the time of Wolsey. Again, it appears
that *Patch* was an appellation given not to one fool only that
belonged to Wolsey. There is an epigram by Heywood, entitled *A saying of Patch my Lord Cardinal's foole*; but in
the epigram itself he is twice called *Sexten,* which was his
real name. In a manuscript life of Wolsey, by his gentleman
usher Cavendish, there is a story of another fool belonging
to the Cardinal, and presented by him to the King. A marginal note states that " this foole was callid *Master Williames,*

owtherwise called *Patch.*"* In Heylin's *History of the reformation,* mention is made of another fool called *Patch,* belonging to Elizabeth. But the name is even older than Wolsey's time; for in some household accounts of Henry the Seventh, there are payments to a fool who is named *Pechie,* and *Packye.* It seems therefore more probable on the whole that fools were nick-named *Patch* from their dress; unless there happen to be a nearer affinity to the Italian *pazzo,* a word that has all the appearance of a descent from *fatuus.* This was the opinion of Mr. Tyrwhitt in a note on *A midsummer night's dream,* Act III. Scene 2. But although in the above instance, as well as in a multitude of others, a *patch* denotes a fool or simpleton, and, by corruption, a clown, it seems to have been occasionally used in the sense of *any low or mean person.* Thus in the passage in *A midsummer night's dream* just referred to, Puck calls Bottom and his companions *a crew of patches, rude mechanicals,* certainly not meaning to compare them to pampered and sleek buffoons. Whether in this sense the term have a simple reference to that class of people whose clothes might be pieced or *patched* with rags; or whether it is derived from the Saxon verb pæcan, to deceive by false appearances, as suggested by the acute and ingenious author of *The diversions of Purley,* must be left to the reader's own discernment.

Scene 7.   Page 450.

MOR. . . . . . They have in England
        A coin that bears the figure of an Angel
        Stamped in gold; but that's *insculp'd upon* ;
        But here an angel in a golden bed
        Lies all *within.*

To insculp, as Mr. Steevens has observed, means *to engrave,* but is here put in opposition to it, and simply denotes to

---

* It may be worth remarking that the historian Stowe has made great use of this curious and valuable Life of Wolsey, without naming the author. It has been several times printed, but the manuscript copies have greatly the advantage in fullness and accuracy.

carve in relief. The angel on the coin was *raised*; on the casket *indented.* The word *insculp* was however formerly used with great latitude of meaning. Shakspeare might have caught it from the casket story in the *Gesta Romanorum,* where it is rightly used : " the third vessell was made of lead, and thereupon was *insculpt* this posey, &c."

SCENE 7.   Page 450.

MOR. *Gilded tombs* do worms infold.

The old editions read *gilded timber*; and however specious the alteration in the text, on the ground of redundancy of measure or defect in grammar, it might have been dispensed with. *To infold* is *to inwrap or contain any thing*; and therefore, unless we conclude that *do* is an error of the press for *doth*, we must adopt the other sense, however ungrammatically expressed, and suppose the sentiment to be, that *timber though fenced or protected with gilding is still liable to the worm's invasion.* The lines cited by Mr. Steevens from the *Arcadia* supports the original reading, as do the following from Silvester's *Works,* edit. 1633, p. 649 :

> " Wealth on a cottage can a palace build,
>   New paint old walls, and *rotten timber guild.*"

SCENE 8.   Page 453.

SALAR. And for the Jew's bond, which he hath of me,
  Let it not enter in your *mind of love.*

Dr. Johnson suspects a corruption. Mr. Langton would place a comma after *mind.* The expression seems equivalent to a *loving* or affectionate *mind*, a mind made up of love.

SCENE 9.   Page 458.

AR. What's here? the portrait of a blinking ideot,
  Presenting me a schedule.

This idea suggests the story of a Jew apothecary, who, to ridicule the Mayersbachs of his time, placed in the front of his shop the figure of a grinning fool holding out an urinal. See Pancirollus *De rebus deperditis,* lib. ii. tit. 1.

ACT III.

SCENE 1.   Page 465.

SHY. 'It was my *turquoise*.

If the reason last assigned in Mr. Steevens's note for the value which Shylock professes for the turquoise be entitled to any preference, the information whereon it rests must be referred to the right owner, who is Anselm de Boot, Nicols being only the translator of his work.

SCENE 2.   Page 469.

POR. . . . he makes a *swan-like* end.
Fading in musick.

That the swan uttered musical sounds at the approach of death was credited by Plato, Chrysippus, Aristotle, Euripides, Philostratus, Cicero, Seneca, and Martial. Pliny, Ælian, and Athenæus, among the ancients, and Sir Thomas More, among the moderns, treat this opinion as a vulgar error. Luther believed in it. See his *Colloquia*, par. 2, p. 125, edit. 1571, 8vo. Our countryman Bartholomew Glantville thus mentions the singing of the swan : " And whan she shal dye and that a fether is pyght in the brayn, then she syngethe, as Ambrose sayth," *De propr. rer.* l. xii. c. 11. Monsieur Morin has written a dissertation on this subject in vol. v. of the *Mem. de l'acad. des inscript.* There are likewise some curious remarks on it in Weston's *Specimens of the conformity of the European languages with the Oriental,* p. 135; in Seelen *Miscellanea,* tom. i. 298; and in Pinkerton's *Recollections of Paris,* ii. 336.

SCENE 2.   Page 472.

BASS. Nor none of thee, thou *pale and common drudge*
'Tween man and man.

The greatest part of the current coin being of *silver*, this metal is here emphatically called the common drudge in the more frequent transactions among men.

Scene 2.   Page 472.

Bass. Thy *plainness* moves me more than eloquence.

However elegant this emendation by Dr. Warburton, it must yield to the decisive reasoning of Dr. Farmer and Mr. Malone, in favour of *paleness*, which ought to have been adopted in the text.

Scene 2.   Page 474.

Bass. Fair Portia's *counterfeit?*

A further illustration occurs in the beginning of Lilie's dedication to his *Euphues*, " Parasius drawing the *counterfeit* of Hellen, made the attire of her head loose." In Littelton's *English and Latin dictionary*, we have " A counterfeit of a picture, *ectypum.*"

Scene 2.   Page 480.

Gra. We are the Jasons, we have won the fleece.

The meaning is " Antonio with his *argosie* is not the successful Jason; we are the persons who have won the fleece." See the note in p. 153.

Scene 2.   Page 480.

Por. . . . . else nothing in the world
Could turn so much the constitution
Of any *constant* man.

This word occasionally signified *grave*, as in the present instance. In Withall's *Shorte dictionarie*, 1599, 4to, fo. 105, we have " sadde, *grave*, constant,—*gravis.*" So in *Twelfth night*, when Malvolio is under confinement, he says, " I am no more mad than you are; make the trial of it in any *constant question.*"

ACT IV.

Scene 1.   Page 501.

Shy. Why he a *swollen* bagpipe.

We have here one of the too frequent instances of *con-*

jectural readings; but it is to be hoped that all future editors will restore the original *woollen,* after weighing not only what has been already urged in its support, but the additional and accurate testimony of Dr. Leyden, who in his edition of *The complaynt of Scotland,* p. 149, informs us that the Lowland bagpipe commonly had the bag or sack covered with *woollen cloth* of a green colour, a practice which, he adds, prevailed in the northern counties of England.

Scene 1.   Page 506.

Bass. Why dost thou *whet thy knife* so earnestly?

This incident occurs in the ballad of *Gernutus,* whence there is reason to suppose it was borrowed.   In 1597 was acted at Cambridge a Latin play called *Machiavellus,* in which there is a Jew, but very unlike Shylock.   He is a shrewd intriguing fellow of considerable humour, who, to obtain possession of a girl, puts a number of tricks on the Machiavel of the piece, and generally outwits him.   In one scene he overhears his rival despairing of success with the father of his mistress, and expressing a wish that he had some instrument wherewith to put an end to his misery.   On this he lays a *knife* in his way, but first takes care *to whet it.*   To *The merchant of Venice* or to *Gernutus* the Latin play was indebted.   If to the former, then Shakspeare's play must have been acted before 1597; if to the latter, it strengthens the above conjecture that he borrowed from the ballad. Should Gosson's *Jew shown at the Bull* ever make its appearance, all would be set right.

Scene 1.   Page 507.

Gra. And, whilst thou *lay'st* in thy unhallow'd dam.

Is not this a very common misprint for *lay'dst,* where the preterite is intended?

Scene 1.   Page 509.

Por. But mercy is above this scepter'd sway,
        It is enthroned in the hearts of *kings*,
        It is *an attribute to God* himself,
        And earthly power doth then show likest God's
        When *mercy* seasons justice.

This beautiful sentiment accords very much with the following speech made by Sir James Melvil to the queen of Scots, and printed in his *Memoirs*, p. 149, edit. 1752, 8vo. These, however, were not published till a considerable time after his death. " For as princes are called divine persons, so no *prince* can pretend to this title, but he who *draws near the nature of God* by godliness and good government, being slow to vengeance, and *ready to forgive.*"

Scene 1.   Page 518.

Gra. Had I been judge thou should'st have had *ten* more
        To bring thee to the gallows.

We had already had an English trial by jury at Vienna. See p. 78.   Here we have one at Venice.

ACT V.

Scene 1.   Page 523.

Lor. Stood Dido with a willow in her hand.

On this passage Mr. Steevens founds an argument that Shakspeare *was no reader of the classics.*   It is true that no classical authority for the above circumstance relating to Dido can be found, and that other instances of our poet's errors in classical matters might be adduced; but this will not prove his ignorance of Greek and Roman writers.   On the contrary, do not the numerous quotations from them in the notes of his commentators afford sufficient testimony that he had read many ancient authors through the medium of English translations ?   If this had not been the case, to what end has the useful and interesting list of such translations been drawn up and published by the above learned critic ? Wherever Shakspeare met with the image in question, it has reference to the popular superstitions relating to the willow, which will be more fully illustrated in some remarks on a passage in Othello.

SCENE 1.   Page 529.

LOR. You shall perceive them make a mutual *stand*,
   Their savage eyes turn'd to a modest *gaze*.

This is spoken of young *colts,* but the speech is only a poetical amplification of a phrase that seems more properly to belong to *deer.* In the *Noble arte of venerie or hunting,* ascribed to Turbervile, the author or translator, speaking of the hart, says, " when he stayeth to looke at any thing, then he *standeth at gaze* ;" and again, " he loveth to hear instruments and assureth himselfe when he heareth a flute or any other sweete noyse. He marvelleth at all things, and taketh pleasure to *gaze* at them." See likewise Holland's translation of *Pliny,* tom. i. p. 213.

SCENE 1.   Page 530.

LOR. The man that hath no musick in himself,
   Nor is not mov'd with concord of sweet sounds,
   Is fit for treasons, stratagems, and spoils ;
   The motions of his spirit, &c.

Had the sentiments in the note on this passage been expressed by Dr. Johnson, disorganized as he was for the enjoyment of music, it would not have been matter to wonder at : but that such a man as Mr. Steevens, whose ordinary speech was melody, and whose correct and elegant ear for poetical concord is so frequently manifested in the course of his Shakspearean labours, should have shown himself a very Timon in music, can only be accounted for by supposing that he regarded the speech in question as a libel on his great colleague's organization. He has here assumed a task, which Dr. Johnson would for obvious reasons have declined ; and with the feeble aid of an illiberal passage from Lord Chesterfield's *Letters,* has most disingenuously endeavoured to cast an odium on a science which from its intimate and natural connexion with poetry and painting, deserves the highest attention and respect. He that is happily qualified to appreciate the *better parts* of music, will never seek them in the society so emphatically reprobated by the noble lord, nor altogether in the way he recommends. He will not lend an ear to the vulgarity and tumultuous roar of the tavern catch, or the delusive sounds of martial clangour; but he will enjoy this heavenly gift, this exquisite and soul-delighting sensation, in the temples of his God, or in the peaceful circles of domestic happiness : he will pursue the blessings and advantages of it with ardour, and turn aside from its abuses.

The quotation which Mr. Steevens has given from Peacham, is in reality an *encomium* on music as practised in the time of Shakspeare. It indicates that gentlemen then associated with their equals only in the pursuit of this innocent recreation; and the same writer would have furnished many other observations that tend to place the science of music in an amiable, or at least in a harmless point of view. Mr. Steevens might have also recollected that Cicero has called it "Stabilem thesaurum, qui *mores* instituit, componitque, ac mollit irarum ardores." It will be readily conceded that Shakspeare has overcharged the speech before us, and that it by no means follows that a man who is unmusical must be a traitor, a Machiavel, a robber; or that he is deserving of no confidence. This, however, is all that should have occupied the commentator's notice; and herein his castigation would have been really meritorious. The Italians too have a proverb that is equally reprehensible: "Whom God loves not, that man loves not music." Let such extravagancies be consigned to the censure they deserve !

SCENE 1.   Page 542.

GRA. . . The first *intergatory*
That my Nerissa shall besworn on——

This word being nothing more than a contraction of *interrogatory*, should be elliptically printed, *inter'gatory*.

THE CLOWN.

There is not a single circumstance through the whole of this play which constitutes Lancelot an *allowed fool or jester*; and yet there is some reason for supposing that Shakspeare intended him as such, from his being called *a patch*, a *fool* of Hagar's offspring, and in one place *the* fool. It is not reasonable, however, to conclude that a person like Shylock would entertain a domestic of this description; and it is possible that the foregoing terms may be merely designed as synonymous with the appellation of *clown*, as in *Love's labour's lost*. On the whole, we have here a proof that Shakspeare has not observed that nice discrimination of character in his clowns for which some have given him credit.

ON THE SOURCES FROM WHICH THE STORY OF THIS PLAY HAS BEEN DERIVED.

The present subject, notwithstanding it has been already discussed with considerable labour and ingenuity, may still be said to rest in much obscurity. This has partly arisen from some confusion in the mode of stating the information conveyed in the several notes wherein it has been discussed. To render this position the more intelligible, it will be necessary to say a few words on each commentator's opinion : and first on that of Dr. Farmer. He states that the *story* was taken from an old translation of the *Gesta Romanorum, first printed* by Wynkyn de Worde; and that Shakspeare has closely copied some of the language. The Doctor's use of the word *story* is not consistent with his usual accuracy, because, in what follows, he speaks only of the incident of the caskets, which forms in reality but *a part of the story*. It is much to be wished, for reasons which will hereafter appear, that Dr. Farmer had been more particular in his account of the edition of the *Gesta Romanorum* which he says was printed by Wynkyn de Worde, none such having, after much inquiry, been discovered; and it is to be feared that he had trusted to a previous statement of his friend the accomplished and elegant historian of English poetry, whose accuracy is unhappily known to have been by no means commensurate with his taste. The Doctor's assertion, that Shakspeare " closely copied some of the language," cannot be maintained until it be first ascertained if any use had been made of the *Gesta Romanorum* by the author of the old play of the *Jew*, mentioned by Gosson, and also in what particulars Shakspeare followed him. It is proper to take notice in this place of the mistake that has been committed by those who speak of Shakspeare's *imitations* of the sources of this play, and who forget that one on the same subject had already appeared, and which might have furnished him with the *whole* of the plot. It is however probable that he improved it by means of other novels, as will be seen hereafter.

The next critic to be noticed is the truly learned and judicious Mr. Tyrwhitt. He informs us that the *two principal incidents* of this play occur in the *Gesta Romanorum*, and produces some extracts from a *Latin manuscript* of that work in the British museum. Admitting that the incident of the *caskets* might have been taken from the *English Gesta Romanorum*, as mentioned by Dr. Farmer, he cautiously gives it as his opinion that both the stories in the *Gesta Romanorum* quoted by himself are the remote originals of Shakspeare's play; for he had also forgotten the elder drama mentioned by Gosson. He thinks, however, that the bond story might have come to Shakspeare from the *Pecorone*, but suspects on the whole that he followed some hitherto unknown novelist, who had saved him the trouble of working up the two stories into one. Aware also that Shakspeare's small acquaintance with the Latin language would scarcely enable him to consult the manuscript *Gesta Romanorum*, he has very properly used the expression *remote originals*; and the rather, because he had probably examined the printed English editions without finding the story of the bond, which would hardly have escaped the diligent researches of Dr. Farmer, had it really been there. The fact however is, that the bond story did exist in English long before Shakspeare's time, and it is extremely probable that the original author of the *Jew* used some English *Gesta Romanorum* for the *whole* of his plot. There is more stress to be laid on this opinion so far as it regards the original dramatist, because it seems most probable that Shakspeare, on account of the closer resemblance of the story in the *Pecorone* to *his* incident of the bond, had, with great advantage, made use of some translation of it now irrecoverably lost. For this reason, with all due respect for Mr. Tyrwhitt's opinion, it is improbable that Shakspeare followed some unknown novelist *who had saved him the trouble of working up the two stories into one*; unless it be conceded that such person was the author of the elder play.

The last opinion to be noticed is that of Dr. Johnson; and he remarks that the modern translator of the *Pecorone* thought the incident of the caskets was borrowed from Boccaccio. This shall be examined presently. The Doctor thinks, however, that Shakspeare had some other novel in view, a conjecture which Mr. Malone very properly supports by a reference to Dr. Farmer's note.

In offering some additional observations on the stories that are connected with the *Merchant of Venice*, it will be necessary, for the purpose of avoiding confusion, to speak separately of the two main incidents on which that play is constructed.

STORY OF THE CASKETS.

The novel of Boccaccio that has been cited on this occasion, together with some other tales that resemble it, have, it is conceived, no manner of connexion with the play. The curious reader will find one of these stories, and perhaps the most ancient of them, in the lives of Barlaam and Josaphat, as related in the Golden legend, though compiled at a period much anterior to that amusing work. Another is in Gower's *Confessio amantis*, fo. 96, edit. 1532 : and a third in the same work, fo. 96, verso. The latter has been related in a more ample and ingenious manner in the *Cento novelle antiche*, nov. 65.

In chap. 109 of *the Latin printed copy* of the *Gesta Romanorum*, a very different work from that referred to by Dr. Farmer and Mr. Tyrwhitt, there is the following story :   A smith had lost a chest of money, which being carried by the sea to the shores of a distant country, was taken up by an inn-keeper, who, not suspecting that it contained any thing, threw it carelessly aside. Having occasion one day for some fuel to warm his guests, he broke up the chest, and finding the money, laid it by safely, till some one should arrive to claim it. The smith soon afterwards appeared; and having publicly declared his loss, the inn-keeper resolved to ascertain if it were the will of Providence that he should make restitution. He therefore caused three pasties to be made; the first he filled with earth, the second with dead men's bones, and the third with money. He then invited the smith to dinner, and gave him the choice of the pasties. The smith fixed on those with the earth and bones, and relinquished the other. The host now concluded that it was not the will of Heaven that he should restore the money; he therefore called in the blind and the lame, opened the other pasty in their presence, and divided the treasure between them.

But the work to which the play stands immediately indebted, is a *Gesta Romanorum* in English, *never printed in Latin*, and of which the earliest edition that could be procured on the present occasion was printed by Thomas Est, in 1595, 12mo, and several times afterwards. The latter part

only of the 32nd history has been used. This has already
been given in English by Dr. Farmer, and in Latin by Mr.
Tyrwhitt. It has undoubtedly furnished the author of the
play with the incident of the caskets; but he has transposed
the mottoes of the gold and silver ones, and substituted
another for that of lead.

THE BOND STORY.

The character of Leti as an historian warrants an opinion
that *his* story is a mere fabrication, grafted on one of those
that he had met with on the same subject. The tale itself is
most probably of Eastern origin. Besides that given by Mr.
Malone from Ensign Munro's manuscript, a similar one is
related in Gladwin's *Persian Moonshee*, story 13 ; and another
likewise from an oriental source, in the *British magazine* for
1800, page 159.

In Tyron, *Recueil de plusieures plaisantes nouvelles*, &c.,
Anvers, 1590, 18mo, a Christian borrows 500 ducats of a
Jew at Constantinople, on condition of paying two ounces of
flesh for usury. At the expiration of the term the Christian
refuses to pay more than the principal. The matter is
brought before the Emperor Solyman, who orders a razor to
be brought, and admonishes the Jew not to cut off more or
less than the two ounces on pain of death. The Jew gives
up the point. The same story occurs in *Roger Bontemps en
belle humeur*; in the *Tresor des recreations*, Douay, 1625,
18mo, p. 27 ; in *Doctæ nugæ Gaudensij Jocosi*, 1713, 12mo,
p. 23 ; in the *Courier facetieux*, Lyon, 1650, 8vo, p. 109; in
the *Chasse ennuy*, Paris, 1645, 18mo, p. 49 ; in Corrozet
Divers propos memorables, &c., 1557, 12mo, p. 77, of which
work there is an English translation under the title of
*Memorable conceits of divers noble and famous personages of
Christendome*, &c., 1602, 24mo ; in *Apophthegmes, ou La recreation de la jeunesse*, p. 155. It agrees also with the story

related by Gracian in his *Hero*.   See Steevens's *Shakspeare*,
V. 515.

It has been imitated by Antony Munday in his *Astræpho*,
being the third part of Zelauto, or The fountaine of fame,
1580, 4to.   This writer had found it in Silvayn's *Orator*,
which, as we have already seen, he translated.   Instead of
the cutting off a pound of flesh, it is agreed that one of
the party's eyes shall be pulled out.   Besides the ballad of
Gernutus the Jew of Venice, printed in Dr. Percy's Reliques,
there is another less ancient, under the title of *The cruel Jew's
garland*, in which the story is varied, and with some ingenuity.

A part of the novel in the *Pecorone* is most likely of
Oriental origin, and might have been transmitted to Ser
Giovanni from the same source that supplied Boccaccio and
many of the French minstrels with their stories, viz. the
crusades.

As the Bond Story in the *Gesta Romanorum* is not known
to exist at present in any printed edition, though it might in
Shakspeare's time, and as the Latin original mentioned by
Mr. Tyrwhitt *has never been printed*, it is therefore offered
to the reader's notice, and will afford besides an interesting
specimen of ancient English.   It occurs in a manuscript
preserved in the Harleian collection, No. 7333, written in the
reign of Henry the Sixth. The language is of the same period.

" Selestinus reignid a wyse emperoure in Rome, and he
had a faire dowter; and in his tyme ther was a knyȝte that
lovid this dowter, but he thowte in himselfe that he dud al
in veyne, for he thouȝt as forsothe that the emperoure
wolde not late him to have hir, for he was unworthi therto ;
nevertheles he thought yf he myght be any wey have love of
the damiselle it were inowe to me.   He yede ofte tyme to
the damisell and aspied hir wille ; and she said to him ayene
that he travaylid al in veyne, for trowist thow, quod she,
with thi deseyvable of faire wordes to begile me ?   Nay sir,

be my soule, hit shal not be so. Thenne saide the kniȝte,
What shal I yeve to the and late me lye by the a nyght?
Not thowh thou woldest yeve me an C marke of florens, quod
she, thou shalt not lye by me a nyght. Then hit shal be as
thou wilte, quod he. What dude he but purveyde him of so
muche mony, s. an C. marke of floreyns, and yaf hir.
Whenne nyght come the kniȝte enterid into the bed of the
mayde, and anoon he was aslepe, and she dude of hir harnes,
and come and laye downe by him. So the kniȝte laye slepynge
al the nyght. On the morow she ros, and did on hir clothis,
and wishe hir hondes. And the kniȝte awoke of his slepe,
and thenne he said, Come hedir to me that I may do my wille
with the. Nay, by the helth of my fadir, that wolle I not,
quod she; for frende, I do the no wronge. Thow accordiste
with me that I shulde lye with the al nyght, and so it is
idon; for I lay by the al nyght, and thou sleptest and
preferdest me no solace, and therrfore blame thi selfe, and
not me. And the kniȝte was hevy, and seide, What shal
I yeve to the and lete me lygge by the another nyght? As
much, quod she, as thou did afor, and no lesse. I assente,
seide he, And the kniȝte yede and solde alle his movable
goodes, and made redy an C. marke of floreynse. But se
now a marvelouse case; for right as hit was the furste nyght,
so hit was in the secounde. Thenne the kniȝte mervaylid mor
thanne man may suppose, and hevy he was, and saide, Allas,
for now have I spend al my godes withoute spede; and therfore thow I shulle dye therefor I woll make another ende, how
moch shall I yeve the, and late us be togeder the thirde
nyght, quod the kniȝte to the damisell. Sothely, she saide,
yf thou have me, as thou paide afore, *fiat voluntas tua.* I
assent, quod he, thou shalte have thin askynge and thi wille.
The kniȝte yede into fer contree, til he come to a grete citee,
in the whiche wer many marchaunts and many philosophers,
amonge the wiche was master Virgile the philesopher. Then
the kniȝte yede to a grete marchaunt, and saide, I have

[nede] of monye, and yf thou wolt lende me an C marke
unto a certeyne day, I wolle ley to the al my londes undir this
conducion that if I holde not my day thow shalt have my
londes for evere. Thenne seyde the marchaunt, Der frend,
I sette not so muche be thi londes, but yf thow wolt make
this covenaunt, that I shal sey to the, I wolle fulfill thi wille.
This saide he I am redy to do thi wille, yf thou wolt do my
petucion. Thenne, seide he, when this covenaunt is made
that I shalle seye unto the, thenne I shalle fulfille thyne askynge ; and the covenaunt shalle be this, that thou make to
me a charter of thine owne blood, in conducion that yf thowe
kepe not thi day of payment, hit shalle be lefulle to me for
to draw awey alle the flesh of thi body froo the bone with a
sharp swerde, and yf thow wolt assent herto, I shalle fulfille
thi wille. The kniȝte lovid the damisell so moch that he
grauntid al this, and made a charter of his owne bloode, and
selid it, and after the selyng this marchaunt toke him the
money that he askid. When he had the moneye, he thoute
to him selfe, yf I gete my wylle by this moneye, I am but
dede ; nay, nay, it may not be so. When he harde tell of
the grete name of maister Virgile, he yede to him, and seide,
Gode sir, I have previ counseill to speke a twene us too, and
I beseche yow of your wise counseill in this cas. Sey on,
quod Virgile, and I shalle telle the aftir my discrecion. Sir, I
love the dowter of the emperoure more than ye wolle trowe,
and I accordid with her for a certen sum of money. I have
be disceyvid two nyghts in swiche maner ; and tolde alle the
cas as welle as he coude, and sir nowe I have borowed of a
marchaunt so much moneye for the same cas to be fulfillid,
and undir this conducion, that yf I holde not my day of
payment, hit shalle thenne be lefulle to him to helde of alle
the skynne of my body with his swerde, and then I am but
dede, and therfor sir, I am com to you to have counsaill and
wyt how I may bothe have helpe ayenste swiche a parill, and
also to have the love of that lovely lady. Thou hast made a

lewde covenaunt, seide Virgile, for as a man bindithe him with his owne wille, right so he shall be servid be lawe of the emperoure ; and therefore thou shalt do wysely for to kepe the day of thi payment alle things lefte. And towchinge the damesell I shall yeve the a tale of truthe. Bitwene her shete and her coverlyte of hir bed is a letter of swiche vertu, that whoso ever gothe with hir to bed, he shall anon falle into a dede slepe ; and he shalle not wake til time that hit be put awey : and therfor when thou comest to hir bed, seche a twene the shete and the coverlyte, and thow shalt fynde the letter ; and when thow hast founde hit caste hit fer from the bedde, and then entre into the bed, for thou shalte not slepe til tyme that thow haste doon thi wille with the damiselle, and that shalle torne to the gret honour and joye. The kniȝte toke his leve at Virgile, and thonkid him moche of his hie counseill and yede to the damysell, and yafe hir the monye. When nyȝt come the kniȝt enterid the chaumber, and preveli putte his honde bitwene the coverlite and the shete, and there he fonde the letter ; and whenne he hadde hit he caste hit fer fro the bedde, and lay downe and feynid as he hadde islepte, and thenne the damiselle knowing that he had yslepte as he dude afor, she caste of hir clothis, and went to bedde. Anon the kniȝte sette hande to hir as is the maner of bed, and she perceyved that, and prayd him of grace, and to save hir maydinhede, and I shall dobble al the monye that thow hast yevin to me and yeve it to the.   .   .   .   .

And aftur he lovid hir so muche that he drow so moche to hir compane that he forȝate the marchaunt and the day of payment was passid by the space of xiiii dayes. And as he lay in a certen nyght in his bed, hit come to his mynde the day that he made to the marchaunt, and alle his bowells wer storid therewithe, and thenne said to her, Alas woman that ever I saw the, for I am but dede. I borowed for thi love swiche a some of mony for to pay at a certeyne day bi this conducion, that yf I pay not at my day he shall have full

power for to hilde of the fleshe of my body without contra-
diccion ; and now my day is passid fourtenyte ago, so hih I
sette myn hert in the.   Then seide she, Sorowithe not so
moche, gothe to him, and debbelithe the mony to him, and
yf he wolle not, aske howe moche he wolle have, and I shalle
paye it.   Tho was the kniʒte comfortid.   He yede to the
citee, and there he mette with the marchaunt in the stret, and
lowly he saluid him.   Tho saide the marchaunt, So sey I
not to the.   Thenne seyde the kniʒte, Sir, for the trespas
that I have made ayenste youre convencion I wolle dowble
the payment.   Naye seide the marchaunt, that spake we not
of, I wolle have right as thou dudest bynde the to me.   Aske
of me, quod the knight, as much mony as thou wolte, and
thowe shalt be paide for my trespas.   It is veyne that thow
spekist, quod the marchaunt, for thowhe thou geve to me al
the gode of thi citee, I wolle have the covenaunt I holde,
and non othere wolle I have of the than as the charter
asselid makith mencioun of ; and anon he made the kniʒt
to be itake and lad to the castell, and sette him in a safe
ward, abyding the justice.   When the juge was come and
satte in the dome, the kniʒt come to barr among other
prisoners, and the marchaunt shewid his lettire afor the
juge.   Anoon as the juge sawe there his owne dede, he
said to alle that stode aboute, Sirs, ye know welle it is the law
of the emperour that yf enye man bynde him by his owne
freewille he shal resseyve as he servithe, and therefore this
marchaunt shalle have covenaunt as lawe wolle.   Now in al
this tyme the damysell his love had sent kniʒts for to aspie
and enquer how the law was pursued ayenst him, and whenne
she harde telle that the lawe passid ayenst him, she kytte of
al the longe her of hir hede, and cladde hir in precious clothing like to a man, and yede to the palys there as hir lemon
was to be demyd, and saluyd the justice, and all they trowid
that she had be a kniʒte ; and the juge enquerid of what
contree she was, and what she had to do ther.   She said, I

am a kniȝte, and come of fer contree, and her tithings that
there is a kniȝte amonge yowe that shuld be demid to dethe
for an obligacion that he made to a marchaunt, and therefor I
am come to deliver him. Thenne the juge said, It is lawe of
the emperoure that who so ever byndethe him with his owne
propre wille and consent withoute enye constraynynge he
shulde be servid so ayene. When the damisell harde this
she turnid to the marchaunt and saide, Der frende, what
profite is it to the that this kniȝte that stondithe her redy to
the dome be slayne? it wer [better] to the to have monye
than to have him slayne. Thou spekest al in veyne, quod
the marchaunt, for withoute doute I wolle have the lawe sithe
he bonde him so frely, and therefor he shalle have noon other
grace than lawe wolle, for he come to me, and I not tȯ him.
I desirid him not thereto ayenste his wille. Thenne saide
she, I praye the howe moche shall I yeve to have my petucion? I shalle yeve the thi monye double, and yf that be not
plesynge to the, aske of me what thou wolte, and Thou shalt
have. Then saide he, thow harde me never seye but that I
wolde have my covenaunte kept. Sothely, seyde she, and
thou shalt trowe me afor your [you] sir juge, and afor yowe
alle, I sey now sir juge ywithe a right wisdome of that that I
shal seye to yowe; ye have ihard howe moche I have proferid
this marchaunt for the lyf of this kniȝte, and he forsakithe
all, and askithe the lawe, and that likith me moche; and
therfore lordinges that beye her, herithe me what I shalle
seye. Ye knowithe welle that the kniȝt bonde him never by
letter but that the marchaunt shulde have power to kutte his
fleshe fro the boons, but there was no covenaunt made of
sheding of blode, thereof was nothing ispoke, and therefor late
him set hond on him anoon, and yf he shede ony bloode with
his shavinge of the fleshe forsothe then shalle the kynge have
goode lawe upon him. And when the marchaunt harde this
he said, Yef me my monye, and I foryeve my accion. Ffor-
sothe, quod she, thou shalt not have oo penye, for afor al this

companye I proferid to the al that I myght, and thou forsoke hit, and saydist with a lowde wyse, I shalle have my covenaunte; and therfor do thi beste with him, but loke that thow shede no blode I charge the; for it is not thin, ne no covenaunt was thereof. Thenne the marchaunt seynge this yede away confus. And so was the Kniȝt's lyf savid, and no penye ipayde. And she yede home ayene, and dude of that clothinge, and clothid hit as she was afor like to a woman. And the kniȝte yede home ayene, and the damisell turnid and met him, and askid howe he had ispedde, as thowhe she had not knowen therof. A, lady, quod he, this day was I in poynt to be dede for thy love, but as I was in point to be dampned, there come in sodeynlye a knite, a fair and well ishape, the whiche I saw never afor, and he delivirid me by his exellent wisdom bothe from dethe and eke from payment of moneye. Thenne were thowhe, quod she, unkynde that woldest nat bidde that kniȝte to mete, that so faire had savid the. He aunswerde therto, and saide that he come sodeinly and sodenly yede. Thenne seide she, Knowiste thow him if thou seye him? Yee, quod he, right wele. She yede up and cladde hir as she dide afore, and then she yede forthe. And the kniȝte knew her thenne wele, and for joye fel doune upon hire, and said, Blessid be thow, and the houre in the whiche I fyrste knew the. And he wepte, and aftir he weddid hir and livid and deyde in the service of God, and yelde to God goode sowlis."

On the whole, then, it is conceived that the outline of the *bond story* is of Oriental origin; * that the author of the old play of *The Jew*, and Shakspeare in his Merchant of Venice,

---

* If the horrible incident of the cutting off the flesh had not occurred in the several Oriental stories that have been mentioned, one should have supposed that it had been suggested by that atrocious decemviral law of the Twelve Tables, which empowered a creditor to mangle the living body of his debtor without fear of punishment for cutting more or less than the magistrate allowed. For the honour of the Roman law, it is not recorded that the above inhuman decree was ever enforced.

have not confined themselves to one source only in the construction of their plot; but that the *Pecorone*, the *Gesta Romanorum*, and perhaps the old *Ballad of Gernutus*, have been respectively resorted to. It is however most probable that the original play was indebted chiefly, if not altogether, to the *Gesta Romanorum*, which contained both the main incidents; and that Shakspeare expanded and improved them, partly from his own genius, and partly, as to the bond, from the *Pecorone*, where the coincidences are too manifest to leave any doubt. Thus, the scene being laid at Venice; the residence of the lady at Belmont; the introduction of a person bound for the principal; the double infraction of the bond, viz., the taking more or less than a pound of flesh and the shedding of blood, together with the after-incident of the ring, are common to the novel and the play. The whetting of the knife might perhaps have been taken from the *Ballad of Gernutus*. Shakspeare was likewise indebted to an authority that could not have occurred to the original author of the play in an English form; this was, Silvayn's *Orator*, as translated by Munday. From that work Shylock's reasoning before the senate is evidently borrowed; but at the same time it has been most skilfully improved.

The frequent allusions to the *different Gesta Romanorum* may have excited a wish to be more familiarly acquainted with that singular and interesting work; but as the discussion of the subject in this place would have augmented the tediousness of the note, it has been thought better to make the attempt in a separate dissertation, where it is hoped that any obscurity in the preceding remarks will be removed.

It is much to be lamented that this exquisitely beautiful drama can neither be read nor performed, without exciting in every humane and liberal mind an abhorrence of its professed design to vilify an ancient and respectable, but persecuted, nation. It should be remembered that contempt and intolerance must naturally excite hatred; that to provoke revenge is, in fact, to become responsible for the crimes it may occasion; that to those who would degrade and oppress us, it is but justice to oppose craft; and that nature has supplied even the brute creation with the means of resisting persecution.   It will be readily conceded that there happily exist in the present moment but few remains of the illiberal prejudices complained of, the asperity of which has been greatly mitigated by the laudable and successful exertions of a modern dramatic writer, to whom the Jewish people are under the highest obligations.

AS YOU LIKE IT.

ACT I.

Scene 2. Page 16.

Cel. This is not fortune's work neither, but *nature's*, who perceiving our *natural* wits too dull to reason of such Goddesses,
hath sent this *natural* for our whetstone.

It must be observed that Touchstone is here called a *natural*
merely for the sake of alliteration and a punning jingle of
words; for he is undoubtedly an artificial fool.

Scene 2. Page 29.

Le Beau. More suits you to conceive, *than me* to speak of.

The old copy had, *than I.* These grammatical errors in
the use of the personal pronoun should either be *uniformly*
corrected or left entirely to themselves. Mr. Steevens in
p. 9, note 7, seems to regard them as the anomalies of the
play-house editors; but Mr. Malone, probably with more
reason, is inclined to place them to the author's own account. If the present correction by Mr. Rowe be retained
in future editions, we ought not to find such expressions as
" hates nothing more than *he*," p. 14; " no child but *I*,"
p. 15, and *who* for *whom* perpetually.

ACT II.

Scene 1. Page 37.

Duke S. Which like the toad, ugly and venomous,
Wears yet a precious *jewel* in his head.

What that stone which many people suppose to come
from the head of a toad really was, would be no easy task

at present to determine. Various conjectures have made it the *batrachites, chelonites, brontia, ceraunia, glossopetra*, &c. Neither is it certain that the text alludes to a *stone*; for Gesner informs us that in his time, and *in England more particularly,* the common people made superstitious uses of a *real jewel* that always could be found in a toad's head, viz., its *forehead bone.* To obtain this they severed the animal in two parts, and exposed it to be devoured by ants; by which means it presently became a skeleton. The above author carefully distinguishes this bone from the toadstone, and from Pliny's bone mentioned in Mr. Steevens's note. He has likewise with great industry, as on all occasions, collected much that relates to the subject of the toadstone. See his work *De quadrup. ovipar.* p. 65. It must be owned that better naturalists than Shakspeare believed in the common accounts of the toadstone. Batman in his edition to the article relating to the *botrax* or *rubeta* in Bartholomæus *De propr. rerum,* informs us that " some toads that breed in Italy and about Naples, have in their heads a stone called a *crapo,* of bignes like a big peach, but flat, of colour gray, with a browne spot in the midst *said to be of vertue.* In times past they were much worne, and used in ringes, as the forewarning against venime." Another learned divine who is often very witty, but on this occasion perfectly grave, has told us that " some report that the toad before her death sucks up (if not prevented with sudden surprisal) the precious stone (as yet but a jelly) in her head, grudging mankind the good thereof."—Fuller's *Church history,* p. 151. In a medical work too we are informed that " in the head of a greate tode there is a stone, which stone being stampt and geven to the pacyent to drinke in warme wine, maketh him to pise the stone out incontinent," &c.—Lloyd's *Treasure of helth,* pr. by Copland, n. d. 12mo. The notion of jewels in the heads of animals is very widely spread. Mr. Wilkins has informed us that it is a vulgar notion in India that some species of serpents have precious stones in their heads. *Hectopades*, p. 302. The best account of the different sorts of toadstones, so far as regards the illustration of the above superstitious notions, is in Topsell's *History of serpents*, 1608, folio, p. 188.

Scene 1. Page 39.

> 1. LORD. To the which place a poor sequester'd stag
> Did come to languish . . . . .
> . . . . . and *the big round tears*
> Cours'd one another down his innocent nose
> In piteous chase.

The stag is said to possess a very large secretion of tears. " When the hart is arered, he fleethe to a ryver or ponde, and roreth cryeth and *wepeth* when he is take."—Bartholomæus *De propriet. rerum*, l. xviii. c. 30. Batman, in his commentary on that work, adds, from Gesner, that " when the hart is sick and hath eaten many serpents for his recoverie, he is brought unto so great a heate, that he hasteth to the water, and their covereth his body unto the very eares and eyes, at which time *distilleth many teares* from which the [Bezoar] stone is gendered," &c. The translator of *The noble arte of Venerie* makes the hart thus address the hunter :

> " O cruell, be content, to take in worth my *teares*,
> Which growe to gumme, and fall from me : content thee with my heares,
> Content thee with my hornes, which every yeare I mew,
> Since all these three make medicines, some sicknesse to eschew.
> My *teares* congeal'd to gumme, by peeces from me fall,
> And thee preserve from pestilence, in pomander or ball.
> Such wholesome *teares* shedde I, when thou pursewest me so."

Compare also Virgil's description of the wounded stag in the seventh book of the Æneid.

Scene 2. Page 43.

> DUKE. And let not search and inquisition *quail*
> To bring again these foolish runaways.

" To *quail*," says Mr. Steevens, " is to *faint*, to sink into dejection ;" and so it certainly is, but not in this instance ; for neither search nor inquisition could very well faint or become dejected. They might indeed *slacken, relax,* or *diminish,* and such is really the present meaning of the word. Thus "Hunger cureth love, for love *quaileth* when good cheare faileth."—*The choise of change,* 1585, 4to, sign. L. i. *To quail* is also used in the several senses of *to sink, abate, deaden, enfeeble, press down,* and *oppress*; all of which might be exemplified from the writings of authors contemporary with Shakspeare, and some of them from his own. It seems to be a modification of to quell, i. e. to destroy altogether, to kill, from the Saxon cᵖellan.

SCENE 2. Page 54.

> JAQ. But that they call compliment, is like the encounter of two *dog-apes.*

Bartholomæus, speaking of apes, says, "some be called *cenophe*; and be lyke to an *hounde* in the face, and in the body lyke to an *ape.*"—Lib. xviii. c. 96.

SCENE 5. Page 55.

> JAQ. Ducdáme, ducdáme, ducdáme.

The stanza which the facetious old squire sang before Dr. Farmer has occurred in the following shape; but where is the Œdipus who shall unfold the connexion of either with Jaques's song?

> " O *damy* what makes my *ducks* to die?
> What can ail them, Oh!
> They eat their victuals and down they lie,
> What can ail them, Oh!"

SCENE 7. Page 66.

> JAQ. . . . . All the world 's a stage,
> And all the men and women merely players.

Mr. Steevens refers to the *totus mundus exerceat histrioniam* of Petronius, with whom probably the sentiment originated; but this author had not been translated in Shakspeare's time. The play of *Damon and Pythias,* which Mr. Malone has cited, might have furnished the observation. There are likewise two other probable sources that are worthy of notice on this occasion. The first is Withal's *Short dictionarie in Latine and English,* several times printed in the reign of Elizabeth, where in fo. 69 of the edit. 1599, is the following passage: " This life is a certain enterlude or *plaie. The world is a stage* full of chang everie way, *everie man is a plaier.*" The other is Pettie's translation of Guazzo's *Civile conversation,* 1586, 4to, where one of the parties introduces the saying of some philosopher " that this *world* was a *stage,* we the *players* which present the comedie." Shakspeare had himself used nearly the same language in the first act of *The merchant of Venice* :

> " I hold the world, but as the world, Gratiano,
> A stage, where every man must play a part."

A portion of Jaques's speech has been imitated in some lines by Thomas Heywood among the commendatory verses prefixed to his *Actors vindication,* 1658, 4to :

> " The world 's a theater, the earth a stage,
> Which God and nature doth with actors fill;
> All men have parts, and each man acts his own," &c.

Scene 7. Page 66.

Jaq. And one man in his time plays many parts,
  His acts being seven ages.

A print of the seven ages of men like those referred to by Messrs. Henley and Steevens may be seen in Comenius's *Orbis pictus,* tit. xxxvii., in which are found *the infant, the boy,* and *the decrepid old man* : the rest of Shakspeare's characters seem to be of his own invention. There is a division of the seven ages of man in Arnolde's *Chronicle,* fo. lix. verso, agreeing, except in the arrangement of years, with that given by Mr. Malone from *The treasury of ancient and modern times.*

Scene 7. Page 69.

Jaq. *Sans* teeth, sans eyes, sans taste, sans every thing.

This word, introduced into our language as early as the time of Chaucer, has sometimes received on the stage a

French pronunciation, which in the time of Shakspeare it certainly had not. The old orthography will serve to verify this position :

> " I none dislike, I fancie some,
>   But yet of all the rest,
>   *Sance* envie, let my verdite passe,
>   Lord Buckhurst is the best."

Turbervile's verses before his
Tragical tales, 1587, 4to.

ACT III.

SCENE 2.   Page 82.

Ros. I'll graff it with you, and then I shall graff it with a medlar : then it will be the *earliest* fruit in the country, for you'll be rotten ere you be half ripe, and that's the right virtue of the medlar.

On this Mr. Steevens observes that Shakspeare had little knowledge of gardening, the medlar being one of the latest fruits, and uneatable till the end of November. But is not the charge, at least in this instance, unfounded ; and has not the learned commentator misunderstood the poet's meaning ? It is well known that the medlar is only edible when *apparently* rotten. This is what Shakspeare calls its *right virtue.* If a fruit be fit to be eaten when rotten and *before it be ripe,* it may in one sense be termed *the earliest.* The inaccuracy seems to be in making the medlar rotten before it is ripe, the rottenness being, as it is conceived, the ripeness.

SCENE 2.   Page 93.

Orl. I pray you, mar no more of my verses with reading them ill-favouredly.

This very much resembles the *sed male cum recitas, incipit esse tuum,* in one of Martial's epigrams, lib. i. ep. 39, of which the following translation was made by Timothy Kendall, in his *Flowers of epigrammes,* 1577, 12mo :

" The booke which thou doest read, it is
    Frende Fidentinus myne ;
    But when thou ill doest read it, then
    Beginns it to bee thyne.'

Scene 4. Page 111.

Cel. He hath bought a pair of *cast* lips of Diana : a nun of winter's
    sisterhood kisses not more religiously ; the very ice of chas-
    tity is in them.

Theobald explains *cast* lips " a pair *left off* by Diana."
It is not easy to conceive how the goddess could *leave off* her
lips ; or how, being left off, Orlando could purchase them.
Celia seems rather to allude to a statue *cast in plaister or metal*, the lips of which might well be said to possess *the ice* of
chastity.

As to the " nun of winter's sisterhood," Warburton might
have contented himself with censuring the dullness of Theobald. His own *sisterhoods of the seasons* are by much too refined and pedantic, and in every respect objectionable.
Shakspeare poetically feigns a new order of nuns, most appropriate to his subject, and wholly devoid of obscurity.

Scene 5. Page 115.

Sil. . . . The common executioner
    Falls not the axe upon the humbled neck.

There is no doubt that the expression *to fall the axe* may
with propriety refer to the usual mode of decapitation ; but if
it could be shown that in the reign of Elizabeth this punishment was inflicted in England by an instrument resembling
the French guillotine, which though merciful in the discharge
of its office, has justly excited abhorrence from the number
of innocent victims that have suffered by it, the expression
would perhaps seem rather more appropriate. Among the cuts
to the first edition of Holinshed's chronicle such a machine is
twice introduced ; and as it does not appear that in either instance there was any cause for the particular use of it, we
may reasonably infer that it was at least sometimes adopted.

Every one has heard of the *Halifax gibbet*, which was just
such another instrument, and certainly introduced into that
town, for reasons that do not appear, long before the time in
which Holinshed was printed. It is said that the Earl of
Morton, the Scotish regent, saw it at Halifax, and that he introduced it into Scotland, where it was used for a considerable
time afterwards.* In that country it was called *the maiden*,
and Morton himself actually suffered by it, when condemned
as an accomplice in the murder of Lord Darnley. In the
best edition of Holinshed, Thynne's continuation of Hector
Boethius's history is printed, in which there is an account of
the conference between the Earl and the Ministers of Edinburgh, under the title of *The examination and answers of the
Earl of Morton before his death, but after his condemnation*.
Thynne seems to say that the above account was delivered over
to him, but he has omitted to state the particulars. In a manuscript of this conference, written at the time, and in the possession of the author of these observations, it is called *The
some of all the conferrence that was betweene the Earle Morton and John Dury and Mr. Walker the same daye that he
suffered which was the 2 June* 1581, and differs in several
places from the other. In both, at the end, there is an account of the Earl's last moments, in which it is stated (the
MS. being here quoted) that he " layde his head *under the
axe*, his handes being unbounde, Mr. Walker cried in his
eare, Lord Jesus receive thy spirite, he saide Jesus receive
my sowle, which wordes he was speaking while *the axe fell
on his necke*." This extract would alone be sufficient to decide on the mode in which Morton was beheaded ; but in the
MS. there is a neat drawing of the machine itself, resembling
the cut in the earliest edition of Holinshed, except that in
the latter the axe is suspended to the top of the frame by a

* See Hume's hist. of the houses of Douglas and Angus, 1644, folio,
p. 356. There are good reasons for supposing that the instrument in question was invented in Germany.

string which the executioner cuts with a knife, whilst in the other, a peg, to which the string is attached, is drawn out of one of the sides.

It may be worth adding that in *King Henry VI. part 2,* Eleanor says to her husband the duke of Gloucester,

> " But be thou mild, and blush not at my shame,
> Nor stir at nothing, till the axe of death
> *Hang over thee——*"

SCENE 5. Page 118.

> Ros. . . What though you have *more* beauty
> (As by my faith, I see no more in you
> Than without candle may go dark to bed)

The old copy reads *no beauty.* Mr. Malone substitutes *mo,* i. e. *more,* and supports his alteration by making Rosalind allow that Phœbe had *more* beauty than her lover; but she soon afterwards asserts the contrary in the most positive terms. The omission of the disputed monosyllable, which in the old copy might have caught the compositor's eye in the ensuing line and occasioned the mistake, will certainly correct the present redundancy in the line, and perhaps restore the author's original language. *As* in the next line appears to have the power of *though*; a word that could not be used on account of its introduction in the preceding line.

ACT IV.

SCENE 1. Page 130.

> Ros. I will laugh like a *hyen,* and that when thou art inclined to *sleep.*

" He commeth to houses *by night,* and feineth *mannes voyce* as he maye," &c.—Bartholomæus *De propriet. rer.* lib. xviii. c. 61. *De Hiena.*

SCENE 3. Page 142.

> Oli. . . for 'tis
> The royal disposition of that beast,
> To prey on nothing that doth seem as dead.

This property of the lion, whether true or false, was acknowledged by our forefathers. Thus in *The choise of change containing the divinitie, philosophie, and poetrie,*" &c., 1585, 4to, a work evidently constructed on the model of the Welsh triads, we find the following passage : " three things shew that there is a great clemencie in lions; *they will not hurt them that lie groveling,*" &c. Bartholomæus says, " their mercie is known by many and oft ensamples: *for they spare them that lye on the ground.*" Shakspeare again alludes to the lion's generosity in *Troilus and Cressida,* Act V. Scene 3 :

> " Brother, you have a vice of mercy in you
> Which better fits a lion than a man."

ACT V.

Scene 2.   Page 152.

Ros. By my life, I do; which I tender dearly, though I say I am a magician.

Of the two constructions of this speech, that by Mr. Stee-vens seems deserving of the preference; but the grounds on which it stands require examination.   A statute against witchcraft was made in the first year of king James.   Now if, as Dr. Warburton conceives, it is to this that Rosalind alludes, the play must have been written after 1603.   Mr. Malone, whose opinion is supported by very solid reasons, thinks it was written in 1600 ; and therefore to reconcile the explanation given by Mr. Steevens, we must suppose that the foregoing allusion is to some prior statutes of Henry the Eighth and Elizabeth, which punished those who practised witchcraft with death.

Scene 2.   Page 154.

Ros. I will satisfy you if ever I *satisfy'd* man.

The context seems to require that we should read *satisfy* ; and it was the genius of Shakspeare's age to write so.

THE CLOWN.

Touchstone is the domestic fool of Frederick the duke's brother, and belongs to the class of witty or allowed fools. He is threatened with the whip, a mode of chastisement which was often inflicted on this motley personage. His dress should be a party-coloured garment. He should occasionally carry a bauble in his hand, and wear asses' ears to his hood, which is probably the head dress intended by Shakspeare, there being no allusion whatever to a cock's head or comb. The three-cornered hat which Touchstone is made to wear on the modern stage is an innovation, and totally unconnected with the genuine costume of the domestic fool.

ALL'S WELL THAT ENDS WELL.

In the *dramatis personæ* of this play the "gentle astringer" is omitted, who, though he says but little, has a better claim to be inserted than Violenta, who says nothing. Mr. Steevens remarks that her name was borrowed from an old *metrical history* entitled *Didaco and Violenta*; but Shakspeare more probably saw it in the running title of Painter's *Palace of pleasure*, whence he got his plot of this play, and where the above history occurs in *prose*. The title is borrowed from a proverbial saying much older than the time of Shakspeare. Knyghton has preserved some of the speeches of Jack Straw and his brother insurgents; and in that of Jack Carter we have this expression : *for if the ende be wele than is alle wele*. The orations of these heroes were made up of proverbial saws, a proof of the great influence they must have had with the common people. See the *Decem scriptores* by Twysden, col. 2637.

ACT I.

Scene 1. Page 187.

Laf. A fistula, my Lord.

What Mr. Steevens calls the *inelegance* of the king's disorder is not to be placed to Shakspeare's account; for it is specifically mentioned both in Painter's story of *Giletta*, and in Boccaccio himself. It is singular that the learned critic should not have remembered this.

Scene 1. Page 188.

Count. Where an unclean mind carries virtuous qualities, there com-
mendations go with pity; they are virtues and traitors
too.

The explanations of this speech appear to be too refined;
and Dr. Warburton's, as usual, particularly so. The meaning
is simply this :—*where strong and useful talents are combined
with an evil disposition, we feel regret even in commending
them ; because, in such a mind, however good in themselves,
their use and application are always to be suspected.*

Scene 3. Page 217.

Clo. A *prophet* I madam.

A reconsideration of these words have suggested the necessity of cancelling *both* the notes, for the clown is not a
natural, but an *artificial* fool.

Scene 3. Page 224.

Hel. Indeed, my mother! or were you *both our mothers.*

This strange and faulty language deserved notice. It
should have been, *or were you so to both.*

ACT II.

Scene 1. Page 234.

Ber. I shall stay here the *forehorse to a smock*
Creaking my shoes on the plain masonry
Till honour be brought up, and *no sword worn,*
But one to dance with.

He means that he shall remain at home to *lead out ladies*
in the dance, till honour, &c. In *Titus Andronicus*, Act II.
Scene 1, Demetrius speaks of *a dancing rapier.* The custom
of wearing swords in the dancing schools is exemplified in
a curious story related in *Newes from the North*, 1579, 4to,
where " Pierce Plowman sheweth how his neighbour and

hee went to the tavern and to *the dauncing schoole* and what hapned there," in these words : " Now was there one man of our company that was as deaf as a doore naile. When we were come into the schoole ; the musitions were playing and one dauncing of a galiard, and even at our entring hee was beginning a trick as I remember of sixteens or seventeens, I doo not very wel remember, but wunderfully hee leaped, flung and took on, which the deaf man beholding, and not hearing any noyse of the musick, thought verily that hee had been stark mad and out of his wit, and of pure pittie and compassion ran to him and caught him in his armes and held him hard and fast. The dauncer not knowing his good meaning, and taking it to the wurst, and having *a dagger* drew it out, and smot the man a great blowe upon the hed, and brake his hed very sore." Another illustration of the subject is too interesting from the picture of ancient manners which it exhibits to stand in need of any apology for its insertion. It is from Stafforde's *Briefe conceipt of English pollicy*, 1581, 4to. " I thinke wee were as much dread or more of our enemies, when our gentlemen went simply and our serving men plainely, without cuts or gards, bearing their heavy swordes and buckelers on their thighes insted of cuts and gardes and *light daunsing swordes*; and when they rode carrying good speares in theyr hands in stede of white rods, which they cary now more like ladies or gentlewomen then men ; all which delicacyes maketh our men cleane effeminate and without strength."

SCENE 2.   Page 249.

CLO. As Tib's rush for Tom's forefinger.

The covert allusion mentioned by Mr. Ritson is, in all probability, the right solution of this passage; but the practice of marrying with a rush ring may admit of some additional remarks. Sir John Hawkins had already, in a very curious and interesting note, illustrated the subject; and it must appear very extraordinary that *one of the subsequent notes* should question the practice of marrying with a rush ring, on the grounds that *no authority* had been produced in support of it. This must therefore be explained. The fact is, that the author of the doubts had never seen Sir John Hawkins's *entire* note, which had originally appeared in the edition of 1778, but was injudiciously suppressed in that of 1785. In the edition of 1790 there is only a brief and general statement of Sir John's opinion, and this led to the doubts expressed. In 1793 Mr. Steevens restores a note which he had already cancelled, and *with all its authorities before him,* permits them to be questioned; but there are many who will comprehend his motive.

The information from Du Breul (not Breval, as misprinted) *Theâtre des antiquitez de Paris,* 1612, 4to, is worth stating more at large. The author tells us that in the official court of the church of Saint Marinus, those who have lived unchastely are conducted to the church by two officers, in case they refuse to go of their own accord, and there married by the curate with a *rush ring.* They are likewise enjoined to live in peace and friendship, thereby to preserve the honour of their friends and relations, and their own souls from the danger they had incurred. This is only practised where no other method of saving the honour of the parties and their connexions can be devised. A modern French writer remarks on this ceremony; " pour faire observer, sans doute, au mari, combien etoit *fragile la vertu* de celle qu'il choisissait."

With respect to the constitutions of the bishop of Salisbury in 1217, which forbid the putting of *rush rings* on women's fingers, there seems to be an *error* in the reason for this prohibition as stated by Sir John Hawkins, but for which he is not perhaps responsible. He says it is insinuated by the bishop, " that there were some people weak enough to believe, that what was thus done in jest, was a real marriage."

The original words, as in Spelman's *councils,* are these : " ne dum jocari se putat, honoribus matrimonialibus se *abstringat.*" Now unless we read "*adstringat*" there is a difficulty in making sense of the passage, which seems to mean, *least, whilst he thinks he is only practising a joke, he may be tying himself in the matrimonial noose.*" It is to be observed that this consequence was not limited to the deception of putting *a rush ring only* on the woman's finger, but any ring whatever, whether of vile or of precious materials.

In Greene's *Menaphon* is this passage: " Well, 'twas a good worlde when such simplicitie was used, sayes the old women of our time, when a *ring of a rush* would tie as much love together as a gimmon of golde." But *rush rings* were sometimes innocently used. Thus in Spenser's *Shepherds calendar,* eclog. xi. mention is made of " the knotted *rush rings,* and gilt rosemaree " of the deceased shepherdess. Again in Fletcher's *Two noble kinsmen,* Act iv. ;

> " . . . . . . *Rings* she made
> Of *rushes* that grew by, and to 'em spoke
> The prettiest posies: *thus our true love's ty'd ;*
> *This you may loose, not me ;* and many a one."

Tib and *Tom* were names for any low or vulgar persons, and they are usually mentioned together in the same manner as *Jack* and *Gill,* &c. In the morality of *Like will to like quoth the devil to the collier,* Nicholas Newfangle says,

> " By the mas for thee he is so fit a mate
> As *Tom* and *Tib* for Kit and Kate."

In the old song of *The shepheard's holyday,* we have,

> " Jetting Gill,
> Jumping Will,
> O'r the floore will have their measure ;
> Kit and Kate
> There will waite,
> *Tib* and *Tom* will take their pleasure."

Thomas Drant in his translation of Horace's *Arte of poetrye,* 1567, 4to, has Englished *fricti ciceris et nucis*

emptor, by *Tom and Tib,* &c.; and in *A satyr against Satyrs,*
or St. Peter's vision transubstantiated, 1680, 4to, are these
lines :

> " O' th same bead-string with fryar hang'd a nun,
> What, would not you have *Tib* to follow *Tom?*"

SCENE 3. Page 257.

HEL. To each of you one fair and virtuous mistress
Fall, when love please ! *marry to each, but one !*

Mr. Tyrwhitt regards the latter exclamation as ludicrous,
in consequence of Helena's limitation of *one* mistress to each
lord, and would therefore give it to Parolles. Mr. Mason,
on the contrary, is of opinion that the words *but one,* mean
except one ; that the person excepted is Bertram, whose mistress Helena hoped she herself should be ; and that she
makes the exception out of modesty, as otherwise it would
extend to herself. Of these two opinions the first is the
most probable, deriving considerable support from the *one* in
the preceding line ; for if Shakspeare had meant *except one,*
he would have written "*a* fair and virtuous mistress." Helena's
exception as stated by Mr. Mason might indeed have been
made on the score of modesty so far as regarded her beauty ;
but she could not with propriety admit that she had no
virtue.

SCENE 3. Page 257.

LAF. I'd give bay *Curtal.*

Mr. Steevens should have added that this was a proper
name for a horse, as well as an appellation for a dock'd one.
" Their knavery is on this manner; they have always good
geldings and trusty, which they can make *curtailes* when they
list, and againe set too large tailes, hanging to the fetlockes at
their pleasure."—*Martin Marhall's apologie to the belman of
London,* 1610, sign. G. *Curtail* is not from *cur* and *tail,* as
stated in some dictionaries, but from the French *tailler
court.*

ACT III.

Scene 6.   Page 298.

2. Lord. If you give him not *John Drum's entertainment.*

The meaning of this phrase has been very well ascertained, but its origin remains to be traced. Is it a metaphor borrowed from the *beating* of a drum, or does it allude to the drumming a person out of a regiment? There can be no reference to a real person, because in many old writers we find both *Jack* and *Tom* Drum.

ACT IV.

Scene 3.   Page 323.

1. Lord. *Hoodman* comes!

An allusion to the game of blindman's buff, formerly called *hoodman blind.*

Scene 3.   Page 326.

Par. He was whipp'd for getting the *sheriff's fool* with child.

Mr. Ritson will not admit this to be a fool kept by the sheriff for diversion, but supposes her one of those idiots whose care, as he says, devolved on the sheriff when they had not been begged of the king on account of the value of their lands. Now if this was the law, the sheriff must have usually had more than one idiot in his custody; and had Shakspeare alluded to one of these persons, he would not have chosen so definite an expression as that in question; he would rather have said, " *a* sheriff's fool." Female idiots were retained in families for diversion as well as male, though not so commonly; and there would be as much reason to expect one of the former in the sheriff's household as in that of any other person. It is not impossible that our author might have in view some real event that had just happened.

Scene 3.   Page 327.

Ber. I know his brains are forfeit to the next *tile* that falls.

In Whitney's *Emblems,* a book certainly known to Shak-speare, there is a story of three women who threw dice to ascertain which of them should first die.   She who lost affected to laugh at the decrees of fate, when *a tile suddenly falling,* put an end to her existence.

Scene 3.   Page 329.

Par. . . a dangerous and lascivious boy, who is *a whale to virginity.*

This is an allusion to the story of *Andromeda* in old prints, where the monster is very frequently represented as a *whale.*

Scene 3.   Page 333.

Par. For a *quart d'ecu* he will sell the fee simple of his salvation.

The quart d'ecu, or as it was sometimes written *cardecue,* was a French piece of money first coined in the reign of Henry III.   It was the fourth part of the *gold* crown, and worth fifteen sols.   It is a fact not generally known, that many foreign coins were current at this time in England; some English coins were likewise circulated on the continent. The French crown and its parts passed by weight only.

Scene 4.   Page 339.

Hel. All's well that ends well: still *the fine's a crown.*

In *King Henry VI. part* 2. Act V. we have " la fin couronne les œuvres."   Both phrases are from the Latin *finis coronat opus.*   In this sense we still use the expression to *crown,* for to *finish* or *make perfect.   Coronidem imponere* is a metaphor well known to the ancients, and supposed to have originated from the practice of finishing buildings by placing a crown at their top as an ornament; and for this reason the words *crown, top* and *head* are become synonymous in most lan-guages.

There is reason for believing that the ancients placed a

crescent at the beginning, and a crown, or some ornament that resembled it, at the end of their books.   In support of the first usage we have a poem by Ausonius entitled CORONIS which begins in this manner :

> " Quos legis à prima deductos *menide* libri."

And of the other, these lines in Martial, lib. x. ep. 1 :

> " Si nimius videor, seraque *coronide* longus
> Esse liber : legito pauca, libellus ero."

The mark which was used in later times for the *coronis* has been preserved in the etymologies of Isidore, lib. i. c. 20. It is this, $\mathcal{G}$; and in some manuscripts of that writer $\hbar$ and $\hbar$.   In other places it has these forms, $\mathcal{B}7\mathcal{L}$.

SCENE 5.   Page 343.

CLO. But sure, he is *the prince of the world.*

The Devil is often called so by Saint John.

ACT V.

SCENE 2.   Page 349.

PAR. Good Monsieur *Lavatch.*

" This," says Mr Steevens, " is an undoubted and perhaps *irremediable* corruption of some French word." Yet the name is obviously *La vache*, which, whether really belonging to the clown or not, seems well adapted to such a character.

SCENE 2.   Page 351.

CLO. Here is a *pur* of fortune's sir, or of fortune's cat.

The text is perfectly intelligible, and requires no conjectural amendment.   The clown calls Parolles's letter a *pur* ; because, like the purring of the sycophant cat, it was calculated to procure favour and protection.

THE CLOWN.

He is a domestic fool of the same kind as Touchstone.

TAMING OF THE SHREW.

INDUCTION.

SCENE 1. Page 386.

SLY. Therefore, *paucas pallabris.*

PERHAPS these words are part of an old Spanish proverb, corresponding with the Portuguese, "A o hom entendedor *poucas palavras,*" i. e. to an intelligent man, few words. Most of the modern European languages have a proverb like our "word to the wise." In Ben Jonson's *Masque of Augures,* Vangoose is made to exclaim "hochos-pochos, *paucos pala-bros.*"

SCENE 1. Page 394.

LORD. And when he says he is—, say that he dreams.

Of the various modes of filling up this blank suggested in the notes, that of Dr. Johnson, who would insert *sly*, is the most probable. Mr. Steevens asks, "how should the Lord know the beggar's name to be Sly?" This is very true; yet Shakspeare might as well forget himself in this place as he certainly did a few pages afterwards, where he makes the Lord's servant talk of *Cicely* Hacket, &c.

ACT I.

SCENE 1. Page 414.

KATH. I pray you, sir, is it your will
To make a *stale* of me amongst these *mates.*

She means to say, "do you intend to make a strumpet of me among these companions?" but the expression seems to have been suggested by the chess-term of *stale mate*, which is used when the game is ended by the king being alone and unchecked, and then forced into a situation from which he is unable to move without going into check. This is a dishonourable termination to the adversary, who thereby loses the game. Thus in Lord Verulam's twelfth essay, " They stand still like a *stale* at chess, where it is no *mate*, but yet the game cannot stir."

SCENE 2.   Page 427.

PET. Be she as foul as was Florentius' love.

Dr. Farmer's note might have been omitted, as it refers to a story which has no manner of connection with that to which Petruchio alludes.

SCENE 2.   Page 436.

PET. Tush, tush, *fear* boys with *bugs*.

To *fear* is to frighten. In Mathews's *Bible*, psalm xci. v. 5, is thus rendered : " Thou shalt not nede to be afraied for any *bugs* by night." In the Hebrew it is " *terror* of the night;" a curious passage, evidently alluding to that horrible sensation the night-mare, which in all ages has been regarded as the operation of evil spirits. Thus much seemed necessary in explanation or defence of the above most excellent old translation, which we have retained with very little change in the language; for the expression, from its influence on a modern ear, might have been liable to a very ludicrous construction. The word *bug* is originally Celtic, *bwg*, a ghost or goblin, and hence *bug-bear*, *boggerd*, *bogle*, *boggy-bo*, and perhaps *pug*, an old name for the Devil. *Boggy-bo* seems to signify the *spirit Bo*, and has been thought, with some probability, to refer to a warrior of that name, the son of Odin, and of great celebrity among the ancient Danes and Norwegians. His name is said to have struck his enemies with terror, and might have been used by the nurses of those times to frighten children, as that of Marlborough was in

France on the same occasion.   It is remarkable that the Italian women use *bau bau,* for this purpose, and the French *ba-bo.*   It should seem as if *bug* had been metaphorically applied to the *cimex,* that insect being in all respects *a terror of the night.*   Nor was the word used in this sense till late in the seventeenth century, the old names for the house bug being, *wall-louse, wig-louse, chinch, punie,* and *puneez ;* the two last from the French.

ACT II.

Scene 1.   Page 442.

KATH. And, for your love to her, *lead apes in hell.*

It is perhaps an ill-natured, though a very common, presumption, that the single state of old maids originates either in prudery or in real aversion to the male sex, and that consequently they deserve some kind of punishment in the next world.   It is therefore not a matter of wonder that some of our waggish forefathers, impressed with this idea, should have maintained that these obdurate damsels would be condemned to lead apes in the inferior regions, instead, as Mr. Steevens has ingeniously suggested, of children ; or perhaps with a view to compel them to bestow such attention on these deformed animals as they had formerly denied to men.   So in Rabelais' hell, Alexander the great is condemned, for his ambition, to mend old stockings, and Cleopatra, for her pride, to cry onions.

It is said that homicides and adulterers were in ancient times compelled by way of punishment to lead an ape by the neck, with their mouths affixed in a very unseemly manner to the animal's tail.   The fact is mentioned in the early Latin dictionary entitled *Vocabularius breviloquus,* and in the *Catholicon* of Johannes Januensis, both printed at the end of the

fifteenth century, under the article *anulus*. It is added, that
the above punishment being found too opprobrious was com-
muted for wearing a ring on the finger, which the higher
classes caused to be made of gold or silver; and this is further
stated to have been the reason why the general practice of
wearing rings declined. After all it may be a mere fabrication
for the purpose of introducing an etymology of the word
annulus, that cannot here be repeated.

Scene 1.   Page 450.

Hor. And, *twangling Jack.*

It is the author's desire to withdraw a former note on this
passage, which, as well as a few others of a confidential nature,
was not intended for publication. To *twangle* means to make
any sharp shrill noise on a stringed instrument, as a bad
player would do. A *Jack* denotes a low or mean person, and
is occasionally used as a term of reproach. Thus Horatio
is afterwards called " swearing *Jack*." *Twangling Jack* may
sometimes allude to that little machine in harpsichords and
spinnets in which the quill is placed that strikes the wires.
The *jangling Jack* mentioned in Mr. Steevens's note is not
connected with the other. He is a mere *prating fellow.*
Thus in Drant's translation of Horace's ninth satire, 1567, 4to:

> " A *prater* shal becom his death,
> Therefore, let him alwayes,
> If he be wise, shun *jangling jackes*,
> After his youthful dayes."

Scene 1.   Page 461.

Gre. My hangings all of *Tyrian tapestry.*

Whether the purple of Tyre be here alluded to is doubtful.
There is a Turkish city of some celebrity in Natolia called
Tiria, where, according to the account of Paul Lucas, carpets
are manufactured; and in the *Comedy of errors*, Act IV.
Scene 1, mention is made of *Turkish tapestry.*

ACT III.

SCENE 1. Page 470.

LUC. . . . . for, *but* I be deceiv'd.

Mr. Malone has well explained this word as meaning *unless*, in which sense it is often used by Shakspeare. It is the Saxon buton, *nisi*. Sometimes it was used with *if*, as " I wol breake thy heed *but if* thou get the hense ;" from Terence's " Diminuam ego tibi caput, *nisi* abis," Udall's *Floures from Latine*, 1533, 12mo.

SCENE 2. Page 487.

PET. Go to the feast, revel and *domineer*.

So in Tarlton's *Jests*, " T. having been *domineering* very late at night with two of his friends." In these instances to *domineer* is to *bluster*.

SCENE 2. Page 487.

PET. She is my goods, my chattels; she is my house,
My houshold stuff, my field, my barn,
My horse, my ox, my ass, my any thing.

In the anonymous play of *A knacke to knowe a knave*, 1594, one of the old men says, " My house? why, 'tis my goods, my wyfe, my land, my horse, my ass, or any thing that is his." If Mr. Malone's conjecture respecting the date of *The taming of the shrew* be well founded, it is difficult to say whether Shakspeare is the borrower, in this instance, or not.

ACT IV.

SCENE 1. Page 494.

CRU. . . . . their *blue coats* brushed——

Thus in Nashe's *Have with you to Saffron Walden, or Gabriell Harvey's hunt is up*, when this foul-mouth'd writer has accused his adversary Harvey of defrauding Wolfe his printer of thirty-six pounds, he adds, that he borrowed of him a *blue coat* for his man; " and yet Wolfe did not so much as *brush* it, when he lent it him, or presse out the print where the *badge* had been." In another place, alluding to the same transaction, he states that Wolfe "lent him one of his prentises for a serving creature to grace him, clapping an old *blue coate* on his backe, which was one of my Lord of Harford's liveries (he pulling the *badge* off)."

The practice of giving liveries to menial servants has not originated in modern times. It is mentioned in some of the statutes made in the reign of Richard the Second. In that of Edward the Fourth the terms *livery* and *badge* appear to have been synonymous, the former having no doubt been borrowed from the French language, and signifying a thing *delivered*. The badge consisted of the master's device, crest, or arms, on a separate piece of cloth, or sometimes silver, in the form of a shield, fastened to the left sleeve. Greene, in his *Quip for an upstart courtier*, speaking of some servingmen, says, "their cognizance, as I remember, was a peacocke without a tayle." In queen Elizabeth's time the nobility gave silver badges, as appears from Hentzner's *Travels*, p. 156, edit. Norimb. 1612, 4to. " Angli magnifici domi forisque magna assectantium famulorum agmini secum trahunt, quibus in *sinistro brachio scuta ex argento focta* appendunt." But this foolish extravagance was not limited to persons of high rank. Fynes Moryson, speaking of the English apparel, informs us that " the servants of *gentlemen* were wont to weare *blew coates,* with their masters badge of silver on the left sleeve, but now they most commonly weare clokes garded with lace, all the servants of one family wearing the same liverie for colour and ornament:" we are therefore to suppose that the sleeve badge was left off in the reign of James I. Yet the badge was at one time so general an accompaniment to a blue coat, that when any thing wanted its usual appendage, it was *proverbially* said to be *like a blue coat without a badge.*

The custom of clothing persons in liveries and badges was not confined to menial servants. Another class of men called *retainers,* who appear to have been of no small importance among our ancestors, were habited in a similar manner. They were a sort of servants, not residing in the master's house like other menial domestics, but attending occasionally for the purpose of ostentation, and *retained* by the annual donation of a livery consisting of a hat or hood, a badge, and a suit of clothes. As they were frequently kept for the purpose of maintaining quarrels and committing other excesses, it became necessary to impose heavy penalties on the offenders, both masters and retainers. In process of time they were licensed. Strype complains of the too great indulgence of queen Mary in this respect. " She granted," says he, " more by half in her short five years than her sister and successor in thirteen. For in all that time there were but fifteen licenses of retainer granted, whereas queen Mary had granted nine and thirty. She was more liberal also in yielding the number of retainers to each person, which sometimes amounted to two hundred. Whereas Q. Elizabeth never yielded above an hundred to any person of the greatest quality, and that rarely too. But Bishop Gardiner began that ill example, who retained two hundred men : whereas under Q. Elizabeth the Duke of Norfolk retained but an hundred ; and Parker, archbishop of Canterbury, but forty." He has added a list of the persons to whom Mary granted licenses, and the number of persons retained. *Eccl. memorials,* iii. 479.

Nor did these retainers always consist of men of low condition. The entertaining author of a book entitled *A health to the gentlemanly profession of serving men, or the serving man's comfort,* 1598, 4to, (to whom these notes have occasionally been indebted, and who with good reason is supposed to have been Jervis Markham,) has certainly alluded to them in the following curious passage, wherein he is consoling the objects of his labour : " Amongst what sort of people should then this serving man be sought for ?   Even the duke's sonne preferred page to the prince, the earles seconde sonne attendant upon the duke, the knights seconde sonne the earles servant, the esquires sonne *to weare the knightes lyverie,* and the gentlemans sonne the esquiers serving man : Yea I know at this day, gentlemen younger brothers, that weares their elder brothers *blew coate* and badge, attending him with as reverend regard and duetifull obedience, as if he were their prince or soveraigne." Let us congratulate ourselves that we no longer endure such insolent aggressions, the result of family pride and ignorance, and which had been too often permitted to degrade the natural liberties and independence of mankind.   The excellent old ballad of *Times alteration,* has the following illustrative stanza of the coats and badges in question :

> " The nobles of our land
>   Were much delighted then,
>   To have at their command
>   A crew of lusty men ;
>   Which by their coats were known
>   Of tawny, red or blue,
>   With crests on their sleeves shown,
>   When this old cap was new."

Before we dismiss the present subject, it will be necessary to observe that the *badge* occurs in all the old representations of posts or messengers.   On the latter of these characters it may be seen in the 52nd plate of Mr. Strutt's first volume of *The dress and habits of the people of England,* where, as in the most ancient instances, the badge is affixed to the girdle ; but it is often seen on the shoulder, and even on the hat or cap.   These figures extend as far back as the thirteenth century, and many old German engravings exhibit both the characters with a badge that has sometimes the device or arms of the town to which the post belongs.   He has generally a spear in his hand, not only for personal security, but for repelling any nuisance that might interrupt his progress. Among ourselves the remains of the ancient badge are still preserved in the dresses of porters, firemen, and watermen, and perhaps in the shoulder-knots of footmen. The blue coat and badge still remain with the parish and hospital boys. The following figure of a person of a higher class with a badge, is copied from the view of Windsor in *Braunii civitates orbis terrarum*, 1573.

SCENE 1.   Page 496.

PET. Where be these knaves? what no man *at door*.

Although *door* might in the *middle* of a line be pronounced as a dissyllable, it is submitted that it cannot, with any propriety, at the *end*.   It were better to suppose an omission at the press, and read " at *the* door."

SCENE 2.   Page 506.

TRA. That teacheth tricks *eleven and twenty* long.

We have here a very uncommon and perhaps unique expression; but it seems to mean no more than that the tricks were of an extraordinary kind. *Eleven and twenty* is the same as *eleven score*, which signified a great length or number as applied to the exertions of a few or even of a single person.   Thus in the old ballad of *The low country soldier*,

> "Myself and seven more
> We fought *eleven score*."

SCENE 3.   Page 513.

KATH. Why then the beef, and let the mustard rest, &c.

This part of the dialogue was in all probability suggested by the following whimsical story in *Wits, fittes and fancies,* 1595, 4to :—" A clowne having surfeited of beefe, and being therewith extreame sicke, vow'd never whiles he liv'd to eat beefe more, if it pleas'd God he might escape for that once : Shortlie after having his perfect health again, he would needs have eaten beefe, and his sister putting him in mind of his vow, hee answered : True (sister) not without mustard (good L.) not without mustard."   This is not the only use that Shakspeare has made of this curious book, which was, in part, translated from a Spanish work, entitled *La floresta Spagnola*, by Anthony Copley, who was the author of a poem printed at the end, called *Love's owle: In dialogue-wise betweene love and an olde man.*   Of this poem Copley thus speaks in his dedication : " As for my *Loves owle*, I am content that Momus turne it to a tennis-ball if he can, and bandy it quite away : namelie, I desire M. *Daniel*, M. *Spencer*, and other the Prime Poets of our time, to pardon it with as easie a frowne as they please, for that I give them to understand, that an Universitie Muse never pend it, though humbly devoted thereunto."

SCENE 3.   Page 514.

PET. And all my pains is *sorted to no proof.*

This is explained by Dr. Johnson, " and all my labour has *proved* nothing."   It rather means, " all my labour is *adapted* to no *approof*," or " I have taken all this pains without *approbation.*   *Approof* is used by Shakspeare in this sense, and should be here printed with an apostrophe, *'proof.*

SCENE 4.   Page 529.

BION. Take your assurance of her *cum privilegio ad imprimendum solum.*

This is not the only instance in which our poet has borrowed his broad metaphors from the typographical art.

In *The winter's tale,* Act V. Scene 1, we have, " Your mother was most true to wedlock, prince ; for she did *print* your royal father off, conceiving you."

To the stories already mentioned in the notes to this play as resembling that of the *induction,* the following are to be added :—1. *The sleeper awakened,* in the Arabian nights. This is probably the original of all the rest.   2. A similar incident in the story of *Xailoun* in the *Continuation of the Arabian nights.*   3. In *The apophthegms of King James, King Charles, the marquess of Worcester,* &c., 1658, 12mo, there is the story of an old bachelor named *Thomas Deputy,* who at the marriage of Edward Lord Herbert taking a fancy to one of the bride's waiting-maids, was persuaded by the old Marquess of Worcester to marry her at the same time.   Thomas, being overpowered on this occasion with the joy he felt from the liberal donations of the noble assistants at the wedding, and also with the good wine that was freely circulated, became altogether incapable of consummating his marriage ; and the Marquess, after relating to the company " the story of the begger who was made to believe he did but dream of the happiness that was really acted," determined to make the experiment in the person of old Thomas, and accordingly ordered that he " should be disrobed of his new wedding garment, the rest of his fine cloaths taken from him, and himself carried unto his old lodging in the porter's lodge, and his wife to respite the solemnization of the marriage bed untill his comportment should deserve so fair an admission : which was done accordingly.   The next morning made the experiment to answer the height of all their expectations; for news was brought unto the Marquesse, all the rest of the lords and ladies standing by, that *Thom.* took all yesterdayes work but for a dream, or at least seemed to do so, to humour the fancy." 4. Winstanley, in his *Historical rarities,* 1684, 8vo, has a story of Aladine the Persian, called the old man of the mountain, who built a magnificent palace near a city called *Mulebet,* and filled it with every sort of luxury and delight. " Hither he brought all the lusty youths he could light on, casting them into prison, where they endured much sorrow and woe. And when he thought good, he caused a certain drink to be given them, which cast them into a dead sleep : then he caused them to be carried into divers chambers of the said palaces, where they saw the things aforesaid as soon as they awaked ; each of them having those damsels to minister meats and excellent drinks, and all varieties of pleasures to them, insomuch, that the fools thought themselves to be in paradise indeed. Having enjoyed this happiness a whole day, they were in a like sleep conveyed to their irons again ; after which, he caused them to be brought into his presence, and questioned where they had been ; which answered, by your grace, in paradise, and recounted all the particulars before mentioned." Winstanley has also given the story of Philip duke of Burgundy. 5. A similar incident in the penny history of *The frolicksome courtier and the jovial tinker.*

The author of the story in the Tatler might have used a novel in the *Piacevoli notti* of Straparola, nott. 8, fab. 2. and the outline of the *Taming of the shrew* may be found in a Spanish work entitled *El conde Lucanor,* 1643, 4to, composed by Don Juan Manuel, nephew to Ferdinand the fourth king of *Castile.*

The character of Petruchio bears some resemblance to that of Pisardo in Straparola's *Novels,* night 8, fab. 7.

WINTER'S TALE.

ACT I.

SCENE 2. Page 27.

LEON. And his pond fish'd by his next neighbour.

THIS is not the only gross and offensive metaphor of the kind that our poet has used. In *Measure for measure,* we have "groping for trouts in a peculiar river."

SCENE 2. Page 30.

LEON. . . . I have trusted thee Camillo,
With all the nearest things to my *heart*——
. . . . . wherein, priest-like thou
Hast cleans'd my bosom.

So in Macbeth we have,

" *Cleanse the stuff'd bosom* of that perilous stuff,
Which weighs upon the *heart.*"

SCENE 2. Page 39.

CAM. . . . If I could find example
Of thousands that had struck anointed kings
And *flourish'd after,* I'd not do't.

If, as Mr. Blackstone supposes, this be an allusion to the death of the queen of Scots, it exhibits Shakspeare in the character of a cringing flatterer accommodating himself to existing circumstances, and is moreover an extremely severe one. But the perpetrator of that atrocious murder *did flourish* many years afterwards. May it not rather be designed as a compliment to King James on his escape from the Gowrie conspiracy, an event often brought to the people's recollection during his reign, from the day on which it happened being made a day of thanksgiving ? See *Osborne's traditionall memoyres,* and the almanacks of the time under the 5th of August.

SCENE 2.   Page 41.

POL. In whose success we are *gentle.*

So in Act V. Scene 2, the old shepherd says, "we must be gentle now we are gentlemen." What our ancestors conceived to be the true definition of a gentleman may be seen at large in *The booke of honor and armes,* 1594, 4to, book iii. In Morgan's *Sphere of gentry,* the silly author has gravely stated that *Jesus Christ* was a *gentleman* and bore arms. Of the latter assertion he has given no proof, though he might have adduced a sort of armorial bearing made up from the implements of the passion, and often exhibited as such in some of the *horæ* and other service books of the church, before the reformation. Such a coat of arms was likewise used as a stamp on the covers of old books, with the motto RE-DEMPTORIS MUNDI ARMA. *Gentle gentlemen* is an alliteration that is very frequent in writers of the age of Shakspeare. In the preface to Gerard Leigh's *Accedence of armorie,* 1597, 4to, three sorts of *ungentiles* are described, "the first whereof are *gentle ungentle.* Such be they as wil rather sweare armes then beare armes. Who of negligence stop mustard pots with their fathers pedegrees, or otherwise abuse them. The second sort are *ungentle gentlemen,* who being enhaunced to honor by their fathers, on whom (though it were to their owne worship) yet can they not keepe so much money from the dice, as to make worshipful obsequies for their sad fathers with any point of armory. The third sort, and worst of all, are neither *gentle ungentle,* or *ungentle gentile,* but verie stubble curs, and be neither doers, sufferers, or wel speakers of honors tokens."

SCENE 2.   Page 42.

CAM. I am appointed *him* to murder you.

" *i. e.*" says Mr. Steevens, "I am the person appointed to murder you." This is certainly the meaning, but the grammatical construction is, " I am appointed the person to murder you." The lines quoted from *King Henry VI.* are ungrammatical, and not, as is conceived, an exemplification of the foregoing passage.

SCENE 2.   Page 42.

POL. . . . . and my name
Be yok'd with his that did betray the best.

Mr. Henderson's conjecture that Judas is here meant is certainly well founded. A clause in the sentence against excommunicated persons was, " let them *have part with Judas that betrayed Christ.* Amen;" and this is here imitated.

ACT II.

SCENE 3.   Page 73.

LEON. And *lozel,* thou art worthy to be hang'd.

The derivation of *lozel* cited from Verstegan is arbitrary, and deduced from a mere resemblance of sound. The word has been apparently corrupted from the Saxon *lorel,* used by Chaucer for a worthless fellow. See Mr. Tyrwhitt's glossary. The corruption may have originated in the similitude of the letters *r* and *z* in ancient manuscripts.

ACT III.

SCENE 2.   Page 82.

HER. . . . . since he came,
With what encounter so uncurrent I
Have strain'd to appear thus.

Dr. Johnson, not understanding these lines, " with the licence of all editors," pronounces them unintelligible. However strange the language may appear in the mouth of a lady, there is hardly a doubt that it is a metaphor taken from tilting. Hermione means to say, *I appeal to your own conscience whether since Polixenes came, I have made any violent or irregular encounter unlike that of a fair courser*; or, in plainer terms, *whether I have deviated from the paths of honour and* forcibly *obtruded myself on this tribunal.* Those who made an encounter at justs were called *runners*; and were said, occasionally, to *run foul.* This may serve to explain what is meant by *uncurrent.*

ACT IV.

Scene 2.   Page 107.

Aut. When daffodils begin to peer, &c.

Mr. Steevens, to give himself an opportunity of introducing a neat retort on an attack which his favourite author had sustained, has quoted a remark by Dr. Burney that Autolycus " is the *true ancient minstrel,* as described in the old fabliaux." With great deference to this learned and elegant writer, the observation is inaccurate. Autolycus has nothing in common with the character of a minstrel but the singing of a song or two. He is a mere *rogue,* assuming various shapes, and is specifically called so in the *dramatis personæ*; but it will not surely be contended that all rogues were minstrels, because a cruel and illiberal statute has made all minstrels rogues. It is true that Autolycus declares he had been an *ape-bearer*; but this was no part of the minstrel profession in Shakspeare's time, though it had been so formerly. As this circumstance however has not been noticed, or at least very slightly, by any of the writers on the subject of the ancient minstrels, it may be worth while to exhibit the following curious story from the second book of *The dialogues of Saint Gregory,* who lived in the sixth century. At the celebration of the feast of Saint Proculus the martyr, a nobleman named Fortunatus having prevailed on Bishop

Boniface to eat with him after celebrating the service of the day, it happened that before the holy prelate had pronounced the usual benediction at table, *a minstrel leading an ape and playing on a cymbal* arrived. This very much discomposed the good bishop, who exclaimed, Alas! alas! the wretched man is dead; behold, I have not yet opened my lips to praise God, and he is here with his ape and playing on his instrument. He then desired the servants to carry some victuals to the unhappy man, which when he had eaten, a stone fell from the house top and killed him.

Scene 2. Page 109.

Aut. The lark that *tirra-lirra* chants.

The tire-lire was not, it seems, peculiar to the lark. In Skelton's *Colin Cloute* we have,

> ". . howe Cupide shaked
> His darte and bente hys bowe,
> For to shote a *crowe*,
> At her *tyrly tyrlowe*."

And in one of the Coventry pageants there is the following old song sung by the shepherds at the birth of Christ, which is further remarkable for its use of the very uncommon word *endenes,* from the Saxon enꝺenehȝꞇ, *the last.*

> " As I out rode this endenes night,
> Of three joli shepherds I sawe a syght,
> And all aboute there fold a stare shone bright:
> They sang *terli terlow,*
> So mereli the sheppards there pipes can blow."

Scene 2. Page 111.

Aut. My father named me Autolycus, &c.

It is necessary on this occasion to lay before the reader Dr. Warburton's own words. " Mr. Theobald says, *the allusion is unquestionably to Ovid.* He is mistaken. Not only the allusion, but the whole speech is taken from Lucian, who appears to have been one of our poet's favourite authors, as may be collected from several places of his works. It is from *his discourse on judicial astrology,* where Autolycus talks much in the same manner, &c."

Now if any one will take the trouble of comparing what Ovid and Lucian have respectively said concerning Autolycus, he will, it is presumed, be altogether disposed to give the preference to Theobald's opinion. Dr. Warburton must have been exclusively fortunate in discovering that *the whole speech is taken from Lucian;* that he was *one of our poet's favourite authors;* and that, in the *dialogue* alluded to, *Autolycus talks much in the same manner.* He must have used some edition of Lucian's works vastly preferable to those which now remain. The reader will be pleased to consult the eleventh book of Ovid's *Metamorphoses,* in the translation (if he have it) by Golding.

SCENE 2.   Page 113.

CLOWN.   .   .   *three-man* songmen all.

" They have also *Cornish three-mens* songs, cunningly contrived for the ditty, and pleasantly for the note." Carew's *Survey of Cornwall,* fo. 72.

SCENE 2.   Page 113.

CLOWN. .   .   but one Puritan amongst them, and he sings psalms to hornpipes.

An allusion to a practice, common at this time among the Puritans, of burlesquing the *plein chant* of the Papists, by adapting vulgar and ludicrous music to psalms and pious compositions.

SCENE 3.   Page 123.

PER. For you there 's *rosemary,* and rue ;
    Grace and *remembrance* be to you both.

The following lines are from a song entitled, *A noseguie alwaies sweet for lovers to send for tokens of love at newyere's tide, or for fairings, as they in their minds shall be disposed to*

write, printed in Robinson's *Handefull of pleasant delites,*
1584, 16mo :—

> " Rosemarie is for remembrance,
> Betweene us daie and night,
> Wishing that I might alwaies have
> You present in my sight."

This plant, as being thought to strengthen the memory,
was therefore *given to friends,* as in the present instance.
See Parkinson's *Flower garden,* p. 426. Thus Ophelia says
to her brother, " There's rosemary ; that's for remembrance,
pray you, love, remember." The reason for calling rue *herb
of grace* is best explained in the notes on a subsequent speech
of Ophelia. See vol. xv. p. 276.

SCENE 3. Page 124.

> PER. . . . . and streak'd gilliflowers,
> Which some call nature's bastards : of that kind
> Our rustick garden's barren ; and I care not
> To get slips of them.
> POL.   Wherefore, gentle maiden,
> Do you neglect them ?
> PER.   For I have heard it said,
> There is an art which in their piedness, shares
> With great creating nature.

The solution of the riddle in these lines that has em-
barrassed Mr. Steevens is probably this : the gilly-flower
or carnation is streaked, as every one knows, with white and
red. In this respect it is a proper emblem of a *painted* or
immodest woman, and therefore Perdita declines to meddle
with it. She connects the gardener's *art* of varying the
colours of the above flowers with the art of painting the face,
a fashion very prevalent in Shakspeare's time. This conclusion is justified by what she says in her next speech but one.

SCENE 3. Page 126.

> PER. The marigold, that goes to bed with the sun
> And with him rises weeping.

" So upon occasions past, David found it true that he

should not have bene heretofore at any time, and therefore professeth, that, for the time to come, he would be no *marigold-servant of God, to open with the sun, and shut with the dewe.*"—Prime's *Consolations of David applied to Queene Elizabeth : in a sermon preached in Oxford the* 17 *of November*, 1588, 12mo.　Lord Howard, in his *Defensative against the poyson of supposed prophecies*, 1583, 4to, says that " *the marie-golde* dooth close and open with the sunne, &c.*"

Scene 3.　Page 131.

Per. . . . . . I 'll swear for 'em.

Dr. Johnson would transfer this speech to the king, and Mr. Ritson would read " swear for *one*," or at least have some alteration ; but in reality no change is necessary.　Florizel had just said, " so *turtles* pair that never mean to part," on which Perdita very naturally observes, " I 'll swear for 'em."　This is no more than a common phrase of acquiescence, as we likewise say, " I'll *warrant* you."

Scene 3.　Page 137.

Aut. . . . . poking-sticks of steel.

To Mr. Steevens's curious note on these implements for stiffening the ruffs formerly worn by persons of both sexes, it may be worth adding that this fashion being carried to a great extremity, became the subject of many satirical prints. One of the oldest was engraved in 1580, by Matthias Quad, and represents the Devil's ruff-shop, he being called the *kragen-setzer* or *ruff-setter*.　A young gallant has brought his mistress to have her ruff set.　The Devil is engaged in this operation whilst an assistant is heating fresh poking-sticks in a brasier.　Another print of this sort by Galle, is copied from a design by Martin de Vos, and entitled *Diaboli partus superbia*.　It has this inscription relating to the *poking-sticks* : " Avec ces fers chauds qu'on vous icy appreste, En enfer puny seras, O layde beste."　Other prints represent several monkeys habited in ruffs, and busily employed in poking and starching them, &c.

SCENE 3. Page 138.

CLOWN. *Clamour* your tongues, and not a word more.

The word is difficult, and, it is feared, likely to afford nothing but conjecture.

Dr. Warburton asserts that the phrase is from ringing; that to clamour bells is to repeat the stroke quicker than before, previously to *ceasing* them. On the contrary, Dr. Grey maintains that to clamour bells is a *continued* ringing, and Mr. Malone, with great probability, suspects that what Warburton has said is *gratis dictum.* Dr. Johnson says that " to clam a bell is to cover the clapper with felt, which drowns the blow, and hinders the sound ;" and Mr. Nicholls, that *a good clam* is a peal of all the bells at once. According to the treatise on ringing in *The school of recreation,* 1684, 12mo, " *clamming* is when each concord strikes together, which being done true, the 8 will strike but as four bells, and make a melodious harmony." The accounts of bell-clamming are therefore so discordant that it seems but fair to give up entirely this sense of the word.

The clown evidently wishes to keep the damsels' tongues from wagging. Now to *clam, clem,* or *cleam* are provincial words, signifying to glue together or fasten with glue, and, metonymically, to starve by contraction. Thus,

<blockquote>
" . . . . . my entrails
Are *clam'd* with keeping a continual fast."
Massinger's *Roman actor.*
</blockquote>

And we still use *clammy,* for sticking together. All the Northern languages have an equivalent term. ·The Germans have *klemmen,* to tie, and in the old Icelandic we find *klæmman* in the same sense. Ihre, *Lexicon Suio-Goth.* In Saxon clam, ligamen, clæmınʒ, a stiffening. Somner *Gloss.* Littelton has *to clamm,* or hunger-starve, and Rider to *clamme,*

to *stop*. The latter is indeed more to the present purpose
than any or all of the others : because by supposing, what is
extremely probable, an error of the press, all will be set right.
On the other hand, *clamour* is the reverse of what is required.
Thus in *Macbeth*, Act II. Scene 3, we have, " The obscure
bird *clamour'd* the live-long night," and we are not to suppose that Shakspeare could have used the same word in
senses so extremely opposite.

SCENE 3.   Page 148.

Re-enter servant, with twelve rusticks habited like *satyrs*. They *dance*,
and then exeunt.

In the old collection of songs set by Thomas Ravenscroft
and others, already quoted in p. 11, there is one called *The
satyres daunce*. It is for four voices, and as follows :—

> " Round a round, a rounda, keepe your ring
> To the glorious sunne we sing;
>   Hoe, hoe !
>
> He that weares the flaming rayes,
> And the imperiall crowne of bayes,
> Him, with him, with shoutes and songs we praise.
>   Hoe, hoe !
>
> That in his bountee would vouchsafe to grace
> The humble sylvanes and their shaggy race."

SCENE 3.   Page 154.

SHEP. Some hangman must put on my shroud, and lay me
Where no priest shovels in dust.

i. e. *I must be buried as a common malefactor, out of the
pale of consecrated ground, and without the usual rites of the
dead*; a whimsical anachronism, when it is considered that
the old shepherd was a Pagan, a worshipper of Jupiter and
Apollo. But Shakspeare seldom cares about blending the
manners of distant ages.

Dr. Farmer has remarked that the *priest's* office above
mentioned might be remembered in Shakspeare's time, which
is very probable : the mention of it here is one of the
numerous instances of his intimate acquaintance with the

ceremonies of the Romish church.   Before the introduction
of the new form of burial service by Edward the Sixth, it was
the custom for the priest to throw earth on the body in the
form of a cross, and then to sprinkle it with holy water; but
this was not done *in pronouncing* the words *earth to earth,*
according to a learned commentator: that part of the ceremony was postponed till after a psalm had been sung, the
body being previously covered up.   An antiphone next
followed; and then the priest said these words: " I commend thy soul to God the father omnipotent: earth to earth,
ashes to ashes, dust to dust," &c.

ACT V.

Scene 1.   Page 182.

Flo.   .   .   .   .   Good my lord,
        She came from *Libya.*

Perdita is here transformed into a *Moor*; and although
this play among others affords the most unequivocal proofs
of Shakspeare's want of skill in the science of geography, it
is at least possible that an error of the press has substituted
Libya for *Lydia* or *Lycia.*

Scene 2.   Page 194.

Clown.   *Give me the lie,* do; and try whether I am not now *a gentle-
        man born.*

This is a satire on certain ridiculous punctilios very much
in use at this time.   Thus in *The booke of honor and armes,*
1590, 4to, " In saying *a gentleman borne,* we meane he must
be descended from three degrees of gentry, both on the
mother's and father's side."   The same work has many
particulars relating to the circumstances in which *the giving
the lie* is to be resented.   See likewise Vincent Saviolo *On
honor and honorable quarrels,* book ii.

THE CLOWN.

He is a mere country booby.

———————

The observation by Dr. Warburton, that *The winter's tale* with all its absurdities is very entertaining, though stated by Dr. Johnson to be just, must be allowed at the same time to be extremely frigid. In point of fine writing it may be ranked among Shakspeare's best efforts. The absurdities pointed at by Warburton, together with the whimsical anachronisms of Whitson pastorals, Christian burial, an emperor of Russia, and an Italian painter of the fifteenth century, are no real drawbacks on the superlative merits of this charming drama. The character of Perdita will remain for ages unrivalled; for where shall such language be found as she is made to utter?

COMEDY OF ERRORS.

ACT II.

Scene 1. Page 228.

Dro. E. Will you come *home*? quoth I; my gold, quoth he.

The word *home*, which the metre requires, is said to have been suggested by Capell, but it had been already adopted by Sir Thomas Hanmer.

Scene 2. Page 234.

Ant. S. If you will jest with me, know my *aspéct*.

Mr. Steevens explains this, *study my countenance.* It seems rather to be an astrological phrase, and to mean, *ascertain whether my aspect be malignant or benign.* He had just before mentioned the sun. Thus in 1 *Henry IV.* Act I. Scene 1, "Malevolent to you in all *aspécts.*"

Scene 2. Page 241.

Adr. Thou art an *elm* my husband, I a *vine* ;
        If aught possess thee from me, it is dross,
        Usurping Ivy, briar or idle moss.

So in *A midsummer night's dream,* Act IV. Scene 1, "The female *ivy* so enrings the barky fingers of the *elm.*" There is something extremely beautiful in making the vine the lawful spouse of the elm, and the *parasite* plants here named its concubines.

ACT III.

Scene 1. Page 248.

Dro. S. *Mome*, malthorse, capon, coxcomb, idiot, patch!

Sir J. Hawkins would derive *mome* from the French *mo-*

mon, the challenge at dice made by a mummer or silent person disguised in masquerade. It more probably came to us from one of those similar words that are found in many languages signifying something foolish. *Momar* is used by Plautus for a fool, whence the French *mommeur*. The Greeks too had μομος and μορμος in the same sense.

SCENE 2. Page 257.

> ANT. S. Less in your knowledge and your grace, you show not,
> Than *our earth's wonder, more than earth divine.*

This play abounds so much in anachronisms, that there will be no impropriety in supposing the above simile to have been designed as a compliment to the reigning sovereign. Pronounced with emphasis, it would not fail to make a due impression on the audience.

ACT IV.

SCENE 3. Page 280.

> DRO. S. What, have you got *the picture of old Adam new apparell'd?*

Here seems to be an allusion to some well-known contemporary painting, perhaps of a sign. " Adam whom God dyd fyrst create, made the fyrst *lether coates* for himself and his wyfe Eve our old mother, leavyng thereby a patron to al his posterite of that crafte." Polydore Vergil *de rer. invent.* translated by Langley, fo. lxix. Similar instances had before occurred in *the picture of we three,* and *Mistress Mall.*

MACBETH.

ACT I.

SCENE 1. Page 327.

ALL. *Paddock* calls.

MR. Steevens has remarked that "in Shakspeare a paddock certainly means a toad." Indeed it *properly* does everywhere; and when applied to the frog, seems either to have been mistakenly used, or to have signified the *rubeta* or *rana bufo,* a frog of a venomous kind. The word comes to us from the Saxon Paba, and a toad is still called by a similar term in most of the Teutonic languages. It may be likewise observed that witches have nothing to do with frogs, an animal always regarded as perfectly harmless, though perhaps not more so in reality than the unjustly persecuted toad.

SCENE 2. Page 331.

SOLD. And fortune on his damned *quarrel* smiling.

The old copy has *quarry,* which Dr. Johnson has changed to *quarrel,* a reading that had already been adopted by Hanmer. Chance may hereafter determine that *quarry* was an *occasional* mode of orthography, *euphoniæ gratiâ,* as we find *perrie* for *perril.* See Howard's *Defensative against the poyson of supposed prophesies,* 1583, 4to, sig. A iij. The word too which expresses a square-headed arrow and a pane of glass is written both *quarry* and *quarrel.*

SCENE 2. Page 335.

DUN.   Dismay'd not this
        Our captains, Macbeth and Banquo?
SOLD.   Yes.

Mr. Steevens, adverting to the apparent defect of metre in

the last line, concludes that some word has been omitted in
the old copy; and Hanmer reads, *brave* Macbeth, &c. No
other change is necessary than in orthography; for Shakspeare had, no doubt, written *capitaynes*, a common mode of
spelling the word in his time; and the fault lay either in the
printer or transcriber for the press.

Scene 2.   Page 339.

Rosse. Till that Bellóna's *bridegroom*, lapt in proof.

Shakspeare is here accused of ignorantly making Bellona
wife to the *God of war*; but, strictly speaking, this is not
the case. He has not called Macbeth, to whom he alludes,
the *God of war*; and there seems no great impropriety in
poetically supposing that a warlike hero might be *newly married* to the Goddess of war. Mr. Steevens's objection appears to have been founded on a conclusion that Shakspeare
meant to compare Macbeth to Mars, and that of the other
learned and ingenious critic, on the impropriety of considering Bellona as a married goddess.

Scene 3.   Page 341.

1. Witch. *Aroint* thee witch!

The reference to Hearne's print from an old calendar, in
his edition of Fordun, is very appositely introduced by Dr.
Johnson in illustration of *aroint*; but his explanation of the
print is in many respects erroneous. He is particularly mistaken in supposing it to represent *Saint Patrick visiting hell*;
for it is manifestly the very trite subject of Christ delivering
souls from purgatory, often painted by Albert Durer and
other ancient artists. The Doctor neglected to examine not
only the inscription on the print, but Hearne's own account
of it; and his eye having accidentally caught the name of
Saint Patrick, of whom Hearne had been speaking, his imagination suggested the common story of the visit to purgatory
(not hell). There is no doubt that *aroint* signifies *away*!

run! and that it is of Saxon origin. The original Saxon verb has not been preserved in any other way, but the glossaries supply *ryne* for running; and in the old Islandic, *runka* signifies *to agitate, to move*. Mr. Grose is certainly wrong in his explanation of the proverb, " *Rynt* you witch! quoth Besse Locket to her mother," when he says it means " by your leave, stand handsomely." See his *Provincial glossary*.

Scene 3. Page 353.

BAN. Or have we 'eaten of the *insane* root,
That takes the *reason* prisoner ?

Mr. Steevens conceives that *hemlock* is the root in question; whilst Mr. Malone, after noticing the trouble which the commentators have given themselves, introduces a quotation from Plutarch's life of Antony, (" which," says he, " our author must have diligently read,") that leads him to conclude the name to have been unknown even to Shakspeare himself. There is however another book which has in the course of these notes been shown to have been also read and even studied by the poet, and wherein, it is presumed, he actually found the *name* of the above root. This will appear from the following passage: " *Henbane* . . . is called *Insana*, mad, for the use thereof is perillous; for if it be eate or dronke, it breedeth madnesse, or slow lykenesse of sleepe. Therefore this hearb is called commonly *Mirilidium*, for it taketh away wit and *reason*." Batman *Uppon Bartholome de propriet. rerum*, lib. xvii. ch. 87.

Scene 5. Page 373.

ATTEN. One of my fellows had the speed of him ;
Who *almost dead for breath*, had scarcely more
Than would make up his message.
LADY M.   Give him tending,
He brings great news. *The raven himself is hoarse*
That croaks the fatal entrance of Duncan.

The last lines may appear less difficult, if the reader will suppose that at the moment in which the attendant finishes his speech, the raven's voice is heard on the battlements of the castle; when Lady Macbeth, adverting to the situation in which the messenger had just been described, most naturally exclaims, "the raven *himself* is hoarse," &c. *Entrance* must be here pronounced as a trisyllable, which is better than to read Dŭncān.

SCENE 5.   Page 374.

LADY M. Under my battlements. Come *come* you spirits.

The second *come* has been added by Mr. Steevens. On this it may be permitted to remark, that although Shakspeare's versification is unquestionably more smooth and melodious than that of most of his contemporaries, he has on many occasions exhibited more carelessness in this respect than can well be accounted for, unless by supposing the errors to belong to the printers or editors. If the above line was defective, many others of similar construction are still equally so; as for example, this in p. 378,

"This ignorant present, and I feel now,"

which Mr. Steevens strangely maintains to be complete, though undoubtedly as discordant to the ear as the other. Both, strictly speaking, have the full number of syllables; a mode of construction which it is to be feared our elder poets regarded as sufficient in general to give perfection to a line.

SCENE 6.   Page 384.

DUN. We cours'd him at the heels, and had a purpose
      To be his *purveyor.*

The duty of the purveyor, an officer belonging to the court, was to make a general provision for the royal household. It was the office also of this person to travel before the king whenever he made his progresses to different parts of the realm, and to see that every thing was duly provided. The right of purveyance and pre-emption having become extremely oppressive to the subject, was included, among other objects of regulation, under the stat. of 12 Car. II.

Scene 7. Page 395.

Lady M. But screw your courage to the *sticking-place*.

Mr. Steevens has suggested two metaphors, neither of which seems to advance the explanation. If it could be shown that the stop of a pile-driver, or the bed of a violin peg were ever called *sticking-places,* one might indeed suspect a miserable pun: but it is submitted that all the metaphor lies in the *screwing.* Another learned commentator states that Davenant misunderstood the sense when he supposed that *stabbing* is alluded to; and yet there are grounds for thinking his opinion correct. Lady Macbeth, after remarking that the enterprise would not fail if her husband would but exert his courage to the commission of the *murder,* proceeds to suggest the particular manner in which it was to be accomplished. In short, if there be a metaphor, abstractedly considered, it signifies nothing; for what would be the use of Macbeth's courage, if, according to Mr. Steevens, it were *to remain fast in that sticking-place from which it was not to move?* The Scots have a proverb, " *Sticking* goes not by strength, but by guiding of the gooly," *i. e.* the knife.

ACT II.

Scene 1. Page 401.

Ban. This diamond he greets your wife withal,
By the name of most kind hostess; *and shut up*
In measureless content.

As the last sentence stands, it is at once ungrammatical and obscure; and neither Mr. Steevens's construction of *shut up* in the sense of *to conclude,* as referring to the speaker, nor Hanmer's reading *and is shut up,* as connected with Duncan, will render it intelligible. It should seem as if Banquo meant to say that the king was immured in happiness; but then it is obvious that some preceding words have been lost.

Scene 3.   Page 428.

Enter Macduff.

Duff in the Erse language signifies a captain; *Macduff,*
the son of a captain.

Scene 3.   Page 433.

Macd. Shake off this downy sleep, death's counterfeit.

This simile has been elsewhere used by Shakspeare. Thus
in *Cymbeline,* he calls sleep *the ape of death.* In *A midsummer night's dream,* he has *death counterfeiting sleep.* It
might indeed from its extreme obviousness have occurred to
writers of weaker imagination than our poet; yet as he is
known to have borrowed so much, it is not impossible that
he might in this instance have been indebted to Marlow's
translation of a line in Ovid's *Elegies,* book ii. el. 9 :

" Foole what is sleepe, but image of cold death ?"

or to another version of the same line in Cardanus's *Comfort*:

" Is not our sleepe (O foole) of death an image playne ?"

Whoever will take the trouble of reading over the whole of
Cardanus's second book as translated by Bedingfield, and
printed by T. Marshe, 1576, 4to, will soon be convinced that
it had been perused by Shakspeare.

Scene 3.   Page 438.

Macb. . . . . . *their daggers*
Unmannerly breech'd with gore.

Mr. Steevens's explanation must be objected to.   Finding
that the *lower end* of a cannon is called its *breech,* he concludes that the *hilt* or *handle* of a dagger must be here intended by the like appellation.   But is not this literally to
mistake the *top* for the *bottom* ?   It is conceived that the
present expression, though in itself something *unmannerly,*
simply means *covered as with breeches.*   The idea, uncouth
and perhaps inaccurate as it is, might have been suggested
from the resemblance of daggers to the legs and thighs of a

man. The sentiments of Dr. Farmer on this, as on all occasions, are ingenious, and deserving of the highest respect;
but it is hardly possible that Shakspeare could have been deceived in the way he states. To give colour to his opinion,
he is obliged in his quotation from Erondell's *French garden*
to print the word *master's* as a genitive case singular, in order
to apply the pronoun *their* to *daggers*; but without the aid
of the French text, the word *their* is *in the original* equally
applicable to *masters*. Indeed the subsequent mention of
stockings, hose and garters, would have satisfied a person of
much less penetration than Shakspeare, that *breeches* were
there intended as an article of dress.

The above conjecture that the term *breech'd* might signify
cover'd, suggests the mention of a circumstance from which it
may on the whole be thought to derive support.

It is well known that some ridicule has been cast on one
of our translations of the Bible from the Genevan French
edition, on account of the following words, " And they sewed
fig-tree leaves together and made themselves *breeches*," Gen.
iii. 7; whence it has been called the *Breeches Bible*, and
sometimes sold for a high price. It is generally conceived
that this peculiarity belongs exclusively to the above Bible,
but it is a mistake. The Saxon version by Ælfric has
ꞇ ꞃıꝼoꝺon ꝼıcleaꝼ ꞇ poꞃhꞇon hım pæꝺbꞃꞃec, *and sewed fig-leaves
and worked them* WEED-BREECH, *or cloaths for the breech*.
Wicliffe also translates " and maden hem *breechis*;" and
it is singular that Littelton in his excellent dictionary explains *perizomata*, the word used in the Vulgate, by *breeches*.
In the manuscript French translation of Petrus Comestor's
commentary on the Bible, made by Guiars des Moulins in
the thirteenth century, we have " couvertures tout autressint
comme unnes petites *braies*."

ACT III.

SCENE 4.   Page 476.

MACB. . . Get thee gone; to-morrow
　　We 'll hear, *ourselves again.*

i. e. *when I have recovered from my fit, and am once more
myself.*   It is an ablative absolute.   *Ourselves* is much more
properly used than *ourself,* the modern language of royalty.

SCENE 4.   Page 482.

MACB. If trembling I *inhibit* thee, protest me
　　The baby of girl.

Every partaker of the rational *Diversions of Purley* will
here call to mind what has been advanced on the subject of
this difficult and much contested passage; but with all the
respect and admiration that are due to their profound and ingenious writer, will he feel himself altogether satisfied?   It
were to be wished that not only the above grammarian but
another gentleman not less eminently qualified to illustrate
any subject he undertakes, had favoured us with some example of the *neutral* use of *inhabit* in the sense of *to house* or
remain at home.   Until this be done, or even then, it may be
boldly said, and without much difficulty maintained, that *inhibit,* in point of meaning, was Shakspeare's word.   Nor is it
a paradox to affirm that *inhabit,* the *original* reading, is also
right; because this may be only one of the numerous instances during the former unsettled state of orthography,
where the same word has been spelled in different ways.
Mr. Malone has already supplied instances of *inhabit* for *inhibit* in a passage from *All's well that ends well,* in all the
folios except the first, and another from Stowe's *Survey of
London.*   In the edition of the *Shepherd's calendar,* printed
without date by Wynkyn de Worde in 4to, there is this
sentence in chap. xxi.: " Correccyon is for to *inhabyte* &
defende by the bridle of reason all errowres," &c.   Later

editions have *inhibit*. Are we then to suppose that *all* these examples are typographical mistakes, rather than a varied orthography?

The difficulty remains to extract a sense from *inhibit* adapted to the occasion. Mr. Steevens has justly said, " to inhibit is to *forbid*;" but this cannot be the present signification. A man cannot well be said to *forbid* another who has challenged him. He might indeed *keep back or hesitate* in such a case, which is the *neutral* sense now offered, but it must be confessed with nearly the same diffidence in its accuracy which has been expressed as to that of the others.

With respect to the punctuation, it is conceived, that considering the mode in which these plays were published, the authority of Shakspeare is almost out of the question; and therefore a judicious modern editor is entitled to use a great deal of discretion in corrections of this kind. In the present instance there is no great objection to the old pointing, though the comma should seem better *after* " inhibit," and may render the line more emphatic. " If trembling, I keep back, *then* protest me," &c. After all, this is one of the many instances in which the real meaning of the author cannot be satisfactorily obtained.

<h2 style="text-align:center">Scene 5. Page 490.</h2>

Enter Hecate.

Mr. Tollett has already vindicated Shakspeare from the supposed impropriety of introducing Hecate among *modern* witches. The fact seems to be, that acquainted, as he has elsewhere shown himself to have been, with the classical connection which this deity had with witchcraft, but knowing also, as Mr. Tollett's quotation from Scot indicates, that *Diana* was the name by which she was invoked in modern times, he has preferred the former rather than the latter name of the goddess, for reasons that were best known to himself.

That there existed during the middle ages numerous superstitions relating to a connection that witches were imagined to have had with Diana, it will be no difficult task to prove. From an ecclesiastical statute, promulgated during the reign of Louis II., king of France, it appears that certain mischievous women professed their belief in that goddess, obeying her as their mistress; and that accompanied by her and a great multitude of other females, they travelled over immense spaces of the earth at midnight, mounted upon various animals. Many other ecclesiastical regulations, and some of the councils, notice these superstitions, and denounce very severe vengeance against those persons who were thought to practise them. In one we find the following declaration: "Nulla mulier se nocturnis equitare cum *Diana* dea Paganorum, vel cum *Herodiade* seu *Benzoria* et innumera mulierum multitudine profiteatur; hæc enim dæmoniaca est illusio."— Ducange, *Gloss.* v. Diana. These witches sometimes assembled at the river Jordan, the favourite spot of Diana or Herodias. The Jesuit Delrio very gravely denies the possibility of the above pranks, remarking that there is in reality no Diana, and that Herodias the dancer, whom he here confounds with her daughter, is at present in hell. *Disquisit. magic.* lib. ii. quæst. 16. Eccard, in his preface to Leibnitz's *Collectanea etymologica*, relates that in a journey through Misnia in Saxony, he discovered traces of the German *Hecate* among the peasants in their *frauholde* or *frau faute,* i. e. *lady fate.* John Herold or Herolt, a German friar of the fifteenth century, in one of his Sermons exclaims against those "qui deam, quam quidam *Dianam* nominant, in vulgari *die fraurve unhold* dicunt cum suo exercitu ambulare."—*Sermones discipuli,* serm. xi. He states this practice to have taken place at Christmas time. See likewise Carpentier *Suppl. ad Ducangii glossar.* v. holda. His majesty King James the First, author of that most sapient work entitled *Dæmonologie,* informs his readers that the spirits whom the gentiles called *Diana and her wandering court,* were known among his countrymen by the name of *pharie.* Other appellations of this personage are likewise to be met with, as *Hera, Nicneven,* and *Dame Habunde;* all as the chief or queen of the witches, whom she generally accompanied in their nocturnal dances and excursions through the air.

For the name of *Herodias* it is not easy to account. It may not be deemed a very extravagant conjecture, that the common people had converted Herod's wife into a witch from their abhorrence of her cruelty towards Saint John the Baptist; for the old mysteries have preserved to us the indignant manner in which they treated Pontius Pilate. The circumstance too of her daughter's dancing, compared with the predilection of witches for that amusement, might contribute to the idea. The learned Schiller thinks that *Herodias* was the same as *Juno.* He founds this opinion on the testimony of Gobelinus Persona, a Monk of Paderborn in the fifteenth century, who in his general history of the world had asserted that the Saxons worshipped Juno under the Greek name of *Hera,* and that the common people still believed in the flight of the *lady Hera* through the air about the time of Christmas; a superstition which seems to have been derived from an older notion, that Juno presided over that element. Ducange imagined he had found the name in *Hera Diana;* but he has not brought forward any instance of the use of such an expression. With respect to *Benzoria* or *Bensozia,* very little is known. Carpentier, in his Supplement to Ducange's glossary, conjectures that she was designed for the daughter of Herodias, and to assist in the magic dances. It is not improbable that this character is in some way or other connected with the Irish *Banshee* or *Benshi,* a kind of fairy. In these subjects we can perceive many corruptions which it is impossible to account for.

Dr. Leyden, in p. 318 of the glossary to his edition of *The complaynt of Scotland,* mentions the " gyre carling, the queen of fairies, the great hag *Hecate,* or mother witch of peasants," and cites Polwart's *Flyting of Montgomery* for " *Nicneven* and her nymphs." In the fragment of an old Scotish poem in Lord Hyndford's manuscript, in strict conformity with what has been just advanced concerning *Juno,* she is termed " quene of Jowis." See *Ancient Scot. poems,* 1768, p. 231.

As *Dame Habunde* or *Abunde* has been classed among the names given to the president of the witches, it becomes necessary to take some further notice of her, though a character of an opposite description to those already mentioned. She appears to have been *the genuine queen of fairies,* and of a most innocuous and benevolent disposition, bestowing happiness and *abundance* on all her votaries. In the passage before mentioned in Gobelinus Persona, *Hera* is spoken of as conferring temporal abundance; and although she is represented as flying through the air, it is not by night, nor accompanied by others. Ducange has therefore improperly assimilated her to Diana and her tribe of mischief, and of course his etymology of *Herodias* is rendered very improbable. In an ancient fabliau by Haisiau, never *entirely* printed, *Dame Abunde* is thus introduced :

> " Ceste richesce nus abonde
> Nos lavon de par *Dame Avonde.*"

She is also mentioned in the works of William Auvergne, bishop of Paris, in the fourteenth century, as a spirit enriching the houses that she visited. Delrio adds, that on her coming with the rest of the *good ladies,* the superstitious old women used to provide plenty of victuals for them, leaving all the dishes and wine-vessels uncovered to prevent any obstruction to their getting at the food, and expecting on the occasion nothing but plenty and prosperity. See *Disquisit. magic.* l. ii. quæst. 27. sect. 2. In the life of Saint Germain, bishop of Auxerre, we find these dames paying their respects to the holy man ; and as the story is misrepresented in its most ma-

terial part by Caxton's translation of the *Golden legend,* it shall
be given from a valuable manuscript of the same work much
older than his time. " Narratio. In a tyme he was her-
boured in a place wher men made redy the borde for to go to
dyner aftir he had soupid, and he was gretli merveiled, and
asked for whom the borde was sette aȝen; and thei seide for
the good women that walke by nyȝte; and than Seinte Ger-
mayne ordeyned that nyȝte to be waked. And than at a cer-
teyn hour gret multitude of feendis come to the borde in
liknesse of men and of women. And than Germayn
comaundid him that thei shold not passe thens, and than he
awoke al the meyne, and asked yf thei knewe eny of thoo
persones, and they seide that thei wer her neyȝebores, and
than he sente to her housis, and thei wer alle founde in bedde,
and than thei alle had gret merveile and thouȝte wel that thei
were feendis that had so longe scorned hem."

The *Samogitæ,* a people formerly inhabiting the shores of
the Baltic, and who remained idolaters so late as the fifteenth
century, believed in the existence of a sort of demi-fairies
about a palm high, with beards, whom they called *Kaukie.*
To these little beings they made an offering of all kinds of
food to avert their displeasure. They likewise invoked a deity
called *Putscet* to send them the *Barstuccæ* to live with them
and make them fortunate. To effect this, they placed every
night in the barn a table covered with bread, butter, cheese,
and ale ; and if these were taken away before morning, they
they looked for good fortune, but if left, for nothing but ill
luck. See Lasicius *De diis Samagitarum,* 1615, 4to, pp. 51,
55. A similar superstition prevailed in England, and is thus
recorded in Browne's *Britannia's pastorals,* book i. song 2.

> " Within one of these rounds was to be seene
> A hillocke rise, where oft the *Fairie queene*
> At twy-light sate, and did command her elves
> To pinch those maids that had not swept their shelves :
> And further, if by maidens oversight,
> *Within doores water were not brought at night ;*

Or if they spread no table, set no bread,
They should have nips from toe unto the head :
And for the maid that had perform'd each thing,
She in the water-paile bad leave a ring."

Mr. Bell, in his *Description of the condition and manners of the Irish peasantry*, relates that the fairies or *good people* were supposed to enter habitations after the family retired to rest, to indulge in sportive gambols, and particularly to wash themselves in clean water ; but if there were no water in the house, to play some mischievous tricks in revenge.

Fairies were also, from their supposed place of residence, denominated *waternymphs*, in the Teutonic languages, *wasserfrauwen, wassernixen, nocka, necker,* and *nicker*, terms, excepting the first, manifestly connected with the Scotish *nicneven*, and most probably with our *old nick*. Very great confusion seems to have arisen in the change of sex and appellation among these supernatural beings. This may have been occasioned by the numerous Pagan superstitions to which the common people were still attached long after the promulgation of Christianity, as well as from their excessive ignorance and credulity, which led them to convert the deities of the heathens into phantoms of their own creation. Thus Diana and Minerva were degraded into witches, and Mercury became the prince of fairies. Neptune was metamorphosed into a *waterfairy*, of whom a most curious account is preserved in the *Otia imperii* of Gervase of Tilbury, published in Leibnitz's *Scriptores rerum Brunsvic.* p. 980, and partly copied into Mr. Tyrwhitt's edition of Chaucer's Canterbury tales, vol. iv. 268. It seems probable that the name of Neptune is merely disguised in the Scotish *Nicneven*. Some of the Teutonic glossaries render the word *necker* by *dæmon aquaticus, Neptunus.* A further account of him may be found in Wormii *Monumenta Danica*, p. 17, and in Keysler *Antiquitat. select. septentr.* p. 261, where the etymology of *necker,* viz. from the Latin *necare*, strengthens the preceding conjecture as to that of *Nicneven*, and resolves it into the *destroying or dæmoniacal Neptune*. The reader may likewise consult Wachter's *German glossary* under the word *necker,* where it would have been of some use to the learned author to have known that this mischievous fairy was remarkable for drowning people, and was called *Nocka,* the Danish term, as he states on another occasion, for *suffocating.* Nor would the contrast of character between this being and the *beneficent queen of fairy* amount to any solid objection against the proposed etymology. Whoever may attempt an investigation of the fairy system will be sure of finding the greatest disorder and confusion; nor is it possible at this time to offer any reason that will be quite satisfactory why different qualities were ascribed to beings of similar names by different people. We must rest contented with possession of the fact. Thus *Dame Abunde* has been made to preside over the *white nymphs, white ladies,* or *witte wyven,* who all appear to have been of a mischievous disposition, committing nocturnal depredations on men and cattle, but more particularly on pregnant women and infants, whom they shut up in their subterraneous abodes, from which groans and lamentations, and occasionally melodious sounds were often heard to issue. See Kempius *De orig. Frisiæ,* p. 341. Ben Jonson in his *Sad shepherd* makes the *white faies* to reside in stocks of trees.

But let us now return from this digression to the subject of Hecate or Diana. Under the reign of Hadrian, Saint Taurinus is said to have converted the inhabitants of Evreux in Normandy to the Christian faith, but this was not accomplished until the Devil had been fairly expelled from Diana's temple in the above city. For this purpose, he was with great solemnity enjoined to appear in the presence of all the people, who, as heathens, were extremely terrified, especially as the evil spirit came forth under the form of an Ethiopian, dark as soot, with a long beard, and fire issuing from his mouth. An angel then tied his hands behind him and led him away. This dæmon is believed still to remain at Evreux, frequently appearing to the inhabitants, but is said to be per-

fectly harmless.   He is called *Goblin* by the common people,
who believe that he is restrained from mischief by the merits
of Saint Taurinus.   The reason why he was not at once consigned to the infernal regions, is, that at the command of the
holy bishop he assisted in destroying the idols of the city;
but he is supposed to have received sufficient punishment
in beholding those persons in a state of salvation, whom
during his power he had insultingly regarded as his victims.
See Ordericus Vitalis, p. 555.   In England it appears that
the common people not only feared Diana as a witch, but
that they had on many occasions paid her reverential honours
as a goddess.   This is confirmed by the remains of such
animals as were used in her sacrifices, and also by her own
images found on rebuilding Saint Paul's cathedral.   These
have been particularly described in Dr. Woodward's letter to Sir Christopher Wren in the eighth volume of Leland's *Itinerary*; from which circumstance the doctor very
plausibly inferred that a Roman temple of Diana had been
formerly erected on this spot.   There is preserved a most
curious sermon by Saint Maximus bishop of Turin in the
fifth century, replete with the superstitions that existed in
his time relating to the worship of Diana; nor can it be controverted that she was equally reverenced in this country long
after the introduction of Christianity, when we find from the
testimony of Richard Sporling, a Monk of Westminster in
1450, and a diligent collector of ancient materials, that during
the persecution of Diocletian the inhabitants of London
sacrificed to Diana, whilst those of Thorney, now Westminster, were offering incense to Apollo.   Sir William Dugdale
records that a commutation grant was made in the reign of
Edward I., by Sir William Le Baud, to the dean and canons
of Saint Paul, of a doe in winter on the day of the saint's
conversion, and of a fat buck in summer on that of his com-
memoration, to be offered at the high altar, and distributed
among the canons.   To this ceremony Erasmus has alluded

in his book *De ratione concionandi,* when he describes the
custom which the Londoners had of going in procession to
St. Paul's cathedral with a deer's head fixed upon a spear, accompanied with men blowing hunting-horns.   Mr. Strype
likewise, in his *Ecclesiastical memorials,* vol. iii. p. 378, has
preserved a notice of the custom as practised in Queen Mary's
time, with this addition, that the priest of every parish in
the city arrayed in his cope, and the bishop of London in
his mitre, assisted on the occasion.   Camden had likewise
seen it when a boy, and had heard that the canons of the
cathedral attended in their sacred vestments, wearing garlands
of flowers on their heads.   As to Mr. Selden's *witty conceit*
on the subject, which bishop Gibson inclines to adopt, it is
enough to allude to it, being most certainly unworthy of a
serious confutation.

Some of the above remarks have been offered as hints only
for a more ample investigation of the fairy superstitions of
the middle ages, *so far as they are connected with the religion
of the ancient Romans*; a subject of intrinsic curiosity, and
well deserving the attention of those who may feel interest
in the history of the human mind.

ACT IV.

Scene 1.   Page 497.

1. Witch. Thrice the *brinded cat* hath mew'd.

Dr. Warburton has adduced classical authority for the
connexion between Hecate and this animal, with a view to
trace the reason why it was the agent and favourite of modern
witches.   It may be added, that among the Egyptians the
cat was sacred to Isis or the Moon, their Hecate or Diana,
and accordingly worshipped with great honour.   Many cat
idols are still preserved in the cabinets of the curious, and
the sistrum or rattle used by the priests of Isis is generally

ornamented with the figure of a cat with a crescent on its head. We know also that the Egyptians typified the Moon by this animal, as the Chinese and some of the people of India do now by the rabbit ; but the cause is as likely to remain a mystery as their hieroglyphic mode of writing. Some of the ancients have amused themselves with guessing at the reason. They have supposed that the cat became fat or lean with the increase or wane of the Moon; that it usually brought forth as many young as there are days in a lunar period ; and that the pupils of its eyes dilated or contracted according to the changes of the planet.

Scene 1.   Page 503.

3. Witch. . . . .   slips of yew.

The reason for introducing this tree is, that it was reckoned poisonous. See Batman *Uppon Bartholome*, l. xvii. c. 161.

Scene 1.   Page 505.

Macb. Though you untie the winds, and let them fight
Against the churches.

The influence of witches over the winds had been already discussed by Mr. Steevens in a former note on Act I. Scene 3, and it might be well supposed that their formidable power would be occasionally directed by these mischievous beings against *religious edifices*. It is therefore by no means improbable that in order to counteract this imaginary danger, the superstitious caution of our ancestors might have planted the yew-tree in their church-yards, preferring this tree not only on account of its vigour as an evergreen, but as independently connected, in some now forgotten manner, with the influence of evil powers. Accordingly in a statute made in the latter part of the reign of Edward I., to prevent rectors from cutting down trees in church-yards, we find the following passage : " verum arbores ipsæ, *propter ventorum impetus ne ecclesiis noceant*, sæpe plantantur." This is at least sufficient for the purpose of disproving what has been so often asserted respecting the plantation of yews in church-yards for the purpose of making bows; for although these weapons were sometimes made of English yew, the more common materials employed were elm and hazel, either on account of the comparative scarcity of English yew, or more probably from its inadequacy, in point of toughness, for constructing such bows as our robust and skilful archers were famed for using. Indeed modern experience has proved the truth of the latter supposition; and therefore, whenever yew was used for making the best sort of bows, it was of foreign growth: many of our ancient statutes very carefully provide for the importation of that commodity, which appears to have been chiefly Italian, with other merchandise.

Scene 1. Page 506.

1. WITCH. . . . grease that's sweaten
From the murderer's gibbet.

Apuleius in describing the process used by the witch, Milo's wife, for transforming herself into a bird, says that " she cut the lumps of flesh of such as were hanged." See Adlington's translation, p. 49, edit. 1596, 4to, a book certainly used by Shakspeare on other occasions.

Scene 3. Page 540.

ROSSE. . . . . to relate the manner,
Were, on the *quarry* of these murder'd deer,
To add the death of you.

" *Quarry*," says Mr. Steevens, " is a term used both in hunting and falconry. In both sports it means the game after it is killed." So far this is just, and serves *partly* to explain the passage before us, as well as this in *Coriolanus*, Act I. Scene 1:

" And let me use my sword, I'd make a *quarry*
With thousands of these quarter'd slaves, as high
As I could pitch my lance."

What follows respecting the etymology of the word may not appear quite so correct. Mr. Steevens cites the MS.

Mayster of game, in which the old English term *querre* is
used for the *square* spot wherein the dead game was deposited.
It is simply the French *carré,* but not, as Mr. Steevens
conceived, the origin of *quarry.* It is necessary to state that
quarry not only signified the game that was killed, but, in
falconry, the bird that was pursued or sought after. The
same term is used to express the flight of the hawk after its
prey. In these senses it is probable that the word has been
formed from the French *querir, to seek after,* and that the game
sought after would be called in that language *querie,* whence
our English *quarrie,* the old and correct orthography. The
more modern French term in falconry for pursuing the game
is *charrier.* See René François, *Essay des merveilles de
nature,* 1626, 4to, p. 48.

It is conceived therefore that in both the passages in
Shakspeare *quarry* signifies the spot or *square* in which the
heaps of dead game were placed. Not so in the quotation
from Massinger's *Guardian*; for there *quarry* is evidently
the bird pursued to death.

ACT V.

Scene 5.   Page 570.

Macb. The way to *dusty* death.

Perhaps no quotation can be better calculated to show the
propriety of this epithet than the following grand lines in
The vision of Pierce Plowman, a work which Shakspeare
might have seen :

> " *Death* came drivynge after, and all to *dust* pashed
> Kynges and kaysers, knightes and popes.''

Scriptural language and a passage in the burial service
might have likewise suggested the epithet.

KING JOHN.

ACT I.

Scene 1. Page 19.

Bast. *Good den*, sir Richard.

See former note, p. 139.

Scene 1. Page 26.

Bast. . . . . *Basilisco* like.

This braggadocio character must have been very popular, as his oaths became proverbial. Thus in Fennor's *Compter's commonwealth*, 1617, 4to, we have, "three-pil'd, huge *Basilisco* oaths that would have torn a roring-boyes eares in a thousand shatters."

ACT II.

Scene 1. Page 39.

Ell. His mother shames him so, poor boy, he weeps.
Const. Now shame upon you, whether *she* does, or no!

Mr. Ritson proposes to read, *whether* he *does or no!* i. e. *whether he weeps or not*; and he adds that Constance, so far from admitting, expressly denies that she shames him. It may be answered, that this reading is *equally* objectionable; for Constance admits also that her son wept. In either case there is ambiguity; but the words as they stand are infinitely more natural, and even defensible, according to common usage.

Scene 1.   Page 44.

K. John. Have brought a *countercheck* before your gates.

Mr. Steevens thinks this one of the *old* terms used at chess, but none such occurs in any of the treatises on that game.   It is presumed to be simply a military word.   Thus the Bastard afterwards asks, " shall a silken wanton brave our fields and find no *check* ?" and we still say, " the enemy has received a *check*."

Scene 1.   Page 47.

K. Phi. Command the rest to stand.—*God, and our right* !

An English motto is here improperly put into the mouth of a Frenchman.   Richard the First is said to have originally used DIEU ET MON DROIT.

Scene 2.   Page 64.

K. Phi. . .   Young princes close your hands
Aust.   *And your lips too* ; for, I am well assur'd,
That I did so, when I was first assur'd.

The kiss was a part of the ceremony of affiancing.   Thus in *Twelfth night* :

> " A contract of eternal bond of love,
> Attested by the *holy close of lips*."

See the note in page 67.

ACT III.

Scene 4.   Page 107.

Const. And *buss* thee as thy wife.

In former times there was no vulgarity in this word, as the two first quotations by Mr Steevens demonstrate; but he is peculiarly unfortunate in his last example, which may without detriment be omitted in future editions.   The singular vulgarity of Stanihurst's language cannot with propriety be used to exemplify the undegraded use of any word whatever.

No further proof of the justice of this remark is necessary

than the mention of his " dandiprat cockney Cupido," or the
" *blubbering* Andromache," whom he describes as " stuttering
and stammering to *fumble* out an answer to her sweeting de-
licat Hector ;" and numerous expressions of a similar nature
occur in his eccentric translation of the pure and elegant Virgil. *To buss* is either from the French *baiser,* or from some
radical word common to both languages, and was formerly
written *bass.* Thus Stanihurst, whom it may be allowable to
quote on this occasion ;

" That when Queen Dido shall col thee and smacklye *bebasse* thee :"

And the duke of Orleans, in one of his love poems written
in the time of King Henry the Fifth ;

" Lend me your praty mouth madame
I wis dere hart to *basse* it swete."

SCENE 4. Page 115.

PAND. No natural exhalation in the sky,
No *scape* of nature, no distempered day,
No common wind, no customed event,
But they will pluck away his natural cause,
And call them meteors, prodigies and signs,
Abortives, presages, and tongues of heaven.

The old copy reads *scope* of nature. The alteration was
made by Pope, and plausibly commented on by Warburton,
who seems to have influenced Mr. Malone to adopt it. The
speaker's design is to show that all the *common effects of nature* which he mentions would be *perverted* by the people ;
but an *escape* of nature would be very *properly* deemed *an
abortive.* The original reading is therefore correct; nor could
an apter word have been selected. Thus in *King Henry the
Fourth, Part I.* :

" And curbs himself even of his *natural scope.*"

ACT IV.

Scene 2.   Page 128.

Pemb. If what in *rest* you have, in right you hold.

Mr. Steevens would read *wrest*, which he explains to be *violence*. But surely " the murmuring lips of discontent" would not insinuate that John was an usurper; because the subsequent words, " in right you hold," would then be contradictory. One could not say, " if, being an usurper, you reign by right." The construction may therefore be more simple : " If the power you now possess in *quiet* be held by right, why should your fears," &c. The explanation given by Mr. Malone might have sufficed.

Scene 2.   Page 137.

K. John. It is the curse of kings to be attended
By slaves that take their humours for a warrant
To break within the bloody house of life.

Mr. Malone ingeniously conceives this to be a covert apology for Elizabeth's conduct to the queen of Scots; yet it may be doubted whether any such apology would be thought necessary during the life of Elizabeth. May it not rather allude to the death of the earl of Essex ? If this conjecture be well founded, it will serve to ascertain the date of the composition of the play, and to show that Meres had mistaken the older piece for Shakspeare's.

Scene 2.   Page 139.

K. John. Or turn'd an eye of doubt upon my face,
As bid me tell my tale in express words.

And, and *or,* have been proposed instead of *as,* but without necessity. The words are elliptical in Shakspeare's manner, and only mean, " or turn'd *such* an eye of doubt *as* bid me," &c.

Scene 3.   Page 142.

Sal. Two long days journey lords, *or e'er* we meet.

Dr. Percy has judiciously remarked that *ever* or *e'er* in this phrase is a useless augmentative, *or* being of itself equivalent to *before*. The corruption is not much older than Shakspeare's time. In some of the editions of Cranmer's Bible, *Ecclesiastes* xii. 6 is rendered, " *Or ever* the silver lace be taken away, and *or ever* the golden well be broken." In others the second *ever* is omitted. Wicliffe's translation, an invaluable monument of our language, has it, " *er* be to broke the silveren corde," &c. This is pure Saxon æn or eɲ; and so is our modern *ere*, often erroneously spelled *e'er*, as a supposed contraction of *ever*. Yet in Chaucer's time it had become *or*;

> " For, par amour, I loved hir first *or* thou."
> Knight's tale, v. 1155.

though some copies, both manuscript and printed, read *er* in this place as well as in others. Mr. Steevens seems properly to object to the orthography of *ore*.

ACT V.

Scene 1. Page 155.

Bast. Away then, with good courage; yet I know,
Our party may well meet a *prouder* foe.

Mr. Steevens has noticed Dr. Johnson's misconception of this passage; yet it may be doubted whether he has sufficiently simplified the meaning, which is, " yet I know that our party is fully competent to engage a more *valiant* foe." *Prouder* has in this place the signification of the old French word *preux*.

KING RICHARD II.

ACT III.

SCENE 2. Page 272.

K. RICH. That when the searching eye of heaven is hid
    Behind the globe, *and* lights *the lower world.*

THE slight but necessary emendation of *and* for *that* ascribed
to Johnson, had already been made by Hanmer. *Lower
world* simply means *lower hemisphere.*

SCENE 2. Page 279.

K. RICH. Our lands, our lives, and all are Bolingbroke's,
    And nothing can we call our own, but death.

This resembles Wolsey's speech;

" To the last penny 'tis the king's; my robe
    And my integrity to heav'n, is all
    I dare now call my own."

SCENE 2. Page 279.

K. RICH. And that small *model* of the barren earth.

Model or *module*, for they were the same in Shakspeare's
time, seems to mean in this place, a *measure, portion,* or
quantity.

SCENE 2. Page 280.

K. RICH. . . . . For within the hollow crown
    That rounds the mortal temples of a king
    Keeps death his court; and there the antick sits,
    Scoffing his state, and *grinning* at his pomp.

Some part of this fine description might have been suggested from the seventh print in the *Imagines mortis,* a celebrated series of wooden cuts which have been improperly
attributed to Holbein.   It is probable that Shakspeare might

have seen some spurious edition of this work; for the great scarcity of the original in this country in former times is apparent, when Hollar could not procure the use of it for his *copy* of the dance of death. This note, which more properly belongs to the present place, had been inadvertently inserted in the first part of *Henry the Sixth.* See Act IV. Scene 7, in Mr. Steevens's edition.

SCENE 3. Page 283.

NORTH. Your grace mistakes me; only to be brief
    Left I his *title* out.
YORK.   The time hath been,
    Would you have been so brief with him, he would
    Have been so brief with you, to shorten you,
    For *taking so the head,* your whole head's length.

" *To take the head,*" says Dr. Johnson, " is to act without restraint; to take undue liberties." It is presumed it rather means to take away or omit the sovereign's *chief* and usual *title*; a construction which considerably augments the play on words that is here intended.

KING HENRY IV.

PART I.

ACT I.

Scene 1.   Page 357.

K. Hen. To be commenced in *stronds* afar remote.

This antiquated word, signifying *shores*, seems to have been entitled to some notice by the editors, as it cannot be familiar to every reader.   We have now, perhaps accidentally, restored the original Saxon ᵹcᵣanb.

Scene 1.   Page 357.

K. Hen. No more the thirsty *Erinnys* of this soil
        Shall daub her lips with her own childrens blood.

The original reads *entrance,* which is supported by Mr. Malone and also by Mr. Ritson, to whose authorities might be added the line in Spenser's *Shepherds calendar*;

    "Quenching the *gasping furrowes thirst* with rayne."

The present reading was ingeniously suggested by Mr. Mason, and has been adopted by Mr. Steevens, who, vigorously maintaining its propriety, throws the gauntlet of defiance to all adversaries : but let us not be appalled !

To the assertion that a just and striking personification is all that is wanted on this emergency, the answer is, that we have it already.   *Soil* is personified ; they are *her* lips, and *her* children that are alluded to.   With respect to *Erinnys,* notwithstanding the examples of typographical errors that are adduced, it is highly improbable that it should have been mistaken for *entrance,* a word which has three letters that are wanting in the other.   Again, are the instances common, or

rather do they exist at all, where the *capital letter* of a proper name has been lost in a corruption ? And, lastly, to turn
in part Mr. Steevens's own words against himself, it is not
probable that Shakspeare would have " opened his play with
a speech, the fifth line of which is obscure enough to demand
a series of comments thrice as long as the dialogue to which
it is appended;" or, it may be added, which contained a
name of such unfrequent occurrence, and certainly unintelligible to the greatest part of the audience.

It is often expected, though perhaps rather unreasonably,
that where an opinion is controverted, a *better* should be substituted; yet it does seem just that something at least, in
value equal or nearly so, should be produced, and on this
ground the following new reading is very diffidently offered :

> " No more the thirsty *entrails* of this soil."

In *Titus Andronicus* we have the expression, " the ragged
entrails of this pit."   And in the *Third part of King Henry VI.,*

> " What, hath thy fiery heart so *parch'd* thine *entrails* ? "

Nothing that has been here advanced is calculated to maintain that the name of *Erinnys* must have been obscure to
Shakspeare.   One or two quotations have been already given
from authorities that might have supplied him, to which the
following shall now be added :

> " *Erinnis* rage is growen so fel and fearce."
>> *Last part of the mirour for magistrates,*
>> 1578, fo. 153.

> " On me, ye swarth *Erinnyes*, fling the flames."
>> Turbervile's *Ovid's epistles,*
>> sign. K. ij.

SCENE 2.   Page 367.

FAL. . . . not by Phœbus,—he, *that wandering knight so fair.*

Falstaff, with great propriety, according to vulgar astro-
nomy, calls the sun *a wandering knight,* and by this expression evidently alludes to some hero of romance.   Now though
the *knight of the sun* mentioned by Mr. Steevens, was doubt-

less a great wanderer, he was not more so than others of his profession; and therefore it is possible that Falstaff may refer to another person particularly known by the name of *the wandering knight,* and the hero of a spiritual romance translated in Shakspeare's time from the French by William Goodyeare, under the last-named title. It may be worth mentioning that in all probability John Bunyan used this work in the composition of his *Pilgrim's progress.*

SCENE 2. Page 376.

FAL. 'S blood, I am as melancholy as a *gib cat.*

Captain Grose in his *Dictionary of the vulgar tongue* informs us that a *gib cat* is so called from *Gilbert,* the northern name for a *he cat;* and this is corroborated by the manner in which Chaucer has used the word in question;

> " I mean but gyle, and follow that,
> For right no more than *Gibbe our cat*
> That awaiteth mice and rattes to killen."
> *Rom. of the rose.*

The original French has " dam *Thibert* le chas," which proves that *Gib* was a proper name in Chaucer's time, whatever change it may have since undergone in its feline application. We see too the reason why a *gib* is a *male* cat. The melancholy of this animal has been sufficiently explained. Another quality belonging to him is thus ironically mentioned in the anonymous play of *The politick whore,* 1680; " as *modest* as a *gib-cat* at midnight."

SCENE 2. Page 381.

POINS. What says sir John *Sack-and-sugar?*

In aid of Mr. Malone's conjecture that sack was so called as being a *dry* wine, *vin sec,* it may be remarked that the old orthography was *secke* and not *sack.* Dr. Boorde in his *Regimente of health,* 1562, 12mo, calls it so. In Hollyband's *French schoolemaister,* 1619, 12mo, we have " *secke,* du vin sec." Again, " Some of you chaplaines, get my lorde a cup of *secke,* to comfort his spirites." Ponet's *Treatise of politike power,* 1556, 12mo ; and Cotgrave in his *Dictionary,* makes *sack* to be *vin sec.* This plausible etymology might have been wholly relied on, if an ingenious female traveller in speaking of the Tatar *koumis,* a preparation of mare's milk, had not informed us that she could not choose to partake of it out of the goatskin *sacks* in which it is carried "as the Spaniards," says she, "do their wine ; which, by the by, is a practice so common in Spain, *as to give the name of sack* to a species of sweet wine once highly prized in Great Britain."—Guthrie's *Tour through the Crimea,* 1802, 4to, page 229. More stress is to be laid on this matter from a remarkable coincidence mentioned by Isidore of Seville, in his *Etymologies,* book iii. ch. 4, where he states *saccatum* to be a liquor made from water and the dregs of wine passed through a sack. See also Ducange *Gloss.* v. *Saccatum,* and Carpentier's supplement, v. *Saquatum.*

Whatever has been said in the course of the scattered notes concerning Falstaff's *sack* is so confused and contradictory, that it will be the duty of a future editor, either to concentrate them for the purpose of enabling the reader to deduce his own inference ; or, rejecting them altogether in their present form, to extract from the materials they supply, the best opinion he may be able to form. There are two principal questions on the subject : 1. Whether sack was known in this country in the time of Henry the Fourth ? 2. Whether it was a dry or a sweet wine when this play was written ? The first is very easily solved ; for there appears to be no mention of it till the 23rd year of Henry the Eighth, when a regulation was made that no malmseys, romineis, *sackes* nor *other sweet* wines, should be sold for more than three-pence a quart. The other question is full of difficulties, and the evidence relating to it very contradictory. We see it was a *sweet* wine before Shakspeare's time, a circumstance that may be noticed as adverse to the etymology of *sec.* But if it was sweet, whence the use of sugar, which we do not find to have been added to other sweet wines? The testimony of Dr. Venner proves that sack was drunk either with or without sugar, *according to the palate*. The quality of this wine, originally sweet and luscious, might have undergone a change, or else some other *Spanish* wine less saccharine in its nature might have obtained the name of sack.

Scene 2. Page 385.

Poins. . . and *sirrah*, I have cases of buckram, &c.

Mr. Malone has in this and some other places maintained that *sirrah* was not used as a term of disrespect in Shakspeare's time; but the learned commentator would probably have revised his opinion had he recollected the quarrel between Vernon and Basset in the first part of Henry the Sixth, where, in the most opprobrious manner, *sirrah* is answered by *villain*. It seems to have been used much in the same way as at present, sometimes expressing anger and contempt, yet more frequently in a milder way when addressed to children and servants. It was even applied to women.

Scene 3. Page 399.

Hot. And if the Devil come and *roar* for them.

This line would be highly relished by an audience accustomed in Shakspeare's time to "Satan's chaunt," on some of the minor stages. On the theatrical *roaring* of the Devil, see the notes of Messrs. Steevens and Malone in *King Henry V.* Act IV.

Scene 3. Page 403.

Wor. As to o'er-walk a current, roaring loud,
On the unsteadfast footing of a spear.

He seems to allude to the practice of making a bridge by means of a sword or a spear sometimes adopted by the heroes of ancient chivalry. See *Lancelot of the lake*, and other similar romances. Such an incident is represented on an ivory chest engraved in the first volume of Mr. Carter's *Specimens of ancient sculpture and painting.*

Scene 3. Page 407.

Hot. And that same *sword-and-buckler* prince of Wales.

To convey to the reader a complete idea of a sword-and-buckler man of Shakspeare's time, the following print of a young Englishman is exhibited. It is taken from the collection of dresses designed by Titian, and said to have been engraved on wood by his brother Cesar Vecelli, the editor of which remarks that the English youths then made great use of the sword and buckler. A similar figure occurs in the frontispiece to Cranmer's Bible, designed by Holbein, which has been most unfaithfully copied in Lewis's *History of the translations of the bible.* Mr. Strutt has given more correct copies of the man with the buckler in his *Manners and customs of the inhabitants of England,* vol. iii. pl. xii. and in his *Dress and habits of the people of England,* pl. cxxxviii.

The subject receives much illustration from a passage in *Stowe's chronicle*, p. 869, edit. 1634 : " Untill about the twelfe or thirteenth yeere of Queene Elizabeth the auncient English fight of sword and buckler was onely had in use : the bucklers then being but a foote broad, with a pike of foure or five inches long. Then they began to make them full halfe ell broad with sharpe pikes ten or twelve inches long wherewith they meant either to breake the swords of their enemies, if it hit upon the pike, or els suddenly to run within them and stabbe, and thrust their buckler with the pike, into the face, arme or body of their adversary ; but this continued not long. Every haberdasher then sold bucklers." The above historian had, no doubt, good authority for what he says respecting the length of the *pike* ; but it is certain that in the eighth year of Elizabeth a proclamation was issued by which no person was permitted to wear any sword or rapier that should exceed the length of one yard and half a quarter in the blade, nor any dagger above the length of twelve inches in the blade, *nor any buckler with a poiut or pike exceeding the length of two inches.* The mode of wearing the buckler at the back may be seen in the cut p. 209.

Scene 3.   Page 407.

Hot. I'd have him poison'd with a pot of ale.

Mr. Steevens suggests that this speech has reference to the prince of Wales's pot companions, and Dr. Grey to the manner of King John's death.   It will indeed suit either of those circumstances.   But this remark has been principally made for the purpose of correcting an error of long standing with respect to what has been generally called *Caxton's chronicle*. Dr. Grey, relying perhaps on Bale or Nicolson, has inaccurately cited Caxton's *Fructus temporum* for the account of King John's death ; yet this work was never printed by Caxton under that title.   It was professedly compiled by a schoolmaster of Saint Alban's, and originally printed in that city in 1483. In this form it is properly called *The Saint Alban's chronicle*, and is in fact a republication of one attributed to Caxton, with some additions at the beginning and end. The original often occurs in manuscript both in French and English ; and, from the evidence of an ancient note in one copy preserved among the Harleian manuscripts, appears to have been composed by a monk of Glastonbury, named Douglas, who in the early part of it has copied Geoffrey of Monmouth. This work has been commonly ascribed to Caxton, and is often cited, even by old writers, under the name of *his* chronicle, though he only made a trifling addition by a continuation to his own time. It is likewise supposed to have been *originally printed* by him, but this is in all probability a mistake ; for there is an edition undoubtedly printed by William Machlinia without date, which had escaped the observation of the correct and industrious Herbert. The type is the same as that used in the *Speculum Christiani*. This is presumed to be the prior edition which is spoken of in the prologue to that which Caxton printed in 1480, and there is no proof whatever that he printed any edition before that year.

ACT II.

Scene 3.   Page 436.

Lady Per. Of *basilisks*, of cannon, *culverin*.

In the note we are only told that " a *basilisk* is a cannon of a particular kind." It is well known that there was a serpent so called, perhaps an imaginary one ; and this animal with others of a like nature being sculptured on the ancient pieces of artillery, supplied them with the various appellations of *serpentines, culverines,* (from the French *couleuvre,*) *flying dragons,* &c. Of these the *basilisk* was the largest. It was sometimes called a *double culverine,* and was much used about the middle of the sixteenth century, especially by the Turks.

It must have been of a prodigious size, as it carried a ball of near two hundred pounds weight. Coryat mentions that he saw in the citadel of Milan "an exceeding huge basiliske which was so great that it would easily contayne the body of a very corpulent man."—*Crudities*, p. 104, quarto edition. Father Maffei, in his History of the Indies, relates that Badur, king of Cambay, had at the siege of Chitor four basilisks of so large a size that each was drawn by a hundred yoke of oxen, so that the ground trembled beneath them.

SCENE 3.   Page 438.

LADY PER. In faith *I'll break thy little finger, Harry.*

This "token of amorous dalliance" is more particularly exemplified in an ancient song, entitled *Beware my lyttyl fynger*, reprinted by Mr. Ritson from Sir John Hawkins's History of music.

As the learned historian has not stated whence he procured this piece, it may be worth adding that it occurs in a small oblong quarto volume of songs with music, printed, according to appearance, by Wynkyn de Worde, in 1530; but as it varies in some instances from the reading in Sir John's work it is possible that he might have used some other authority.

SCENE 4.   Page 442.

P. HEN. I am no proud Jack, like Falstaff; but a *Corinthian*, a lad of mettle.

The celebrity of Lais, the Corinthian courtezan, is said to have occasioned the proverb cited in Mr. Steevens's note, because from the extravagance of the lady's demands *every one could not afford to go to Corinth*, which, says Taverner, in his *Proverbs or adagies of Erasmus*, 1569, 12mo, is of like sense with our English proverb, *Every man may not be a lord*. We are told by Strabo that the temple of Venus at Corinth was furnished with a thousand young girls who performed the rites of the goddess. In short, that city appears to have been so notorious for its luxury, that ancient writers are full of allusions on this subject. See particularly Aristophanes's *Plutus*, Act I. Scene 2, and Saint Paul's first epistle to the *Corinthians*, ch. v. verse 1. This may serve to explain why *wenchers* were called *Corinthians*.

Scene 4. Page 444.

FRAN. Anon, anon, sir.

This was the *coming, sir,* of the waiters in Shakspeare's time. In *Summer's last will and testament,* Harvest says, " Why, friend, I am no *tapster* to say, *anon, anon, sir.*

Scene 4. Page 461.

P. HEN. Thou *knotty-pated* fool.

Although it certainly stands thus in the old copy, the word should be changed without scruple to *nott-pated,* i. e. polled or cropped. The prince had a little before bestowed the same epithet on the drawer. In this place it may refer to the practice of nicking or cropping naturals.

Scene 4. Page 461.

FAL. What upon compulsion ? No ; were I at the *strappado,* or all the racks in the world, I would not tell you on compulsion.

As the *strappado* has been elsewhere improperly defined " a chastisement by blows," under an idea that a strap was used on the occasion, it may be necessary to take further notice of it on this occasion. It *was* a military punishment, by which the unfortunate sufferer was most inhumanly tortured in the following manner :—a rope being fastened under his arms, he was drawn up by a pulley to the top of a high beam, and then suddenly let down with a jerk. The consequence usually was a dislocation of the shoulder blade. Representations of this nefarious process may be seen in Breughel's print of *The punishments of the law* ; in one of Gerini's fine *Views of Florence,* and in Callot's *Miseries of war.* The term is evidently taken from the Italian *strappare,* to pull or draw with violence. At Paris there was a spot called *l'estrapade* in the fauxbourg St. Jaques, where soldiers received this punishment. The machine, whence the place took its name, remained fixed like a perpetual gallows.

Scene 4. Page 468.

FAL. . . . he of Wales, that gave *Amaimon* the bastinado.

Amaimon, king of the East, was one of the *principal devils* who might be bound or restrained from doing hurt from the third hour till noon, and from the ninth hour till evening. See Scot's *Discovery of witchcraft,* B. xv. ch. 3.

ACT III.

Scene 1. Page 487.

GLEN. The front of heaven was full of fiery shapes
Of burning *cressets*.

A cresset light was the same as a beacon light, but occasionally portable. It consisted of a wreathed rope smeared with pitch and placed in a cage of iron like a trivet, which was suspended on pivots in a kind of fork. The light sometimes issued from a hollow pan filled with combustibles. The term is not, as Hanmer and others have stated, from the French *croissette,* a little cross, but rather from *croiset,* a cruet or earthen pot; yet as the French language furnishes no similar word for the cresset itself, we might prefer a different etymology. Our Saxon glossaries afford no equivalent term, but it may perhaps exhibit a Teutonic origin in the German *kerze,* a light or candle, or even in the French *cierge,* from *cereus,* because the original materials were of wax. Stowe the historian has left us some account of the marching watches that formerly paraded many of the streets of London, in which he says that "the whole way ordered for this watch extended to two thousand three hundred taylors yards of assize, for the furniture wherof with lights there were ap-

pointed *seven hundred cressets*, five hundred of them being
found by the companies, the other two hundred by the chamber of London.   Besides the which lights every constable in
London, in number more than two hundred and forty, had his
cresset, the charge of every *cresset* was in light two shillings
fourepence, and every *cresset* had two men, one to beare or
hold it, another to beare a bagge with light, and to serve it :
so that the poore men pertaining to the *cressets*, taking wages,
besides that every one had a strawne hat, with a badge painted,
and his breakfast in the morning, amounted in number to
almost two thousand."—*Survay of London*, 1618, 4to, p. 160.
The following representations of *ancient cressets* have been
collected from various prints and drawings.

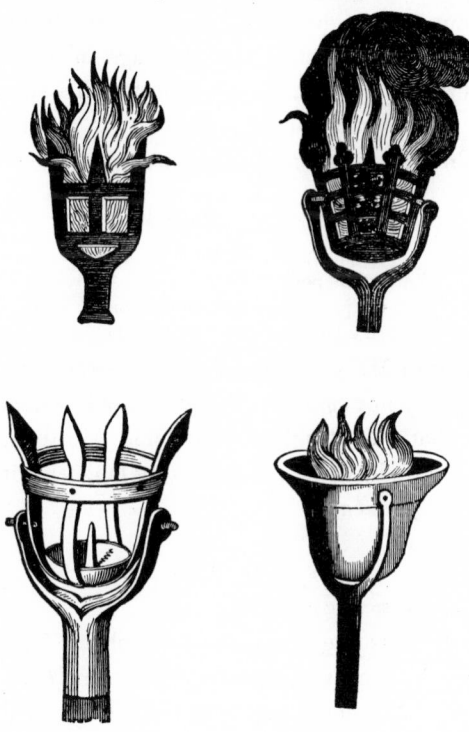

SCENE 1.   Page 492.

HOT. And cuts me from the best of all my land,
> A huge half-moon, a monstrous *cantle*.

The word in its *strict* sense, signifies a *small* piece of any
thing, but here a portion or parcel.   The French have *chan-
teau* and *chantel*, from the Latin *quantulum*.

SCENE 1.   Page 494.

GLEN. . . . I framed to the harp
> Many an English ditty, lovely well,
> And gave *the tongue* a helpful ornament,
> A virtue that was never seen in you.

" Glendower means," says Mr. Ritson, " that he graced
his *own* tongue with the art of singing."   This is surely wrong.
The meaning is, that, by setting the English ditties to Welsh
music, he had embellished the language in a manner that
Hotspur had never done, the roughness of his speech affording neither poetry nor music.   *Tongue* was rightly explained
by Dr. Johnson, *the English language*.

SCENE 1.   Page 499.

MORT. . . . that pretty Welsh
> Which thou pourest down from these *swelling heavens*
> I am too perfect in ; and but for shame,
> In such a parley would I answer thee.

According to Mr. Steevens, *swelling heavens* are prominent
lips.   Are they not *eyes swollen with tears* ?   Glendower had
just said that his daughter wept ; and Mortimer tells his
wife that he would answer the melting language of her eyes,
if it were not *for shame*.

SCENE 2.   Page 508.

P. HEN. By smiling *pick-thanks*.

A pick-thank is one who gathers or collects favour, thanks,
or applause, by means of flattery.   " Cave ne *falsam gratiam*
studes inire."   Terence ; which is thus Englished by Udall

in his *Floures for Latine spekynge*, 1533, 12mo, fo. 137 :—
" Beware that thou desire not to *pyke* or to have a *thanke* of
me undeserved."

SCENE 3.   Page 522.

FAL. I never see thy face, but I think upon hell-fire.

Falstaff's wit at the expense of poor Bardolph's ruby face
is inexhaustible.   The same subject is treated with considerable humour in the following passage in Melton's *Astrologas-
ter*, 1620, 4to : " But that which most grieves me, is, most
of the varlets belonging to the citie colledges (I meane both
the prodigious compters) have *fierie red faces*, that they cannot put a cup of Nippitato to their *snowts*, but with the extreme heat that doth glow from them, they make it cry hisse
again, as if there were a gadd of burning steele flung into the
pot," &c.

SCENE 3.   Page 528.

FAL. There's no more truth in thee, than in a *drawn fox*.

The quotation from Olaus Magnus does not support Mr.
Steevens's assertion that the fox when *drawn* out of his hole
was supposed to counterfeit death ; for it is stated by that
writer, and indeed by others, that he uses this device when
hungry, to attract the birds, who mistake him for carrion.
The following passage from Turbervile's *Noble arte of venery
or hunting* is offered, but with no great confidence, as a possible illustration of the phrase in question : " Foxes which
have been beaten have this *subtletie*, to *drawe* unto the largest
part of the burrow where three or foure angles meete together, and there to stand at baye with the terriers, to the ende
they may afterwardes shift and goe to which chamber they
list."

SCENE 3.   Page 535.

P. HEN. Go bear this letter to lord John of Lancaster, &c.

The first seven lines of this speech are undoubtedly prose,
and should be so printed, like the preceding speeches of the
Prince. No correct ear will ever receive them as blank verse,

notwithstanding the efforts that have been or shall be made
to convert them into metre.

ACT IV.

Scene 1.   Page 543.

Ver. All plum'd like *estridges*, that *wing* the wind
     Bated like eagles having lately bath'd :

The evident corruption or mutilation in these lines, has
rendered any attempt to explain them a task of great difficulty.   It will be necessary in the first place to ascertain
the exact sense of the word *estridge*; and although it is admitted that the *ostrich* was occasionally so denominated by
our old writers, it is by no means certain that this bird is
meant in the present instance.   It may seem a very obvious
comparison between the feathers of a crested helmet and
those of the ostrich; and had the expression *plum'd like estridges* stood *singly*, no doubt whatever could have arisen.
It is what follows that occasions the difficulty.

The old copies read, *with the wind* : now if the ostrich had
been here alluded to, the conjectural substitution of *wing*
would have been absolutely requisite; but the line which follows cannot by any possible construction be made to apply to
that bird.   It relates altogether to falconry, a sport to which
Shakspeare is perpetually referring.   Throughout the many
observations on these difficult lines, it has been quite overlooked that *estridge* signifies a *goshawk*.   In this sense the
word is used in *Antony and Cleopatra*, Act III. Scene 2 :

  " And in that mood [of fury] the dove will peck the *estridge*."

There is likewise a similar passage in the third part of
King Henry VI., which may serve as a commentary on the
above line :

      " So cowards fight, when they can fly no further;
       So *doves* do peck the *faulcon's* piercing talons."

It would be absurd to talk of a dove pecking an ostrich; the allusion is to the practice of flying falcons at pigeons. Thus Golding in his translation of *Ovid's metamorphoses,* fo. 9 :

" With flittering feather sielie *doves* so from the *gosshawk* flie."

The manor of Radeclyve in Nottinghamshire was held by the service of " mewing a goshawk ;" in the original charter, "mutandi unum *estricium*." In the romance of *Guy earl of Warwick* we have,

" *Estrich falcons,* of great mounde."

Falconers are often called *ostregers* and *ostringers* in the old books of falconry, and elsewhere. *Estridge* for *ostrich* or *ostridge* is a corrupt spelling that crept into the language at the commencement of Queen Elizabeth's reign, and it appears that after that period the two words were very often confounded together, and used one for the other.

The explanation of *to bate,* as cited from *Minsheu* in one of the notes, cannot apply to *ostriches,* though it does, very properly, to a bird of prey like the falcon.

After all, there is certainly a line lost, as Mr. Malone has very justly and ingeniously conjectured; but the place should rather seem to have been *after* the word *bath'd,* than *before.* The sense of the old copies, as to what remains, will then be tolerably perspicuous :

" All plum'd like estridges, that with the wind
Bated, like eagles having lately bath'd
*　*　*　*　*　*　* "

i. e. plumed like falcons, which, their feathers being ruffled with the wind, like eagles that have recently bathed, *make a violent fluttering noise*; the words in Italics being here conjecturally offered as something like the sense of the omitted line.

SCENE 1. Page 546.

VER. I saw young Harry with his *beaver on.*

There are two other passages in Shakspeare's plays that relate to the *beaver*, which it will be best to insert here for the purpose of avoiding confusion, and to afford likewise the means of assembling together the various and discordant opinions of the commentators. These are, 1. in *King Henry IV.* Part II. Act IV. Scene 1, " their beavers *down* ;" and 2. in *Hamlet*, Act I. Scene 2, " he wore his beaver *up*."

In the first of these passages Dr. Warburton would read *with his beaver up* ; and he remarks that " the *beaver* is only the *visiere* of the helmet, which, let down, covers the face. When the soldier was not upon action, he wore it *up*, so that his face might be seen, but when upon [in] action, it was let down to cover and secure the face." All this is correct, except that the beaver is certainly not the visor.

Dr. Johnson says, " there is no need of all this note ; for beaver may be a helmet." This too is very just ; the beaver, a part only of the helmet strictly speaking, is frequently used to express a helmet generally. Thus, in the first scene of the third part of *King Henry VI.*, " I cleft his *beaver* with a downright blow." The latter part of the doctor's note was unnecessary, and its inference apparently wrong.

Mr. Malone remarks that " Dr. Warburton seems not to have observed, that Vernon only says, he saw *youny Harry*, not that he saw his *face*." But surely, Dr Warburton having contended for the reading *beaver up*, could not have misconceived Vernon's meaning as above.

Dr. Lort contents himself with distinguishing and explaining the beaver and visor. He is however wrong in stating that the beaver was *let down* to enable the wearer to drink.

Mr. Malone's second note relating to *Hamlet*, will be considered in the third passage.

In the second passage, Mr. Malone remarks that the *beaver* " is confounded both here and in *Hamlet* with visor, or used for *helmet* in general," but that " Shakspeare is not answerable for any confusion on this subject, as he used *beaver* in the same sense in which it was used by all his contemporaries."

The latter part of this note applies very justly to the first passage, *beaver on,* where it is used generally for a *helmet,* but not to the present; *beavers down* being perfectly accurate. It is submitted that the former part of the note, which relates to a supposed confusion both here and in Hamlet between *beaver* and *visor,* is not quite accurate, as may hereafter appear.

In the third passage Mr. Malone says, "though *beaver* properly signified that part of the helmet which was *let down,* to enable the wearer to drink, Shakspeare always uses the word as denoting that part of the helmet which, when raised up, exposed the face of the wearer; and such was the popular signification of the word in his time. In Bullokar's *English expositor,* 8vo, 1616, *beaver* is defined thus:—' In armour it signifies that part of the helmet which may be *lifted up* to take the breath more freely.' " On this passage Mr. Malone had also before remarked that Shakspeare confounded the *beaver* and *visor;* for in *Hamlet* Horatio says that he saw the old king's face, because he wore his *beaver up;* and yet the learned commentator inadvertently quotes Bullokar's definition, which is adverse to his own opinion. Another observation that suggests itself on Mr. Malone's note on *Hamlet* is, that Shakspeare does *not always* use *beaver* to denote that part of the *helmet* which, when raised up, exposed the face of the wearer; because we have just seen that he *sometimes,* as other writers do, applies it to the *whole* of the helmet.

And lastly, as to preceding notes; the present writer had, in defending Shakspeare's accuracy, expressed himself in most faulty and inaccurate terms, when he said that " the beaver was as often made to lift up as to let down." A great deal of confusion has arisen from the want of due attention to these words.

There is a chance that the reader, unless he have paid more attention to what has already been stated than it perhaps deserves, may have got into a labyrinth; from which it shall be the endeavour of the rest of this note to extricate him.

In the first place, no want of accuracy whatever is imputable to Shakspeare.

The *beaver* of a helmet is frequently used by writers, improperly enough, to express the helmet itself. It is in reality the lower part of it, adapted to the purpose of giving the wearer an opportunity of taking breath when oppressed with heat, or, without putting off the helmet, of taking his repast. As it was *raised up* for this purpose, it could of course be *let down* again; but it could not be *let down* on either of the before-mentioned occasions. The *visiere* or *visor* was another moveable part in the front of a helmet, and placed above the beaver in order to protect the upper part of the face; and being perforated with many holes, afforded the wearer an opportunity of *discerning* objects : and thence its name. It was made also to *lift up* when the party either wanted more air, or was desirous of seeing more distinctly. It was perhaps never down but in actual combat; whilst the beaver would be thrown up or *kept* down at the wearer's discretion, without much difference, except that in battle it would be closed, and at meals, or for additional coolness, thrown up. In short, the visor or beaver could only be *let down* after they had been already lifted up; and when a writer speaks of their being *down*, it is generally meant that the helmet is closed.

To exemplify the above remarks, correct representations of a real helmet and its parts are here given. See likewise Grose's *Treatise on ancient armour*, plates 10, 26, 30.

Fig. 1. The helmet closed.
Fig. 2. The visor thrown up, the beaver down.
Fig. 3. The visor and beaver thrown up.
Fig. 4. The visor detached.
Fig. 5. The beaver detached.

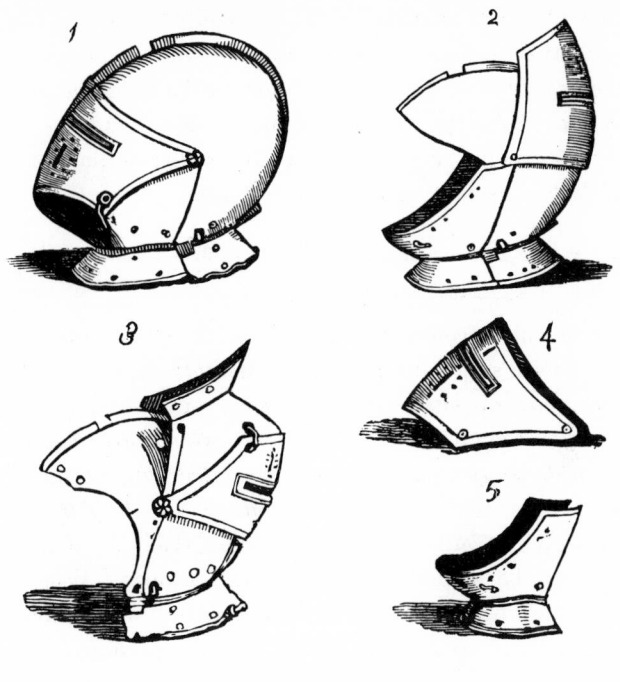

ACT V.

SCENE 1. Page 567.

P. HEN. Of fickle changelings, and poor discontents,
Which gape and *rub the elbow*, at the news
Of hurly burly innovation.

The *itching of the elbow*, according to popular belief, denoted an approaching change of some kind or other.

SCENE 4. Page 587.

HOT. . . . . . and life *time's fool.*

Mr. Steevens could not very easily have supported his
opinion, that the allusion here is to the fool in the ancient
farces, or in the representations called the *Dance of death*;

a character which has been altogether misconceived in the course of the annotations on Shakspeare. Dr. Johnson's interpretation is much more natural and intelligible, and the allusion is certainly to the common or domestic fool, who was retained for the express purpose of affording *sport* to his still more foolish employers. In this sense our author uses *death's fool, fortune's fool*, and *fate's fool*.

SCENE 5. Page 589.

P. HEN. *Embowel'd* will I see thee by and by.

An ingenious commentator on Mr. Mason's supplement to Dr. Johnson's dictionary, (see the *Monthly magazine*, vol. xii. p. 299,) has disputed the usual sense of *embowel'd* in this speech, on the ground that the prince would not be guilty of such *brutality* as to see Falstaff *eviscerated*; and he therefore contends that the meaning is, *put into the bowels of the earth*. But surely the prince designs no more than that Falstaff's body shall be embalmed in the usual manner. When the knight rises, he exclaims, " if thou embowel me to day, I 'll give you leave to *powder me*, and eat me to-morrow," evidently alluding to the practice of evisceration and subsequent treatment of a dead body by strewing aromatics over it for preservation. If the body were to be *put into the bowels of the earth*, as the commentator contends, Falstaff's " eat me to-morrow " would manifestly be an absurd expression. That the present writer may not be suspected of plagiarism on this occasion, he feels himself obliged to lay claim to the above opinion in answer to the commentator, as it appeared in the before-mentioned periodical publication.

But the following curious extract from the arraignment of Hugh Le Despenser, the favourite of Edward II., will set the question at rest for ever : " *Hugh* contraytour este trove, par quoy vous agardent touz lez bonez gentz de realme, meyndrez et greyndres, ryches et povrez par comun assent, que vous come larone estes trove, par quey vous serrez pendue. Et contreytour estez trove, par quey vous serrez *treynez** et quarterecez, et envoye parmy le realme. Et pur ceo que vous fuistez utlage par nostre seignour le roy et par commune assent, et estez revenue en courte sanz garrant, vous serrez decollez. Et pur ceo que vous abbestatez et procurastez discorde entre nostre seignour le roy et la royne et lez altrez del realme, si serret *enbouelleez*, et puis ils serront ars. Retrayez vous traytour, tyrant reneyee, si alez vostre juyse prendre. Traytour malveys et attaynte." In English. " *Hugh Le Despencer*, you have been found an arch-traitor, for which cause all good people of the realm, great and small, rich and poor, by common consent, award you a convicted felon; *therefore you shall be hanged.* And forasmuch as you have been found a traitor, *you shall be drawn and quartered, and [your limbs] dispersed throughout the kingdom.* And having been outlawed by our lord the king, and by common assent, you have unwarrantably returned into court ; *and therefore you shall be beheaded.* And because you have procured and abetted discord between our lord the king, and the queen, and others of the realm, *you shall be embowelled, and [your bowels] afterwards burnt.* Begone traitorous renegade tyrant, and await the execution of your sentence. Wicked and attainted traitor !"—Knighton, inter *Historiæ Anglicanæ decem scriptores,* col. 2549.

The author of *Aulicus coquinariæ,* 1650, speaking of the opening of King James the First's body, has these words : "The next day was solemnly appointed for *imbowelling* the corps, in the presence of some of the counsell, all the physicians, chirurgions, apothecaries, and the Palsgrave's physician."

We got this word from the *old* French *eboeler,* the orthography of which at once declares its meaning. With us

---

* This word may serve to correct a mistake in a note in *King Richard III.,* Act V. Scene 2, by Dr. Johnson, who had supposed that *drawn* was the same as *exenterated.*

it might perhaps be more properly written *ebowel,* if the ear were not likely to be offended by the change.

Foote has borrowed some hints from Falstaff's speeches, in his admirably drawn character of Mother Cole. Among others take the following:—" Now am I, if a man should speak truly, little better than one of the wicked. I must give over this life, and I will give it over." He immediately changes his praying into pursetaking. See particularly the beginning of the third scene in the third act. Our English Aristophanes seems to have been likewise indebted to a story related in Lord Bacon's *Apophthegms,* of an old bawd who on her death-bed was interrogated by a customer whether a wench whom she had provided for him was in all respects as she had promised; to which she answered, *that she was; and further left it to him to judge with what comfort and confidence she could expect to meet her Saviour, if she should leave the world with a lie in her mouth.*

KING HENRY IV.
PART II.

ACT I.

SCENE 1. Page 11.

TRA. Up to the *rowel head.*

DR. JOHNSON had either forgotten the precise meaning of the word *rowel*, or has made choice of inaccurate language in applying it to the *single spiked spur* which he had seen in old prints. The former signifies the moveable spiked *wheel* at the end of a spur, such as was actually used in the time of Henry the Fourth, and long before the other was laid aside. Shakspeare certainly meant the spur of his own time.

SCENE 1. Page 13.

NORTH. Even such a man so faint so spiritless,
So dull, so dead in look, so *woe-begone*,
Drew Priam's curtain in the dead of night, &c.

Dr. Bentley's proposed substitution of *Ucalegon* for *woe-begone*, is a most striking example of the uselessness of learning when unaccompanied with judgment to direct it. Where too had the doctor found that Ucalegon drew Priam's curtain? and, it may be added, where did Shakspeare find that any one did so? It is not very uncommon for our poet to forget his reading, and make events change places. Thus a little further on, he has confounded Althea's firebrand with Hecuba's; and it is not improbable that in the present instance he might have misapplied the vision of Hector to Æneas so finely described in the second book of the Æneid.

SCENE 3. Page 46.

HAST. The *duke* of Lancaster and Westmorland.

Mr. Malone's note on this anachronism would be more

perfect if this slight addition were made to it, " and then not duke of *Lancaster* but of *Bedford*." Mr. Ritson seems to have traced the source of Shakspeare's error in calling prince John of Lancaster *duke* of Lancaster, in Stowe's *Annales*; but he has omitted to remark that even then Shakspeare had forgotten that prince John was not the *second* son of Henry the Fourth. The blunder of the industrious historian is unaccountable. See the seal of Henry the Fifth as prince of Wales and duke of Lancaster in Sandford's *Genealogical history*.

ACT II.

Scene 1. Page 49.

> Host. A hundred mark is a long *loan* for a poor lone woman to bear.

The old copy reads long *one*, and the above alteration has, on the suggestion of Theobald, been very improperly and unnecessarily made. The hostess means to say that a hundred mark is a long *mark*, that is *score, reckoning*, for her to bear. The use of mark in the singular number in familiar language admits very well of this equivoque.

Scene 2. Page 64.

> Page. Marry, my Lord, Althea dream'd she was delivered of a fire-brand.

Dr. Johnson has properly noticed the error concerning Althea's firebrand. This mythological fable is *accurately* alluded to in 2 *Henry VI.* Act I. Scene 1; a circumstance that may perhaps furnish an additional argument, though a slight one, that that play was not written by Shakspeare.

Scene 4. Page 91.

> Pist. Have we not *Hiren* here.

The notes on this expression have left it a matter of doubt whether Pistol is speaking of his sword or of a woman; but the fact is, after all, that the word Hiren was purposely designed by the author to be ambiguous, though used by Pistol with reference *only* to his sword. When the hostess replies, " There's none such here, do you think I would deny her ?" she evidently conceives that he is calling for some wench. Pistol, not regarding her blunder, *continues to handle his sword, and in his next speech* reads the motto on it—SI FORTUNA ME TORMENTA, SPERATO ME CONTENTA. It is to be observed that most of the ancient swords had inscriptions on them, and there is no doubt that if diligent search were made, the one before us, in a less corrupted state, would be found. In the mean time the reader is presented with the figure of an old French *rapier,* in the author's possession, on which these lines are engraved: SI FORTUNE ME TOURMENTE L'ESPERANCE ME CONTENTE.

In further illustration, the following story from *Wits, fits and fancies,* 1614, 4to, is added :—" Haniball Gonsaga being in the low countries overthrowne from his horse by an English captaine, and commanded to yeeld himselfe prisoner: *kist his sword* and gave it the Englishman saying: *Si fortuna me tormenta, il speranza me contenta.*" Part of this story had already been quoted by Dr. Farmer, but not for a similar purpose.

SCENE 4.   Page 94.

FAL. Quoit him down, Bardolph, like a *shove-groat* shilling.

Mr. Steevens supposes the *shove-groat* shilling to have been used in the game of shovel-board, by which he seems to infer that the games of *shove-groat* and *shovel-board* were the same; but this is apparently a mistake. The former was invented during the reign of Henry the Eighth ; for in the statutes of his 33rd year, chap. ix., it is called a *new* game. It was also known by the several appellations of *slide-groat*, *slide-board, slide-thrift*, and *slip-thrift*, the first of which was probably adopted from the game being originally played with the silver groats of the time, then nearly as large as modern shillings. When the broad shillings of Edward the Sixth were coined, they were substituted for the groats in this game, and used also at that of *shovel-board*, which seems to have been only a variation of the other on a larger scale. Nothing has occurred to carry it beyond the time of Henry the Eighth ; and from the want of such a term as a *shovel-groat*, it is probably not older than the reign of Edward the Sixth, who first coined the shilling piece. *Shovel-board* is already two well known to require any description of it in this place ; but of the other little seems recorded, or not sufficient to discover the manner in which it was played. Holinshed, or rather Stanihurst, in his history of Ireland, speaking of a mandate for the execution of the Earl of Kildare in the reign of Henry the Eighth, says, that " one night when the lieutenant and he for their disport were playing at *slidegrote* or *shofleboorde*, sodainly commeth from the Cardinall (Wolsey) a mandatum to execute Kyldare on the morrow. The earle marking the lieutenant's deepe sigh, By S. Bryde, Lieutenant, quoth he, there is some made game in that scrole ; but fall how it will, *this throwe is for a huddle.*" Here the writer has either confounded the two games, or might only mean to state that the Earl was playing at one or the other of them. Rice the puritan, in his *Invective against vices*, black letter, no date, 12mo, speaks of " paysed [weighed] *groates* to plaie at slip-thrifte ;" and in another place he asks whether God sent Adam into Paradise to play at it. There is a modern game called *Justice Jervis*, which is supposed by Mr. Strutt, who has described it at large, to bear some resemblance to *shove-groat.* See his *Sports and pastimes*, p. 225.

SCENE 4.   Page 94.

PIST.   Why then let grievous, ghastly, gaping *wounds*
       Untwine the sisters three.   Come *Atropos,* I say!

This is manifestly in ridicule of Sackvile's *Complaynt of Henry Duke of Buckingham,* in *The mirour for magistrates* :

   " Where eke my graundsire, Duke of Buckingham
     Was *wounded* sore, and hardly scapt untane.
     But what may boote to stay the *sisters three?*
     When *Atropos* perforce will cut the *thred.*"

                                  Stanzas 5 and 6.

SCENE 4.   Page 96.

PAGE.   The musick is come, sir.
FAL.   Let them play ;—play, sirs.

This music was, in all probability, that belonging to one of those dances called *passameasures* ; and it appears to have afterwards travelled by some means or other to *Barbadoes* : for Ligon, in his entertaining account of that island, where he was in 1647, tells us that he heard it played there by an *old fellow.* Ligon, no doubt, remembered it on the stage, and it is very likely to have been the *original* music of Shakspeare's time ; but the above writer has very ignorantly supposed it to have been " a tune in great esteem in Harry the Fourth's dayes."

SCENE 4.   Page 98.

FAL.   Drinks off candles ends for *flap-dragons* ; and *rides the wild mare* with the boys.

A *flap-dragon* is a sport among choice spirits, by putting nuts or raisins into a bowl of brandy, which being set on fire, the nuts are snatched out hastily and swallowed, the party usually burning his mouth and fingers. In this way men formerly drank healths to their mistresses. It is likewise a Christmas gambol among young people, at which, instead of brandy, spirits of wine are used. It is sometimes called *slap-dragon* and *snap-dragon.* In *The laws of drinking,* 1617, 12mo, p. 147, a person is said to be " as familiar as *slap-dragons* with the *Flemming.*"

Riding the wild mare, is another name for the childish sport of *see-saw,* or what the French call *bascule* and *balançoire.*

<h3 style="text-align:center">SCENE 4. Page 100.</h3>

FAL. . . and breeds no bate with telling of *discreet* stories.

Dr. Warburton would most unnecessarily read *indiscreet.* Mr. Steevens supposes that " by *discreet stories* is meant what suspicious masters and mistresses of families would call *prudential information*; i. e. what ought to be known, and yet is disgraceful to the teller." But Poins, of whom Falstaff is speaking, had no masters or mistresses; and if it be recollected with what sort of companions he was likely to associate, Falstaff's meaning will appear to be, that *he excites no censure for telling them modest stories*; or in plain English, that he tells them nothing but *immodest* ones.

<h3 style="text-align:center">SCENE 4. Page 102.</h3>

FAL. What stuff wilt have a *kirtle* of?

Notwithstanding this word has excited as much conjecture as almost any other in the language, it will still admit of discussion. *Kirtel* is pure Saxon, and signifies, generally, a *covering,* i. e. over all the other garments; in which sense it will always be found to have been [properly] used. In Littelton's Dictionary it is Latinized *supparum.* See likewise Ducange's *Glossary,* and a multitude of other authorities. Hence probably *covercle.* From the circumstance of its occurring as often in the sense of a long as of a short garment, it is more probable that the root of the word should denote that which *covers,* simply, than something that is *short, curtus.* In one of the notes, Cotgrave is cited as making *kirtle* and *petticoat* synonymous; but this definition is at variance with the line in the comedy of *Ignoramus,*

" Gownos, silkcotos, *kirtellos* et *peticotos.*"

It is admitted, however, that this word has been used with

great latitude of meaning. Randle Holme makes it the same with the apron.

SCENE 4. Page 104.

FAL. Ha! a bastard son of the king's?—And art not thou *Poins his brother?*

Mr. Ritson explains this *the brother of Poins.* But where is the use of asking the *prince* such a question? It must be remembered that the prince and Poins have just made their appearance, and Falstaff has a question for *each.* The sense therefore is, " Art not thou Poins, the brother of this bastard?"

ACT III.

SCENE 2. Page 135.

BULL. . . . here is four *Harry ten shillings* in French crowns for you.

This is an anachronism; there were no coins of ten shillings value in the reign of Henry the Fourth. Shakspeare's *Harry ten shillings* were those of Henry the Seventh or Eighth, but he thought these might do for any other Harry.

SCENE 2. Page 140.

SHAL. I was then Sir Dagonet in Arthur's show.

The question whether Shallow represented Sir Dagonet at Mile-end green, or Clement's inn, although it has been maintained on either side with great plausibility, must ever remain undecided; but Mr. Malone's acute and ingenious conjecture that *Arthur's show* was an *exhibition of archery,* and not an *interlude,* will no longer admit of any doubt. The truth of both these positions will appear from the following circumstances: In 1682 there was published " A remembrance of the worthy *show* and shooting by the Duke of Shoreditch and his associates the worshipful citizens of London upon Tuesday the 17th of September 1583, set forth according to the truth thereof to the everlasting honour of the game of shooting in the long bow. By W. M." in p. 40 of which book is this passage: "The prince of famous memory King Henry the Eighth, having red in the chronicles of England, and seen in his own time how armies mixed with good archers have evermore so galled the enemy, that it hath been great cause of the victory, he being one day *at Mile-end when prince Arthur and his knights were there shooting* did greatly commend the game, and allowed thereof, lauding them to their encouragement." One should be very much inclined to suppose this decisive of the first question, and that these *shows* were usually held at *Mile-end*; but this is by no means the case. The work proceeds to state that King Henry the Eighth, keeping at one time a princely court at Windsor, caused sundry matches to be made concerning shooting with the long bow; at which one Barlo, who belonged to his majesty's guard, remaining to shoot, the king said to him, "Win thou all, and thou shalt be duke over all archers." Barlo drew his bow and won the match ; whereat the king being pleased, commended him for his good archery; and the man dwelling in Shoreditch, the king named him *Duke of Shoreditch*. One of the successors to this duke appointed a *show* on the 17th of September 1583, to be held in Smithfield and other parts of the city, which is here very circumstantially described ; and among many other curious particulars it is mentioned that the citizens and inhabitants of Fleetbridge, &c. followed with a *show* worth beholding of seemly archers ; "then the odd devise of *Saint Clements parish*, which but ten days before had made the same *show* in their own parish, in setting up the queen's majesties stake in Holborn fields, which stakemaster Knevit, one of the gentlemen of her majesties chamber, gave unto them at his cost and charges ; and a *gunn* worth three pound, made of gold, to be given unto him that best deserved it by shooting in a peece at the mark which was set up on purpose at Saint Jame's wall." This however was not solely a shoot-

ing with fire-arms, but also with bows : for in the account of
the *show* itself, which immediately follows, men bearing
" shields and shafts" are mentioned, and " a worthy *show of
archers following.*" In the continuation of the description of
the Smithfield *show*, mention is made of "the baron *Stirrop*,
whose costly stake will be in memorys after he is dead, now
standing at *Mile-end*;" and again, "And this one thing is
worthy of memory: that upon the day of *Prince Arthur's
shooting*, which was five weeks before this show, the duke,
willing to beautifie the same in some seemly sort, sent a buck
of that season by the marquess *Barlo*, (the name of this person was kept up long after his decease,) accompanied with
many goldsmiths, who coming in satten dublets and chains
of gold about their bodies, with horns at their backs, did all
the way wind their horns, and presented the same to *prince
Arthur*, who was at his tent, which was at *Mile-end-green*."

We see therefore that Shakspeare having *both these shows*
in his recollection, has made Shallow, a talkative simpleton,
refer to them indistinctly, and that probably by design, and
with a due attention to the nature of his character. What
Shallow afterwards says about the management of the *little
quiver fellow's* piece, or *caliver*, will not weigh in either scale ;
because in all these *shows* there were musketeers. In that
at Smithfield the feryers marched, consisting of " one hundred handsome fellowes with *calivers* on their necks, all trimly
decked with white feathers in their hats." *Maister Thomas
Smith*, who in Mr. Malone's note is said to have personated
Prince Arthur, was "chiefe customer to her majesty in the
port of London ;" and to him Richard Robinson, a translator
of several books in the reign of Elizabeth, dedicated his
*Auncient order, societie and unitie laudable of Prince Arthure
and his knightly armory of the round table, with a threefold
assertion frendly in favour and furtherance of English archery
at this day*, 1583, 4to. Such part of this work as regards

Prince Arthur is chiefly a translation from the French, being a description of the arms of the knights of the round table; the rest is a panegyric in verse by Robinson himself in praise of archery. It appears from the dedication that King Henry VIII. confirmed by charter to the citizens of London, the " famous order of knightes of prince Arthur's round table or society: like as in his life time when he sawe a good archer in deede, he chose him and ordained such a one for a knight of the same order." Hearne says this book was so scarce in his time that he could never get a copy of it. See preface to Leland's *Collectanea*, p. liii.

Whatever part Sir Dagonet took in this show would doubtless be borrowed from Mallory's romance of the *Mort Arture*, which had been compiled in the reign of Henry VII. What there occurs relating to Sir Dagonet was extracted from the excellent and ancient story of *Tristan de Leonnois*, in which Dagonet is represented as the fool of king Arthur. He is sometimes dressed up in armour and set on to attack the knights of Cornwall, who are uniformly described as cowards. It once happened that a certain knight, who for a particular reason had been called *Sir Cotte mal taillée* by Sir Kay, king Arthur's seneschal, was, at the instance of Sir Kay, attacked by poor Dagonet; but the latter was very soon made to repent of his rashness and thrown over his horse's crupper. On another occasion Tristan himself, in the disguise of a fool, handles Sir Dagonet very roughly; but he, regardless of these tricks of fortune, is afterwards persuaded to attack Mark the king of Cornwall, who is in reality a coward of the first magnitude. Mark, supposing him to be Lancelot of the lake, runs away, and is pursued by the other; but the persons who had set on Sir Dagonet, becoming apprehensive for the consequences, followed them, as " they would not," says the romance, " for no good, that Sir Dagonet were hurt; for king Arthur loved him passing well, and made him knight .

with his owne hands." King Mark at length meets with another knight, who, perceiving his cowardice, attacks Dagonet and tumbles him from his horse.

In the romance of *Sir Perceval li Gallois*, Kay, the seneschal of Arthur, being offended with Dagonet for insinuating that he was not the most valorous of knights, kicks him into the fire. So much for the hero personated by Master Justice Shallow.

Scene 2. Page 146.

Fal. . . . . this *Vice's* dagger——

To each of the proposed etymologies of *Vice* in the note there seem to be solid objections.

Hanmer's derivation from the French *visdase*, is unsupported by any thing like authority. This word occurs in no ancient French writer as a theatrical character, and has only been used by modern ones in the sense of ass or fool, and then probably by corruption; there being good reason to suppose that it was originally a very obscene expression. It is seldom, if ever, that an English term is made up from a French one, unless the thing itself so expressed be likewise borrowed; and it is certain that in the old French moralities and comedies there is no character similar to the *Vice*.

Mr. Warton says it is an abbreviation of *device*, because in the old dramatical shows this character was nothing more than a *puppet moved by machinery*, and then originally called a *device*. But where is the proof of these assertions, and why should *one puppet in particular* be termed a *device*? As to what he states concerning the name of the smith's machine, the answer is, that it is immediately derived from the French *vis*, a screw, and neither probably from *device*; for the machine in question is not more a device than many other mechanical contrivances. Mr. Warton has likewise informed us that the vice had appeared as a puppet *before* he was introduced into the early comedies; but it would be no easy task to maintain such an opinion. Nor is it by any means

clear that Hamlet, in calling his uncle a *vice,* means to compare him to a *puppet* or *factitious* image of majesty; but
rather simply to a *buffoon,* or, as he afterwards expresses it,
a *king of shreds and patches.* The puppet shows had, probably,
kings as well as *vices* in their dramas; and Hamlet might as
well have called his uncle at once, a *puppet king.*

What Mr. Steevens has said on this subject in a note to
Twelfth night, vol. iv. 146, deserves a little more consideration.
He states, but without having favoured us with proof, that
the vice *was always acted in a mask;* herein probably recollecting that of the modern Harlequin, the *illegitimate* successor to the old vice. But the mask of the former could
have nothing to do with that of the latter, if he really wore
any. Admitting however that he might, it is improbable that
he should take his name from such a circumstance; and even
then, it would be unnecessary to resort, with Mr. Steevens,
to the French word *vis,* which, by the bye, never signified a
mask, when our own *visard,* i. e. a covering for the *visage,*
would have suited much better.

A successful investigation of the origin and peculiarities of
this singular theatrical personage would be a subject of extreme curiosity. The etymology of the word itself is all that
we have here to attend to; and when the *vicious* qualities
annexed to the names of the above character in our old dramas, together with the mischievous nature of his general
conduct and deportment, be considered, there will scarcely
remain a doubt that the word in question must be taken *in its
literal and common acceptation.* It may be worth while just
to state some of these curious appellations, such as *shift,
ambidexter, sin, fraud, vanity, covetousness, iniquity, prodigality, infidelity, inclination;* and many others that are either
entirely lost, or still lurk amidst the impenetrable stores of
our ancient dramatic compositions.

ACT IV.

SCENE 3. Page 174.

COLE. I am a knight, sir; and my name is *Colevile of the dale.*

" At the king's coming to *Durham,* the Lord Hastings, *Sir John Colevile of the dale,* &c., being convicted of the conspiracy, were *there* beheaded."—Holinshed, p. 530.

The above quotation has not been appositely made by Mr. Steevens. It appears very soon afterwards in this scene that *Colevile* and his confederates were sent by prince John to *York* to be beheaded.

It is to be observed that there are two accounts of the termination of the archbishop of York's conspiracy, *both* of which are given by Holinshed, who likewise states that on the archbishop and the earl marshal's submission to the king and to his son prince John, there present, " their troupes skaled and fledde their wayes, but being pursued, many were taken, many slain, &c., the archbishop and earl marshal were brought to Pomfret to the king, who from thence went *to Yorke whyther the prisoners were also brought and there beheaded.*" It is this account that Shakspeare has followed, but with some variation; for the names of Hastings and Colevile are not mentioned among those who were so beheaded at York.

Mr. Ritson, in an additional note, says it is not clear that *Hastings and Colevile* were taken prisoners in *this* battle; meaning, it is presumed, the skirmishes with " the scattered stray" whom prince John had ordered to be pursued, including Hastings and Colevile. It is however *quite clear* from the testimony of the parliament rolls, that *they were taken prisoners* in their flight from *Topcliffe,* on the borders of *Galtree forest,* where they had made head against the king's army, and were dispersed by prince John and the earl of Westmoreland.

Scene 3. Page 176.

Fal. . . if you do not all shew like *gilt two-pences* to me——

He means to say, " you will seem no more in comparison to me than a gilt two-pence does to a coin of real gold." It was the practice to gild the smaller pieces of silver coin in the reign of Elizabeth.

Scene 3. Page 178.

Fal. . . 'twere better than your *dukedom*.

Mr. Ritson justly observes that prince John had no dukedom, and in a former note pointed out a passage in Stowe's annals which had misled Shakspeare. The annalist repeated his error, strange as it is, in the account of the conspiracy. Holinshed always names prince John properly.

ACT V.

Scene 1. Page 207.

Shal. By *cock and pye*, sir, you shall not away to night.

This oath has been supposed to refer to the sacred name, and to that service book of the Romish church which in England, before the reformation, was denominated a *pie*; but it is improbable that a volume with which the common people would scarcely be acquainted, and exclusively intended for the use of the clergy, could have suggested a popular adjuration.

It will, no doubt, be recollected, that in the days of ancient chivalry it was the practice to make solemn vows or engagements for the performance of some considerable enterprise. This ceremony was usually performed during some grand feast or entertainment, at which a roasted peacock or pheasant, being served up by ladies in a dish of gold or silver, was thus presented to each knight, who then made the particular vow which he had chosen, with great solemnity. When this custom had fallen into disuse, the peacock nevertheless continued to be a favourite dish, and was introduced on the table in a *pie*, the head, with gilded beak, being proudly elevated above the crust, and the splendid tail expanded. Other birds of smaller value were introduced in the same manner, and the recollection of the old peacock vows might occasion the less serious, or even burlesque, imitation of swearing not only by the bird itself but also by the *pie*; and hence probably the oath *by cock and pie*, for the use of which no very old authority can be found. The vow to the peacock had even got into the mouths of such as had no pretensions to knighthood. Thus in *The merchant's second tale, or the history of Beryn,* the host is made to say,

> "*I make a vowe to the pecock* there shal wake a foul mist."

There is an alehouse sign of the *cock and magpie,* which seems a corruption of the *peacock pie.* Although the latter still preserved its genuine appellation of *the cock and pie,* the magic art of modern painters would not fail to produce a metamorphosis like that which we have witnessed on many other occasions.

Scene 1. Page 211.

Fal. . . . if to his men, I would *curry* with Master Shallow——

To curry is the same as to *curry favour,* to flatter, to please. *To curry,* in its genuine acceptation, is, as every one knows, to rub or dress leather, in French *courroyer,* from *cuir*; and in this sense it was applied to rubbing down a horse's hide, a process that conveys a sensation of pleasure to the animal. The rest of the phrase is corrupt, as will appear from the ancient orthography, which is, to curry *favel.* Thus in the old story *How a merchande dyd hys wyfe betray,* we have,

> "There sche *currayed favell* well;"

and in the prologue to *The merchant's tale of Beryn,* in **Urry's** Chaucer, p. 597,

> "As though he had lerned *cury favel* of some old frere."

Now the name of *Favel* was anciently given to yellow-coloured horses, in like manner as *Bayard, Blanchard,* and *Lyard* were to brown, white, or gray.   One of Richard the First's horses was so called, as we learn from Robert of Brunne's *Chronicle,* p. 175 :

> " Sithen at Japhet [Jaffa] was slayn *faurelle* his stede,
> The romance tellis grete pas ther of his douhty dede :"

and see Warton's *Hist. of Engl. poetry,* vol. i. p. 161.   It must be obvious, therefore, that the phrase *to curry favel* was a metaphorical expression adopted from the stable.

Puttenham informs us that moderation of words tending to flattery, or soothing, or excusing, is expressed by the figure *paradiastole,* " which therefore," says he, " nothing improperly we call *curry favell,* as when we make the best of a thing," &c.—*Arte of English poesie,* p. 154.   There is likewise a pro- verb, " He that will in court dwell, must needes *currie fabel;*" the meaning of which was not well understood, even in the time of Elizabeth ; for Taverner speaking of it says, " Ye shal understand that fabel is an olde Englishe worde, and signified as much as favour doth now a dayes."—*Proverbes or adagies gathered out of the Chiliades of Erasmus,* 1569, 18mo, fo. 44. Much about this time began the corruption from *favel* to *favour,* of which an example may be seen in Forrest's transla- tion of *Isocrates,* 1580, 4to, fo. 23.

It is necessary to add that *favel* is also an old word that ex- presses *deceit,* from the French *favele,* fabula ; and is so used by Skelton : but this will not invalidate the foregoing ety- mology.   As to Skinner's derivation of *curry favour* from the French *querir faveur,*—if an equivalent phrase had existed in the French language, it might at least have been plausible : but there is no instance of *cury,* or rather *curray,* the proper word, being used alone in the sense of *to seek* ; nor does it appear from *ancient* authority that *favel* ever denoted *favour.*

Scene 2.   Page 217.

Cᴴ. Jᴜsᴛ. And struck me in my very seat of justice.

In a note on this passage, the anachronism of continuing

Gascoine chief justice in the reign of Henry the Fifth has been adverted to. The fault is properly to be ascribed to the author of the old play of *Henry the Fifth,* from which Shakspeare inadvertently adopted it.

SCENE 3.　Page 229.

SIL. And dub me knight.

The following addition to the ceremony of dubbing topers knights *on their knees* in Shakspeare's time, from a contemporary pamphlet, may not be unacceptable: " The divell will suffer no dissensions amongst them untill they have executed his wil in the deepest degree of drinking, and made their sacrifice unto him, and most commonly that is done *upon their knees being bare.* The prophaneness whereof is most lamentable and detestable, being duely considered by a Christian, to think that that member of the body which is appointed for the service of God is too often abused with the adoration of a harlot, or a base drunkard, as I. myself have been (and to my griefe of conscience) may now say have in presence, yea and amongst others, been an actor in the business, when *upon our knees,* after healthes to many private punkes, a health have been drunke to all the whoores in the world."—Young's *England's bane,* or the *description of drunkennesse,* 1617, quarto.

SCENE 4.　Page 238.

DOL. You *blue-bottle* rogue.

This allusion to the dress of the beadle is further confirmed by the *two beadles in blew gownes* who are introduced in the fourth act of the old play of *Promos and Cassandra,* which at the same time furnishes additional illustration of Mr. Steevens's remark on the strumpet's dress, as Polina is there exhibited doing penance in a *blue habit.*

SCENE 5.　Page 241.

1. GROOM. More rushes, more rushes.

Dr. Bullein, who speaks much in general commendation of

the rush for its utility, informs us, that " rushes that grow
upon dry groundes be good to strew in halles, chambers and
galleries, to walke upon, *defending apparell, as traynes of
gownes and kertles from dust.* Rushes be olde courtiers, and
when they be nothing worth, then they be cast out of the
doores; so be many that do treade upon them."—*Bulwarke
of defence,* 1579, fol. 21. The *length* of the *kirtle* is here
ascertained, and Mr. Malone's account of it in this respect
fully confirmed. See his note in Act II. Scene 4, of this
play.

SCENE 5.   Page 248.

CH. JUST. Go, carry Sir John Falstaff to the Fleet.

Every body will agree with Dr. Johnson in the impropriety
of Falstaff's cruel and unnecessary commitment to prison.
The king had already given him a fit admonition as to his
future conduct, and banished him to a proper distance from
the court. We must suppose therefore that the chief justice
had far exceeded his royal master's commands on this occasion, or that the king had repented of his lenity. The latter
circumstance would indeed augur but unfavourably of the
sovereign's future regard to justice; for had he not himself
been a partaker, and consequently an encourager, of Falstaff's
excesses ? On the stage this scene may very well be spared.
The audience will be better pleased at the poor knight's
retiring with his companions under the impression that the
king's behaviour to him has been necessarily disguised. No
one will wish to see him *punished.*

KING HENRY V.

Page 263.

CHORUS. O for a muse of fire, &c.

"THIS," says Dr. Warburton, "goes upon the notion of the Peripatetic system, which imagines several heavens, one above another; the last and highest of which was one of fire." We have here one of the very best specimens of the doctor's flights of fancy. Shakspeare, in all probability, knew nothing of the Peripatetic philosophy; he simply wishes for poetic fire, and a due portion of inventive genius. The other explanation by Dr. Johnson seems likewise too refined.

Page 264.

CHORUS. . . . Can this cock-pit hold
The vasty fields of France? or may we cram
Within this wooden O, the very casques
That did affright the air at Agincourt?

Dr. Johnson has elsewhere remarked that Shakspeare was fully sensible of the absurdity of showing battles on the theatre, which, says he, is never done but tragedy becomes a farce. The whole of this chorus receives considerable illustration from a passage in Sir Philip Sidney's *Defence of poesie*, where, speaking of the inartificial management of time and place in the theatres of his time, he thus proceeds: "where you shall have Asia of the one side and Affricke of the other, and so many other under-kingdoms, that the player when he comes in, must ever begin with telling where hee is, or else the tale will not be conceived. Now shall you have three ladies walke to gather flowers, and then we must beleeve the stage to bee a garden. By and by we heare newes of shipwracke in the same place, then we are too blame if we accept it not for a rocke.   Upon the backe of that comes out a hidious monster with fire and smoke, and then the miserable beholders are bound to take it for a cave : *while in the meane time two armies flie in, represented with foure swordes and bucklers, and then what hard hart will not receive it for a pitched field ?*   Now of time they are much more liberal.   For ordinarie it is that two young princes fall in love, and after many traverses she is got with child, delivered of a faire boy ; he is lost, groweth a man, falleth in love, and is ready to get another child ; and all this in two houres space : which how absurd it is in sence, even sence may imagine : and art hath taught, and all ancient examples justified, and at this day the ordinary players in Italie will not erre in."   These remarks might with great propriety be applied to the play before us, to the *Winter's tale,* to *Pericles,* and some others of Shakspeare's dramas.   In France, the contemporary play-wrights were commonly more observant of the unities, though many charges to the contrary might be brought against them.

ACT I.

Scene 2.   Page 277.

K. Hen. Therefore take heed how you impawn *our* person,
How you awake the sleeping sword of war.

Dr. Johnson would read *your person,* and then explain it, " take heed how you pledge your honour, &c. in support of bad advice."   The archbishop might indeed pledge his *opinion* in this case ; but *person* must in all events belong to the *king.* It was he who had the prerogative of making war ; and as the impawning of a thing is generally attended with a risk of its future loss, so the king may here allude to the danger of his own person, which, from the practice at that time of sove-reigns to engage in battle, might not be inconsiderable.

Scene 2. Page 281.

CANT. . . . Also king Lewis the *tenth*.

Shakspeare having here adopted *Holinshed's error* in substituting Lewis the *Tenth* for Lewis the *Ninth*, Mr. Malone has faithfully discharged his editorial duty in permitting it to remain. It was sufficient to point out the mistake in a note; and therefore Mr. Ritson's genealogy, designed to vindicate the text, but *manifestly erroneous*, should be omitted.

Scene 2. Page 291.

CANT. They have a king, and officers of *sorts*.

Sorts, if the true reading, rather means *portions* or *companies*, than *of different kinds*, according to Mr. Steevens; and such is the sense of the word in Mr. Reed's quotation, " drummes and *sortes* of musicke," though adduced in support of Mr. Steevens. In that much disputed verse 13 of the 68th psalm, the Greek word *cleros*, very strangely introduced into the *Vulgate translation*, is rendered by Wicliffe *sortis*; and in another old translation, *lottes*.

Scene 2. Page 295.

K. HEN. . . . . . . or else our grave
Like Turkish mute, shall have a tongueless mouth,
Not worship'd with a *waxen* epitaph.

The question is whether *paper*, the reading of the quarto, or *waxen* of the folio, should be adopted. Mr. Malone very justly remarks that the passage has been misunderstood, and, not finding any construction of waxen that agrees with the sense required, seems disposed to give the preference to *paper* of which epithet he has offered a very ingenious explanation. The alteration in the folio was doubtless occasioned by some dissatisfaction with the former word, and made with a view to improvement: but no satisfactory meaning can be gathered from the term *waxen*, as connected with the noun *wax*; and the passages adduced by Mr. Steevens afford a sense entirely opposite to what is required. It seems to have been forgotten that *waxen* is the participle to *wax*, to grow, to increase, to *expand*. Thus in *Hamlet*, Act I. Scene 3, we have,

> " . . . . but as this temple *waxes*,
> The inward service of the mind and soul
> *Grows* wide withall——"

In *A Mids. N. Dream*, Act II. Scene 1,

> " And then the whole quire hold their lips and loffe,
> And *waxen* in their mirth——"

In *Titus Andronicus*, Act III. Scene 1,

> " Who marks the *waxing* tide *grow* wave by wave."

A *waxen* epitaph may be therefore a *long* or *protracted* one, such as a king would expect.

SCENE 2.   Page 298.

> K. HEN. Tell him he hath made a match with such a *wrangler*,
> That all the courts of France will be disturb'd
> With *chaces*.

Dr. Johnson informs us that *chace* is a term at tennis. It is *often*, not always, necessary to know more of a term than that it belongs to some particular science. A *chace* at tennis then is that spot where a ball falls, beyond which the adversary must strike his ball to gain a point or chace. At long tennis it is the spot where the ball leaves off rolling. We see therefore why the king has called himself a *wrangler*.

ACT II.

Page 304.

> CHOR. And by their hands this grace of kings must die
> (If hell and treason hold their promises,)
> Ere he take ship for France, and in Southampton.
> Linger your patience on; and well digest
> The abuse of distance, while we force a play.
> The sum is paid; the traitors are agreed;
> The king is set from London; and the scene
> Is now transported, gentles, to Southampton.

An unnecessary transposition of these *most plain and intelligible* lines has been offered by Dr. Johnson, on *his* supposition that every one who reads them "looks about for a meaning which he cannot find." In confirmation of their original arrangement, we learn from Stowe and Holinshed, the historians whom Shakspeare followed, and Dr. Johnson perhaps never thought worth consulting, that the plot against the king was laid by the conspirators at Southampton; a circumstance that is weakened, if not altogether cancelled, by the proposed alteration. See a speech by King Henry in the ensuing act.

SCENE 1. Page 314.

PIST. No; to the *spital* go,
  And from the powdering tub of infamy
  Fetch forth the *lazar kite of Cressid's kind*
  Doll Tear-sheet, she by name——

This alludes to the punishment of Cressida for her faisehood to Troilus. She was afflicted with the leprosy, "like a *Lazarous*," and sent to the "spittel hous." See Chaucer's *Testament of Creseide.*

SCENE 2. Page 324.

K. HEN. If that same dæmon, that hath gull'd thee thus,
  Should with his *lion gait* walk the whole world——

This very uncommon comparison of the devil to a lion seems to have been suggested by 1 Pet. v. 8. "The devil as a roaring *lion walketh about*, seeking whom he may devour."

SCENE 3. Page 329.

QUICK. 'A made a finer end, and went away, an it had been any *christom* child.

It was the ancient practice at baptism not only to use water, but oil, which from the Greek was denominated chrism, whence the name of the *chrisome* or white cloth in question. The priest first made the sign of the cross with the holy oil on the child's breast and between the shoulders, saying, " I anoint thee with the oil of health, in Christ Jesus our lord, that thou mayest inherit eternal life. Amen." After the usual immersion in water, he made another cross on its head with the oil. Then the chrisome was put on, the priest asking at the same time the child's name, and saying, " Receive this white, pure and holy vestment which thou shalt wear before the tribunal of our lord Jesus Christ that thou mayest inherit eternal life. Amen." This chrisome might be used a second time on a similar occasion, and then it was not to be applied to any common use, but brought back and deposited in the church. The *chrisome* was an emblem of the Christian purity communicated by baptism, and which it was expected the party should maintain during life; and it might also, as Ducange conjectures, have been used for the purpose of preventing the oil from running off. It was sometimes ornamented with a sort of crown worked in crimson thread, alluding to the passion of Christ, and the crown or reward of eternal life obtained by his sacrifice. It was to be worn seven days, being taken off on the eighth, as symbolical of the seven ages of man's life; or, according to others, of the passage from the sabbath of mortal life to that of eternity. It was also thought to refer to the influence of the seven planets. The above ceremony took place *before* the reformation; afterwards several changes were made. The use of oil was omitted, and the chrisome worn by the child till the mother's purification by the ceremony of churching, when it was returned to the church. If the child died before the latter rite, it was buried in the chrisome; and this is probably the reason why children were called chrisoms in the bills of mortality. Dame Quickly simply compares the manner of Falstaff's exit to that of a young infant.

ACT III.

SCENE 5. Page 369.

BOUR. They bid us—to the English dancing schools,
    And teach *lavoltas high*, and swift corantoes.

The *lavolta*, as the name implies, is of Italian origin. The man *turns* the woman round several times, and then assists her in making a *high* spring or cabriole. This dance passed from Italy into Provence and the rest of France, and thence into England. Monsieur Bodin, an advocate in the parliament of Paris, and a very savage and credulous writer on demonology, has gravely ascribed its importation from Italy into France, to the power of witches. The *naiveté* with which that part of the *lavolta* which concerns the management of the lady in making the *volta* is described by Thoinot Arbeau, an author already quoted, is extremely well worth transcribing, particularly as the book is seldom to be met with. " Quand vouldrez torner, laissés libre la main gaulche de la damoiselle, et gettés vostre bras gaulche sur son dos, en la prenant et serrant de vostre main gaulche par le faulx du corps au dessus de sa hanche droicte, et en mesme instant getterez vostre main droicte au dessoubz de son busq pour layder à saulter quand la pousserez devant vous avec vostre cuisse gaulche : Elle de sa part mettra sa main droicte sur vostre dos, ou sur vostre collet, et mettra sa main gaulche sur sa cuisse pour tenir ferme sa cotte ou sa robbe, affin que cueillant le vent, elle ne monstre sa chemise ou sa cuisse nue : Ce fait vous ferez par ensemble les tours de la *volte,* comme cy dessus a esté dit : Et après avoir tournoyé par tant de cadances qu'il vous plaira, restituerez la damoiselle en sa place, ou elle sentira (quelque bonne contenance qu'elle face) son cerveau esbranlé, plain de vertigues et tornoyements de teste, et vous n'en aurez peult estre pas moins : Je vous laisse à considerer si cest chose bien seante à une jeusne fille de faire de grands pas et ouvertures de jambes : et si en ceste volte l'honneur et la santé y sont pas hazardez et interessez." And again : " Si vous voulez une aultre fois dancer la volte à main droicte, vous fauldra mettre vostre main droicte sur le doz de la damoiselle, et la main gaulche soubz son busq, et en la poussant de la cuisse droicte soubz la fesse, torner le revers de la tabulature cy dessus. Et nottez qu'il y a dex-

terité à empoigner et serrer contre vous la damoiselle, car il
faut ce faire en deux mesures ternaires, desmarchant sur la
premiere mésure pour vous planter devant elle, et sur la fin
de la deuxieme mésure, luy mettant l'une des mains sur la
hanche, et l'aultre soubs le busq pour à la troisième mésure
commencer à torner selon les pas contenus en la tabulature."

Scene 6.   Page 379.

PIST. Die and be damn'd ; and *figo* for thy friendship.

The practice of thrusting out the thumb between the first
and second fingers to express the feelings of insult and contempt has prevailed very generally among the nations of
Europe, and for many ages been denominated *making the fig,*
or described at least by some equivalent expression.   There
is good reason for believing that it was known to the ancient
Romans.   Winckelman in his letter from Herculaneum has
described a bronze satyr as actually making the fig with his
fingers, and such a character is among the engravings in the
king of Naples's magnificent publication on the antiquities
of the above city.   The upper part of a similar bronze in a
private collection is here copied in the last figure below.   It
is more likely that *making the fig* was borrowed from this
Roman custom, than from another with which it has been
sometimes confounded.   This is the *infamis digitus* of
Persius; or the thrusting out the middle finger, on that
account called *verpus.*   In many private as well as public collections of Roman antiquities there are still preserved certain
figures in bronze, ivory, coral, and other materials, of the
following forms.

These however are well known to have been used · as
amulets against fascination in general, but more particularly
against that of the *evil eye.*   They are sometimes accompanied with the common symbol of Priapus, but often consist of it exclusively.   The connexion which this phallic
figure had with the above-mentioned superstition is known

to every classical reader. The introduction of the crescent or moon is not so easily explained. If these amulets were borrowed from the Egyptians, as some have supposed, the

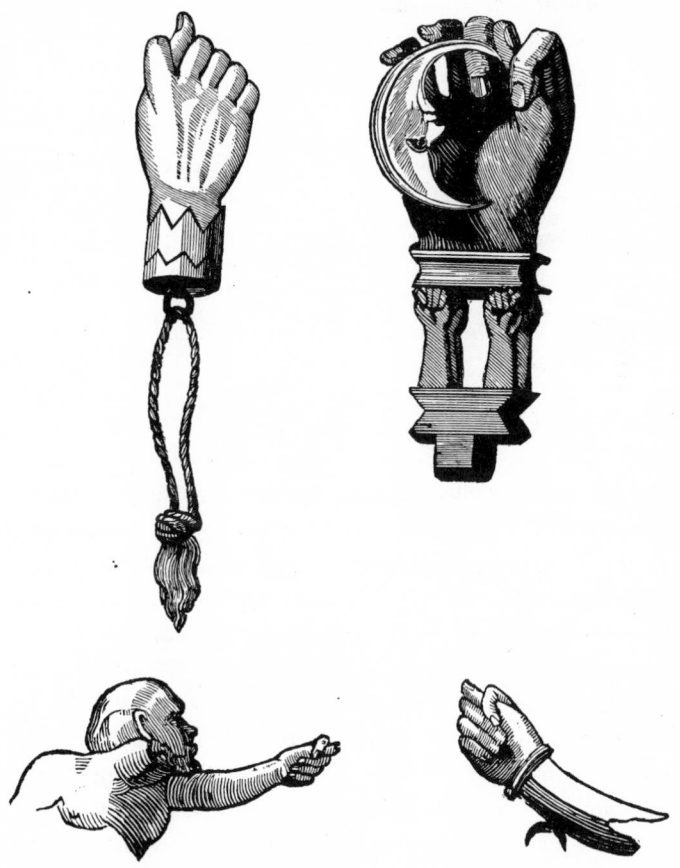

crescent may denote the influence of Isis or Venus, and the two symbols united may represent nature, or what the Hindus intend by their sacred Lingam: but every thing on this subject must be conjectural, the very essence of it being mysterious.

The Italian *fica* seems more intimately and etymologically

connected with the obscure disease known to the Romans by
the name of *ficus*; a term, with its appendages, rather to be
conceived than fully explained in this place. It has afforded
matter for some of Martial's Epigrams. In one of these he
thus dashes his mirth against an unlucky sinner:

> " Gestari junctis nisi desinis, Ædyle, capris,
>   Qui modo ficus eras, jam caprificus eris."
>
> lib. iv. ep. 52.

In another he instructs those who delight in the chase how
to avoid this affliction:

> " Stragula succincti venator sume veredi:
>   Nam solet a nudo surgere ficus equo."
>
> lib. xiv. ep. 86.

And lastly, he thus expresses himself immediately to the
present purpose:

> " Ut pueros emeret Labienus, vendidit hortos:
>   Nil nisi ficetum nunc Labienus habet."
>
> lib. xii. ep. 32.

No one who has lived among Italians will fail to perceive
the force of these quotations as applied to the feelings excited by this most offensive gesticulation, which is justly
held in the greatest abhorrence. Whether it be abstractedly
a symbol of the *ficus* itself, and, in the use, connected with
the very worst of its causes; whether it be the genuine remains of a custom actually known among the Romans; or
whether a corruption of the *infamis digitus*, must be left to
every one's own determination. The complicated ambiguity
of the word *fica* must be likewise attended to; and whoever
is at a loss on this occasion may consult the *early* Italian
dictionaries.

The author of these remarks, pursuing the opinions of
others, had already offered another explanation, viz. the story
of the Milanese revolt against the Emperor Frederick Bar-
barossa. This he desires to withdraw, as resting on the very
weak authority of Albert Crantz, a credulous, and comparatively modern, historian; neither is it probable that an inci-

dent so local would have spread so widely throughout Europe. Again, whoever will take the trouble of comparing the Hebrew word *techor* with the story itself, will feel very much inclined to reject the whole as a fabrication.

The earliest Italian authority for the use of this phrase is the *Inferno* of Dante. In the twenty-fifth canto are the following lines:

> " Al fine delle sue parole, il ladro
> Le mani alzò, con ambeduo *le fiche*
> Gridando: togli Dio, ch'a te le squadro."

The miscreant who utters this blasphemy, refines on the gesticulation, and doubles the measure of it. It is also to be found in Sacchetti's hundred and fifteenth novel, and in the *Cento novelle antiche*, nov. 55.

Villani, in his Chronicle, relates that in 1228 the inhabitants of Carmignano insulted the Florentines by setting up a statue on a rock with the hand making the *fig*, and turned towards the city of Florence. Pope Paul II. made a law against this insult, which punished the offending party by a fine of twenty soldi.

In France the use of it may be traced to a very early period. It occurs in a satire by Guyot de Provins, a poet of the twelfth century. The Spaniards, in all probability, got it from the Romans. They use the phrase *higa para vos* as a term of contemptuous insult and also as a spell against the consequences of satirical applause. See *Menckenii dissertationes*, p.52. Amulets against fascination, or the evil eye, are still used in Spain by women and children, precisely in the same manner as formerly among the Romans. These are made of ivory, but more frequently of jet. A figure of one of the latter, from an original, is here exhibited.

It furnishes a very extraordinary combination of subjects: figures of the holy Virgin and the infant Jesus; the *manus lasciva* or phallic hand; and a lunar crescent. It is indeed an obvious remnant of the ancient Roman amulet, the potency of which is strengthened by the addition of a Christian mystery. These things are said to be sometimes met with in nunneries, but the use which is there made of them does not seem generally known. One of these modern hands, well carved in ivory, and converted to the purpose of a snuff-box, was lately picked up by a curious traveller in Russia.

A very learned Spaniard, Ramirez de Prado, the author of a commentary on Martial and other ingenious works, adopting the opinion of Doctor Francis Penna Castellon, has fallen into a strange error respecting the etymology of *higa*. Speaking of it as well known among the Spanish women and children, he derives the name from *iynx*, the bird called the wryneck, concerning which the ancients had certain superstitions. From the *Pharmaceutria* of Theocritus, it appears to have been regarded as a love philtre. The similitude of sound has doubtless contributed to this error. See Laurentij Ramirez de Prado ΠΕΝΤΗΚΟΝΤΑΡΧΟΣ, 1612, 4to, p. 248.

The Germans, the Dutch, and perhaps other Northern nations, possess equivalent terms; and it is remarkable that in those languages the signification of the Roman *ficus*, as a disease, has been preserved. How the phrase of *making the fig* first came into the English language does not appear; it may perhaps be found only in translation. The Saxons had a term for the *ficus*, which they called ʀ1c-aƀle. With us the expression has happily dwindled altogether into a more innocent meaning. *Not to care a fig for one*, literally applies to the fruit so called, according to modern acceptation. In this sense it is sometimes used by Shakspeare, who makes Pistol say, " A *fico* for the phrase."—*M. Wives of Windsor.* " And *figo* for thy friendship."—*Henry the Fifth.* Again, in the *Second Part of Henry the Sixth*, we have, " A *fig* for

Peter." And in *Othello*, " Virtue? a *fig*!" In the *Second Part of Henry the Fourth*, Pistol says,

> " When Pistol lies *do this*; and *fig me*, like
> The bragging Spaniard."

Here the phrase seems accompanied by some kind of gesticulation, which might either be the thrusting out of the thumb, or the putting of it into the mouth so as to press out the cheek, another mode of insult that perhaps originally alluded to the *ficus*, by presenting something like its form. Thus in Lodge's *Wit's miserie*, " Behold I see contempt marching forth, giving mee the *fico with his thombe in his mouth*."

In the present play, ancient Pistol, after spurting out his "*figo* for thy friendship," as if he were not satisfied with the *measure* of the contempt expressed, more emphatically adds, " the fig of *Spain*." This undoubtedly alludes to the poisoned figs mentioned in Mr. Steevens's note, because the quartos read, " the fig of Spain *within thy jaw*," and " the fig within thy *bowels and thy dirty maw*." Or, as in many other instances, the allusion may be twofold; for the *Spanish fig*, as a term of contempt only, must have been very familiar in England in Shakspeare's time, otherwise the translator of Della Casa's *Galateo* would not, in the passage cited by Mr. Reed, have used such an expression, when it was neither in his original nor in Dante; a very strong circumstance in favour of Mr. Reed's opinion.

On the whole, there is no other way of extricating ourselves from the difficulties and ambiguities that attend the present subject, than by supposing some little confusion of ideas in our poet's mind, a weakness not more uncommon with him than with many of his commentators. Or, his phraseology might have been inaccurate; and it is to be feared that too much time and conjecture have been frequently expended on passages originally faulty, and which it might have been sufficient to have stated as such, to the exclusion of further comment or useless explanation.

ACT IV.

Page 399.

Cho. The armourers accomplishing the knights,
With busy hammers closing *rivets* up.

This does not solely refer to the business of rivetting the plate armour before it was put on, but as to part when it was on. Thus the top of the cuirass had a little projecting bit of iron, that passed through a hole pierced through the bottom of the casque. When both were put on, the smith or armourer presented himself, with his rivetting hammer, *to close the rivet up,* so that the party's head should remain steady notwithstanding the force of any blow that might be given on the cuirass or helmet. This custom more particularly prevailed in tournaments. See *Varietés historiques,* 1752, 12mo, tom. ii. p. 73.

Scene 2.   Page 424.

Grand. Their horsemen sit like *fixed candlesticks,*
With torch-staves in their hands.

This fashion is of great antiquity, being mentioned in Homer's description of the palace of Alcinous. *Odys.* book 7.

" Youths forg'd of gold, at every table there,
Stood holding flaming torches, that in night
Gave through the house, each honour'd guest his light."

It is likewise thus alluded to in Lucretius, lib. ii.

" Si non aurea sunt juvenum simulacra per ædeis
Lampadas igniferas manibus retinentia dextris,
Lumina nocturnis epulis ut suppeditentur."

The practice might originate in a supposed indelicacy of placing candlesticks on a table. Gregory of Tours relates a story of a French nobleman named Rauching, who disgraced himself by an act of wanton and excessive cruelty. When a servant *held a candle before him* at his supper, he made him uncover his legs, and drop the burning wax on them ; if the man offered to move, the cruel master was ready with his sword to run him through ; and the more the unfortunate sufferer lamented, the more his persecutor convulsed himself with savage laughter.   Gregor. Turon. *Hist.* lib. v. cap. 3.

The favourite forms of these inanimate *candle-holders* were those of armed warriors.   Sometimes they were hairy savages, a fool kneeling on one knee, &c.

Scene 4.   Page 439.

Pist. Quality, call you me ?—Construe me, art thou a gentleman?

The old copy reads *qualitee, calmie custure me,* and has been corrected or rather *corrupted anew* into its present form. The proposed reading of Mr. Malone deserves a decided preference, as founded on the ingenious conjecture that Pistol is quoting, as he has elsewhere done, the fragment of an old ballad.   It is exceedingly probable that, whenever chance shall disclose this ballad, we shall find in it this whole line,

" Calen, o custure me, art thou a gentleman."

Calen may be some proper name ; the ballad itself may be provincial, and *custure* the representative of *construe*.   Nothing is more probable than that *calmie* should be a misprint of *calen o.*

Scene 4.   Page 441.

Fr. Sol. . . . ayez pitié de *moy* !
Pist. *Moy* shall not serve, I will have forty *moys.*
Fr. Sol. O pardonnez *moy* !
Pist. Say'st thou me so ? is that a *ton of moys* ?

Dr. Johnson says that " *moy* is a piece of money, whence moi-d'or, or moi of gold."   But where had the doctor made this discovery ?   His etymology of *moidor* is certainly incorrect.   *Moidore* is an English corruption of the Portuguese *moeda d'ouro*, i. e. *money* of gold ; but there were no moidores in the time of Shakspeare.

We are therefore still to seek for Pistol's *moy*. Now a *moyos* or *moy* was a measure of corn; in French *muy* or *muid*, Lat. *modius*, a bushel. It appears that 27 moys were equal to a last or two *tons*. To understand this more fully, the curious reader may consult Malyne's *Lex mercatoria*, 1622, p. 45, and Roberts's *Marchant's Mapp of commerce*, 1638, chap. 272.

SCENE 4.   Page 442.

FR. SOL. Est il impossible d'eschapper la force de ton *bras*?
PIST. *Brass*, cur.
  Thou damned and luxurious mountain goat,
  Offer'st me *brass*.

A question having arisen concerning the pronunciation of the French word *bras* in the time of Shakspeare, it was observed in a former note that some remarks by the Rev. Mr. Bowle, in another place, had contributed at least to leave the matter open to discussion. That gentleman has certainly offered some evidence from Pasquier, that in the *middle* of words the *s* was pronounced where now it is silent; but on the other hand there is positive proof that the contrary practice prevailed in 1572, when De la Ramée published his French grammar. At page 19, he says, " Premierement nous sommes prodigues en lescripture de *s*, *sans la prononcer* comme en *maistre, mesler, oster, soustenir.*" This writer has expatiated on the difficulty which foreigners have in pronouncing the French language on account of its orthography, and offered a new mode by which it may be avoided. In the course of this specimen, he has, fortunately for the present occasion, printed the word *bras* without the *s*, (see p. 61,) and thereby supplied the means of deciding the present question, which, after all, was scarcely worth a controversy. Whoever wrote this dialogue was unacquainted with the true pronunciation of the French language, as Mr. Malone has already remarked, and framed Pistol's reply accordingly. In Eliot's *Orthoepia Gallica*, 1593, 4to, mentioned in Dr. Farmer's note, there is a passage which seems to have escaped the doctor's notice. In page 61, the author directs the sentence " vous avez un *bras* de fer," to be pronounced " voo-za-ve-zewn *bra* de fer."

SCENE 5. Page 448.

BOUR. Let him go hence, and with his cap in hand,
    Like a base pander, hold the chamber door, &c.

This is an allusion to the conduct of Pandarus when he introduced Troilus to his niece Cressida's chamber. See the story as related by Chaucer.

ACT V.

Page 470.

CHOR. . . Like a mighty *whiffler*, 'fore the king
    Seems to prepare his way.

Some errors have crept into the remarks on this word which require correction. It is by no means, as Hanmer had conceived, a corruption from the French *huissier*. He was apparently misled by the resemblance which the office of a whiffler bore in modern times to that of an usher. The term is undoubtedly borrowed from *whiffle*, another name for a *fife* or small flute ; for whifflers were originally those who preceded armies or processions as fifers or pipers. Representations of them occur among the prints of the magnificent triumph of Maximilian I. In a note on *Othello*, Act III. Scene 2, Mr. Warton had supposed that *whiffler* came from what he calls " *the old* French *viffleur* ;" but it is presumed that that language does not supply any such word, and that the use of it in the quotation from Rymer's *fœdera* is nothing more than a vitiated orthography. In process of time the term *whiffler*, which had always been used in the sense of a *fifer*, came to signify any person who went before in a procession. Minsheu, in his *Dictionary*, 1617, defines him to be a club or staff-bearer. Sometimes the whifflers carried white staves, as in the annual feast of the printers, founders, and ink-makers, so curiously described in Randle Holme's *Academy of armory*, book iii. ch. 3, where one of them is stated to have carried in his right hand a great bowl of white wine and sugar. Another mistake occurs in Mr. Warton's note, when he says, that "by degrees the word *whiffler* hence acquired the metaphorical meaning which it at present obtains in common speech, and became an appellation of contempt." This is by no means the case, for *whiffler*, in its sense of a *babbler*, *trifler*, or *versatile person*, is pure Saxon, pæꝼleꞃe, *blatero*.

KING HENRY VI.

PART I.

ACT I.

BED. And with them scourge the bad revolting stars,
      That have consented unto Henry's death.

It is conceived that most readers, after perusing the several notes on these lines, will be of opinion that some further elucidation is necessary. The first attempt should be to ascertain the respective significations of the words *concent* and *consent,* which can only be effected by an attention to their Latin etymology.

Concent, in its simple and primitive acceptation, is nothing more than a *singing together harmoniously*; but because in such harmony there is an *agreement* of sounds, the word was sometimes metaphorically used to express *concord or agreement generally.* *Consent* never means *union of sounds,* but *agreement generally,* or an union of *sense* or *opinion.* Cicero has most carefully distinguished them when he says, " Ubi enim perspecta vis est rationis ejus qua causæ rerum atque exitus cognoscuntur, mirus quidam omnium quasi *consensus* doctrinarum, *concentusque* reperitur."—De oratore, lib. iii. Among English writers, the similitude in sound and an inattention to orthography have contributed to their common and promiscuous use.

Mr. Steevens inclines to the meaning above given of *concent,* and yet he adopts *consent* in his text; nor are his instances uniform. Thus in the quotation from Cicero *De nat. deorum,* concentus simply means *concord* or *agreement.* In the passage from Milton, *consent* evidently denotes the same thing. The rest of his quotations relate to *musical concent*.

Mr. Mason, in his own words, assents to Mr. Steevens's explanation ; yet his instances are all unfortunately calculated to illustrate the other sense of *barely agreeing*.

The books of Elizabeth's time indiscriminately use both modes of orthography. Thus we have, " Broughton's *concent* of Scripture," for *consent* ; though, as is shown already, either will serve for *agreement*.

In the two passages cited by Mr. Steevens from Spenser, the orthography varies, though the meaning is evidently the same, i. e. *musical concent*. His expectations will be often disappointed who shall seek an exact meaning from some particular mode of orthography in ancient writers. ˙ There does not perhaps exist a more fallible rule; and it was reserved for the superior accuracy of modern times to affix any thing like uniformity of spelling, and consequently of sense, to our language.

It is impossible at this time to collect precisely what the author of the lines in question intended. The only guide we have is the passage quoted by Mr. Malone from another part of this play, " You all *consented* unto Salisbury's death." Yet, had the poet written *concented*, the sense in both places might be, *you all acted in concert, or jointly in unison, to accomplish the death, &c.* This accords with the following passage in *Pericles*, Act I. Scene 1 : —

> " The Senate house of planets *all did sit*
> To knit in her their best perfections."

An opportunity here presents itself of remarking how injudiciously we have discarded the more expressive and legitimate term *consort*, as a company of musicians playing together, for the new-fangled Italian *concert*. The other would be vulgar to a modern ear, and is now marked in our dictionaries as a *corrupt spelling*.

ACT III.

SCENE 1. Page 584.

MAY. The bishop's and the duke of Gloster's men,
Forbidden late to carry any weapon,
Have fill'd their pockets full of *pebble stones,* &c.

This fact is borrowed, with some variation, from Stowe or Fabian. " Men being forbidden to bring swords or other weapons, brought great battes and staves on their neckes; and when *those weapons were inhibited them,* they took *stones* and plomets of lead, &c."

SCENE 1. Page 587.

WAR. Sweet king!—the bishop hath a *kindly gird.*

Mr. Steevens has on this occasion, for the sake of the last word, introduced two notes which might very well have been spared. There is no doubt that Warwick means to say that the young king has given Winchester a gentle reproof. This is the plain and obvious meaning of *gird.* Dr. Johnson is wide, very wide, of the mark.

ACT V.

SCENE 3. Page 645.

Puc. You speedy helpers, that are substitutes
Under the lordly *monarch of the north,*
Appear.

The *monarch of the North* was Zimimar, one of the four principal devils invoked by witches. The others were, Amaimon king of the East, Gorson king of the South, and Goap king of the West. Under these devil kings were devil marquesses, dukes, prelates, knights, presidents and earls. They are all enumerated, from Wier *De præstigiis dæmonum,* in Scot's *Discoverie of witchcraft,* book xv. c. 2 and 3.

KING HENRY VI.

PART II.

ACT I.

SCENE 2. Page 20.

DUCH. With *Margery Jourdain,* the cunning witch.

IT appears from Rymer's *Fœdera,* vol. x. p. 505, that in the tenth year of King Henry the Sixth, *Margery Jourdemayn,* John Virley clerk, and friar John Ashwell, were, on the ninth of May 1433, brought from Windsor by the constable of the castle, to which they had been committed for sorcery, before the council at Westminster, and afterwards, by an order of council, delivered into the custody of the Lord Chancellor. The same day it was ordered by the lords of council that whenever the said Virley and Ashwell should find security for their good behaviour they should be set at liberty, and in like manner that Jourdemayn should be discharged on her husband's finding security. This woman was afterwards burned in Smithfield, as stated in the play and also in the chronicles.

ACT II.

SCENE 3. Page 64.

PET. Here Robin, an if I die, I give thee my *apron.*

Minsheu and others conceived that this word was derived from *afore one,* an etymology that perfectly accords with the

burlesque manner of Dean Swift. It has been also deduced
from the Greek words προ and περι; the Latin *porro* and
operio, &c. &c. Skinner, with more plausibility, has suggested
the Saxon apopan. After all, *an apron* is no more than a corruption of *a napron*, the old and genuine orthography. Thus
in *The mery adventure of the pardonere and tapstere*:

> " . . . . and therwith to wepe
> She made, and with her *napron* feir and white ywash
> She wypid soft hir eyen for teris that she outlash
> As grete as any mylstone——"
>
> *Urry's Chaucer*, p. 594.

We have borrowed the word from the old French *naperon*,
a large cloth. See Carpentier *Suppl. ad Cangium*, v. *Naperii*.
So *napkin*, which has perplexed our dictionary-makers, is only
a *little* cloth, from *nappe*.

SCENE 3. Page 66.

Hor. Hold Peter, hold; I confess treason.
[*Dies.*

The real names of these combatants were *John Daveys* and
William Catour, as appears from the original precept to the
sheriffs still remaining in the Exchequer, commanding them
to prepare the barriers in Smithfield for the combat. The
names of the sheriffs were Godfrey Boloyne and Robert
Horne; and the latter, which occurs in the page of Fabian's
chronicle that records the duel, might have suggested the
name of *Horner* to Shakspeare. Stowe is the only historian
who has preserved the servant's name, which was *David*.
Annexed to the before mentioned precept is the account of
expenses incurred on this occasion, duly returned into the
Exchequer. From this it further appears that the erection
of the barriers, the combat itself, and the subsequent execution of the armourer, occupied the space of six or seven
days; that the barriers had been brought to Smithfield in a
cart from Westminster; that a large quantity of sand and
gravel was consumed on the occasion, and that the place of

battle was strewed with rushes. Mr. Steevens has inferred from the above record that *the armourer was not killed by his opponent, but worsted, and immediately afterwards hanged.* This, however, is in direct contradiction to *all* the historians that have mentioned the circumstance, who, though they differ in some particulars, are certainly agreed as to the death of the accused by the hands of his servant. Halle's words are, " whose *body* was drawn to Tyborn and there hanged and beheaded ;" a mode of expression which, though ambiguous, seems rather to refer to the previous death of the party. Fabian, Grafton, Stowe, and Holinshed, state that he was slain. It is possible that Mr. Steevens, in making the above inference, conceived that because the man was hanged he must necessarily have been alive at the time of his execution : but the *mercy* of the law on this occasion certainly made no such distinction ; and *the dead body of the vanquished was equally adjudged to the punishment of a convicted traitor, in order that his posterity might participate in his infamy.* Indeed, the record itself seems decisive ; for it states that the dead man was watched *after the battle was done,* and this probably means before it was conveyed to Tyborn for execution and decapitation. The same rule was observed in cases of appeal for murder, as we learn from the laws or assizes of Jerusalem made there in the fourteenth century ; by which he that was *slain* or vanquished from cowardice in the field of battle, was adjudged to be *drawn and hanged* ; his horse and arms being given to the constable. See Thaumassiere *Assises de Jerusalem,* ch. 104, and Selden's *Duello,* p. 30. The hanging and beheading were confined to cases of murder and treason ; in a simple affair of arms the vanquished party was only disarmed and led forth ignominiously from the lists.

Since this note was written, the whole of the curious record in the Exchequer has been printed in Mr. Nicholls's valuable and interesting work entitled, " *Illustrations of the manners and expences of antient times in England,* 1797, 4to. As intimately connected with the present subject, the following extract cannot fail of being acceptable. It is taken from Gaguin, *Gestes Romains,* printed at paris by Ant. Verard, without date, in folio, a volume of extreme rarity, and is part of the ceremony of an appeal for treason as regulated by Thomas Duke of Gloucester, high constable to Richard the Second. " Et si la dicte bataille est cause de traison, celluy qui est vaincu et desconfit sera desarmé dedans les lices, et par le commandement du conestable sera mis en un cornet et en reprehencion de luy sera traisné hors avec chevaulx du lieu mesme ou il est ainsi desarmé parmy les lices jusques au lieu de justice, ou sera decolé ou pendu selon lusaige du pays, laquelle chose appartient au mareschal veoir par fournir par son office, et le mettre a execution," fo. 148 :—that is, " If the said battle be on account of treason, he that is vanquished and discomfited shall be disarmed within the lists, and by the authority of the constable put into a little cart; then having received a proper reprimand he shall be drawn by horses from the spot where he has been disarmed, through the lists, to the place of public execution, and there hanged or beheaded according to the custom of the country : which matter the marshal, by virtue of his office, is to see performed and executed."

ACT III.

Scene 1. Page 74.

Suf. I think, I should have told your *grace's* tale.

On this expression Dr. Johnson remarks that " *majesty* was not the settled title till the time of King James the First." In a note to vol. i. p. 97, of the lives of *Leland, Hearne, and Wood,* it is said that our kings had not the title of *majesty* in the reign of Henry the Eighth ; and another note in Dr. Warburton's edition of the Dunciad, b. iv. l. 176, states that

James was the first who assumed the title of *sacred majesty*; all which information is unsupported by authority.

On the other hand, Camden more correctly says, that "*majesty* came hither in the time of King Henry the Eighth, as *sacred majesty* lately in our memory."—*Remains concerning Britain*, p. 198, edit. 1674, 8vo. Selden, referring to this passage, wishes it to be understood so far as it relates to the title being "commonly in use and properly to the king applied," because he adduces an instance of the use of *majesty* so early as the reign of Henry the Second. In a letter from queen Elizabeth to Edward the Sixth, she signs "Your *majesties* humble sister," and addresses it "To the kinges most excellent *majestie*."—Harl. MS. No. 6986. In the same volume is a most extraordinary letter in Italian to Elizabeth, beginning, "Serenissima et *sacratissima maesta*," which shows that Camden, who wrote what he says above early in 1603, must rather refer to Elizabeth than James the First.

The use of *majesty* is ascribed by the learned authors of the *Nouveau traité de diplomatique* to Gondemar king of the Visigoths, and to the kings of Lorraine in the seventh century; but in France it is not traceable before the year 1360, about which time Raoul de Presle, in the dedication to his translation of Saint Augustin *De civitate Dei*, thus addresses Charles the Fifth: "si supplie à vostre *royalle majesté*." It was however but sparingly used till the reign of Louis XI. In the treaty of Créssy the emperor Charles V. is called *imperial majesty*, and Francis I. *royal majesty*. In that of Château Cambresis, Henry II. is entitled *most christian majesty*, and Philip II. *catholic majesty*. Pasquier has some very curious remarks in reprobation of the use of *majesty*. See *Recherches de la France*, liv. viii. ch. 5.

Both Camden and Selden agree that the title of *Grace* began about the time of Henry the Fourth, and of *excellent Grace* under Henry the Sixth.

Scene 1. Page 91.

YORK. . . . . I have seen him
Caper upright like a wild *Mórisco*,
Shaking the bloody darts as he his bells.

However just Dr. Johnson's explanation of Morisco may be in an etymological point of view, it is at least doubtful whether it mean in this place a real or even personated *Moor*. Nothing more may be intended than simply a performer in a morris dance. It may be likewise doubted whether in the English morris dance, a single Moorish character was ever introduced. The quotation from Junius is extremely perplexing; yet it must be remembered that he was a foreigner, and speaking perhaps conjecturally.

Scene 2. Page 96.

K. HEN. . . . . Come, *basilisk*,
And kill the innocent gazer with thy *sight*.

Bartholomæus, with whom it has been shown that Shakspeare was well acquainted, speaking of the basilisk or cockatrice, says, " In his *sight* no fowle nor birde passeth harmelesse, and though he be farre from the foule, yet it is burnt and devoured by his mouth . . . . Plinius also sayth there is a wilde beast called Catobletas [which is] great noyeng to mankinde : *for all that see his eyen should dye anone, and the same kinde hath the cockatrice*."—*De propriet. rer.* lib. xviii. c. 16. The same property is also mentioned by Pliny of the basilisk, but Holland's translation was not printed till after this play was written. It is true that if Shakspeare did not write the lines in question, the original author might have used a Latin Pliny.

Scene 2. Page 103.

WAR. Oft have I seen a *timely-parted* ghost.

It has been very plausibly suggested that *timely-parted* signifies *in proper time*, as opposed to *timeless*; yet in this place

it seems to mean *early, recently, newly.* Thus in *Macbeth,*
Act II. Scene 3,

> " He did command me to call *timely* on him."

Again, in *The unfaithful lover's garland,*

> " Says he, I'll rise ; says she, I scorn
>   To be so *timely parted."*

Porter, in his comedy of the *Two angry women of Abingdon,* 1599, 4to, seems to have had Warwick's speech in view
when he wrote these lines :

> " Oft have I heard a *timely married* girl
>   That *newly* left to call her mother mam, &c."

SCENE 2.   Page 105.

WAR. But see, his face is black and full of blood.

The accounts given by the English historians of the Duke
of Gloucester's death are very discordant and unsatisfactory.
They relate that he was smothered between feather-beds ;
that he was found dead in his bed ; that a red hot spit was
thrust through him ; and that he died of grief. There is
another account of this event, which, as it seems to have been
quite unnoticed in our histories, and may deserve as much attention as either of the foregoing, shall here be given.

George Chastellain, a celebrated soldier, poet, and historian, was by birth a Flemming, and is said to have been in
the service of Philip duke of Burgundy. He travelled into
various countries, and wrote an account of what he had seen,
under the title of *The wonderful occurrences of his time.*
Speaking of his visit to England, he says,

> " Passant par Angleterre
>   Ie veis en grant tourment
>   Les seigneurs de la terre .
>   S'entretuer forment
>   Avec un tel deluge
>   Qui cueurs esbahissoit
>   Que a peine y eut refuge
>   Ou mort n'apparoissoit.

> Ung nouveau roy creerent
> Par despiteux vouloir
> Le viel en debouterent
> Et son legitime hoir
> Qui fuytif alla prendre
> Descosse le garand,
> De tous siécles le mendre
> Et le plus tollerant."

This alludes to the flight of Henry the Sixth into Scotland. In another place he speaks as an eye witness of. the death of duke Humphrey, and relates that *he was strangled in a cask of wine,* adding also the reason,

> " Par fortune senestre
> Veiz a l'oeil vifvement
> Le grant *duc de Clocestre*
> Meurdrir piteusement
> *En vin plein une cuve*
> *Failloit que estranglé fust,*
> *Cuydant par celle estuve,*
> *Que la mort ny parut.*"

What credit he may deserve may be worth the inquiry of some future historian. His work in general will strike every reader as a strange mixture of veracity and credulity.

The above singular mode of inflicting death seems to have prevailed about this time; for we find not long afterwards another instance of it in the execution of George duke of Clarence, who, as is generally agreed, was drowned in a butt of Malmsey wine. He appears to have chosen the manner of his death, on which Mr. Hume makes the following observation : " A whimsical choice, which implies that *he had an extraordinary passion for that liquor.*" *   It should rather be inferred that the punishment in question was more frequent than is commonly known, and made use of for culprits of

---

* One should almost suppose that the historian had recollected Cyrano de Bergerac's dream of a visit to the infernal regions, where he saw the Duke of Clarence, " who," says he, " *voluntarily drowned himself in a barrel of Malmsey,* seeking for Diogenes, in hopes of getting half his tub to lodge in."

rank and eminence when dispatched in secret.   Jean Molinet, the continuator of the above work of Chastellain, has thus described this event:

> " Jay veu *duc de Clarence*
> Bouté en une tour
> Qui queroit apparence
> De regner a son tour;
> De mort preadvisee
> *Le roy le feist noyer*
> *Dedans mallevoisee*
> *Pour le moins ennuyer.*"

Scene 2.   Page 116.

Q. Mar. Away! though parting be a fretful *corrosive.*

A learned commentator has stated that this word was *generally* written *corsive* in Shakspeare's time, and he has indeed proved that it was so written *sometimes.*   The fact is, it was written as at present in prose, and in poetry either way, as occasion required.   Thus Drant in his translation of *Horace's satyres,* 1566, 4to:

> " Wote you not why? *corrosyve* style
> Is *corsey* to the eye."

In the text it should be printed *cor'sive.*

Scene 3.   Page 116.

K. Hen. O beat away the busy meddling fiend
That lays strong siege unto this wretch's soul.

It was the belief of our pious ancestors, that when a man was on his death-bed the devil or his agents attended in the hope of getting possession of the soul, if it should happen that the party died without receiving the sacrament of the eucharist, or without confessing his sins.   Accordingly in the ancient representations of this subject, and more particularly in those which occur in such printed services of the church as contain the vigils or office of the dead, these *busy meddling fiends* appear, and with great anxiety besiege the dying man; but on the approach of the priest and his attendants, they betray symptoms of horrible despair at their impending discomfiture.   In an ancient manuscript book of devotions, written in the reign of Henry the Sixth, there is a prayer addressed to Saint George, with the following very singular passage: " Judge for me whan the moste hedyous and damnable dragons of helle shall be redy to take my poore soule and engloute it in to theyr infernall belyes."

Shakspeare, who in many instances has proved himself to have been well acquainted with the forms and ceremonies of the Romish church, has, without doubt, on the present occasion availed himself of the above opinion.   Whether this had happened to that pre-eminent painter, who, among the numerous monuments of his excellence that have immortalized himself and done honour to his country, has depicted the last moments of Cardinal Beaufort with all the powers of his art, cannot now be easily ascertained.   He has been censured for personifying the fiend, on the supposition that the poet's language is merely figurative ; with what justice this note may perhaps assist in deciding.   Some might disapprove the renovation of Popish ideas ; whilst others, more attentive to ancient costume, and regardless of popular or other prejudices, might be disposed to defend the painter on the ground of strict adherence to the manners of the times.

The reader may not be displeased at being introduced to a more intimate acquaintance with the *ancient* mode of representing a dying man as above referred to.   It is copied from a print in a later edition of the *Ars moriendi,* one of those books on which the citizens of Haarlem found their claim to the invention of printing; whereas it is in fact no more than a collection of wooden engravings made for pious purposes, and explained by writing cut on the same blocks, and by no means a real specimen of the above art.   To this is added another exhibition of the same subject, but very superior in

point of art.   It is copied from an engraving in wood by an
unknown artist of considerable merit; and from the striking
resemblance which it bears to the picture of our great painter
above alluded to, much cannot be hazarded in supposing that
he might have taken some hints from it, as it is well known
that he collected many prints with the view of making such
use of preceding excellence as the most exalted genius will
ever condescend to do.

The Greeks, when persons were dying, drove away evil
spirits by placing at the door branches of bramble or buck-
thorn.   They likewise made a noise by beating brazen vessels
for the same purpose.

ACT IV.

Scene 2. Page 139.

Cade. . . . the *three-hoop'd* pot shall have ten hoops.

The note here is not sufficiently explanatory. The old drinking pots, being of wood, were bound together, as barrels are, with hoops; whence they were called *hoops*. Cade promises that every can which now had three hoops shall be increased in size so as to require ten. What follows in the notes about "burning of cans," does not appear to relate to the subject.

Scene 2. Page 140.

Smith. The clerk of Chatham.

This person is a nonentity in history, and in all probability a character invented by the writer of the play. It is presumed that few will be inclined to agree with Mr. Ritson in supposing him to have been Thomas Bayly, *a necromancer at Whitechapel,* and Cade's bosom friend.

Scene 7.   Page 161.

CADE. Then break into his son in law's house, Sir *James* Cromer.

Mr. Ritson cites William of Worcester to show that this sheriff's name was *William.* The author of the play, if wrong, may be justified by the examples of Halle, Grafton, Stowe, in his early editions, and Holinshed, who call him *James.* Fabian, as if doubtful, leaves a blank for Crowmer's Christian name. As to the fact itself, the evidence of William of Worcester, a contemporary writer, is entitled to the preference. Fuller's list of the sheriffs of Kent likewise makes the name *William.*

Scene 10.   Page 173.

CADE. I think this word sallet was born to do me good : for many a time, but for a *sallet,* my brain-pan had been cleft with a brown bill.

The notes on this occasion may admit of correction as well as curtailment. It is possible that we have borrowed *sallet* from the French *salade,* in the sense of a helmet : but the original word is the old Teutonic *schale,* which signifies generally *a covering.* Hence *shell, scale, scull, shield,* &c. Wicliffe does not use *brain-pan* for scull, in Judges ix. 53, as Mr. Whalley supposes, but *brain,* simply.

KING HENRY VI.

PART III.

ACT I.

Scene 1. Page 223.

Exe. Here comes the queen whose looks *bewray* her anger.

Although the word *bewray* has received very proper illustration on the present and other occasions, it remains to observe that its simple and original meaning was to *discover* or *disclose*; that it has been confounded with *betray*, which is used, though not exclusively, for *to discover for bad or treacherous purposes*, a sense in which bewray is never *properly* found. Of this position take the following proof: " If you do so, saide the other, then you ought to let me knowe what so ever you know your selfe: unless you thinke that yourself will *bewray* yourself, except you doubt yourself will deceive yourself, and unless you thinke that yourself will *betray* your self."—Lupton's *Siuqila*, 1580, 4to, sign. L 4. b.

Scene 1. Page 224.

Q. Mar. *Rather* than made that savage duke thine heir.

The note which follows Mr. Steevens's was *not* inadvertently introduced by that gentleman, though it certainly should not have been retained *as the text now stands*.

Scene 4. Page 242.

Q. Mar. [Putting a *paper* crown on his head.]

Mr. Ritson has not shown, as he conceived he had, that the preceding commentator was *certainly mistaken*: for the author of the play, if he be accountable for the stage direction, could not have "followed history with the utmost precision," when he makes *queen Margaret* put a *paper* crown on York's head; whereas Holinshed, the black-letter chronicler whom Mr. Ritson should have first consulted, and who only follows Whethamstede, relates that a garland of *bulrushes* was placed on York's head, which was afterwards stricken off and presented to the queen. Nor is there historical evidence that the queen herself put on the crown. Shakspeare has continued the same error in *King Richard the Third*, where he makes Gloucester say to queen Margaret,

> " The curse my noble father laid on thee
> When thou didst crown his noble brows with *paper*."

He was therefore, in this instance, misled by the author of *King Henry the Sixth*; or he must have written the queen's speech himself.

Scene 4.   Page 244.

York. Whose tongue more poisons than the adder's tooth.

Again in *Cymbeline*, Act III. Scene 4 ;

> " Whose tongue outvenoms all the worms of Nile."

ACT III.

Scene 2.   Page 310.

L. Grey. But, mighty lord, this merry inclination
Accords not with the *sadness* of my suit.

The following is offered as a very select instance of the use of *sadness* for *seriousness*. It is from Tom Coriat's speech that he made to a Mahometan who had called him an infidel. " But I pray thee tell me thou Mahometan, dost thou in *sadness* call me *Giaur*? That I doe, quoth he. Then quoth I, in very *sober sadness* I retort that shameful word in thy throate."

Scene 2.   Page 314.

Glo. Like to a chaos, or an *unlick'd bear-whelp.*

The common opinion which Dr. Johnson mentions of the

bear bringing forth unformed lumps of animated flesh, and afterwards licking them into proper shape, has been very properly exposed and confuted by Sir Thomas Brown in his *Enquiries into vulgar errors*, book iii. ch. 6. His adversary Ross, in his *Arcana microcosmi*, p. 115, has attempted a solution of this matter, by stating it as a fact that bears bring forth their young deformed and mis-shapen, by reason of the thick membrane in which they are wrapped, that is, covered over with a mucous and phlegmatick matter. This, he says, the dam contracts in the winter time, by lying in hollow caves without motion, so that to the eye the cub appears like an unformed lump. The above mucilage is afterwards licked away by the dam, and the membrane broken, whereby that which before seemed to be unformed appears now in its right shape. And this, he contends, against Dr. Brown, is all that the ancients meant. See more on the subject of the old opinion in Bartholomæus *De proprietat. rerum*, lib. xviii. c. 112.

ACT IV.

Scene 7.   Page 359.

Glo. For many men that *stumble at the threshold.*

To understand this phrase rightly, it must be remembered that some of the old thresholds or steps under the door, were, like the hearths, raised a little, so that a person might stumble over them unless proper care was taken. A very whimsical reason for this practice is given in a curious little tract by Sir Balthazar Gerbier, entitled, *Councel and advice to all builders*, 1663, 24mo, in these words, " A good surveyour shuns also the ordering of doores with *stumbling-block-thresholds*, though our forefathers affected them, perchance to perpetuate the antient custome of bridegroomes, when formerly at their return from church [they] did use to lift

up their bride, and to knock their head against that of the
doore, for a remembrance, that they were not to passe the
threshold of their house without their leave."

ACT V.

Scene 7.   Page 403.

CLAR. What will your grace have done with Margaret?
  Reignier her father, to the king of France
  Hath pawn'd the Sicils and Jerusalem,
  And hither have they sent *it* for her ransom.

Unless there be some omission in this speech, it must
either be regarded as improperly elliptical, or as ungrammatical. *It* refers to the sum of money borrowed by Margaret's
father, which is mentioned by the French historians to have
been fifty thousand crowns. The author of the play followed
Holinshed.

THE right accentuation of Hĕcătē, as well as the proper
description of Althea's torch, which Shakspeare, in *King
Henry the Fourth,* had misrepresented, are additional arguments that he did *not* write the whole of these plays; but
that they were composed by some person who had more
classical knowledge, but infinitely less genius than our
author.

KING RICHARD III.

ACT I.

ACT I.

SCENE 1. Page 461.

SCENE 1. Page 461.

GLO. *He capers* nimbly in a lady's chamber
To the lascivious pleasing of a lute.

THE question with Dr. Johnson is, whether it be *war* that
capers, or *York*; and he justly remarks that if the latter, the
antecedent is at an almost forgotten distance. The amorous
temper of Edward the Fourth is well known; and there
cannot be a doubt that by *the lascivious pleasing of a lute,* he
is directly alluded to. The subsequent description likewise
that Richard gives of himself is in comparison with the *king.*
Dr. Johnson thought the image of *war capering* poetical; yet
it is not easy to conceive how *grimvisag'd war* could *caper in
a lady's chamber.*

SCENE 1. Page 462.

GLO. Cheated of feature by *dissembling* nature.

The poet by this expression seems to mean no more than
that nature had made for Richard features *unlike* those of
other men. To dissemble, both here and in the passage
quoted from *King John,* signifies the reverse of to *resemble,*
in its active sense, and is not used as *dissimulare* in Latin.

ACT II.

SCENE 3. Page 540.

2 CIT. Ill news by'r lady; *seldom comes the better.*

Well might the author of the book quoted by Mr. Reed

say " that proverb indeed is auncient," as will appear from the following curious account of its origin extracted from a manuscript collection of stories compiled about the time of king Henry the Third:—

" Quidam abbas dedit monachis suis tria fercula. Dixerunt monachi, Iste parum dat nobis. Rogemus Deum ut cito moriatur. Et sive ex hac causa, sive ex alia, mortuus est. Substitutus est alius, qui eis tamen dedit duo fercula. Irati monachi contristati dixerunt, Nunc magis est orandum, quia unum ferculum subtractum est, Deus subtrahat ei vitam suam. Tandem mortuus est. Substitutus est tertius, qui duo fercula subtraxit. Irati monachi dixerunt, Iste pessimus est inter omnes, quia fame nos interficit; rogemus Deum quod cito moriatur. Dixit unus monachus, Rogo Deum quod det ei vitam longam, et manu teneat eum nobis. Alii admirati querebant quare hoc diceret; qui ait, Vide quod primus fuit malus, secundus pejor, iste pessimus; timeo quod cum mortuus fuerit alius pejor succedet, qui penitus nos fame perimet. Unde solet dici, *Seilde comed se betere.*"

Scene 4.   Page 546.

Q. ELIZ. A *parlous* boy.

" Parlous," says Mr. Steevens, "is keen, shrewd." Mr. Ritson is of a different opinion, and thinks it a corruption of *perilous,* dangerous. Both parties are right; but it is probably used here as *perilous,* in like manner as the nurse in *Romeo and Juliet* talks of " a *parlous* knock," and as it is also to be taken in *A midsummer night's dream,* where Mr. Steevens had properly explained it; and the instance which he has given on the present occasion does, in fact, corroborate his former note. *Parlous* is likewise made synonymous with *shrewd* by Littelton. See his Latin dict. v. *importunus.* In Middleton's play of *The changeling,* we have " a *parlous* fool," i. e. *shrewd,* " he must sit in the fourth form at least." Yet a few pages further the same word is as clearly used for *perilous.* After all there is little or no difference in the senses of it, for in shrewdness there is certainly peril. He that meets with a *shrew,* may well be said to be *in danger.* Some might think that this word is the same as *talkative,* in which case it must have been borrowed from the French; but that language does not furnish an adjective of the kind. The original corruption was *perlious.* Thus in an unpublished work by William of Nassyngton, a poet of the fifteenth century, who wrote on the Lord's prayer, &c., we have, "Methinks this maner is *perlious.*"

ACT III.

SCENE 1. Page 561.

YORK. Uncle, my brother mocks both you and me;
Because that I am little, like an *ape,*
He thinks that you should *bear me on your shoulders.*

Mr. M. Mason contends that this is simply an allusion to Richard's deformity, and is not inclined to admit the propriety of Dr. Johnson's supposition that York means to call his uncle a *bear.* From a quotation given by the former gentleman, it is clear that Shakspeare, when alluding to Richard's deformity, mentions his *back*; and it is therefore probable that he would have used the same term in the present instance, had he adverted to the duke's shape. For this reason Dr. Johnson's opinion seems preferable; yet something more might have been intended. The practice of keeping apes or domestic monkeys was formerly much more common than at present. Many old prints and paintings corroborate this observation,* and in some the monkey appears chained to a large globe or roller of wood, which, whilst it permitted the animal to shift his situation, prevented him from making his escape. It is almost unnecessary to add that the monkey, as the intimate companion of the domestic

* See the fine frontispiece by Coriolano to Vesalius's Anatomy.

fool, would often get upon his shoulders. There is a fine picture, by Holbein, of Henry the Eighth and some of his family, which by favour of his majesty now decorates the meeting room of the Society of Antiquaries. In it is an admirable portrait of Will Somers, the king's fool, with a monkey clinging to his neck, and apparently occupied in rendering his friend William a very essential piece of service, wherein this animal is remarkably dexterous, the fool reclining his head in a manner that indicates his sense of the obligation. York may therefore mean to call his uncle a fool, and this, after all, may be the *scorn* that Buckingham afterwards refers to.

Every one is acquainted with the propensity of the monkey to climbing upon other animals. Gervase Markham in his *Cavalerice,* a treatise on horsemanship, already referred to, devotes a chapter to inform his readers "how a horse may be taught to doe any tricke done by *Bankes* his curtall," in which he says, "I will shew you by the example of two or three trickes, how you shall make your horse to doe any other action as well as any dog or *ape* whatsoever, except it be *leaping upon your shoulders.*" The curious reader may find more illustration of the subject in the specimen of Dr. Boucher's *Supplement to Johnson's dictionary,* article *ape ;* but the learned and ingenious author was certainly mistaken in supposing that fools carried the *representations of apes on their shoulders,* and probably in what he says concerning the origin of the phrase of putting an *ape* in a man's hood.

ACT IV.

SCENE 2.   Page 621.

K. RICH. Because that like a *Jack,* thou keep'st the *stroke.*

At Horsham church, in Sussex, there was a figure dressed in scarlet and gold, that struck the quarters. He was called

Jack o' the clock-house. The French term for this kind of automaton is *jaquemar,* the etymology of which is very fanciful and uncertain.

ACT V.

SCENE 1.   Page 660.

Buck. *Holy* king Henry——

This epithet is not applied without good reason. King Henry the Sixth, though never actually canonized, was regarded as a saint, and miracles were supposed to have been performed by him. In some of our church service-books before the Reformation, there are prayers which are said to have been of his composition, and one in particular that is addressed to him is entitled, " A prayer to *holy* king Henry."

SCENE 3.   Page 665.

K. RICH. Besides, the king's name is a tower of strength.

Borrowed from *Proverbs,* xviii. v. 10.   " The *name* of the Lord is *a strong tower.*"

SCENE 3.   Page 667.

CATE. . . . . It's supper time, my lord;
It's *nine* o'clock.

" A supper at so late an hour as nine o'clock in the year 1485," says Mr. Steevens, "would have been a prodigy." It certainly would, and even at the time when this play was written, the period to which the criticism more justly belongs. In either instance there was a reason for preferring the text of the quarto copy, and yet the unnecessary alteration is retained.

SCENE 3.   Page 688.

K. RICH. This and Saint George *to boot.*

Dr. Johnson is undoubtedly right against both his opponents, one of whom has adduced the phrase *St. George to borrow,* unintentionally in support of him.   *To borrow* is no more a verb than *to boot*; it means *as a pledge or security,* *borrow* being the Saxon term for *a pledge.*   The phrase is an invocation to the saint to act as a protector.   *Saint George to thrive* is evidently a misconceived paraphrase of the old mode of expression, by improperly changing the substantive to a verb.   Holinshed, in the speech of Richard before the battle, introduces " *St. George to borrowe.*"

Scene 3.   Page 690.

K. Rich.   Long kept in Bretagne at our *mother's* cost.

It has already been stated by Dr. Farmer that the mistake here of *mother* for *brother* must be placed to the account of the book which Shakspeare followed, viz. Holinshed's chronicle; but the doctor has omitted to notice that in the *first edition* of Holinshed the word is rightly printed *brother.*   It is no otherwise worth while to mention this fact, than that it points out the particular edition of the above historian which Shakspeare used.   Nothing can be more judicious nor decisive than Mr. Malone's argument for retaining the historical errors of Shakspeare, and Mr. Ritson's desire of changing the text does not correspond with those principles of accuracy on which he laid so much stress.

Scene 3.   Page 691.

K. Rich.   A *milksop,* &c.

This is from Holinshed, " To begyn with the earle of Richmonde capitayne of this rebellion, he is a *Welsh milksoppe,*" &c.

KING HENRY VIII.

ACT I.

Scene 1. Page 21.

Buck. . . . . but this top-proud fellow
(Whom from the flow of gall I *name not*, but
From *sincere motions*)

Dr. Johnson explains *sincere motions* to be *honest indignation*; and, for *name not*, would substitute *blame not*. But is not the following the plain sense, without any alteration? " this top-proud fellow, whom I call so, not from an excess of bitterness, but from a genuine *impulse* of the mind."

Scene 1. Page 26.

Buck. I am the shadow of poor Buckingham,
Whose figure even this instant cloud puts on,
By dark'ning my clear sun.

It is no easy matter on some occasions to comprehend the precise meaning of Shakspeare's metaphors, which are often careless and confused; and of this position the present lines are, doubtless, an example. We have here a double comparison. Buckingham is first made to say that he is but a shadow; in other terms, a dead man. He then adverts to the *sudden* cloud of misfortune that overwhelms him, and, like a shadow, obscures his prosperity.

Scene 3. Page 42.

Cham. Is it possible the spells of France should juggle
Men into such strange *mysteries*?

Dr. Johnson's explanation is much too fanciful. Mysteries are *arts*, and here *artificial fashions*.

ACT II.

Scene 2.   Page 71.

Nor. I 'll venture one *heave* at him.

The first folio reads " I 'll venture one ; *have* at him," and this, except as to the punctuation, is right.   *Have at you* was a common phrase ; it is used by Surrey in the ensuing act, and afterwards by Cromwell.

Scene 2.   Page 73.

Cam. . . . which so griev'd him, [Doctor Pace]
That he ran mad and died.

This is from Holinshed.   " Aboute this time the king received into favor doctor Stephen Gardiner, whose service he used in matters of great secrecie and weighte, admitting him in the room of Doctor Pace, the which being continually abrode in ambassades, and the same oftentymes not much necessarie, by the Cardinalles appointment, at length he toke such greefe therwith, that he fell out of his right wittes."

Scene 3.   Page 75.

Anne. . . . . 't is a sufferance panging
As soul and body's severing.

Of the parallel passages already cited, this is not the least so, from *Measure for measure* ;

" . . . in *corporal sufferance* feels a *pang* as great
As when a giant dies.

Scene 4.   Page 98.

[*they rise to depart.*

Mr. Ridley's note is very judiciously introduced to get rid of the interpolated stage direction inserted by some of the editors, and to account for the king's apostrophe to Cranmer. He might have adduced an earlier exemplification of his remark from the ensuing scene, where Norfolk asks, *when Cranmer returns*?   The archbishop of Canterbury, who attends the procession to Blackfriars, was William Warham.

ACT III.

SCENE 2. Page 112.

SUF. . . . I persuade me, from her
    Will fall some blessing to this land, which shall
    In it be memoriz'd.

This is, no doubt, a compliment to queen Elizabeth.

SCENE 2. Page 126.

SUR. . . . . I'll startle you
    Worse than the sacring bell, when the brown wench
    Lay kissing in your arms, lord cardinal.

Was there any Skeltonical tradition to this effect in Shakspeare's time, or has he only taken a hint from one of the articles against Wolsey, which is conceived in the following terms ? " Also the said Lord Cardinall did call before him Sir John Stanly knight which had taken a farm by Covent seal of the Abbot of Chester and afterwards by his power and might contrary to right committed the said Sir John Stanly to the prison of Fleet by the space of a year unto such time as he compelled the said Sir John to release his Covent seal to one Leghe of Adlington, which married one Lark's daughter, *which woman the said Lord Cardinall kept, and had with her two children,*" &c.

SCENE 2. Page 127.

SUR. First, that, without the king's assent, or knowledge,
    You wrought to be a legate ; by which power
    You maim'd the jurisdiction of all bishops.

We have here in substance the first of the articles exhibited by the lords of the privy council and two of the judges against Wolsey. They had been unfaithfully recorded in some of our histories, but were at length printed by Lord Coke from the originals in his fourth Institute, chap. 8.

SCENE 2. Page 127.

NOR. Then, that, in all you writ to Rome, or else
    To foreign princes, *Ego et rex meus*
    Was still inscrib'd ; in which you brought the king
    To be your servant.

The nature of this supposed offence has been apparently

misconceived by Shakspeare and others whom he might have followed. The original article against Wolsey, states, that " the Lord Cardinall of his presumptuous mind, in divers and many of his letters and instructions sent out of this realme to outward parts had joyned himself with your Grace, as in saying and writing, *The king and I would ye should do thus. The king and I doe give unto you our hearty thankes.* Whereby it is apparent that he used himself more like a fellow to your Highnes, then like a subject." Wolsey's crime therefore was not in degrading the king beneath himself, but in assuming a degree of consequence that seemed to place him on a level with his sovereign. The offensive language when put into Latin would be more striking and apt to deceive; but the idiom of the language required the above arrangement of the words.

SCENE 2. Page 128.

SUF. Then that without the knowledge
　　Either of king or council, when you went
　　Ambassador to the emperor, you made bold
　　To carry into Flanders the great seal.
SUR. Item, you sent a large commission
　　To Gregory de Cassalis, to conclude,
　　Without the king's will, or the state's allowance,
　　A league between his highness and Ferrara.

Both these charges seem included in the third article. " Also the said Lord Cardinall being your ambassador in France, sent a commission to Sir Gregory de Cassalis under your great seale in your grace's name to conclude a treaty of amity with the Duke of Ferrara, without any commandment or warrant of your highnes, nor your said highnesse advertised or made privy to the same."

SCENE 2. Page 129.

SUF. That out of mere ambition you have caus'd
　　Your holy hat to be stamp'd on the king's coin.

An absurd and frivolous allegation against the unfortunate Cardinal, being the substance of the fortieth article. The episcopal privileges of coining money had been long esta-

blished, and were conceded in this reign to Bainbrigge and
Lee the predecessor and successor of Wolsey, as well as to
the archbishops of Canterbury, Warham and Cranmer. But
the great offence was placing the *Cardinal's hat* under the
king's arms, " which like deed," says the article, " hath not
been seen to be done by any subject within your realm before
this time." It may be asked how could it, Wolsey being the
only English cardinal to whom the privilege of striking money
had been granted ? Nor could there be any substantial reason
for regarding the cardinal's hat as more offensive than the
bishop's mitre, which had already appeared on the coins of
Durham.

Scene 2.   Page 129.

Suf. Lord Cardinal, the king's further pleasure is,—
Because all those things, you have done of late
By your power legatine within this kingdom,
Fall into the compass of a *præmunire*,—
That therefore such a writ be sued against you.

The poet was under the necessity of introducing the
præmunire immediately after the articles ; but we learn from
Cavendish that " Maister Cromwell inveighed against the byll
of articles with such wittie persuasions and depe reasons that
the same could take none effect. *Then were his enemyes con-
strained to indite him in a* PREMUNIRE," &c.

Scene 2.   Page 131.

Wol. And when he falls, he falls like *Lucifer.*

Manifestly borrowed from that fine passage in *Isaiah,* xiv.
ver. 12 : " How art thou *fallen* from heaven, O *Lucifer,* son
of the morning !"

Scene 2.   Page 135.

Wol. And sleep in *dull cold* marble.

Mr. Gray seems to have remembered this line in his
elegy,—

" Or flattery sooth the *dull cold* ear of death."

Scene 2.   Page 137.

Wol. Had I but serv'd my God with half the zeal
I serv'd my king, he would not in mine age
Have left me naked to mine enemies.

Dr. Johnson remarks, that "this sentence was really uttered by Wolsey." The *substance* of it certainly was. The words themselves have been preserved in the valuable Life of Wolsey by *George* Cavendish his gentleman usher, which Shakspeare might have used either in Stowe's chronicle or in manuscript; for several copies are still remaining that were transcribed in the reign of Elizabeth. Mr. Malone has already taken due notice of their very superior value, and of the omissions and interpolations in the printed editions. In the latter, the work has been abridged of many details of great curiosity with respect to the manners of the times. A new and correct edition would be well deserving of the patronage of an enlightened public. The real words uttered by Wolsey were these; "Yf I hadd served God as diligently as I have done the kinge, he wolde not have geven me over in my graye heares."

ACT V.

Scene 3.   Page 193.

Man. . . and hit that woman, who cry'd out, *Clubs!*

It has been observed, in illustration of this practice of crying out *clubs*, that it was usually adopted in any quarrel or tumult in the streets; but it remains to point out the persons that were so called, because the watchmen's weapon was the *bill.* Stowe informs us, that "when prentizes and journeymen attended upon their masters and mistresses in the night, they went before them carrying a lanthorne and candle in their hands, and a *great long club on their neckes.*"—*Annales,* p. 1040, edit. 1631. The frequency of this exclamation in nocturnal quarrels might in process of time adapt the expression to general occasion.

SCENE 4. Page 199.

It is submitted that the stage exhibition of Elizabeth's christening should be conducted according to the curious and circumstantial details of the manner in which it was really performed, to be found in Halle's *Chronicle,* and copied from him by Stowe into his *Annales.*

TROILUS AND CRESSIDA.

PROLOGUE.

. . . . . Priam's six-gated city.

In this, as well as in **Dr.** Farmer's subsequent note, it might have been better to have quoted Caxton's translation of the *Recuyles or destruction of Troy,* instead of *Lydgate.* In the edition of 1607 of the former work, which, in all probability, is that used by the author of the play, the gates of Troy are thus named; *Dardan, Timbria, Helias, Chetas, Troyen, Antenorides.* These are nearer to the text than those in the other quotation from Lydgate, whose work the author does not seem to have consulted. Should the curious reader be desirous of seeing the manner in which Troy was formerly represented, he may be gratified by an inspection of it in its full glory; the gates inscribed with their names, and fortified with portcullises, in the edition of Jaques Milot's *Mystere de la destruction de Troye,* Lyon, 1544, folio; or in Raoul le Fevre's *Recueil des hystoires Troyennes,* Lyon, 1510, folio. This was also a favourite subject in old tapestry, a very fine and ancient specimen of which remained a long time in the painted chamber that separates the two houses of parliament, till it was removed during the repairs of Saint Stephen's chapel for the accommodation of the Irish members. A copy of it was fortunately taken by that ingenious artist, Mr. John Carter, draughtsman to the Society of Antiquaries.

ACT I.

Scene 1. Page 223.

Tro. Thou lay'st in every gash that love hath given me
The *knife* that made it.

When poets speak of the wounds inflicted by love, they

generally make the instrument to be an *arrow*; how a *knife* came here to be introduced is not easy to account for. Is it possible that our author has transposed the old saying that *a knife cuts love*?

SCENE 3. Page 245.

NEST. . . . . . and, anon, behold
 The strong-ribb'd bark through liquid mountains cut,
 Bounding between the two moist elements,
 Like *Perseus' horse*.

Mr. Steevens, admitting the curiosity of his colleague's note on this passage, is unwilling to allow that its design to prove the horse of Perseus a ship, and not an animal, has been accomplished. The learned editor observes, that " Shakspeare would not have contented himself with merely comparing one ship to another;" and that " unallegorized *Pegasus* might be fairly stiled *Perseus'* horse, because the heroism of *Perseus* had given him existence." That one thing is compared to another which resembles it, can surely be no solid objection to the justice of a comparison; and though the birth of the unallegorized Pegasus was doubtless the result of Perseus's bravery in conquering Medusa, it was incumbent on the objector to have demonstrated how this *horse of Perseus* had " bounded between two moist elements," to have made good the poet's comparison. There can be no doubt that the author of the simile has alluded to the fact concerning the *ship* Pegasus adduced by Mr. Malone; and every thing leads to the supposition that he used the *authority* of Caxton's Troy book, though, as will be seen presently, *that* was not the most ancient of the kind.

It is undoubtedly a well justified poetical license to compare a ship to a horse, on account of its speed. In the translation of an old Celtic ballad called *The maid's tragedy*, the monarch who pursues the flying damsel is sometimes said to traverse the waves on *an enchanted steed*; " which," say

the Edinburgh reviewers, "probably arises from some equivo-
cal expression in the original, as the Scalds term a ship the
rider, and sometimes the horse of the ocean."—*Edinb. review*,
1805, p. 439.

Mr. Malone has stated in the beginning of his valuable
note, that we nowhere hear of Perseus's horse;" and that
"Pegasus was the property not of Perseus but of Bellerophon."
This is not quite accurate. It is certain that *Ovid* has *not*
mounted Perseus on any horse in his combat with the monster
which was to devour Andromeda; and therefore it is matter
of wonder that the mythological dictionary of Chompré, and
particularly that most excellent one by Lempriere, should
positively affirm that he has. This error has been likewise
adopted by other writers. But though classic authority be
wanting that Perseus made use of a horse, Boccaccio, in his
Genealogia Deorum, lib. xii. c. 25, has quoted Lactantius as
saying, that when Perseus undertook his expedition against
Gorgon, at the instance of king Polydectus, he was accompanied by the winged horse Pegasus, but not that he used
him in delivering Andromeda. Boccaccio adds that others
were of opinion that he had a *ship* called Pegasus. The
liberties which the old French translators of Ovid's Metamorphoses have taken, and their interpolations, are unaccountable. Some have caused Perseus at the instant of his birth,
to bestride Pegasus, and travel away to Helicon. In the cuts
to many of the early editions of Ovid, the designers have
not only placed him on Pegasus in the adventure with Andromeda, but even in his attack upon Atlas. These facts
may serve to account for the multiplied errors of artists, who,
neglecting to consult proper authorities, have trusted to the
erroneous examples of their predecessors. Achilles Tatius,
in his third book of *The loves of Clitophon and Leucippe*, has
described a picture of Perseus delivering Andromeda, in which
he is made to descend by means of wings to his feet; and

another on the same subject is spoken of by Lucian in his description of a house. In neither of these is there any mention of a horse.

ACT II.

Scene 1.   Page 276.

THER. . . . an *assinego* may tutor thee.

Some doubt having arisen whether an *assinego* is an *ass* or an *ass-driver*, the following passages from Ligon's *History of Barbadoes*, 1673, will serve to decide the question in favour of the *four-legged animal*; and demonstrate at the same time that the above term is not exclusively applied to a male ass, as Mr. Ritson had supposed. " We found it was far better for a man that had money, goods, or credit, to purchase a plantation there ready furnish'd, and stockt with servants, slaves, horses, cattle, *assinigoes*, camels, &c." And again, " And though I found at Barbadoes some who had musical minds; yet I found others, whose souls were so fixt upon, and so riveted to the earth, and the profits that arise out of it, as their souls were lifted no higher; and those men think, and have been heard to say, that three whip-sawes going all at once in a frame or pit, is the best and sweetest musick that can enter their ears; and to hear a cow of their own low, or an *assinigo bray*, no sound can please them better."— pp. 22, 107.

Scene 3.   Page 309.

ULYSS. Praise him that got thee, *she* that gave thee suck.

This ungrammatical line, though perhaps the property of Shakspeare, might as well be corrected.

Scene 3.   Page 309.

ULYSS. Let Mars divide eternity in twain
        And give him half.

How Mars was to accomplish this the metaphysicians must

decide. The idea is an odd compound of grandeur and absurdity. It might have turned to some account in the hands of the ingenious Edgworths.

ACT III.

SCENE 2.   Page 329.

CRES. . . . For to be wise, and love,
Exceeds man's might; that dwells with gods above.

If this be Shakspeare's, he got it from Taverner's translation of *Publius Syrus*, at the end of *Catonis disticha*, 1553, 12mo, where it stands thus, " To be in love and to be wyse is scarce graunted to God. It is not one man's propertie both to love and also to be of a sounde mynde."

SCENE 2.   Page 333.

PAN. . . . let all pitiful *goers-between* be call'd to the world's end after my name, call them all *Pandars*.

Although the above is, no doubt, the real etymology of the word *pandar*, the original use of it does not rest with Shakspeare. An earlier instance occurs in Gabriel Harvey's *Pierce's supererogation*, 1593, 4to, in which " the pandars stew" is mentioned. All other derivations must be rejected, because the term occurs in no language but our own. Nashe, in his *Have with you to Saffron Walden*, has most extravagantly deduced it from *Pandora*; and he adds that Sir Philip Sidney fetches it from Plautus. In Sir Philip's *Defence of poesie*, the author, speaking of Terence's *Gnatho* and Chaucer's *Pandar*, says, " we now use their names to signifie their trades."

SCENE 3.   Page 338.

CAL. . . . . But this Antenor
I know is such a *wrest* in their affairs.

If a former explanation should be thought to stand in need of further authority, the following may suffice.

In *A treatise between trouth and information,* by W. Cornishe, printed among the works of Skelton, are these lines:

> " A harpe geveth sounde as it is sette,
> The harper may *wrest* it untunablye;
> A harper with his *wrest* may tune the harpe wrong,
> Mystunyng of an instrument shal hurt a true songe."

The same instrument was used for tuning other stringed instruments, as appears from the same poem:

> " The claricord hath a tunely kynde,
> As the wyre is *wrested* hye and lowe;
> So it turnyth to the players mynde,
> For as it is *wrested* so must it nedes showe,
> Any instrument mystunyd shall hurt a trew song,
> Yet blame not the claricord the *wrester* doth wrong."

Again,

> " With golden strings such harmonie
> His harpe so sweet did *wrest*;
> That he reliev'd his phrenesie
> Whom wicked sprites possest."
>
> Archb. Parker's *Psalter,* sign. B. 1. b.

In King James's edict against combats, &c., p. 45, is this passage, " this small instrument the tongue being kept in tune by the *wrest* of awe," &c.

And in Swetnam's *Arraignment of women,* 1615, 4to, " They are always tempering their wits, as fidlers do their strings, who *wrest* them so high, that many times they stretch them beyond time, tune, and reason."

ACT IV.

SCENE 5.　Page 383.

ULYSS. . . . . set them down
For sluttish spoils of opportunity,
And *daughters of the game.*

This expression seems borrowed from the *maister of the game,* the ancient title of the king's game-keeper. There was also a treatise on hunting, so called, which Shakspeare had often read of, or might perhaps have seen.

ACT V.

Scene 3. Page 425.

TRO. Brother, you have a vice of mercy in you
Which better fits a *lion* than a man.

See a preceding note pp. 189, 190.

Scene 9. Page 444.

HECT. I am unarm'd; forego this vantage, Greek.

The author of this play, in his account of the death of Hector, has undoubtedly departed from his original; and, as it should seem, without necessity. Mr. Steevens, on this occasion, takes notice of *Lydgate's* vehement reprehension of Homer's praise of Achilles, and of his gross violation of the characters drawn by the Grecian poet; but he has censured the wrong person. Lydgate has only followed his predecessor Guido of Colonna, who, (or perhaps the original writer Benoit de Saint More,) adopting the statement in the prologue to Dares Phrygius, appears to regard the latter as a more correct and veracious historian than Homer.

Scene 9. Page 451.

PAN. Some *galled goose of Winchester* would hiss.

If Mr. Mason had accidentally consulted the English part of Littelton's excellent dictionary, he would not have doubted that " any symptom of the venereal disease was called a Winchester goose."

ON THE STORY OF THIS PLAY.

OF Lollius, the supposed inventor of this story, it will become every one to speak with diffidence. Until something decisive relating to him shall occur, it is better to conclude with Mr. Tyrwhitt, that Chaucer borrowed the greatest part of his admirable story from Boccaccio's Philostrato; and that he either invented the rest altogether, or obtained it from some completer copy of the Philostrato than that which we now possess. What Dryden has said of Lollius is entirely destitute of proof, and appears to be nothing more than an inference from Chaucer's own expressions.

It would be a matter of extreme difficulty to ascertain, with any sort of precision, when and in what manner the story of Troilus and Cressida first made its appearance. Whether the author of the Philostrato was the first who detailed it so minutely as it is there found, remains to be decided; but it is certain that so much of it as relates to the departure of Cressida from Troy, and her subsequent amour with Diomed, did exist long before the time of Boccaccio. The work in which it is most known at present is the *Troy book* of Guido of Colonna, composed in 1287, and, *as he states,* from Dares Phrygius, and Dictys Cretensis, neither of whom mentions the name of Cressida. Mr. Tyrwhitt, as it has eventually proved, had, with his usual penetration and critical acuteness, suspected that Guido's Dares was in reality an old Norman French poet named *Benoit de Saint More,* who wrote in the reign of our Henry the Second, and who himself made use of Dares. This work seems to be the earliest authority now remaining. The task which Mr. Tyrwhitt had declined, has on this occasion been submitted to; and the comparison has shown that Guido, whose performance had long been regarded as original, has only translated the Norman writer into Latin. It is most probable that he found *Benoit's* work when he came into England, as he is recorded to have done; and that pursuing a practice too prevalent in the middle ages, he dishonestly suppressed the mention of his real original. What has been advanced by Mr. Warton and some other writers respecting an old

2 A

French romance under the name of Troilus and Cressida, will not carry the story a moment higher; because this French romance is in fact nothing more than a much later performance, about the year 1400, compiled by *Pierre de Beauvau* from the Philostrato itself. This has been strangely confounded with several other French works on the Troy story related with great variety of circumstance, all or most of which were modelled on that of Guido of Colonna or his original; citing, as they had done, the supposititious histories of Dictys and Dares. It is worth while to embrace this opportunity of mentioning, for the first time, that there is a *prose* French version of *Benoit's* metrical romance; but when made, or by whom, does not appear in a MS. of it transcribed at Verona in 1320.

Lydgate professedly followed Guido of Colonna, occasionally making use of and citing other authorities. In a short time afterwards *Raoul le Fevre* compiled from various materials his *Recueil des histoires de Troye,* which was translated into English and published by Caxton; but neither of these authors has given more of the story of Troilus and Cressida than any of the other romances on the war of Troy; Lydgate contenting himself with referring to Chaucer. Of *Raoul le Fevre's* work, often printed, there is a fine MS. in the British museum, Bibl. Reg. 17, E. II., under the title of *Hercules,* that must have belonged to Edward the Fourth, in which *Raoul's* name is entirely and unaccountably suppressed. The above may serve as a slight sketch of the romances on the history of the wars of Troy; to describe them all particularly would fill a volume.

It remains to inquire concerning the materials that were used in the construction of this play. Mr. Steevens informs us that Shakspeare received the greatest part of them from the *Troy book of Lydgate.* It is presumed that the learned commentator would have been nearer the fact had he substituted the *Troy book or recueyl* translated by *Caxton* from

Raoul le Fevre; which, together with a translation of Homer, supplied the incidents of the Trojan war. Lydgate's work was becoming obsolete, whilst the other was at this time in the prime of its vigour. From its first publication to the year 1619, it had passed through six editions, and continued to be popular even in the eighteenth century. Mr. Steevens is still less accurate in stating *Le Fevre's* work to be a translation from Guido of Colonna; for it is only in the latter part that he has made any use of him. Yet Guido actually had a French Translator before the time of Raoul: which translation, though never printed, is remaining in MS. under the whimsical title of " La *vie* de la *piteuse destruction* de la noble et supellative cité de Troye le grant. Translatée en Francois lan MCCCLXXX;" and at the end it is called, " Listoire *tres plaisant* de la destruction de Troye la grant." Such part of our play as relates to the loves of Troilus and Cressida was most probably taken from Chaucer, as no other work, accessible to Shakspeare, could have supplied him with what was necessary.

TIMON OF ATHENS.

ACT I.

Scene 1. Page 481.

Enter Apemantus.

" See this character of a cynic finely drawn by Lucian in his *Auction of the philosophers* ; and how well Shakspeare has *copied* it," says Dr. Warburton; who took it for granted that · our author could read Lucian *out of English.* Until this can be proved, or that any English translation of the above piece existed in Shakspeare's time, we are at liberty to doubt how far Apemantus is a copy from Lucian, or rather to believe that he is a highly finished portrait after a very slight sketch by Plutarch.

ACT IV.

Scene 3. Page 587.

Tim. She, [her] whom the spital-house and ulcerous sores
Would cast the gorge at, this embalms and spices
To the *April day* again.

It had been better to have withdrawn Dr. Johnson's note, for he has entirely misconceived the meaning of this part of Timon's speech. He has mistaken the *person* who was to be *embalmed to the April day again,* and supposed, without reason, that the wedding day is here called *April* or *fools day.* Mr. Tollett has already corrected the first of these errors, and properly explained the *April day* to mean the *freshness* of youth. See a description of April from an old calendar in

p. 45. The word *day* in this instance is equivalent with *time*.

SCENE 3. Page 593.

TIM. To the *tub-fast* and the *diet*.

What this *diet* was may be seen at large in Dr. Bullein's *Bulwarke of defence,* fo. 57 b. and in his *Booke of compoundes,* fo. 42, 43.

In a former note a conclusion was too hastily drawn, concerning the origin of *Cornelius's tub.* It was stated that it took its name from the hero of Randolph's pleasant comedy of *Cornelianum dolium*; but the term is much older, being mentioned in Lodge's *Wit's miserie,* 1599, 4to, sig. F iiij b. Its origin therefore remains in a state of uncertainty; for what Davenant has left us in his *Platonick lover* can only be regarded as a piece of pleasantry.

> SCIOLT. As for *Diogenes* that fasted much, and took his habitation in a tub, to make the world believe he lov'd a strict and severe life, he took the diet, sir, and in that very tub swet for the French disease.
>
> FRED. And some unlearned apothecary since, mistaking 's name, called it *Cornelius tub.*
>
> Act iii.

There is yet another passage which may be worth inserting, as it throws a gleam of light on this obscure term. It is from *The law of drinking,* 1617, 12mo, p. 55. " Like ivie they cling close about *Cornelius' bulke*; till sleepe surprize them, oblivion divide them, and *brave Cornelius* guide them to his *tub.*"

SCENE 3. Page 624,

TIM. The sea 's a thief, whose liquid surge resolves
The moon into salt tears.

Some difficulty has arisen in the course of the notes on this passage to account for the manner in which the sea could despoil the moon of its moisture and change it into saline tears. It has been judiciously remarked by one of the commentators, that we are not to attend on these occasions merely to philosophical truth, but to consider what might have been the received or vulgar notions of the time: yet no example of such notions applicable to the present occasion has been produced. The following may perhaps serve to supply this defect, and to establish at the same time the genuineness of the text: " The moone gathereth deawe in the aire, for she printeth the vertue of hir moysture in the aire, and chaungeth the ayre in a manner that is unseene, and breedeth and gendereth deawe in the utter part thereof."—Bartholomæus *De propriet. rerum,* lib. viii. c. 29.

ACT V.

Scene 5.   Page 658.

Alcib. Here lies a *wretched* corse, &c.

There is a *fourth* epitaph on Timon, which is scarcely worth mentioning, but as it perhaps completes the list, and might even, as well as that in Kendal and Painter, have suggested the slight alteration made by Shakspeare. It is in Pettie's translation of Guazzo's *Civile conversation,* 1586, 4to, fo. 5, as follows :

" Here doe I lie, ne am the same
I heretofore was wont to bee ;
Thou reader never aske my name,
A *wretched* end God send to thee."

THE FOOL.

The fool in this play is a very obscure and insignificant character. Dr. Johnson's conjecture that he belongs to one of Alcibiades's mistresses is extremely probable. Many ancient prints conduce to show that women of this description were attended by buffoons ; and there is good reason for supposing, partly from the same kind of evidence, that in most brothels such characters were maintained to amuse the guests by their broad jokes and seasonable antics. In *Measure for measure* we have such a person, who is also a tapster; and in *Antony and Cleopatra*, Act I. Scene 1, we hear of a *strumpet's fool*.

The dress, in the present instance, should be a party-coloured garment, with a hood and asses' ears, and a cock's comb. He might also carry a bauble.

CORIOLANUS.

ACT I.

SCENE 1. Page 12.

MEN. Even to the court, the heart,—to the seat o' the brain.

MR. MALONE has most ingeniously shown that the *heart* here signifies the *seat of the brain*, that is, of the understanding; and this is conformable to the old philosophy. Thus our English Pliny, Bartholomew Glanville, informs us, from Aristotle, that the substance of the brain being cold, it is placed before the well of heat, which is, the heart; and that small veins proceed from the heart, of which is made a marvellous caul wherein the brain is wrapped. *De propr. rerum*, lib. v. c. 3. On this ground, the heart has been very appositely made the seat of reason; and accordingly in another place, Glanville tells us that in the heart is " all business and knowing."

If the above able commentator be right in his chronology of this play, and there appears to be no reason for doubting that he is so, the present lines must have been imitated by a contemporary writer of great ability and poetical talents, though undeservedly .obscure. This is W. Parkes, who calls himself a student of Barnard's inn. In his work entitled *The curtaine-drawer of the world,* 1612, 4to, he has two passages which bear so strong a resemblance, that a mere coincidence of thought is entirely out of the question. This is the first, in p. 6: " If any vice arise from the *court*, as from the *head*, it immediately discends to the cittie, *as the heart*, from thence drawes downe to the country, as the heele: and so like an endlesse issue or theame, runs through the whole land." The other is in p. 13: " For whereas that member was ordained for a light and window, and as a true interpreter to expresse and expound the consultations, and councels, and purposes of that hidden dumbe and secret privy-councellour that *sits within the throne and breast* and bosome of every living man, it many times doth belye, and forge, and flatter, and speaks then most faire when the deepest deceit and treachery is intended: not the foot, nor the finger, nor the whole hand: no not the whole body, nor all the members thereof, either severally, by themselves, or joyntly together (this one onely excepted) that doth so stretch, and draw, and finger, and fold and unfold this curtaine or canopy to the daily use and deceit of itselfe and others, as it alone doth."

It is rather extraordinary that none of Shakspeare's commentators should have noticed the skilful manner in which he has diversified and expanded the well known apologue of *the belly and the members,* the origin of which it may be neither unentertaining nor unprofitable to investigate, as well as the manner in which it has been used, and by whom.

The composition has been generally ascribed to Menenius Agrippa; but as it occurs in a very ancient collection of Æsopian fables, there may be as much reason for supposing it the invention of Æsop as there is for making him the parent of many others. The first person who has introduced Menenius as reciting this fable is Dionysius of Halicarnassus, book 6. Then follow Livy, lib. 2; Plutarch, in the life of Coriolanus; Florus, lib. 1. cap. 23; each of whom gives it in his own manner. During the middle ages there appeared a collection of Latin fables in hexameter verse, that has agitated the opinions of the learned to little purpose in their endeavours to ascertain the real name of the compiler or versifier. He has been called Romulus, Accius and Salo. Nor is the time when he lived at all known. These fables are sometimes called *anonymous,* and have been published in

various forms. An excellent edition by Nilant appeared in
1709, 12mo. Many of them were translated into French
verse in the eleventh century by a French lady who calls herself *Marie de France*, in which form they have been happily
preserved with many others extremely curious composed by
the same ingenious person, on whose life and writings a most
valuable memoir has been communicated to the Society of
Antiquaries, by the author's truly learned and amiable friend
the Abbé Gervase de la Rue, professor of history in the
university of Caen. William Herman of Gouda, in Holland,
reduced them into Latin prose about the year 1500, omitting
some, and adding others. The works of Romulus and Herman of Gouda, have been published in a great variety of
forms and languages, and constitute the set of Æsopian
fables which commences with that of the cock and the precious
stone; in all which the apologue of the belly and the members
is to be found, and sometimes with considerable variation.
What Camden has given is from John of Salisbury, who wrote
in the reign of Henry the Second, and professes to have received
it from Pope Hadrian IV. See his *Polycraticon, sive de nugis
curialium*, l. vi. c. 24. Camden has omitted the latter part;
and the learned reader will do well to consult the original,
where he will find some verses by Q. Serenus Sammonicus,
a physician in the reign of Caracalla, that allude to the fable.
John of Salisbury has himself composed two hundred Latin
lines *De membris conspirantibus*, which are in the *first edition*
of his *Polycraticon* printed at Brussels, without date, about
1470. These were reprinted by Andreas Rivinus at Leipsic,
1655, 8vo; and likewise at the end of the fourth volume of
Fabricius's *Bibliotheca mediæ et infimæ ætatis*, Hamburg, 1735,
8vo. They are, most probably, the lines which are called in
Sinner's catalogue of the MSS. at Berne, " Carmen *Ovidii* de
altercatione ventris et artuum," vol. iii. p. 116. Nor was this
fable unknown in the Eastern world. Syntipas, a Persian
fabulist, has placed it in his work, published, for the first time,

from a MS. at Moscow, by Matthæus. Lips. 1781, 8vo. Lafontaine has related it in his own inimitable manner; and lastly, the editor of Baskerville and Dodsley's *Æsop* has given it in a style not inferior perhaps to that of any of his predecessors.

Scene 4. Page 35.

Mar. All the contagion of the *south* light on you.

See the note on Caliban's similar wish, " A *south*-west blow on you," p. 5.

ACT II.

Scene 1. Page 77.

Bru. The *napless* vesture of humility.

" The players read the *Naples,*" says Mr. Steevens; but the players are right, and the fault was with the printer in giving the word with a capital letter. The termination *less* in old books is very frequently spelled with a single *s*; so that Mr. Rowe's change scarcely deserves the name of *a correction.*

ACT IV.

Scene 1. Page 159.

Cor. I shall be lov'd when I am lack'd.

Thus Cæsar in *Antony and Cleopatra,* Act I. Scene 4, " And the ebb'd man comes dear'd by being lack'd." We have still preserved this proverbial saying in another form. Mother Cole says, " When people are miss'd, then they are mourn'd." It is, in fact, Horace's " extinctus amabitur idem."

JULIUS CÆSAR.

ACT I.

Scene 2.   Page 254.

Cas. Now is it Rome indeed, and *room* enough.

This jingle of words is deserving of notice on no other account than as it shows the pronunciation of *Rome* in Shakspeare's time.

Scene 3.   Page 266.

Cas. Why old men fools, and children calculate.

In this manner has the former punctuation of the line, which had a comma after *men,* been disturbed at the suggestion of Sir W. Blackstone, and thereby rendered extremely uncouth if not unintelligible.   He observes that there is no prodigy in old men's calculating from their past experience; but the poet means old dotards in a second state of childhood.   With the supposed power of divination in *fools,* few are unacquainted.   He that happens to be so may consult the popular history of Nixon, the Cheshire prophet.

ACT II.

Scene 2.   Page 299.

Cal. When beggars die, there are no comets seen;
The heavens themselves blaze forth the death of princes.

This might have been suggested by what Suetonius has related of the blazing star which appeared for seven days together, during the celebration of games instituted by Augustus in honour of Julius. The common people believed that this comet indicated his reception among the gods; and not only his statues were accordingly ornamented with its figure, but medals were struck on which it was represented. One of these, struck by Augustus, is here exhibited.

Pliny relates that a comet appeared before the death of Claudius, lib. ii. c. 25 ; and Geffrey of Monmouth speaks of one that preceded the death of Aurelius Ambrosius; but the comets would have appeared though the men had not died, and the men would not have lived longer had the comets never been seen.

SCENE 2. Page 300.

SER. Plucking the entrails of an offering forth
    They could not find a heart within the beast.
CÆS. The gods do this in shame of cowardice :
    Cæsar should be a beast without a heart,
    If he should stay at home to day, for fear.

Dr. Johnson remarks on this occasion, that "the ancients did not place courage in the heart." He had forgotten his classics strangely.

" Nunc animis opus, Ænea, nunc *pectore firmo*."   *Æn.* vi. 261.

" . . . . . . Juvenes, *fortissima* frustra
  Pectora—— ."   *Æn.* ii. 263.

" . . . . Teucrûm minantur *inertia corda*."   *Æn.* ix. 55.

" . . . . excute, dicens,
  Corde metum——"   Ovid. *Metam.* lib. iii. 689.

" *Corda pavent* comitum, mihi mens interrita mansit."
                              Ovid. *Metam.* lib. xv. 514.

" *Cor pavet* admonitu temeratæ sanguine noctis."
                              Ovid. *Epist.* xiv. 16.

" Nescio quæ *pavidum* frigora *pectus* habent."
                              Ovid. *Epist.* xix. 192.

ACT III.

Scene 1.   Page 329.

Ant. .   .   .   .   . . for mine eyes,
       Seeing those beads of sorrow stand in thine,
       Began to water.

We have a similar expression in *The tempest*, Act V.
Scene 1, where Prospero says,

" Holy Gonzalo, honourable man,
    Mine eyes even sociable to the shew of thine,
    Fall fellowly drops."

ANTONY AND CLEOPATRA.

ACT I.

Scene 1. Page 410.

Ant. Let Rome in Tiber melt! and the *wide arch*
Of the *rang'd* empire fall! Here is my space.

As *range* signifies *compass, extent,* so the verb seems to be used, rather licentiously, in the present instance, in the sense of *spread, extended.* It may be doubted, at least, whether there be any allusion to a triumphal arch, as Dr. Warburton supposed, or even of a fabric standing on pillars, according to Dr. Johnson. The *wide arch* may refer to the vast concave of the Roman world, its wide domains covered by *the arch of heaven,* which has been beautifully styled by some oriental writer " the star-built arch of heaven." See *The tales of Inatulla* by Dow, vol. i. p. 78.

Scene 3. Page 440.

Cleo. O my oblivion is a very Antony
And I am *all* forgotten.

She compares her memory to Antony, and says she is treacherously abandoned and neglected by *both.* Mr. Steevens's explanation of the first line is satisfactory; but one cannot well agree with him or Mason, that " I am all forgotten" can possibly mean, " I forget myself, or every thing."

ACT II.

Scene 4. Page 490.

Ant. . . . . . and his quails
Ever beat mine, *inhoop'd* at odds.

It may be doubted whether quail-fighting was practised in Shakspeare's time, though Dr. Farmer appears to have thought so; but when our poet speaks of their being *inhoop'd*, he might suppose that Cæsar's or Antony's quails, which he found in Plutarch, were trained to battle like game cocks in a *ring* or *circle*. Hanmer plausibly reads *incoop'd*, but no change is necessary.

Quail combats were well known among the ancients, and especially at Athens. Julius Pollux relates that a circle was made in which the birds were placed, and he whose quail was driven out of this circle lost the stake, which was sometimes money, and occasionally the quails themselves. Another practice was to produce one of these birds, which being first smitten or filliped with the middle finger, a feather was then plucked from its head: if the quail bore this operation without flinching, his master gained the stake, but lost it if he ran away. The Chinese have been always extremely fond of quail-fighting, as appears from most of the accounts of that people, and particularly in Mr. Bell's excellent relation of his travels to China, where the reader will find much curious matter on the subject. See vol. i. p. 424, edit. in 8vo. We are told by Mr. Marsden that the Sumatrans likewise use these birds in the manner of game cocks. The annexed copy from an elegant Chinese miniature painting represents some ladies engaged at this amusement, where the quails are actually *inhoop'd*.

SCENE 5.   Page 493.

CHAR. . . . . 'T was merry, when
You wager'd on your angling; when your diver
Did hang a salt-fish on his hook, which he
With fervency drew up.

This incident, which, as Mr. Steevens has already remarked, was borrowed from Plutarch, probably suggested a story related by Nashe, " of a scholler in Cambridge, that standing angling on the towne bridge there, as the country people on the market day passed by, secretly bayted his hooke wyth a red herring wyth a bell about the necke, and so conveying it into the water that no man perceived it, all on the sodayn, when he had a competent throng gathered about hym, up he twicht it agayne, and layd it openly before them, whereat the gaping rurall fooles, driven into no lesse admiration than the common people about London some few yeares since were at the bubbling of Moore-ditch, sware by their christendomes that as many dayes and yeeres as they had lived, they never saw such a myracle of·a red herring taken in the fresh water before."—*Lenten stuffe, or praise of the red herring*, 1599, 4to, p. 60. But Cleopatra's trick was of a different nature. Antony had fished unsuccessfully in her presence, and she had laughed at him. The next time therefore he directed the boatman to dive under the water and attach a fish to his hook. The queen perceived the stratagem, but affecting not to notice it, congratulated him on his success. Another time, however, she determined to laugh at him once more, and gave orders to her own people to get the start of his divers, and put some dried *salt-fish* on his hook.

SCENE 5. Page 499.

CLEO. Some innocents 'scape not the thunder bolt.

This alludes to a superstitious notion among the ancients, that they who were stricken with lightning were honoured by Jupiter, and therefore to be accounted holy. Their bodies were supposed not to putrify; and after having been shown for a certain time to the people, were not burned in the usual manner, but buried on the spot where the lightning fell, and a monument erected over them. Some, however, held a contrary opinion. See the various notes on the line in Persius,

" Triste jaces lucis, evitandumque bidental," *Sat.* ii.

The ground also that had been smitten by a thunderbolt was accounted sacred, and afterwards inclosed: nor did any one presume to walk on it. This we learn from Festus, " fulguritum, id quod est fulmine ictum; qui locus statim fieri

putabatur religiosus, quod eum Deus sibi dicasse videretur."
These places were therefore consecrated to the gods, and
could not in future become the property of any one.

SCENE 7.　Page 512.

> 2. SER. I had as lief have a reed that will do me no service, as a
> *partizan* I could not heave.

Dr. Johnson says the partizan is a pike, and so say many
of our dictionaries; but it was in reality a weapon between a
pike and a halbert.　Not being so long as the former, it was
made use of in trenches, in mounting a breach, and in attacking or defending a lodgment; on all which occasions the
pike would have been unmanageable.　Its upper extremity
resembled that of a halbert, but was longer and broader.　In
more modern times it wanted the cutting axe which belongs
to the halbert, though in that used by the old Switzers and
Germans it seems to have had it.　The etymology of the
word has been much controverted, but appears to lie between
the Latin *pertica* and the German *bart,* an axe, whence *bar-
dike,* a little axe.　Shakspeare himself has distinguished it
from the pike, " Let us make him with our *pikes and parti-
zans* a grave."—*Cymbeline,* Act IV. Scene 2.

SCENE 7.　Page 518.

> ENO. Drink thou; increase the *reels.*

Here is some corruption, and unless it was originally *revels,*
the sense is irretrievable.　In all events Mr. Steevens has
erred in saying that " *reel* was not, in our author's time, employed to signify a dance."　The following passage in a book
with which the learned editor was well acquainted, and which
had escaped his excellent memory, proves the contrary:—
" Agnis Tompson was after brought againe before the king's
majestie and confessed that upon the night of Allhollon even
last, she was accompanied with a great many witches to the
number of two hundreth; and that all they together went by

sea each one in a riddle or cive, and went in the same very
substantially with flaggons of wine making merrie and drinking by the waye in the same riddles or cives, to the kerke of
North Barrick in Lowthian, and that after they had landed,
tooke hands on the land, and daunced this *reill or short daunce,*
singing all with one voice,

> ‘ Commer goe ye before, commer goe ye,
> Gif ye will not goe before, commer let me.’

At which time she confessed, that Geilles Duncane did goe
before them playing this *reill or daunce* upon a small trump,
call a Jewes trump, untill they entered into the kerk of North
Barrick.”—*Newes from Scotland declaring the damnable life
and death of doctor Fian, a notable sorcerer, who was burned
at Edenbrough in January last,* 1591, sign. B iij.

ACT III.

Scene 6.   Page 543.

Cæs. . . . . . The wife of Antony
 Should have an army for an *usher.*

An *usher* is a person who introduces others ceremoniously,
though originally a door-keeper, from the French *huissier,*
and that from *huis, ostium.* This is no otherwise worth the
mention, than to mark the corrupt orthography of the word,
which ought to be written *husher.* Thus Spencer,

> “ A gentle *husher,* vanitie by name,
> Made roome, and passage for them did prepare.”
> *Fairy queen,* B. i. Canto 4, st. 13.

Cavendish, the servant of Cardinal Wolsey, speaking of his
master’s arrest by the Earl of Northumberland, says, “ he
toke the Earle by the hande, and led him in to his bed-cham-
ber. And they being there all alone, save onely I *who kept
the dore according to my dutye, being gentleman ussher,* &c.”
—*Life of Wolsey,* MS.

Scene 6.   Page 544.

> Cæs. . . . . and have prevented
> The *ostent* of our love.

Mr. Steevens, in claiming the merit of this necessary change from *ostentation*, had forgotten that it had been already made by Sir Thomas Hanmer.

Scene 6.   Page 544.

> Cæs. . . . Which soon he granted,
> Being an *obstruct* 'tween his lust and him.

The change was made by Dr. Warburton from *abstract*, which he declares to be absurd; but, as an eminent critic has remarked, it has been made very unnecessarily. The canon somewhere laid down, viz. that where the old text is capable of a meaning, no alteration should be hazarded, ought to have been observed in this instance. The sense is obviously, " Octavia drew away or *abstracted* Cleopatra from Antony," and she might therefore be very properly called, in Shakspeare's bold language, an *abstract*.

Another reason for retaining the old reading is, that, generally speaking, Dr. Warburton's *emendations* are inadmissible.

Scene 11.   Page 587.

> Ant. If from the field I shall return once more
> To kiss these lips, I will appear in blood—
> I will be treble-sinew'd, hearted, breath'd,
> And fight maliciously: for when mine hours
> Were *nice* and lucky, men did ransom lives
> Of me for jests——

The word *nice*, sometimes used by Shakspeare in a sense bordering on that of *amorous* or *wanton*, seems in the present instance to have precisely that meaning. Antony says that his former *luxurious* hours with Cleopatra were fortunate to those who asked his favours, but that now he will appear in blood. The historian Stowe, in recording an accident that happened to one Mary Breame in the year 1583, says that she " had beene *accused* by her husband to bee a *nice woman of her body.*" We have also an old play entitled *The nice wanton.*

SCENE 11.　Page 589.

ENO.　.　.　.　.　.　.　and in that mood,
　　　The dove will peck the *estridge.*

i. e. the *falcon.*　See note p. 268, &c.

ACT IV.

SCENE 9.　Page 611.

1. SOLD. .　.　.　.　.　.　.　so bad a prayer
　　　Was never yet for *sleeping.*
2. SOLD.　　　　　　　　　　Go we to him.

In the old copy *sleep.* The alteration is by Mr. Steevens, and, as he says, for the sake of *measure* ; but that was already complete. The *harmony* is certainly improved, as the accent is to be laid on *to* in the ensuing line.

SCENE 12.　Page 624.

ANT.　My good *knave*, Eros, now thy captain is
　　　Even such a body : here I am Antony ;
　　　Yet cannot hold this visible shape, my *knave.*
　　　I made these wars for Egypt ; and the *queen*,—
　　　Whose *heart*, I thought, I had, for she had mine ;
　　　.　.　.　.　.　.　.　.　.　she, Eros, has
　　　Pack'd cards with Cæsar, and *false play'd* my glory
　　　Unto an enemy's *triumph.*

One should really suppose that Shakspeare had written this speech just after having lost a game at cards, and before the manner in which it had been played was out of his mind. Dr. Warburton's explanation is too superficial to merit the commendation which Dr. Johnson has bestowed on it. That of Mr. Malone is much more judicious and satisfactory ; but it has not been perceived that a marked and particular allusion is intended. This is to the old card game of *trump*, which

bore a very strong resemblance to our modern whist. It was
played by two against two, and sometimes by three against
three. It is thus mentioned in *Gammer Gurton's needle,*
Act II. Scene 2 : " We be fast set at *trump* man, hard by
the fire ;" and like wise in Dekkar's *Belman of London,* among
other card games. In Eliot's *Fruits for the French,* 1593,
p. 53, it is called " a verie common alehouse game in England ;" and Rice, in his *Invective against vices,* 12mo, b. l. n. d.
but printed before 1600, speaking of sharpers' tricks at cards,
mentions " renouncyng the *trompe* and comming in againe."
The Italians call it *triomphetto* ; see Florio's dictionary. In
Capitolo's poem on Primero, another card game, 1526, 8vo,
it is called *trionfi,* and consigned to the peasants. Minsheu,
in his *Spanish dialogues,* p. 25, makes it a game for old men.
We, in all probability, received it from the French *triomphe,*
which occurs in Rabelais as one of Gargantua's games. The
term indicates a winning or *triumphant* card ; and therefore
there can be no pretence for deriving it from *tromper,* whatever
Ben Jonson might have thought to the contrary, who, in
reality, seems only to indulge in a pun upon the word.

SCENE 12.   Page 627.

ANT. I will o'ertake thee, Cleopatra, and
       Weep for my pardon.   So it must be, for now
       All *length* is torture.

Mr. Steevens suspects that the author wrote *life* ; surely
without reason. Length is *extension* or *protraction of life.*

THE CLOWN.

He is a mere country fellow ; but Shakspeare, in compliance with the usual expectations of the audience, has bestowed on him a due portion of wit and satire.

CYMBELINE.

ACT I.

SCENE 2. Page 18.

IMO. . . . . he is
  A man worth any woman; overbuys me
  Almost the sum he pays.

THIS has already been so ingeniously interpreted, that there is considerable hazard in the offer of any other conjecture on the subject; yet, may not Imogen mean, " the possession of me is much too dearly bought by the *banishment* to which you sentence him; he has almost nothing for so large a price."

SCENE 5. Page 27.

Enter PHILARIO, IACHIMO, &c.

Mr. Malone having shown that this name is borrowed from the Italian *Giacomo*, it should be printed *Jachimo*, in order to prevent any mistake in the pronunciation.

ACT II.

SCENE 2. Page 65.

IMO. From fairies and the tempters of the night,
  Guard me, beseech ye!

See p. 128.

SCENE 3. Page 72.

Hark, hark, the lark at heaven's gate sings.

The frequent mention of the lark, especially among our older poets, has been already exemplified in a variety of corresponding passages with the above, which either Shakspeare

might have imitated, or which are imitations from him.   To
these the following may be added :—

> " On morowe tho the dai sprong
> And the larke bigan her song."
>
> Romance of Sir Oluel. MS.

> " Even at the twelyght in the dawnynge
> Whan the larke of custome gynneth synge
> For to salue in her heavenly laye
> The lusty goddesse of the morowe graye."
>
> Lydgate's Sege of Troye, B. i.

> " Whan the larke messager of day
> Of custome aye Aurora doth salue,
> With sondry notes hir sorowe to transmue,
> Or Phebus ryse to joye and gladnesse."
>
> Lydgate's Sege of Troye, B. iii.

> " Upsprang the golden candle matutyne,
> With cleir depurit bemys chrystallyne,
> Glading the mirry fowlis in thair nest:
> Or Phebus was in purpour kaip revest
> Upsprang the lark, the hevene's mynstral syne
> In may intill a morrow mirth fullest."
>
> Dunbar's Golden terge.

> " With merry note her loud salutes the mounting lark."
>
> Spenser's Fairy queen, B. I. Canto xi. st. 51.

> " Early, cheerful, mounting lark,
> Light's gentle usher, morning's clerk,
>   In merry notes delighting ;
> Stint awhile thy song, and hark,
>   And learn my new inditing.
> " Bear up this hymn, to heav'n it bear
> E'en up to heav'n, and sing it there," &c.
>
> Davies's Acrostick hymns, 1599.

> " . . . . . . and then my state,
> (Like to the lark, at break of day arising
> From sullen earth) sings hymns at heaven's gate."
>
> Shakspeare's 29th Sonnet.

> " The larke that left her food, her nest, her yong,
> And early mounting, first with her sweet song
> Saluted heaven."
>
> Niccolls's London Artillery, 1616, 4to.

> " And the lark from out the furrow,
> Soars upright on matin wings,
> And at the gate of heaven sings."
>
> Penshurst.   In Dodsley's collection, vol. iv.

Scene 4. Page 88.

Iach.   The roof o' the chamber
With *golden cherubims* is fretted; her andirons
(I had forgot them) were two winking Cupids
Of silver, each on one foot standing, nicely
Depending on their brands.

Mr. Steevens calls the *golden cherubims* a tawdry image, and proceeds, justly enough, to ridicule an idle representation of the heavenly choirs; but the poet must be cleared from any imputation of blame. He is not accountable for the fashions or follies of his age, and has, in this instance, given a faithful description of the mode in which the rooms in great houses were sometimes ornamented. That *brands* were those parts of the andirons which supported the wood, according to Mr. Whalley, remains to be proved. The Cupids would not lean or hang over these bars, but rather stand with their faces turned from them, and opposite to the spectator. The brands are more likely to have been the inverted torches mentioned by Mr. Steevens.

Scene 5. Page 94.

Post. Me of my lawful pleasure she restrain'd,
    And pray'd me, oft, forbearance: did it
    With a pudency so rosy, &c.

A useless note on this speech, which would make our poet equally vulgar and obscene, when he was expressing a sentiment of the most refined delicacy, may be well dispensed with in any future edition.

ACT III.

Scene 1. Page 99.

Cym. Our ancestor was that Mulmutius, which
    Ordain'd our laws . . . .
    . . . . Mulmutius,
    Who was the first of Britain, &c.

The judicious and necessary omission of the words "made

our laws," after the second Mulmutius, originally belongs to
Sir Thomas Hanmer, who would have deserved more thanks
from his readers for his regulations of Shakspeare's metre, if
they had not been too frequently made without a proper regard to the accuracy of the text.

SCENE 1. Page 100.

CYM. Thy Cæsar *knighted* me.

Although our old writers frequently make mention of
Roman knights, that is, military chieftains, it is very much to
be apprehended that the present expression must be regarded
as a downright anachronism, as well as another similar passage, in p. 213, where Cymbeline addresses Belarius and his
sons: " Bow your knees; arise my *knights* of the battle, &c."
The word *knight* was formerly used with great latitude.
Dr. Bullein calls Dioscorides " that olde famous Egyptian
knyghte."

SCENE 2. Page 105.

IMO. (Some griefs are med'cinable ;) that is one of them,
For it doth physick love ;——

The *whole* of this should be included in the parenthesis,
as in Mr. Malone's edition. No reason has been assigned
by Mr. Steevens for the variation, which may be an error of
the press.

SCENE 3. Page 117.

BEL. . ` . . . . *Euriphile,*
Thou wast their nurse——

The above name might have been borrowed from the story
of Amphiaraus and *Eriphile,* in Pettie's *Petite palace,* 1598,
4to.

SCENE 4. Page 120.

PIS. . . . . . whose tongue
Outvenoms all the worms of Nile.

So in the anonymous play of *Wily beguilde,*

" Whose tongue more venom than the serpent's sting."

It is difficult to say which is the imitation.

ACT IV.

SCENE 2.   Page 154.

GUI. But his neat *cookery*.

This speech has exercised the talents of a certain ingenious female *illustrator* of Shakspeare, who has endeavoured to ridicule the character of Imogen, and indeed the whole of the play.   She degrades our heroine into a mere kitchen wench, and adverts to what she calls her *œconomical education*.   Now what is this but to expose her own ignorance of ancient manners ?   If she had missed the advantage of qualifying herself as a commentator on Shakspeare's plots by a perusal of our old romances, she ought at least to have remembered, what every well informed woman of the present age is acquainted with, the education of the princesses in Homer's *Odyssey*. It is idle to attempt to judge of ancient simplicity by a mere knowledge of modern manners; and such fastidious critics had better close the book of Shakspeare for ever.   In another part of her critique on this play, she condemns the giving of the drug to Imogen which Pisanio had received from the queen, from an idea that he was sufficiently warned of its soporific quality ; and she positively states that the physician had, by a whisper, informed Pisanio of its property; not one word of which is to be found in Shakspeare.   So much for the criticism and accuracy of a work to which Dr. Johnson condescended to write a dedication.   He has likewise too often confided in its opinions in the course of several of his remarks on Shakspeare's plays.

SCENE 2.   Page 156.

CLO. Know'st me not by my clothes ?
GUI.   *No*, nor thy tailor, rascal.

Mr. Steevens's correct ear has on this, perhaps single, occasion been deceived.   He objects to the negation *no*, as " at once superfluous and injurious to the metre ;" yet it is impossible to read the line harmoniously without it. Nor does it constitute the superfluity of the metre, which has, exclusively, two redundant syllables. If any alteration were allowable, it might be the following:—

> " Know'st not my clothes?   No, nor thy tailor, rascal."

SCENE 2.   Page 164.

BEL.   O thou goddess,
        Thou divine nature, *how* thyself thou blazon'st——

This judicious emendation from *thou* thyself, &c., claimed by one learned gentleman and adopted by another, is the original property of Sir Thomas Hanmer.

SCENE 2.   Page 168.

GUI. With *female* fairies will his tomb be haunted.

i. e. harmless and protecting spirits, not fairies of a mischievous nature.

SCENE 2.   Page 169.

GUI. And worms will not come to *thee.*

Mr. Steevens imputes *great violence* to this change of person, and would read " come to *him;*" but there is no impropriety in Guiderius's sudden address to the *body itself.* It might indeed be ascribed to our author's careless manner, of which an instance like the present occurs at the beginning of the next act, where Posthumus says,

> ". . . . . . . *you* married ones,
> If each of *you* would take this course, how many
> Must murder wives much better than *themselves.*"

SCENE 2.   Page 169.

ARV. . . . . . the ruddock would,
        With charitable bill,—bring thee all this;
        Yea and furr'd moss besides, when flowers are none
        To *winter-ground* thy corse.

The question made by Dr. Percy, whether the notion of the redbreast covering dead bodies be older than the celebrated ballad of the babes of the wood, has been satisfactorily an-

swered in the affirmative by Mr. Reed's note.   In Dekker's
Villanies discovered by lanthorn and candle light, 1616, 4to, it
is said, " They that cheere up a prisoner but with their sight,
are Robin red breasts that bring strawes in their bils to cover
a dead man in extremitie."   See chap. xv.

With respect to *winter-ground* ; until some other example
of the use of this word be produced, there will be no impropriety in offering a substitute in *winter-green,* that is, " to preserve thy tomb green with moss in the winter season, when
there will be no flowers wherewith to deck it."   Such a verb
might have been suggested to Shakspeare, who often coins in
this way, by the plant *winter-green,* the *pyrola.*

Ruddock was the Saxon name ꞃubbuc, for the red-breast,
and long continued to be so.   In Bullokar's *Æsop,* 1585,
12mo, there is a fable " Of a fowlor and the bird cale'd
Robin-red-brest," which concludes in these words : " Then
the fowlor, hop of-taking many being lost, when it waz now
tym too-rest, drawing the netz, he cauht only on *Robin-rud-
dok,* which being unhappy [unlucky] had abydd stil in the
shrap."

Scene 2.   Page 175.

Imo. 'Od's pittikins !

Mr. Steevens's derivation from God's *my* pity, is not quite
correct.   It is rather from *God's pity,* diminutively used by
the addition of *kin.*   In this manner we have *'od's bodikins.*

ON THE STORY OF THIS PLAY.

For the plot of Cymbeline, Shakspeare has been almost
exclusively indebted to Boccaccio's novel of Bernabo Lomel-
lin, Day 2, novel 9, as Mr. Malone has proved beyond the
possibility of doubt. Unless we suppose, what is not probable,
that Shakspeare was acquainted with the Italian language, or
that he had heard the above novel read by some person in

English, a difficulty arises in accounting for the manner in which he got access to it. The earliest English translation of the *whole of the Decameron* was first printed in 1620, by Isaac Jaggard, in folio, and in two parts, the first of which was re-published under the title of *The modell of wit, mirth, eloquence, and conversation, framed in ten days of an hundred curious pieces, by seven honourable ladies, and three noble gentlemen, preserved to posterity by the renowned John Boccacio, the first refiner of Italian prose, and now translated into English,* 1625, in folio. See more on this subject in a preceding note, p. 102. Had Shakspeare been intimately acquainted with Boccaccio's *Decameron,* one should have expected that he would have made considerable use of that work; but this is the only play in which the most material part of the plot has been extracted from it. There are indeed one or two instances in which a very slight use has been made of it, but then evidently through the medium of an English translation. Is it not possible that our author might have known French enough to have occasionally read the Decameron in that language?

TITUS ANDRONICUS.

ACT II.

SCENE 1. Page 276.

AAR. And faster bound to Aaron's *charming* eyes.

HE is not here commending the *beauty* of his eyes, but adverting to their power of *fascination*. This was anciently supposed a peculiar quality of the eye, and many remedies or amulets were used to charm away its power.

SCENE 3. Page 287.

TAM. While hounds, and horns, and sweet melodious birds,
Be unto us, as is a nurse's song
Of *lullaby*, to bring her babe asleep.

We have here a curious lullaby note, which, as well as the present, may possibly have a drowsy effect on all readers but staunch antiquaries and etymologists. For the benefit therefore of the latter it may be observed, that Dr. Johnson is probably mistaken in supposing that the nurse's word *by* signifies sleep, otherwise than as a contraction of *lullaby*. It is to be wished that Mr. Holt White had favoured us with some proof that to *lull* originally signified to *sleep*, and that its present sense, *to compose to sleep by a pleasing sound*, is but a secondary one, retained after the primitive import had become obsolete. The same ingenious critic proceeds to state that *by* means *house*, and therefore *lullaby* is to *go to house or cradle*. There is so much plausibility in this conjecture that it is almost a pity to be obliged to dissent from it. Though it cannot be disputed that *by* signifies a *dwelling*, it is presumed that this sense is as unconnected with the word in question as Dr. Johnson's *sleep*. It would be a hopeless task to trace the origin of the northern verb *to lull*, which means *to sing gently* ; but it is evidently connected with the Greek λαλεω, loquor, or λαλλη, the sound made by the beach at sea. Thus much is certain, that the Roman nurses used the word *lalla* to quiet their children, and that they feigned a deity called *Lallus*, whom they invoked on that occasion ; the lullaby or tune itself was called by the same name. As *lallare* meant to *sing lalla*, to *lull* might in like manner denote the singing of the nurse's lullaby to induce the child to sleep. Thus in an ancient carol composed in the fifteenth century, and preserved among the Sloane MSS. No. 2593 :

> " che song a slepe w^t. her *lullynge*
> here dere sone our savyoure."

In another old ballad printed by Mr. Ritson in his *Ancient songs*, p. 198, the burden is " lully, lully, lullaby, lullyby, sweete baby, &c. ;" from which it seems probable that *lullaby* is only a comparatively modern contraction of *lully baby*, the first word being the legitimate offspring of the Roman *lalla*. In another of these pieces still more ancient, and printed in the same collection, we have, " lullay, lullow, lully, *bewy*, lulla baw baw." The welsh appear to have been famous for their lullaby songs. Jones, in his *Arte and science of preserving bodie and soule*, 1579, 4to, says, " The best nurses, but especially the trim and skilfull Welch women, doe use to sing some preaty sonets, wherwith their copious tong is plentifully stoared of divers pretie tunes and pleasaunt ditties, that the children disquieted might be brought to reste : but translated never so well, they want their grace in Englishe, for lacke of proper words : so that I will omit them, as I wishe they would theyr ·lascivious *Dymes*, wanton *Lullies*, and amorous *Englins*."

Mr. White, in reviewing his opinion of the etymology of *good-by*, will perhaps incline to think it a contraction, when properly written *good b'ye,* of *God be with you,* and not " may your *house* prosper !"

To add to the stock of our old lullaby songs, two are here subjoined. The first is from a pageant of *The slaughter of the innocents,* acted at Coventry in the reign of Henry the Eighth, by the taylors and shearers of that city, and most obligingly communicated by Mr. Sharpe. The other is from the curious volume of songs mentioned before in p. 262. Both exhibit the simplicity of ancient manners.

" Lully, lulla, thou littell tine childe,
　　By by lully lullay,
Lully lullay thou littell tyne child,
　　By by lully lullay.

O sisters too, how may we do,
　　For to preserve this day
This pore yongling, for whom we do singe
　　By by lully lullay.

Herod the king, in his raging,
　　Chargid he hath this day ;
His men of might, in his owne sight,
　　All yonge children to slay.

That wo is me, pore child for thee,
　　And ever morne and say ;
For thi parting, nether say nor sing,
　　By by lully lullay."

" By by lullaby
Rockyd I my chyld
In a drē late as I lay
Me thought I hard a maydyn say
And spak thes wordys mylde,
My lytil sone with the I play
And ever she song by lullay.
Thus rockyd she hyr chyld
By by lullabi,
Rockid I my child by by.
Then merveld I ryght sore of thys
A mayde to have a chyld I wys,
By by lullay.
Thus rockyd she her chyld
By by lullaby, rockyd I my chyld." Finis.

2 c

Scene 3.   Page 290.

Tam. O'ercome with moss and *baleful* misletoe.

This epithet is extremely appropriate either conformably to an ancient, but erroneous, opinion, that the berries of the misletoe were poisonous ; or on account of the use made of this plant by the Druids during their detestable human sacrifices.

ACT III.

Scene 1.   Page 305.

Tit. Speak my Lavinia, what accursed hand
    Hath made thee handless in thy father's *sight?*

Dr. Warburton says, " we should read *spight* ;" but there is no reason for a change for the worse.   Titus had made no attempt to *prevent* the mutilation of his unhappy daughter, nor had it taken place in *despite,* i. e. contempt or hatred of him.

ACT IV.

Scene 3.   Page 338.

Tit. And sith there is no justice in earth nor hell,
    We will solicit heaven, and move the Gods.

Notwithstanding the difference in arrangement, it will hardly be questioned that the author is here indebted to Virgil's

" Flectere si nequeo superos, Acheronta movebo."

This may be added to the list of classical allusions at the end of the play.

ACT V.

Scene 1.   Page 351.

Aar. An idiot holds his *bauble* for a God,
    And keeps the oath which by that God he swears.

Even though the bauble here mentioned had been actually

of that kind which is alluded to in the course of a note in *All's well that ends well*, Act IV., his imagination would be deemed not a little fanciful, who would connect it with the object of the singular oath in *Genesis* xxiv. 9. There cannot however be a doubt that Aaron refers to that sort of bauble or sceptre which was usually carried in the hand by natural idiots and allowed jesters, and by which, it may be supposed, they would sometimes swear. The resemblance which it bore to an image or idol suggested the poet's comparison.

SCENE 2. Page 363.

TIT. So, now bring them in, for I will play the cook.

This redundant line ought to be thus arranged and printed :

So,
Now bring them in, for I will play the cook.

SCENE 3. Page 364.

MAR. Rome's emperor, and nephew, *break* the parle.

Dr. Johnson makes the sense " *begin* the parley." Is it not rather " *break off* this sort of discourse !" ? for Lucius and Saturninus had already *begun* the parley by sparring language : to prevent the continuance of it Marcus interferes, by declaring that their quarrels must be adjusted by gentle *words*.

Throughout this play the name *Andrŏnĭcus* is improperly accented. It should have been *Andronīcus*.

THE CLOWN.

HE is nothing more than a shrewd rustic, performing the office of a messenger.

PERICLES.

Page 388.

Pentapolis.]

" THIS," says Mr. Steevens, " is an imaginary *city*, and its
name might have been borrowed from some romance. We
meet, indeed, in history with *Pentapolitana regio*, a country
in Africa, and from thence perhaps some novelist furnished
the sounding title of *Pentapolis*," &c. But there was no absolute reason for supposing it a *city* in this play, as Gower in
the *Confessio amantis* had done, a circumstance which had
probably misled Mr. Steevens. In the original Latin romance
of Apollonius Tyrius, it is most accurately called *Pentapolis
Cyrenorum*, and was, as both Strabo and Ptolemy inform us,
a *district* of Cyrenaica in Africa, comprising *five cities*, of
which Cyrene was one.

ACT I.

GOWER. To sing a song *of old* was sung.

The editor, having very properly adopted Mr. Malone's
amendment in the text, has forgotten to mention that the
former reading was *that old*, and the note is consequently rendered obscure.

SCENE 1. Page 397.

PER. See where she comes, apparell'd like the spring,
Graces her subjects, and her thoughts the king
Of every virtue——

A transposition of *spring* and *king* has been suggested, but
on no solid foundation ; nor, it is presumed, is the passage

incurably depraved, or even any change necessary. Mr. Steevens asks, " With what propriety can a lady's thoughts be styled the king of every virtue? " For this the poet must answer, who evidently designed an antithesis in *king* and *subjects.*

SCENE 1. Page 402.

ANT. Read the *conclusion* then;
 Which read and not expounded, 'tis decreed,
 As these before thee, thou thyself shalt bleed.

Conclusion, which formerly signified a trial or *experiment,* is here put for *riddle,* itself a trial of skill. The practice of proposing such riddles, with the penalty for not expounding them, is borrowed from ancient romances. In that of *Tristan de Leonnois,* there is a giant who detains all passengers that he meets, and puts them to the test of unfolding a riddle. If they fail, he kills them. A hero at length presents himself, who, after explaining the riddle, proposes one in his turn; the giant not being able to expound it, is himself put to death. The construction of these riddles is the same as that in the play, as will appear from the following specimen :—

 " Je d'un arbre jouy jadis
 Que j'aimois mieux que paradis ;
 C'est arbre bel fruict m'apporta
 Que sa grand' beauté m'entorta
 Tellement que la fleur en pris :
 Et puis du fruist tant je mespris
 Qu'a le manger fu irrité.
 Dy moy du cas la verité,
 La me disant la vie auras ;
 Si non sois seur que tu mourras."

SCENE 1. Page 402.

DAUGH. *In all save that,* may'st thou prove prosperous!

This reading has been adopted in preference to that of the old copy, which was, *of all said yet* ; and in support of it Mr. Mason has offered the following argument.

She cannot wish him more prosperous in expounding the riddle than those who had preceded him ; because his success

would cause the publication of her own shame. Feeling a re-
gard for the prince, she deprecates his fate, and wishes he may
not succeed in solving the riddle; but that his failure may be
attended with prosperous consequences. Now she must have
very well known that the failure in question could be attended
with no other consequences than the forfeiture of his life, a
condition that had been just before expressly declared. Nor
was such a wish on the part of the lady likely to operate
as an inducement to the prince to try his chance. The words
" save that" appear to have no regular antecedent. Would
it not therefore be more charitable towards the lady to suppose that her mind revolted at the guilty situation she was
placed in; and that a sudden affection for the prince, and a
desire to be honourably united to such a man, might take
possession of her mind, and induce her to wish, according to
a sense which may be extracted from the old reading, that, *as*
to all which had been uttered, he might prove successful? It
should be remembered too, that this idea corresponds entirely
with the character of the princess in Gower. Should this
interpretation be thought just, the present speech must be
supposed to be *privately* addressed to the prince.

Scene 1.   Page 410.

Per. . . . . . . for wisdom sees, those men
        Blush not in actions blacker than the night,
        Will *shun* no course to keep them from the light.

The old reading was *show* no course, which is equivalent
with *take no means*; and the construction is, " they who blush
not for bad actions will take no means to conceal them."

Scene 2.   Page 413.

Per. Let none disturb us: why this *charge* of thoughts?

Both the old editions have *change*, which, as Mr. Mason
has shown, may very well stand; and even the redundant
word *should*, in the old copies, might be retained without
diminishing the harmony of the line. The sense would then

be, " Let none disturb us : why should this change of sentiment [disturb us] ?"

SCENE 4. Page 426.

> CLE. If *heaven* slumber while *their* creatures want,
> They may awake *their* helps to comfort them.

As these lines stand they are ungrammatical. The original
reading was, no doubt, *if the Gods slumber*, which was altered
by the licencer of the press. This should either be restored,
or the whole rendered correct.

ACT II.

Page 438.

> Gow. . . . . . what shall be next,
> Pardon old Gower; this *longs* the text.

Which Mr. Steevens thus explains : " Excuse old Gower
from telling you what follows. The very text to it has proved
of too considerable a length already." But has he not missed
the meaning of this elliptical mode of expression, which seems
to be, " Excuse old Gower from relating what follows ; this
belongs to the text, i. e. the play itself, not to me the commentator ?" In the third Act he uses a similar speech,

> " I will relate ; action may
> Conveniently the rest convey."

Longs should be printed *'longs*, as we have *'lated* for *belated*
in *Macbeth*, Act. III. Scene 3.

SCENE 1. Page 450.

> PER. . . . . . I yet am unprovided
> Of a pair of *bases.*

These were a sort of petticoat that hung down to the knees,
and were suggested by the Roman military dress, in which
they seem to have been separate and parallel slips of cloth or
leather. Gayton in his *Festivous notes on Don Quixote*, p. 218,
says, that " all heroick persons are *pictured* in *bases* and bus-

kins." In the celebrated story of *Friar John and Friar Richard*, as related in Heywood's *History of women*, p. 253, the skirts of the *armed* friar's gown are made to serve as *bases*. At the justs that were held in honour of Queen Catherine in the second year of Henry VIII., some of the knights had " their *basses* and trappers of cloth of golde, every of them his name embroudered on his *basse* and trapper."—Halle's *Chronicle*. But here the term seems applied to the furniture of the horses. The bases appear to have been made of various materials. If in tilting they fell to the ground, the heralds claimed them as a fee, unless redeemed by money; this indeed was the case with respect to any piece of armour that happened to be detached from the owner. Sometimes *bases* denoted the hose merely; as in the comedy of *Lingua*, 1607, where *Auditus*, one of the characters, is dressed in " a cloth of silver mantle upon a pair of sattin *bases*." In Rider's Latin Dictionary, 1659, *bases* are rendered *palliolum curtum*. The term seems to have been borrowed from the French, who at a very early period used *bache* for a woman's petticoat. —See Carpentier *Glossar. medii ævi*.

SCENE 2. Page 454.

THAISA. And his device, a *wreath* of chivalry
The word, *Me pompæ provexit apex*.

Pompæ, and not *Pompei*, is undoubtedly the true word; and the whole of Mr. Steevens's reasoning in favour of the latter is at once disposed of by referring to the work which appears to have furnished the author of the play with this and the two subsequent devices of the knights. It is a scarce little volume entitled, *The heroicall devises of M. Claudius Paradin canon of Beaujeu, whereunto are added the lord Gabriel Symeon's and others. Translated out of Latin into English,* by *P. S.* 1591, 24mo. The *sixth* device, from its peculiar reference to the situation of Pericles, may perhaps have been altered from one in the same collection used by Diana of Poictiers. It is a green branch issuing from a tomb with the

motto SOLA VIVIT IN ILLO. The following are what have
been immediately borrowed from Paradin; but it is also proper to state that the torch and the hand issuing from a cloud
are to be found in Whitney's *Emblems*, 1586, 4to. As they
are all more elegantly engraved in the original editions of
Paradin and Symeon than in the English book above mentioned, the copies here given have been made from the former.

ACT III.

Scene 2.　Page 498.

1. Gent.　Or tie my treasure up in silken bags,
　　　　To please *the fool and death.*

The notes on this passage having got into some little
confusion by the introduction of the lines in *Measure for
measure* which relate to the *fool and death* and the supple-
mental remarks on it, it will be necessary in all future editions to keep them separate, as it seems almost certain that
they have no connection with each other.

Cerimon in most express terms declares that he feels
more real satisfaction in his liberal employment as a physician, than he should in the uncertain pursuit of honour, or
in the mere accumulation of wealth; which would assimilate
him to a miser, the result of whose labour is merely to entertain the fool and death.　But how was such amusement as
this to affect those personages in the *other* instance, where
the vain attempts of a fool to escape the jaws of his adversary
form the whole of the subject?　The allusion therefore is to
some such print as Mr. Steevens happily remembered to have

seen, in which death plunders the miser of his money bags, whilst the fool is grinning at the process. It may be presumed that these subjects were common in Shakspeare's time. They might have ornamented the poor man's cottage in the shape of rude prints, or have been introduced into halfpenny ballads long since consigned to oblivion. The miser is at all times fair game; and to prove that this is not a chimerical opinion, and at the same time to show the extensive range of this popular subject, a few prints of the kind shall be mentioned. 1. Death and the two misers, by Michael Pregel. 2. An old couple counting their money, death and two devils attending, a mezzotint by Vander Bruggen. 3. A similar mezzotint by Meheux without the devils. 4. An old print on a *single sheet* of a dance of death, on which both the *miser* and the *fool* are exhibited in the clutches of the grim monarch.

The rear may be closed with the same subject as represented in the various *dances of death* that still remain. Nor should it be concluded that because these prints exhibit no fool to grin at the impending scene, others might not have done so. The satirical introduction of this character on many occasions supports the probability that they did. Thus in a painting of the school of Holbein, an old man makes love to a girl, attended by a fool and death, to show, in the first instance, the folly of the thing, and in the next, its consequences. It is unnecessary to pursue the argument, as every print of the above kind that may in future occur, will itself speak much more forcibly than any thing which can here be added.

ACT IV.

SCENE 3. Page 539.

The two last lines in the quotation from *The wife for a month* should be printed thus:

Hung up *my* picture in a market place,
And sold *me* to vile bawds.

Scene 3.   Page 540.

Bawd. . . .   to scatter his *crowns in the sun*.

"There is here," says Mr. Malone, "perhaps, some allusion to the *lues venerea,* though the words *French crowns* in their literal acceptation were certainly also in Boult's thoughts." Mr. Mason sees no allusion whatever to the ·above disease. That a French crown did signify the *lues venerea* cannot be doubted; but Mr. Mason's difference of opinion might be further supported by reflecting that if the Frenchman came to *renovate** his malady, he could not well be said to scatter it. It must therefore be inferred that he was to scatter nothing but his money. As Mr. Mason has not favoured us with an explanation of the coins in question, it is necessary to state that they were *crowns of the sun* specifically so called, *écus du soleil*; and in this instance, for the sake of antithesis, termed crowns *in* the sun. They were of gold, originally coined by Louis XI. Their name was derived from the mint mark of a sun; and they were current in this kingdom by weight, in the same manner as certain English coins were in France.

Scene 3.   Page 541.

Boult. . . .   we should lodge them with *this sign*.

This sign is properly referred by Mr. Malone to the person of Marina, and cannot, for the reasons in the last note, allude to the *sun*, according to Mr. Mason's second explanation. Nor is this gentleman's argument supported by the instance adduced of the sun having been used as the sign of a brothel. It was by no means exclusively, or even particularly so. The following passage from Dekker's *Villanies discovered, or the belman's night walks,* may throw some light on the subject before us. "He saw the doores of notorious *carted bawdes* (like hell gates) stand night and day

* It is necessary that the reader should review Mr. Malone's preceding and satisfactory note.

wide open, with *a paire of harlots* in taffata gownes (like two painted posts) garnishing out those doores, being better to the house then a *double signe*."

SCENE 6. Page 567.

MAR. Thou 'rt the damn'd door-keeper to every coystrel
That hither comes enquiring for his *tib*.

Mr. Malone thinks *Tib* a contraction of Tabitha; but quære if not of Isabel? In all events it was a name given to any lewd woman. In *Pasquil's mad cappe*, 1626, 4to, an excellent satire, mention is made of *a tinker and his tibbe*. Why this name was exclusively applied to a loose woman, or how it got into the game of gleek, does not appear.

ACT V.

SCENE 3. Page 607.

PER. Heav'ns make a *star* of him!

So in 1 *Henry VI.* Act I.

" A far more glorious star thy soul will make
Than Julius Cæsar——"

This notion is borrowed from the ancients, who expressed their mode of conferring divine honours and immortality on men, by placing them among the stars. Thus on a medal of Hadrian the adopted son of Trajan and Plotina, the divinity of his parents is expressed by placing a star over their heads; and in like manner the consecration medals of Faustina the elder exhibit her on an eagle, her head surrounded with stars. Other similar medals have the moon and stars; and some of Faustina the younger the inscription SIDERIBVS RECEPTA.

THE CLOWN.

ALTHOUGH Boult, the servant to the pandar and his wife, is not termed a *clown* in the *dramatis personæ*, it should seem that he has an equal claim to the appellation with several other low characters that have been introduced into plays for the purpose of amusing the audience. He bears some affinity to the tapster in *Measure for measure*; but there is nothing that immediately constitutes him the jester to a brothel. See what has been said on such a character in the article relating to the clown in *Measure for measure*.

ON THE STORY OF PERICLES.

As the very great popularity of this play in former times may be supposed to have originated rather from the interest which the *story*, replete with incident, must have excited, than from any intrinsic merit as *a dramatic composition*, it may be worth while, and even interesting to many, to give the subject more ample discussion. To trace it beyond the period in which the favourite romance of *Apollonius Tyrius* was composed, would be a vain attempt. That was the probable original; but of its author nothing decisive has been discovered. The following circumstance, however, has led to a conjecture concerning him, which shall be stated with as much brevity as possible. When Tarsia, the Marina of Pericles, has finished the song which she addresses to her unknown father Apollonius, she receives from him a hundred pieces of gold, with a command to leave him. Athenagoras, the Lysimachus of Pericles, afterwards meets her, gives her two hundred pieces, and prevails on her to make another effort to sooth the melancholy of Apollonius. She returns to him, requests permission to renew their conversation, and insists on his taking back his money, unless he can expound certain riddles which she proceeds to state. Now these riddles, three in number, are to be found in a work entitled *Symposii ænigmata*. The original editor of this book, Pierre Pithou, thought fit, without the smallest authority, to entitle the supposed author Cælius Firmianus Symposius. Heuman, a subsequent editor, placing implicit confidence in this name, maintained that this person could be no other than the celebrated father of the church Cælius Firmianus Lactantius; for having found that he had written a work, now lost, under the title of *Symposium*, he concluded that the name of *Symposius*, which occurs at the beginning of the ænigmas, was a mistake, and that he had therefore proved his point. But this futile reasoning was easily subverted by the superior critical talents of the truly learned Fabricius, who demonstrated the impossibility of such an error, and that Heuman had even misconceived the meaning of the word *Symposium*, which could not apply to a work like the ænigmas. Besides, the evidence of Saint Jerome remained to show that the symposium was not written, like the ænigmas, in hexameter verses. Lactantius is therefore out of the question; and though there is no immediate proof respecting the time in which Symposius lived, it appears that it must have been before the eighth century, as bishop Aldhelm, who died in 709, quotes the ænigmas *as composed by Symposius the poet*. This, and many other circumstances, sufficiently identify him against the ill-founded assertions of Heuman, who regarded him as a nonentity. Aldhelm himself wrote ænigmas so much in the manner of Symposius, that one might reasonably enough infer there was no great difference in their respective ages. The learned Barthius (see his *Adversaria*, lib. lviii. c. 1.), fully persuaded of the reality of Symposius, and acquainted with the occurrence of the riddles in the history of *Apollonius Tyrius*, concluded, with other learned men, that Symposius wrote the latter; and he justly terms the author *dulcis scriptor et eruditus,* as will be evident to any one who will take the trouble of reading it in Velser's edition, which is printed from a better manuscript than those used in the *Gesta Romanorum.* If, as Velser maintains, and Barthius admits, it was originally written in Greek, a difficulty arises with respect to Symposius, unless he be regarded as the translator. But, to say the truth, there does not appear to be any solid reason for supposing him the author, or even translator. It is not very probable that in either character he would have introduced his own matter from another work ; and therefore, until some more fortunate discovery shall occur, the romance of Apollonius Tyrius must remain anonymous.

With respect to the language in which it was composed, Velser was of opinion, from certain Græco-Latin words which it contains, that this was Greek, and he speaks rather obscurely of a manuscript of it in that language at Constantinople. He seems to think that the translator was a Christian, living about the period of the decline of the Roman empire. Barthius conceived him to have been a monk of the sixth century. The *Saxon* translation mentioned in Wanley's list of manuscripts, and now in Bennett College, Cambridge, is doubtless from the Latin, and is alone a sufficient testimony of the antiquity of the work. At what time it was made must be left to the decision of those who are critically skilled in the Saxon language. One Constantine is said to have translated it into modern Greek verse about the year 1500; and this is probably the manuscript mentioned in Dufresne's index of authors, and afterwards printed at Venice in 1563. Mr. Tyrwhitt has observed that Velser was not aware of its having been already published in the *Gesta Romanorum*; and it may be added that it had been printed separately at Augsburg in 1471, perhaps as early as in the *Gesta Romanorum*; a fact that cannot well be ascertained, because there are editions of the latter without date which might have been printed

before.   Mr. Warton has committed a slight mistake in supposing that Alamannus Rinucinus made a Latin translation
corrected by Beroaldus about the year 1520.* Vossius, whom
he had misconceived, was speaking of a translation of Philostratus's life of Apollonius *Tyaneus.*   What Mr. Malone
has said of the *English* translations precludes the necessity
of any further notice of them; but with respect to that
gentleman's supposition, that there might have been an early
prose translation from the *Gesta Romanorum, in which the
name of Apollonius was changed to Pericles,* it becomes necessary to state that there are very good reasons for concluding
that the story of *Apollonius Tyrius,* from the *Gesta Romanorum,* never was translated into English ; and even that the
Gesta Romanorum in question did not appear in our language
till the beginning of the eighteenth century, and then but a
small portion of it.† The name of Pericles has been very
well accounted for by Mr. Steevens.

To render this article as complete as possible, and to facilitate the reference to a story once so celebrated, a list of the
various manuscripts and printed copies is subjoined.

MANUSCRIPTS.

Those in *Latin* are, two in Bennett Coll. Cambridge; see
Nasmith's *Catal.* Nos. cccxviii. ccccli.—Two in the Bodleian
libr. Nos. 2435, 2540; see *Catal. MSS. Angliæ,* pp. 125, 134.
Mr. Warton mentions a third, in *H. E. Poetry,* vol. i. p. 350,
note h.   A fourth is in the same library among Archb. Laud's
MSS. No. 1302, *Catal. MSS. Angliæ,* p. 70 ; on what authority this is said to have been translated from the Greek, remains to be examined.

In Magdal. Coll. Ox. No. 2191, *Catal. MSS. Angliæ,* p. 72.
—In Vossius's collection, No. 2409, *Catal. MSS. Angliæ,*
p. 64.—In the Norfolk collection, now in the library of the

---

* Hist. of Engl. poetry, III. lxiv.
† See the subsequent Dissertation on the Gesta Romanorum.

Royal Society, No. 3181, *Catal. MSS. Angliæ*, p. 80.—Two
in the Sloanian library; see Ascough's *Catal.* p. 854.—Two
in the Vatican. See Montfaucon *Bibl. bibliothecarum*, i. 20,
Nos. 275, 284.—In the Medicean library, Montfaucon *Bibl.
bibl.* i. 372, No. xl.—In the royal library at Paris; Montfaucon *Bibl. bibl.* ii. 756, No. 5251.

A *Saxon* translation. Bennett Coll. Camb. See Nasmith's
Catal. No. cci. and Wanley, Libror. vett. septentrional. catal.
apud Hickesij *Thesaur.* p. 146.

A *French* translation is among the royal MSS. in the British
museum, 20 c. ii. evidently made from the Latin about the
15th century.

A fragment in old *English* verse, probably by Thomas
Vicary of Wimborn minster in Dorsetshire, on the story of
Apollonius Tyrius, was in the possession of the late reverend and learned Dr. Farmer of Cambridge. See it noticed
in the present vol. of Mr. Steevens's Shakspeare, pp. 381,
609.

PRINTED COPIES.

Apollonii Tyrii historia, no date, but before 1500, 8vo.

The same published by Velser, 1595, 4to.

In modern Greek verse. Venice, 1563, 1601, 1696, 8vo.

In Italian rime. Venice, 1486, and without place, 1489,
4to.

In Italian prose, *reformed*; and published for the benefit of
the common people, *per piacer del popolo*, Milan, 1492, 4to.

In Spanish, in the *Patrañas* of Juan Timoneda, Alcala,
1576, and Bilbao, 1580, 8vo. This translation may be presumed to have been made from the *Gesta Romanorum*, as
other stories from it are in the same work.

In German, Augsburg, 1471, folio, and 1476, 4to.

In Dutch, Delft, 1493, 4to.

In French, b. l. Geneva, 4to, n. d. Again, transl. by Gilles
Corrozet, Paris, 1530, 8vo. Again, Amst. 1710, *Paris*, 1711,
12mo, modernized by M. Le Brun. It is abridged in *Me-*

langes tirées d'une grande ·bibliotheque, vol. lxiv. p. 265. It is also among the *Hist. tragiques* de Belleforest, tom. vii. 1604, 12mo.

In Engl. transl. by Rob. Copland from the French, and printed by Wynkyn de Worde, 1510.

The patterne of painful adventures &c. that befell unto Prince APPOLONIUS, *&c.* translated by T. Twine, 1607, Originally published by W. Howe, 1576.

In Gower's *Confessio amantis,* 1483, 1532, and 1554, folio, from Godfrey of Viterbo.

In the *Pantheon* or *universal chronicle* of Godfrey of Viterbo, compiled in Latin in the 12th century. First printed at Basil, 1569, folio, and afterwards in Pistorius's collection of German historians.

And lastly, in *most* of the editions of the *Gesta Romanorum,* in which it makes the 153rd chapter. In comparing this with Velser's work, it will be perceived that it is the same, making allowance for the usual difference of manuscripts. In short, there is but one story.

A few years after the publication of this play, there appeared on the French stage a tragi-comedy on the same story, entitled *Les heureuses infortunes.* It is in two parts, each of five acts, and composed by Francois Bernier de la Brousse. It might be worth while to examine whether he had made any use of the English Pericles.

However unworthy of Shakspeare's pen this drama, as an *entire* composition, may be considered, many will be of opinion that it contains more that *he might have written* than either *Love's labour's lost,* or *All's well that ends well.*

KING LEAR.

ACT I.

Scene 1.   Page 11.

Cor.   .   .   .   .   I am sure, my love's
More richer than *my* tongue.

Dr. Warburton would have it *their* tongue, meaning her sisters', which would be very good sense. Dr. Johnson is content with the present reading, but gives no explanation. Cordelia means to say, " My love is greater than my powers of language can express." In like manner she soon afterwards says, " I cannot heave my heart into my mouth."

Scene 1.   Page 12.

Lear. Nothing can come of nothing.

In the fourth Scene of this Act, Lear uses the same expression in answer to the fool, who had asked him if he could " make no use of nothing." For this ancient saying of one of the philosophers, Shakspeare might have been indebted to the following passage in *The prayse of nothing*, by E. D. 1585, 4to. " The prophane antiquitie therefore, unlesse by casuall meanes, entreated little hereof, as of that which by their rule, that *nihil ex nihilo fit*, conteined not matter of profit or commendation: for which those philosophers hunted, as ambicious men for dominion and empire."

Scene 4.   Page 60.

Fool. That such a king should play *bo-peep*.

Mr. Steevens remarks that little more of this *game* than its mere denomination remains. He had forgotten the amusements of his nursery. In Sherwood's *Dictionary* it is defined,

" Jeu d'enfant; ou (plustost) des nourrices aux petits enfans; se cachans le visage et puis se monstrant." The Italians say *far bau bau,* or *baco baco,* and *bauccare;* which shows that there must at some time or other have been a connexion between the nurse's *terriculamentum,* the *boggle or buggy bo,* and the present expression. See the note in p. 202. Minsheu's derivation of *bo-peep* from the noise which chickens make when they come out of the shell, is more whimsical than just.

SCENE 4. Page 65.

LEAR. Lear's shadow?

We are told that " the folio has given these words to the fool." And so they certainly should be, without the mark of interrogation. They are of no use whatever in Lear's speech; and without this arrangement, the fool's next words, " which they will make an obedient father," are unintelligible. It will likewise dispose of Mr. Steevens's subsequent charge against Shakspeare, of inattention to the rules of grammar.

ACT II.

SCENE 2. Page 92.

KENT. I'll make a *sop o' the moonshine* of you.

It is certain that an equivoque is here intended by an allusion to the old dish of *eggs in moonshine,* which was eggs broken and boiled in salad oil till the yolks became hard. They were eaten with *slices* of onions fried in oil, butter, verjuice, nutmeg and salt.

SCENE 3. Page 109.

EDG. Pins, *wooden pricks,* &c.

Rightly explained *skewers.* Greene, in his admirable satire, *A quip for an upstart courtier,* speaking of the tricks played by the butchers in his time, makes one of his characters exclaim, " I pray you, goodman Kilcalfe, have you not your artificial knaveries to set out your meate with *pricks?*" The brewers and bakers come in also for their share of abuse.

Scene 3.   Page 110.

EDGAR. Poor Turlygood!

Warburton would read *Turlupin,* and Hanmer *Turluru;* but there is a better reason for rejecting both these terms than for preferring either; viz. that *Turlygood* is the *corrupted* word in *our* language.   The Turlupins were a fanatical sect that overran France, Italy, and Germany, in the thirteenth and fourteenth centuries.   They were at first known by the names of *Beghards* or *Beghins,* and brethren and sisters of the free spirit.   Their manners and appearance exhibited the strongest indications of lunacy and distraction.   The common people alone called them *Turlupins*; a name which, though it has excited much doubt and controversy, seems obviously to be connected with the *wolvish howlings* which these people in all probability would make when influenced by their religious ravings.   Their subsequent appellation of *the fraternity of poor men* might have been the cause why the wandering rogues called *Bedlam beggars,* and one of whom Edgar personates, assumed or obtained the title of *Turlupins* or *Turlygoods,* especially if their mode of asking alms was accompanied by the gesticulations of madmen.   *Turlupino* and *Turluru* are old Italian terms for a fool or madman; and the Flemings had a proverb, *As unfortunate as Turlupin and his children.*

Scene 4.   Page 113.

LEAR. To do upon respect such violent outrage.

Explained by Dr. Johnson, " to violate the character of a messenger from the king."   It is rather " to do outrage to that respect which is due to the king."   This, in part, agrees with the ensuing note.

Scene 4. Page 114.

Kent. They summon'd up their *meiny*.

Meiny, signifying *a family, household,* or *retinue of servants,* is certainly from the French *meinie,* or, as it was anciently and more properly written, *mesnie;* which word has been regarded, with great probability, by a celebrated French glossarist and antiquary, as equivalent with *mesonie* or *maisonie,* from *maison*: in modern French *ménage.* See glossary to Villehardouin, edit. 1657, folio.

Mr. Holt White has cited Dryden's line,

" The *many* rend the skies with loud applause,"

as supplying the use of *many* in Kent's sense of *train* or *retinue.* With great deference, the word is quite unconnected with *meiny,* and simply denotes any *multitude* or collection of people. It is not only used at present in its common adjective form for *several, divers, multi,* but even substantively: for in the Northern parts of England they still say *a many,* and *a many people,* i. e. *of* people. In this sense it is never found in the French language; but we have received it directly, as an adjective, from the Saxon manı manıჳ, and as a substantive from menıu, mænıჳeo, menıჳo, &c. &c.; for in that language the word is found written not less than twenty different ways. It is the same as the Latin *manus.* Horace uses *manus poetarum*; and Quintilian *oratorum ingens manus.* It does not appear that the Saxons used *many* for a *family* or household.

Scene 4. Page 121.

Fool. Cry to it nuncle, as the *cockney* did to the eels.

The difficulties that have attended all inquiries concerning this term, have been not a little augmented by an expectation of finding an uniformity which it does not possess, and by not reflecting that it is in reality susceptible of very different explanations.

There is hardly a doubt that it originates in an Utopian region of indolence and luxury, formerly denominated the country of *cocaigne*,* which, as some have thought, was intimately connected with the art of *cookery* ; whilst others, with equal plausibility, relate that the little pellets of woad, a commodity in which Languedoc was remarkably fertile, being called by the above name, the province itself acquired the appellation of the kingdom of *cocaigne* or of plenty, where the inhabitants lived in the utmost happiness, and exempt from every sort of care and anxiety. Hence the name came to be applied to any rich country. Boileau calls Paris *un pays de cocagne*. The French have likewise some theatrical pieces under this title. The Italians have many allusions to it ; and there is said to be a small district between Rome and Loretto so called from its cheapness and fertility. With us the lines cited by Camden in his *Britannia*, vol. i. col. 451,

> " Were I in my castle of Bungey
> Upon the river of Waveney
> I would ne care for the king of *Cockeney*,"

whencesoever they come, indicate that London was formerly known by this satirical name ; *and hence a Londoner came to be called a cockney*. The French have an equivalent word, *coqueliner*, to pamper, cherish, or dandle, whence our *cocker*.

From the above circumstances it is probable that a cockney became at length a term of contempt ; one of the earliest proofs of which is Chaucer's use of it in the *Reve's tale*, v. 4206 : " I shall be halden a daffe or a *cokenay*." In the *Promptuarium parvulorum*, 1516, 4to, it is explained to be a term of derision. In Shakspeare's time it signified a child tenderly brought up, a dearling, a wanton. See Barret's

---

* This country has been humorously described by an old French fablier, from whose work an extract may be found in Mons. Legrand's entertaining collection of *Fabliaux*, tom. i. p. 251 ; and which verifies Mr. Tyrwhitt's conjecture, that the old English poem first published by Hickes, *G. A. Sax.* p. 231, was a translation from the French. See *Cant. tales*, vol. iv. p. 254.

Alvearie ; and a little before it had been used in a bad sense, from an obvious corruption. See Hulæt's *Abcedarium*, 1552, folio. In this place too Mr. Steevens's quotations from Meres and Deckar might be introduced.

The next sense in which *cockney* was used seems to be conveyed in the line cited by Mr. Tyrwhitt from *Pierce Plowman's Visions* :

> " And yet I say by my soule I have no salt bacon,
> Ne no *cokeney* by Christe coloppes to make :"

as well as in those from the tournament of Tottenham ;

> " At that feast were they served in rich array,
> Every five and five had a *cokeney* :"

where in both instances, with deference to the respectable authorities of Dr. Percy and Mr. Tyrwhitt, it signifies a *little cock*. In the latter quotation it might mean a peacock, a favourite dish among our ancestors ; and this conjecture is countenanced by the words *served in rich array*. This mode of forming a diminutive with respect to animals is not unfrequent. Thus in the *Canterbury tales*, l. 3267 : " She was a primerole, a *piggesnie*." And here again some apology may be necessary for differing from Mr. Tyrwhitt, who supposes that Chaucer " meant no more than *ocellus*, the eyes of that animal being remarkably small, and the Romans using *oculus* as a term of endearment." But the objection to this ingenious explanation is, that *nie* cannot well be put for *eye*; that in this case the word would have been *pigseye*, and that it is rather formed from the A. S. pi3a, a girl. See Lye's *Saxon dict*. Similar words were afterwards constructed, but without due regard to the above etymology. For example, " Prythee sweet *birdsnye*, be content."—Davenport's *City night cap*, Act III. Scene 1. " Jella, why frownst thou ? say sweet *biddiesnie* ?"—Davies's *Scourge of folly*. " Ay *birdsneys*, she's a quean."—Shadwell's *Virtuoso*, Act III. And in Congreve's *Old bachelor*, Fondlewife calls his mate *cockey*.

It is observable that in all the above instances these ap-

pellations are only used to females. It is not improbable
therefore, that, in an abstract sense, *cockney* might sometimes
be used in speaking to male children as a term of endearment ; and it may be necessary to make this remark here,
for the purpose of anticipating any suggestion that it is connected with the present subject.

It remains only to notice the *cockneys* or *sugar pellets*
which Mr. Steevens's old lady remembered to have eaten in
her childhood. The French formerly used a kind of perfumed pastry made of the powdered Iris flower, sugar, musk,
and rose-water ; these were called *pastilles* ; and from the similitude of the word to *pastel*, or the Languedoc woad mentioned at the beginning of this note as the produce of the *pays
de cocagne*, it is not improbable that some latent affinity may
exist. The animal involved in the English term might indeed be thought sufficient to indicate the form. Had the old
lady, happily for us, described the shape of these comfits, and
which motives of delicacy might have prevented, we could
possibly have traced them from our Gallic neighbours in another descent of a very singular nature. The following extract
from *Legrand's Vie privée des Francois,* tom. ii. p. 268, will
explain this : " Croira-t-on qu'il a existé en France un tems
ou l'on a donné aux menues pâtisseries de table les formes les
plus obscenes, et les noms les plus infâmes ? Croira-t-on que
cet incroyable excés de depravation a duré plus de deux
siécles ? Aussi sont ce moins les noms de ces pâtisseries
qu'il faut blâmer que les formes qu'on leur donnait. Cham-
pier, apres avoir décrit les differentes pâtisseries usitées de son
temps, dit, *Quædam pudenda muliebria, aliæ virilia (si diis
placet) representant. Sunt quos c . . . . saccharatos
appellitent. Adeò degeneravere boni mores, ut etiam Christi-
anis obscœna et pudenda in cibis placeant.*"

Minsheu's tale of the cock neighing, and Casaubon's derivation of cockney from οικογενης, i. e. domi natus, may
serve to increase those smiles of compassion which it is to be

feared some of the present remarks may have already excited.

It is worth remarking, although not immediately connected with the present subject, that in the Celtic languages *coeg*, and *kok*, signified anything foolish or good for nothing. They seem connected with the radical word for a *cuckow*, a silly bird, which has thus transmitted its appellation to persons of a similar nature. See the words *cog* in the Welsh dictionaries, and *cok* in Pryce's Cornish vocabulary. In the North they call the cuckow a gowk, whence *genkit*, foolish, and *gawky*. Our term *cokes*, for a fool, is of the same family, and, perhaps, *cuckold*.

Scene 4. Page 132.

Lear. Thou art a *boil*.

The note on this word states that it was written *byle* in the old copies, which all the modern editors have too strictly followed; that the mistake arose from the word *boil* being often pronounced as if written *bile*; and that in the folio we find in *Coriolanus* the same *false* spelling as here.—But this charge against the editors seems to have originated in a misconception. The ancient and true orthography is *byle* and *bile*, and such was the common pronunciation. The modern *boyl* and *boil* are corruptions. Thus in the *Promptuarium parvulorum*, 1516, we have " *Byle* sore,—Pustula." In Mathews's bible, 1551, " Satan smote Job with marvelous soore *byles*." In Whetstone's *Mirour for magestrates of cyties*, 1584, 4to, " Dicyng houses are of the substance of other buildinges, but within are the botches and *byles* of abhomination." *Bile* is pure Saxon, and is so given in most of the old dictionaries.

Scene 4. Page 135.

Lear. . . . . but this heart
  Shall break into a hundred thousand *flaws*.

On the word *flaws* we have the following note: " A *flaw*,

signifying a crack or other similar imperfection; our author, with his accustomed license, uses the word here for a *small broken particle.* So again in the fifth Act,

> '.   .   .   .   but his *flaw'd* heart
> Burst smilingly.'"

Now there is some reason for supposing that *flaw* might signify a *fragment* in Shakspeare's time, as well as a mere crack; because among the Saxons it certainly had that meaning, as may be seen in Somner's *Diction. Saxon.* voce ᵹloh. It is to be observed that the quartos read *flowes,* approaching nearer to the original. In the above quotation *flaw'd* seems to be used in the *modern* sense.

ACT III.

Scene 2.   Page 147.

Fool. Marry, here 's grace, and a *cod-piece*; that 's a wise man and a *fool.*

Shakspeare has with some humour applied the above name to the fool, who, for obvious reasons, was usually provided with this unseemly part of dress in a more remarkable manner than other persons. To the custom Gayton thus alludes, when speaking of the decline of the stage: " No fooles with *Harry codpieces appeare.*"—*Festivous notes upon Don Quixote,* p. 270.

Scene 2.   Page 150.

Fool. No hereticks *burn'd* but wenches suitors.

Dr. Johnson has very well explained why *wenches suitors* were *burned*; but Mr. Steevens's quotation from Isaiah iii. 24, " —and *burning* instead of beauty," has not been applied on this occasion with his usual discernment. Not to mention the improbability that the *burning* in question should have existed in the time of Isaiah, the expression itself is involved in the deepest obscurity. Saint Jerome has entirely omitted it; and if the Hebrew word, which in some translations has been rendered *adustio*, be susceptible of any fair meaning, it is that of *shrivelled* or *dried up by heat*. It is, therefore, in the bishop's bible and some foreign translations paraphrastically given, "and for their bewty witherednesse and *sunne burning*." The manuscript regulations for the stews in Southwark, printed but abridged in Stowe's Annals, would have furnished the learned commentator with a far more apposite illustration. In these it is said, "no stewholder shall keep any woman that hath the perilous infirmity of *burning*."

Scene 4.   Page 160.

EDG. *Pillicock* sat on pillicock's hill.

In the metrical romance of *Sir Gawain and Sir Galaron*, there is this line,

"His polemous with *pelicocus* were poudred to pay."

Pinkerton's *Scotish poems*, vol. iii. 214.

In the comedy of *Ignoramus* by Ruggles, Act III. Scene 6, Cupes talks of "quimbiblos, indenturas, *pilicoccos*, calimancas;" where it is perhaps a new-fangled term for any kind of stuff or cloth. There is an attempt to explain the word in Warner's *Letter to Garrick*, p. 30; but whoever would be certain of finding the exact meaning, may consult, besides the article in Minsheu, 9299, the following books: Durfey's *Pills to purge melancholy*, iv. 311.—The *Nightingale*, (a collection of songs) 1738, p. 380.—Lyndsay's *Works*, as edited by Mr. Chalmers, ii. 145, and the excellent glossary.— Florio's *Italian dictionary*, 1611, under the articles *piviolo*, and *rozzone*.

Scene 4.   Page 162.

EDG. Keep thy pen from *lenders books*.

When spendthrifts and distressed persons resorted to

usurers or tradesmen for the purpose of raising money by means of shop-goods or *brown paper commodities,* they usually entered their promissory notes or other similar obligations in books kept for that purpose. It is to this practice that Edgar alludes.

In Lodge's *Looking-glasse for London and Englande,* 1598, 4to, a usurer says to a gentleman, " I have thy hand set to my book that thou received'st fortie pounds of me in money." To which the other answers, " It was your device, to colour the statute, but your conscience knowes what I had." Parke, in his *Curtaine-drawer of the world,* speaking of a country gentleman, alludes to the extravagance of his back, which had got him into *the mercer's book.*

SCENE 4.   Page 163.

EDG. . . . ha, no nonny.

This was the burden of many old songs. One of these, being connected with Mr. Henley's curious note, is here presented to the reader. It is taken from a scarce collection, entitled *Melismata. Musicall phansies, fitting the court, citie and countrey humours, To 3, 4, and 5 voyces,* 1611, 4to. In Playford's *Musical companion,* p. 55, the words are set to a different tune.

E that will an Ale-house keepe must have three things in store,

a Chamber and a feather Bed, a Chimney and a hey no-ny no-ny

hay no-ny no-ny, hey nony no, hey nony no, hey nony no.

Scene 4.   Page 164.

LEAR. . . . . unaccommodated man is no more but such a poor,
bare, *forked* animal as thou art.

Forked is a very strange epithet, but must be taken literally. See a note by Mr. Steevens in Act IV. Scene 6, of this play. The Chinese in their *written* language represent a man by the following character.

Scene 6.   Page 176.

FOOL. He's mad that trusts in the tameness of a wolf, a horse's
health, a boy's love, or a whore's oath.

Though *health* will certainly do, it has probably been substituted for *heels*, by some person who regarded it as an improved reading. There are several proverbs of this kind. That in the text has not been found elsewhere, and may be the invention of Shakspeare. The Italians say, *Of a woman beware before, of a mule beware behind, and of a monk beware on all sides*; the French, *Beware of a bull's front, of a mule's hinder parts, and of all sides of a woman.* In Samuel Rowland's excellent and amusing work, entitled *The choice of change, containing the triplicity of divinitie, philosophie, and poetrie,* 1585, 4to, we meet with this proverbial saying, "Trust not 3 thinges, dogs teeth, horses feete, womens protestations."

Scene 6.   Page 184.

EDG. Poor Tom, *thy horn is dry.*

On this speech Dr. Johnson has remarked that men who begged under pretence of lunacy, used formerly to carry a horn and blow it through the streets. To account for Edgar's horn being *dry*, we must likewise suppose that the lunatics in

question made use of this utensil to drink out of, which seems
preferable to the opinion of Mr. Steevens, that these words
are "a proverbial expression, introduced when a man has nothing further to offer, when he has said all he has to say,"
the learned commentator not having adduced any example of
its use. An opportunity here presents itself of suggesting a
more correct mode of exhibiting the theatrical dress of Poor
Tom than we usually see, on the authority of Randle Holme
in his most curious and useful work *The academy of armory*,
book III. ch. iii. p. 161, where he says that the *Bedlam*
has "a long staff and a cow or ox-horn by his side; his
cloathing fantastic and ridiculous; for being a madman, he is
madly decked and dressed all over with rubins, feathers, cut-
tings of cloth, and what not, to make him seem a madman or
one distracted, when he is no other than a dissembling
knave." It is said that about the year 1760 a poor idiot called *Cude Yeddy*, went about the streets of Hawick in Scotland habited much in the above manner, and rattling a cow's
horn against his teeth. Something like this costume may be
seen in the portrait of that precious knave *Mull'd Sack*, who
carries a *drinking horn* on his staff. See Caulfield's *Portraits,
memoirs, and characters of remarkable persons,* vol. ii.

ACT IV.

SCENE 2.   Page 209.

ALB. Humanity must perforce *prey on itself*,
    Like monsters of the deep.

"Fishes," says Dr. Johnson, "are the *only* animals that
are known to prey upon their own species." But Shakspeare
did not mean to insinuate this; for he has elsewhere spoken
of "cannibals that each other eat." He only wanted a comparison. Many of the insect tribes prey on their own
species, as spiders, scorpions, beetles, earwigs, blattæ, &c.

Scene 4. Page 233.

Lear. That fellow handles his bow like a *crow keeper.*

The notes on this passage serve only to *identify the cha-racter* of a crow-keeper; but the *comparison* still remains to be explained. On this occasion we must consult our sole preceptor in the manly and too much neglected science of archery, the venerable Ascham. In speaking of awkward shooters he says, " Another coureth downe and layeth out his buttockes, as thoughe hee should *shoote at crowes.*"

Scene 4. Page 234.

Lear. O well-flown bird !

The notes are at variance as to whether Lear allude to archery or falconry. Certainly to the latter. In an old song on hawking, set for four voices by Thomas Ravenscroft, *O well flown* is a frequent address to the hawk.

Scene 4. Page 239.

Lear. Hark, in thine ear : change places; and *handy-dandy,* which is the justice, which is the thief?

Mr. Malone's explanation of this children's sport is con-firmed by the following extract from *A free discourse touching the murmurers of the tymes,* MS. " They hould safe your childrens patrymony, and play with your majestie as men play with little children at *handye dandye, which hand will you have,* when they are disposed to keep any thinge from them." The above *discourse* is a very bold and libellous address to King James I. on his pacific character, written, anonymously, with great powers of composition.

Scene 4. Page 240.

Lear. There thou might'st behold the great image of authority : a dog 's obey'd in office.——
Thou rascal beadle, hold thy bloody hand :
Why dost thou lash that whore? Strip thine own back ;
Thou hotly lust'st to use her in that kind,
For which thou whip'st her. The usurer hangs the cozener.
Through tatter'd clothes small vices do appear;
Robes and furr'd gowns hide all.

This admirable speech has a remarkable coincidence with

the following passage from " Parke's *Curtaine-drawer of the world*," 1612, 4to, p. 16, a work of very considerable merit. " The potency and power of magnificence and greatnesse dare looke sinne openly in the face in the very market place, and the eye of authority never takes notice thereof: the poore harlot must be stript and whipt for the crime that the courtly wanton and the citie-sinner ruffle out, and passe over and glory in, and account as nothing. The poore thiefe is hanged many times that hath stolne but the prise of a dinner, when sometimes hee that robbes both church and commonwealth is seene to ride on his footecloth." If this book was written according to its date, and Mr. Malone be right as to that of Lear, a fact which is not meant to be controverted, the merit of originality will rest with Shakspeare.

Scene 4.   Page 241.

EDG.   O, matter and *impertinency* mix'd.

This word was not used in its modern and corrupted sense of *sauciness* or *intrusion*, but merely to express *something not belonging to the subject*. Thus, an old collection of domestic recipes, &c., entitled, *The treasurie of commodious conceits*, 1594, is said to be " not *impertinent* for every good huswife to use in her house amongst her own familie." It does not seem to have been used in the sense of *rude* or *unmannerly* till the middle of the seventeenth century; nor in that of *saucy* till a considerable time afterwards.

Scene 4.   Page 241.

LEAR. . . . . . . we came crying hither.
　　　　　Thou know'st, the first time that we smell the air,
　　　　　We *wawl and cry* :——

Evidently taken from Pliny as translated by Philemon Holland. " Man alone, poor wretch [nature] hath laid all naked upon the bare earth, even on his birth day *to cry and wrawle* presently from the very first houre that he is borne into this world."—*Proeme* to book 7.

THE FOOL.

The fool in this play is the genuine domestic buffoon: but notwithstanding his sarcastical flashes of wit, for which we must give the poet credit, and ascribe them in some degree to what is called stage effect, he is a mere *natural* with a considerable share of cunning. Thus Edgar calls him *an innocent*, and every one will immediately distinguish him from such a character as Touchstone. His dress on the stage should be parti-coloured; his hood crested either with a cock's comb, to which he often alludes, or with the cock's head and neck. His bauble should have a head like his own with a grinning countenance, for the purpose of exciting mirth in those to whom he occasionally presents it.

The kindness which Lear manifests towards his fool, and the latter's extreme familiarity with his master in the midst of the most poignant grief and affliction, may excite surprise in those who are not intimately acquainted with the simple manners of our forefathers. An almost contemporary writer has preserved to us a curious anecdote of William duke of Normandy, afterwards William I. of England, whose life was saved by the attachment and address of his fool. An ancient Flemish chronicle among the royal MSS. in the British Museum, 16, F. iii., commences with the exile of Salvard lord of Roussillon and his family from Burgundy. In passing through a forest they are attacked by a cruel giant, who kills Salvard and several of his people; his wife Emergard and a few others only escaping. This scene the illuminator of the manuscript, which is of the fifteenth century, has chosen to exhibit. He has represented Emergard as driven away in a covered cart or waggon by one of the servants. She is attended by a female, and in the front of the cart is placed her fool, with a countenance expressive of the utmost alarm at the impending danger. Nor would it be difficult to adduce, if necessary, similar instances of the reciprocal affection between these singular personages and those who retained them.

ON THE STORY OF THIS PLAY.

To the account already given of the materials which Shakspeare used, nothing perhaps of any moment can be added; but for the sake of rendering this article more complete, it may be worth while to add that the *unpublished Latin Gesta Romanorum* contains the history of Lear and his daughters under different names, and with some little variety of circumstance. As it is not tedious, and has never been printed, at least as far as we know at present, it is here subjoined in its English form. The manuscript used on this occasion is No. 7333, in the Harleian collection.

" Theodosius regned, a wys emperour in the cite of Rome and myghti he was of power; the whiche emperour had thre doughters. So hit liked to this emperour to knowe which of his doughters lovid him best. And tho he seid to the eldest doughter, how moche lovist thou me? fforsoth, quod she, more than I do myself, therfore, quod he, thou shalt be hily avaunsed, and maried her to a riche and myghti kyng. Tho he cam to the secund, and seid to her, doughter, how moche lovist thou me? As moche forsoth, she seid, as I do myself. So the emperour maried her to a duc. And tho he seid to the thrid doughter, how moche lovist thou me? fforsoth, quod she, as moche as ye beth worthi, and no more. Tho seid the emperour, doughter, sith thou lovist me no more, thou shalt not be maried so richely as thi susters beth. And tho he maried her to an erle. Aftir this it happid that the emperour held bataile ayend the king of Egypt. And the kyng drove the emperour oute of the empire, in so moche that the emperour had no place to abide ynne. So he wrote lettres ensealed with his ryng to his first doughter that seid

that she lovid him more than herself, for to pray her of
socouryng in that grete nede, bycause he was put oute of his
empire. And when the doughter had red thes lettres, she
told hit to the kyng her husbond. Tho, quod the kyng, it is
good that we socour him in this nede. I shal, quod he,
gadern an host and help him in all that I can or may, and
that will not be do withoute grete costage. Yee, quod she,
hit were sufficiant if that we wold graunt him V knyghts to
be in felashyp wᵗ him while he is oute of his empire. And
so hit was ydo indede. And the doughter wrote ayen to the
fader, that other help myght he not have but V knyghts of
the kyng to be in his felashyp at the cost of the kyng her
husbond. And when the emperour herd this, he was hevy
in his hert, and seid, alas! alas! all my trust was in her, for
she seid she lovid me more than herself, and therfore I
avaunced her so hye.

"Then he wrote to the seconde that seid she lovid him as
moche as hirself, and when she had herd his lettres, she
shewid his erand to hir husbond, and yaf him in counseil that
he siuld fynde him mete and drink and clothing honestly, as
for the state of such a lorde during tyme of his nede. And
when this was graunted, she wrote lettres agein to hir fadir.
The emperour was hevy wᵗ this answere, and seid, sith my
two doughters have thus yhevid me, sothely I shal preve the
third. And so he wrote to the thrid that seid she lovid him
as moche as he was worthi, and praied her of socour in his
nede, and tolde her the answere of her two sustris. So the
thrid doughter when she had considered the myschief of her
ffader, she told her husbond in this fourme : my worshipfull
lord do socour me now in this grete nede, my fadir is put
oute of his empire and his heritage. Then spake he, what
were thi will I did therto. That ye gadre a grete oste, quod
she, and helpe him to fight ayens his enemys. I shal fulfill
thi will, seide the erle, and gaderid a grete oste and yede with
the emperoure at his owne costage to the bataile, and had

the victorye, and set the emperour ayen in his heritage. And then seid the emperour, blessed be the hour I gate my yongist doughter: I lovid her lesse than eni of the othir, and now in my nede she hath socoured me, and the othir have yfailed me; and therefore aftir my deth she shal have myn empire. And so hit was ydo in dede; for aftir the deth of the emperour, the yongist doughter regned in his sted and ended pesibly."

The same story is to be found in the formerly celebrated English chronicle erroneously supposed to have been written by Caxton, the early part of which was copied from Geoffrey of Monmouth. The circumstance of its having been printed by Caxton more than once, with a continuation to his own time, probably by himself, seems to have occasioned the mistake. See what has been said of it before, p. 261.

ROMEO AND JULIET.

ACT I.

Scene 1. Page 325.

Sam. Gregory, o' my word, we 'll not *carry coals*.
Gre. No, for then we should be colliers.

Of the various conjectures on the origin and real meaning of this phrase, that by Mr. Steevens seems deserving of the preference. In a rare little pamphlet entitled *The cold yeare*, 1614, 4to, being a dialogue in which the casualties that happened in the great fall of snow are enumerated, one of the interlocutors, a North-country man, relates that on his approach to London he overtooke a collier and his team, " walking as stately as if they scorned to *carry coales*." It was therefore a term of reproach to be called a collier; and thence, to *carry coals* was metaphorically used for any low or servile action. Barnaby Googe, in his *New yeares gift to the Pope's holinesse*, 1579, 4to, says he " had rather be a *collyer at Croydon* than a Pope at Rome."

A hint had been given, by a gentleman whose opinions are on all occasions entitled to the highest respect and attention, that the phrase in question might have originated from Proverbs xxv. 22. " If thine enemy be hungry, give him bread to eat; and if he be thirsty, give him water to drink; for thou shalt *heap coals* of fire upon his head." But this is a metaphor expressive of the pain which a man shall suffer from the reproaches of his conscience, and as such, has been adopted into our language. Thus, in *Newes from the North*, otherwise called *The conference between Simon Certain and Pierce Plowman*, 1579, 4to, " Now God forbid that ever a lawyer should *heap coales upon a merchant's head,* or that a merchant should not be as willing and as ready to doo a goodly deed as a lawyer."

SCENE 2.   Page 347.

> CAP. Such comfort, as do *lusty young men feel*
> When well-apparell'd *April* on the heel
> Of limping winter treads.

Two of the commentators would read *lusty yeomen,* and make the passage refer to the sensations of the farmer on the return of spring.   One of them, Dr. Johnson, to render the present text objectionable, has been obliged to *invert* the comparison.   Capulet, in speaking of the delight which Paris is to receive in the society of the young ladies invited to his house, compares it to that which the month of April usually afforded to the youth of both sexes, when assembled in the green fields to enjoy their accustomed recreations.   Independently of the frequent allusions in the writings of our old poets to April, as the season of youthful pleasures, and which probably occurred to Shakspeare's recollection, he might besides have had in view the decorations which accompany the above month in some of the manuscript and printed calendars, where the young folks are represented as sitting together on the grass; the men ornamenting the girls with chaplets of flowers.   From the following lines in one of these, the passage in question seems to derive considerable illustration.

> " The next VI. yere maketh foure and twenty
> And fygured is to *joly Apryll*
> The tyme of pleasures man hath moost plenty
> Fresshe and lovyng his *lustes* to fulfyll."

SCENE 4.   Pages 364, 367.

> ROM. Give me a torch——
> I'll be a candle-holder, and look on.

Froissart, describing a dinner on Christmas day in the hall of the castle of Gaston Earl of Foix, at Ortern, in the year 1388, has these words : " At mydnyght when he came out of his chambre into the halle to supper, he had ever before hym *twelve torches* brennyng, *borne by twelve varlettes* standyng before his table all supper." In Rankin's *Mirrour of monsters*, 1587, 4to, is the following passage : " This *maske* thus ended, wyth visardes accordingly appointed, there were certain petty fellows ready, as the custome is, *in maskes to carry torches*, &c." In the *Weiss kunig*, being a collection of wood engravings representing the actions of Maximilian the First, there is a very curious exhibition of a masque before the emperor, in which the performers appear with their visards, and one of them holds a torch in his hand. There is another print on the same subject by Albert Durer. The practice of carrying torch lights at entertainments continued even after the time of Shakspeare. See a future note on Hamlet, Act III. Scene 2.

SCENE 4. Page 368.

MER. If thou art dun, we'll draw thee from the mire.

There is no doubt that this is an allusion to some now forgotten sport or game, which gave rise to a proverbial expression, *Dun is in the mire*, used when a person was at a stand, or plunged into any difficulty. We find it as early as Chaucer's time in the Manciple's prologue :

> " Ther gan our hoste to jape and to play,
> And sayde; sires, what? *Dun is in the mire.*"

How the above sport was practised we have still to learn. *Dun* is, no doubt, the name of a horse or an ass. There is an equivalent phrase, *Nothing is bolder than blynde Bayard which falleth oft in the mire*. See Dr. Bullein's *dialogue between soarenesse and chirurgi*, fo. 10 ; and there is also a proverb, *As dull as Dun in the mire*.

SCENE 4. Page 376.

MER. . . . . This is that very Mab
That plats the manes of horses in the night.

No attempt has hitherto been made to explain this line,

which alludes to a very singular superstition not yet forgotten in some parts of the country. It was believed that certain malignant spirits, whose delight was to wander in groves and pleasant places, assumed occasionally the likenesses of women clothed in white; that in this character they sometimes haunted stables in the night time, carrying in their hands tapers of wax, which they dropped on the horses' manes, thereby plaiting them in inextricable knots, to the great annoyance of the poor animals, and vexation of their masters. These hags are mentioned in the works of William of Auvergne, bishop of Paris in the 13th century. There is a very uncommon old print by Hans Burgmair relating to this subject. A witch enters the stable with a lighted torch: and previously to the operation of entangling the horse's mane, practises her enchantments on the groom, who is lying asleep on his back, and apparently influenced by the night-mare. The *Belemnites,* or elf-stones, were regarded as charms against the last-mentioned disease, and against evil spirits of all kinds; but the *ceraunice* or *bætuli,* and all perforated flint-stones, were not only used for the same purpose, but more particularly for the protection of horses and other cattle, by suspending them in stables, or tying them round the necks of the animals.

The next line,

"And bakes the elf-locks in foul sluttish hairs,"

seems to be unconnected with the preceding, and to mark a superstition which, as Dr. Warburton has observed, may have originated from the *plica Polonica,* which was supposed to be the operation of wicked elves; whence the clotted hair was called *elf-locks* and *elf-knots.* Thus Edgar talks of "*elfing* all his hair in *knots.*" Lodge, in his *Wit's miserie,* 1599, 4to, describing a devil whom he names *Brawling-contention,* says, "his ordinary apparell is a little low-crown'd hat with a fether in it like a forehorse; his haires are curld, and full of *elves locks* and nitty for want of kembing."

ACT II.

SCENE 2. Page 398.

ROM. It is the East, and Juliet is the sun.

This line in particular, and perhaps the whole of the Scene, has been imitated by the ingenious author of the Latin comedy of *Labyrinthus.* In Act III. Scene 4, two lovers meet at night, and the Romeo of the piece says to his mistress, " Quid mihi noctem commemoras, mea salus? Splendens nunc subitò illuxit dies, ubi tu primum, mea lux, oculorum radiis hasce dispulisti tenebras." This excellent play was acted before King James I. at Cambridge, and for bustle and contrivance has perhaps never been exceeded.

SCENE 2. Page 398.

JUL. Thou art thyself *though*, not a Montagu.

Dr. Johnson would have substituted *then* for *though*; but without necessity, because *in that sense* the latter word was anciently written *tho* : unskilful printers, deceived by sound, substituted *though*; whence the ambiguity has arisen. Thus Chaucer in his *Canterbury tales,* v. 2214,

> " Yet sang the larke, and Palamon right *tho*
> With holy herte and with a high corāge
> He rose."

And again, v. 2392,

> " For thilk sorrow that was *tho* in thyn herte."

Thus much in explanation of *though*, if put here for *then*, which is by no means clear. Mr. Malone's quotations on the other side of the question carry great weight with them.

SCENE 2. Page 400.

ROM. When he bestrides the lazy-pacing clouds
And sails upon the bosom of the air.

On this occasion Shakspeare recollected the 104th *psalm*, " Who maketh the clouds his charet, who walketh upon the wings of the winde."

Scene 2.   Page 405.

Jul. . . . . . at lovers perjuries,
They say, Jove laughs.

This Shakspeare found in Ovid's *Art of love,* perhaps in Marlow's translation, book I,

" For Jove himself sits in the azure skies,
And laughs below at lovers perjuries."

With the following beautiful antithesis to the above lines, every reader of taste will be gratified. It is given *memoriter* from some old play, the name of which is forgotten;

" *When lovers swear true faith,* the list'ning angels
Stand on the golden battlements of heaven,
And waft their vows to the eternal throne."

Scene 2.   Page 410.

Rom. How *silver-sweet* sound lovers tongues by night.

In *Pericles,* Act V., we have *silver-voic'd.* Perhaps these epithets have been formed from the common notion that silver mixed with bells softens and improves their tone. We say likewise that a person is *silver-tongued.*

Scene 3.   Page 414.

Fri. O mickle is the powerful grace, that lies
In herbs, plants, stones, and their true qualities:
For nought so vile that on the earth doth live,
But to the earth some special good doth give;
Nor aught so good, but strain'd from that fair use
Revolts from true birth, stumbling on abuse.

Thus all the copies. But in Swan's *Speculum mundi,* the first edition of which was published in 1635, they are quoted with the following variations;

" O mickle is the powerful *good* that lies
In herbs, *trees,* stones, and their true qualities:
For nought so vile that on the earth doth live,
But to the earth some *secret* good doth give.
And nought so rich on either rock or shelf;
But, if unknown, lies uselesse to itself."

Scene 4. Page 427.

MER. . . . for this driveling love is like a great natural, that
runs lolling up and down *to hide his bauble in a hole.*

When the physical conformation of idiots is considered,
the latent but obscene allusion which this speech conveys will
be instantly perceived. What follows is still less worthy of
particular illustration. Mercutio riots in this sort of language. The epithet *driveling* is applied to love as a *slavering
idiot*; but Sir Philip Sidney has made Cupid an *old drivell.*
See the lines quoted from the Arcadia by Dr. Farmer, *Much
ado about nothing,* Act III. Scene 2.

Scene 4. Page 431.

NURSE. I pray you sir, what *saucy merchant* was this, that was so
full of his *ropery*?

Mr. Steevens has justly observed that the term *merchant*
was anciently used in contradistinction to *gentleman.* *Whetstone,* in his *Mirour for majestrates of cyties,* 1584, 4to, speaking of the usurious practices of the citizens of London who
attended the gaming-houses for the purpose of supplying the
gentlemen players with money, has the following remark :
" The extremity of these mens dealings hath beene and is so
cruell as there is a natural malice generally impressed in the
hearts of the gentlemen of England towards the citizens of
London, insomuch as if they odiously name a man, they
foorthwith call him, a *trimme merchaunt.* In like despight the
citizen calleth every rascall *a joly gentleman.* And truly this
mortall envie betweene these two woorthie estates, was first
engendred of the cruell usage of covetous merchaunts in hard
bargaines gotten of gentlemen, and nourished with malitious
words and revenges taken of both parties."

With respect to *ropery*,—the word seems to have been
deemed unworthy of a place in our early dictionaries, and was
probably coined in the mint of the slang or canting crew. It sa-
vours strongly of the halter, and appears to have signified a low

kind of knavish waggery. From some other words of similar import, it may derive illustration. Thus a *rope-rype* is
defined in Hulæt's *Abcedarium* to be " an ungracious waghal-
ter, *nequam* ;" and in Minshæu's dictionary, " one ripe for a
rope, or for whom the gallowes grones." A *roper* has nearly
the same definition in the English vocabulary at the end of
Thomasii *Dictionarium*, 1615, 4to ; but the word occasionally
denoted a crafty fellow, or one who would practise a fraud
against another (for which he might deserve hanging). So
in the book of blasing of arms or coat armour, ascribed to
Dame Juliana Bernes, the author says, " which crosse I saw
but late in tharmes of a noble man : the whiche in very dede
was somtyme *a crafty man, a roper*, as he himself sayd," sig.
Aij. b. *Roper* had also another sense, which, though rather
foreign to the present purpose, is so quaintly expressed in
one of our old dictionaries, that the insertion of it will doubtless be excused :—" Roper, *restio*, is he that loketh in at John
Roper's window by translation, he that hangeth himselfe."
—Hulæt's *Abcedarium* Anglico-Latinum, 1552, folio. *Rope-
tricks*, elsewhere used by Shakspeare, belongs also to this
family.

SCENE 4. Page 431.

NURSE. I am none of his skains-mates.

This has been explained *cut-throat companions*, and *fre-
quenters of the fencing school*, from *skein*, a knife or dagger.
The objection to this interpretation is, that the nurse could
not very well compare herself with characters which it is presumed would scarcely be found among females of any description. One commentator thinks that she uses *skains-mates*
for *kins-mates*, and *ropery* for *roguery* ; but the latter words
have been already shown to be synonymous, and the existence of such a term as *kins-mate* may be questioned. Besides, the nurse blunders only in the use of less obvious
words.

The following conjecture is therefore offered, but not with

entire confidence in its propriety. It will be recollected that there are *skains of thread*; so that the good nurse may perhaps mean nothing more than *sempstresses*, a word not always used in the most honourable acceptation. She had before stated that she was " none of his flirt-gills."

ACT III.

Scene 1. Page 452.

Rom. O! I am fortune's fool!

" I am always running in the way of evil fortune, *like the fool in the play*," says Dr. Johnson. There is certainly no allusion to any *play*. See the note in p. 146.

Scene 2. Page 456.

Jul. That *run-away's eyes* may wink.

A great deal of ingenious criticism has been expended in endeavouring to ascertain the meaning of this expression. Dr. Warburton thought the *runaway* in question was the *sun*; but Mr. Heath has most completely disproved this opinion. Mr. Steevens considers the passage as extremely elliptical, and regards the *night* as the *runaway*; making Juliet wish that its eyes, the stars, might retire to prevent discovery. Mr. Justice Blackstone can perceive nothing *optative* in the lines, but simply a *reason* for Juliet's wish for a cloudy night; yet according to this construction of the passage, the grammar of it is not very easily to be discovered.

Whoever attentively reads over Juliet's speech will be inclined to think, or even be altogether satisfied, that the *whole tenor* of it is *optative*. With respect to the calling night a runaway, one might surely ask how it can possibly be so termed in *an abstract point of view*? Is it a greater fugitive than the morning, the noon, or the evening? Mr. Steevens lays great stress on Shakspeare's having before called the night a runaway in *The Merchant of Venice*,

" For the close night doth play the *runaway*;"

but there it was already far advanced, and might therefore with great propriety be said to *play the runaway*; here it was not begun. The same remark will apply to the other passage cited by Mr. Steevens from *The fair maid of the Exchange.* Where then is this *runaway* to be found? or can it be Juliet herself? She who had just been secretly married to the enemy of her parents might with some propriety be termed a *runaway from her duty*; but she had not abandoned her native pudency. She therefore invokes the night to veil those rites which she was about to perform, and to bring her Romeo to her arms in darkness and in silence. The lines that immediately follow may be thought to favour this interpretation; and the whole Scene may possibly bring to the reader's recollection an interesting part in the beautiful story of Cupid and Psyche.

Scene 5. Page 483.

Jul. Hunting thee hence with *hunt's-up* to the day.

Of the notes on this line, that by Mr. Malone is most to the point. He has shown from Cotgrave, that the *hunt's-up* was " a morning song to a new married woman, &c.;" and it was, no doubt, an imitation of the tune to wake the hunters, noticed by Mr. Steevens, as was that in the celebrated Scotish *booke of godly and spirituall songs,* beginning,

> " With hunts up, with huntis up,
> It is now perfite day:
> Jesus our king is gane in hunting,
> Quha likes to speed they may."

It is not improbable that the following was the identical song composed by the person of the name of Gray mentioned in Mr. Ritson's note. It occurs in a collection entitled *Hunting, hawking, &c.,* already cited in the course of the remarks on *The merry wives of Windsor.* There was likewise a country dance with a similar title.

C<small>HO</small>. $\begin{cases}\text{The hunt is up, the hunt is up,}\\ \text{Sing merrily wee, the hunt is up;}\end{cases}$
    The birds they sing,
    The Deare they fling,
        Hey, nony nony-no:
    The hounds they crye,
    The hunters flye,
        Hey trolilo, trololilo.
                        The hunt is up, *ut supra.*

    The wood resounds
    To heere the hounds,
        Hey, nony nony-no:
    The rocks report
    This merry sport,
        Hey, trolilo, trololilo.
C<small>HO</small>. $\begin{cases}\text{The hunt is up, the hunt is up,}\\ \text{Sing merrily wee, the hunt is up.}\end{cases}$

    Then hye apace,
    Unto the chase,
        Hey nony, nony-no;
    Whilst every thing
    Doth sweetly sing,
        Hey trolilo, trololilo.
C<small>HO</small>. $\begin{cases}\text{The hunt is up, the hunt is up,}\\ \text{Sing merrily wee, the hunt is up.}\end{cases}$

S<small>CENE</small> 5. Page 496.

N<small>URSE</small>. . . . . . an eagle, madam,
    Hath not so *green*, so quick, so fair an eye.

Besides the authorities already produced in favour of *green*
eyes, and which show the impropriety of Hanmer's alteration
to *keen*, a hundred others might, if necessary, be given. The
early French poets are extremely fond of alluding to them
under the title of *yeux vers*, which Mons. Le Grand has in
vain attempted to convert into *yeux vairs*, or grey eyes.* It
must be confessed that the scarcity, if not total absence of
such eyes in modern times, might well have excited the
doubts of the above intelligent and agreeable writer. For
this let naturalists, if they can, account. It is certain that

---

* Fabliaux ou contes, tom. iv. p. 215.

green eyes were found among the ancients. Plautus thus alludes to them in his *Curculio* :

> " Qui hic est homo
> Cum collativo ventre, atque oculis *herbeis?*"

Lord Verulam says, " Great eyes with a *green circle* between the white and the white of the eye, signify long life."—*Hist. of life and death*, p. 124. Villa Real, a Portuguese, has written a treatise in praise of them, and they are even said to exist now among his countrymen. See Pinkerton's *Geography*, vol. i. p. 556, and Steevens's Shakspeare, vol. v. 164, 203.

ACT IV.

SCENE 2.   Page 508.

CAP. Where have you been *gadding?*

Mr. Steevens remarks that " the primitive sense of this word was to straggle from house to house and collect money under pretence of singing carols to the blessed Virgin ;" and he quotes a note on Milton's Lycidas by Mr. Warton : but this derivation seems too refined. Mr. Warton's authority is an old register at Gadderston, in these words : " Receyvid at the *gadyng* with Saynte Mary songe at Crismas." If the original were attentively examined, it would perhaps turn out that the word in question has some mark of contraction over it, which would convert it into *gaderyng*, i. e. gathering or collecting money, and not simply *going about from house to house* according to Mr. Warton's explanation.

SCENE 5.   Page 525.

FRI. . .   .   .   and stick your *rosemary*
On this fair corse——

This plant was used in various ways at funerals. Being an

evergreen, it was regarded as an emblem of the soul's immortality. Thus in Cartwright's *Ordinary,* Act V. Scene 1 :

> " . . . . . If there be
> Any so kind as to accompany
> My body to the earth, let them not want
> For entertainment; pr'ythee see they have
> A *sprig of rosemary* dip'd in common water
> To smell to as they walk along the streets."

In an obituary kept by Mr. Smith, secondary of one of the Compters, and preserved among the Sloanian MSS. in the British Museum, No. 886, is the following entry : " Jan[y]. 2. 1671. Mr. Cornelius Bee bookseller in Little Britain died; buried Jan. 4. at Great St. Bartholomew's without a sermon, without wine or wafers, only gloves and *rosmary.*"

And Mr. Gay, when describing Blouzelinda's funeral, records that

> " Sprigg'd rosemary the lads and lasses bore."

SCENE 5.   Page 528.

PET. No money, on my faith; but the *gleek* : I will *give* you the minstrel.

From what has been said in page 118, it becomes necessary to withdraw so much of a former note as relates to the *game* of gleek. *To give the minstrel,* is no more than a punning phrase for *giving the gleek.* Minstrels and jesters were anciently called *gleekmen* or *gligmen.*

SCENE 5.   Page 529.

PET. When *griping grief* the heart doth wound
And *doleful dumps* the mind oppress.

The following stanza from one of Whitney's *Emblems,* 1586, 4to, is not very dissimilar from that of Richard Edwards, communicated in the note by Sir John Hawkins, and may serve to confirm the propriety of Mr. Steevens's observation, that the epithet *griping* was not calculated to excite laughter in the time of Shakspeare.

> " If griping greifes have harbour in thie breste
> And pininge cares laie seige unto the same,
> Or straunge conceiptes doe reave thee of thie rest,
> And daie and nighte do bringe thee out of frame :
>   Then choose a freinde, and doe his counsaile crave,
>   Least secret sighes, doe bringe untimelie grave."

Griping griefs and *doleful dumps* are very thickly interspersed in Grange's *Golden Aphroditis*, 1577, 4to, and in many other places. They were great favourites; but griefs were not always *griping*. Thus in Turbervile's translation of *Ovid's epistle from Hero to Leander*;

> " Which if I heard, of troth
> For *grunting* griefe I die."

ACT V.

Scene 1.   Page 536.

Rom. An *alligator* stuff'd——

Our dictionaries supply no materials towards the etymology of this word, which was probably introduced into the language by some of our early voyagers to the Spanish or Portuguese settlements in the newly discovered world. They would hear the Spaniards discoursing of the animal by the name of *el lagarto*, or the lizard; Lat. *lacerta*; and on their return home, they would inform their countrymen that this sort of crocodile was called an *alligator*. It would not be difficult to trace other corrupted words in a similar manner.

STORY OF THE PLAY.

It has hitherto remained unnoticed, that one of the material incidents in this drama is to be found in *The love adventures of Abrocomas and Anthia,* usually called the *Ephesiacs* of

Xenophon of Ephesus. The heroine of this romance, separated, by a series of misfortunes, from her husband, falls into the hands of robbers, from whom she is rescued by a young nobleman called Perilaus. He becomes enamoured of her; and she, fearing violence, affects to consent to marry him; but on the arrival of the appointed time, swallows a poisonous draught which she had procured from Eudoxus, an old physician and the friend of Perilaus, to whom she had communicated the secret of her history. Much lamentation is made for her death, and she is conveyed with great pomp to a sepulchre. As she had only taken a sleeping potion, she soon awakes in the tomb, which, on account of the riches it contained, is plundered by some thieves, who also carry her off. This work was certainly not published nor translated in the time of Luigi da Porto, the original narrator of the story of *Romeo and Juliet*; but there is no reason why he might not have seen a copy of the original in manuscript.

Two incidents in this Greek romance are likewise to be found in *Cymbeline*; one of which is the following: Antha a having become the slave of Manto and her husband, he is captivated with her beauty; and this coming to the knowledge of the jealous Manto, she orders a trusty servant to carry Anthia into a wood and put her to death. This man, like the servant in Boccaccio, and Pisanio in Shakspeare, commiserates the situation of Anthia, spares her life, and provides the means for her future safety. A similar occurrence is introduced into some of the tales of the middle ages. The other is the above-mentioned draught of poison swallowed by Imogen, as by Anthia, though not with precisely the same effect. As it is not to be found either in Boccaccio or in the old story-book of *Westward for smelts,* one might suspect that some novel, imitated from the *Ephesiacs,* was existing in the time of Shakspeare, though now unknown.

HAMLET.

ACT I.

Scene 1. Page 9.

Mar. Thou art a *scholar*, speak to it, Horatio.

The reason why the common people believed that ghosts were only to be addressed by scholars seems to have been, that the exorcisms of troublesome spirits were usually performed in *Latin*.

Scene 1. Page 21.

Hor. The *cock* that is the *trumpet to the morn*,
  Doth with his lofty and shrill-sounding throat
  Awake the God of day; and at his warning,
  Whether in sea or fire, in earth or air,
  The extravagant and erring spirit hies
  To his confine.

Besides the hymn of Prudentius referred to in Dr. Farmer's note, there is another said to have been composed by Saint Ambrose, and formerly used in the Salisbury service. It contains the following lines, which so much resemble Horatio's speech, that one might almost suppose Shakspeare had seen them :

  " *Preco diei jam sonat,*
  Noctis profundæ pervigil ;
  Nocturna lux viantibus,
  A nocte noctem segregans.
  Hoc excitatus Lucifer,
  Solvit polum caligine ;
  Hoc omnis errorum chorus
  Viam nocendi deserit.
  Gallo canente spes redit, &c."

See *Expositio hymnorum secundum usum Sarum*, pr. by R.

Pynson, n. d. 4to, fo. vii. b. The epithets *extravagant* and *erring* are highly poetical and appropriate, and seem to prove that Shakspeare was not altogether ignorant of the Latin language.

SCENE 2. Page 35.

HAM. Or that the Everlasting had not fix'd
His *canon* 'gainst self slaughter.

Mr. Steevens says, " there are yet those who suppose the old reading (cannon, in the sense of artillery) to be the true one." He himself was not of the number. It must be owned that *fixing a cannon* is an odd mode of vengeance on the part of the Deity ; yet it is still more difficult to conceive in what manner this instrument could operate in avenging *suicide*. The pedants of Hierocles, who were the Gothamites of their time, might, if now existing, be competent to explain all this; or, indeed, we might ourselves suppose that suicides could be blown into atoms as the seapoys sometimes are, by tying them to the cannon's mouth, a method equally humane with the practice of driving stakes through their bodies. Mr. Malone's happy quotation has for ever *fixed* the proper meaning.

SCENE 2. Page 40.

HAM. . . . . the *funeral bak'd meats*
Did coldly furnish forth the marriage tables.

The practice of making entertainments at funerals which prevailed in this and other countries, and which is not even at present quite disused in some of the northern counties of England, was certainly borrowed from the *cœna feralis* of the Romans, alluded to in Juvenal's fifth satire, and in the laws of the twelve tables. It consisted of an offering of a small plate of milk, honey, wine, flowers, &c., to the ghost of the deceased. In the instances of heroes and other great characters, the same custom appears to have prevailed among the Greeks. With us the appetites of the living are consulted on this occasion. In the North this feast is called an *arval* or *arvil-*

supper; and the loaves that are sometimes distributed among the poor, *arval-bread*. Not many years since one of these arvals was celebrated in a village in Yorkshire at a public-house, the sign of which was the family arms of a nobleman whose motto is VIRTUS POST FUNERA VIVIT. The undertaker, who, though a clerk, was no scholar, requested a gentleman present to explain to him the meaning of these Latin words, which he readily and facetiously did in the following manner: *Virtus*, a parish clerk, *vivit*, lives well, *post funera*, at an *arval*. The latter word is apparently derived from some lost Teutonic term that indicated a funeral pile on which the body was burned in times of Paganism. Thus *ærill* in Islandic signifies the inside of an oven. The common parent seems to have been *ar*, fire; whence *ara*, an altar of fire, *ardeo, aridus*, &c. &c. So the pile itself was called *ara* by Virgil, Æn. vi. 177 :

> " Haud mora, festinant flentes ; *aramque sepulchri*
> Congerere arboribus, cœloque educere certant."

SCENE 2. Page 41.

HAM. He was a man, take him for all in all,
I shall not look upon his like again.

In further support of the proposed elegant emendation, " *Eye* shall not look, &c.," this passage in 1 Corinth. ch ii. v. 9, may be adduced, " *Eye* hath not seen, nor ear heard, the things which he hath prepared for them that love him." An objection of some weight may however be made to this change; which is, that in recitation some ambiguity might arise, or at least the force of it would not be perceived; whereas the other reading could not be mistaken.

SCENE 3. Page 51.

POL. But do not dull thy palm with entertainment
Of each new-hatch'd, unfledg'd comrade.

In Taverner's *Proverbes or Adagies, gathered out of the Chiliades of Erasmus*, 1569, 12mo, is the following adage:

" *Ne cuivis porrigas dexteram.* Holde not forth thy hande to every man. He meaneth wee should not unadvisedlie admitte every body into our frendship and familiaritie." In the margin of the copy from which this extract is made, some person has *written* the above lines from Hamlet, on which the whole serves as an excellent comment, supporting **Dr.** Johnson's explanation of them in a remarkable manner.

Scene 4. Page 59.

HAM. The king doth wake to-night, and takes his *rouse.*

This word is used in the various significations of a riotous noise, a drunken debauch, and a large portion of liquor. We had it probably from our Saxon or Danish progenitors; and though the original word is lost it remains in the German *rausch.* Hence our *carouse; roister* is of the same family, and perhaps the word *row,* which was very much used a few years since. The Greeks too had their καρωσις, *nimia ebrietas.*

Scene 4. Page 60.

HAM. And as he drains his draughts of Rhenish down,
  The kettle-drum and trumpet thus bray out
  The triumph of his pledge.

Thus Cleaveland in his *Fuscara, or The bee errant,*

  " Tuning his draughts with drowsie hums
   As Danes carowse by kettle-drums."

Scene 4. Page 60.

HAM. Keeps *wassel*——

As the whole that appertains to this ancient, and, as connected with convivial manners, interesting word, lies scattered in various places, and has been detailed by writers whose opinions are extremely discordant, an attempt seemed necessary to digest within a reasonable compass the most valuable of the materials on the subject. There cannot be the smallest doubt that the term itself is to be sought for in the well-known story of Vortigern and Rowena, or Ronix, the daughter of Hengist; the earliest authority for which is that of

Walter Calenius, who supplied the materials for Geoffrey of Monmouth's history. He relates that on Vortigern's first interview with the lady, she kneeled before him, and presenting a cup of wine, said to him, " Lord king, *wacht heil*," or in purer Saxon *wæs hæl*; literally, be health, or health be to you! As the king was unacquainted with the Saxon language, he inquired the meaning of these words; and being told that they wished him health, and that he should answer them by saying *drinc heil,* he did so, and commanded Rowena to drink. Then, taking the cup from her hand, he kissed the damsel and pledged her. The historian adds, that from that time to his own the custom remained in Britain that whoever drank to another at a feast said *wacht heil,* and he that immediately after received the cup answered *drinc heil.* Robert of Brunne, in translating this part of Geoffrey of Monmouth, has preserved a curious addition to it. He states that Vortigern, not comprehending the words of Rowena, demanded their meaning from one of his Britons, who immediately explained to him the Saxon custom as follows:

> " This es ther custom and ther gest,
> Whan thei are at the ale or fest,
> Ilk man that lovis qware him think,
> Salle say *Wosseille,* and to him drink.
> He that bidis salle say, *Wassaile* ;
> The tother salle say again, *Drink haille.*
> That sais *Wosseille* drinkis of the cop,
> Kissand his felaw he gives it up;
> *Drinheille,* he sais, and drinks therof,
> Kissand him in bourd and skof.
> The king said as the knight gan ken
> *Drinkheille,* smiland on Rouewen,
> Rouwen drank as hire list,
> And gave the king, sine him kist.
> There was the first wassaille in dede
> And that first of fame yede
> Of that wassaille men told grete tale,
> And wassaille whan thei were at ale
> And drinkheille to tham that drank
> Thus was wassaille tane to thank."

An old metrical fragment preserved by Hearne in his

glossary to Robert of Gloucester's chronicle, carries the practice of wassailing much higher, even to the time of Saint Alban in the third century:

> " In that tyme weteth welle,
> Cam ferst wassayle and drynkehayl
> In to this londe, withowte wene,
> Thurghe a mayde, brygh and schene
> Sche was cleput mayde Ynge."

The chronicler proceeds to relate a story of this Ynge, who quitted Saxony with several others of her countrymen on account of hunger, and, arriving in Britain, obtained of the king as much land as she should be able to cover with a bull's hide. She afterwards invited the king and his nobles to a feast, and *giving him wassel,* treacherously slew him, her companions following the example by murdering the nobles. By these means she obtained possession of the whole kingdom, which was from her afterwards called *Yngland.* This statement is unworthy of notice in an historical point of view, being manifestly a corrupt account of the arrival of Hengist as related by Geoffrey of Monmouth. But the story of Vortigern is not improbable, and has at least furnished the origin of the words *wæs hæl* and *drinc hæl,* as used at convivial meetings in this country; for whatever may have been said or imagined concerning any previous custom of health-drinking among the Saxons or other German nations, it is certain that no equivalent term with our *wassel* is to be found in any of the Teutonic dialects.

Among other valuable remarks that have already been made in some notes on this word by Messrs. Steevens and Malone, it has been observed that the *wassel* bowl was particularly used at the season of Christmas, and that in process of time *wassel* came to signify not only meetings of rustic mirth, but also general riot, intemperance, and festivity. In the eleventh volume of *Archæologia,* the learned Dr. Milner has exhibited and described an ancient oaken cup, formerly belonging to the abbey of Glastonbury, which with great probability he supposes to be of Saxon times, and to have been used for wasselling. In *The antiquarian repertory*, vol. i. p. 217, there is an account, accompanied with an engraving, of an oaken chimney-piece in a very old house at Berlen near Snodland in Kent, on which is carved a wassel bowl resting on the branches of an apple-tree, alluding, probably, to part of the materials of which the liquor was composed. On one side is the word ꞗaſſꞗeil, and on the other ꞗꞃincꞗeile. This is certainly a very great curiosity of its kind, and at least as old as the fourteenth century. Edmund Mortimer, Earl of March, in his will gave to Sir John Briddlewood a silver cup called *wassail*; and it appears that John Duke of Bedford, the regent, by his first will bequeathed to John Barton, his maitre d'hotel, a silver cup and cover, on which was inscribed WAS-HAYL. During the Christmas holidays these wassel-bowls were often carried from house to house by the common people with a view to collect money. There are, besides, other significations of the word *wassel* that deserve to be noticed. These are, 1. A drinking song sung on the eve of Twelfth-day. 2. A custom of throwing toast to apple-trees for the purpose of procuring a fruitful year; which, says Mr. Grose, who has mentioned this practice in his provincial glossary, seems to be a relic of the heathen sacrifice to Pomona. 3. The contents of the wassel-cup, which were of different materials, as spiced wine or ale, with roasted apples and sugar, mead, or metheglin, &c. There was also what was called *wassel*, or more properly *wastel-bread*, which may be deserving of particular notice, as there is much diversity of opinion among those who have mentioned it. Bishop Lowth, in his Life of William Wykeham, had supposed that the term was derived from the *wastell, vessell or basket in which the bread was made, or carried or weighed*; an etymology which is with great reason contested by Dr. Milner in his paper on the Glastonbury cup. The latter writer is of opinion, that during the times of wasselling a finer sort of bread was provided, which on that account was called *wassel-bread*; and other persons had already conceived that the bread in question took its name from being dipped in the wassel-bowl. As a preliminary objection to these conjectures, it must be observed that the genuine orthography of the word is *wastel*, and not *wassel*, which is undoubtedly a corruption, and has led to much misconception. The earliest instance in which mention is made of wastel-bread is the statute 51 Henry III., entitled *Assisa panis et cerevisiæ*; where it is coupled with the *simnel bread*, which was made of the very finest flour, and twice baked. It appears from the same statute that *wastel-bread* was next in fineness to the simnel, and is described as *white bread well baked*. There does not seem therefore any reason for concluding that the wastel-bread was in *particular*, but in *general use at all seasons*. We are told by Hoveden the historian, that at an interview which took place between William king of Scotland and Richard the First, at Northampton, a charter was granted to the Scotish monarch, in which it was agreed, that, whenever he should be summoned to the English court for the performance of homage, his daily allowance, among other things, should consist of twelve simnels and as many *wastels*. In Matthew Paris's history of the abbots of Saint Alban's, p. 141, it is said of the abbot; "Solus in refectorio prandebit supremus, habens *vastellum*." It is surprising how Mr. Watts the editor should misconceive the meaning of this word so much as to call it a *canopy*; nor is it indeed much less extraordinary that Dr. Milner, who is so well skilled in ecclesiastical antiquities, should have supposed it to signify a *wassel-bowl*. The regulation is general, and it had escaped the learned writer's recollection that wasselling was of a particular season; for it could not be applied in its subordinate sense of revelling or rioting, to so grave a person as an abbot. The Doctor might have been misled by the authority of Mr. Blount in his edition of Cowel's law dictionary, where the conjecture on the part of Mr. Somner, that the wastel bread might have been derived from *pastillus*, is termed *unlucky* ; but, as it is presumed, without sufficient reason, although it may not be the exact origin of the expression. Chaucer, speaking of his Prioress, says,

> " Of smale houndes hadde she, that she fedde
> With rosted flesh, and milk, and *wastel-brede*."

We cannot suppose that these animals would have been regaled with a food which was set apart for particular festivities, but rather with what was to be procured at all times, though of a more delicate and expensive nature. In short, what seems to be the most probable original of this much disputed word is the French *gasteau*, anciently written *gastel*, in the Picard language *ouastel* or *watel*, and signifying *a cake*; a name which might with great propriety have been applied to this sort of bread on account of its superior quality, in like manner as the *simnel* bread was so termed from the Latin *simila*, the finest part of the flour. The cake-like form, too, of this kind of bread seems to be alluded to in the following extract from the register of William of Wykeham, which has been quoted by Bishop Lowth for a very different, but, as it is submitted, inapplicable purpose : " Octo panes *in wastellis*, ponderis cujuslibet wastelli unius miche conventualis," i. e. eight loaves in the form of *wastels* or cakes, the weight of each being that of a conventual manchet. And to conclude this part of the subject, in the old French language the term *wastelier* is used for a pastry-cook or maker of *wastiaux*, where it is not likely that there could have been any connection with our *wassel* in its Saxon and legitimate construction. What the heralds call *torteauxes*, in reality little cakes, from the French *tourte*, were likewise termed *wastels*, as we learn from the old book on coat armour ascribed to Dame Juliana Bernes, the celebrated abbess of Sopewell near Saint Albans.

The *wassel songs* were sung during the festivities of Christmas, and, in earlier times, principally by those itinerant minstrels who frequented the houses of the gentry, where they were always certain of the most welcome reception. It has indeed been the chief purpose in discussing the present subject, to introduce to the reader's notice a composition of this kind, which is perhaps at the same time to be regarded as the most ancient drinking song, composed in England, that is extant. This singular curiosity has been written on a spare leaf in the middle of a valuable miscellaneous manuscript of the fourteenth century, preserved in the British Museum, Bibl. Reg. 16, E. viii. It is probably more than a century older than the manuscript itself, and must have been composed at a time when the Norman language was very familiar in England. In the endeavour to translate it, some difficulties were to be encountered; but it has been an object to preserve the whole and sometimes literal sense of the original, whilst from the nature of the English stanza it was impossible to dispense with amplification.

AN ANGLO-NORMAN SONG.

Seignors ore entendez a nus,
De loinz sumes venuz a wous,
    Pur quere NOEL;
Car lem nus dit que en cest hostel
Soleit tenir sa feste anuel
    A hi cest jur.
        Deu doint a tus icels joie d'amurs
        Qi a DANZ NOEL ferunt honors.

Seignors jo vus di por veir
Ke DANZ NOEL ne velt aveir
    Si joie non;
E repleni sa maison,
De payn, de char & de peison,
    Por faire honor
        Deu doint a tuz ces joie damur.

Seignors il est crié en lost,
Qe cil qui despent bien et tost,
    E largement;
E fet les granz honors sovent
Deu li duble quanque il despent
    Por faire honor.
        Deu doint a.

Seignors escriez les malveis,
Car vus nel les troverez jameis
          De bone part :
Botun, batun, ferun gruinard,
Car tot dis a le quer cuuard
          Por faire honor.
                    Deu doint.

Noel beyt bien li vin Engleis
E li Gascoin & li Franceys
          E l'Angevin :
Noel fait beivre son veisin,
Si quil se dort, le chief enclin,
          Sovent le jor.
                    Deu doint a tuz cels.

Seignors jo vus di par Noel,
E par li sires de cest hostel,
          Car bevez ben :
E jo primes beurai le men,
Et pois apres chescon le soen,
          Par mon conseil,
Si jo vus di trestoz *Wesseyl*
Dehaiz eit qui ne dirra *Drincheyl* !

TRANSLATION.

Lordings, from a distant home,
To seek old Christmas we are come,
          Who loves our minstrelsy :
And here, unless report mis-say,
The grey-beard dwells; and on this day
Keeps yearly wassel, ever gay,
          With festive mirth and glee.

To all who honour Christmas, and commend our lays,
Love will his blessings send, and crown with joy their days.*

Lordings list, for we tell you true;
Christmas loves the jolly crew
          That cloudy care defy :
His liberal board is deftly spread
With manchet loaves and wastel-bread;
His guests with fish and flesh are fed,
          Nor lack the stately pye.†

---

* These two lines seem intended, in the original, as a kind of burden or chorus at the end of each stanza; but as they only intrude upon the measure, the translation were perhaps better without them.

† It was the custom at this time to serve up at entertainments peacock

Lordings, you know that far and near
The saying is, " Who gives good cheer,
   And freely spends his treasure;
On him will bounteous heaven bestow
Twice treble blessings here below,
His happy hours shall sweetly flow
   In never-ceasing pleasure."

Lordings, believe us, knaves abound;
In every place are flatterers found;
   May all their arts be vain!
But chiefly from these scenes of joy
Chase sordid souls that mirth annoy,
And all who with their base alloy
   Turn pleasure into pain.

CHRISTMAS quaffs our English wines,*
Nor Gascoigne juice, nor French declines,
   Nor liquor of Anjou:
He puts th' insidious goblet round,
Till all the guests in sleep are drown'd,
Then wakes 'em with the tabor's sound,
   And plays the prank anew.

Lordings, it is our host's command,
And CHRISTMAS joins him hand in hand,
   To drain the brimming bowl :
And I 'll be foremost to obey;
Then pledge me sirs, and drink away,
For CHRISTMAS revels here to day,
   And sways without control.

Now WASSEL to you all! and merry may ye be !
But foul that wight befall, who DRINKS not HEALTH to me !

SCENE 4.   Page 60.

HAM. This heavy-headed revel, east and west,
   Makes us traduc'd, and tax'd of other nations :
   They clepe us drunkards.

Dr. Johnson has noticed the frequent allusions in this play
to the king's intemperance, a failing that seems to have been

---

and pheasant pies, the forms of those elegant birds being externally preserved, and much pomp bestowed on their appearance. See what has been
already said on this subject in p. 291.

   * This is a stubborn fact against the opinion of those who maintain that
wine was not made in England. See the controversy on this subject in
Archæologia, vol. iii.

too common among the Danish sovereigns as well as their subjects. A lively French traveller being asked what he had seen in Denmark, replied, " rien de singulier, sinon qu'on y chante tous les jours, *le roy boit*;" alluding to the French mode of celebrating Twelfth-day. See De Brieux, *Origines de quelques coutûmes,* p. 56. Heywood in his *Philocothonista, or The drunkard opened, dissected, and anatomized,* 1635, 4to, speaking of what he calls the *vinosity of nations,* says of the Danes, that " they have made a profession thereof from antiquity, and are the first upon record that brought their wassell-bowles and elbowe-deep healthes into this land."

Scene 4. Page 68.

Ham. That thou, dead corse, again, in *cómplete* steel——

This word is accented in both ways by our old poets as suited the metre. Thus in Sylvester's *Du Bartas*, edit. folio, 1621, p. 120 :

" Who arms himself so cómplete every way."

But in *King John*, Act II., we have,

" Such as she is, in beauty, virtue, birth,
Is the young Dauphin, every way compléte :
If not compléte, oh say, he is not she."

Scene 4. Page 68.

Ham. Say why is this, wherefore, *what should we do?*

This interrogation is perfectly consistent with the opinions entertained by our forefathers concerning ghosts, which they believed had some particular motive for quitting the mansions of the dead; such as a desire that their bodies, if unburied, should receive Christian rites of sepulture; that a murderer might be brought to due punishment, as in the present instance; with various other reasons. On this account Horatio had already thus invoked the ghost :

" If there be any good thing to be done,
That may *do ease to thee* and grace to me,
Speak to me."

Some of the superstitions have been transmitted from the

earliest times. It was the established opinion among the ancient Greeks, that such as had not received the funeral rites would be excluded from Elysium, and that on this account the departed spirits continued in a restless state until their bodies underwent the usual ceremony. Thus the wandering and rejected shade of Patroclus appears to Achilles in his sleep, and demands the performance of his funeral. The Hecuba of Euripides supplies another instance of a troubled ghost. In like manner the unburied Palinurus complains to Æneas.* In Plautus's *Mostellaria,* the cunning servant endeavours to persuade his master that the house is haunted by the ghost of a man who had been murdered, and whose body remained without sepulture. The younger Pliny has a story of a haunted house at Athens, in which a ghost played many pranks on account of his funeral rites being neglected. Nor were ghosts supposed to be less turbulent, even after burial, whenever the party had died a premature death, as we learn from Tertullian, in his treatise *De anima,* cap. 56, where he says, "Aiunt et immatura morte præventos eousque vagari isthic, donec reliquatio compleatur ætatis qua cum pervixissent si non intempestivé obiissent."

SCENE 5. Page 72.

HAM. Speak, I am bound to hear.
GHOST. So art thou to revenge when thou shalt hear.

These words have been turned into ridicule by Fletcher in his *Woman-hater,* Act II.;

" LAZ. Speak, I am bound.
" COUNT. So art thou to revenge when thou shalt hear the fish-head is gone, and we know not whither."

---

* The late Rev. Mr. Hole of Faringdon in Devonshire, whose loss is deplored by all who knew him, has left an essay on the character of Ulysses, which has been recently published by some kind and grateful friends. In this elegant morsel the learned author has noticed the anxiety which Homer's favourite heroes constantly manifest to give their enemies a prey to dogs, and thereby prevent the advantage of obtaining admission into the regions of happiness.

Scene 5. Page 72.

GHOST. And for the day, confin'd *to fast in fires,*
'Till the foul crimes, &c.

A member of the church of Rome might be disposed to regard this expression as simply referring to a *mental* privation of all intercourse with the Deity. Such an idea would remove the inconsistency of ascribing corporeal sensations to the ghost, and might derive support from these lines in an ancient Christian hymn. See *Expositio hymnorum,* sec. usum Sarum.

> " Sic corpus extra conteri,
>   Dona per abstinentiam,
>   *Jejunet ut mens sobria*
>   *A labe prorsus criminum.*"

The whole of the ghost's speech is remarkable for its terrific grandeur.

Scene 5. Page 75.

GHOST. And *duller* should'st thou be than the fat weed
That rots itself in ease on *Lethe's* wharf.

The plant here alluded to might have been *henbane,* of which Gerarde says that it causes drowsiness, and stupefies and *dulls* the senses.

Scene 5. Page 76.

HAM. O, my prophetick soul ! my uncle !

Copied, perhaps maliciously, in Beaumont and Fletcher's *Double marriage,* Act II.

" SES. Oh my prophetique soul!"

Scene 5. Page 77.

GHOST. But soft, methinks I scent the morning air—
The glow-worm shows the matin to be near.

It was the popular belief that ghosts could not endure the light, and consequently disappeared at the dawn of day. This superstition is derived from our northern ancestors, who held that the sun and every thing containing *light or fire* had the property of expelling demons and spirits of all kinds. With them it seems to have originated in the stories that are related in the Edda concerning the battles of Thor against the giants and evil demons, wherein he made use of his dreadful mallet of iron, which he hurled against them as Jupiter did his thunderbolts against the Titans. Many of the *transparent* precious stones were supposed to have the power of expelling evil spirits ; and the flint and other stones found in the tombs of the northern nations, and from which fire might be extracted, were imagined, in like manner, to be efficacious in confining the manes of the dead to their proper habitations. They were called Thor's hammers.

Scene 5.   Page 77.

GHOST. With juice of cursed *hebenon* in a vial,
And in the porches of mine ear did pour, &c.

Dr. Grey had ingeniously supposed this word to be a *metathesis* for *henebon* or *henbane*; but the best part of his note on the subject has been omitted, which is his reference to Pliny, who says that the oil of henbane *dropped into the ears* disturbs the brain. Yet it does not appear that henbane was ever called *henebon.* The line cited by Mr. Steevens from Marlow's *Jew of Malta,* shows that the *juice* of *hebon,* i. e. *ebony,* was accounted poisonous ; and in the English edition by Batman, of *Bartholomæus de proprietatibus rerum,* so often cited in these observations as a Shakspearean book, the article for the wood ebony is entitled, " Of *Ebeno,* chap. 52." This comes so near to the text, that it is presumed very little doubt will now remain on the occasion. It is not surprising that the *dropping into the ears* should occur, because Shakspeare was perfectly well acquainted with the supposed properties of henbane as recorded in Holland's translation of Pliny and elsewhere, and might apply this mode of use to any other poison.

Scene 5.   Page 77.

GHOST. . . . . . it doth posset
And curd, like *eager* droppings into milk.

Many readers may require to be told that *eager* means *sour*, from the French *aigre*. In the preceding Scene it is used in the sense of *sharp*, and is there properly so explained; but the quotation of the present passage on that occasion seems misapplied.

Scene 5.   Page 79.

GHOST. . . . . and sent to my account
With all my imperfections on my head.

Heywood, a contemporary writer, has imitated this in his play of *A woman kill'd with kindness*;

" . . . . . and send them, laden
With all their scarlet sins upon their backs
Unto a fearful judgment."

Scene 5.   Page 81.

HAM. My tables,—meet it is, I set it down.

It is remarkable that neither public nor private museums should furnish any specimens of these table-books, which seem to have been very common in the time of Shakspeare; nor does any attempt appear to have been made towards ascertaining exactly the materials of which they were composed. Certain it is, however, that they were sometimes made of slate in the form of a small portable book with leaves and  clasps. Such a one is fortunately engraved in Gesner's treatise *De rerum fossilium figuris*, &c. Tigur. 1565, 12mo, which is not to be found in the folio collection of his works on natural history. The learned author thus describes it: " Pugillaris è laminis saxi nigri fissilis, cum stylo ex eodem." His figure of it is here copied.

To such a table-book the Archbishop of York seems thus to allude in *The second part of King Henry IV.*, Act IV. Scene 1 :

> " And therefore will he *wipe his tables clean*
> And keep no tell-tale to his memory——"

In the middle ages the leaves of these table-books were made of ivory. Montfaucon has engraved one of them in the third volume of his " Antiquities," plate cxciv., the subject of which clearly shows that the learned writer has committed an error in ascribing them to remoter times. In Chaucer's *Sompnour's tale* one of the friars is provided with

> " A pair of tables all of *ivory*,
> And a pointel ypolished fetishly,
> And wrote alway the names, as he stood,
> Of alle folk that yave hem any good."

The Roman practice of writing on wax tablets with a stile was continued also during the middle-ages. In several of the monastic libraries in France specimens of wooden tables filled with wax and constructed in the fourteenth century were preserved. Some of these contained the household expenses of the sovereigns, &c., and consisted of as many as twenty pages, formed into a book by means of parchment bands glued to the backs of the leaves. One remaining in the abbey of St. Germain des préz at Paris, recorded the expenses of Philip le Bel, during a journey that he made in the year 1307, on a visit to Pope Clement V. A single leaf of this table-book is exhibited in the *Nouveau traité de diplomatique*, tom. i. p. 468.

SCENE 5.   Page 85

HAM. Swear by my sword.

In consequence of the practice of occasionally swearing by a sword, or rather by the cross or upper end of it, the name of *Jesus* was sometimes inscribed on the handle or some other part. Such an instance occurs on the monument of a crusader in the vestry of the church at Winchelsea. See likewise the tomb of John duke of Somerset engraved in Sandford's *Genealogical history,* p. 314, and Gough's *Sepulchral monuments,* Pref. ccxiii. Introd. cxlviii. vol. i. p. 171, vol. ii. p. 362.

ACT II.

Scene 2.　Page 115.

Pol. Though this be madness, yet there's method in it.

This is precisely Horace's,

"Insanire paret certo ratione modoque."

Scene 2.　Page 121.

Ham. The clown shall make those laugh whose lungs are *tickled o' the sere.*

Sere is *dry.* Thus in *Macbeth,*

"He is deformed, crooked, old and *sere.*"

Among the Saxons June was called the *sere* month. In the present instance *sere* appears to be used as a substantive. The same expression occurs in Howard's *Defensative against the poyson of supposed prophecies,* 1620, folio: "Discovering the moods and humors of the vulgar sort to be so loose and *tickle of the seare,*" &c., fo. 31. Every one has felt that dry tickling in the throat and lungs which excites coughing. Hamlet's meaning may therefore be, *the clown by his merriment shall convert even their coughing into laughter.*

Scene 2.　Page 131.

Ham. Buz, Buz.

Minsheu says, "To *buzze,* or hum as bees, *buzze, buzze;*" and again, in his Spanish dictionary, "when two standing or kneeling together, holding their hands upon their cheekes and ears, and so cry, *buzze buzze,* and hitting one another a good box on the eare, if he pull not his head away quickly." Selden in his *Table talk,* speaking of witches, says, "If any

should profess that by turning his hat thrice, and crying *buz,*
he could take away a man's life, (though in truth he could do
no such thing) yet this were a just law made by the state, that
whosoever should turn his hat thrice, and cry *buz,* with an
intention to take away a man's life, shall be put to death."
The expression has already exercised the skill of the critics,
and may continue to do so, if they are disposed to pursue the
game through the following mazes: "Anno DCCCXL Ludo-
vicus imperator ad mortem infirmatur, cujus cibus per XL dies
solummodo die dominica dominicum corpus fecit. Cum
vidisset dæmonem astare, dixit *buez, buez,* quod significat
foras, foras."—Alberici monachi trium fontium *chronicon,*
Leips. 1698. Ducange under the article *Buzi,* says, "Inter-
pretatur despectus vel contemptus. Papias. [Ab Hebraico
Bus vel *bouz,* sprevit.]"

Scene 2. Page 135.

HAM. Your ladyship is nearer to heaven, than when I saw you last,
by the altitude of a *chopine.*

In Raymond's *Voyage through Italy,* 1648, 12mo, a work
which is said to have been partly written by Dr. Bargrave,
prebendary of Canterbury, the following curious account of
the *chopine* occurs: "This place [Venice] is much frequented
by the walking may poles, I meane the women. They weare
their coats halfe too long for their bodies, being mounted on
their *chippeens,* (which are as high as a man's leg) they walke
between two handmaids, majestickly deliberating of every
step they take. This fashion was invented and appropriated
to the noble Venetians wives, to bee constant to distinguish
them from the courtesans, who goe covered in a vaile of white
taffety."

James Howell, speaking of the Venetian women, says,
"They are low and of small statures for the most part, which
makes them to rayse their bodies upon high shoes called
chapins, which gave one occasion to say that the Venetian

ladies were made of three things, one part of them was wood, meaning their chapins, another part was their apparrell, and the third part was a woman; The Senat hath often endeavour'd to take away the wearing of those high shooes, but all women are so passionately delighted with this kind of state that no law can weane them from it."

Some have supposed that the jealousy of Italian husbands gave rise to the invention of the *chopine*. Limojon de Saint Didier, a lively French writer on the republic of Venice, mentions a conversation with some of the doge's counsellors of state on this subject, in which it was remarked that smaller shoes would certainly be found more convenient; which induced one of the counsellors to say, putting on at the same time a very austere look, *pur troppo commodi, pur troppo.* The first ladies who rejected the use of the chopine were the daughters of the Doge Dominico Contareno, about the year 1670. It was impossible to set one foot before the other without leaning on the shoulders of two waiting women, and those who used them must have stalked along like boys in stilts.

The choppine or some kind of high shoe was occasionally used in England. Bulwer in his *Artificial changeling*, p. 550, complains of this fashion as a monstrous affectation, and says that his countrywomen therein imitated the Venetian and Persian ladies. In Sandys's travels, 1615, there is a figure of a Turkish lady with chopines; and it is not improbable that the Venetians might have borrowed them from the *Greek* islands in the Archipelago. We know that something similar was in use among the ancient Greeks. Xenophon in his œconomics, introduces the wife of Ischomachus, as having high shoes for the purpose of increasing her stature. They are still worn by the women in many parts of Turkey, but more particularly at Aleppo. As the figure of an object is often better than twenty pages of description, one is here given from a real Venetian chopine.

SCENE 2. Page 135.

HAM. Pray God, your voice, like a piece of uncurrent gold, be not *crack'd within the ring.*

It is to be observed, that there was a ring or circle on the coin, within which the sovereign's head was placed ; if the crack extended from the edge beyond this ring, the coin was rendered unfit for currency. Such pieces were hoarded by the usurers of the time, and lent out as lawful money. Of this we are informed by Roger Fenton in his *Treatise of usury,* 1611, 4to, p. 23. " A poore man desireth a goldsmith to lend him such a summe, but he is not able to pay him interest. If such as I can spare (saith the goldsmith) will pleasure you, you shall have it for three or foure moneths. Now, hee hath a number of light, clipt, *crackt* peeces (for such he useth to take in change with consideration for their defects :) this summe of money is repaid by the poore man at the time appointed in good and lawfull money. This is usurie." And again, " It is a common custome of his [the usurer's] to buy up *crackt angels* at nine shillings the piece. Now sir, if a gentleman (on good assurance) request him of mony, Good sir (saith hee, with a counterfait sigh) I would be glad to please your worship, but my *good* mony is abroad, and that I have, I dare not put in your hands. The gentleman thinking this conscience, where it is subtilty, and being beside that in some necessity, ventures on the *crackt angels*, some of which cannot flie, for soldering, and paies double interest to the miser under the cloake of honesty."—Lodge's *Wit's miserie*, 1596, 4to, p. 28. So much for the cracked gold. The cracking of the *human voice* proceeded from some alteration in the larynx, which is here compared to a ring.

As metaphors are sometimes double, the present may be of that kind. A piece of cracked metal is spoiled for the *ringing of it*; so the human voice, when cracked, may be said to lose the clearness of its *tone*. All Mr. Steevens's quotations, except the last, are obscene, and none of them apply to Hamlet's simile.

Scene 2. Page 137.

Ham. 't was *caviare* to the general.

This word has been frequently mispronounced *caveer* on the stage. The other mode of spelling it in Mr. Reed's note, viz. *caveary*, as well as the Italian term in the text, which should rather be *caviaro*, would have been sufficient for the purpose of demonstrating how it should be accented; but the following line from Sir J. Harrington's 33rd epigram of the third book leaves no uncertainty in the matter:

" And căvĕārĕ, but it little boots."

Dr. Ramsey, physician to King Charles the Second, wrote a curious treatise on the worms of the human body, in which he says, " *Caviale* also is a fond dish of the Italians, made of the roes of sturgion, and altogether as unwholsome, if not much worse; invented by idle brains, and fansied by none but such as are ignorant what it is; wherefore I would have them consider the Italian proverb,

Chi mangia di *Caviale*,
Mangia moschi, merdi, & sale.

Which may be Englished thus,

He that eats Cavialies,
Eats salt, dung, and flies.

For it is only (as was said) the roes of sturgion powdred, pickled, and finely denominated *Caviale,* to be a bait for such woodcocks and dotrils that account every exotick fansie a real good." This commodity is still common in the North of Europe, and was formerly a considerable article of commerce between England and Russia.

Scene 2. Page 145.

1 Play. Would have made *milch* the burning eyes of heaven.

i. e. would have drawn tears from them. *Milche-hearted,* in Hulæt's *Abcedarium,* 1552, is rendered *lemosus ;* and in *Bibliotheca Eliotæ,* 1545, we find " *lemosi,* they that *wepe* lyghtly." The word is from the Saxon melce, milky.

ACT III.

Scene 1. Page 158.

Ham. . . . To die,—to sleep,—
No more ;——

There is a good deal on this subject in Cardanus's *Comforte,* 1576, 4to, a book which Shakspeare had certainly read. In fo. 30, it is said, " In the holy scripture, death is not accompted other than sleape, and to dye is sayde to sleape."

Scene 1. Page 162.

Ham. The undiscovered country, from whose bourn
No traveller returns.

The resemblance of this passage to the lines cited by Mr. Steevens from Catullus is very remarkable, yet no translation of that author into English is known to have been made. It is true, they might have occurred to our poet in his native language through the medium of some quotation; yet it is equally possible that both the writers have casually adopted the same sentiment. This is a circumstance that more frequently happens than they are aware of who hunt after imitations even in writers of the most original genius. Many of Shakspeare's commentators might seem to be implicated in this charge, if it were not that they have rather designed to mark coincidence than imitation. On the present occasion our author alludes to a country altogether unknown to mortals. That of the Pagan poet is happily illustrated by Seneca, who cites the lines from Catullus, when he causes Mercury to drag the emperor Claudius into the *infernal regions.* " Nec mora, Cyllenius illum collo obtorto trahit *ad inferos.*"—*Lud. de morte Claudii.*

Dekker, in his *Seven deadlie sinns of London,* 1606, 4to, apostrophizing that city, exclaims, " Art thou now not cruell against thyselfe, in not providing (before the land-waters of affliction come downe againe upon thee) more and more convenient cabins to lay those in, *that are to goe into such farre countries, who never looke to come back againe*? If thou should'st deny it, the graves when they open, will be witnesses against thee."

In the *History of Valentine and Orson,* p. 63, edit. 1694, 4to, is this passage: " I shall send some of you here present *into such a country, that you shall scarcely ever return again* to bring tydings of your valour." As Watson, the translator of this romance, translated also *The ship of fools* into prose, which was printed by Wynkyn de Worde, it is probable that there was an edition of *Valentine and Orson* in Shakspeare's time, though none such is supposed now to remain. Perhaps the oldest we know of is that of 1649, printed by Robert Ibbitson. In 1586, *The old book of Valentine and Orson* was licensed to T. Purfoot.

SCENE 1.   Page 166.

> HAM. I have heard of your *paintings* too, well enough; God hath given you one *face,* and you make yourselves another; you jig, you amble, and you lisp and nickname God's creatures, and make your wantonness your ignorance.

The folio reads *prattlings,* and *pace*; the quarto as in the text, which **Dr.** Johnson thinks best, though he admits that Shakspeare might have written both. Other very good reasons have been given for preferring the present reading; yet whoever will reflect on the typographical errors for which the quarto plays of Shakspeare are remarkable, may be disposed to think that the folio editors had good reason for their variation. Our author's bible might here, as in many other instances, have furnished his materials. " Moreover thus saith the Lorde : seyng the daughters of Sion are become so proude and come in with stretched oute neckes, and with vayne wanton eyes ; seynge they come in trippynge so nicely with their fete ; therefore, &c."—Isaiah, ch. iii. ver. 16. It has not been observed that *lisp* seems to refer to *prattling,* as *jig* and *amble* do to *pace.*

SCENE 2.   Page 173.

HAM. .   .   . it out-herods Herod.

The violence of Herod in the old mysteries has been already exemplified by some extracts from the Chester and Coventry plays. One of the latter, of which some account has been given in the preceding pages, may truly be said on the present occasion to completely *out-herod* the others. It exhibits the fury of the monarch to so much advantage, that every zealous amateur of theatrical manners must be gratified with the following extracts.

His majesty's entrance is announced by a herald in the vilest French jargon that can be conceived. He commences by enjoining silence on the part of the spectators, and ends with sending them all to the devil. " La gran deaboly vos umport." He then makes a speech, which begins in bad Latin, and thus proceeds :

" [I am] the myghtyst conquerowre that ever walkid on grownd,
  For I am evyn he that made bothe hevin and hell,
  And of my myghte power holdith up the world rownd ;
  Magog and *Madroke* bothe thes did I confownde,

And in this bryght bronde* there bonis I brak on sunder,
That all the wyde worlde on those rappis † did wonder.
I am the cawse of this grett lyght and thunder ;
Yt ys throgh my fure ‡ that the § soche noyse doth make ;
My feyrefull contenance the cloudis so doth incumber,
That oftymes for drede therof the verre ‖ yerth doth quake.
Loke when I with males ¶ this bryght brond doth shake,
All the whole world from the north to the sowthe,
I ma them dystroie with won worde of my mouthe.
To recownt unto you myn inewmerabull substance,
Thatt were to moche for any tong to tell ;
For all the whole orent ** ys under myn obbeydeance,
And prince am I of purgatorre and chef capten of hell ;
And thase tyranees trayturs be force ma I compell
Myne enemys to vanquese, and evyn to duste them dryve,
And with a twynke of myn iee not won to be left alyve.
Behald my contenance and my colur,
Bryghter than the sun in the meddis of the dey.
Where can you have a more grettur succur
Then to behold my person that ys so gaye ?
My fawcun †† and my fassion with my gorgis ‡‡ araye ?
He that had the grace allwey theron to thynke,
Lyve the myght allwey withowt othur meyte or drynke ;
And thys my tryomfande fame most hylist doth abownde
Throgh owt this world in all reygeons abrod,
Reysemelyng the favour of that most myght *Mahownd.*
From *Jubytor* be desent §§ and cosyn to the grett God,
And namyd the most reydowndid ‖‖ kyng *Eyrodde,*
Wycche that all pryncis hath undr subjeccion,
And all their whole powar undur my proteccion ;
And therefore my hareode ¶¶, here called *Calcas,*
Warne thow eyvyry porte that noo schyppis aryve ;
Nor also aloond *** stranger throgh my realme pas,
But the for there truage do pay markis fyve.
Now spede the forthe hastele,
For the that wyll the contrare,
Upon a galowse hangid schal be,
And be *Mahownde* of me they gett noo grace."

---

* sword.	† raps, blows.	‡ fury.
§ they.	‖ very.	¶ malice.
** orient.	†† falcon, or perhaps falchion.	‡‡ gorgeous.
§§ I am descended.	‖‖ renowned. ¶¶ herald.	*** allow.

When he hears of the flight of the messengers, he exclaims,

> " I stampe, I stare, I loke all abowt,
> Myght I them take I schuld them bren at a glede *,
> I ren, I rawe †, and now I am wode ‡,
> A that these velen trayturs hath mard this my mode
> The schal be hangid yf I ma cum them to."

The stage direction is, " Here *Erode* ragis in the pagond and in the strete also." He consults with his knights on putting the children to death; and on their dissuading him from it as likely to excite an insurrection, he says,

> " A rysyng, owt, owt, owt."

" There *Erode* ragis ageyne and then seyth thus :

> " Out velen wrychis har apon § you I cry,
> My wyll utturly loke that yt be wroght,
> Or apon a gallowse bothe you schall dye
> Be *Mahownde* most myghtyst that me dere hath boght."

At length the knights consent to slay the children, and *Herod* says,

> " And then wyll I for fayne trypp lyke a doo."

The bodies of the children are brought to him in carts; but he is told that all his deeds are come to nothing, as the child whom he particularly sought after had escaped into Egypt. He once more falls into a violent passion, orders his palfrey to be saddled, and hurries away in pursuit of the infant. Here the piece ends. It was performed by the taylors and shearmen in the year 1534 ; but the composition is of much greater antiquity.

SCENE 2. Page 179.

> HAM. . . . . Give me that man
> That is not passion's slave, and I will wear him
> In my heart's core, ay in my heart of heart.

From this speech Anthony Scoloker, in his *Daiphantus, or The passions of love,* 1604, 4to, has stolen the following line :

> " Oh, I would weare her in my heart's-heart-gore."

---

* burn on live coals.   † rave.

‡ mad.   § here upon, or perhaps *haro* !

2 H

SCENE 2.   Page 179.

HAM. It is a *damned* ghost that we have seen.

i. e. the ghost of a person sentenced for his wickedness to damnation, and which has in this instance deceived us. Thus Spenser,

> " What voice of *damned ghost* from Limbo lake
>   Or *guileful spright* wandering in empty ayre,
>   Sends to my *doubtful eares* these speeches rare ?"
>   *Fairy Queen*, book i. canto 2, st. 32.

>   " He show'd him painted in a table plain
>   The *damned ghosts*——"
> " Nor *damned ghosts* cald up with mightie spels."
>   *Epithalamion*, st. 19.

SCENE 2.   Page 182.

HAM. Lady, shall I lie in your lap?
        [*Lying down at* OPHELIA's *feet.*]

Mr. Steevens has noticed the practice of lying at the feet of a mistress during dramatic representations; yet we are not to conclude that it prevailed at the public theatres. The instances which have occurred seem to be confined to entertainments at the houses of the nobility and gentry. These were plays, masques, masquerades, balls, concerts, &c. Many old pictures and engravings furnish examples of the above custom, the young men being often seen sitting or lying on the ground in conversation with their mistresses, and sometimes in Hamlet's situation. One of these shall be described more particularly. It is an extremely neat little print, belonging to a set designed to contrast the sufferings of Christ with the vanities of the world. The scene is a ball-room. In the background are the musicians and torch-bearers. In front a lady and gentleman are performing a dance before some standing spectators. In various parts of the room pairs of young gallants and their mistresses are seated on the floor, apparently more attentive to their own concerns than to the dancing; and one youth is sitting on the spread petticoat of his companion. The costume is French, and of the time of Louis the Thirteenth.

SCENE 2. Page 198.

HAM. With two *provencial roses* on my razed shoes.

The old copies read *provincial*, which led Mr. Warton to ask, why provincial roses? and to conclude that roses of *Provence* were meant, on which conclusion the text has been *most unnecessarily* changed; because the old reading was certainly correct. There is no evidence to show that *Provence* was ever remarkable for its roses; but it is well known that *Provins*, in *La Basse Brie*, about forty miles from Paris, was formerly very celebrated for the growth of this flower, of which the best cataplasms are said to have been made. It was, according to tradition, imported into that country from Syria, by a count De Brie. See Guillemeau *Histoire naturelle de la rose*. It is probable that this kind of rose, which in our old herbals is called the Great Holland or *Province* rose, was imported into this country both from Holland and France, from which latter country the Dutch might have first procured it. There is an elegant cut of the Provins rose, with a good account of it, in the first edition of Pomet *Hist. des drogues*, 1694, folio, p. 174.

SCENE 2. Page 200.

HAM. A very, very, —*peacock*.

The word that was in the original of Hamlet's quotation would have been too coarse to be applied to royalty; and therefore he substitutes another, which there is good reason to suppose was *peacock*. Dr. Farmer has given proof that this term was proverbial for a fool. Reginald Scot, speaking of Pope Julius the Third, says that he blasphemed Christ, and cursed his mother for a *peacock*. *Disc. of witchcraft*, b. 2, ch. viii. The bird in question is at once *proud* and *silly*.

SCENE 2. Page 205.

Enter the players with *recorders*.

" i. e." says Mr. Steevens, " a kind of *large* flute." Yet the former note, to which he refers, vol. v. p. 149, describes this instrument as a *small* flute. Sir J. Hawkins, in vol. iv. p. 479, of his valuable History of music, has offered very good proofs that the recorder was a *flagelet*, and he maintains that the flute was improperly termed a recorder, and that the expressions have been confounded: yet his opinion that the books of instructions entitled ' for the recorder' belong in reality to the flute, seems rather doubtful.   The confusion is in having blended the genus with the species.   In the *Promptuarium parvulorum*, 1516, 4to, a recorder is defined to be a "lytell pype."   In *Udall's flowres for Latine spekyng selected oute of Terence*, 1532, 12mo, the line from Virgil's Bucolics,

" Nec te pœniteat *calamo* trivisse labellum,"

is rendered, " and thynke it not a smalle thynge to have lerned to playe on the *pype* or the *recorder*:" and it is not a little curious that in modern cant language the recorders of corporations are termed *flutes*. The following story in *Wits fits and fancies*, 1595, 4to, shows that the pipe and recorder were different; such is the uncertainty of definition among old writers: " A merrie recorder of London mistaking the name of one *Pepper*, call'd him *Piper*: whereunto the partie excepting, and saying : Sir, you mistake, my name is *Pepper*, not *Piper*: hee answered : Why, what difference is there (I pray thee) between *Piper* in Latin, and *Pepper* in English; is it not all one? No, sir (reply'd the other) there is even as much difference betweene them, as is between a *Pipe* and a *Recorder*."

SCENE 2.   Page 207.

> HAM. Do you think I am easier to be play'd on than a pipe? Call me what instrument you will, though you can *fret* me, you cannot play upon me.

A *fret* is the stop or key of a musical instrument, and consequently here is a play on words, and a double meaning. Hamlet says, *though you can vex me, you cannot impose on me; though you can stop the instrument, you cannot play on it.*

Scene 3. Page 216.

Ham. . . that his soul may be as damn'd and black
As hell, whereto it goes.

To the stories collected in the notes that illustrate Hamlet's shocking design of killing the king at his prayers, may be added one in Howel's *Parley of the beasts*, p. 91, and another related in Chetwind's *Historical collections*, p. 77.

Scene 4. Page·231.

Ham. . . . a *vice* of kings.

" A low mimick of kings. The vice is the fool of a *farce*, from whence the modern *punch* is descended." Thus far Dr. Johnson. The first position in his note is questionable, the others erroneous. The *vice* belonged to the old moralities; and the modern *Punch* is most certainly not descended from him, but legitimately from a character well known in the theatres of ancient Rome. *We* have borrowed him from the Italian *Polichinello*. With respect to the former part of the note, Hamlet's expression may be quite literal. Thus in *King Henry the Fifth*, we have " this *grace* of kings." Afterwards indeed, Shakspeare, in his usual manner, recollecting the ambiguity of the term, takes up another simile, and makes Hamlet call his uncle *a king of shreds and patches*. See a former note in p. 287.

ACT IV.

Scene 2. Page 248.

Ham. The body is with the king, but the king is not with the body.

Hamlet's riddle seems still unresolved. Can this be its meaning? Instead of giving a direct answer to the inquiry after the body of Polonius, he seizes the opportunity of venting his sarcasm against the king, by saying that the body, i. e. the external appearance or person of the monarch, is with his uncle; but that the real and lawful king is not in that body.

SCENE 5.   Page 262.

OPH. To be your *Valentine.*

The custom of choosing *Valentines* is of very long standing, and, like many others of a popular nature, is no more than a corruption of something similar that had prevailed in the times of paganism.   It was the practice in ancient Rome, during a great part of the month of February, to celebrate the *Lupercalia,* which were feasts in honour of Pan and Juno, whence the latter deity was named *februata, februalis,* and *februlla.*   On this occasion, amidst a variety of ceremonies, the names of young women were put into a box, from which they were drawn by the men as chance directed.   The pastors of the early Christian church, who by every possible means endeavoured to eradicate the vestiges of Pagan superstitions, and chiefly by some commutation of their forms, substituted, in the present instance, the names of particular saints, instead of those of the women: and as the festival of the *Lupercalia* had commenced about the middle of February, they appear to have chosen Saint Valentine's day for celebrating the new feast; because it occurred nearly at the same time.   This is, in part, the opinion of a learned and rational compiler of the lives of the saints, the Reverend Alban Butler.   It should seem, however, that it was utterly impossible to extirpate altogether any ceremony to which the common people had been much accustomed; a fact which it were easy to prove in tracing the origin of various other popular superstitions: and accordingly the outline of the ancient ceremonies was preserved, but modified by some adaptation to the Christian system.   It is reasonable to suppose that the above practice of choosing mates would gradually become reciprocal in the sexes; and that all persons so chosen would be called *Valentines,* from the day on which the ceremony took place. There is another opinion on the origin of choosing *Valentines,* which has been formed on a tradition among the common people, that at the above season of the year birds choose their mates, a circumstance that is frequently alluded to by poets, and particularly by Chaucer ; yet this seems to be a mere poetical idea, borrowed in all probability from the practice in question. Again, it has been supposed that the custom originated in the following manner : During carnival time, which usually happens about Saint Valentine's day, great numbers of knights assembled together in the various courts of Europe to entertain the ladies with feasts and tournaments, when each lady made choice of a knight who usually enlisted in her service for a whole year, during which period he bound himself to perform, at the instance of his mistress, whatever was consistent with propriety. One employment was the writing verses full of tenderness; not that it was requisite for the heart to be at all concerned in the matter. A little reflection, however, may serve to show that even this practice is only derivative from the older one.

It is presumed that the earliest specimens remaining of poetical *Valentines* are those preserved in the works of Charles duke of Orleans, a prince of high accomplishments, and the father of Louis the Twelfth of France. He was taken prisoner at the battle of Agincourt, and remained a captive in this country twenty-five years, during which time he wrote several thousand lines of poetry, a few of them in English. Many of these poems are written on Saint *Valentine's* day, and in some of them his mistress is called his *Valentine*. In the Royal library of manuscripts, now in the British museum, there is a magnificent volume containing probably all that the duke wrote whilst in England. It belonged to King Henry the Seventh, for whom it had been copied from some older manuscript, and is beautifully illuminated. In one of the paintings the duke is represented in the White tower sitting at a writing table with guards attending him. In another part of it he is looking out of a window; and in a third he is

going out of the tower to meet some person who has just
alighted from his horse.   At a distance is London bridge with
the houses on it, and the curious chapel, all very distinct, and
probably faithful copies.   Besides the above work, this fine
manuscript contains some compositions by the celebrated
Eloisa, and other matters of less consequence.

In one of the duke's poems, he feigns that on Saint Valentine's day *Youth* appears to him with an invitation to the temple of love.   On the same day he devotes himself to the
service of several ladies, according to what he states to have
been the custom in England.   The following extracts from
some of his poems are given, as containing allusions to the
subject immediately before us :

> " A ce jour de Saint *Valentin*
> Que chascun doit choisir son per,
> Amours demourrai-je non per
> Sans partir à vostre butin ?
> A mon reveillier au matin
> Je n'y ay cessè de penser
> A ce jour de saint *Valentin*."

It appears from the following songs, that when Ash Wed-
nesday happened to fall on Saint Valentine's day, the knights
and their ladies assembled only in the afternoon, the morning
being necessarily devoted to pious purposes.

> " Saint *Valentin* quant vous venez
> En caresme au commencement,
> Receu ne serez vrayement
> Ainsi que accoustumè avez
>
> Saint *Valentin* dit, veez me ça,
> Et apporte pers a choysir :
> Viegne qui y devra venir,
> C'est la coustume de pieça.
> Quand le jour des cendres, hola,
> Respond, auquel doit-on faillir ?
> Saint *Valentin* dit, veez me ça,
> Et apporte pers à choysir.
> Au fort au matin convendra
> En devotion se tenir,

> Et après disner à loysir,
> Choysisse qui choisir vouldra ;
> Saint *Valentin* dit, veez me ça,
> Et apporte pers à choysir."

Another French *Valentine,* composed by John Gower, is quoted by Mr. Warton in his *History of English poetry,* add. to vol. ii. p. 31, from a manuscript in the library of Lord Gower. In this the poet tells his mistress that in choosing her he had followed the example of the birds.

Madame Royale, the daughter of Henry the Fourth of France, built a palace near Turin which was called *the Valentine,* on account of the great veneration in which the saint was held in that country. At the first entertainment given there by the princess, who was naturally of a gallant disposition, she directed that the ladies should choose their lovers *for the year* by lots. The only difference with respect to herself was, that she should be at liberty to fix on her own partner. At every ball during the year each lady received from her gallant a nosegay ; and at every tournament the lady furnished his horse's trappings, the prize obtained being hers. From this circumstance Monsieur Menage, to whom we are indebted for the above information, infers that in Piedmont, the parties were called *Valentines* ; but the learned writer was not aware of the circumstances already stated, nor of the antiquity of the custom in his own country. See Menage *Dict. étymologique,* art. *Valentin.*

In an old English ballad the lasses are directed to pray *cross-legged* to Saint *Valentine,* for good luck. For the modern ceremonies on choosing *Valentines,* the reader may consult Brand's *Popular antiquities,* and No. 56 of *The connoisseur.*

Scene 5. Page 263.

Oph. Let in the maid, that out a maid,
    Never departed more.

In an Album that belonged in 1598 to a Dutch lady named

Theodora Van Wassenaer, there is the following pretty French ballad addressed to her.   The conclusion resembles the above lines in Ophelia's song :

" Au jardin de mon pere
Un oranger il y a,
Qui est si chargè d'orenges
Je croy qu'il en rompra.
        Mignone tant je vous ayme,
        Mais vous ne m'aymez pas.

Elle demanda à son pere
Quand on le cueillera,
Ma fille, ma fille,
Quand la saison viendra.
        Mignone, &c.

La saison est venue
Le cueillerons nous pas ?
Elle prend une echelle,
Un panier à son bras.
        Mignone, &c.

Elle cueillit les plus meures,
Les verds elle y laissa ;
Elle les alloit porter vendre
Au marcher de Damas.
        Mignone, &c.

En son chemin rencontroit
Le fils d'un avocat ;
Que portez vous la belle
Dans ce panier couvert ?
        Mignone, &c.

Monsieur ce sont des orenges
Ne vous en plait-il pas ?
Il en prend une couple,
Dans son sein il les metta.
        Mignone, &c.

Venez vous en la belle,
On vous les payera ;
Elle y entra pucelle
Grossette elle en sorta.
        Mignone tant je vous ayme,
        Mais vous ne m'aymez pas.''

Scene 5. Page 263.

Oph. By *Gis,* and by Saint Charity.

The frequent occurrence of this adjuration sufficiently proves that Dr. Johnson's proposed change to *Cis* is unnecessary; nor indeed would the name of Saint Cecilia be proper to swear by. Mr. Ritson's *Gislen,* an obscure *Irish* saint, is equally out of the question. In the interlude of *Mary Magdelain,* she is made to say,

> " Nay by Gis, twentie shillings I dare holde
> That there is not a gentlewoman in this land
> More propre than I in the waste, I dare be bolde."

In *Promos and Cassandra,* Dalia swears by *Gys*; and in *Gammer Gurton's needle* and some other old plays, the same expression occurs. Mr. Ridley's conjecture that *Jesus* is the corrupted word is the true one; but the corruption is not in the way that he has stated. The letters IHS would not be pronounced *Gis,* even by those who understood them as a Greek contraction.

ACT V.

Scene 1. Page 297.

2 Clo. . . . therefore make her grave *straight.*

Dr. Johnson thought this meant " From East to West, in a direct line parallel to the church; not from North to South, athwart the regular line." The frequency of the above mode of expression in Shakspeare's plays sufficiently indicates that if he had alluded to the mode of burial contended for by Dr. Johnson, he would have adopted some other. It has occurred upwards of a hundred times already in the sense of *immediately.* Nor would it be easy to show that to make a grave *straight,* or in a direct line, was to make it East and West;

or that it was the designation of Christian burial. The first clown rather adverts to the *place* where the grave should be made than to its *form*. Suicides were buried on the North side of the church, in ground purposely *unconsecrated*.

Much of this scene has been imitated in the *Valiant Welshman,* by R. A. [q. Robert Armin] 1663. See Act IV.

Scene 1.   Page 299.

> 2. Clo. If this had not been a gentlewoman, she should have been bury'd out of Christian burial.

We have here a manifest satire on the partial verdicts of coroners' juries, where the suicide has been above the common condition of life. Judge Blackstone has hinted at them in his Commentaries. Nothing, however, but the partiality is reprehensible; the rest is an amiable tenderness towards the living, calculated to resist a law that justly deserves to be abhorred for a savage and impotent revenge so far as it regards the dead.

Scene 1.   Page 299.

> 1 Clo. Come; my *spade*. There is no ancient gentlemen but gardeners, ditchers and grave-makers; they hold up *Adam's* profession.
> 2 Clo. Was he a *gentleman?*
> 1 Clo. He was the first that ever bore arms.

This is undoubtedly in ridicule of heraldry. Gerard Leigh, one of the oldest writers on that subject, speaks of " Jesus Christ, a *gentleman* of great linage, and king of the Jewes." And again, " For that it might be known that even anon after the creation of Adam, there was both *gentlenes,* and *ungentlenes,* you shall understand that the second man that was born was a *gentleman,* whose name was Abell. I say a gentleman both of vertue and of lignage, with whose sacrifice God was much pleased. His brother Cain was *ungentle,* for he offered God the worst of his fruites," &c.—*Accedence of armorie,* 1591, 4to, fo. 13. Another morsel of satire against the above science lurks in the very ancient proverbial saying,

> " When Adam delv'd and Eve span,
> Where was then the gentleman ?"

which is found in almost every European language. It was the text on which the rebel priest John Balle preached his sermon during the insurrection of Wat Tyler. Although the first clown afterwards explains why Adam bore arms, by means of a punning allusion to his digging with arms, there is still a concealed piece of wit with respect to the *spade.* Adam's spade is set down in some of the books of heraldry as *the most ancient form of escutcheons* : nor is it improbable that the lower part of this utensil suggested the well-known form of the old triangular shields ; whilst from the spindle of Eve might have originated the lozenge-like escutcheon on which the arms of females are usually emblazoned.

SCENE 1.   Page 308.

HAM. . . the age is grown so *picked,* that the toe of the peasant, &c.

Mr. Malone's note, in exclusion of the others, is sufficiently satisfactory. The fashion of wearing pointed shoes, to which Hamlet had been supposed to allude, had ceased long before the time of Shakspeare ; nor is it probable that he would have transferred it to the age of Hamlet. We still say *a person treads close on the heels of another,* in the same signification as in the text.

SCENE 1.   Page 310.

1 CLO. This same scull, sir, was *Yorick's* scull, the king's jester.

The frequency of such names as *Eric* and *Roric* in the Danish history, might have suggested that of the jester in question, but in a manner that may not very easily be discovered. *Roric* was the name of the king of Denmark contemporary with Hamlet, according to Saxo Grammaticus.

SCENE 1. Page 311.

> HAM. Now get you to my lady's chamber, and tell her, let her paint an inch thick, to this favour she must come ; make her laugh at that.——

There is good reason for supposing that Shakspeare borrowed this thought from some print or picture that he had seen. There are several which represent a lady at her toilet, and an old man presenting a scull before the mirror. A print by Goltzius exhibits *Vanity* as a lady sitting in her chamber with jewels, &c. before her, and surprised by the appearance of Death. In one of Henry the Eighth's wardrobe accounts, a picture at Westminster is thus described: " Item a table with the picture of a woman playing upon a lute, and an olde manne holding a glasse in th'one hande and a deadde mannes headde in th'other hande."—Harl. MS. No. 1419.

IN a poem written by Anthony Scoloker, a printer, entitled *Daiphantus, or The passions of love, comicall to reade, but tragicall to act, as full of wit, as experience,* 1604, 4to, and recently quoted in p. 465, there are the following allusions to the play of *Hamlet*: In a quaint dedication he says, " It [the epistle] should be like the *never-too-well read Arcadia,* where the *prose* and *verse* (*matter* and *words*) are like his *mistresses* eyes, one still excelling another and without Corivall: or to come home to the vulgars element, like *friendly Shake-speare's tragedies*, where the *commedian* rides, when the *tragedian* stands on tiptoe : *Faith it should please all, like prince Hamlet.* But in sadnesse, then it were to be feared *he would runne mad.* In sooth I will not be moonesicke, to please: nor out of my wits though I displeased all."

" His breath he thinkes the smoke ; his tongue a cole,
  Then calls for bottell ale ; to quench his thirst.
  Runs to his Inke pot, drinkes, then stops the hole,
  And thus growes madder, then he was at first.
     Tasso he finds, by that of *Hamlet*, thinkes,
     Tearmes him a *mad-man* ; than of his Inkhorne drinks.

" *Calls players fooles*, the foole he judgeth wisest,
  Will learne them action, out of Chaucers Pander :
  Proves of their poets bawdes even in the highest,
  Then drinkes a health ; and sweares it is no slander,
     Puts off his cloathes ; his shirt he onely weares,
     Much like *mad-Hamlet* ; thus as passion teares."

OTHELLO.

ACT I.

Scene 3. Page 422.

OTH. Wherein of antres vast and desarts *idle*.

DR. JOHNSON has very properly taken notice of Mr. Pope's *inadvertency* in substituting *wild* for *idle*; but whether he is strictly right in regarding this word as " poetically beautiful," according to Shakspeare's use of it, may admit of some doubt. Perhaps in a modern writer it would be poetical, where designed to express *infertility*. It may be worth while to examine how it was originally used.

In Ælfric's version of Genesis, ch. i. ver. 1, the *inanis et vacua* of the Vulgate is rendered ẏbel ꞇ æmꞇiꞃ. Now it is conceived that *inanis* never signified *infertile*, but *useless, unprofitable*; and such appears to be the meaning of *idle*. In two or three of the early Latin and English dictionaries, *inanis* is rendered *idle*; and in this sense the latter word is used by Shakspeare in *Richard the third*, Act III.:

" You said that *idle weeds* were fast in growth."

It is clear that in the last instance *infertility* is out of the question: but *useless* and *unprofitable* well denote the poet's meaning, or rather that of the inventor of the proverb, which was afterwards corrupted into " *ill* weeds," &c.

It is conceived therefore that Dr. Johnson is not accurate in his opinion, that *idle* in the before-cited Saxon translation is an epithet expressive of the *infertility* of the chaotic state. Wicliffe has not adopted this term; he has preferred *vain*: but in the first page of the English *Golden legend*, which contains a part of the first chapter of Genesis, we have—" the erth was *ydle* and voyde." Here Caxton the translator must have followed the *Vulgate*, corroborating what is already stated on the construction of *idle*. The learned reader will not want to be informed why this term could not occur in any of the subsequent English versions of the Bible.

Scene 3. Page 447.

Iago. . . the food that to him now is as luscious as locusts, shall be to him shortly as bitter as coloquintida.

There is another phrase of this kind, viz. *to exchange Herb John for coloquintida.* It is used in Osborne's *Memoirs of James I.,* and elsewhere. The pedantic Tomlinson, in his translation of Renodæus's *Dispensatory,* says, that many superstitious persons call mugwort Saint John's herb, "wherewith he circumcinged his loyns on holidays," p. 317. Shakspeare, who was extremely well acquainted with popular superstitions, might have recollected this circumstance, when, for reasons best known to himself, he chose to vary the phrase by substituting the *luscious locusts* of the Baptist. Whether these were the fruit of the tree so called, or the well known insect, is not likely to be determined.

ACT III.

Scene 4. Page 556.

Des. . . . I had rather have lost my purse
Full of *cruzadoes.*

The following account of this Portuguese coin is presumed to be more correct than that already given. The cruzado was not current, as it should seem, at Venice, though it certainly was in England in the time of Shakspeare, who has here indulged his usual practice of departing from national costume. It was of gold, and weighed two penny-weights six grains, or nine shillings English. The following varieties of it as to type, are given from an English almanac of the year 1586, whence also the weight has been taken. The sovereigns who struck this coin were Emanuel and his son John.

Scene 4.   Page 558.

Oth.   .   .   The hearts, of old, gave hands;
But now new heraldry is—hands, not hearts.

There cannot be a doubt that the text is right, and that there is a punning allusion to the *new heraldry of hands* in the baronets' arms. The plain meaning is—*formerly the heart gave away the hand in marriage; but now, as in the new heraldy, we have hands only: no cordiality nor affection.* In *The tempest,* Ferdinand says to Miranda, " Here's my hand;" to which she answers, " And mine *with my heart in it.*" In this latter instance, Shakspeare, not Miranda, might recollect the gemmel rings, some of which had engraven on them a hand with a heart in it.

ACT IV.

Scene 2.   Page 601.

Oth. The bawdy wind, that kisses all it meets.

The same image occurs more delicately, but less strongly, in a beautiful " Song to a forsaken mistresse," written by an anonymous author, about the time of Charles the First, and published in Playford's *Select ayres,* 1659, folio. As most persons of taste already possess the whole of it in Mr Ellis's *Specimens of the early English poets,* it is unnecessary to give more in this place than the stanza in which the above image occurs:

"I do confess thou'rt sweet, yet find
Thee such an unthrift of thy sweets;
Thy favours are but *like the wind*,
Which kisseth every thing it meets:
And since thou can'st with more than one,
Th'art worthy to be kiss'd by none."

SCENE 2.   Page 635.

OTH. Had all his hairs been lives, my great revenge
Had stomach for them all.

The same sentiment occurs in the third part of *King Henry the Sixth*, where Clifford says,

"Had I thy brethren here, their lives and thine,
Were not revenge sufficient for me."

SCENE 2.   Page 653.

OTH. *Blow me about in winds!* roast me in sulphur!

Again, in *Measure for measure,*

"To be imprison'd in the viewless winds,
And blown with restless violence round about
The pendent world."

THE CLOWN.

HE appears but twice in the play, and was certainly intended to be an allowed or domestic *fool* in the service of Othello and Desdemona.

ADDITIONS TO THE NOTES.

PAGE 37. The *tune* of the old ballad of *Green sleeves* may be seen in Sir John Hawkins's *Hist. of musick*, vol. v. Append., and is still used in *The beggar's opera*, in the song of "Since laws were made for every degree."

Page 53. Cupid's *golden shaft* is again mentioned in the *Midsummer night's dream*, Act I. Scene 1:

"HERM. by his *best* arrow with the *golden head*."

Page 96. To the list of imitations, &c. of the story of *Measure for measure*, add the novel of *Waldburgh and Belanca*, in Reynolds's *God's revenge against adultery*. This is the substance of it: In the reign of Gustavus Adolphus king of Sweden, Moruffi, a Danish general, in attacking the castle of Colmar, was taken prisoner by the governor count Waldbourg. Belanca, the wife of Moruffi, obtained a promise from the count to liberate her husband on the terms of her submitting to his unlawful desires. The unfortunate woman was afterwards inhumanly presented with the head of her husband. When Gustavus heard of the fact, he compelled the count to marry the injured lady, and then condemned him to death. Reynolds pretended that all his stories in this and his other once celebrated work, *God's revenge against murder*, were originals, and that he had collected the materials for them in the course of his travels.

Page 119. The recipe here given for making men seem like horses or asses, from Scot's *Discoverie of witchcraft*, where Shakspeare might have seen it, is the real property of Baptista Porta, in the serious refutation of whom the Jesuit

Kircher has wasted too much time. See his treatise *De luce et umbra.*

In the *Prodromo apologetico alli studi Chircheriani* of Petrucci, there are similar receipts, and especially one in which an oil is directed to be made from the semen of a horse, which being used in a lamp, the company present will appear to have horses' heads. It is accompanied with a curious engraving of a Houyhnhnm party engaged in conversation, among whom there is the figure of an *equus togatus,* that will not fail to make a due impression on such readers as are acquainted with the trick put by Mr. Spence, the author of *Polymetis,* on Dr. Cooke, the provost of King's College Cambridge, a sour pedant who had offended him. See the tailpiece to the 17th dialogue in the *first* edition of the above work.

Page 123. The blessing of the bridal bed had doubtless, during the dark ages that preceded the promulgation of the gospel in many parts of Europe, been deemed the immediate office of fairies and other supernatural beings. The object of it was to make the issue of the marriage happy, and to avert deformity. In this, as in numerous other instances, the priests felt themselves obliged, in their attempt to do away a Pagan superstition, which, as we see, continued notwithstanding to maintain its influence, to substitute some congenial ceremony that should console the deluded people; but their particular enmity to fairies on the present occasion seems manifest in the passage cited from the Salisbury manual, in the words "ab omnibus fantasmaticis demonum illusionibus;" unless they should be thought rather to allude to the subject which is particularly noticed in the subsequent remarks on the night-spells.

The above ceremony is thus mentioned by Chaucer in his description of the marriage of January and May:

> " The bride is brought a-bed as stil as ston;
> And whan the bed was with the preest yblessed,
> Out of the chambre hath every wight him·dressed."
>
> *Marchantes tale,* v. 9692.

On the evidence relating to the consummation of the marriage between prince Arthur and the Lady Catharine, Robert Viscount Fitzwater deposed that " the prince was then about fifteen, and queen Katherine elder, and that the next day after being in bed together (*which he remembred after they entered to have been solemnly bless'd*), he waited at breakfast on prince Arthur, &c."—Lord Herbert's *Life of Henry the Eighth*, p. 243.   It is said that some vestiges of this custom still remain among the Presbyterians in Scotland.

Page 169. There is a story of *two* caskets, &c., in Morlini *novellæ*, nov. 5.

Quære if the general construction of all these stories have not been borrowed from the trick related to have been put by Prometheus on Jupiter with the two bull-skins filled with flesh and bones ?

Page 178 (note). Dr. Taylor, in his treatise *De inope debitore in partes dissecando,* has offered some strong arguments against the supposed mutilation of the debtor's body, and endeavoured to show that the law in question demanded nothing more than that the produce of his servitude should be divided among the creditors. Yet Aulus Gellius was of a different opinion At a very early period, among the Jews, the creditor had a right to make a slave of the debtor. See 2 Kings, chap. iv. ver. 1.

Page 185. To the explanation of *sans*, add that in the early editions of the dictionaries of Coles and Littelton the word is printed *sance*.

Page 214. Morgan the herald must be acquitted of having conveyed to us the *original* information that " Jesus Christ was a gentleman and bore arms." He was indebted for it to Dame Julian Berners, who, in her treatise on coat armour, speaks of " the gentyl Jesus," and states that " Cryst [was] a gentylman of his mother's behalf and bare cote armure." She also tells us that " Cain became a churl from the curse of God, and Seth a *gentleman* through his father and mother's blessing." So that we find J. C. was not the *first* gentleman.

Page 317. In further confirmation of the opinion here expressed, the curious reader is referred to Wlson de Colombiere's *Vray theatre d'honneur*, vol. ii. p. 313, for the account of a duel on appeal for murder which was fought at Valenciennes in the year 1454, where the dead body of the vanquished party was adjudged to be hanged on a gallows as a convicted murderer.

The frequent use which has been made in the course of these remarks of a work cited under the title of Bartholomæus *de proprietatibus rerum*, may require that a more particular description of it should be given. It is a general history of nature, composed in Latin by Bartholomew Glanvile, an English Minorite or Franciscan, of the family of the earls of Suffolk. He flourished about the year 1360, and appears to have been the Pliny of his time. It was several times printed abroad in the infancy of the typographic art, and translated into the English, French, Dutch, and Spanish languages. The English version was made by John Trevisa, a Cornish man, and vicar of Barkley in Gloucestershire, at the request of his patron Thomas Lord Barkley, in the year 1398, and originally printed by Wynkyn de Worde; for there is no evidence that it came from Caxton's press in English, though it has been so asserted. Neither is the date of Wynkyn de Worde's edition, if it ever had any, been ascertained. The next edition was printed in 1535, by Thomas Berthelette, in folio. The last was published under the title of *Batman uppon Bartholome*, his *Booke de proprietatibus rerum*, &c. Printed by Thomas East, 1582, in folio. Stephen Batman appears to have been a worthy and pious character, and was chaplain to Lord Hunsdon. His additions were compiled from Gesner and other writers of his own time. In a manuscript diary of expenses in the reign of Elizabeth, the price of this book is stated to have been eight shillings.

THE ANACHRONISMS

SOME OTHER INCONGRUITIES

SHAKSPEARE.

THE transgressions against the rules of chronology committed by those who, in recording the events of preceding ages, introduce matters which have originated in subsequent periods, seem almost exclusively to belong to authors whose works, in point of date, are to be separated from those admirable compositions which are usually styled the Classics. In the latter, such instances seldom, if ever, occur; whilst in the writers, as well as the artists, of the middle ages, they are innumerable. Nor do these absurdities diminish as we approach periods more enlightened as to general science. From the time of Chaucer to that of Shakspeare, there is scarcely an author to be found who is not implicated in this accusation; and about the age of Elizabeth, the dramatists in particular seem to have been remarkably inattentive to the unities of time and place. It has been observed that Ben Jonson is almost the only writer against whom the charge of uniting dissimilar manners and discordant periods is not to be laid; and though the poets of the ensuing century are not wholly free from the imputation in question, it is certain that from about the reign of king James the First more care was taken to preserve a due attention to the manners and customs of particular ages, or at least to avoid any very palpable anachronisms, than had already been done. But whilst the compositions of dramatic writers remained pretty free from these blemishes, the directors of the theatres continued to practise their, perhaps innocent, impostures on the public; and every absurdity that could be devised, or distortion of reality in costume, still continued to disgrace the stage. We were not indeed more absurd in this respect than other European nations, nor was it until a short time before the late revolution that the French theatre had reformed itself in this respect. Many persons now recollect the state of the English stage in Garrick's time, when that excellent performer used to exhibit his Hamlet in a common French suit of black velvet and a cocked hat, and his Macbeth in a scarlet coat with broad gold lace like the uniform of a modern general. Quin is said to have played Othello in a flowing powdered periwig. How Shakspeare's characters were habited on the stage in his time, would be difficult or even impossible to ascertain with accuracy at present, except in a few instances; but we have no reason to suppose that much propriety was manifested on the occasion. Unluckily for us it was not then the practice to decorate the printed plays with frontispieces; and the theatrical prints and pictures even of succeeding times are not very commonly to be met with. It is on this account that the cuts to Mr. Rowe's edition of Shakspeare, and those to the first octavo edition of the works of Beaumont and Fletcher, are at present extremely valuable, as they serve to record many pleasant absurdities that will not fail to excite a smile in the beholder.

It was reserved for the great actor who to the scenic talents of a Garrick unites that managerial skill and judgment in the costume of nations which the other wanted, to reform these follies; and, by exhibiting to us times as they were, to render the stage what it should be, a true and perfect mirror of history and manners.

The above very slight notice of the subject before us may perhaps be sufficient for the purpose of introducing the mention of those anachronisms that are ascribable to Shakspeare : and this has not been done with any view to exhibit him as more culpable in this respect than most of his contemporaries, but solely for the purpose of collecting them together as an object of amusement : nothing however could have been less judicious than the conduct of Mr. Pope when he placed them to the account of the publishers. Nor is the catalogue offered as a complete one ; the diligent and critical reader will discover some that are here unnoticed.

But the negligence of writers in the due observance of costume is but trifling, when compared with what is to be laid to the charge of painters and other artists. Volumes have been professedly filled, and the number might still be augmented, with the errors of even the best of the old painters. Nor are the modern by any means to be acquitted on this score. We too frequently see works of the greatest intrinsic worth, both in composition and execution, depreciated by the most absurd violations of historical accuracy and a want of adherence to the manners of the times they refer to. In this case they are not what they profess to be ; and whilst they delight the eye, they delude the understanding. It is extremely pleasing to observe the zeal which manifests itself among the leading artists of the present day to obtain correct notions of the manners of former times whenever they have occasion to depict them. The works of many of our best painters will not only excite the admiration but the gratitude of posterity for the faithful delineation of their subjects, and the labours of future antiquaries will be reduced in proportion as pictures of this kind shall increase.*

* Mr. Stothard, the most unassuming of men, but with every claim to superior talent, has recently finished a painting of the procession of Chaucer's Canterbury pilgrims, which may be classed among the choicest morsels of its kind. The attention to accuracy of costume which it displays has never been exceeded, and but very seldom so well directed.

To return to Shakspeare. In the *dramatis personæ* of many of his plays we find a medley of ancient and modern names that is often extremely ridiculous. At Ephesus we meet with *Pinch*, a schoolmaster; at Mitylene with *Boult*, a clown; and at Athens with *Snug, Bottom, Snout, Quince,* &c. In his later stories English names are given to foreigners. Thus at Vienna we have *Froth* and *Elbow*; in Navarre, *Dull, Costard,* and *Moth*; and in Illyria, *Sir Toby Belch* and *Sir Andrew Aguecheek.* But these, strictly speaking, are not anachronisms, but, on the whole, justifiable licences; for it would have been impossible to transmit the humour of such characters as the above to an English audience under the disguise of foreign names, though it must be admitted that mere English characters as well as names are sometimes introduced. Nor is Shakspeare always responsible for such whimsicalities, for they are occasionally to be traced in the materials whereof his plays were constructed; and others belong to those authors whom he had only assisted in dramas the whole composition of which had been improperly ascribed to him.

MERRY WIVES OF WINDSOR.

The incidents in this play are supposed to belong to the reign of Henry the Fourth, and consequently the introduction of the *shillings of Edward the Sixth*, and the mention of *Machiavel,* are improper; as well as the then newly-introduced terms of the fencing-school ridiculed by Shallow. Perhaps *Ancient* Pistol and *Corporal* Nym are objectionable titles. The allusions to *Guiana* and the *West Indies* by Falstaff are obvious anachronisms.

TWELFTH NIGHT.

The introduction of the *bed of Ware* may be justified, because it is referred to as in England; but the same defence cannot be made for *the bells of Saint Bennet,* as they are specifically alluded to.

MEASURE FOR MEASURE.

We have here an English jury in a German court of justice.

MIDSUMMER NIGHT'S DREAM.

The scene of this play lies at Athens, in the time of Theseus, but we find the mention of *guns*; of *French-crowns* and *French-crown-coloured beards*; of *church-yards* and *coats in heraldry*; of clean *linen,* new *ribbons to pumps,* and *masks*; of *Jack and Gill,* the *nine-mens morris,* and *blessing the bridal bed.* *Carols,* inasmuch as they are applicable to songs in general, and, in an antiquated sense, to dances, may be doubtful, though the allusion was in all probability to Christmas carols. Hermia is made to speak of the fire which burned the *Carthage queen.*

MERCHANT OF VENICE.

English juries are introduced into the Venetian republic.

WINTER'S TALE.

The transactions of this play arise in Sicily and Bohemia; and though the characters are imaginary, they are supposed to exist in Pagan times. Notwithstanding this we have *Whitson* pastorals, *Christian* burial, a *hobby-horse,* an emperor of *Russia,* and an Italian printer of the *fifteenth century.*

COMEDY OF ERRORS.

In the *ancient* city of Ephesus we have *ducats, marks,* and *guilders,* and the *abbess of a nunnery.* Mention is also made of several *modern* European kingdoms, and of *America*; of *Henry the Fourth of France*, of *Turkish* tapestry, a *rapier*, and a *striking clock*; of *Lapland* sorcerers, *Satan*, and even of *Adam* and *Noah*. In one place Antipholis calls himself a *Christian*. As we are unacquainted with the immediate source whence this play was derived, it is impossible to ascertain whether Shakspeare is responsible for these anachronisms.

MACBETH.

The errors here are confined to the introduction of *cannon* and of *dollars*.

KING JOHN.

In this play we also find *cannon*, with *angels, half-fac'd groats,* and *three-farthing pieces. Cards* too are introduced, and *Basilisco*, a character of the time of Shakspeare.

KING HENRY THE FOURTH.

The anachronisms are very numerous in the plays on this reign. We have *pistols* and *silk* stockings; *gilt two-pences,* and *ten-shilling-pieces*; a ballad with a *picture* on it, evidently alluding to the wood-cuts on those compositions; the game of *shove-groat* or *slide shrift*, which was not invented before the reign of Henry the Eighth. Mention is also made of *John* Scogan jester to Edward the Fourth, and of *Arthur's show*, though not introduced till a long time afterwards.

KING HENRY THE FIFTH.

The Turks are put into possession of Constantinople, which did not fall into their hands till upwards of thirty years after Henry's death.

KING HENRY THE SIXTH.

Machiavel, who was not born till 1469, is twice introduced in these plays.   Printing is also prematurely mentioned.

KING HENRY THE EIGHTH.

An old woman is made to talk of bow'd *three-pences*; but these pieces were not known in England till the reign of Edward the Sixth, though some are said to have been coined in Ireland during that of Edward the Fourth.

TROILUS AND CRESSIDA.

Hector quotes *Aristotle*; Ulysses speaks of the bull-bearing *Milo*, and Pandarus of a man born in *April. Friday* and *Sunday*, and even *minced-pies* with dates in them are introduced.

TIMON OF ATHENS.

Paper is mentioned in this play.   In a Roman drama it might have passed; but we have no evidence that the Greeks used the papyrus plant at this early period.

CORIOLANUS.

Alexander, Cato, and *Galen,* are improperly alluded to, all being posterior to the time of Coriolanus.   Other anachronisms are—the mention of graves in a holy *church-yard*; *groats, mummers, lockram,* and a kitchen *malkin.*   Coriolanus describes the populace by the names of *Hob and Dick.*

JULIUS CÆSAR.

Cassius speaks of a *masker* and *reveller,* and of the *clock striking three.*

ANTONY AND CLEOPATRA.

Antony talks of *packing cards,* and deals out his *knaves, queens, hearts,* and *trumps,* as if he were a whist-player. His bestowing the epithet of *gipsy* on Cleopatra is whimsical, but may perhaps admit of defence.

CYMBELINE.

The British tribute being estimated at three thousand pounds, strikes on the ear as a modern computation. Imogen calls her supposed master, a valiant ancient Briton, by the name of *Richard Du Champ.* We find mention of the re-creation of *bowling;* of *paper;* of *rushes* strewed in apartments; of a *striking clock;* of *cherubims,* and a *chapel* as a *burial place.* Cymbeline is made to knight Bellario and his sons on the field of battle by *dubbing* them according to the fashion of the middle ages.

TITUS ANDRONICUS.

The period in which the incidents in this play are supposed to have happened (for they are all fictitious) is difficult to ascertain. There was an usurper called Saturninus during the reigns of Gallien and Aurelian, but he was not the son of any Roman emperor, as stated in the *dramatis personæ.* From the introduction of the Goths, the author perhaps adverted to the time of the above sovereigns. In all events the play has many absurdities to answer for. A child is sent to Aaron the Moor to be *christened* by him. He accuses Lucius of twenty *Popish* tricks; talks of an *idiot's bauble*: and says he can blush " like a black dog, as the saying is." A clown invokes " God and *Saint Stephen.*" Aaron calls for *clubs,* as if addressing the *London 'prentices*; and Demetrius speaks of a *dancing rapier.* *Cards* and a *monastery* are also introduced.

PERICLES.

The story, though altogether fabulous, belongs to a period a little antecedent to the Christian æra; and therefore it is a manifest inconsistency to introduce *crowns of the sun*; *sequins*; a *pistol*; *cambrick*; a *Spanish ruff*; *signs* of inns; *Monsieur Veroles a French knight*; a *Spanish* name and motto, and the *lues Venerea*. Amidst numerous invocations to Heathen Gods, there is an immediate allusion to the unity of the Deity.

KING LEAR.

We have here a plentiful crop of blunders. Kent talks, like a good Protestant, of *eating no fish*; and Gloster, of not standing in need of *spectacles*. We have *Turks, Bedlam* beggars, *child Roland, Saint Withold*, a *Marshal of France, steeples, dollars, paper, holy water*, and the *French disease*. There is an allusion to the old theatrical *moralities*; and *Nero*, who did not live till several hundred years after Lear, is mentioned by Edgar as an angler in the lake of darkness.

HAMLET.

The Danish history has placed Hamlet in fabulous times, long before the introduction of Christianity into the North of Europe; and therefore there is great impropriety in the frequent allusion to Christian customs. Hamlet swears by *Saint Patrick*; and converses with Guildenstern on the *children of the chapel of Saint Paul's*. In several places *cannon* are introduced, and a good deal of the theatrical manners of Shakspeare's own time. We have a Danish *seal royal* long before seals were used; a *university* at Wittemberg; *Swiss* guards; *serjeants* or *bailiffs*; *bells*; *ducats*; *crown-pieces*; *modern heraldry*; *rapiers*, and terms of *modern fencing*.

DISSERTATION I.

ON THE CLOWNS AND FOOLS OF SHAKSPEARE.

THE ensuing dissertation originated from the opinion of a late eminent critic and antiquary that the subject was deserving of particular consideration. How imperfectly it must be executed will best be felt by those who are already accustomed to obscure inquiries; and little more can here be offered, or reasonably expected, than some attempt to arrange a few materials that have occurred during a course of reading immediately connected with the history of ancient manners. The critic above alluded to had remarked, that Shakspeare has most judiciously varied and discriminated his fools.* Without doubting that great writer's capacity to have done so, it certainly remains to be proved that he has; or it might even be maintained that on some occasions he has left his sketches so imperfect as to render it by no means an easy matter to comprehend them. It has already been thought better to make the attempt in a separate note to the plays in which a clown or fool is introduced, and to direct what is now offered to a more general view of the subject.

It is so exceedingly clear that the terms *clown* and *fool* were used, however improperly, as synonymous by our old writers, that it would be an unnecessary occupation of the reader's time to adduce examples. Their confused introduction in the dramatis personæ might indeed render this position doubtful to any one who had not well considered the

* See a note by Mr. Ritson in *Twelfth night*, Act II. Scene 3, edit. Steevens, vol. iv. p. 53.

matter; but although the *fool* of our old plays denoted either a mere idiot or natural, or else a witty hireling or artificial fool, both retained for the purpose of making sport for their employers, the *clown* was certainly a character of much greater variety. He occasionally represented one of the above personages; sometimes he was a mere rustic, and very often no more than a shrewd and witty domestic. There are some instances in which any low character in a play served to amuse the audience with his sallies of coarse buffoonery, and thus became the *clown* of the piece. In short, the theatrical clown or fool seems to have been a kind of heterogeneous character, drawn in part from real life, but very considerably heightened in order to produce stage effect; an opinion that derives considerable support from what Shakspeare has put into the mouth of Hamlet, when he makes him admonish those who play the clowns to speak no more than is set down for them. Indeed, the great dramatist himself cannot be absolved from the imputation of having given too high a colouring to the characters in question, unless we suppose, what is extremely probable, that his plays have been very much interpolated with the extemporaneous nonsense of the players. To this licentious practice the author of an excellent and well written satire, entitled *Pasquil's mad-cappe, throwne at the corruptions of these times*, 1626, 4to, alludes in the following lines:

> "Tell country players, that old paltry jests
>   Pronounced in a painted motley coate,
>   Filles all the world so full of cuckoes nests,
>   That nightingales can scarcely sing a note:
>   Oh bid them turne their minds to better meanings;
>   Fields are ill sowne that give no better gleanings."

Among other grave writers of the age, Sir Philip Sidney has reprobated the practice of introducing fools on the theatre. He remarks that the plays of his time were neither right tragedies nor right comedies, but that the authors mingled kings and clowns, "not," says he, "because the matter so carieth it, but thrust in the *clowne* by head and shoulders to play a part in majestical matters, with neither decencie nor discretion: so as neither the admiration and commiseration, nor the right sportfulnesse is by their mongrell tragi-comedie obtained."* William Rankin, a puritan, and contemporary with Shakspeare, has left us a most virulent attack on plays, and players, whom he calls monsters : " And whie monsters," says he, " Bicause under colour of humanitie they present nothing but prodigious vanitie. These are wels without water, dead branches fit for fuell, cockle amongst corne, unwhole-some weedes amongst sweete hearbes, and finallie, feends that are crept into the worlde by stealth, and holde possession by subtill invasion." In another place, describing the perfor-mers at a fictitious banquet in Terralbon, [England] he says, " Some transformed themselves to roges, other to ruffians, some other to *clownes*, a fourth to *fooles* . . . . the roges were ready, the ruffians were rude, *theyr clownes cladde* as well with country condition, as in ruffe russet; theyr *fooles as fonde as might be*," &c.† The latter passage is inter-esting, because the clown is properly distinguished from the fool, as he always should have been.

It may be the means of affording a clearer view of the present subject, if something like a classification of the diffe-rent sorts of fools and clowns be given. The following is therefore offered as a substitute for a better.

I. *The general domestic fool*, often, but as it should seem improperly, termed a clown. He was, 1. a mere natural, or idiot. 2. Silly by nature, yet cunning and sarcastical. 3. Ar-tificial. Puttenham, speaking of the latter, says, " A buffoune or counterfet foole, to here him speake wisely which is like himselfe, it is no sport at all; but for such a counterfait to talke and looke foolishly it maketh us laugh, because it is no

* Defence of poesie, near the end.
† Mirrour of monsters, 1587, 4to, fo. 7.

part of his naturall."* All these officiated occasionally as menial servants.

II. *The clown,* who was, 1. a mere country booby. 2. A witty rustic. 3. Any servant of a shrewd and witty disposition, and who, like a similar character in our modern plays, was made to treat his master with great familiarity in order to produce stage effect.

III. *The female fool,* who was generally an idiot.

IV. *The city or corporation fool,* whose office was to assist at public entertainments and in pageants. To this class belong perhaps the Lord Mayor's state fool, and those employed by the companies of trades, &c.

V. *Tavern fools.* These seem to have been retained to amuse the customers. We learn from one of Ben Jonson's plays that they exhibited with a Jew's harp, mounted on a joint-stool,† and in another of them he has preserved the name of such a character :‡ they were sometimes qualified to sing after the Italian manner.§ Fools were also employed in the common brothels.‖

VI. *The fool of the ancient theatrical mysteries and moralities.* He was, more properly speaking, the *Vice,* a singular character, that would afford sufficient matter for much better dissertations than those of Warburton or Upton. Being generally dressed in a fool's habit, he appears to have been gradually and undistinguishably blended with the domestic fool; yet he was certainly a buffoon of a different sort. He was always a bitter enemy to the Devil, and a part of his employment consisted in teazing and tormenting the poor fiend on every occasion. He ceased to be in fashion at the end of the sixteenth century.¶

---

* Arte of English poesie, 1589, 4to, fo. 243.
† *The devil is an ass,* Sc. 1.   ‡ *The fox,* Act II. Sc. 1.
§ Marston's *Malcontent,* Sc. 7.   ‖ See p. 94.
¶ *The devil is an ass,* Sc. 1.

VII. *The fool in the old dumb shows exhibited at fairs and perhaps at inns,* in which he was generally engaged in a struggle with Death ; a fact that seems alluded to more than once in Shakspeare's plays. It is possible that some casual vestiges of this species of entertainment might have suggested the modern English pantomimes.

VIII. *The fool in the Whitsun ales and Morris dance.*

IX. *The mountebank's fool, or merry Andrew.*

There may be others introduced into our old dramas of an indefinite and irregular kind, and not reducible to any of the above classes; but to exemplify these or many of the above by a specific reference to authorities is not within the scope of the present essay. It is hoped that what has been just stated may contribute to assist the readers of old plays in forming some judgment of their own whenever the necessity shall arise.

A general investigation of that most singular and eccentric character, the real domestic fool, would occupy more space than could here have been spared. It would indeed extend to a length that few will conceive; but should the same laudable spirit of curiosity respecting the manners of former times which at present constitutes much of the amusement of an enlightened public continue to maintain its influence, encouragement would not be wanting to resume the subject more at large. In the mean time it may be sufficient to re-mark that the practice of retaining fools can be traced in very remote times throughout almost all civilized and even among some barbarous nations. It prevailed from the palace to the brothel. The pope had his fool, and the bawd her's ; and ladies entertained them of both sexes. With respect to the antiquity of this custom in our own country, there is reason to suppose that it existed even during the period of our Saxon history; but we are quite certain of the fact in the reign of William the Conqueror. An almost contemporary historian, Maitre Wace, has left us a curious account of the preservation of William's life when he was only duke of Normandy by his fool *Goles*.* Mention is made in Domesday of *Berdic joculator regis*; and although this term was unquestionably applied in numerous instances to denote a minstrel, much evidence might be adduced to show that on this occasion it signified a buffoon. Latin terms were used by the middle-age writers so licentiously and with such extreme carelessness, that in many cases it is difficult to obtain a precise idea of their meaning. Thus the jesters and minstrels were indefinitely expressed by the words *joculator, scurra, mimus, ministrallus,* &c., a practice that may admit of justification when we consider that in early times the minstrel and buffoon characters were sometimes united in one person. It must be allowed, however, that in an etymological point of view the term *joculator* is much better adapted to the jester than the minstrel.

The accounts of the household expenses of our sovereigns contain many payments and rewards to fools both foreign and domestic, the motives for which do not appear, but might perhaps have been some witty speech or comic action that had pleased the donors. Some of these payments are annual gifts at Christmas. Dr. Fuller, speaking of the court jester, whom he says some count a necessary evil, remarks, in his usual quaint manner, that it is an office which none but he that hath wit can perform, and none but he that wants it will perform.† A great many names of these buffoons have been preserved; and sufficient materials remain to furnish a separate biography of them, which might afford even more amusement than can be found in the lives of many of their betters. They continued an appurtenance to the English court to a late period. Muckle John, the fool of Charles the First, and the successor of Archee Armstrong, is perhaps the

---

* Roman des ducs de Normandie, MS. Reg. 4, C. xi.
† Holy state, p. 182.

last regular personage of the kind.* The national troubles
that produced the downfall of regal power, and the puritanical manners that ensued, at once determined the existence of
an office that had so long maintained its ground at court:
and when Charles the Second resumed the throne, it was probably deemed a matter of no moment to restore it. The
common stories that relate to Killigrew as jester to Charles,
rest on no sufficient authority; and although he might have
contributed to amuse the witty monarch with his jokes, it is
certain that he had no regular appointment to such an office.
Mr. Granger has justly observed that the wit of the buffoons
became the highest recommendation of a courtier in the time
of Charles the Second.†

The discontinuance of the court fool had a considerable influence on the manners of private life; and we learn from
one of Shadwell's plays, that it was then " out of fashion for
great men to keep fools."‡ But the practice was by no
means abolished; it maintained its ground in this country so
late as the beginning of the last century; and we have an
epitaph, written by Dean Swift, on Dicky Pearce the Earl of
Suffolk's fool, who was buried in Berkley church-yard,
June 18, 1728.§ This person was an idiot. Lord Chancellor Talbot kept a Welsh jester named Rees Pengelding.
He was a very shrewd fellow, and rented a farm of his master. Being distrained on for his rent by an oppressive steward, who had been a tailor and bore him a grudge, the surly
fellow said to him on this occasion, " I 'll fit you, sirrah."

* This person was probably the subject of the following lines in Bancroft's
Epigrams, 1639, 4to :

> " How plumpe's the libertine! how rich and trimme !
> He jests with others, fortune jests with him."

Mr. Garrard, in a letter to lord Strafford, says, " There is a new fool in
his [Archee's] place, Muckle John, but he will ne'er be so rich, for he cannot abide money."—*Strafford papers*, ii. 154.

† Biogr. hist. of England, i. 116.		‡ *The woman captain*, 1680, Sc. i.
§ Bigland's *Collect. for Gloucest.*

" Then," replied Rees, " it will be the first time in your life
that you ever fitted any one." Another Welshman called
Will the taborer was retained in a similar capacity, about the
beginning of the last century, by Sir Edward Stradling, of
St. Donat's castle, in Glamorganshire. He is said to have
been a very witty fellow, and man of strong intellects. Lord
Bussy Mansel, of Margam, had likewise in his service one Robin Rush, an idiot by nature, but who often said very witty
things. There are people now alive in Wales, or lately were,
who well remembered him.

The sort of entertainment that fools were expected to afford, may be collected in great variety from our old plays,
and particularly from those of Shakspeare; but perhaps no
better idea can be formed of their general mode of conduct
than from the following passage in a singular tract by Lodge,
entitled *Wit's miserie*, 1599, 4to: " Immoderate and disordinate joy became incorporate in the bodie of a jeaster; this
fellow in person is comely, in apparell courtly, but in behaviour a very ape, and no man; his studie is to coine bitter
jeasts, or to shew antique motions, or to sing baudie sonnets
and ballads : give him a little wine in his head, he is continually flearing and making of mouthes: he laughs intempe-
rately at every little occasion, and dances about the house,
leaps over tables, out-skips mens heads, trips up his companions heeles, burns sack with a candle, and hath all the feats
of a lord of misrule in the countrie : feed him in his humor,
you shall have his heart, in meere kindness he will hug you
in his armes, kisse you on the cheeke, and rapping out an
horrible oth, crie God's soule Tum, I love you, you know my
poore heart, come to my chamber for a pipe of tabacco, there
lives not a man in this world that I more honor. In these
ceremonies you shall know his courting, and it is a speciall
mark of him at the table, he sits and makes faces: keep not
this fellow company, for in *jugling* with him, your wardropes
shall be wasted, your credits crackt, your crownes consumed,

and time (the most precious riches of the world) utterly lost." This is the picture of a real hireling or artificial fool.

As the profession of these hirelings required a considerable degree of skill and dexterity to amuse their employers, so it would in some instances fail of success, and the want of the above talents would excite considerable disgust and dissatisfaction. Cardinal Perron being one day in company with the duke of Mantua, the latter, speaking of his fool, said that he was *un magro buffone & non haver spirito.* The cardinal remarked that nevertheless he had wit. "Why so?" demanded the duke. "Because," replied the other, "he lives by a trade which he does not understand."* The liberties allowed them were necessarily very great; but this was not always a protection to them. Every one knows the disgracefully severe conduct of archbishop Laud to poor Archee. The duke d'Espernon, though a man of great haughtiness of spirit, conducted himself on a similar occasion with much more discretion. His Gascon accent was a constant subject of raillery on the part of Maret, the fool of Louis XIII., whose great talent lay in mimicry. Cardinal Richelieu, who took upon him to give the duke some pointed admonitions, ordered him among other things to endeavour to get rid of his provincial tones, at the same time counterfeiting his speech, and sarcastically intreating him not to take his advice in bad part. "But why should I," replied the duke, "when I bear as much every day from the king's fool, who mocks me in your presence?"† Selden has remarked, on a similar occasion, that a gallant man is above ill words, and has left us a story of the forbearance of the old lord Salisbury, whom he calls a great wise man, towards Stone, a celebrated fool in the reign of James the First.‡ Fools, however, did not always escape

* Perroniana, inter Scaligerana, &c. i. 115.
† Vigneul de Marville, Mélanges. ii. 50.
‡ Table talk, Art. Evil-speaking.

with impunity; they were liable to, and often experienced, very severe domestic castigation. Whipping was the punishment generally inflicted.* On the other hand they appear to have been sometimes used with great tenderness. This is very feelingly exemplified in the conduct of Lear. Stafford in his *Guide of honour*, 1634, 18mo, tells us, that he "had knowne a great and competently wise man who would much respect any man that was good to his foole." An opportunity here presents itself of explaining the old proverb of "five pounds; you've bled a fool," which, adverting to the usual privilege or allowance belonging to this character, seems to demand a forfeit from whoever had infringed it by inflicting an improper and unlawful chastisement. This exposition derives support from a passage in Ben Jonson's *Fox*, and also contributes to its illustration. In the second Act there is a song describing a fool, in which it is said that he "speaks truth free from slaughter." This has been with some ingenuity supposed to mean "*free* from hurting any one." The other construction may perhaps be thought as plausible.

* This appears from many of our old plays. Lear threatens his fool with the whip, Act I. Scene 4; and see *As you like it*, Act I. Scene 2. In Dr. Turner's *New booke of spirituall physik*, 1555, 12mo, fo. 8, there is a very curious story of John of Low, the king of Scotland's fool, which throws light on the subject in question. Yet the chastising of the poor fools seems to have been a very unfair practice, when it is considered that they were a privileged class with respect to their wit and satire. Olivia, in *Twelfth night*, says, that "there is no slander in an allowed fool though he do nothing but rail;" and Jaques, in *As you like it*, alludes to the above privilege. See likewise other instances in Reed's *Old plays*, iii. 253, and xi. 417. Yet in cases where the free discourse of fools gave just offence to the ears of modest females they seem to have been treated without mercy, and to have forfeited their usual privilege. This we learn from Brantôme, who, at the end of his *Dames galantes*, relates a story of a fool belonging to Elizabeth of France, who got a whipping in the kitchen for a licentious speech to his mistress. A representation of the manner in which the flagellation of fools was performed may be seen in a German edition of Petrarch *De remediis utriusque fortunæ*, published more than once at Frankfort, in the sixteenth century, part ii. chap. 100.

With respect to his office on the stage, we may suppose it would be nearly the same as in reality ; the difference might be that his wit was more highly seasoned. Mr. Malone has already cited a very curious passage on this subject from the play of *The careless shepherdess*, 1656.* In Middleton's *Mayor of Quinborough*, a company of actors with a clown make their appearance, and the following dialogue ensues :

FIRST CHEATER.

This is our clown, sir.

SIMON.

Fye, fye, your company
Must fall upon him and beat him ; he 's too fair, i' faith
To make the people laugh.

FIRST CHEATER.

Not as he may be dress'd sir.

SIMON.

'Faith, dress him how you will, I 'll give him
That gift, he will never look half scurvily enough.
Oh, the clowns that I have seen in my time.
The very peeping out of one of them would have
Made a young heir laugh, though his father lay a dying ;
A man undone in law the day before
(The saddest case that can be) might for his second
Have burst himself with laughing, and ended all
His miseries. Here was a merry world, my masters !
Some talk of things of state, of puling stuff;
There 's nothing in a play like to a clown,
If he have the grace to hit on it, that 's the thing indeed.

SIMON.

Away then, shift ; clown to thy *motley* crupper.

Whoever is desirous of obtaining general and accurate information concerning the great variety of dresses that belong to some of the characters in question at different periods, must study ancient prints and paintings, and especially the miniatures that embellish manuscripts. These will afford sufficient specimens ; but the difficulty of ascertaining how the *theatrical fools and clowns* of Shakspeare's time were

* See his note in *All 's well that ends well*, Act I. Scene 3.

always habited, is insuperable.   In some instances the plays themselves assist by peculiar references that leave but little doubt; but this is not the case in general.   It is to be lamented that our artists did not appropriate more of their labours to the representation of theatrical subjects, and the fortunate discovery of a single ancient painting of this kind would be of more importance than a volume of conjectural dissertations.   As it may be presumed that former theatrical managers exhibited with fidelity on the stage, the manners of their own times, a reference to the materials which remain to illustrate the dress of the real fools, may supply the defect before alluded to.

It may be collected both from the plays themselves, and from various other authorities, that the costume of the domestic fool in Shakspeare's time was of two sorts.   In the first of these the coat was motley or parti-coloured, and attached to the body by a girdle, with bells at the skirts and elbows, though not always.   The breeches and hose close, and sometimes each leg of a different colour.   A hood resembling a monk's cowl, which, at a very early period, it was certainly designed to imitate, covered the head entirely, and fell down over part of the breast and shoulders.   It was sometimes decorated with asses ears, or else terminated in the neck and head of a cock,* a fashion as old as the fourteenth century. It often had the comb or crest only of the animal,† whence the term *cockscomb* or *coxcomb* was afterwards used to denote any silly upstart.   This fool usually carried in his hand an official scepter or bauble, which was a short stick ornamented at the end with the figure of a fool's head, or sometimes with that of a doll or puppet.‡   To this instrument there was fre-

* Plate II. fig. 1; also figs. 2 and 3, p. 516; and fig. 4, p. 517.

† Plate II. fig. 3.

‡ Plate III. figs. 7, 8, 9; also the centre fig. in Plate II. Hence the French call a bauble *marotte*, from *Marionnette*, or little Mary; but if the learned reader should prefer to derive the word from the Greek μορος, or the Latin *morio*, he is at full liberty to do so; and indeed such preference would be

quently annexed an inflated skin or bladder, with which the
fool belaboured those who offended him, or with whom he
was inclined to make sport; this was often used by itself, in
lieu, as it should seem, of a bauble.* The form of it varied,
and in some instances was obscene in the highest degree. It
was not always filled with air, but occasionally with sand, or
peas. Sometimes a strong bat or club was substituted for
the bauble.† In the second tale of the priests of Peblis, a
man who counterfeits a fool is described " with *club* and bel
and partie cote with eiris;" but it afterwards appears that he
had both a club and a bauble. In an inventory of the goods
of the ancient company of Saint George at Norwich, mention
is made of " two habits, one for the *club-bearer*, another for
his man, who are now called fools;"‡ and the author of
Tarlton's newes out of purgatory, 1630, 4to, describes a dream
in which he saw " one attired in russet with a button'd cap
on his head, a great bag by his side, and a *strong bat* in his
hand, so artificially attired for a clowne, as I began to call
Tarlton's woonted shape to remembrance."

In some old prints the fool is represented with a sort of
flapper or rattle ornamented with bells. It seems to have
been constructed of two round and flat pieces of wood or
pasteboard, and is no doubt a vestige of the crotalum used
by the Roman mimes or dancers.§ This implement was used

supported by the comparatively modern figure of the child's head, which the
term *marotte* might have suggested. The bauble originally used in King Lear
is said to have been extant so late as the time of Garrick, and the figure of it
would certainly have been worth preserving. To supply its place a representation is given of the head of a real bauble very finely carved in ivory. See
Plate IV. figs. 3, 4. A bauble is very often improperly put into the hands
of Momus.

* Plate III. figs. 2, 6, 7. 9; also figs. 1 and 3, p. 516.

† Plate III. fig. 4; and see Strutt's *Dress and habits of the people of
England*, Plate LXXI.

‡ Blomefield's *History of Norfolk*, ii. 737.

§ Plate III. fig. 1. In the Imperial library at Vienna, there is a manuscript calendar, said to have been written in the time of Constantius the
son of Constantine the great, with drawings of the twelve months. April

for the same purpose as the bladder, and occasionally for correcting the fool himself whenever he behaved with too much licentiousness.   Such a castigation is actually exhibited in one ancient German edition of the *Ship of fools*, by Sebastian Brandt; but the usual punishment on this occasion was a simple whipping.   In some old plays the fool's *dagger* is mentioned, perhaps the same instrument as was carried by the *Vice* or buffoon of the Moralities; and it may be as well to observe in this place that the domestic fool is sometimes, though it is presumed improperly, called the Vice.*   The dagger of the latter was made of a thin piece of lath; and the use he generally made of it was to belabour the Devil.   It appears that in Queen Elizabeth's time the archbishop of Canterbury's fool had a wooden dagger and coxcomb.†   In Greene's play of *Fryer Bacon*, the fool speaks of his dagger. In Beaumont and Fletcher's *Noble gentleman*, a person being compared to a fool, it is added that he should wear a guarded coat and a *great wooden dagger*.   In Chapman's *Widows tears*, an upstart governor is termed " a wooden dagger *gilded* o'er ;" and Rabelais has made Panurge give Triboulet the fool a wooden sword.   In an old German print a fool is represented with a sword like a *saw*.‡

The other dress, and which seems to have been more common in the time of Shakspeare, was the long petticoat.§ This originally appertained to the idiot or natural fool, and was obviously adopted for the purposes of cleanliness and concealment.   Why it came to be used for the allowed fool is

---

is represented as a man dancing with a *crotalum* in each hand.   This instrument was probably constructed of brass, in order to make a rattling noise.   See it represented in Plate III. fig. 3, which is copied from a print in *Lambecii Bibl. Cæsar. Vindobon.* tom. iv. p. 291.   These months are also given in Montfaucon's antiquities.

* See Ben Jonson's *Devil is an ass*, Scene 1.

† Penry's *O read over John Bridges*, fo. 48.

‡ Plate III. fig. 5. copied from Schopperi ΠΑΝΟΠΛΙΑ, *omnium illiberalium artium genera continens*, &c.   Francof. 1568, 12mo, sign. O. 8.

§ Figs. 1 and 2, p. 516.

not so apparent. It was, like the first, of various colours, the materials often costly, as of velvet, and guarded or fringed with yellow.* In one instance we have a *yellow leather* doublet.† In Bancroft's *Epigrams*, 1639, quarto, there is one addressed " to a giglot with her greene sicknesse," in which are these lines,

> " Thy sicknesse mocks thy pride, that 's seldom seene
> But in *foole's yellow*, and the lover's greene."

And a manuscript note in the time of the commonwealth states yellow to have been the *fool's colour*. This petticoat dress continued to a late period, and has been seen not many years since in some of the interludes exhibited in Wales.

But the above were by no means the only modes in which the domestic fools were habited. Many variations can be traced. The hood was not always surmounted with the cocks comb, in lieu of which a single bell and occasionally more appeared.‡ Sometimes a feather was added to the comb.§ In the old morality of *The longer thou livest the more foole thou art*, Moros the fool says,

> " By my trouth the thing that I desire most
> Is in my cappe to have a *goodly feather*."

The head was frequently shaved in imitation or perhaps ridicule of a monk's crown. This practice is very ancient, and can be traced to the twelfth century. In one instance the hair exhibits a sort of triple or Papal crown.‖ The tails of foxes or squirrels were often suspended to the garment. Godfrey Gobilive, the fool in Hawes's *Pastime of pleasure*, 1517, 4to, is described as so habited. In *The pope's funerall*, 1605, 4to, the author says, " I shall prove him such a noddy before I leave him that all the world will deeme him worthy to weare in his forehead a coxcombe for his foolishness, and

---

* Prologue to *King Henry the Eighth*. Marston's *Malcontent*, Act I. Scene 7, and Act III. Scene 1.

† Malone's Shakspeare, vol. i. part ii. p. 301.

‡ Plate II. fig. 4. Plate IV. fig. 1.

    Plate IV. fig. 1.   ‖ Plate II. fig. 2.

on his back, a *fox tayle* for his badge." It was likewise the
dress of the fool in the plough pageant and morris dance.*
One might almost conclude that this custom was designed to
ridicule a fashion that prevailed among the ladies in the reign
of Edward the Third, and which is mentioned by the author
of the old chronicle of England, erroneously ascribed to
Caxton the printer, in the following terms : " And the women
more nysely yet passed the men in aray and coriouslaker, for
they were so streyt clothed that they let hange *fox tailles*
sowed bineth within hir clothes for to hele and hide thir a—,
the which disguysinges and pride paradventure afterward
brouzt forth and encaused many myshappes and meschief in
the reame of Englond." The idiot or natural was often
clothed in a calf or sheep's skin.†

A large purse or wallet at the girdle is a very ancient part
of the fool's dress. Tarlton, who personated the clowns in
Shakspeare's time, appears to have worn it.‡ The budget
given by Panurge to Triboulet the fool is described as made
of a tortoise shell.§

We may suppose that the same variety of dress was observed on the stage which we know to have actually prevailed
in common life. The fools, however, did not always appear
in a discriminative habit, and some of their portraits still remaining confirm this observation. A very fine painting by
Holbein, in Kensington palace, represents Will Somers the

---

* Coryat's *Crudities*, p. 9. edit. 1611, 4to.   Brand's *Observ. on popular
antiquities*, p. 176.

† See the notes on a passage in *King John.* Steevens's *Shakspeare*, viii.
p. 79, edit. 1793. " The scribe claims the manor of Noverinte, by providing *sheep-skins and calves skins to wrappe his highness wards* and idiotts
in."—*Gesta Grayorum*, 1688, 4to.

‡ See the quotation from Tarlton's *Newes out of purgatory* given in a
preceding page (509). The portrait of Tarlton in Hardinge's *Biographical
mirror*, and a print in the title of Greene's *Tu quoque, or the cittie gallant*,
show the costume of the purse and feather. See likewise Plate IV. fig. 2 ;
and the centre fig. in Plate II.

§ Rabelais, book iii. ch 45.

fool of Henry the Eighth, in a common dress.* In a wardrobe account of that sovereign, we find these articles : " For
making a dubblette of wursteede lyned with canvas and cotton,
for William Som'ar oure foole. Item for making of a coote
and a cappe of grene clothe fringed with red crule and lyned
with fryse, for our saide foole. Item for making of a dub-
lette of fustian, lyned with cotton and canvas for oure same
foole." Yet he sometimes wore the usual hood instead of a
cap; for in the same account is an article " For making of
a coote of grene clothe with a *hoode* to the same, fringed
with white crule lyned with fryse and bokerham, for oure foole
aforesaid;"† and there is a print of him after a picture by
Holbein, in which he is represented in a long tunic with a chain
and horn in his hand.‡ In the celebrated picture of Sir Thomas
More's family by Holbein, Patenson the fool is not distinguished by any peculiarity of dress, and, in one instance at
least, the same remark applies to Archy, the fool of James I.§
In those families where the fool acted as a menial servant, it
is possible that he might have reserved his official habit for

* This picture is very well engraven in Caulfield's *Portraits of remarkable persons*, vol. ii. There is a beautifully illuminated psalter preserved
among the royal manuscripts in the British Museum, 2 A xvi, written by
John Mallard the chaplain and secretary of Henry the Eighth, with several
marginal notes in the king's own hand-writing, some of which are in pencil.
Prefixed to psalm 52, " Dixit insipiens," according to a very ancient custom,
are the figures of king David and a fool, in this instance evidently the portraits of Henry and his favourite Will Somers. That of the latter person is
here copied in Plate IV. fig. 2, but rather enlarged. The countenance bears
a strong resemblance to that of the figure in Holbein's picture of Henry
the Eighth and his family, already noticed in p. 336.

† Archæologia, ix. p. 249.

‡ In Tatham's play of *The Scot's figgaries*, 1652, 4to, the king's fool is
described as habited in a long coat with a gold rope or chain about his
neck.

§ See the print of Archy engraved by Cecill and prefixed to his *Jests*, in
which, unless Mr. Granger could have been certain with respect to what he
has called " a parti-coloured tunic," there is nothing discriminative of the
fool's dress. This portrait has been copied in Caulfield's above-cited
work.

particular occasions. The paucity of materials that illustrate the theatrical character in question, must necessarily leave this part of the subject still more imperfect than the rest; but the plays of Shakspeare have furnished more information than those of any other writer. It is surprising, on the whole, that the character of the domestic fool is so seldom found in the old dramas that remain; because it was not only capable of affording considerable mirth to the unrefined part of the audience, but of giving the authors an opportunity of displaying a great deal of ingenuity so far as regarded extemporary wit. It is certain that the fools in Shakspeare's plays were pre-eminent above all others. For this we have the authority of Shadwell, who makes one of his characters say that they had more wit than any of the wits and critics of his time.* Beaumont and Fletcher have but rarely introduced them; Ben Jonson and Massinger never. Indeed, the originals had rapidly declined at the period in which most of their plays were written, and another character of a mixed nature been substituted in their room. This was the witty servant or clown (Class II. No. 3.), and of course his dress was not distinguished by any peculiarity.

The practice of introducing the fools and clowns between the acts and scenes, and after the play was finished, to amuse the audience with extemporaneous wit and buffoonery, has been so well illustrated by the able historian of the English stage, that very little can remain to be said on the subject.† It has been traced from the Greek and Roman theatres; and, as their usages were undoubtedly preserved in those of the middle ages that belonged to the countries where Roman influence had been spread, it would not of course be peculiar to the early stage in England. Indeed, the records of the French theatre amply demonstrate the truth of this position, and furnish several examples of the practice in question. In the

---

* *The woman captain*, Scene I.
† See Mr. Malone's *Historical account of the English Stage.*

mystery of *Saint Barbara* we find this stage direction, " Pausa. Vadant, et Stultus loquitur;" and he is several times introduced in like manner between the scenes, in order that the amusement of the spectators might not be suspended whilst something was in agitation for the further prosecution of the piece.* Perhaps the most singular *pause* in any dramatic composition whatsoever is one which occurs in the very rare morality of *La condamnacion des banquetz* in the following words : " Pause pour pisser le fol. Il prent ung coffinet en lieu de orinal & pisse dedans, et tout coule par bas," sign. M iiij. Nor was the English stage in Shakspeare's time allowed to remain empty. Lupton has related a story of the clown at the Red Bull theatre, who was suddenly called for between the acts, and forgot his fool's cap.† Puttenham, speaking of verses that rhime in the middle and end, observes that " they were more commodiously uttered by the buffoons or vices in plays than by any other person."‡ It was likewise part of the stage fool's office to introduce at his own discretion a great many old songs, or at least the fragments of them.§

The first symptoms of the decline of the domestic fools, and the causes of it, have been already touched on ; and the same reasons may partly be assigned for their exile from the stage. In the præludium to Goffe's *Careless shepherdess,* 1656, 4to, there is a panegyric on them,‖ and some concern is manifested for the fool's absence in the play itself. It is likewise expressly stated that " the motly coat was banish'd with trunk-hose." Yet during the reign of Charles the Second occasional efforts were made to restore the character. In the tragedy of *Thorney abbey, or the London maid,* 1662, 12mo,

---

* Parfait, *Histoire du theatre François,* II. pp. 27, 46, 62.

† See Mr. Steevens's note at the end of the second act of *The taming of the shrew.*

‡ Arte of English poesie, 69.

§ See Mr. Steevens's note in *King Lear,* Act III. Scene 6.

‖ See Mr. Malone's note in *All's well that ends well,* Act I. Scene 3.

the prologue is spoken by a fool who uses these words, " the poet's a fool who made the tragedy to tell a story of a king and a court and leave a fool out on't, when in Pacy's and Sommer's and Patche's and Archee's times, my venerable predecessours, a fool was alwaies the principal verb." Shadwell's play of *The woman captain,* 1680, is perhaps the last in which a regular fool is introduced, and even there his master is made to say that the character was then exploded on the stage.

The following is some additional and necessary explanation of the cuts belonging to this dissertation.

Plate II. fig. 1, is from *Catzii emblemata.* Fig. 2 is the duke of Suffolk's fool in the time of Henry VIII., copied from a print in Mr. Brydges's *Memoirs of the peers of England.* Figs. 3 and 4 are from paintings in the author's possession. The centre fig. is from a print by Breughel.

Plate III. All these instruments, excepting fig. 3, before described, are taken from various Dutch and German prints.

Plate IV. fig. 1, is from an old German print by an unknown master.

Figs. 1 and 3 below are from *A booke of Christian prayers,* &c., 1590, 4to, being figures belonging to a dance of Death. Fig. 2 is from the frontispiece to Heywood's comedy of *The*

1   2   3

fair maid of the exchange. Similar figures of the costume of
fools in the time of James I., or Charles I., may be seen in
The life of Will Summers, compiled long after his time. Figs.
4 and 5 are from *La grant danse Macabre,* printed at Troyes
without date, but about the year 1500, in folio, a book of un-

common rarity and curiosity. Fig. 6 is from the *Stultarum
virginum scaphæ seu naviculæ* of Badius Ascensius, another
work of much rarity, and far exceeding that of the ship of
fools by Sebastian Brandt. In all the editions of the latter,
a great variety of the fools of the fifteenth century will be
found. Fig. 7 is from a French translation of St. Augustine
on the city of God, printed at Abbeville 1486. It exemplifies
the use of the tabor and pipe by fools; a practice that seems
to have been revived by Tarlton in the time of Elizabeth.

Figures 3, 4, and 6, have been introduced to show the costume of female fools.   Among others of this kind that might
deserve notice is a very interesting one in the picture, by
Holbein, of Henry the Eighth's family already mentioned.

Published by T. Tegg, Cheapside. Sept.r 1839.

Plate III.

Plate IV.

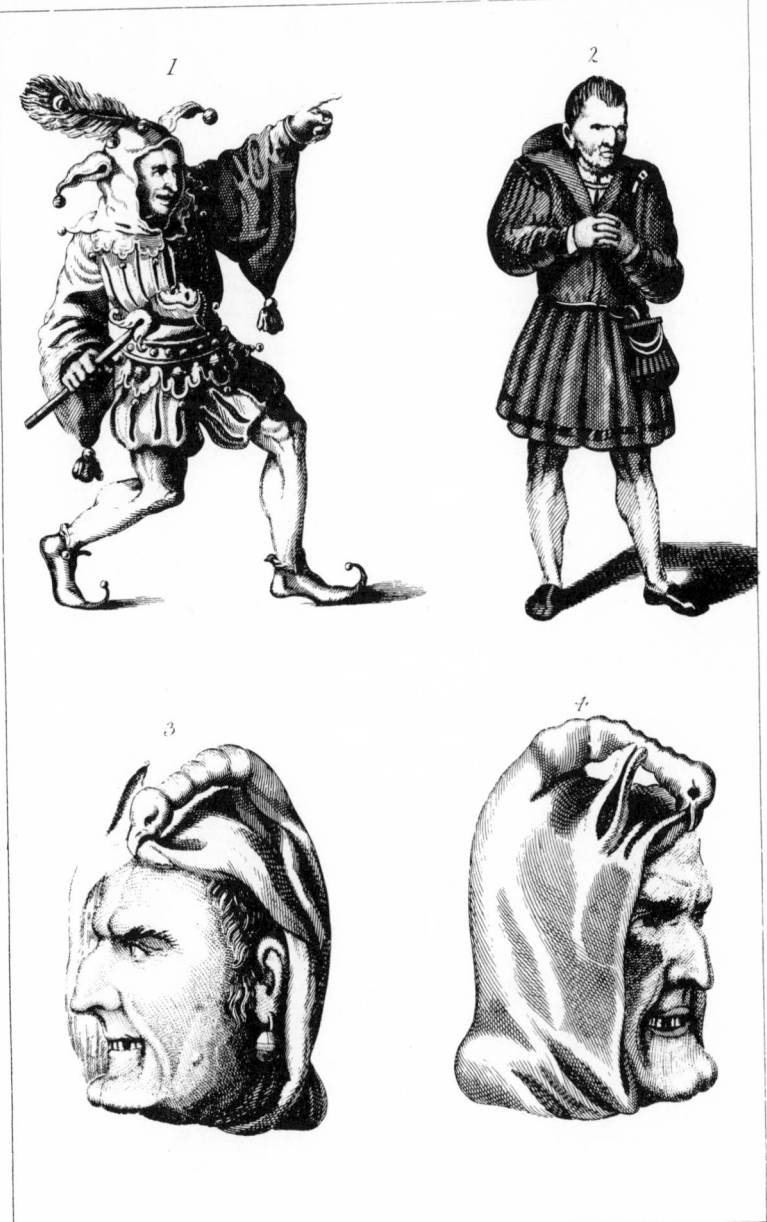

Published by T. Tegg, Cheapside, Sept.r 1839.

DISSERTATION II.

ON THE GESTA ROMANORUM.

ENQUIRIES like the present, however unimportant to the generality of readers, will not fail of being duly appreciated by those who take an interest in tracing the origin and progress of literary genius, which has perhaps been never more successfully, and even laudably, employed, than in the composition of such works as combine amusement with instruction. Of these the simple and engaging apologues of many ancient writers form a considerable portion, and have always been justly and generally esteemed. This mode of conveying instruction became so attractive in the middle ages, that the ecclesiastics themselves were under the necessity of introducing narrations both historical and imaginary into their discourses, in order to acquire that degree of popularity and attention which might otherwise have been wanting, and also for the purpose of enforcing their morality by such examples as should touch the feelings of the hearers, and operate, with respect at least to ruder minds, more efficaciously than precept. The work before us was designed to answer these purposes; and it not only proceeded on this ground in common with others of a similar nature, but has even furnished the materials to some of the best writers, and more especially poets, of ancient and modern times.

It will perhaps be expected that some reason should be assigned why the present essay has been attempted, after the labours of Mr. Warton on the same subject, which some may think has been amply and satisfactorily treated, if not exhausted; and if the judgment and accuracy of that pleasing and elegant writer had been commensurate with his taste and industry, the expectation had been exceedingly well founded. This however is, unfortunately, not the case. He has, in this and many other instances, left much to be done and undone; but we ought to feel very grateful to him for having founded a school that has already produced some accomplished pupils, and will, no doubt, contribute to form many a future one. Thus much seems due to an amiable man and excellent character, who has been most undeservedly insulted for errors of small moment, and censured for opinions of the most innocuous kind. Even his antiquarian dullness and perseverance have been arraigned, as if in a work like the history of English poetry, genius should have occupied the place of industry, and have created those facts which honest men are content to discover; a method not uncommon with some writers who have derived too much of their importance from the indolence and superficiality of their readers, and who are unwilling to submit to those laws of providence which justly impose on man the duty of penetrating to the mine before he be permitted to enjoy the precious metal. Such was not Warton. His taste and research will remain the admiration of future ages, when the flimsy compositions of some of his opponents shall be totally forgotten. He has effected, however imperfectly, more for the illustration of English poetry than any or all of his predecessors, or than has hitherto been accomplished for the poetry of other nations, by any writer whatever.

Mr. Warton's dissertation would, no doubt, have been rendered more perfect, had he been aware of a fact which had not only escaped his own attention, but even that of Mr. Tyrwhitt. Neither of these gentlemen, in consulting the manuscripts of the *Gesta Romanorum*, had perceived that there were *two* works so entitled, totally distinct from each other, except as to imitation, and certainly compiled by different persons. Of that treated of by Mr. Warton, it is presumed *no manuscript has been yet described*; of the other several manuscripts remain, *but it has never been printed, except in some translated extracts.* It will be better to postpone for the present any further mention of the latter, and to proceed to submit some additional remarks on the other. And first of its use and design.

A particular mode of instruction from the pulpit has been already hinted at, and will admit of some enlargement. Mr. Warton has mentioned one of the earliest instances of introducing Æsop's fables, as recorded by Vincent of Beauvais in the thirteenth century.* Supplies of another kind were furnished to those who might be more scrupulous as to the use of profane examples, not only in that great repertory of pious fictions, *The golden legend,* but in multitudes of similar stories, denominated in France *contes devots,* and composed for the purpose of counteracting the great influence which the witty and licentious stories of the minstrels had obtained, of which they were palpable imitations both in construction and versification. Most of these were founded on miracles supposed to have been operated by the Virgin Mary. The earliest known specimens of them were composed in the twelfth century by Hugues Farsi, a monk of St. John de Vignes at Soissons, who was soon followed by many imitators both in prose and verse.† His own work was turned into French verse by Gautier de Coinsi, another monk of Soissons, about 1230. A similar collec tion is the *Lives of the holy fathers,* chiefly from Saint Jerome, and anonymously composed in

---

* p. j. For the benefit of those who may have an opportunity of consulting the original, a mistake in Mr. Warton's reference to the *Speculum historiale* is corrected, which should be lib. IV. c. viii.

† A fine collection of them, in verse, was in the library of the Duke de la Valliere. One volume is in MS., Harl. 4401, two others in the author's possession, as well as a third in prose, beautifully painted in camaieu gris. Some of those in prose have been printed. See a memoir by Racine in the *Acad. des inscript.* tom. xviii. p. 360. Specimens of them may be seen in the fifth volume of that very entertaining work, the *Fabliaux et contes* of M. Le Grand.

French verse by some person whose name deserved to have been recorded on account of the great merit of the work, which would be deemed an ornament to any period, for the excellence of the poetry.

The promptuary of examples for the use of preachers, at the end of Herolt's *Sermones discipuli*, composed in 1418, has been already mentioned by Mr. Warton, who has given a curious and correct account of that work ; but he has omitted to notice, that, among a multitude of pious authors cited in it, the name of Ovid appears. This practice of indiscriminate quotation became afterwards very common. It was, indeed, sanctioned by a preceding custom, among religious writers, of *moralizing* works of all denominations. Thus, to mention only a few, Thomas Walleys, a Welsh Dominican friar, had published his moralizations of Ovid's metamorphoses, in the fourteenth century.* The *Bestiarium*, a treatise on animals, is, as well as the *Gesta Romanorum*, perhaps an earlier instance. Afterwards the celebrated, but licentious, *Romance of the rose* was moralized by Jean Molinet. Even the game of chess was moralized; for the reader who may take up Caxton's translation of Jacobus de Cæsolis, will be grievously disappointed should he expect to find any didactic or even historical information. We are not to wonder, therefore, if on the restoration of letters, a system of morality was extracted from Æsop and other fabulists ; and, accordingly, some of the early printed editions of Æsop were published under the title of

* There is a great deal of confusion respecting this man, some making him an English Jacobin of the fourteenth century. He has been mistaken for other persons of the same name, and his works are by no means well ascertained, being often confounded with those of Nicolas Trivet and others. In his Ovid he has been indebted to a preceding work by Alexander Neckam. Another allegorical work on Ovid's metamorphoses was written about 1370, by Giovanni Buonsignore di Castello, and a tropological explanation of them was published by Pierre Lavigne, about 1500. There is also a manuscript in the Royal library at Paris, entitled *Ovidii metamorphosis moralisata, per Johannem Bourgauldum.* See Labbe *nova bibl. MSS.*, p. 321.

Æsopus moralizatus, and this, no doubt, led the way to the moral applications to his fables which afterwards appeared in other languages.

Among the preachers who interspersed their sermons with narrations of various kinds, a Carthusian monk of the fifteenth century deserves particular mention. With as much quaintness as humility, he styles himself *'Guillelmus Hilacensis quondam simplex cordatus pauperculus discalciatus ac contemptibilis denudatus, sapientissimorum rudissimus, electorum infimus, et minorum minimus.* He has left a volume of sermons on the Lord's prayer, with stories in every page.* In the British Museum there is a very curious collection of Latin sermons, compiled about the reign of Henry the Sixth, by a person who calls himself a vicar of Magdalen college, Oxford. They abound with stories from Æsop, Cicero, Seneca, Valerius Maximus, Saint Austin, venerable Bede, &c.† Stephen Baron, an English Minorite in the reign of Henry the Eighth, has left a similar volume of sermons preached before the university of Cambridge.‡

Among the most remarkable persons of this description who soon followed, were fathers Menot, Maillard, Barelete, Raulin, Vincent Ferrier, Pierre de Boves, &c., whose discourses are filled with quotations from Virgil, Valerius Maximus, Apuleius, Dante, Petrarch, and the *Gesta Romanorum.* Erasmus, ridiculing the absurdities of some of the theologians, mentions their practice of quoting the *Speculum historiale* and *Gesta Romanorum.*§ Schelhorn speaks of a copy of the latter

---

* It was printed at Paris, 1494, in 12mo, by Geringard Rembolt.

† MS. Harl. 5396. This manuscript contains another similar collection; and these are the more worthy of being noticed, as we have very few of the kind printed in England.

‡ These were printed by Wynkyn de Worde, and at Paris, without date.

§ " Hic mihi stultam aliquam et indoctam fabulam, ex Speculo opinor historiali, aut Gestis Romanorum, in medium adferunt, et eandem interpretantur allegoricè, tropologicè, et anagogicè."—*Stultitiæ laus.* Basil. 1780, 8vo, p. 261.

in his possession, dated 1499, in which some former possessor had marked against many of the stories the year in which he had used them in his sermons.*   Even in the eighteenth century the Italians had not left off this custom. Grosley states, that he heard a buffoon preacher at Rome, who stuffed his discourse with a thousand tales, among which was that of father Philip's geese, from Boccaccio.†

There is a remarkable work to which the preachers of the middle ages appear to have been indebted, and which deserves mention here not only on that account, but also from its having hitherto remained in unmerited obscurity. This may be partly owing to its having never been printed. It is a collection of tales and fables that has been ascribed to Odo de Ceriton, Shirton, or Ciringron, for all these names are mentioned, a Cistercian monk of the twelfth century. In one manuscript they are called *proverbs*, and given to Hugo de Sancto Victore, of the monastery of Saint Victoire at Paris, and who lived much about the last-named period.‡   There is perhaps no task more difficult than that of ascertaining the real authors of many works of the middle ages, especially where, as in the present instance, there occurs any thing satirical against religious abuses. The evidence with respect to authorship is in favour of the Englishman, because in some

---

* Amœnit. eccles., i. 807.   † Observ. on Italy, ii. 108.

‡ This MS. is in the author's possession, as well as another of the same work with considerable variations. A third is in the library of the Royal Society, No. 292, and there ascribed to Odo de Ceriton. Concerning this person, who was tutor in theology to the celebrated John of Salisbury, see Bale, *Script. Brytann. catal.* pars i. p. 221, edit. 1559. Tanner, *Bibl. Britannico-Hibernic.* p. 560. A great deal of confusion, and yet not more than is often found on similar occasions, has been made concerning this work and its author. It has been confounded with a moral treatise on natural history called *Bestiarium*, from which it is totally different. If the reader be desirous of perplexing himself with further inquiries concerning this subject, he may consult Fabricius, *Bibl. med. ætat.*, i. 93, & v. 466, edit. 1734. Cave, *Script. eccles.* p. 572. Pitts, p. 245. There is another similar but anonymous work among the Harl. MSS., No. 219, that has some fables not in the others, and wants many in both.

of the stories English sentences are found.   Nor do the sarcasms against the clergy militate in the least against ecclesiastical manufacture.   Numerous instances could be brought
to show the satirical spirit of the clergy, frequently towards
each other, and generally against the church of Rome.

The work in question is an extraordinary mixture of Æsopian fables with pious and profane histories in great variety.
One or two specimens have been already given,* but the
reader may not regret the trouble of perusing the following in
addition.   "There is a kind of wren, named after Saint Martin, with very long and slender legs.   This bird sitting one
day in a tree, in the fullness of his pride suddenly exclaimed;
' It matters not to me though the heavens fall; for with the
aid of my strong legs I shall be able to support them.'   Presently a leaf fell upon the foolish boaster, who immediately flew
away in great terror, exclaiming, ' O Saint Martin, Saint Martin, help your poor bird !'"   The moral compares Saint Peter
denying Christ to this wren, which it also assimilates to certain
pot-valiant soldiers, who boast, in their cups, that each of them
can beat three of the stoutest Frenchmen.   Again: "Isengrin the wolf, to expiate his sins, became a monk.   His brethren endeavoured to teach him his letters, that he might say
Pater noster; but all that they were able to get from him was,
'lamb, lamb.'   They told him to look up to the cross, but
could never make him turn his eyes from the sheep.   In like
manner do the monks cry out for good wine, and fix their
eyes on dainty viands and full trenchers; whence the English
proverb, *Yf alle that the wolf unto the prest worthe and be
sette on to boke salmes to ler, ȝit is ever hys onne eye to the
wodeward.*†   To conclude with one more, "The wolf being
dead, the lion assembled the rest of the beasts to celebrate

* See pp. 157, 334.

† That is, " Though the wolf come to the priest, and be set to his book
to learn psalms, yet is one of his eyes ever turned towards the wood."   A
similar fable is among those composed by Marie de France in the twelfth

his obsequies. The hare carried the holy water, and the hedge-hogs the wax tapers. The goats tolled the bells; the badger dug the grave; the fox carried the coffin; Berengarius the bear celebrated mass; the ox read the gospels, and the ass the epistles. Mass being finished, and Isengrin duly buried, the beasts partook of a splendid feast, the expense of which was defrayed out of the deceased's property. The parties wished for nothing better than a similar ceremony. So, says the moral, on the death of any rich usurer, the abbots assemble all the *beasts* of the monastery; for in general, the black and white monks are really brutes, that is, lions in pride; foxes in cunning; hogs in gluttony; goats in luxury; asses in sloth; and hares in cowardice."

Besides the storehouses of this sort of knowledge that have been already described, there were doubtless many others that are now lost; but there is one that ought not to be passed over without some notice. It is the *Summa prædicantium* of John Bromyard, an English preacher, and a violent opponent of Wicliffe. It is an immense repertory of matter for the use of the clergy, every page containing stories and examples in all possible variety.* It is divided into classes of such subjects as were adapted to the pulpit, and must have been a work of immense labour, and the result of much reading. In the article *rapina* he has a story resembling chap. viii. of the *Gesta Romanorum,* which he probably cites under the title of *Antiqua gesta.*

century. A curate having tamed a wolf, undertook to teach him to read. " Now," says he to the scholar, " repeat after me, A." The wolf articulated A. " Good," says the curate; " now say B." The wolf cried " bee, bee ;" but thinking he heard the bleating of the sheep, away he ran to the fold. This apologue is probably from the East. See the story of *Bohetzad and his ten vizirs* in the continuation of the Arabian nights' entertainments. The other seems to have been borrowed from the celebrated and interesting romance of Reynard the Fox, evidently composed long before the twelfth century.

* Printed at Nuremberg, 1485. Paris, 1500. Basil, sine anno, in folio.

Although most of these works were undoubtedly composed for the immediate purpose of assisting the preachers, it by no means follows that they were exclusively so, or that other uses might not be made of some of them. Not that they could be accessible to the laity in any great degree, inasmuch as they were wrapped up in a learned language. But the private readings of the monks would not be always of a serious and ascetic nature. They might be disposed occasionally to recreate their minds with subjects of a lighter and more amusing nature; and what could be more innocent or delightful than the stories of the *Gesta Romanorum*? They might even have indulged in this kind of recreation during their continuance in the refectory after meals. For this purpose one of the fraternity, more eminently qualified than the rest, might entertain them with the recital of matters that would admit of some moral application to be made by the reader, or which was already attached to the subject. The word *carissimi*, so frequently to be found in the moralizations, seems as much adapted to this purpose, as to the addressing of an auditory from the pulpit. Perhaps the same idea had occurred to him who chose to apply the term *liber monasticus* to the *Gesta Romanorum*.*

The excellent analytical account that has been given of this work would admit of no other improvement than some augmentation of the sources of the stories, and of their several imitations; but with respect to the author of it, some further inquiry may be necessary. Mr. Warton has attempted to show, with considerable ingenuity as well as plausibility, that the *Gesta Romanorum* was composed by Peter Bercheur, a native of Poitou, and prior of the convent of Saint Eloy at Paris, where he died in 1362.† He has founded this opinion on a passage in the *Philologia sacra* of Salomon Glassius, who, in his chapter *de allegoriis fabularum,* after censuring those

---

* Michael Neander, apud Schelhorn. *Amœnit. ecclesiast.* i. 798.

† Diss. on the Gesta Romanorum, p. lxxxvi.

writers who not only employed themselves in allegorizing the
scriptures, but affected to discover in profane stories and
poetical fictions certain matters that seemed to illustrate the
mysteries of the Christian faith, makes the following observation: " Hoc in studio excelluit quidam *Petrus Berchorius*
Pictaviensis, ordinis Divi Benedicti: qui *peculiari* libro, *Gesta
Romanorum*, necnon legendas patrum, aliasque aniles fabulas
allegoricè ac mysticè exposuit." On this single testimony,
or rather assertion, which is unaccompanied by any proof or
reference to authority, Mr. Warton proceeds to assign *his*
reasons for concluding that Bercheur was the author of the
Gesta, and they are principally these: 1. A general coincidence between the manner and execution of the works of
Bercheur and the *Gesta*. 2. A resemblance in their titles
3. The introduction of some of the stories of the *Gesta* into
the *Repertorium morale* of Bercheur.* 4. His having allegorized the Metamorphoses of Ovid. And 5. His writings
being full of allusions to the Roman history. To these might
have been added the quotations common to both the *Gesta*
and the *Repertorium* from Pliny, Seneca, Solinus, and Gervase
of Tilbury, and the time in which Berchorius lived, which
certainly corresponds with that of the composition of the
Gesta Romanorum, as far as can be collected from internal
evidence. It may be remarked in this place, that Mr. Tyrwhitt, in supposing it to have been written at the end of the
12th or the beginning of the 13th century, has fixed on too
early a date.† It could not have been written before 1256,

---

* The *Repertorium* or *Reductorium morale* is an extraordinary performance for the time in which it was composed. It contains a system of
natural history that may be consulted with advantage, even by modern
students; but it is obscured by unlimited credulity and the grossest absurdities, which may nevertheless have their use in exhibiting the folly of
learning when unaccompanied by judgment. The good monk is even occasionally witty, but without design. In speaking of the noise which frogs
make, he compares them to the lawyers, " Tales sunt causidici et advocati
quod vero isti sunt *clamosi*, quia clamando litigant ad invicem."
    † Canterbury tales, iv. 331.

because the chronicle of Albertus, which is cited in one of the chapters, terminates with that year.

It might be supposed that very little could be urged in opposition to the foregoing reasons, nor is it here intended to deny absolutely that Bercheur was the author of the *Gesta*; but certain doubts having arisen on the subject, they shall be submitted to the reader, that he may then be enabled to use his own judgment and discretion in deciding the question. With respect to the similitude between the works of Berchorius and the *Gesta Romanorum*, no one would think of maintaining, on this ground alone, that any two compositions, the one anonymous, were written by the same author. It shows, generally speaking, nothing more than coincidence, or, what is more likely, simple imitation ; and it is as probable that the author of one of the works should have imitated the other, as that one person should have written both. Perhaps the other reasons might be disposed of in the same way, but it will be better to state specific objections to them ; and here Mr. Warton's own evidence might be turned against himself. He had stated on a former occasion,* his having seen a manuscript of the *Gesta in almost Saxon characters*; but it is certain that this manuscript had doubly deceived him, and that his eye had caught one or two of the Saxon letters which continued to be used in writing long after Saxon times.

In the preface to the *Repertorium morale* Bercheur tells us that he was by birth a Frenchman, a Benedictine monk, and the familiar servant of Cardinal de Pratis, or Des Prez, to whom he was indebted for books and other necessaries towards the completion of his works. Now throughout the ponderous tomes that have been consulted for this purpose, there are no Gallicisms to be traced, nor any other symptom of French authorship. On the other hand, there are strong marks that the *Gesta Romanorum* was composed by a German. In the

* Vol. ii. p. 14.

2 M

moralization to chapter 144, there is, in most of the early editions, a German proverb; and, in chapter 142, several German names of Dogs. Many of the stories are extracted from German authors, as Cesarius, Albert of Stade, and Gervase of Tilbury, who wrote his book *De otiis imperialibus*, in Germany. In this country likewise the earliest editions of the *Gesta* were printed.

Mr. Warton, anticipating an objection that might be taken from the omission of any mention of the *Gesta* by the biographers of Bercheur, has remarked, that it might have been among his smaller pieces, or proscribed by graver writers, or even discarded by its author as a juvenile performance, unsuitable to his character and abounding in fantastic and unedifying narration. But this description does not accord with the *general* use that we know to have been made of it in the pulpit; nor can it come under the denomination of a work that is not altogether grave, serious, and moral, nor likely to have been the effusion of a glowing or youthful mind. Besides, the biographers of Bercheur are not alone silent as to the *Gesta*; the editors of his printed works were entirely unacquainted with it as his composition, and they were more likely to have been better informed on the subject than Glassius, whose opinion, like Mr. Warton's, seems to have been mere inference, and unsupported by any evidence. But what is more to the point, Bercheur has himself, in the prologue to his *Repertorium*, and in the preface to a French translation of Livy, given a very particular account of his works, among which his moralizations of the *Fabulæ poetarum*, never printed, are mentioned; yet this is certainly not the *Gesta Romanorum*, any more than the *Chronicon* mentioned by Mr. Warton.* Again; most of the known works of Bercheur are still existing in manuscript, but not a single manuscript that can be pronounced to be the *Gesta Romanorum in question* has

* Diss. on the Gesta Romanorum, p. xc.

occurred after the most diligent research. Such indeed might be supplied from the libraries in Germany, and possibly throw new light on this difficult and mysterious inquiry. Some stress has been laid on the circumstance of four of the stories in the *Gesta* being related in the *Repertorium morale*,* but they are not told in the same words, and the moralizations are entirely different. This has very much the appearance of different authorship. The title of *Reductorium* to some of the editions of the *Gesta*, together with many other matters, might have been borrowed from the writings of Bercheur by some German Monk, whose name has been irretrievably consigned to oblivion. It is scarcely worth while to mention the blunder that Foppens has committed in ascribing the composition instead of the printing of the *Gesta*, to Gerard De Leeu, of Gouda in Holland.†

It remains to offer some account of the various forms in which this once popular and celebrated work has appeared; and the rather, because what has been said on this subject is widely scattered, unconnected, and frequently erroneous.

MANUSCRIPTS.—It is a fact as remarkable as the obscurity which exists concerning the author of the *Gesta*, that no manuscript of this work, that can with certainty be pronounced as such, has been hitherto described. If the vast stores of manuscripts that are contained in the monastic and other libraries of Germany, Switzerland, Italy, and Spain, were examined, there is scarcely a doubt that some original of a work so often printed would be discovered. Father Montfaucon has indeed mentioned a manuscript *Gesta Romanorum* in the Vatican;‡ but it may be either a transcript from the printed copy, or a different work under the same title, that will presently be noticed.

---

* Ubi supr. p. lxxxviii. † Biblioth. Belgic. i. 353.
‡ Biblioth. MSS. tom. i. p. 17. No. 172.

PRINTED EDITIONS.—The titles of these are different, and are as follows :

No. 1. " Incipiunt hystorie collecte ex gestis romanorum et quibusdam aliis libris cum applicationibus eorundem."
The colophon.   " Et sic est finis."

No. 2. " Incipiunt historie notabiles atque magis principales collecte ex gestis romanorum et quibusdam aliis notabilibus gestis cum moralizationibus eorundem."
The colophon.   " Et sic est finis."

No. 3.   " Ex gestis romanorum hystorie notabiles de viciis virtutibusque tractantes cum applicacionibus moralisatis et misticis incipiunt feliciter."
The colophon.   " Gesta romanorum cum quibus aliis historiis eisdem annexis ad moralitates dilucide reducta hic finem habent.   Que diligenter correctis aliorum viciis impressit Johannes de Westphalia &c."

No. 4. " Recollectorium ex gestis romanorum cum pluribus applicatis historiis."

No. 5. " Ex gestis romanorum hystorie notabiles collecte de viciis virtutibusque tractantes cum applicacionibus moralisatis et mysticis incipiunt *fideliter.*"   (sometimes *feliciter.*)
The colophon.   " Ex gestis Romanorum cum pluribus applicatis hystoriis de virtutibus et viciis mystice ad intellectum transumptis recollectorii finis."

It is impossible to speak with certainty as to the *first edition,* on account of the omission of dates, places, and printers' names in some of the early copies.   There are two editions so circumstanced, with the titles No. 1 and 2, in folio, and containing 152 chapters only.   There is a third printed without date by Nicolas Ketelaer and Gerard de Leempt at Utrecht, in folio, with 152 chapters, to which Lambinet has inaccurately assigned the date of 1473.*   One of these three is probably the first edition.   They are all excessively rare, and a copy containing 152 chapters only would not easily be found in this country.

Of the editions without date, place, or printer, that contain 181 chapters, there are three, and perhaps more.   One of

* Recherches sur l'origine de l'imprimerie.   Bruxelles, an vii. 8vo, p. 246.

these, in folio, is in the British Museum, but imperfect. It was certainly printed with the types used by Ulric Zell, about 1475. Two others, the one in folio, the other in quarto, were printed without date at Louvain, by John of Westphalia. He is said to have printed one edition with the date 1473; but this is probably a mistake copied from one book into another, as Lambinet assures us that the copy in the royal library at Paris has the above date, but in *manuscript only*.* The following editions with dates can be spoken of with more confidence.

1. 1480, no place, nor printer. In folio.
2. 1480, at Gouda, by Gerard Leeu. In folio.
3. 1481, at Hasselt, no printer. In folio.
4. 1482, no place, nor printer. In quarto. This is doubtful, being taken from a bookseller's catalogue.
5. 1488, no place, nor printer. In folio.
6. 1489, no place, nor printer. In folio.
7. 1489, at Strasburg, no printer. In folio.
8. 1490, at Gouda, by Gerard Leeu. In folio.
9. 1493, no place, nor printer. In folio.
10. 1494, no place, nor printer. In quarto.
11. 1494, at Louvain, no printer. . . . .
12. 1497, no place, nor printer. In quarto.
13. 1497, at Strasburg, by John Knoblouch. In quarto.
14. 1498, no place, nor printer. In folio.
15. 1499, no place, nor printer. In folio.
16. 1499, at Paris, no printer. In quarto.
17. 1506, at Paris, by Jean Petit. In 12mo.
18. 1508, at Hagenau, by Henry Gran. In folio.
19. 1509, at Paris, by Francois Regnault. In 12mo.
20. 1512, at Venice, no printer. In 12mo.
21. 1515, at Paris, by Jean Petit. In 12mo.
22. 1516, at Venice, by George de Rusconibus. In 8vo.
23. 1517, at Paris, no printer. In 12mo.
24. 1517, at Hagenau, by Henry Gran. In folio.
25. 1520, at Venice, by A. de Bindonis. In 8vo.
26. 1521, at Paris, by Jean Petit. In 12mo.
27. 1521, at Rouen. . . . .
28. 1555, at Lyons, no printer. In 12mo.

GERMAN TRANSLATION.—Of this only one edition has

---

* *Recherches*, &c. p. 205.

occurred, printed at Augsburg, by John Schopser, 1489, in folio.

DUTCH TRANSLATION.—Two editions are mentioned, the one printed at Gouda, by Gerard Leeu, 1481, and the other at Zwollis, by Peter Van Os, 1484 ; both in folio.

FRENCH TRANSLATION.—It does not appear who was the author of the translation into this language, which is entitled *Le violier* des hystoires Rommaines : moralisez sur les nobles gestes faitz vertueulx et anciennes chroniques de toutes nations de gens, fort recreatif et moral.* It contains only one hundred and forty-nine stories. About the year 1516, Pierre Gringore, herald to the duke of Lorraine, and the author of several moralities and other works, published a book called *Les fantasies de mere sote,* which is only a translation in prose, intermixed with verse, of some twenty or thirty stories in the *Gesta Romanorum,* with their moralizations. He has suppressed all mention of his original, and insinuated in the privilege that he was himself the inventor. This work seems to have preceded the anonymous translation above mentioned, of which it is possible that Gringore might have likewise been the author. There is another French *Gestes Romaines* by Gaguin the historian, which has been mistaken for a translation of the *Gesta* ; but it is nothing more than an extract from the history of the Roman republic. The editions of the *Violier* are, 1. without date, printed at Paris, by Philip Le Noir, in quarto ; 2. 1521, printed at Paris, by Jean de la Garde, in folio ; and 3. 1529, printed also at Paris, for Denis Janot, in quarto.

ENGLISH TRANSLATION.—In 1703 was published a little volume entitled *Gesta Romanorum :* or *Forty-five histories originally (as 't is said) collected from the Roman records, with applications or morals for the suppressing vice, and encouraging virtue and the love of God.* Vol. I. *newly and with*

---

* An obsolete word that signifies a flower-pot.

care translated from the Latin edition, printed, A.D. M.D.XIV.
This seems to be the first English translation, and the translator B. P. has remarked in his preface that most of the
matters contained in his book had, as he understood, appeared already in the English tongue; and therefore he
desires the reader, if he should discover a great difference in
names, sense, and expression, to compare each work with the
Latin copy, by which comparison he conceives it will be
found that *his* translation is faithful.   He was not aware that
the preceding translation to which he alludes had been made
from a different work.   The stories are here extracted without attention to the original arrangement, but with a reference
in each to the Latin copy.   The editor, whoever he was,
designed an extension of his labours to other volumes.   Next
followed an edition of the same work, without date, 18mo,
but printed about 1720.   It wants the references to the Latin
copy, and the former preface is abridged.   It contains four-
teen additional stories that do not belong to the *original Gesta.*
Of this another edition, with the language much altered, was
printed in 1722, 18mo, with the same number of stories.   The
editor signs himself A. B., perhaps Bettesworth the printer.

It is now time to proceed to the description of *another
Gesta Romanorum,* and which has indeed been the principal
cause of the present dissertation.   This work was undoubtedly composed in England in imitation of the other; and
therefore it will be necessary for the future to distinguish the
two works by the respective appellations of the *original* and
the *English Gesta.*

It is remarkable that neither Mr. Tyrwhitt nor Mr. Warton, both of whom had frequent occasion to inspect the work
in question, and to notice certain variations between what
they have too loosely termed the *printed copies* and the *manuscripts,* should not have perceived that the latter were in
reality a different performance.   Mr. Tyrwhitt indeed, for
want of this perception, has made use of certain English

features in the manuscripts as an argument to prove that the *original Gesta* was composed in England.*

From the great celebrity of the *original Gesta*, it could not fail of being known to the English clergy, and accordingly we find that it was used by them in the pulpit as in other countries. If the numerous volumes of the sermons of the middle ages that still remain in our college and cathedral libraries were examined, a task by no means here recommended, it would, no doubt, be found, that they had been indebted to it among other similar authorities for many of their *examples*; and to show that this is not a mere conjecture, there is a collection of ancient sermons in the British Museum that affords a solitary instance of the introduction of a story from the *original Gesta*.† It is the thirty-ninth story, of two brothers at enmity with each other. Though anonymous, there is no doubt that these sermons were composed by some Englishman, who has cited a multitude of authors, and among other matters the well-known story of the Jew who refused to be delivered from a jakes into which he had fallen on the sabbath day.

It is natural to suppose that a work like the *original Gesta* would stimulate some person to the compilation of one that should emulate if not altogether supersede it; and accordingly this design was accomplished at a very early period by some Englishman, in all probability a monk. There is a considerable difficulty even in forming a conjecture as to the precise time in which this was done. One of the earliest manuscripts appears to have been written about the reign of Richard the Second, nor is there any internal evidence in this work that places its composition below that period. That its purpose was similar to that of the other is manifest from its being quoted no less than five times in a collection of sermons by a preacher at Magdalen college already mentioned,

---

* Cant. tales, IV. 331.   † MS. Harl. 5396.

who has likewise introduced the moralizations generally in the very words of his original. If additional proofs were wanting of the English origin of the work before us, it might be stated, 1. That no manuscript of it appears to exist in any of the catalogues of continental libraries; whereas there are many in those of this country.* 2. That in one of the chapters there are some English verses,† and in another some English proper names.‡ 3. That it has a few English terms and modes of speech, as *parliament, livery of seizin,* &c.

The construction resembles that of the *original Gesta,* from which a great many stories have been retained; but these are always newly written, and sometimes materially altered. The moralizations are uniformly different, and the proper names generally changed. The best manuscripts contain one hundred and two stories, out of which there are upwards of forty that are not in the original work, none of which have been ever printed in the *Latin* of this *Gesta,* and but few of them in an English translation. The sources from which many of them were taken cannot easily be traced, whilst others are extracted from works that will hereafter be mentioned.

In the following analysis of the additional stories to this *Gesta,* the plan of Mr. Warton has been adopted. Though it should fail in exciting much pleasurable sensation in the reader, it may at least serve to throw a ray or two of light on the manners of the middle ages. The arrangement of the chapters is from MS. Harl. 2270, but the copy used is one of equal value in the author's possession. The variety in these is very inconsiderable.

Chap. i.—The emperor Anselmus bore a silver shield with five red roses. He had three sons equally beloved by him.

---

* There may perhaps be one exception in the Vatican MS. mentioned before in p. 531.

† MS. Harl. 2270, chap. 53.

‡ MS. Harl. 5259, chap. 28; but in most of the MSS. they are omitted.

His continual wars with the king of Egypt had reduced him so low, that of all his temporal goods only a single tree remained. Being mortally wounded in one of his battles, he called his sons before him, and bequeathed to the eldest all that was under the earth and above the earth belonging to the tree; to the second, all that was great and small in it; and to the youngest, all that was wet and dry in it. On the king's death a dispute arose between his sons concerning the possession of the tree, which by mutual consent was referred for decision to the king of Reason. He caused all the young men to be bled, and ordered that a bone, taken from the breast of their dead father, should be dipped in the blood and afterwards washed. The blood of the two elder sons was easily discharged, but that of the youngest remained. The king declared that he was of the true blood and nature of the bone, and the others bastards; to him therefore the tree was adjudged.

CHAP. II.—The emperor Diocletian, desirous to know what bird had the greatest affection for its young, goes into a wood and returns to his palace with an ostrich's nest, which he places under a glass vessel. The dam follows him, and finding it impossible to get at her offspring, proceeds to a desert, where she remains thirty-four days, and then comes home with a worm called Thurnar; this she kills on the vessel, which being broken by the blood of the animal, her young ones are set at liberty. At this conduct of the bird Diocletian expresses much pleasure.

CHAP. IV.—The emperor Gauterus, reflecting on the vanities of the world, resolves to find a situation where there is nothing but happiness. He leaves his kingdom, and meets a beautiful woman who had lost her husband. She offers him marriage, and abundance of wealth; but on inspecting the nuptial chamber, the emperor is startled and disgusted at the appearance of several serpents and a lion that threaten him with destruction. The lady informs him that he may pos-

sibly survive a night or two, but that the animals will afterwards devour him, as they had her husband. The emperor
declines the honour of this marriage, and proceeds to another
country, where the nobles are desirous to elect him king in
the room of their deceased monarch; but finding a bed-
chamber like the former, he instantly departs, and arrives at
a third place, where he is offered the kingdom on similar
terms. At length he meets an old man, sitting near a ladder
with three steps raised against a wall. He is interrogated as
to his wishes, and answers that he sought three things, viz.
joy without sorrow, abundance without want, and light without darkness. He is desired to ascend the ladder, when he
finds what he had wished for, and continues on the spot
during the rest of his life. This is, in substance, the 101st
story in the other *Gesta*, but here related with much variety.

Chap. xviii.—A knight falls in love with Aglae, the
daughter of the emperor Polentius, and being obliged to be
absent in the Holy Land for seven years, the lady agrees not
to marry till his return. In the mean time the emperor promises his daughter to the king of Hungary, who being deeply
in love with her, consents, at her request, to postpone the
marriage. On the day before the appointed time, the king
of Hungary, riding to the emperor's court in great pomp to
celebrate his nuptials, is met by the knight, with whom he
enters into conversation, and a violent rain coming on, the
king's fine clothes are presently spoiled. The knight remarks
that he should have brought his house with him. The king
is struck with the singularity of the admonition. They arrive
at a deep water, and the king plunging in with his horse, is
nearly drowned. The knight tells him that he should have
brought his bridge with him. Shortly after the king inquires
what time of day it is; his companion replies that it is time
to eat, and offers a cake, which is accepted. He then
observes to the king that he had acted unwisely in omitting
to bring his father and mother with him. As they approach

the emperor's palace, the knight requests leave of the king to take another road, meaning to get to the court by a nearer way that was known to him, and carry off the lady before the king should arrive. On being asked what road he intended to take, he declares he will speak the truth. He says, that on that day seven years he had spread a net in a certain place to which he was then going; that if he should find it broken he shall leave it, but if whole, that he shall take it with him. The king arrives at the palace, and is kindly entertained. The emperor interrogates him concerning the particulars of his journey, and on hearing the strange observations that the knight had made, commends him as a wise man, and informs the king that by the house he had meant nothing more than a cloak; that the bridge he talked of, signified the attendants who should have been sent before to ascertain the depth of the water; and that by the king's father and mother, he intimated the bread and wine that he should have brought with him. But when the emperor came to reflect on the meaning of the net which had been spread seven years since, he perceived that his daughter was in danger, and on commanding her chamber to be examined, found his suspicions verified. The king being deceived by the knight and the damsel, returned in disgrace to his own country.

CHAP. XXI.—This is the story of king Lear under the name of Theodosius, emperor of Rome. It has been already given from the old English translation in manuscript. See page 420.

CHAP. XXIV.—Antonius made a law at Rome, that whenever a fire happened in the city a sentinel should cry out to the people to ring all the bells, and secure the gates. A certain warrior was desirous of becoming master of the city, and, apprised of this law, consulted with his companions how it should be evaded. One advised that they should enter the city peaceably, and proclaim a general feast, at which a certain liquor should be used that would set all the guests asleep. The stratagem is adopted, the city fired, the inhabitants carried off, and not one person left to comply with the emperor's edict.

CHAP. xxv.—A certain knight is unjustly accused before an emperor, who, when he finds that the accusation cannot be maintained, endeavours to perplex him with intricate questions, which he is obliged to answer on pain of death. Among these are, the distance of a sigh from the heart? the number of flaggons of salt water in the sea? the depth of it? which are the most honourable and poorest professions? &c. These are all answered satisfactorily, and the knight dismissed with commendation.

CHAP. xxvi.—A sick emperor sends into a foreign country for the physician Averrhoes, who cures him of his disease. This excites the envy of three other physicians, and they resolve to effect his ruin. For this purpose they deceive him into a belief that he is become leprous, and he returns with great sorrow to the emperor, to acquaint him with his misfortune. Being offered all the consolation that the emperor can afford him, he requests that he may have the use of a bath made of goat's blood. By this remedy he is restored to health; and the emperor, wondering at the suddenness with which he had been attacked, is informed by Averrhoes that three leprous persons of his own profession had terrified him, and thereby communicated their disease. They are immediately punished with death.

CHAP. xxvii.—Antony, emperor of Rome, is fond of chess. Playing once at this game, he observed that when the men were replaced as usual in the bag, the king was indiscriminately confounded with the rest of the pieces. This suggests to him his mortal state, and that he himself shall be eventually blended with others in the grave. He divides his kingdom into three parts; one he gives to the king of Jerusalem, another to his nobles, and the third to the poor. He then retires to the Holy Land to end his days in peace.

CHAP. XXX.—The emperor Averrhoes proclaims a tournament, and that the conquerer shall marry his daughter after his decease. Decius, a knight who excelled in arms, had two infant sons. Hearing of the proclamation, he goes one morning into a forest where a nightingale was singing very sweetly. He expresses a wish to know the meaning of the song, and an old man, suddenly appearing to him, explains it. The bird had directed him to go to the tournament, but in his way thither he is to meet with some heavy misfortune, which he is recommended to support with constancy and patience, because, eventually, his sorrow is to be turned to joy. The old man then disappears, and the nightingale flies away. Decius returns home and acquaints his wife with the adventure. She advises him to go to the tournament with herself and children; and he had no sooner finished the preparations for his journey, than his house and all his goods are consumed by fire. Not discouraged, he embarks on board a vessel, and on his arrival in the country to which he was going, the captain of the ship demands the price of his passage. The knight confesses his present inability to comply with the requisition, but promises on his return from the tournament to satisfy him fully. The captain, who had in the meantime conceived an improper passion for the lady, demands her as an hostage, refusing an offer of the children. The poor knight, finding no remedy, affectionately takes leave of his wife, and departs in great sorrow with his children. The mariner in vain attempts the accomplishment of his purpose with the lady, and after having accompanied her to some strange country, dies. She is reduced to great misery, and obliged to beg her bread from door to door. The story then returns to the knight, who, proceeding in his journey to the emperor's palace, meets with a deep piece of water, which it was necessary to cross. Not being able to carry over both the children together, he leaves one of them on the ground. On his return for his child, a lion springs from a wood, seizes the infant before he could arrive at the spot, and carries it away. He endeavours in vain to pursue the ravisher, and at length goes back to his other child. But here again his ill fortune attends him ; a bear had seized it, and was in the act of carrying it to a neighbouring forest. He now gives way to his grief, and exclaims bitterly against the nightingale and her song, but resolves to proceed to the tournament. Here he has better luck, and repeatedly carries away the prize. The emperor takes him into great favour, and places him at the head of his armies. Walking one day through a certain city, he finds a precious stone of three colours. On carrying it to a lapidary, he is informed that he possesses a great treasure ; that the stone has the power of making the owner completely happy, of enabling him to find what he might have lost, and of converting his poverty into wealth, and his sorrows into joy. Soon afterwards he has occasion to raise troops for the emperor's service, and in the course of the war two young soldiers eminently distinguish themselves by their valour. As they are sitting one night at supper, they make inquiries of each other respecting their parents; and from certain matters that are detailed, they are recognized by their mother, who happens to be present. This discovery soon leads to that of their father, who is known by his wife, from a particular mark in his forehead. All the parties return to their own country, and end their days happily.

The burning of the knight's house, and the manner in which he was deprived of his children, have been borrowed from the romance of *Sir Isumbras.**

CHAP. XXXI.—A law was made at Rome that the sentinels of the city should each night examine what was passing in all the houses, so that no private murders might be committed, nor any thing done whereby the city should be endangered. It happened that an old knight named Josias had

* See Mr. Ellis's *Metrical romances*, voi. iii. pp. 155, 157.

married a young and beautiful woman, who, by the sweetness of her singing, attracted many persons to his house, several of whom came for the purpose of making love to her. Among these were three young men who were high in the emperor's favour. They respectively agreed with the woman for a private assignation for which she was to receive twenty marks. She discloses the matter to her husband, but not choosing to give up the money, prevails on him to consent to the murder of the gallants, and the robbing of their persons. This is accomplished, and the bodies deposited in a cellar. The woman, mindful of the new law that had been made, sends for one of the sentinels, who was her brother, pretends that her husband had killed a man in a quarrel, and prevails on him, for a reward, to dispose of the dead body. She then delivers to him the first of the young men, whom he puts into a sack and throws into the sea. On his return to the sister, she pretends to go into the cellar to draw wine, and cries out for help. When the sentinel comes to her, she tells him that the dead man is returned. At this he of course expresses much surprise, but putting the second body into his sack ties a stone round its neck and plunges it into the sea. Returning once more, the woman, with additional arts, plays the same part again. Again he is deceived, and taking away the third body, carries it into a forest, makes a fire, and consumes it. During this operation he has occasion to retire, and in the meantime a knight on horseback, who was going to a tournament, passes by, and alights to warm himself at the fire. On the other's return the knight is mistaken for the dead man, and with many bitter words thrown into the fire, horse and all. The sentinel goes back to his sister, and receives the stipulated reward. A hue and cry had now been made after the young men who were missing. The husband and wife engage in a quarrel, and the murder is of course discovered.

This story has been immediately taken from *The seven wise*

masters, where it forms the *example* of the sixth master.
The ground-work is, no doubt, oriental, and may be found,
perhaps in its most ancient form, in *The little hunchbacked
taylor* of *The Arabian nights.* It was imported into Europe
very early, and fell into the hands of the lively and entertaining French minstrels, who have treated it in various ways,
as may be seen in Le Grand, *Fabliaux et contes,* tom. iv.,
where it is related five times. The several imitations of it
from *The seven wise masters* may be found in all the editions
of *Prince Erastus,* an Italian modification of the *Wise masters.*
It forms the substance of a well constructed and entertaining
story of two friars, John and Richard, who are said to have
resided at Norwich in the reign of Henry the Fifth. This is
related in Heywood's *History of women* under the title of
The faire ladie of Norwich,* and has crept into Blomefield's
History of Norfolk in a very extraordinary manner, unaccompanied with any comment, but with the addition of the murderer's name, who is unaccountably stated to be Sir Thomas
Erpingham, a well-known character.† In the Bodleian library there is an old English poem entitled *A merry jest of
Dane Hew munk of Leicestre, and how he was foure times
slain and once hanged.* Printed at London by J. Allde, in
4to, without date. This is probably the same story, which
has certainly been borrowed from one of those related by the
Norman minstrels.‡

* P. 253, folio edit.

† Vol. iii. p. 647. Mr. Gough speaks of it as separately printed. *Brit.
Topogr.* ii. 27. It is also copied in Burton's *Unparallelled varieties,*
p. 159*, edit. 1699, 12mo, and *The gentleman's magazine,* vol. l. p. 310. It
has been twice versified: 1. anonymously, under the title of *A hue and cry
after the priest, or the convent, a tale,* 1749, 8vo; and 2. by Mr. Jodrell
under that of *The knight and friars,* 1785, 4to.

‡ The curious reader may also consult the following authorities, where
he will find the above story in some shape or other. Fauchet, *Anciens
poetes Francois,* chap. lxxxix. Barbasan, *Fabliaux et contes,* ii. 125. The
first novel of Masuccio. Straparole, *Piacevole notte,* N. v. fab. 3. *Pa-
tranas* di Timoneda, patr. 3. *Comptes du monde adventureux,* 1595, 18mo,
compte xxiii. Guellette *Contes Tartares,* in the story of *Les 3 bossus de*

CHAP. XXXII.—Folliculus, a knight, was fond of hunting and tournaments. He had an only son, for whom three nurses were provided. Next to this child he loved his falcon and his greyhound. It happened one day that he was called to a tournament, whither his wife and domestics went also, leaving the child in a cradle, the greyhound lying by him, and the falcon on his perch. A serpent that inhabited a hole near the castle, taking advantage of the profound silence that reigned, crept from his habitation, and advanced towards the cradle to devour the child. The falcon, perceiving the danger, fluttered with his wings till he awoke the dog, who instantly attacked the invader, and after a fierce conflict, in which he was sorely wounded, killed him. He then lay down on the ground to lick and heal his wounds. When the nurses returned they found the cradle overturned, the child thrown out, and the ground covered with blood as well as the dog, who they immediately concluded had killed the child. Terrified at the idea of meeting the anger of the parents, they determined to escape, but in their flight fell in with their mistress, to whom they were compelled to relate the supposed murder of the child by the greyhound. The knight soon arrived to hear the sad story, and, maddened with fury, rushed forward to the spot. The poor wounded and faithful animal made an effort to rise, and welcome his master with his accustomed fondness; but the enraged knight received him on the point of his sword, and he fell lifeless to the ground. On examination of the cradle the infant was found alive and unhurt, and the dead serpent lying by him. The knight now perceived what had happened, lamented bitterly over his faithful dog, and blamed himself for having depended

---

Damas. Histoire des larrons, tom. i. pp. 2, 239. *Biblioth. amus. et instructive*, tom. ii. p. 14. *Bibl.* de Du Verdier et La croix du Maine, par Juvigny, tom. iv. p. 376. *Pasquil's Jests, or Mother Bunch's merriments*, p. 51; and Marlow's *Jew of Malta*, in Reed's *Old plays*, vol. viii. p. 366.

too hastily on the words of his wife. Abandoning the profession of arms he broke his lance into three pieces, and vowed a pilgrimage to the Holy Land, where he spent the rest of his days in peace.

This tale is likewise borrowed by the compiler of the *Gesta*, from the Seven wise masters, and of oriental construction. It is originally in Pilpay's fables, being that of *The Santon and the broken pitcher*.*

There is a very extraordinary tradition in North Wales, of an incident resembling that in our story having happened to prince Llewellyn about the year 1205. He is said to have erected a tomb over his faithful dog, still known in Carnarvonshire by the name of *Cilhart's grave*.† This tradition is the subject of an elegant ballad by the honourable Mr. Spencer, privately printed in a single sheet, under the title of *Beth Gêlert, or The grave of the greyhound*. At Abergavenny priory church there is said to be the figure of an armed knight with a dog at his feet; and with this person, whoever he was, the story of *Cilhart* has also been connected. But

---

* This fable is only to be found in Mons. de Cardonne's translation, book V.; Galland's and the English edition having no more than the first 4 books. It occurs also in that exceedingly rare and curious work, the *Directorium vitæ humanæ*, printed in Germany, without date, place, or name of printer, at the end of the fifteenth century; and in its imitation, the *Moral. philosophia* of Doni, part ii. p. 68, in the English translation of which, printed by Denham, 1570, 4to, it has been omitted. It is also in Starkij *Specimen sapientiæ Indorum*, 1697, 12mo, p. 339. The two last works are in fact the fables of Pilpay under different forms, or rather the *Heetopades* of Veeshnu Sarma, the Hindoo fabulist, who appears to be the parent of all.

The same story occurs likewise in the following works. Le Grand, *Fabliaux et contes*, tom. iii. p. 168. Sansovino, *Cento novelle*, giorn. 9, nov. 1. *Les facetieuses journées*, p. 287. Lestrange's *Æsop*, vol. i. fab. 464, 8vo edition. *Asiatic miscellany*, 12mo, 1787, p. 73, from the *Ayar Danish* of Abulfazel, which seems to have been extracted from, or at least much resembles, the oriental work that forms the seventh chapter in the *Directorium humanæ vitæ*.

† Jones's *Relics of the Welsh bards*, p. 75, where there is an old Welsh song, or *Englyn* on the subject.

the dog, as well as other animals, is frequently found at the feet of figures on old monuments. On the whole, the subject appears not undeserving of the consideration of Welsh antiquaries. It would be proper however, on any such occasion, to bear in mind the numerous applications of circumstances altogether fabulous to real persons; one example of which has occurred in the story from the *Gesta* that immediately precedes the present.

It may be thought worth adding that Virgil's *Original Gnat* resembled in its outline, as given by Donatus, the story in the *Gesta*. A shepherd there falls asleep in a marshy spot of ground; a serpent approaches, and is about to kill him. At this moment a gnat settles on the shepherd's face, stings, and awakens him. He instinctively applies his hand to the wounded part, and crushes the gnat. He soon perceives that he had destroyed his benefactor, and, as the only recompense in his power, erects a tomb to his memory.

CHAP. XXXVI.—A king having educated his three sons under a celebrated philosopher, interrogates each of them as to what kind of a God he should prefer; for it was the custom of the country that every man should make his own choice on this occasion. The eldest chooses Jupiter for his power, the second Jupiter also for his wisdom, the third Mercury for his piety and mercy. The king recommends a Deity who should unite all these properties, and who is compared to Jesus Christ, &c.

CHAP. XLVI.—The emperor Alexander made a law that no man should turn a flat-fish on his plate, so as to eat the other side, under pain of death; it being nevertheless permitted him to ask three things before his execution. The son of an offender against this law saves his father's life by his ingenuity, and contrives to marry the emperor's daughter.

CHAP. XLVII.—A law was made that if any child should die, or even be hurt by the negligence of the person to whose care it were committed, such person should suffer death. A knight requested as a reward for some services, that he might have the care of the king's son. This was accordingly granted, and the child delivered over to nurses. In their absence at a fair, a wolf entered the house and carried off the infant towards a wood. A shepherd gathering fruit in an orchard saw the affair and gave the alarm. The child was recovered, but not till it had received a bite that left a mark in its forehead. When the king had received back his son, he discovered the wound, and menaced the knight with the punishment of the law. The knight asserted that he was not a God, nor able to control the effect of nature. The king maintained that the mark was not natural, but produced by accident; and the knight at length confessed the fact, and threw himself on the king's mercy. He was only enjoined to do exclusive homage to the king, and taken into favour.

In the moral, God is the maker of the law. He delivers man's soul to him pure and unspotted, to be nourished in deeds of virtue. The ecclesiastics are the nurses, who instead of attending to their duty, frequent the worldly fairs of wickedness and vanity. The wolf is the devil, who seizes the soul and endeavours to precipitate it into hell; but the good preacher sitting in the arbour of the holy scriptures, gives the alarm, and delivers it from the clutches of the devil, &c.

CHAP. XLVIII.—This story has been given from the old English translation in manuscript, at the end of the notes to the Merchant of Venice. See p. 173.

CHAP. XLIX.—An emperor made a law that whoever violated a Virgin should lose both his eyes. His own son is found guilty of the crime, and the emperor, notwithstanding the entreaties of his nobles, enforces punishment, but consents to divide the loss of sight with the aggressor.

CHAP. L.—This story is in the other *Gesta*, but differently related. A king on some domestic difference with his wife, had been told by her that one only of her three sons was legitimate; but which of them was so she refused to discover.

This gave him much uneasiness ; and his death soon afterwards approaching, he called his children together, and declared in the presence of witnesses, that he left a ring which
had very singular properties to him that should be found to
be his lawful son. On his death a dispute arose between the
youths, and it was at length agreed to refer its decision to the
king of Jerusalem. He immediately ordered that the dead
body of the father should be taken up and tied to a tree :
that each of the sons should shoot an arrow at it, and that he
who penetrated the deepest should have the ring. The eldest shot first, and the arrow went far into the body ; the second shot also, and deeper than the other. The youngest son
stood at a distance, and wept bitterly ; but the king said to
him, " Young man, take your arrow and shoot as your
brothers have done." He answered, " Far be it from me to
commit so great a crime. I would not for the whole
world disfigure the body of my father." The king said,
" Without doubt you are his son, and the others only bastards ; to you therefore I adjudge the ring."

This story has been entitled *The judgment of Solomon,* and is
probably of oriental origin.* It is often represented in that
illumination which in the ancient manuscripts of the French
translation of the Bible by Guiars des Moulins is prefixed to
the proverbs of Solomon, although the story itself does not
occur in that bible, nor in the original commentary by Petrus
Comestor. It appears to have been a great favourite in the middle ages, and was often related from the pulpit.† The original
judgment of Solomom in the first book of Kings had probably

* See Le Grand, *Fabliaux et contes,* ii. 426, who quotes the *Tartarian tales*
for a similar story.

† See the *exempla* at the end of the *Sermones discipuli,* ex. ix. de. B.
The *Sermones fratris Gulielmi Cartusiensis,* 1494, 12mo, sig. V. 7 b. An
ancient collection of Latin sermons in the Harl. coll. No. 5396. See likewise *A christen exhortation unto customable swearers,* at the end of *The
christen state of matrimonye,* 1543, 12mo, p. 28, the author of which cites
the *Preceptorium Johannis Beets,* a German preacher about 1450; and
Burton's *Unparellelled varieties,* p. 21.

reached the continent of India at some very early period, as
it is imitated in the following story which occurs in one of
the books belonging to the kingdom of Pegu. Two women
went out together to bathe, each accompanied by her child.
Whilst they were in the water, the children being left on the
bank of the river, an alligator seized one of them and carried it away. A dispute arose between the women for the
possession of the remaining infant, and they at length agreed
to go before the judge. To determine the controversy, the
judge ordered one of the women to lay hold of the child's
head, and the other of its heels, and thus to pull for it. In
the course of the struggle, the child was hurt, and cried out ;
one of the women instantly quitted her hold, and the other
carried off the prize. The judge ordered her to be brought
back, and told her that as she had manifested so little compassion for the sufferings of the child, she could not possibly
be its mother. The infant was restored to the other woman.*
There is another ingenious adjudication by the emperor Claudius, scarcely inferior to Solomon's. A woman had refused
to acknowledge her son : and, the arguments on each side
being doubtful, Claudius ordered that the parties should be
married. The mother was compelled to a confession. See
Sueton. in Claud. cap. 15.

CHAP. LI.—Archillaus, a Roman emperor of an elegant
person and lofty stature, was desirous to have a shirt made
by the hands of a pure and spotless virgin, in such a skilful
and subtile manner as to prolong the duration of his life.
After the strictest search no such virgin could be found ; or
at least, says the story, no female whose talents were compe-

---

* From *Memorandums in India by John Marshall,* beginning Sep. 11th,
1678, preserved among the Harleian MSS. in the British Museum, No. 4523.
The above person appears to have been a very curious and intelligent traveller, and many of his observations on the manners of the Indians would
be exceedingly well worth publishing. Marshall was educated at Cambridge,
had a great desire to travel, and by the interest of Lord Craven, went out
1667, in the India ship the Unicorn, in the Company's service.

tent to the task. Some time afterwards the emperor walking in his orchard, and meditating on the above matter, was
accosted by a certain person who told him that he believed
there was one young woman remaining in the country who
was in all respects capable of performing what he desired. A
messenger was immediately despatched by the emperor on
this pleasing mission, with instructions to salute the lady
most honourably on his part, and to present her with a particular piece of cloth three inches only in length and breadth,
and to request that she would convert it into the shirt required; with a promise that if she succeeded, she should become his wife. The messenger faithfully executed his instructions; but when the damsel saw the cloth, she told him
that it was impossible with such a quantity to make a shirt
that would fit the emperor in the manner required, but undertook notwithstanding to make one according to the best
of her ability. When the emperor heard the answer he sent
a pure and handsome vessel to the lady, in which she manufactured a shirt that gave him satisfaction. He performed
his promise and married her. This very silly and obscure
story is allegorized into the miraculous conception of the
Virgin Mary.

CHAP. LIV.—Is also in the other *Gesta*, but here related
with much greater variety of circumstance, and in all respects
improved. The story has been very properly termed by
Mr. Warton, a beautiful one; but he has not been equally
accurate in his statement that "Occleve has literally followed
the book before us (i. e. the original *Gesta*,) and has even
translated into English prose the moralisation annexed."
Occleve's immediate model was our English *Gesta*; nor is it
improbable that he might even be the translator of it; the
moralisation also is entirely different.*   Mr. Warton has

---

* The *whole* of Occleve's poem may be seen in MS. Reg. 17 D. vi. with
the moralisation, omitted by Browne, who has otherwise mutilated the
poem.

omitted to notice that this story corresponds with that of
Fortunatus; which, unless itself of oriental origin, might have
been taken from it.*

CHAP. LVI.—An emperor who had only a daughter, hunting one day in a forest, lost his way, and was obliged to seek
shelter in the cottage of a forester.   He was kindly and hospitably received, and after taking some refreshment, retired to
rest without disclosing to the man who he was.   As he lay in
bed he thought he heard a voice that said to him, " take, take,
take ;" presently after, another that cried, "give, give, give ;"
and then a third that still more emphatically pronounced
these words, " fly, fly, fly ; for this night a child is born who
shall succeed to your empire."   When he arose in the morning, he inquired of the forester if any child had been born
during the night, who informed him that his wife had just been
delivered of a son.   The emperor then discovered himself, examined a mark on the child's forehead, and told the man that
he should send for it the next day, as he designed to have it
bred up at his court.   On his return home he directed some
confidential servants to take away the child from the forester's
cottage, to put it to death, and to bring back its heart, that he
might be satisfied that his orders were obeyed.   A contention
arose among the domestics about destroying the infant,† and
one more humane than the rest, proposed the killing of a pig
in its stead, and delivering the heart to the king.   This was at
length acceded to by the others.   The child was wrapped up
in some linen, and placed in a hollow tree for present shelter.
When the emperor received the supposed heart of the child he

* One reason for suspecting it might have originated in the East is that
it forms the subject of one of the old French *fabliaux,* many of which came
in with the Crusades. See Sinner, *Catal. des MSS. de Berne,* iii. 389. It
has been likewise imitated by La Harpe in his *Pied de nez.* Some traces of
resemblance may be found in the stories of *Ahmed, and the enchanted horse*
in the Arabian nights entertainments.

† This incident has been introduced into the popular old ballad of *The
children in the wood.*

cast it into the fire, and mocked the idle dreams that had tormented him. Shortly after, as an earl was hunting in the above forest, the dogs discovered the child, which was taken home and committed to the care of the earl's wife, whom he prevailed on to acknowledge it as their own, and to give out that she had just been delivered of it. When thirteen years had elapsed from this time, the emperor proclaimed a great feast, to which, among others, the earl was invited, who carried the boy with him as a squire to attend his person. When the youth came into the presence of the emperor, the latter instantly perceived the mark on his forehead, and in great anger interrogated the earl so strictly that he confessed the manner in which he had discovered the child. But the emperor's indignation was still more excited against the servants whom he had employed. He sent for them and commanded them on their oaths to speak the truth. The emperor, now satisfied of the identity of the youth, informed the earl that he should retain him at his court, and that he himself was at liberty to return home. It happened that at this time the empress was in a foreign kingdom with her daughter. The emperor therefore sent the youth to her with a letter in which he commanded her to cause him to be put to death in the most cruel and ignominious manner. In the prosecution of his journey, the poor young man came to the castle of a knight whom he humbly entreated to afford him lodging; and being hospitably received, laid himself down to sleep, placing near him a box in which he had deposited the letter. The knight accidentally seeing the box, became anxious to know its contents; and having opened it immediately perceived the emperor's signet. This he very carefully put aside, and, reading the letter, was moved with compassion for the youth. He immediately resolved to save his life, and substituted another letter, in which the king was made to direct the empress to marry her daughter to the young man with great solemnity, and to detain him with her until he should himself arrive. This letter was delivered to the empress, and the supposed directions of the emperor complied with. The youth by his deportment engaged the affections of all. Some time afterwards the emperor resolved to visit the empress, and on his arrival she went out to meet him accompanied by her children. As soon as the emperor saw the young man, he again recognized him; and, beholding his wife with looks of fury and indignation, he demanded of her why she had omitted to obey his commands. She maintained that they had been obeyed by the marriage of the youth to their daughter, who then stood before him, and, as she perceived, with child. The anger of the emperor was now mitigated, and he exclaimed, " The will of the Lord be done, for I see it is in vain to oppose it." He saluted his children with great affection, and they succeeded happily to his throne.

Chap. lxii.—Cornelius seduces an emperor's daughter, murders her infant, and abandons her. The emperor expostulates to no purpose. He then proclaims a tournament in which the wicked knight is overcome. The princess is brought back to her father.

Chap. lxviii.—An emperor in his old age foolishly married a young wife, who carried on an intrigue with a certain knight. He resolved to make a journey to the Holy Land, and, setting out immediately, left his kingdom in the custody of the empress and his nobles. The captain of the ship in which he embarked, having received a large bribe for the purpose, threw the unfortunate emperor into the sea, and returned home with the news of his death, to the great joy of the wicked empress. The old monarch, who had been a good swimmer from his youth, fortunately reached an island which he found inhabited only by wild beasts. The third day after his arrival, he saw in a wood a young lion fighting with a strong and full-grown leopard; and compassionating the lion, who was nearly overpowered by his adversary, he drew his sword and killed the leopard. The grateful lion remained with him, and every day brought him as food some animal that he had hunted, which the emperor dressed by means of a fire that he contrived to make. After some time had elapsed, as he was one day walking on the shore, he perceived a ship, and making signals of distress, was taken on board. The faithful lion plunged after him into the sea, and swam by the side of the vessel, till some of the sailors, perceiving that he was exhausted with fatigue and about to sink, lifted him into the ship. On the emperor's arrival in his own kingdom he handsomely rewarded the captain, and proceeded to his palace accompanied by the lion. When he arrived there, he heard the sound of musical instruments, and perceived other demonstrations of joy. On inquiry he learned that the empress had been just married, and that his subjects believed he had perished in his voyage to the Holy Land. He then applied to one of the domestics of the palace to report him to the new emperor as a minstrel newly arrived, and to request that he might be permitted to entertain him with the tricks of his lion. He was ordered to appear before the new sovereign; whom the lion no sooner beheld than he instantly tore him in pieces, and immediately afterwards the empress. The nobles, astonished at what they saw, were now preparing to make their escape, when the emperor discovered himself, and desired them to lay aside their fear, as the vengeance of God had been accomplished. After relating his adventures, he reassumed his government.

CHAP. LXX.—Josias, a warlike king, was married to the king of Apulia's daughter, who had vowed she would unite herself to that man only who had obtained the victory in all his battles. Walking one day in his garden he saw it written in a star, that he should undertake as many wars for the love of Christ as he had for that of his lady, to whom he communicated the vision. She was extremely afflicted at the news, and threatened to destroy herself and the infant in her womb, but was comforted by her husband with a promise of returning as soon as he had conquered all the enemies of Christ. He then departed in company with Tirius, a valiant knight to whom he was attached, and they shortly arrived in Ethiopia. The king desired his friend to remain there, and subdue the country, whilst he should accomplish other conquests. Tirius requested of the king that he would send him occasional tidings of himself, and directions how to act in his absence. This was promised; and the knight received at the same time a ring from his master, as a pledge whereby to remember him. The king took his departure, and went to the Holy Land. In his absence a certain tyrant named Acharon, made war against Tirius; and finding it impossible to subdue him, accused him of treason to the king of Ethiopia, who deprived him of all his possessions, so that he became very poor and was obliged to beg his bread. Josias soon afterwards returned from the Holy Land to Ethiopia, in the character of a pilgrim, and by chance met Tirius, whom he immediately recognized, but remained himself unknown. He put many questions to his friend, who related to him his misfortunes, and added, that he was in daily expectation of the speedy return of his own sovereign, whose token he still preserved, and whom he described as the better half of his soul. Josias told him that he had travelled far on account of the love he also bore to the same person; that he was exceedingly fatigued, and requested of him to sit down that he might repose his head on his bosom. Tirius answered, that he would do this and much more for him. Whilst Josias was asleep, a white weasel issued from his mouth, and proceeding towards a mountain, walked round it. It then returned, and again entered the mouth of the king. Tirius wondered much at this, and when the king awoke was interrogated as to what he had seen. Josias, on being informed, said, " Let us go to the mountain, perhaps we may behold more wonders." On their coming to a hollow place in the mountain, they found a dragon lying dead, with a large quantity of gold in his belly, and a sharp sword, on which was inscribed, "By my power, and with the king's assistance, the knight Tirius shall once more possess his lands." Josias then discovered himself to his friend, who fell on the ground and kissed his feet. The king gave all the gold to Tirius, but reserved the sword for himself, and commanded the knight not to disclose who he was until they should have accomplished their purpose. Josias then proceeded in his pilgrim's habit to the king's palace, where he found the tyrant Acharon, and sat himself down before the largest table. The king inquired of him whence he came and what tidings he brought. The pilgrim answered, " I come from the Holy Land, where many persons recommend your soul to Christ for having despoiled a worthy knight of his lands on the lying accusation of a tyrant." Acharon then exclaimed, " Why hast thou uttered these things? I would thou wert able to defend thyself, that I might fight with thee." The pilgrim requested leave to accept the challenge, which the king granted, and promised that if he obtained the victory he should not only receive all the lost lands of the knight, but be made the second man in his kingdom. The day of battle was appointed, and the combatants respectively maintained the contest with considerable valour. At length Acharon, exhausted with fatigue, was about to yield, when he said to the pilgrim, " You are doubtless a generous adversary, I die with thirst; suffer me to go once to the river and drink." The pilgrim acquiesced on the like conditions for himself. When Acharon had quenched his thirst, his strength returned; he renewed the combat with vigour, and Josias, in his turn, sorely pressed, requested permission to drink. His treacherous enemy not only refused him, but compelled him to fight his way to the water, into . which he plunged and assuaged his thirst. Having recovered his strength, the battle was continued till the evening; and when Acharon was once more about to yield the victory, the king parted the combatants, and appointed the next day to renew the battle. At night the king sent for the pilgrim, commended his valour, and desired his daughter to take him under her care, and provide him with all necessaries, that he might be able to maintain the combat on the following day. The damsel then led him to a chamber, bathed him,* prepared his supper, and afterwards placed him in a bed with four feet, so that it could be easily moved from place to place. In the mean time Acharon called together his four sons, all of them robust young men ; told them of the danger his life would be in if he should renew the contest with the pilgrim on the ensuing day, and prevailed with them to seize him in his chamber whilst he slept, and throw him into the sea. It happened that a fisherman from his vessel perceived by the light of the moon the floating bed, and to his great astonishment a man lying upon it. Josias also awoke, and wondered much at seeing the stars over his head. The fisherman cried out to the king, and the king to him for assistance, telling him he was the person who had the day before been engaged in combat with the tyrant. The fisherman took him on board his vessel, and afterwards to his dwelling, where he was again put to bed. On the morrow Acharon armed himself and went to the palace, exclaiming aloud, " Bring forth the traitor pilgrim, that I may this day present his head to our lord the king." When the princess was ordered by her father to awake the pilgrim, she was astonished to find him gone, together with the bed; and when the king heard the strange news he was much grieved, for he loved the pilgrim, and detested the tyrant. The fisherman at length appeared and related what had happened. Josias returned to the palace, armed himself, once more attacked his adversary,

* This was a common practice in the times of chivalry, and many examples of it may be found in ancient romances. The ladies not only assisted in bathing the knights, after the fatigues of battle, but administered proper medicines to heal their wounds. Similar instances occur in the writings of Homer. In the Odyssey, Polycaste, one of the daughters of Nestor, bathes Telemachus ; and it appears that Helen herself had performed the like office for Ulysses.

who was by this time quite dejected, and cutting off his head, presented it to the king. He was then desired to name the reward that he wished for, when he requested that the lands which Tirius had acquired by his valour might be again restored to him. Josias afterwards took leave of his friend, returned to his own kingdom, and ended his days in peace.*

CHAP. LXXI.—An emperor committed the education of his only son to one of his knights, who had obtained a victory at a tournament. The child was placed in a chamber, round which the seven liberal sciences were depicted, so that when he lay awake in bed he could be gathering all kinds of knowledge. Near the bed was a fountain, in which the child could bathe, and beyond the fountain a window to admit the sun. It happened that a bear, finding the door open, entered the chamber and washed himself in the fountain, so that the water was much infected with his filth. The knight and his wife soon afterwards drank of the fountain, and became leprous. An eagle also flew in at the window, and carried off the king's son. At length a skilful physician was consulted, who cured the parties of their leprosy, and instructed them how to recover the child.

CHAP. LXXII.—A king hears the song of a nightingale. He is desirous of knowing what it means; and, applying to a wise knight, is informed that it directs him to seek three things, viz. joy without sorrow, abundance without want, and light without darkness. The king sets out in pursuit of them, and arrives in a kingdom where the sovereign was just dead, leaving his throne to his sister. She becomes enamoured of the royal traveller and offers him marriage. Here the story is discontinued, but the narrator refers to chap. iv. as containing the same matter.

---

* The incident of the weasel in this story is manifestly borrowed from a similar relation in the chronicle of Helinandus, a monk of the twelfth century, from which it is inserted in Wierus *De præstigiis dæmonum,* lib. i. cap. 14, as in allusion of the devil.

CHAP. LXXVII.—In the castle of an emperor was a fountain, the water of which had the property of curing drunkenness To this vice, which the emperor particularly detested, one of his knights, named Ydronicus, was much addicted; but whenever he perceived the consequences of his intemperance, he repaired to the fountain, and drinking a hearty draught, recovered himself in such a manner that the emperor, who was extremely attached to him, had never yet discovered his failing. It happened that the emperor had found a bird in his forest which sang so sweetly, that, being fond of melody, he repaired daily to the spot to hear it. The particular attention which the emperor bestowed on these two favourites had excited the envy of his courtiers, among whom one wiser than the rest at length undertook their ruin. He first sealed up the fountain, so that when Ydronicus next became intoxicated he was deprived of his usual remedy; and the emperor, perceiving his condition, was filled with indignation, and instantly decreed his banishment. The insidious courtier then repaired to the forest; and watching attentively the motions of the bird, perceived that her mate often came to visit her, but that in his absence she committed infidelities with strange birds, and then bathing herself in an adjacent well, deceived her mate on his return. He therefore closed up the well, and the unfaithful bird being soon detected by her mate, he tore her to pieces. The latter part of this story seems borrowed from the last chapter of the original *Gesta*.

CHAP. LXXVIII.—A law was made at Rome, that no man should marry for beauty, but for riches only; and that no woman should be united to a poor man, unless he should by some means acquire wealth equal to her own. A certain poor knight solicited the hand of a rich lady, but she reminded him of the law, and desired him to use the best means of complying with it, in order to effect their union. He departed in great sorrow, and after much inquiry, was informed of a rich duke who had been blind from the day of his birth. Him

2 o

he resolved to murder, and obtain his wealth; but found that he was protected in the day-time by several armed domestics, and at night by the vigilance of a faithful dog. He contrived however to kill the dog with an arrow, and immediately afterwards the master, with whose money he returned to the lady. He informed her that he had accomplished his purpose; and being interrogated how this had been done in so short a space of time, he related all that had happened. The lady desired, before the marriage should take place, that he would go to the spot where the duke was buried, lay himself on his tomb, listen to what he might hear, and then report it to her. The knight armed himself, and went accordingly. In the middle of the night he heard a voice saying, " O duke, that liest here, what asketh thou that I can do for thee?" The answer was, " O Jesus, thou upright judge, all that I require is vengeance for my blood unjustly spilt." The voice rejoined, " Thirty years from this time thy wish shall be fulfilled." The knight, extremely terrified, returned with the news to the lady. She reflected that thirty years were a long period, and resolved on the marriage. During the whole of the above time the parties remained in perfect happiness.

When the thirty years were nearly elapsed, the knight built a very strong castle, and over one of the gates, in a conspicuous place, caused the following verses to be written:

> " In my distress, religion's aid I sought;
> But my distress reliev'd, I held it nought.
> The wolf was sick, a lamb he seem'd to be;
> But health restor'd, the wolf again we see."

Interrogated as to the meaning of these enigmatical lines, the knight at once explained them by relating his own story, and added that in eight days time the thirty years would expire. He invited all his friends to a feast at that period; and when the day was arrived, the guests placed at table, and the minstrels attuning their instruments of music, a beautiful bird flew in at the window and began to sing with uncommon sweetness. The knight listened attentively, and said, " I fear this bird prognosticates misfortune." He then took his bow, and shot an arrow into it in the presence of all the company. Instantly the castle divided in two parts, and, with the knight, his wife, and all who were in it, was precipitated to the lowest depth of the infernal regions. The story adds, that on the spot where the castle stood, there is now a spacious lake, on which no substance whatever floats, but is immediately plunged to the bottom.

CHAP. LXXIX.—The emperor Miremius had an only son, on whose birth the wise men being consulted as to his future destiny, declared that he would not live except he were brought up for seven years under ground, where the light of the sun could never come. This was accordingly done ; and at the expiration of the time the young prince was taken out of his subterraneous confinement, and became the admiration of all men for his virtues and good disposition. In due time he was married to a daughter of the king of Hungary. At each corner of the nuptial bed was placed a little dog to watch, and near it a burning lamp, which by the emperor's special command was to be lighted only by the hands of a pure virgin. The prince coming one night into the chamber found the lamp extinguished, and made a solemn vow that he would never more enter the bed until the lamp were re-kindled ; but after many inquiries no virgin could be found for the purpose. The prince determined to make search himself, and taking affectionate leave of his wife, proceeded on his expedition. He presently overtook a lion, whose foot had been wounded by a thorn, which he extracted, and the animal followed him. Arriving at the castle of a king who had a virgin daughter, the prince fell in love with and demanded her in marriage. The king consented, on condition that he would destroy a horrible dragon, who had nearly devoured all the sheep and oxen in the country, and for whose future supply it would soon be necessary to draw lots in the king's own family. The prince agreed to the proposal, and waited till the period arrived when the lot had fallen on the king's daughter. He then became exceedingly terrified, but ventured to attack the dragon, who was on the point of destroying him, when the lion came to his assistance, and speedily killed his adversary. The virgin was delivered to the prince, who took her home to his wife. The lamp was rekindled, to the great joy of the parties, and the virgin treated with all possible kindness and attention. The dog and the lamp in this story are introduced in chap. i. of the other *Gesta*, but the tales have nothing else in common.

CHAP. LXXX.—There was a law at Rome, that every woman at her purification should write some words on the church door, for the edification of the people, and then return home with due solemnity. The empress on this occasion writes, " I am a king governing the age ; all the world is mine." Some time afterwards a noble lady attended by several musicians comes to be purified. She inscribes on the door, " I am an infant at the breast whose milk is wine," and returns home to prepare a feast. The empress is much offended, and sends for her. She procures two serpents, and compels the lady to suckle them, &c. The substance of this story is incorporated with the old ballad of " A warning piece to England, or the fall of queen Eleanor." *

CHAP. LXXXI.—A city is infested with dragons and other venomous animals that destroy the inhabitants. A philosopher advises the emperor to hang a live lion on a cross, and thus terrify the other creatures from molesting the city.

CHAP. LXXXII.—A law was made, that if any one could escape from prison and fly to the king's palace he should receive protection. An imprisoned knight is visited by a bird, who leaves a precious stone, by the touch of which his fetters are loosed and he escapes, &c.

* Coll. of old ballads, vol. i. No. xiii.

Chap. lxxxiv.—A dispute arose between the three sons of an emperor respecting the succession. The nobles decided that they should run a race on horseback, and that he whose horse neighed should inherit the throne. A cunning servant of one of the princes contrived that his master should win, by placing in the horse's way a mare that he remembered. This is the well-known story of Darius.

Chap. xc.—Of a law that whoever violated a virgin without making atonement to her father within a certain time should suffer death.

Chap. xcii.—Of a madman who tore his flesh every day, and was poisoned by his father.

Chap. xciii.—An empress falls in love with a young knight; and becoming extremely sick, the physicians inform her husband that there is no mode of cure, but the bathing her with the knight's blood.

Chap. xciv.—A poor man is promoted by an emperor to great honours, but soon becomes proud, and rebels against his sovereign. He is banished with his accomplices. These invite their successors to a poisoned banquet. The emperor is recommended by his son to apply to a damsel who possesses a well with miraculous powers. By means of its water the dead men are restored to life. The prince is rewarded with a crown of gold.

Chap. xcvii.—Jonathas, having contrived to keep fire and water in his house, at a time when his fellow citizens had been plundered of them by a tyrant named Eulopius, is rewarded by having the education of the emperor of Rome's son committed to him. He builds a chamber for the young prince, and causes various images and inscriptions to be placed in it, which keep him attentive to his charge. He is finally promoted to great honour.

Chap. xcviii.—The emperor Martin had brought up his nephew Fulgentius as his page and cup-bearer; but his steward soon became envious of the young man, and resolved to effect his ruin. For this purpose he prevailed on the emperor to believe that Fulgentius had ungratefully circulated many ill reports of him, and particularly that he was leprous to such a degree that it was unsafe to approach his person or administer his drink to him. He then went to the young man, related to him that the emperor had made great complaint of the foulness of his breath, and advised him, when he performed the duties of his office, to take special care to turn his head aside. The innocent Fulgentius pursued this insidious counsel, and, the emperor's anger being excited, he struck his nephew violently on the breast, and drove him from his presence. He then consulted with the steward how he should deprive the youth of life; and it was settled that some men who lived near at hand, and kept a furnace to burn stones for cement, should immediately be directed to throw into their fire, without the least ceremony, that person who should come early on the morrow, and desire them to fulfil the emperor's commands. Measures were then taken that Fulgentius should be the victim; but in his progress to the lime-kiln he was induced by the sound of a church bell to deviate from his road, and attend the celebration of the mass. During the service he fell asleep, and when it was finished no efforts of the priest could for a very considerable time awake him. In the meanwhile the steward, solicitous to hear of the young man's death, repaired to the spot, and inquiring if the emperor's commands had been executed, was seized by the workmen, who, in spite of all his entreaties and remonstrances, threw him into the furnace. Fulgentius himself soon afterwards arrived, delivered his message, and was surprised to hear of the steward's death, and the miraculous manner in which he himself had escaped. He then returned thanks to God for his preservation, and went back to the palace. The emperor in great anger demanded why he had not executed his commands. Fulgentius related what had happened, and this leading to a mutual explanation, he was restored to his uncle's favour, and ended his days honourably This story may have come from the East.* It is likewise extremely well related in the *Contes devots* or *Miracles of the Virgin*,† and in other places.‡

CHAP. XCIX.—A marriage was proposed between the son of Anselmus, emperor of Rome, and the daughter of the king of Apulia. The young lady in her voyage was shipwrecked and swallowed by a whale. In this situation she contrived to make a fire and to wound the animal with a knife, so that he was driven towards the shore, and slain by an earl named Pirius, who delivered the princess and took her under his protection. On relating her story she was conveyed to the emperor. In order to prove whether she was worthy to receive the hand of his son, he placed before her three vessels. The first was of gold, and filled with dead men's bones ; on it was this inscription ; *who chuses me shall find what he deserves*. The second was of silver filled with earth, and thus inscribed ; *who chuses me shall find what nature covets*. The third vessel was of lead, but filled with precious stones. It had this inscription ; *who chuses me shall find what God hath placed*. The emperor then commanded her to chuse one of the vessels, informing her that if she made choice of that which should profit herself and others, she would obtain his son ; if of what should profit neither herself nor others, she would lose him. The princess after praying to God for assistance, preferred the leaden vessel. The emperor informed her that she had chosen as he wished, and immediately united her with his son. This is obviously the story which had supplied the caskets in the *Merchant of Venice*. See the note at the end of that play, p. 169.

* See Scott's *Tales from the Arabic and Persian*, p. 53, where there is an excellent story of similar construction.

† Le Grand, *Fabliaux*, v. 74.

‡ *Cento novelle antiche*. nov. 68. *Patrañas* de Timoneda, pat. 17. *Dialogus creaturarum moralizatus*, cap. 120. Minsheu's address to the reader, before his *Spanish grammar*, 1623, folio.

CHAP. C.—A king hunting in a forest loses his attendants, and is left alone. He meets a lame lion, who stretches out his foot to him, as if soliciting assistance. The king, perceiving a thorn, extracts it, and binds up the wound with certain herbs. Finding no way out of the wood, he is obliged to take shelter in the lion's den, where he is supplied with food by the grateful animal. After remaining here some time a bear comes to the den. The rest of the story will not admit of being told. What has been stated is evidently grafted on the well-known tale of Androcles.

CHAP. CI.—A certain emperor made a pilgrimage to the Holy Land, leaving the care of the kingdom in his absence to his wife, a wise and beautiful woman. The emperor's brother not only oppressed and persecuted many of his subjects, but had even the temerity to make unlawful love to the empress. On consulting with her counsellors, they advised her to cast him into prison, which was accordingly done. Here he lay until rumours were spread of the emperor's intended return; and fearing that if his unworthy conduct were reported to his brother he should be sentenced to die, he entreated mercy of the empress, and made such solemn promises of future good behaviour that she consented to release him. On the emperor's arrival, his wife and brother went out to meet him; but in passing through a forest, a stag springing up, diverted the attention of the domestics who accompanied them, and they were left entirely by themselves. The wicked brother now renewed his solicitations to the empress; but receiving from her the most positive refusal of compliance, and menaced with the vengeance of her husband, he inhumanly tied her by the hair to a tree, leaving her palfrey by the side of her. He then rejoined the attendants, and pretended that a multitude of armed men had attacked him and carried off the empress. Shortly afterwards the unfortunate lady was discovered by an earl who was hunting in the forest, taken home to his castle, and by her own consent

appointed to superintend the care of his infant daughter.
Here a certain seneschal fell in love with her, but his addresses being rejected, he determined on speedy revenge.
For this purpose he contrived to get into the castle at night,
and proceeding to the earl's chamber, found the empress in
bed and asleep with the child. After murdering the infant,
he placed the bloody knife in the empress's hand. During
the night the earl's wife awoke, and perceiving by the light
of the lamp what had happened, accused the empress of the
murder in the most bitter terms, and entreated her husband
to inflict immediate punishment. The earl, however, thought
fit to spare the empress's life, and contented himself with dis-
missing her from his castle. The poor lady mounted her
palfrey, and had not proceeded far, when she met a robber
going to execution. Her compassion led her to ransom the
man by means of a sum of money ; and, depending on his
gratitude, she sent him before her to the next city to provide
lodging and other necessaries. All the inhabitants of the
place admired her beauty, and many persons in vain solicited
her love. It happened that a ship arrived in the harbour of
this city laden with merchandize, and the empress despatched
her servant to the captain, requesting him to attend her for
the purpose of negociating for the articles she might want.
The captain came, received her orders, and promised to send
the goods ; but he was also captivated with the beauty of the
empress, and desired her servant to follow him. He then offered the man a large reward to assist him in getting his mistress on board the vessel, that he might thus have her in his
power, and carry her away. The fellow consented ; and, telling his lady that the captain would only permit his merchandize to be examined on board the ship, prevailed on her to
accompany him thither, and she immediately became a prisoner. The vessel sailed, the commander earnestly pressed
his unlawful solicitations, and threatened death in case
of refusal. The empress requested a short respite, and ad-

dressed her prayers to heaven for assistance. A tempest instantly arose, the ship sunk to the bottom, and all perished except the empress and the captain. Each of them had clung to a piece of timber, but they were cast on different shores; and the empress, without her knowledge, on that of her own country. Here she soon found shelter in a convent, and applying herself to the study of healing the sick, soon became so skilful that her fame spread throughout the land. About this time the emperor's wicked brother had become a loathsome leper; the earl whose daughter had been killed was blind and paralytic; the treacherous servant became lame and gouty, and otherwise diseased; and the master of the ship had lost his reason. When the emperor heard of the lady's skill in curing diseases, he accompanied his brother to the convent, where the others had also come to be healed. The empress, preserving her disguise, informed them that she had no power of relieving them unless they previously, and in the presence of each other, made a full and solemn confession of their sins, and repented of them sincerely. This was accordingly done; and when the innocence of the empress was clearly manifested, to the great and mutual surprise of all the parties, she first performed her promise to the sick, and then discovered herself to the emperor. He conducted her to the palace with much joy, and they finished their days happily.

Occleve has related this story in verse from the present work,* and it is also to be found in the *Patrañas* of Timoneda.† The outline has been borrowed from one of the *Contes devots*, or miracles of the Virgin Mary.‡ The incident of the bloody knife occurs likewise in Chaucer's *Man of law's tale*, and in a story related by Gower.§

---

* MS. Reg. 17 D. vi. † Patr. 21.

‡ See Vincent de Beauvais, *Specul. historiale*, lib. viii. cap. 90, 91. Herolt, *Sermones discipuli*, par. iii. exempl. i. de mirac. b. Virginis, and Le Grand, *Fabliaux*, v. 164.

§ *Confessio Amantis*, fo. 32.

The author of this *Gesta* has been nowhere recorded; but it may be necessary on this occasion to lay before the reader part of a note prefixed to the Merchant of Venice, in which Dr. Farmer has corrected one mistake, but inadvertently fallen into another. He says, " In a MS. of *Lidgate*, I find a *tale of two marchants of Egipt* and of *Baldad, ex Gestis Romanorum*. *Leland* therefore could not be the original author *as Bishop Tanner suspected*. He lived a century after Lidgate." The inference is perfectly just; but the suspicion was not Bishop Tanner's, who has only retailed that of another writer, Richard Robinson, and he in reality seems to have regarded Leland merely as a *translator*, as will presently appear.* Dr. Farmer had been deceived by the mode of printing Robinson's words, which have much the appearance of belonging to the bishop. There would have been more probability in a conjecture that either Walleis or Bromyard might have been the fabricator of the *English Gesta*. The moralizations to Ovid's metamorphoses, which the former of these persons composed, adapt him extremely well to the purpose; but though the date of his existence is, on the whole, uncertain, he seems to have lived about half a century too early, viz. towards the beginning of the fourteenth century.† From what has already been said of Bromyard, it will appear that he was no less qualified than the other for the authorship of the work in question.

TRANSLATION.—As this work was not circulated in foreign countries, no translation of it appears to have been made in any other language than the English; and in that, not of the whole. There is a very fine manuscript in the

---

* *Biblioth. Britannico-Hibern.* p. 476.

† Dufresnoy, in his catalogue of Roman historians, has this strange article, " *Thomas Walheis* gesta Romanorum, cum applicationibus moralisatis ac mysticis. Paris, 1499, in 4." *Methode pour etudier l'histoire*, xi. 78, edit. 1772, 12mo. It remains to account for this most extraordinary assertion. It is certain that the book itself, which is the *original Gesta*, affords no evidence in support of it.

Harleian collection, written in the reign of Henry the Sixth, containing seventy stories only.* In this manuscript are several pieces by Lydgate, and some tales from Gower's *Confessio amantis*. As the *English Gesta* appears to have been extremely well known to both these writers, and also to Occleve, it is by no means improbable that the above translation was made by one or the other of them. Whether it has ever been *printed* is another question. Mr. Warton has twice mentioned an addition without date by Wynkyn de Worde;† and Dr. Farmer has also, in a note prefixed to the Merchant of Venice, referred to the same edition. It had escaped the researches of the industrious Herbert, who has only mentioned it after Mr. Warton,‡ and has in vain been sought for on the present occasion. The fortunate possessor of it may have the means of ascertaining whether it be the same as the above manuscript, by referring to the stories that have been given in the present volume at the end of the remarks on the plays of King Lear, and the Merchant of Venice.

Among the manuscripts in the Royal Library, now in the British Museum, there is one entitled " *Eupolemia; Archippus and Panoplia*; that ys to say. His good warrfare agenst Satan and his malignant spirites ; his good soldyer agenst the flesh, the lustes and concupiscences therof: And his complet harness agenst the worlde and the wickednes and wretchednes therof. Conteyning a true catalogue of all his pore paynefull laboures, translated, collected, allso printed and published and præsented in English, by authority. Shewyng allso what good Benifactors hee hathe had, for meyntenance of his sayde pore study and peine, and what hynderances hee hathe had othirwyse from the yeare of oure Savyour Christe 1576, untill this yeare 1602, for 26 yeares. Newly written

---

* No. 7333. Out of the seventy stories there are twenty-four of the additional. The whole deserve to be printed, partly as a curious monument of the English language.

† Vol. ii. p. 18, and vol. iii. p. lxxxiii.   ‡ *Typogr. antiq.* p. 233.

oute to the glory of God, honour of the Queenes most excellent
Majesty, comfort of the faythfull and convertion or subvertion
of their enemyes. By *R. Robinson*, London." This strange
work has a great number of scriptural quotations in Latin and
English, in the several margins. The dedication is here given
for its singularity. " Sacrosanctæ beatæque Trinitati, simul-
que serenissimæ ac pientiss. regis majestati sacrum. Pro re-
levio professionis Christianæ ac remedio oppressionis inhu-
manæ. Cum impressione presentis codicilli." Then follows
a dedication to Queen Elizabeth, made up of scraps from the
sacred writings, and from Tibullus, Ovid and Juvenal; next,
another to King James, entirely scriptural and in Latin verse.
Afterwards we have a list of the author's works, which he divides into three columns, the first containing their titles, the
second the allowance and printing, and the third patrons
and benevolences. Among these is the following: " 1577.
A record of ancyent historyes intituled in Latin *Gesta Romanorum*, translated (auctore ut supponitur Johane Leylando
antiquario) by mee perused corrected and bettered. Perused
further by the wardens of the stationers and printed first and
last by Thomas Easte in Aldersgate streete 6 tymes to this
yeare 1601.* cont. 21 shetes. Dedicated for 5 impressions to
the R. honorable Lady Margaret Countess of Lyneux, who
gave me for her booke 13*s*. 4*d*. besydes sale of 25 boks. Dedicated last to the wardens of the Lether sellers,† who with
others have given mee xx*s*. Dedicated last of all anno 1602
to D. Watson B. of Chichester and B. Almoner to the
Queenes Majesty who, (not so thankfull to mee as I de-

---

* This seems a mistake for 1602.

† He had already ated himself a member of their company. Of this
man little more is known than that he lived by his pen. He appears to
have assisted in a translation from *Meteranus* of an account of the civil wars
in the Netherlands, published in 1602, by Thomas Churchyard, who in
the dedication says that he was "a man more debased by many then he
merits of any, so good parts are there in the man."

served) gave me but ij*s*. for my booke dedicatory." * If Leland made any translation of the *Gesta*, it must have been
that printed by Wynkyn de Worde, which Robinson perhaps
alludes to, when he says that he had *perused bettered and
corrected* the work ; for it is very clear that the older translation in the Harleian manuscript was not known to him.

MANUSCRIPTS.—Of these many are still remaining. They
are, in general, written during the reigns of the Fifth and
Sixth Henries, though one or two appear to be as old as that
of Richard the Second. As the work was a great favourite,
many of the stories are found in some of those miscellaneous
volumes, which, in all probability, constituted the private
libraries of the monks. If these were carefully examined,
there is no doubt that many might be added to the following,
necessarily imperfect, list :—

IN THE BRITISH MUSEUM.

1.	Harl.	206. 37. 47. contains	26 stories.
2.		219.	15 stories.
3.		406.	37 stories.
4.		2270.	102 stories.
5.		3132.	81 stories.
6.		5259.	101 stories.
7.		5369.	43 stories.
8.	Sloane, 4029.		95 stories.
9.	Bibl. Reg. 8 F. vi.		

AT OXFORD.

10.	Bodl.	1986. or B. 3. 10.
11.		2760. or MS. sup. O. i. Art. 17.
12.		3826. but query ?
13.	Coll. Lincoln. lib. theolog. 60.	
14.	Magdal.	13.
15.		60.
16.	Joh. Bapt. C. 31.	
17.		G. 48.

* MS. Reg. 18, A. lxvi. In 1576, Robinson appears to have had a
licence to print, *xpmas recreacons of histories and moralizacons aplied for our
solace and consolacons*. See Herbert's typogr. antiq. p. 1023. This might
have been his then intended title for the translation of *Gesta Romanorum*.

MISCELLANEOUS.

18. Worcester Cathedral. 80.
19. Hereford Cathedral. 74.
20. MSS. Rob. Burscough, 82, in Catal. MSS. Angliæ.
21. MSS. Symonds D'Ewes, 150. Catal. MSS. Angliæ.
22. Trin. Coll. Dublin, G. 326.
23. In the author's possession. 101 stories.
24. Ibid. 50 stories.
25. Ibid. 34 stories.

PRINTED EDITIONS.—It has been already stated that the Latin copy of this work has never been printed. The following are all translations into English, No. 1 may be that ascribed to Leland; the rest are by Robinson.

1. No date, printed by Wynkyn de Worde . . . .
2. 1577. T. East. From Robinson's Eupolemia, as above.
3. 1595. T. East. 12mo. In the author's possession. Contains 43 stories.
4. No date. R. Bishop. 12mo.
5. No date. Stansby. 12mo.
6. 1648. R. Bishop. 12mo. 44 stories.
7. 1663. J. B. for A. Crook. 12mo.
8. 1668. A. J. for A. Crook. 12mo. 44 stories.
9. 1672. E. Crowch, for A. Crook. 12mo.
10. 1689. for T. Bassett, &c. 12mo. 44 stories.
11. 1703. for R. Chiswell. 12mo. The same as that of 1668.

DISSERTATION III.

ON THE ANCIENT ENGLISH MORRIS DANCE.

It is the observation of an elegant writer, that disquisitions concerning the manners and conduct of our species in early times, or indeed at any time, are always curious at least, and amusing. An investigation of the subject before us, if completely and successfully performed, would serve to fill up a chasm in the history of our popular antiquities: but this must not be expected. The culpable indifference of historical writers to private manners, and more especially to the recreations and amusements of the common people, has occasioned the difficulties that always attend inquiries of this nature, many of which are involved in impenetrable darkness; whilst others can only receive illustration from detached and scattered facts, accompanied by judicious inferences and opinions.

It will be necessary, in the first place, to attempt some definition of what the Morris dance originally was: this may be best accomplished by the aid of etymology, which will generally be found a faithful guide, when managed with discretion. It seems, however, on the present occasion to have been too slightly treated in a work of considerable labour and ingenuity, the author of which has expressed an opinion that the Morris dance originated from that part of the ancient ceremony of the feast of fools, in which certain persons habited like buffoons, with bells, &c., joined in a dance. He then proceeds as follows: " The word *Morris* applied to the dance is usually derived from *Morisco,* which in the Spanish lan-

AN ANCIENT MORRIS DANCE.

Published by T. Lloyd, Cheapside. Septr. 1834.

guage signifies a *Moor*, as if the dance had been taken from the
Moors : but I cannot help considering this as a mistake ; for
it appears to me that the *Morisco* or Moor dance is exceedingly
different from the morris-dance formerly practised in this
country ; it being performed with the castanets or rattles, at
the ends of the fingers, and not with bells attached to various
parts of the dress.* I shall not pretend to investigate the
derivation of the word *Morris*; though probably it might be
found at home : it seems, however, to have been applied to
the dance in modern times, and, I trust, long after the festival to which it originally belonged was done away and had
nearly sunk into oblivion."†

Now if the term in question had been *exclusively* used in
England, there would have been some weight in these observations ; but when we find it adopted by most of the European nations to express a dance, the origin of which both
English and foreign glossaries uniformly ascribe to the Moors,
we must pause at least before we consent to abandon the
only clue that presents itself to assist us. The genuine
Moorish or Morisco dance was, no doubt, very different from
the European *morris*; but there is scarcely an instance in
which a fashion or amusement that has been borrowed from
a distant region has not in its progress through other countries undergone such alterations as have much obscured its
origin. This remark may be exemplified in chess and cards,
which, beyond all doubt, were invented in India or China,
and spread, by means of the Arabians, progressively throughout Spain, Italy, France, England, and the north of Europe.
But the above writer has cited a passage from the play of
Variety, 1649, in which *Spanish Morisco* the is mentioned ;
and this not only shows the legitimacy of the term *morris*, but
that the real and uncorrupted Moorish dance was to be found

---

* This will hereafter appear to be a mistake.
† Strutt's *Sports and pastimes of the people of England*, p. 171.

in Spain, where it still continues to delight both natives and strangers under the name of the *fandango*. It may be like-wise remarked, that the exquisitely pretty music to this lively dance is undoubtedly Moorish.* The Spanish morris was also danced at puppet-shows by a person habited like a Moor, with castagnets; and Junius [Du Jon] has informed us that the morris dancers usually blackened their faces with soot, that they might the better pass for Moors.†

Some have sought the origin of the morris in the *Pyrrhica saltatio* of the ancients, a military dance which seems to have been invented by the Greeks, and was afterwards adopted by the Salii or priests of Mars. This continued to be practised for many ages, till it became corrupted by figures and gesti-culations foreign to its original purpose. Such a dance was that well known in France and Italy by the name of the dance of fools or *Matachins*, who were habited in short jackets with gilt-paper helmets, long streamers tied to their shoulders, and bells to their legs. They carried in their hands a sword and buckler, with which they made a clashing noise, and per-formed various quick and sprightly evolutions.‡ A species of this sword dance by some means or other got introduced into England, where it has generally and unaccountably been

* Hist. of Musick, vol. iv. 388, by Sir John Hawkins, who was clearly of opinion that the morris dance was derived from the Moors.

† Etymologicum Anglicanum. In further corroboration of this deduction of the morris dance, the following words may be adduced; MORESQUE a kind of grotesque painting, sometimes called Arabesque, and used in em-broidery and damasking. MORISCLE, and MOURICLE, a gold coin used in Spain by the Moors, and called in the barbarous Latin of the fourteenth century *morikinus*. See Carpentier, *Suppl. ad glossar. Ducangian.* v. *Mori-kinus*. MORRIS WAX, called likewise *mores wax*, in the *Garbelling of spices*, 1594, 4to. To these the *morris-pike* may perhaps be added. It is pro-bable that the English terms *morris* and *morice* have been corrupted from *mores*, the older and more genuine orthography.

‡ Tabourot *Orchesographie*, 1589, 4to, p. 97, where the several postures of this dance are described and represented. The Pyrrhic dance appears to have travelled from Greece into the north. See Olaus Magnus, *De gentibus septentrionalibus*, lib. xv. c. 23, 24, 25, 26, 27.

exhibited by women, whose dexterous feats of tumbling and dancing with swords at fairs, and in the minor theatres, are still remembered by many persons.* A very learned writer, speaking of the *Pyrrhica saltatio,* informs us, that " The common people in many parts of England still practise what they call a *Morisco dance,* in a wild manner, and as it were in armour, at proper intervals striking upon each others staves, &c."† This might be found on inquiry to differ from the common morris, and to be a mixture of the old Pyrrhic and Moorish dances. Such a one may be alluded to in *The second part of King Henry the Sixth,* Act III. Scene 1,

> " . . . . . I have seen him
> Caper upright like a *wild Morisco,*
> Shaking the bloody darts, as he his bells."

Before we proceed to an examination of the more immediate object of this essay, the English morris, it may be as well to lay before the reader a short description of the *uncorrupted morris dance,* as practised in France about the beginning of the sixteenth century. It has been preserved by Tabourot, the oldest and by far the most curious writer of any other on the art of dancing.‡ He relates, that in his youthful days it was the custom in good societies for a boy to come into the hall, when supper was finished, with his face blackened, his forehead bound with white or yellow taffeta, and

---

* It is remarkable that the same practice should be found in the island of Ceylon. Knox tells us that " A woman takes two naked swords, under each arm one, and another she holds in her mouth, then fetcheth a run and turns clean over, and never touches the ground till she lights on her feet again holding all her swords fast."—*Hist. of Ceylon,* p. 99.

† Wise's *Enquiries concerning the first inhabitants, language, &c. of Europe,* p. 51.

‡ Jean Tabourot, canon and official of the cathedral of Lengres, published his *Orchesographie et traicté en forme de dialogue par lequel toutes personnes peuvent facilement apprendre et practiquer l'honneste exercice des dances,* 1589, 4to, under the anagrammatized name of *Thoinot Arbeau.* He died in 1595, at the age of 66. His work is equally curious and uncommon.

bells tied to his legs. He then proceeded to dance the *Mo-risco,* the whole length of the hall, backwards and forwards to the great amusement of the company.* He hints that the bells might have been borrowed from the *crotali* of the ancients in the Pyrrhic dance. He then describes the more modern morris dance, which was performed by striking the ground with the forepart of the feet; but, as this was found to be too fatiguing, the motion was afterwards confined to the heel, the toes being kept firm, by which means the dancer con-trived to rattle his bells with more effect. He adds that this mode of dancing fell into disuse, as it was found to bring on gouty complaints. This is the air to which the last-mentioned morris was performed.

It has been supposed that the morris dance was first brought into England in the time of Edward the Third, when John of Gaunt returned from Spain; † but it is much more pro-bable that we had it from our Gallic neighbours, or even from

---

* But the French morris can be traced to a much earlier period. Among other instances of the prodigality of Messire Gilles de Raiz, in 1440, *mor-ris dancers* are specified. Lobineau, *Hist. de Bretagne,* ii. 1069. In the accounts of Olivier le Roux, treasurer to Arthur III. duke of Bretagne in 1457, is this article: " à certains compaignons qui avoient fait plusieurs esbatemens de *morisques* et autres jeux devant le duc à Tours, vi. escus."— Id. 1205. At a splendid feast given by Gaston de Foix at Vendôme in 1458, " foure yong laddes and a damosell attired like savages daunced (by good direction) an excellent *Morisco,* before the assembly."—Favines *Theater of honour,* p. 345; and see Carpentier, *Suppl. ad glossar. Ducan-gian.* v. *Morikinus.* Coquillart, a French poet, who wrote about 1470, says that the Swiss danced the *Morisco* to the beat of the drum. *Œuvres,* p. 127.

† Peck's *Memoirs of Milton,* 135. What this writer has added on the subject of the morris dance is not very interesting; but he is certainly mis-taken in his explanation of *five, seven,* or *nine men's morris.*

the Flemings. Few if any vestiges of it can be traced beyond
the reign of Henry the Seventh; about which time, and particularly in that of Henry the Eighth, the churchwardens' accounts in several parishes afford materials that throw much
light on the subject, and show that the morris dance made
a very considerable figure in the parochial festivals. A late
valuable writer has remarked that in some places the May-
games of Robin Hood were nothing more than a morris
dance, in which *Robin Hood, Little John, Maid Marian,* and
Friar Tuck, were the principal personages, the others being
a clown or fool, the hobby-horse, the taborer, and the dancers,
who were more or less numerous;* but this seems to be a
mistake. The May-games of Robin Hood appear to have
been principally instituted for the encouragement of archery,
and were generally accompanied by morris dancers, who,
nevertheless, formed but a subordinate part of the ceremony.
It is by no means clear that at any time Robin Hood and his
companions were *constituent* characters in the morris. There
were, besides, May-games of a more simple nature, being
merely dances round a May-pole, by the lads and lasses of
the village, and the undoubted remains of the Roman Flo-
ralia.† We find also that other festivals and ceremonies had
their morris, as Holy-Thursday; the Whitsun-ales; the
bride-ales, or weddings,‡ and a sort of play or pageant called
the lord of misrule. Sheriffs too had their morris dance.§
The reader may be amused with the following account of the
lord of misrule, as it contains a description of an attendant
morris. It has been fortunately handed down to us by a puritanical writer of the reign of Elizabeth, whose loud ravings

---

* Ritson's *Robin Hood,* I. cii.

† See particularly Stubbes's *Anatomie of abuses,* p. 109, edit. 1595, 4to.

‡ In Laneham's *Letter from Kenilworth or Killingworth castle,* a bride-
ale is described, in which mention is made of "a lively Moris dauns, according too the auncient manner: six dauncerz, Mawdmarion, and the
fool."

§ See Stowe's *Survay of London,* 1618, 4to, p. 161.

against the fashionable excesses of his countrymen have contributed to furnish posterity with the completest information
respecting a considerable portion of the manners and customs
of the above period that is any where to be found. These
are his words : " First, all the wilde heads of the parish,
flocking togither, chuse them a graund captaine (of mischiefe)
whome they innoble with the title of *my Lord of misrule*,
and him they crowne with great solemnitie, and adopt for
their king. This king annoynted, chooseth foorth twentie,
fourtie, threescore or a hundred lustie guttes like to himselfe
to waite upon his lordly majesty, and to guarde his noble person. Then every one of these his men, he investeth with his
liveries of greene, yellow, or some other light wanton collour.
And as though that were not (bawdy) gawdy ynough, I should
say, they bedecke themselves with scarffes, ribbons and laces
hanged all over with golde ringes, precious stones, and other
jewels : this done, they tie about either legge twentie or fourtie
belles, with rich handkerchiefe in their handes, and sometimes laide a crosse over their shoulders and neckes, borrowed
for the most part of their pretie *Mopsies* and loving *Bessies*,
for bussing them in the darke. Thus all things set in order,
then have they their hobby-horses, their dragons and other
antiques, togither with their baudie *pipers*, and thundering
drummers, to strike up the *Devils Daunce* withall : then
martch this heathen company towards the church and church-
yarde, their pypers pypyng, their drummers thundering, their
stumpes dauncing, their belles iyngling, their handkercheefes
fluttering about their heades like madde men, their hobbie
horses, and other monsters skirmishing amongst the throng :
and in this sorte they goe to the church (though the minister
be at prayer or preaching) dauncing and swinging their hand-
kerchiefes over their heades in the church like Devils incarnate,
with such a confused noise, that no man can heare his owne
voyce. Then the foolish people they looke, they stare, they
laugh, they fleere, and mount upon formes and pewes, to see

these goodly pageants solemnized in this sort. Then after
this about the church they goe againe and againe, and so
foorth into the church yard, where they have commonly
their sommer haules, their bowers, arbours, and banquetting
houses set up, wherein they feast, banquet, and daunce all
that day, and (peradventure) all that night too. And thus these
terrestrial *furies* spend the Sabboth day. Another sort of
fantasticall fooles bring to these helhoundes (the Lord of misrule and his complices) some bread, some good ale, some new
cheese, some olde cheese, some custardes, some cracknels, some
cakes, some flaunes, some tartes, some creame, some meat,
some one thing, some another; but if they knewe that as
often as they bringe anye to the maintenance of these exe-
crable pastimes, they offer sacrifice to the Devill and Sathanas,
they would repent and withdrawe their handes, which God
graunt they may." * Another declaimer of the like kind,
speaking of May games and morris dances, thus holds forth :·
" The abuses which are committed in your may-games are
infinite. The first whereof is this, that you doe use to attyre
in womans apparrell whom you doe most commenly call *may-
marrions,* whereby you infringe that straight commaundement
whiche is given in Deut. xxii. 5, that men must not put on
womens apparrell for feare of enormities. Nay I myself have
seene in a may game a troupe, the greater part wherof hath
been men, and yet have they been attyred so like unto women,
that theyr faces being hidde (as they were indeede) a man
coulde not discerne them from women. The second abuse,
which of all other is the greatest, is this, that it hath been
toulde that your morice dauncers have daunced naked in
nettes : what greater entisement unto naughtines could have
been devised ? The third abuse is, that you (because you will
loose no tyme) doe use commonly to runne into woodes in
the night time, amongst maidens, to fet bowes, in so muche

* Stubbes's *Anatomie of abuses,* p. 107.

as I have hearde of tenne maidens which went to fet May,
and nine of them came home with childe."* He seems likewise to allude to a character of the *Devil* in the May games,
of which no mention is elsewhere made.

In the course of time these several recreations were blended
together so as to become almost indistinguishable. It is,
however, very certain that the May games of Robin Hood, accompanied with the morris, were at first a distinct ceremony
from the simple morris, which when Warner lived was celebrated about the season of Easter, and before the May games:
he thus speaks of them:

" At Paske begun our Morrise, and ere Penticost our May."†

It is probable that when the practice of archery declined,
the May games of *Robin Hood* were discontinued, and that
the morris dance was transferred to the celebration of Whitsuntide, either as connected with the Whitsun ales, or as a
separate amusement. In the latter instance it appears to have
retained one or two of the characters in the May pageants;
but no uniformity was or possibly could be observed, as the
arrangement would vary in different places according to the
humour or convenience of the parties.

The painted glass window belonging to George Tollett,
Esq., at Betley, in Staffordshire, exhibits, in all probability,
the most curious as well as the oldest representation of an
English May game and morris dance, that is any where to be
found.‡ The learned possessor of this curiosity, to whom
the readers of Shakspeare are much indebted not only for this,
but for many other valuable communications, has supposed
that the window might have been painted in the youthful

---

* Fetherston's *Dialogue agaynst light, lewde, and lascivious dauncing,*
1582, 12mo, sign. D. 7. See a passage to the same purpose in Northbrooke's *Treatise against dicing, dancing, &c.* 1597, 4to, fo. 68 b.

† Albion's *England,* 1612, p. 121.

‡ Steevens's *Shakspeare,* at the end of the play of *King Henry IV.
part I.*

days of Henry the Eighth, when he delighted in May games; but it must be observed that the dresses and costume of some of the figures are certainly of an older period, and may, without much hazard, be pronounced to belong to the reign of Edward the Fourth. Among other proofs that could be adduced, it will be sufficient to compare it with the annexed print of another morris dance. This is a copy from an exceedingly scarce engraving on copper by Israel Von Mecheln, or Meckenen, so named from the place of his nativity, a German village on the confines of Flanders, in which latter country this artist appears chiefly to have resided; and therefore in most of his prints we may observe the Flemish costume of his time. From the pointed shoes that we see in one of the figures it must have been executed between the year 1460, and 1470; about which latter period the broadtoed shoes came into fashion in France and Flanders. It seems to have been intended as a pattern for goldsmiths' work, probably a cup or tankard.

The artist, in a fancy representation of foliage, has introduced several figures belonging to a Flemish May game morris, consisting of the lady of the May, the fool, the piper, two morris dancers with bells and streamers, and four other dancing characters, for which appropriate names will not easily be found. The similitude between some of the figures in this print and others in Mr. Tollett's window, is very striking, and shows that the period of execution, as to both, was nearly the same. One objection to this opinion will, no doubt, present itself to the skilful spectator, and that is the shape of the letters which form the inscription A MERY MAY on the pane of glass No. 8. These are comparatively modern, and cannot be carried further back than the time of Elizabeth; but this will be accounted for hereafter.

The above curious *painting* has furnished the means of ascertaining some of the personages of which the May games and morris consisted at the time of its execution. To trace their original forms and numbers, or the progressive changes they underwent, with any degree of accuracy, would be perhaps impossible; because not only the materials for such an attempt are extremely few, but a variety of circumstances contributed to constitute their differences even during the same period. Wherever we turn, nothing but irregularity presents itself. Sometimes we have a lady of the May, *simply*, with a friar Tuck; and in later times a Maid Marian remained without even a Robin Hood or a friar. But consistency is not to be looked for on these occasions, when we find, as has been remarked, that the May games, those of Robin Hood, the ales, and the morris dances, were blended together as convenience or caprice happened to dictate.*

The several characters that seem in more ancient times to have composed the May game and morris were the following: Robin Hood, Little John, Friar Tuck, Maid Marian the queen or lady of the May, the fool, the piper, and several morris dancers habited, as it appears, in various modes. Afterwards a hobby horse and a dragon were added. To avoid the confusion that might otherwise ensue, it will be best to speak of each character by itself.

I. Robin Hood. The history of this celebrated outlaw has been so ably and ingeniously treated by Mr. Ritson, and every fact that relates to him so minutely developed, that it will be long before any novelty shall be discovered of suffi-

---

* There is a remarkable instance of the corruption that has been gradually introduced into popular ceremonies, in the celebration of the gunpowder-plot; in which, formerly, Guy Faux was ignominiously carted, in company with the Pope and the Devil, all of whom were afterwards consigned to the flames: whereas at present we have only the image of a fellow, or sometimes a real boy bedizened with gilded rags, ruffles, and powdered periwig, under the appellation of *Poor Guy*, for whom the attendants seem to crave charity. The Pope had been long dismissed by proclamation or act of parliament; and the Devil is probably forgotten by some, or become an object of too much terror with others to be sported with.

cient importance to deserve attention. It appears that in the May game he sometimes carried a painted standard.*

II. LITTLE JOHN. The faithful companion of Robin Hood, but of whom little that is not fabulous has been handed down to us. He is first mentioned, together with Robin Hood, by Fordun the Scotish historian, who wrote in the fourteenth century, and who speaks of the celebration of the story of these persons in the *theatrical performances* of his time, and of the minstrels' songs relating to them, which he says the common people preferred to all *other romances.*†

III. FRIAR TUCK. There is no very ancient mention of this person, whose history is very uncertain. Drayton has thus recorded him, among other companions of Robin Hood:

> " Of *Tuck the merry friar* which many a sermon made
> In praise of Robin Hood, his outlaws and their trade." ‡

He is known to have formed one of the characters in the May games during the reign of Henry the Eighth, and had been probably introduced into them at a much earlier period. From the occurrence of this name on other occasions, there is good reason for supposing that it was a sort of generic appellation for any friar, and that it originated from the dress of the order, which was *tucked* or folded at the waist by means of a cord or girdle. Thus Chaucer, in his prologue to the *Canterbury tales,* says of the Reve;

> " *Tucked* he was, as is a frere aboute :"

---

* Churchwardens' accounts at Kingston, in Lysons's *Environs of London,* vol. i. p. 227. The learned author of this interesting work has remarked that he had found no entries at Kingston relating to the May games, after the 29 Hen. VIII.; but they certainly continued, as parochial ceremonies, in other places to a much later period. In the churchwardens' accounts of Great Marlow it appears that dresses for the morris dance were lent to neighbouring parishes so late as 1629. See Langley's *Antiquities of Desborough,* 4to, 1797.

† Fordun's *Scotichronicon,* 1759, folio, tom. ii. p. 104.

‡ Polyolbion, song xxvi.

And he describes one of the friars in the Sompnour's tale :

" With scrippe and tipped staff, *ytucked* hie."

This friar maintained his situation in the morris under the reign of Elizabeth, being thus mentioned in Warner's *Albion's England* :

" Tho Robin Hood, liell John, *frier Tucke* and Marian deftly play : "

but is not heard of afterwards. In Ben Jonson's *Masque of gipsies,* the clown takes notice of his omission in the dance.*

IV. MAID MARIAN. None of the materials that constitute the more authentic history of Robin Hood, prove the existence of such a character in the shape of his mistress. There is a pretty French pastoral drama of the eleventh or twelfth century, entitled *Le jeu du berger et de la bergere,* in which the principal characters are *Robin* and *Marion,* a shepherd and shepherdess. Mr. Warton thought that our English Marian might be illustrated from this composition ; but Mr. Ritson is unwilling to assent to this opinion, on the ground that the French Robin and Marion " are not the Robin and Marian of Sherwood." Yet Mr. Warton probably meant no more than that the name of Marian had been suggested from the above drama, which was a great favourite among the common people in France, and performed much about the season at which the May games were celebrated in England. The great intercourse between the countries might have been the means of importing this name amidst an infinite variety of other matters ; and there is indeed no other mode of accounting for the introduction of a name which never occurs in the page of English history.† We have seen that the story of Robin Hood was, at a very early period, of a dramatic cast ; and it was perfectly natural that a

* Ben Jonson's *Works,* 1756, vol. vi. p. 93.

† *Marian,* or as it is more frequently written *Marion,* is not formed, as some French writers have supposed, from Mary and Ann, but more probably from *Mariamne* the wife of Herod, whose name seems borrowed from that

principal character should be transferred from one drama to another. It might be thought likewise that the English Robin deserved his Marian as well as the other. The circumstance of the French Marian being acted by a boy contributes to support the above opinion; the part of the English character having been personated, though not always, in like manner. Little, if any, stress can be laid on the authority of an old play cited by Mr. Steevens to prove that " *Maid Marian* was originally a name assumed by *Matilda,* the daughter of Robert Lord Fitzwater, while Robin Hood remained in a state of outlawry." * This is rather to be considered as a dramatic fiction, designed to explain a character the origin of which had been long forgotten.

Maid Marian not only officiated as the paramour of Robin Hood in the May games, but as the *queen or lady of the May,* who seems to have been introduced long before the games of Robin Hood. In the isle of Man they not only elected a queen of May, but likewise a queen of winter.† Gatherings for the May lady, as anciently for Robin Hood, were lately kept up at Cambridge, but in a corrupted form, the real occasion of this ceremony being, in all probability, quite unknown to the gatherers. There can be no doubt that the queen of

---

of Miriam מרים the prophetess, the sister of Aaron. Miriam is said to come from a Syrian word signifying *mistress,* or from מרר *marar, bitterness.* The name of *Mary,* evidently contracted from *Miriam* or *Mariamne,* does not occur till the time of the daughter of Joachim and Anne, the mother of Christ, at which period we find other *Maries* in the New Testament. It is remarkable that *Maria,* from Marius, should not occur among the Roman names of women, in like manner as we have Julia, Cornelia, Fulvia, Proba, Valeria, &c., from Julius, Cornelius, Fulvius, Probus, and Valerius. The facetious and eccentric Edmund Gayton, in the dedication to his *Festivous notes on Don Quixote,* speaks of *Mayd Myriam.* He perhaps imagined that the morris dance had been suggested by the prophetess and her dancing women with their timbrels.

    * Steevens's *Shaksp.* viii. 530.

    † Waldron's *History of the Isle of Man,* 12mo, p. 95, where he has described the mock battle between the queens.

the May is the legitimate representative of the Goddess Flora in the Roman festival.

The introduction of Robin Hood into the celebration of May probably suggested the addition of a *king* or *lord of the May*. In the year 1306 Robert Bruce caused himself to be crowned at Scone, and a second time by the hands of his mistress, the adulterous wife of the earl of Bowhan, who changed his name to David. It is reported that he said to his own wife on this occasion, " Yesterday we were but earl and countess, to day we are king and queen ;" to which she replied, " True, you are now a *summer king*, but you may not chance to be a winter one." Matthew of Westminster has recorded this fact, and Holinshed, who copies him, makes the lady say, that " she feared they should prove but as *a summer king and queen, such as in country townes the yong folks chose for sport to dance about may-poles.*" In 1557 there was a May game in Fenchurch-street, with a *Lord and Lady of the May*, and a morris dance.* Both these characters are introduced in a morris in Fletcher's play of *The two noble kinsmen*, Act. III.; and, in the *Knight of the burning pestle*, a grocer's apprentice personates a lord of the May dressed out in " scarves, feathers, and rings." He is made to deliver a speech from the conduit to the populace, of which this is a part:

> " London, to thee I do present the merry month of May,
> Let each true subject be content to hear me what I say :
> For from the top of conduit-head, as plainly may appear,
> I will both tell my name to you, and wherefore I came here.
> My name is *Rafe*, by due descent, though not ignoble I,
> Yet far inferiour to the flock of gracious grocery.
> And by the common counsel of my fellows in the Strand,
> With gilded staff, and crossed skarfe, the *May lord* here I stand."

A lord and lady are still preserved in some places where the Whitsun-ales continue to be celebrated, and perhaps in other morrises during the season of May.

---

* Strype's *Eccl. memorials*, iii. 376.

To return to Maid Marian.—She was usually dressed according to the fashion of the time, as we may collect from the figures of her in Mr. Tollett's window, and Israel's engraving. In both the kirtle and petticoat are alike; and the pendent veil is supported by the hand. The English figure holds a flower, and has a fancy coronet as *queen of the May*. The other has apparently an apple in her hand, and her steeple head-dress is what was actually worn in the middle of the fifteenth century by queens and ladies of high rank. Barnaby Rich, who wrote in the reigns of Elizabeth and James I., inveighing against the foppery of men's apparel, exclaims, " And from whence commeth this wearing, and this embroidering of long locks, this curiosity that is used amongst men, in frizeling and curling of their haire, this gentlewoman-like starcht bands, so be-edged and belaced, *fitter for Maid Marion in a Moris dance*, then for him that hath either that spirit or courage that shold be in a gentleman ? " *

It appears that the Lady of the May was sometimes carried in procession on men's shoulders; for Stephen Batman, speaking of the Pope and his ceremonies, states that he is carried on the backs of four deacons, "after the maner of carying whytepot queenes in Western May games."† Her usual gait was nice and affected.‡ Thus in the description of the family visit to the royal guest, in the old ballad of *The miller of Mansfield*:

> " And so they jetted down towards the king's hall:
> The merry old miller, with his hands on his side;
> His wife, like Maid Marian did *mince* at that tide."

But although the May-lady was originally a character of

* The honestie of this age, 1615, 4to, p. 35.

† What these ladies exactly were is not easy to comprehend. *Whitepot* in old cookery was a kind of custard, made in a crust or dish with cream, eggs, pulse of apples, sugar, spices, and sippets of *white* or manchet bread. It is possible therefore that Maid Marian, being occasionally personated by a kitchen malkin or cook wench, obtained the title of a *white-pot queen*.

‡ Golden books of the leaden Goddes, 1577, 4to, fo. 30.

some delicacy and importance, she appears to have afterwards
declined in both respects. In the time of Elizabeth she was
usually represented by some smooth-faced and effeminate
youth.* Falstaff tells the hostess, that " for *womanhood*
Maid Marian may be the Deputy's wife of the ward to her;"
meaning perhaps that she was as masculine in her appearance
as the country clown who personated Maid Marian: and in
Fletcher's *Monsieur Thomas*, Dorothea desires her brother to
conduct himself with more gentleness towards his mistress,
unless he would choose to marry *Malkyn the May Lady*;
another allusion to the degraded state of Maid Marian, who
is here assimilated to a vulgar drudge or scullion both in
name and condition. But during the whole of her existence
mirth and gaiety were her constant companions. The translator of *The hospitall of incurable fooles*, 1600, 4to, speaking
of Acco, the old woman who became mad on beholding her
ugliness in a mirror, says that " one while shee could be *as
merrie as Maid Marrian.*" Nor was this character, even in
later times, *uniformly* vulgar. Every one will call to mind
Nicholas Breton's pretty sonnet of *Phyllida and Corydon*,
where the shepherdess,

> " . . . . with garlands gay
> Was made the Lady of the Maye."

V. The Fool. This character in the morris was the same,
in point of dress, as the domestic buffoon of his time. In
Mr. Tollett's window he has additional bells tied to his arms
and ancles as a morris dancer, but is, in other respects, the
English fool of the fifteenth century. Yet the habit of this
eccentric person was not the same in all countries, nor even
uniform in the same country. Accordingly, he is very differently accoutred in the Flemish print. He has a cap or
hood with asses' ears, and a row of bells for the crest; in his
left hand he carries a bauble, and over his right arm hangs a

---

* Greene's *Quip for an upstart courtier*, sig. D. 3.

cloth or napkin. He wears behind what seems intended for a purse or wallet, with which the fool in the old German prints is generally exhibited. It is certain that there was only one fool in the morris; and therefore Mr. Steevens and Mr. Tollett have erred in supposing the figure No. 1, in the window, to be the *Bavian fool with the bib*. The former gentleman had apparently misconceived the following passage in Fletcher's *Two noble kinsmen*,

> " . . . . and next the fool,
> The *Bavian*, with long tail and eke long tool."

Here are not *two* fools described. The construction is, " next comes the fool, i. e. the Bavian fool," &c. This might have been the *idiot* fool, and so denominated from his wearing a bib, in French *bavon*,* because he drivelled. Thus in *Bonduca*, Act V., Decius talks of a " dull *slavering* fool." The tricks of the Bavian, his tumbling and barking like a dog, suggested perhaps by the conduct of Robert the Devil when disguised as a fool in his well known and once popular romance, were peculiar to the morris dance described in *The two noble kinsmen*, which has some other characters that seem to have been introduced for stage effect, and not to have belonged to the genuine morris. The tail was the fox tail that was sometimes worn by the morris fool; and the long tool will be best understood by referring to the cut of the idiot in the *genuine* copy of the *dance of death* usually, though improperly, ascribed to Holbein, and by reflecting on some peculiar properties and qualifications of the idiot character.

---

* *Bavon* or *bavette*, is from *bave*, spittle. Hence the middle age Latin term for a fool, *bavosus*. See Ducange *Gloss*. This is a very plausible etymology, and might stand well enough by itself; but it must not be concealed that in some of the Northern languages *Bavian* signifies a monkey or *baboon*. Whether Fletcher, who seems the only writer that has made use of this word, applied it to the fool in question on account of the *monkey tricks* that he played, remains to be ascertained. If we could discover the names of the characters in a French, Dutch, or German morris of this time, some light might be thrown on the subject.

What Mr. Tollett has termed a *bib* was in fact no uncommon part of the male dress in the fifteenth century. Some of the contemporary figures of the Beverley minstrels are so habited, as well as others in the representation of the Whitsun ale at Cirencester.* Whatever character the supposed Bavian of the window was, he is also found in the print by Israel on the left hand of the fool, not only in the same habit, but with his hands and feet precisely in similar attitudes. There is no doubt that the morris dance was in some respects a sort of *chironomy*; and Higgins, the English editor of Junius's *Nomenclator*, has actually translated the word *chironomia* by "the morrise dance."† In the absence of some of the other characters of the morris dance, the exertions of the fool appear to have been increased, as we learn from Ben Jonson's *Entertainment at Althrope*:

> " But see the hobby-horse is forgot.
> Foole, it must be your lot,
> To supply his want with faces
> And some other buffon graces.
> You know how."—

Coryat relates that near Montreuil he saw " *a Whitsuntide foole* disguised like a foole, wearing a long coate, wherein there were many severall peeces of cloth of divers colours, at the corners whereof there hanged the tailes of squirrels : he bestowed a little peece of plate, wherein was expressed the effigies of the Virgin Mary, upon every one that gave him money : for he begged money of all travellers for the benefite of the parish church."‡ The romance of *The spiritual Quixote* has a morris fool with a fox's tail depending from his cap, and a sheep bell attached to his hinder parts. In the modern morris dance the fool is continued, but his real character and

---

* See Carter's *Specimens of ancient sculpture and painting*, vol. ii. pl. xiii. Nos. 5 and 13, and pl. xxxvi.

† Edit. 1585, 12mo, p. 299. See likewise the article *chironomus* in p. 521.

‡ Coryat's *Crudities*, 1611, 4to, p. 9.

dress appear to have been long since forgotten. In some places he is called *the Squire*.

VI. THE PIPER. Sometimes called Tom Piper, an obvious and necessary attendant on a morris, and who requires very little illustration. Mr. Steevens has already referred to Drayton for the mention of him; and Spenser, in his third eclogue, speaking of the rimes of bad poets, observes that

" *Tom Piper* makes as little melodie;"

whence we are to infer that his music was not usually of the very best kind. The resemblance, as to attitude and dress, between the figures of this character in Mr. Tollett's painting and the Flemish print, is remarkable. In both we have the sword and feather. What Mr. Tollett has termed his *silver shield* seems a mistake for the lower part or flap of his stomacher.

VII. THE HOBBY-HORSE; of which the earliest vestige now remaining is in the painted window at Betley. It has been already observed that he was often omitted in the morris. During the reign of Elizabeth the Puritans made considerable havoc among the May-games, by their preachings and invectives. Poor Maid Marian was assimilated to the whore of Babylon; friar Tuck was deemed a remnant of Popery, and the Hobby-horse an impious and Pagan superstition; and they were at length most completely put to the rout as the bitterest enemies of religion. King James's book of sports restored the lady and the hobby-horse : but during the commonwealth they were again attacked by a new set of fanatics; and, together with the whole of the May festivities, the Whitsunales, &c., in many parts of England degraded. At the restoration they were once more revived.* The allusions to the

* Yet, in the reign of Charles the Second, Thomas Hall, another puritanical writer, published his *Funebria Floræ, the Downfall of May-games*, 1661, 4to, in which, amidst a great deal of silly declamation against these innocent amusements, he maintains that "Papists are forward to give the people May-poles, and the Pope's holiness with might and main keeps up his

omission of the Hobby-horse are frequent in the old plays, and the line

"For O, for O, the hobby-horse is forgot,"

is termed by Hamlet *an epitaph*, which Mr. Theobald supposed, with great probability, to have been satirical. The following extract from a scene in Beaumont and Fletcher's *Women pleased*, Act IV., will best show the sentiments of the puritans on this occasion, and which the author has deservedly ridiculed:

HOB.

Surely I will dance no more, 'tis most ridiculous,
I find my wife's instructions now mere verities,
My learned wife's, she often hath pronounc'd to me
My safety; *Bomby*, defie these sports, thou art damn'd else.
This beast of Babylon I will never back again,
His pace is sure prophane, and his lewd wi-hees,
The sons of Hymyn and Gymyn, in the wilderness.

FAR.

Fie neighbour *Bomby*, in your fits again?
Your zeal sweats, this is not careful, neighbour,
The *Hobby-horse* is a seemly *Hobby-horse*.

HOB.

The beast is an unseemly, and a lewd beast,
And got at Rome by the Pope's coach-horses,
His mother was the mare of ignorance.

SOTO.

Cobler thou ly'st, and thou wert a thousand coblers
His mother was an honest mare, and a mare of good credit,
Scorn'd any coach-horse the Pope had; thou art foolish,
And thy blind zeal makes thee abuse the beast.

---

superstitious festivals as a prime prop of his tottering kingdome." That "by these sensual sports and carnal-flesh-pleasing wayes of wine, women, dancing, revelling, &c., he hath gained more souls, than by all the tortures and cruel persecutions that he could invent." He adds, "What a sad account will these libertines have to make, when the Lord shall demand of them, where wast thou such a night? why, my Lord, I was with the prophane rabble, stealing May-poles; and where wast thou such a day? why, my Lord, I was drinking, dancing, dallying, ranting, whoring, carousing, &c."

Hob.

I do defie thee and thy foot-cloth too,
And tell thee to thy face, this prophane riding
I feel it in my conscience, and I dare speak it,
This unedified ambling hath brought a scourge upon us.

Far.

Will you dance no more, neighbour?

Hob.

Surely no,
Carry the beast to his crib : I have renounc'd him
And all his works.

Soto.

Shall the Hobby-horse be forgot then?
The hopeful Hobby-horse, shall he lye founder'd ?

Hob.

I cry out on 't,
'Twas the forerunning sin brought in those tilt-staves,
They brandish 'gainst the church, the Devil calls *May poles.*

Soto.

Take up your horse again, and girth him to ye,
And girth him handsomely, good neighbour *Bomby.*

Hob.

I spit at him.

Soto.

Spit in the horse-face, cobler?
Thou out-of-tune psalm-singing slave; spit in his visnomy ?

Hob.

I spit again, and thus I rise against him :
Against this beast, that signify'd destruction,
Foreshew'd i'th' falls of monarchies.

Soto.

I'th' face of him?
Spit such another spit, by this hand cobler,
I'll make ye set a new piece o' your nose there;
Take't up I say, and dance without more bidding,
And dance as you were wont; you have been excellent,
And are still but for this new nicety,
And your wife's learned lectures; take up the Hobby-horse,
Come, 'tis a thing thou hast lov'd with all thy heart, Bomby,
And wouldst do still, but for the round-breech'd brothers.
You were not thus in the morning; take 't up I say,
Do not delay, but do it : you know I am officer,

And I know 'tis unfit all these good fellows
Should wait the cooling of your zealous porridge;
Chuse whether you will dance, or have me execute;
I'll clap your neck i'th' stocks, and there I'll make ye
Dance a whole day, and dance with these at night too.
You mend old shoes well, mend your old manners better,
And suddenly see you leave off this sincereness,
This new hot batch, borrowed from some brown baker,
Some learned brother, or I'll so bait ye for 't,
Take it quickly up.

Hob.

I take my persecution,
And thus I am forc'd a by-word to my brethren.

The Hobby-horse was represented by a man equipped with as much pasteboard as was sufficient to form the head and hinder parts of a horse, the quadrupedal defects being concealed by a long mantle or footcloth that nearly touched the ground. The performer on this occasion exerted all his skill in burlesque horsemanship. In Sampson's play of *The vow-breaker*, 1636, a miller personates the hobby-horse; and being angry that the mayor of the city is put in competition with him, exclaims, " Let the major play the hobby-horse among his brethren, and he will, I hope our towne-lads cannot want a hobby-horse. Have I practic'd my reines, my careeres, my pranckers, my ambles, my false trotts, my smooth ambles and Canterbury paces, and shall master major put me besides the hobby-horse? Have I borrowed the forehorse bells, his plumes and braveries, nay had his mane new shorne and frizl'd, and shall the major put me besides the hobby-horse?"

Whoever happens to recollect the manner in which Mr. Bayes's troops in the *Rehearsal* are exhibited on the stage, will have a tolerably correct notion of a morris hobby-horse. Additional remains of the Pyrrhic or sword dance are preserved in the daggers stuck in the man's cheeks, which constituted one of the hocus-pocus or legerdemain tricks practised by this character, among which were the threading of a needle, and the transferring of an egg from one hand to the other, called by Ben Jonson *the travels of the egg.** To the horse's mouth was suspended a ladle for the purpose of gathering money from the spectators.   In later times the fool appears to have performed this office, as may be collected from Nashe's play of *Summer's last will and testament,* where this stage direction occurs, " Ver goes in and fetcheth out the Hobby-horse and the morris daunce who daunce about." Ver then says, " About, about, lively, put your horse to it, reyne him harder, jerke him with your wand, sit fast, sit fast, man; *foole, holde up your ladle there.*" Will Summers is made to say, " You friend with the hobby-horse, goe not too fast, for feare of wearing out my lord's tyle-stones with your hob-nayles." Afterwards there enter three clowns and three maids, who dance the morris, and at the same time sing the following song :

> " Trip and goe, heave and hoe,
> Up and downe, to and fro,
> From the towne, to the grove,
> Two and two, let us rove,
> A maying, a playing ;
> Love hath no gainsaying :
> So merrily trip and goe."

Lord Orford in his catalogue of English engravers, under the article of Peter Stent, has described two paintings at Lord Fitzwilliam's on Richmond green which came out of the old neighbouring palace.   They were executed by Vincken-boom, about the end of the reign of James I., and exhibit views of the above palace; in one of these pictures a morris dance is introduced, consisting of seven figures, viz. a fool, a hobby-horse, a piper, a Maid Marian, and three other dancers, the rest of the figures being spectators.   Of these the first four and one of the dancers are reduced in the an-nexed plate from a tracing made by the late Captain Grose. The fool has an inflated bladder or eel-skin with a *ladle* at the

---

* *Every man out of his humour,* Act II. Scene 1.

end of it, and with this he is collecting money. The piper is pretty much in his original state; but the hobby-horse wants the legerdemain apparatus, and Maid Marian is not remarkable for the elegance of her person.

Dr. Plott, in his *History of Staffordshire*, p. 434, mentions that within memory, at Abbot's or Paget's Bromley, they had a sort of sport which they celebrated at Christmas, or on new year and twelfth days, called the *Hobby-horse dance*, from a person who carried the image of a horse between his legs made of thin boards, and in his hand a bow and arrow. The latter passing through a hole in the bow, and stopping on a shoulder, made a snapping noise when drawn to and fro, keeping time with the music. With this man danced six others, carrying on their shoulders as many rein-deer heads, with the arms of the chief families to whom the revenues of the town belonged. They danced the heys and other country dances. To the above hobby-horse dance there belonged a pot, which was kept by turns by the reeves of the town, who provided cakes and ale to put into this pot; all people who had any kindness for the good intent of the institution of the sport giving pence a-piece for themselves and families. Foreigners also that came to see it contributed; and the money, after defraying the expense of the cakes and ale, went to repair the church and support the poor; which charges, adds the doctor, are not now perhaps so cheerfully borne.

A short time before the revolution in France, the May games and morris dance were celebrated in many parts of that country, accompanied by a fool and a *hobby-horse*. The latter was termed *un chevalet*; and, if the authority of Minsheu be not questionable, the Spaniards had the same character under the name of *tarasca*.*

VIII. THE DRAGON. The earliest mention of him as a part of the morris dance we have already seen in the extract

* Spanish dictionary.

Published by T. Tegg Cheapside Sep.t 1839.

from Stubbes's *Anatomie of abuses*; and he is likewise introduced in a morris, in Sampson's play of the *Vowbreaker, or
fayre maid of Clifton*, 1633, where a fellow says, " I'll be a
fiery dragon:" on which, another, who had undertaken the
hobby-horse, observes that he will be " a thund'ring *Saint
George* as ever rode on horseback.*" This seems to afford a
clue to the use of this dragon, who was probably attacked in
some ludicrous manner by the hobby-horse saint, and may
perhaps be the *Devil* alluded to in the extract already given
from Fetherstone's *Dialogue against dancing*.

IX. The Morris Dancers. By these are meant the
common dancers in the late morrises, and who were not distinguished by any particular appellation, though in earlier times
it is probable that each individual had his separate title. If
there were any reason for a contrary opinion, it might depend
on the costume of numbers 10 and 11 in Mr. Tollett's window, which may perhaps belong to the present class. There
are likewise two similar figures in the Flemish print; and the
coincidence in their attitudes is no less remarkable than it is in
those of some of the other characters. The circumstance too
of one only wearing a feather in his hat is deserving of notice,
as it is the same in both the representations. The streamers
which proceed from their sleeves and flutter in the wind,
though continued in very modern times, were anciently not
peculiar to morris dancers, examples of them occurring in
many old prints.* In the reign of Henry the Eighth the
morris dancers were dressed in gilt leather and silver paper,
and sometimes in coats of white spangled fustian. They had
purses at their girdles, and garters to which bells were attached.† The latter have been always a part of the furniture
of the more active characters in the morris, and the use of
them is of great antiquity. The *tinkling ornaments of the feet*

---

* See the plate of ancient cards, xxxi. in Strutt's *Sports and pastimes*,
where a *knave* or attendant is dressed in this manner.

† Churchwardens' accounts at Kingston, in Lysons's *Environs of London*,
i. p. 227, 228.

among the Jewish women are reprobated in *Isaiah* iii, 16, 18. Gratius Faliscus, who wrote his poem on hunting in the time of Augustus, has alluded to the practice of dancing with bells on the feet among the Egyptian priests of Canopus, in the following lines:

> " Vix operata suo sacra ad Bubastia lino
> Velatur *sonipes æstivi turba Canopi.*"
>
> *Cynegeticon*, lib. i. 42.

There is good reason for believing that the morris bells were borrowed from the genuine *Moorish dance*; a circumstance that tends to corroborate the opinion that has been already offered with respect to the etymology of the *morris*. Among the beautiful habits of various nations, published by Hans Weigel at Nuremberg, in 1577, there is the figure of an African lady of the kingdom of Fez in the act of dancing, with bells at her feet. A copy of it is here exhibited:

The number of bells round each leg of the morris dancers amounted from twenty to forty.* They had various appel-

---

* Stubbes's *Anatomie of abuses*, ubi supra.

lations, as the fore-bell, the second bell, the treble, the tenor, the base, and the double bell. Sometimes they used trebles only; but these refinements were of later times.* The bells were occasionally jingled by the hands, or placed on the arms or wrists of the parties. Scarves, ribbands, and laces hung all over with gold rings, and even precious stones, are also mentioned in the time of Elizabeth.† The miller, in the play of the *Vowbreaker*, says he is come to borrow " a few ribbandes, bracelets, eare-rings, wyertyers, and silke girdles and handkerchers for a morice and a show before the queene." The handkerchiefs, or napkins‡ as they are sometimes called, were held in the hand, or tied to the shoulders.§ In Shirley's *Lady of pleasure*, 1637, Act I., Aretina thus inveighs against the amusements of the country:

> " . . . . . to observe with what solemnity
> They keep their wakes, and throw for pewter candlestickes,
> How they become the morris, with whose bells
> They ring all into Whitson ales, and sweate
> Through twenty scarffes and napkins, till the Hobby horse
> Tire, and the maide Marrian dissolv'd to a gelly,
> Be kept for spoone meate."

---

* See Rowley's *Witch of Edmonton*, 1658, Act I. Scene 2.

† Stubbes, ubi supra. *Knight of the burning pestle*, Act IV.

‡ Stubbes, ubi supra. Jonson's *Masque of gipsies*. Holme's *Academy of armory*, book iii. p. 169, whence the following cut has been borrowed, which, rude as it is, may serve to convey some idea of the manner in which the handkerchiefs were used.

§ *Knight of the burning pestle*, Act IV.

The early use of the feather in the hat appears both in
Mr. Tollett's window and the Flemish print; a fashion that
was continued a long time afterwards.* Sometimes the hat
was decorated with a nosegay,† or with the herb *thrift*, formerly called *our lady's cushion*.‡

Enough has been said to show that the collective number
of the morris dancers has continually varied according to
circumstances, in the same manner as did their habits. In
Israel's print they are nine: in Mr. Tollett's window, eleven.
Mr. Strutt has observed that on his sixteenth plate there are
only five, exclusive of the two musicians: but it is conceived
that what he refers to is not a morris, but a dance of fools.
There is a pamphlet entitled *Old Meg of Herefordshire for a
Mayd Marian and Hereford town for a morris dance, or* 12
morris dancers in Herefordshire of 1200 *years old*, 1609, 4to.§
In the painting by Vinckenboom, at Richmond, there are
seven figures. In Blount's *Glossographia*, 1656, the *Morisco*
is defined, " a dance wherein there were usually five men and
a boy dressed in a girles habit, whom they call Maid
Marrian." The morris in Fletcher's *Two noble kinsmen* contains some characters, which, as they are nowhere else to be
found, might have been the poet's own invention, and designed
for stage effect:

> " The chambermaid, and serving man by night
> That seek out silent hanging : Then mine host
> And his fat spouse, that welcomes to their cost
> The gauled traveller, and with a beckning
> Informs the tapster to inflame the reck'ning.
> Then the beast-eating clown, and next the fool,
> The *Bavian*, with long tail and eke long tool,
> *Cum multis aliis*, that make a dance."

---

* Vox graculi, 1623, p. 49.
† Fletcher's *Women pleased*, Act IV.
‡ Greene's *Quip for an upstart courtier*, sign. B. 2.
§ This tract is mentioned by Sir William Temple, in his Essay on health
and long life, from the communication of Lord Leicester. Howel, in his
Parly of beasts, 1660, has recorded that " of late years ther were call'd out

Mr. Ritson has taken notice of an old wooden cut "preserved on the title of a penny-history, (*Adam Bell, &c.*) printed at Newcastle in 1772," and which represents, in his opinion, a morris dance consisting of the following personages: 1. A bishop. 2. Robin Hood. 3. The potter or beggar. 4. Little John. 5. Friar Tuck. 6. Maid Marian. He remarks that the execution of the whole is too rude to merit a copy, a position that is not meant to be controverted; but it is necessary to introduce the cut in this place for the purpose of correcting an error into which the above ingenious writer has inadvertently fallen. It is proper to mention that it originally appeared on the title page to the first *known* edition of *Robin Hood's garland,* printed in 1670, 18mo.

Now this cut is certainly *not* the representation of a morris

within three miles compasse ten men that were a thousand years between them, one supplying what the other wanted of a hundred years apiece, and they danc'd the *morris* divers hours together in the market place with a taborer before them 103 years old, and a maid *Mariam* 105."—p. 122. This seems to allude to the same event.

dance, but merely of the principal characters belonging to the garland. These are, Robin Hood, Little John, *queen Catherine*, the bishop, the *curtal frier*, (not Tuck,) and the beggar. Even though it were admitted that Maid Marian and Friar Tuck were intended to be given, it could not be maintained that either the bishop or the beggar made part of a morris.

There still remains some characters in Mr. Tollett's window, of which no description can be here attempted, viz. Nos. 1, 4, 6, and 7. As these are also found in the Flemish print,* they cannot possibly belong to Robin Hood's company; and therefore their learned proprietor would, doubtless, have seen the necessity of re-considering his explanations.† The resemblance between the two ancient representations is sufficiently remarkable to warrant a conjecture that the window has been originally executed by some foreign artist; and that the panes with the English friar, the hobbyhorse, and the may-pole have been since added.

Mr. Waldron has informed us that he saw in the summer of 1783, at Richmond in Surrey, a troop of morris dancers from Abingdon, accompanied by a fool in a motley jacket, who carried in his hand a staff about two feet long, with a blown bladder at the end of it, with which he either buffeted the crowd to keep them at a proper distance from the dancers, or played tricks for the diversion of the spectators. The dancers and the fool were Berkshire husbandmen taking an annual circuit to collect money.§ Mr. Ritson too has noticed

* Compare No. 1, with the left hand figure at bottom in the print; No. 4, with the left hand figure at top; No. 6, with the right hand figure at bottom; and No. 7, with the right hand figure at top. This last character in the Flemish print has a flower in his hat as well as No. 4. Query if that ornament have been accidentally omitted by the *English engraver?*

† This gentleman's death is recorded to have happened Oct. 22nd, 1779. Gough's *Brit. topogr.* ii. 239.

‡ See his continuation to *Ben Jonson's sad shepherd*, 1782, 8vo, p. 255, a work of very considerable merit, and which will materially diminish the regret of all readers of taste that the original was left unfinished.

that morris dancers are yet annually seen in Norfolk, and
make their constant appearance in Lancashire. He has also
preserved a newspaper article respecting some morris dancers
of Pendleton, who paid their annual visit to Salford, in
1792;* and a very few years since, another company of this
kind was seen at Usk in Monmouthshire, which was attended
by a boy Maid Marian, a hobby-horse, and a fool. They
professed to have kept up the ceremony at that place for the
last three hundred years.   It has been thought worth while
to record these modern instances, because it is extremely
probable that from the present rage for refinement and innovation, there will remain, in the course of a short time, but
few vestiges of our popular customs and antiquities.

* *Robin Hood,* I. cviii.

INDEX.

―――――――

" Commoditas homines studiosos invitavit librorum *Indices* comparare, quibus minimo labore ad id quod quisque quæreret, tanquam manu duceretur."—CICERO AD ATTICUM.

―――――――

GLOSSARIAL INDEX.

THE END.